THIRTEENTH EDITION

CRIMINAL INVESTIGATION

BASIC PERSPECTIVES

Charles A. Lushbaugh

Retired Lieutenant, Sacramento County Sheriff's Department, Sacramento, California
Lecturer of Criminal Justice—Emeritus, California State University, Sacramento, California
FBI NA, 185th Session

Paul B. Weston

(Deceased)

PEARSON

Boston   Columbus   Hoboken   Indianapolis   New York   San Francisco   Amsterdam   Cape Town
Dubai   London   Madrid   Milan   Munich   Paris   Montreal   Toronto   Delhi   Mexico City
Sao Paulo   Sydney   Hong Kong   Seoul   Singapore   Taipei   Tokyo

Editorial Director: Andrew Gilfillan
Senior Acquisitions Editor: Gary Bauer
Editorial Assistant: Lynda Cramer
Director of Marketing: David Gesell
Senior Marketing Manager: Thomas Hayward
Senior Marketing Coordinator: Alicia Wozniak
Senior Marketing Assistant: Les Roberts
Project Manager: Susan Hannahs
Program Manager: Tara Horton
Senior Art Director: Diane Ernsberger
Cover Designer: Studio Montage, Melissa Welch
Cover Art: Oriontrail/Shutterstock
Full-Service Project Management and Composition: George Jacob/Integra
Printer/Binder: LSC Communications
Cover Printer: LSC Communications
Text Font: 10/12, Minion Pro Regular

Credits and acknowledgments borrowed from other sources and reproduced, with permission, in this textbook appear on the appropriate page within the text.

Library of Congress Cataloging-in-Publication Data
Lushbaugh, Charles.
Criminal investigation: basic perspectives/Charles A. Lushbaugh, Paul B. Weston.—Thirteenth edition.
    pages cm
  ISBN 978-0-13-351440-7—ISBN 0-13-351440-4
  1. Criminal investigation—United States.   I. Weston, Paul B.   II. Title.
  HV8073.W44 2016
  363.250973—dc23

                                                                                           2014036668

18 2022

ISBN 10:   0-13-351440-4
ISBN 13: 978-0-13-351440-7

This edition is dedicated to those who pointed me in the right direction and kept me on track. First, there were my parents, Helen and Charles, who, despite going no further than the eighth grade in school, valued education and hard work. They were always there to answer my questions and provide valuable insights. For those questions that my parents were hoping I would never ask, I had lifelong friends such as John Miele, Richard Hinman, Anthony Palumbo, and Joseph Nekola. While together we may not have always come up with the right answers to these questions, the process was always informative. Then there were the Westons, Ceal, and Paul, who taught me that not only were education and hard work important but that determination and motivation were also major components in getting ahead in life. Finally there is Sharon, who teaches me the meaning of life on a daily basis, and I would be lost without her.

Contents

PART 2

Investigating Major Crimes

Preface

The thirteenth edition of *Criminal Investigation: Basic Perspectives* was written to keep abreast of changes in the field of criminal investigation. Two new chapters dealing with cybercrime and missing and exploited persons have been added to this edition. In addition, new segments were added to various chapters:

Cell phones, social networking sites and video cameras as investigative leads (Chapter 6, "Basic Investigative Leads").

Cold case investigations, how DNA, improved fingerprint databases, and the passage of time may assist investigators (Chapter 8, "Crimes of Violence").

Home invasion, drug house, and bank robberies and preventive measures (Chapter 11, "Robbery").

Organized retail theft and cargo theft (Chapter 13, "Property Crimes").

The financial aspects of organized crime investigations through money laundering, asset forfeiture, money reporting, and the witness protection program (Chapter 16, "Special Investigations").

The Symbionese Liberation Army, Weatherman, and the lone wolf terrorist (Chapter 17, "Terrorism").

Three new case studies, designed to enhance the learning process, have been added to this edition. The case study method of instruction facilitates learning by linking case content to textbook topics and by encouraging the exchange of opinions and viewpoints among students during discussion sessions. The case studies in this book are designed to contribute to this type of learning process. Each case provides factual information that is likely to promote analysis and discussion and thus aids in developing the student's ability to analyze, evaluate, and reason. The topic of discussion is focused on the facts of each case study, but only the range of student opinions and ideas limits the scope of the discussion.

Some cases are presented in straight narrative style, while others are written in dialogue form as the best means of joining the personalities and the situations of a case study. Each case presents a real-life situation or episode experienced sometime in the past. No "doctoring" has been done to develop points, theories, or problems. However, names, dates, and locations have been altered in some instances to avoid embarrassing any persons or their families.

Also new to this edition is the applied investigative procedures section at the end of each chapter. These scenarios are designed to enhance the learning process by asking the student to apply material presented in the chapter to address real-life investigative issues.

I thank the reviewers for this edition, whose insights and suggestions have made this a better book. They include Vincent Benincasa, Hesser College, David MacDonald, Eastfield College, David Powell, Daymar College, and Jacqueline Smith, Kennesaw State University.

I extend special thanks to David Lushbaugh and Christopher Baker for their assistance.

▶ Supplements

Instructor Supplements

Instructor's Manual with Test Bank. Includes content outlines for classroom discussion, teaching suggestions, and answers to selected end-of-chapter questions from the text. This also contains a Word document version of the test bank.

TestGen. This computerized test generation system gives you maximum flexibility in creating and administering tests on paper, electronically, or online. It provides state-of-the-art features for viewing and editing test bank questions, dragging a selected question into a test you are creating, and printing sleek, formatted tests in a variety of layouts. Select test items from test banks included with TestGen for quick test creation, or write your own questions from scratch. TestGen's random generator provides the option to display different text or calculated number values each time questions are used.

PowerPoint Presentations. Our presentations offer clear, straightforward outlines and notes to use for class lectures or study materials. Photos, illustrations, charts, and tables from the book are included in the presentations when applicable.

To access supplementary materials online, instructors need to request an instructor access code. Go to **www.pearsonhighered.com/irc**, where you can register for an instructor access code. Within 48 hours after registering, you will receive a confirming email, including an instructor access code. Once you have received your code, go to the site and log on for full instructions on downloading the materials you wish to use.

▶ Alternate Versions

eBooks. This text is also available in multiple eBook formats, including Adobe Reader and CourseSmart. *CourseSmart* is an exciting new choice for students looking to save money. As an alternative to purchasing the printed textbook, students can purchase an electronic version of the same content. With a *CourseSmart* eTextbook, students can search the text, make notes online, print out reading assignments that incorporate lecture notes, and bookmark important passages for later review. For more information, or to purchase access to the *CourseSmart* eTextbook, visit **www.coursesmart.com**.

1 Evolution of Policing and Investigation

LEARNING OBJECTIVES

After reading this chapter, you will be able to:

1 *Discuss the evolution of policing in England and how it applies to American policing.*

2 *Evaluate the political climate in the United States at the time the first police departments were being formed and the effect this political climate had on these departments.*

3 *Describe the emergence of the reform movement in American policing and the major tenets of the reform agenda.*

4 *Identify the persons and their scientific discoveries that led to the development of the field of criminalistics.*

5 *Identify the various policing agencies at the local, state, and federal levels and their areas of responsibility.*

Policing as we know it is a relatively new concept as police agencies have only been in existence for less than 200 years. Prior to the introduction of policing, people were responsible for their own personal protection and responded to crime victimization on their own as best they could with the limited recourses at hand. The first policing efforts were rudimentary and these efforts evolved over time to what we have today, a professional policing model. In America this evolutionary process included a reform movement which addressed the failings of our early policing efforts. The move toward professional policing was aided by the scientific community with discoveries that could be applied to criminal investigations. Today criminal investigations are conducted by investigators from various law enforcement agencies at the local, state, and federal levels.

❶ *Discuss the evolution of policing in England and how it applies to American policing.*

▶ Early Response to Crime

A review of the history of policing in England is essential to understand the evolution of policing in the United States. The original British colonists to this country brought with them their customs and their law which was used to form the basis of our own legal system used today. When police agencies were first being formed in this country, they were modelled after the London Metropolitan Police.

Before there was a criminal justice system, comprising the three main components of the police, courts, and corrections, the individual citizen played a much larger role in providing for his or her own personal protection and dealing with any crime victimization. For centuries people depended upon themselves, their family, their neighbors, and their faith for protection. People lived typically in small agrarian communities where everyone knew every one else, which is a deterrent to criminal activity in itself. When threatened, the community responded as one to deal with the threat. Under the principle of *posse comitatus*, which means the power or force of the community to enforce the law, all available citizens were expected to respond to protect the community.

In the event a person was a victim of a crime, that person first had to decide if they personally wanted to do anything about their victimization, or simply accept what happened and move on with their life. If they wanted action taken, they had to do it themselves. As there were no police to call, the victim would have to conduct the investigation, often with the assistance of family and friends. When the culprit was identified, the victim was also responsible for arresting this person. At this point the offender had to be turned over to the local **sheriff**, the chief law enforcement officer who represented the crown. One of the sheriff's duties was to take and hold prisoners for an eventual hearing before a disinterested third party, typically the local lord or magistrate. The reasoning behind this was that the victim was too emotionally involved to fairly adjudicate the case and often, the punishment rendered in such cases did not fit the crime; that is, killing a person who stole from the victim. Such unjust reactions often led to **blood-feuds,** or **vendettas**, where the family of the offender would retaliate against the victim or the victim's family to get even. Such feuds were very destructive to communities and could continue indefinitely.

Night Watch

As populations increased and cities and towns grew in size, the social controls of the small tight-knit agrarian community failed to control crime in these larger communities. In response to this, in 1285 the **Statute of Winchester** was passed requiring all towns to have men on the streets after dark to provide for the safety of travelers and the town's inhabitants. All able-bodied males were required to serve on a rotational basis, without pay, as night watchmen. As part of their service, they manned the village gates and patrolled the streets while on the lookout for disturbances of the peace, crimes in progress, and other threats such as fires. There was no expectation that the night watchmen would conduct investigations or aid the victim in determining who committed the crime; this was still the victim's responsibility. The watchmen were supervised by a **constable**, also a private citizen, who served a voluntary one-year term in this position as part of his civic duty. In addition to supervising the watchmen, the constable had the additional duty of bringing any arrested offenders before a magistrate in the morning.[1] The statute also required citizens to come to the aid of the night watchmen whenever they gave the *hue and cry*, a loud outcry that alerted citizens of a pursuit of a criminal which bound all who heard the cry to join in the pursuit. If the citizens did not respond and assist, they could be considered accomplices to the crime and punished. The statute required all males between the ages of fifteen and sixty to keep arms for the purpose of rendering aid and subduing offenders.[2]

The effectiveness of the night watch waned over time as citizens began to understand the inconvenience of staying up all night, especially if they had jobs to go to or shops to open in the morning. Many people ignored the call to serve, paid the fine, or paid a substitute to serve in their place. Many of the men willing to serve as replacements were often deemed too weak or feeble to effectively suppress crime. Eventually, in order to improve the quality of the service, the night watchmen were paid. However, the amount was not substantial.[3]

► Thief-Takers

As night watchmen patrolled the streets, they did not follow up on crimes to determine who was responsible for the ever-increasing crime problem. To address this issue, parliament, in 1689, established rewards for the conviction of crimes such as robbery, burglary, and counterfeiting. The intent of the legislation was to encourage victims to make an effort to catch and prosecute the persons responsible for these crimes. By 1750 the reward for the conviction of a robbery suspect was increased to 140 pounds, a sum equal to three to four years of income for a skilled workman.

While these rewards were designed to encourage victims to take action—and many did—the unintended consequence was that these rewards also encouraged others to get involved. These thief-takers, as they came to be known, often criminals themselves, were motivated by the reward money and their ability to confiscate the possessions of the criminal. This form of bounty system gave the thief-takers a bad reputation and some were suspected of encouraging crimes for the purpose of solving them.[4]

► Bow Street Runners

By 1748 crime had increased in England and its capital, London, was recognized as one of the most dangerous cities in Europe. That same year Henry Fielding (1707–1754), former novelist, playwright, and attorney, was named magistrate for the Bow Street court. At the time Bow Street was known as one of the worst crime-ridden areas of London. Fielding organized a group of former constables and thief-takers to carry out investigations and bring suspects to trial. Fielding's men received a small stipend and relied on rewards they received for a successful prosecution. These runners, as they came to be known, were also used to guard the King and to investigate various crimes such as robbery and murder.[5]

John Fielding (1721–1780), who took over after his brother passed away in 1754, instituted a number of changes at Bow Street. He organized mounted patrols to protect the highways from robbers and instituted foot patrols on the city streets. At one time Fielding employed between 300 and 400 officers to patrol the Bow Street area. Another one of his innovations was the establishment of the *Police Gazette* which encouraged victims to report crimes to his court. Victims would then receive assistance from the runners in the investigation of these crimes. The gazette also published information about criminal activity, names and descriptions of wanted criminals, and descriptions of stolen property.[6] John Fielding served as magistrate of the Bow Street court for over twenty five years and was knighted for his efforts in fighting crime. Fielding is considered to be the father of the modern police detective.

► London's Metropolitan Police

In 1822 Robert Peel became the British Home Secretary, a position which was responsible for the internal security of England. Peel was a strong advocate of establishing a police force to combat crime. The idea had been presented to parliament several times before but had been rejected over the concerns of the possible loss of individual liberties. Peel repeatedly addressed parliament about the need for policing while ensuring the rights of Englishmen.

In 1829 Peel presented a reform bill that expressly excluded the city of London but provided policing for the metropolitan area surrounding the city. Peel's proposal was for a model police force which, if successful, could be implemented throughout the rest of the country. The bill passed without major opposition and called for the operation of a police force with a twenty-four-hour operation. Peel decided that this police force should be uniformed as to be readily identifiable to the citizenry. The blue uniform was chosen in order to distinguish it from the scarlet military uniform in use at the time. Officers were issued a numbered badge so citizens could properly identify the officers in order to lodge a complaint or praise the service they had received. The police were to be modelled after the highly successful military organizational structure that is still in use today. The metropolitan police force included nearly

3,000 officers who were paid only slightly less than that of a skilled workman. These officers carried only nightsticks for protection, no lethal weapons, and were instructed to be respectful to the public.

When the new police officers came on duty in September of 1829, they were viewed by many citizens as a threat to personal liberty. Turnover was high in the early years largely due to improper conduct. All complaints against an officer were painstakingly investigated. Within the first twenty years of operation the new police gradually won the respect and acceptance from the citizenry they served. Their restraint in the use of force, their professionalism, and civility in dealing with the public established this new police force as an institution of order and protector of liberty. The "peelers" who were both feared and hated soon became the "**bobbies**" a name used in reference to Robert Peel and a term of respect and appreciation.[7] Known today as the father of policing, Peel would go on to become the prime minister of England and would be eventually knighted for his service to his country.

2 *Evaluate the political climate in the United States at the time the first police departments were being formed and the effect this political climate had on these departments.*

▶ American Policing

Much like England, the night-watch system of policing in the United States was overwhelmed with crime as a result of urbanization and immigration. A series of riots in the major cities such as Philadelphia, Boston, and New York showed that the time for policing had come. In 1845 the city of New York established a police force modelled after the London Metropolitan Police and other cities soon followed suit. While these agencies were modelled after the London police, there were some major differences that would cause serious lasting problems. London's police, while local, were administered at the federal level as a model policing effort to be implemented throughout England. In contrast early police departments in America were formed at the city level of government. At the time these departments were formed the cities were under the

1865 depiction of a London police officer.
Source: Bryan Fosten/Peter Newark Pictures/Bridgeman Images

control of corrupt political machines operating under the **spoils system**. Under this system, politicians extorted money from people and companies wanting to do business with the city. Many politicians became rich and this influence corrupted the new police departments as well.

Under this corrupt system a form of **patronage** existed whereby an applicant had to have political friends to become a police officer. Another way to get a job as a police officer was to buy your way in with a payment to the political machine. Unlike the London police, which established strict hiring standards, the American police had no standards; furthermore, upon being hired, recruits received little or no training for their role as police officers.[8]

The emphasis of early policing was to maintain order, which consisted of arresting vagrants, those under the influence of alcohol, and those involved in disturbances of the peace. The police paid little attention to the investigation or prevention of crime and often ignored vice going on around them. Saloons, brothels, and gambling establishments paid the police to look the other way and to leave their operations alone. Since the general public had no way to call the police when they needed them, and officers were often incompetent and corrupt, it is no wonder the police were held with little regard by the public.[9]

3 *Describe the emergence of the reform movement in American policing and the major tenets of the reform agenda.*

▶ The Reform Movement

One of the chief advocates of reforming the police was August Vollmer (1876–1955), chief of police in Berkeley, California, from 1905 to 1932. Vollmer and other reformers advocated the following agenda:

1. Policing should be a profession that serves the community on a nonpartisan basis.
2. Politics should be eliminated from policing.

Seattle police officers in formation in 1910.
Source: © PEMCO/ Webster & Stevens Collection; Museum of History and Industry, Seattle/ CORBIS

3. Law enforcement agencies should be headed by qualified chief executives.

4. Law enforcement agencies should raise the hiring and training standards for new recruits.

5. Agencies should apply modern management principles and advocate centralized command and control of police operations.

6. Agencies should create specialized units such as traffic, juvenile, and vice.[10]

To accomplish many of these goals, reformers advocated the use of the *civil service system* for the selection and promotion of police personnel. Under this system police applicants, and those seeking promotion, would be required to take a test, usually a written examination. Those who passed the test would have their names placed on a list and the police agency was required to hire off the list of qualified applicants. This system ensured that only the best candidates would be hired and promoted by the agency.

Vollmer wrote extensively about the police and became the president of the International Association of Chiefs of Police during the 1920s. In this capacity he was able to spread the message about the need for police professionalism. As a police chief and professor of police administration at the University of California at Berkeley, Vollmer was able to influence the next generation of police professionals as well. Today Vollmer is considered to be the father of modern policing in America.

A major social event that had a tremendous impact on moving policing toward professionalism was the Great Depression of the 1930s. The lack of employment opportunities elsewhere made policing attractive to college-educated people who would not otherwise have considered a career in policing. This new pool of better-educated middle-class applicants enabled police administrators to upgrade the entry-level requirements for police positions. In addition, these better-educated people were more receptive to the concepts of the reform movement. The trend toward higher education and policing continued after World War II when returning veterans took advantage of the GI Bill benefits and enrolled in colleges and universities that, by that time, offered specialized courses in police science and administration.[11]

The reform movement was successful in removing politics from policing and in raising the standards of both new recruits and managers of police departments around the country. Over the years police administrators have taken a hard-line approach to corruption and misconduct. Administrators have vigorously investigated allegations of wrongdoing and have taken

▼

corrective action when these allegations are substantiated, including discipline and prosecution where appropriate. Today, corruption in policing is the exception rather than the rule.

4 *Identify the persons and their scientific discoveries that led to the development of the field of criminalistics.*

▶ Development of Forensic Science

The move toward professional policing has been greatly assisted by developments in various fields of science that can be applied to criminal investigations. The use of science to answer legal questions is known as **forensics**, a field of study that has developed over time. Scientists schooled in a variety of disciplines have made meaningful contributions to the field of **criminalistics**, the application of scientific techniques in collecting and analyzing physical evidence. The following are a few of the contributors to this endeavor.

Mathieu Orfila (1787–1853) is thought by many to be the father of forensic **toxicology**—that is, the study of the effects of poisons. His work on the detection of poisons and their effects on animals established the science of forensic toxicology.

Hans Gross (1848–1915) was the earliest advocate of criminal investigation as a science. Gross was a native of Austria, born in Graz. Educated in law, he became interested in investigation while serving as an examining magistrate. He became a professor of criminology at the University of Vienna. Perhaps it was the legal training, or the education in rational theory joined with the study of law, that made Magistrate Gross unhappy with the lack of science in police investigation. In any event, he deserves credit for developing a system of investigation. His *System der Kriminalistik (Criminal Investigation)*, translated into English and published in 1906, is a classic text in this field. Gross strongly supported scrupulous accuracy and high ethics in criminal investigation. His greatest contribution to the introduction of science in criminal investigation was the advocacy of a parallel system of inquiry based on the crime scene.

Alphonse Bertillon (1853–1914) developed the first means of human identification, known as **anthropometry**. This system involved the taking of eleven measurements of various parts of the body—such as height, reach, head width, and length of left foot—along with a photograph of the subject. Bertillon based his system on the assumption that it would be virtually impossible for two people to look alike and to have the same physical measurements. His system worked well for over two decades until unraveled by the Will West case in 1903. When West was being processed into the

Fort Leavenworth prison, it was discovered that another prisoner, already in custody, had the same measurements and appearance, as if they were identical twins. Bertillon's system was eventually replaced by the identification of individuals through fingerprints, but he is still considered to be the father of criminal identification.

Francis Galton (1822–1911) provided the first definitive study of fingerprints in his book *Finger Prints*. His pioneering efforts in this area led to the creation of a classification system that was capable of filing these prints in a logical searchable sequence.

Albert S. Osborn (1858–1946) authored in 1910 the first significant text in the field of questioned documents. The book remains a primary resource for document examiners and was responsible for the acceptance of documents as scientific evidence by the courts.

Edmond Locard (1877–1966) in 1910 persuaded the police department in Lyons, France, to finance a small police laboratory. Locard's research and accomplishments became known throughout the world. He eventually became the founder and director of the Institute of Criminalistics at the University of Lyons. The institute developed into an international center for the study of and research in forensic science. Locard is perhaps best known today for his **exchange principle**. He believed that when a criminal came in contact with another object or person, a cross-transfer of evidence occurred, primarily of hairs and fibers.

Leone Lattes (1887–1954) expanded upon the discovery that blood can be grouped into four different categories: A, B, AB, and O. Lattes, a professor of medicine in Turin, Italy, devised a procedure for determining the blood group from dried bloodstains and applied this technique to criminal investigations.

Calvin Goddard (1891–1955) was aware that the determination of whether a fired bullet originating from the suspect's weapon required a comparison with a bullet that had been fired and retrieved from the suspect's gun. Goddard refined the techniques for making these determinations by using a comparison microscope.[12]

Alec Jeffreys (1950–) in 1985 conducted an investigation into the structure of the human gene that led to the discovery of deoxyribonucleic acid (DNA) at Leicester University, England. This discovery disclosed that certain genetic markers are as unique to each individual as are fingerprints. This discovery gave the scientific community a means to link biological evidence such as blood, semen, hair, and tissue to a single individual.[13]

Professor Alec Jeffreys, the molecular biologist who discovered the DNA profiling technique in 1984.
Source: David Parker/Science Source

⑤ *Identify the various policing agencies at the local, state, and federal levels and their areas of responsibility.*

▶ Local Policing

Policing at the local level is provided by municipal, or city police departments, or by the county sheriff's department in those areas outside the city limits. According to the U.S. Department of Justice, Bureau of Justice Statistics, there are over 12,600 police departments and over 3,000 sheriff's departments in the United States. These agencies employ over 600,000 sworn officers, the vast majority of which, 73 percent, are employed by city police departments.[14]

City police departments typically provide law enforcement services in three broad areas of patrol, traffic, and detective functions. Patrol enforcement involves officers being out-and-about the community randomly looking for criminal activity or responding to citizens' calls for service. Officers in larger cities may patrol on foot; however, the typical patrol officer is in a marked patrol vehicle. Patrol activities are often augmented by officers in helicopters or boats, on motorcycles or horses, and with k-9s, also known as police dogs. These officers are tasked with dealing with all types of crime—from the relatively minor crime such as traffic offence to major crime such as murder.

Those crimes that require follow-up investigation are typically referred to a detective division. Detectives conduct searches for witnesses and suspects and evidence not located at the scene of the crime. Detectives also conduct specialized investigations such as surveillances and decoy operations.

The traffic division enforces vehicle code regulations and conducts accident investigations. One of the major functions of this division is the enforcement and arrest of those motorists operating a vehicle while under the influence of alcohol or drugs. Thousands of deaths each year in this country are attributable to people who operate a motor vehicle while under the influence of intoxicants.

Sheriff's departments typically provide law enforcement–related functions to those areas in the county that are located outside the jurisdiction of the city police departments. While many sheriffs' departments are in rural settings, many are not, and are dealing with the same crime issues as city police departments. Often the dividing line between the city and the county is the center line of a major street, with one side being in the city and the other in the county. In addition to providing patrol and detective-related services many sheriffs' departments are responsible for the operation of the county jail. Sheriff's personnel may provide security for the courthouse and serve as bailiffs that guard prisoners when they appear in court. Sheriff's departments often provide the county-wide function of civil process. In this capacity sheriff's deputies carry out the orders of the court such as evictions and property seizures.

▶ State Policing

Most states, but not all, may provide law enforcement services in three broad areas: patrol of the state's highways; general law enforcement, including patrol and detective functions, to areas not serviced by a municipal police department or sheriff; or specialized investigations. Agencies such as the California Highway Patrol enforce traffic laws, investigate traffic accidents, and make arrests for any penal code violation they encounter in the course of their duties. Specialized investigations might include statewide enforcement of alcohol beverage control laws, controlled substances or drug investigations, consumer and welfare fraud, and investigative support to any police agency in the state that requests assistance.

▶ Federal Investigative Agencies

Every branch of the federal government has an investigative agency that is responsible for the investigation of violations of the law that come within its jurisdiction. For the sake of brevity this discussion will be limited to those federal agencies that have a high profile and are most readily identifiable to most readers.

▼

Marshal's Service—Created in 1789 with the passage of the first judiciary act, the marshal's service claims to be the oldest federal law enforcement agency. Over the years the marshals have served the country in a variety of law enforcement functions. In the west they were "the law," as Marshal Virgil Earp and his deputies demonstrated at the famous shootout at the OK Corral in Tombstone, Arizona, in 1881.

Today the marshals provide court security for the federal court system and serve as bailiffs to the federal courts. The marshals guard prisoners while they are in court and when convicted transport them to the various correctional facilities. The marshals also enforce federal court orders; it was the U.S. Marshals that guarded the first African American students to be enrolled at Ole Miss in 1962. The marshal's service assumed responsibility for the administration of the witness protection program in 1971. Eight years later they were given the task of investigating and apprehending federal fugitives.[15]

Postal Inspection Service—can trace its roots back to 1830 with the creation of the Office of Instructions and Mail Depredations. Special Agents, as they were known at the time, investigated theft of mail and eventually would be given the responsibility for investigating mail frauds and the shipment of obscene materials through the mail. In 1880 the title of special agent was changed by Congress to post office inspector and changed again in 1954 to postal inspector.

Today in addition to mail frauds and mail theft, postal inspectors have jurisdiction over crimes that occur on postal property, including burglary, robbery, and homicide. In 1984 the inspection service was given the responsibility of investigating the use of the mail to distribute child pornography. Postal inspectors were a key component of the multi-agency task force that investigated the Unabomber case, one of the most extensive criminal investigations in modern history.[16]

Secret Service—was created in 1865 to suppress the counterfeiting of U.S. currency. The agencies responsibilities were broadened over the years to include the detection of criminals perpetrating frauds against the government. As a result, the agency investigated the Ku Klux Klan, nonconforming distillers, smugglers, mail robbers, land frauds, and a number of other federal crimes until other agencies were established to investigate them.

In 1902 congress gave the Secret Service the responsibility of protecting the president following the assassination of President McKinley. This role has been expanded over the years and now the agency provides protection for major presidential candidates, the president-elect, the president's immediate family, the vice president, and former presidents.

In 1984 Congress passed legislation making the use of fraudulent credit cards and debit cards a federal crime and authorized the Secret Service to investigate these violations as well as federal-interest computer fraud, and fraudulent identification documents such as passports. With the passage of the Patriot Act in 2001, Congress authorized the agency to establish nationwide electronic crimes taskforces to detect and suppress computer-based crimes. Since 2003 the Secret Service has been under the Department of Homeland Security. Since the reorganization, the agency has made over 29,000 arrests for counterfeiting, cyber investigations, and other financial crimes. They have seized over $295 million in counterfeit currency and closed financial crimes cases where the actual losses amounted to $3.7 billion.[17]

Federal Bureau of Investigation (FBI)—created in 1908 at a time when there were few federal crimes. With just thirty-four agents the agency investigated crimes involving national banking, bankruptcy, naturalization, antitrust, and land fraud. The first major expansion came in 1910 when the agency became responsible for the enforcement of the Mann Act, which prohibited the transportation of women across a state line for immoral purposes. With the entry of the United States into World War I the Bureau acquired responsibility for the investigation and enforcement of the Espionage Act, the Selective Service Act, and the Sabotage Act.

In 1924 J. Edgar Hoover became the director of the agency and he remained in this position until his death in 1972 just shy of forty-eight years as the director. During his tenure the agency assumed responsibility for the investigation of a variety of crimes, including kidnapping, civil rights violations, threats to national security, and organized crime. In 1932 the Bureau established its crime laboratory. In 1935 the agency changed its name from the Bureau of Investigation to the Federal Bureau of Investigation. Today the FBI has jurisdiction over violations of more than 200 categories of federal law. The agency's responsibilities include national security priorities such as counterterrorism, counterintelligence, and cyber crime. Its criminal priorities include investigations involving public corruption, civil rights, organized crime, white-collar crime, and major thefts.[18]

Bureau of Alcohol, Tobacco, Firearms and Explosives (ATF)—is a tax-collecting, enforcement, and regulatory arm of the U.S. Department of the Treasury. It is one of the youngest tax-collecting agencies, separated from the Internal Revenue Service in 1972. While the agency might be young, it can trace it roots back 200 years when Congress first imposed a tax on imported spirits. In 1863 Congress authorized the hiring of detectives to aid in the prevention, detection, and punishment of tax evaders. In 1875 federal investigators broke up the "Whiskey Ring," an association of grain dealers, politicians, and revenue agents who had defrauded the government of millions of dollars of tax revenue. Ratification of the Eighteenth Amendment to the Constitution in 1919 banned the manufacture or sale of intoxicating liquors in this country. One of the most illustrious "T-men," short for treasury men, involved in the enforcement of this law was Eliot Ness. He was responsible for bringing down Chicago's organized-crime king, Al Capone, on tax evasion charges.

In its original charter the ATF is tasked with the responsibility of enforcing the law relating to alcohol, tobacco, firearms, and explosives. In 1982 Congress passed the Anti-Arson Act declaring that arson is a federal crime and gave the ATF the responsibility for investigation of commercial arson nationwide. The agency has its own crime laboratory to support its field agents and runs the state-of-the-art Integrated Ballistic Identification System, a computerized matching program for weapons and the ammunition fired from them.[19]

Drug Enforcement Administration (DEA) was created by President Nixon through an executive order that merged several agencies into a single unified command to combat the global war on drugs. At the time of its formation the agency had 1,470 special agents and a budget of $75 million. Today the agency has over 5,000 agents and a budget in excess of $2 billion. The DEA has concurrent jurisdiction with the FBI domestically on controlling illegal drugs and has sole responsibility for coordinating these investigations abroad. Accordingly, the agency has eighty-seven foreign offices in sixty-three countries around the world.[20]

CASE STUDY

BETTY'S NEW CAR

Most investigations are reactive in that first a crime occurs, then police are notified, and then the investigation begins. Some investigations, however, are proactive. These investigations are based on facts that would lead an investigator to believe that crime is occurring or is about to occur. The following is an actual recounting of one of these two types of investigations.

It was late on a Friday afternoon in mid-summer and I was looking forward to relaxing over the weekend. I had a trainee all week and needed some alone-time. Before I took off I called the swing shift supervisor at one of the major postal processing facilities in my area of responsibility. This facility accounted for the bulk of the problems in terms of employee thefts of mail, and I liked to keep in touch in order to stay on top of any problems before they got out of hand. I contacted the supervisor and after a few moments of small talk he informed me it had been a slow week with no citizen complaints or discoveries of rifled mail in the restrooms. It is a common tactic for dishonest employees to take the mail into the restrooms, rip it open, steal the contents, and then dispose of the envelopes in the trash. He went on to mention that one of his employees by the name of Betty was driven to work by her husband in their brand new car, a Cadillac. Betty's name was familiar to me as she was a longtime postal employee with about twelve years of service. She had been suspected of employee theft on a number of occasions but these suspicions had not been confirmed through previous investigative efforts by other inspectors. The supervisor went on to state that he thought it was odd that Betty and her husband could afford such a vehicle as the husband was working as a short order cook at a local diner.

After hanging up the phone I started thinking about Betty and her new car. I thought that she would probably need some extra cash to cover the down payment or to make the first payment. I also reasoned that Betty probably thought that this would be a good night to steal whatever she could, because no postal inspector in his right mind would be working on a Friday night. My trainee agreed with this logic and said we should go to the facility and take a look at her. We arrived a few hours before Betty's shift ended. The supervisor was contacted to let him know we were there and he told us where Betty was working in the mail sorting area and gave us a clothing description so we could identify her.

(continued)

From a concealed position we were able to watch Betty while she worked. Her job was to sort the mail; she worked at a mail case that had a number of pigeon holes for the sorted mail. Her particular mail case contained a pigeon hole for a major charity in the area. Through my contacts with this charity I was aware that a large percentage of the donations they received was in the form of cash. It seems that many people, when they receive a solicitation for money, simply take a few bills out of their wallets, stick the bills in the envelope, and send it back to the charity. While watching Betty work, I noted that every once in a while she would take one of the charities' distinctly colored envelopes and place it on her sorting shelf rather that in the pigeon hole where it belonged. However, Betty was not demonstrating any of the other behaviors typical of dishonest employees. Most of the dishonest employees I had seen usually felt the envelopes, or held them up to the light to confirm that they contained cash, and most usually looked around to make sure they were not being watched. Betty did not do these things, but throughout the remainder of the shift the pile of charity letters on her shelf kept growing. At quitting time Betty swooped up all the letters and placed them in her purse and left the area.

My trainee and I met Betty on the sidewalk as she left the facility. She was advised that she was under arrest and escorted back inside the facility. Once in our office the contents of her purse were examined and 115 letters were recovered. The letters were opened and all but two contained cash. The total amount of cash contained in these letters was equal to the combined monthly salary of both Betty and her husband and was more than enough to cover her down payment on her new car. When confronted with the evidence against her, Betty decided to cooperate and supplied a full confession. During our conversation I told Betty we had suspected that she had been stealing from the post office for years. Betty did not respond to this allegation; however, she did not deny it either. Betty subsequently lost her job and pled guilty to a single charge of theft of mail.

CHAPTER REVIEW

Key Terms

anthropometry   *7*
blood-feuds or vendettas   *2*
bobbies   *4*
civil service system   *6*
constable   *2*
criminalistics   *7*

exchange principle   *8*
forensics   *7*
hue and cry   *2*
patronage   *5*
police gazette   *3*

posse comitatus   *2*
sheriff   *2*
spoils system   *5*
statute of winchester   *2*
toxicology   *7*

Review Questions

1. The Statute of Winchester of 1285 required all available citizens to respond to protect the community under what principle?
   a. *Hue and cry*
   b. *Posse comitatus*
   c. Spoils system
   d. Patronage

2. The person who is known today as the father of the modern police detective is:
   a. Sir John Fielding
   b. Sir Robert Peel
   c. August Vollmer
   d. J. Edgar Hoover

3. The person who is now recognized as the father of modern policing in America is:
   a. Sir John Fielding
   b. Sir Robert Peel
   c. August Vollmer
   d. J. Edgar Hoover

4. Early American police agencies typically hired police applicants based on the candidates' political connections rather than their ability to be a good police officer. This system of police hiring was known as:
   a. The spoils system
   b. The civil service system

c. Patronage

d. Corruption

5. The person who first developed a system of human identification, known as anthropometry, was:

a. Alphonse Bertillon

b. Calvin Goddard

c. Edmond Locard

d. Francis Galton

6. The scientist who theorized that when a criminal came into contact with another object or person, a cross-transference of evidence could occur was:

a. Alphonse Bertillon

b. Calvin Goddard

c. Edmond Locard

d. Francis Galton

7. The scientist who refined the technique necessary for the determination of whether or not a bullet was fired from a suspect weapon was:

a. Alphonse Bertillon

b. Calvin Goddard

c. Edmond Locard

d. Francis Galton

8. The study of the effects of poisons on the human body is known as:

a. Forensics

b. Typing

c. Anthropometry

d. Toxicology

9. The use of science to answer legal questions is known as:

a. Toxicology

b. Criminology

c. Forensics

d. Modus operandi

10. The federal law enforcement agency that would have jurisdiction in the event of a terrorist attack similar to the one on 9/11 would be the:

a. Marshal's Service

b. Secret Service

c. Federal Bureau of Investigation

d. Bureau of Alcohol, Tobacco, and Firearms

Application Exercise

Consider yourself to be a U.S. postal inspector and you specialize in employee theft of the mail. You are aware that in your area of responsibility there are several charities that receive a substantial amount of their contributions in the form of cash. The donors to these charities, when asked for a contribution, simply put a few bills in the response envelope and send it back to the charity. The employees at the post office where this mail is finally processed are well aware of the contents of these envelopes, especially the dishonest employees. When an employee does steal this mail, there is often no evidence of the theft and the investigation is therefore proactive rather than reactive. Review the case study and develop a strategy for dealing proactively to this potential problem and explain how you would proceed and who you would contact to assist you in this investigation.

Discussion Questions

1. After reading the case study would you say that this is a reactive or proactive investigation? Explain the reason for your choice.

2. Regarding the case study, what was the reason Betty was able to steal for such a long time without being caught?

3. Thief-takers were criminals who were paid a reward for capturing other criminals. Explain the problems that were associated with the use of these criminals to solve crime.

4. Contrast the early American policing efforts with those of the London Metropolitan Police and the results of these policing efforts.

5. Discuss the agenda of the reform movement in American policing and explain how this agenda was implemented.

6. Discuss the differences and the similarities between a municipal police department and a sheriff's department.

Related Websites

With over 37,000 sworn officers the New York City Police Department (NYPD) is the largest police department in the United States. To learn more about this agency visit their website at www.nyc.www.nypd/html/home/home.shtml

The largest sheriff's department in the United States is the Los Angeles County Sheriff's Department. To learn more about this agency visit their website at www.lasd.org

Want to know more about counterfeit money and the other investigations conducted by the U.S. Secret Service? Visit their website at www.secretservice.gov/index.shtml

Interested in knowing who is on the FBI's ten most wanted list? To find out, visit their website at www.fbi.gov

The California Highway Patrol is one of the best known of all the state law enforcement agencies. To learn more about this agency, visit their website at www.chp.ca.gov

Notes

1. Elaine A. Reynolds, *Before the Bobies, the Night Watch and Police Reform in Metropolitan London, 1720–1830* (Stanford, CA: Stanford University Press, 1998), 9.
2. Lawrence F. Travis and Robert H. Langworthy, *Policing in America: A Balance of Forces* (Upper Saddle River, NJ: Pearson Prentice Hall, 2008), 59–60.
3. John M. Beattie, *Policing and Punishment in London, 1660–1750: Urban Crime and the Limits of Terror* (Oxford, England: Oxford University Press, 2001), 173–177.
4. Clive Emsley and Haia Shpayer-Makov, *Police Detectives in History, 1750–1950* (Burlington, VT: Ashgate Publishing, 2006), 16–17.
5. Leonard A. Steverson, *Policing in America: A Reference Handbook* (Santa Barbara, CA: ABD-CLIO, 2008), 7–8.
6. Travis and Langworthy, *Policing in America,* 64–65.
7. Ibid., 70–71.
8. Samuel Walker and Charles M. Katz, *The Police in America, and Introduction,* 4th ed. (Boston, MA: McGraw Hill, 2002), 28–29.
9. Steverson, *Policing in America,* 15–17.
10. Walker and Katz, *The Police in America,* 33–34.
11. Travis and Langworthy, *Policing in America,* 96–101.
12. Richard Saferstein, *Criminalistics and Introduction to Forensic Science* (Upper Saddle River, NJ: Pearson Prentice Hall, 2004), 2–5.
13. Richard Saferstein, *Forensic Science: From the Crime Scene to the Crime Lab* (Upper Saddle River, NJ: Pearson Prentice Hall, 2009), 465.
14. U.S. Department of Justice, Bureau of Justice Statistics, *Sourcebook of Criminal Justice Statistics 2002* (Washington, DC: Government Printing Office, 2004), 39.
15. www.Usmarshals.gov/history/timeling.html.
16. www.postalinspectors.uspis.gov/aboutus/Histroy.aspx.
17. www.secretservice.gov/history.shtml.
18. www.fbi.gov/libref/historic/history/text.htm.
19. www.atf.gov/about/history/atf-from-1789-1998.html.
20. www.justice.gov/dea/history.htm.

2 Rules of Evidence and Arrest

CHAPTER OUTLINE

LEARNING OBJECTIVES

After reading this chapter, you will be able to:

1 *Define the process for obtaining a search warrant and the information required in the warrant application.*

2 *Recognize that a person may waive the search warrant requirements by consenting to a search.*

3 *Explain the concept of "stop and frisk" and the justifications for taking this action.*

4 *Explain the situations that would place an investigator in a lawful position to view and seize evidence according to the "plain view" exception.*

5 *Discuss the scope of a search incidental to a lawful arrest.*

6 *Discuss the justification for the motor vehicle exception to the search warrant requirement.*

7 *Explain what are considered to be "open fields" and whether these areas are protected by the Fourth Amendment.*

8 *Appreciate what is meant by the term* exigent circumstances *and what justification must exist to allow a warrantless entry and search.*

9 *Contrast the legal justification for a detention versus an arrest.*

10 *Define the guidelines used for the application for an arrest warrant.*

11 *Discuss how broadcast alarms, records inquiries, and wanted notices are used to locate suspects.*

12 *Define the conditions under which additional items of evidence may be gathered at the time of an arrest of a suspect.*

13 *Explain who in the criminal justice system is responsible for making the decision to charge a suspect with a crime and what steps are involved in making this decision.*

14 *Discuss the various reasons an investigation may be closed without making an arrest.*

No evidence is admissible in a court of law unless it is relevant. **Relevance** is the connection between a fact offered in evidence and the issue to be proved. Evidence must also be material. An item of evidence is considered material if it is important or substantial, that is, capable of properly influencing the outcome of the trial. Evidence becomes immaterial when it is so unimportant compared to other easily available evidence that the court should not waste time admitting it. The third and most contentious criterion is that evidence must also be obtained lawfully. A search for evidence must be reasonable, and any search conducted as a result of a lawful warrant is, on its face, reasonable. However, a number of exceptions apply to the search warrant requirement. The court's remedy for the handling of evidence seized illegally is to exclude the evidence from trial.

1 *Define the process for obtaining a search warrant and the information required in the warrant application.*

▶ Search Warrants

The Fourth Amendment to the U.S. Constitution provides protections against unreasonable searches and seizures by all government officials and reads as follows:

> The right of the people to be secure in their persons, houses, papers, and effects, against unreasonable searches and seizures, shall not be violated, and no Warrants shall issue, but upon probable cause, supported by Oath or affirmation, and particularly describing the place to be searched, and the persons or things to be seized.

This amendment is intended to provide a means of balancing society's need to deal with criminals and criminal activity with the need to protect individual rights. The issuance of a warrant makes a search reasonable by placing an unbiased third party—a magistrate or judge—in the process. The role of the magistrate is to review the application for a search warrant and determine if the request is reasonable and meets the guidelines established by the Fourth Amendment. The magistrate will determine reasonableness by considering all the circumstances in each case.

To obtain a search warrant, an investigator must prepare a written application that outlines the probable cause for the search and describes the place to be searched and the person or things to be seized. The investigator must swear, or affirm, to the **magistrate** that the information contained in the warrant application is true.

Probable cause, as used in the warrant requirement, exists when enough facts lead a reasonable and prudent person to believe that criminal activity is fairly probable. This standard of proof is well below what is required at a criminal trial: guilt beyond a reasonable doubt. For example, an undercover police officer making a buy of illegal drugs at a residence would be sufficient probable cause to lead a reasonable and prudent person to believe that controlled substances were being sold at that location.

For the description of the place to be searched, the investigator must provide sufficient detail in the warrant application to identify the location of the requested search. In urban areas, a street address—with an apartment number, if applicable—would be required. In rural areas the court may be more flexible and allow a general description, such as "a yellow house with a detached barn located on Mill Pond Road one half mile north of Highway 212."

For the description of the persons or things to be seized, the investigator must outline exactly what is being sought, as an approved warrant is not a license to rummage through a person's home or personal effects. Usually the type of crime being investigated will dictate where the investigator can search. The investigation of stolen 42-inch plasma TV sets, for example, would allow a search of any area where a TV set could be hidden or stored; the search of smaller areas, such as a dresser, would not be allowed as a TV set could not be hidden there and such a search would, therefore, be unreasonable.

The application for a search warrant must be supported by **oath or affirmation** as required by the Fourth Amendment. This means that the investigator must raise his or her right hand before the magistrate and swear—or affirm, if he or she does not believe in God—that the information is true and correct to the best of his or her knowledge under the penalty of perjury. This means that an investigator could be charged with a crime if he or she knowingly presents false information in a search warrant application.

A plain-clothes detective swearing to the judge that the information contained in a warrant application is true.
Source: © Mikael Karlsson/Alamy

In emergency situations, an investigator can obtain a search warrant by telephone. The investigator must prepare a written application for a warrant as if for an appearance in court. The written warrant request is then read over the telephone to the magistrate, who then transcribes what is read in order to prepare the warrant. The magistrate has the investigator swear to the truthfulness of the application. The authorization for the search warrant, if granted, is authorized over the phone and made available in the magistrate's court the following business day, at which time the investigator must pick up the warrant.

Search warrants must be executed within a prescribed time period, normally within ten days. The magistrate or the legislature, by law, can limit the time of execution to daylight hours only, as well as to no weekend or holiday service. The restrictions of the Fourth Amendment do not apply to private persons as long as they are not acting as agents of the government.[1]

▶ Warrantless Searches

While conducting a search with a lawful warrant is a reasonable process, it is not always practical. Emergency situations, the possible destruction of evidence, and other considerations make obtaining a warrant impractical at times. The U.S. Supreme Court has defined as reasonable some specific searches that may be conducted without a warrant. These exceptions to the warrant requirement include consent searches, stop and frisks, plain view exceptions, searches incident to a lawful arrest, motor vehicle stops, open fields, and emergency circumstances.

❷ *Recognize that a person may waive the search warrant requirements by consenting to a search.*

Consent Search

A person can voluntarily consent to the police to search his or her person, home, and property. Any evidence found as a result of a **consent search** is admissible in court. The consent to search the person of an individual can be given only by that individual. The waiver of the Fourth Amendment is a personal right and can be waived only by the affected individual. Consent to search property can be given only by the actual owner or by a person in charge of that property.

A person has an absolute right to refuse to consent to a search when asked by the police and may revoke consent at any time. When a person agrees to a consent search, the investigator should obtain the consent in writing to substantiate the voluntariness of the consent and subsequent search.

The courts have held that a consent search was unreasonable if the consent was obtained by deceit, trickery, or misrepresentation by investigators. The courts typically justify consent searches by the voluntariness test: the consent was obtained without coercion or promises and was, therefore, reasonable.[2]

❸ *Explain the concept of "stop and frisk" and the justifications for taking this action.*

Stop and Frisk

The U.S. Supreme Court has held that a police officer may temporarily detain a person for questioning if the officer has a reasonable suspicion that criminal activity may be involved. The person may also be patted down for weapons if the officer has the additional **reasonable suspicion** that the pat-down was necessary for officer safety. Such a temporary **stop and frisk** detention is not considered to be an arrest. A temporary detention is based on reasonable suspicion, which is less than the necessary probable cause needed for an arrest.

Reasonable suspicion for a detention must be based on facts that can be articulated in court. The investigator must have a reasonable suspicion that criminal activity is occurring, is about to occur, or has recently occurred, and that the person or vehicle to be detained is related to that criminal activity. The detention must be fairly short in duration and only long enough to clarify the reasons for the detention. Any evidence discovered during this detention would be admissible in court.[3]

4 *Explain the situations that would place an investigator in a lawful position to view and seize evidence according to the "plain view" exception.*

Plain View Exception

The **plain view exception** permits investigators to observe and seize evidence without a warrant if the officer is lawfully in a position to view an object and if the incriminating character of the object is immediately apparent. In a number of situations, law enforcement officers may make a seizure of evidence based on the plain view exception.

- *Effecting an arrest.* An officer may lawfully seize an object that comes into view during a lawfully executed arrest or search incident to arrest.

- *Executing a search warrant.* An officer executing a valid search warrant can legally seize items of evidence lying in plain view even though they were not specifically described in the warrant.

- *Pursuing a fleeing suspect.* Officers who are lawfully on the premises in hot pursuit of a dangerous person may seize items of evidence in plain view.

- *Responding to an emergency.* Officers responding to emergency situations, such as crimes in progress or crimes of violence, shooting, stabbings, etc., may seize items of evidence in plain view.[4]

5 *Discuss the scope of a search incidental to a lawful arrest.*

Search Incident to a Lawful Arrest

The U.S. Supreme Court has recognized that police officers have the authority to conduct a warrantless **search incident to a lawful arrest**. The scope of this search includes the person of the arrestee, including a wallet or purse immediately associated with the arrestee. Also included in the scope of this search is the area into which the arrestee could reach at the time of the arrest to retrieve a weapon or to destroy evidence. The officers may also search adjoining areas for persons posing a threat to the officers or the arrest scene. This search must be made contemporaneously with the arrest, and any items of evidence in plain view may be seized.[5]

 Discuss the justification for the motor vehicle exception to the search warrant requirement.

Motor Vehicle Stop

The U.S. Supreme Court has created an exception to the warrant requirement for motor vehicles due to their mobility; their use as transportation to and from crime scenes; and their use in transporting weapons, stolen goods, and contraband. A lawful search under the **motor vehicle exception** requires the existence of probable cause to believe that the vehicle contains evidence of a crime, or contraband, and that the searching officers have lawful access to the vehicle. Other mobile conveyances, such as motor homes, houseboats, and airplanes, are included in this exception. In the case of *Arizona v. Gant* the court allowed a warrantless search of a vehicle passenger area if the person has access to the vehicle at the time of the search, in other words not detained, and a reasonable belief exists that evidence related to the crime in question may be found in the vehicle.[6]

Locked containers, such as vehicle trunks and suitcases, may also be searched without a warrant, provided probable cause exists relating to these locked containers. In other words, the scope of the warrantless search is no broader or narrower than if a search warrant had been obtained.[7]

In the interest of public safety, vehicles are frequently taken into police custody when the driver is arrested or intoxicated or if the vehicle is used in a crime or has been reported stolen. The impound procedure involves the police taking possession of the vehicle and moving it to a secure area for safekeeping. Once in police custody, the police are potentially liable for the vehicle and its contents. Therefore, the courts allow the inventorying of the vehicle's contents. The inventory procedure is not a search but rather a routine administrative custodial procedure. However, if contraband or items of evidence are observed during the inventory, they may lawfully be seized and are admissible as evidence in court.[8]

 Explain what are considered to be "open fields" and whether these areas are protected by the Fourth Amendment.

Open Fields

The U.S. Supreme Court has held that **open fields** are not protected by the Fourth Amendment and that investigators may enter and search unoccupied or undeveloped areas. The rationale here is that only "homes, person, effects and paper" are protected by the Fourth Amendment and that there is a lesser expectation of privacy in open fields. The term *open fields* includes open lands and forests. Even if ownership of the area is posted, the area may be searched without a warrant. The exception would be the area immediately surrounding a dwelling, known as the **curtilage**.[9]

8 *Appreciate what is meant by the term* exigent circumstances *and what justification must exist to allow a warrantless entry and search.*

Exigent Circumstances

Investigators who have established probable cause that evidence is likely to be at a certain place may make a warrantless entry into the premises if exigent or **emergency circumstances** exist. Such circumstances include the following:

1. A reasonable belief that the evidence may be immediately destroyed
2. Hot pursuit of a suspect whom the investigators reasonably believe is in the area to be searched

3. An immediate need to protect or preserve life
4. A threat to the safety of the officers conducting a protective sweep of the premises, for other suspects[10]

▶ Exclusionary Rule

The **exclusionary rule** is applied when investigators violate a person's constitutional rights by conducting an unlawful search and seizure. This rule prevents illegally obtained evidence from being admitted into evidence. This is the method the courts use to uphold the Fourth Amendment and to control investigator's actions and prevent illegally obtained evidence from being used at trial. An extension of the exclusionary rule is the "fruit of the poisonous tree doctrine," which holds that evidence derived from an illegal search or seizure is inadmissible because of its original taint.

9 *Contrast the legal justification for a detention versus an arrest.*

▶ Arrest vs. Detention

Typically police encounters with the public fall within three categories. The first is the voluntary or consensual stop which is the least intrusive. This encounter is limited in scope by the consent given by the person being encountered and that person can terminate the encounter at any time. The second type of encounter is the investigative detention or stop and frisk encounter discussed previously. In this type of encounter the investigator must have some specific and articulable facts supporting a reasonable suspicion that criminal activity is occurring or about to occur or has recently occurred. This type of detention is limited in time and scope to what is necessary to confirm or refute the suspicion that criminal activity is occurring or about to occur. During this investigative detention the suspect is not free to leave and reasonable force may be used to detain the person.

The third type of encounter is an arrest, which is the most intrusive. A legal arrest must be based on probable cause which is that point in time when an investigator has reason to believe that a crime was or is about to be committed and that the individual to be arrested has engaged in the criminal activity.[11] These types of arrest usually occur when the crime has just occurred and the person to be arrested is in the presence of the investigator. In this type of situation an arrest warrant is not necessary.

⑩ *Define the guidelines used for the application for an arrest warrant.*

▶ Arrest Warrants

Arrest warrants are necessary when a person to be arrested is unavailable or his or her identity is not known at the time. The arrest warrant empowers any officer to make an arrest upon confirmation of the warrant even though the officer is unaware of the particulars of the crime. The procedure of obtaining an arrest warrant is similar to the procedure for obtaining a search warrant. A presentation is made to a judge, in writing, stating the known facts which establish the existence of the probable cause for the issuance of the arrest warrant. The following are the guidelines for the application of an arrest warrant.

1. The warrant must describe the offense charged and contain the name of the accused, or if the name is unknown, a description of the accused.
2. The warrant must also indicate the time of issuance, the city or county and state where it is issued, and the duty of the arresting officer to bring the defendant before the magistrate.
3. It is directed to, and thus may be acted on, by any peace officer in the jurisdiction. A warrant issued in a state court is enforceable by any peace officer in that state.
4. Arrest warrants, unlike search warrants, are valid until they are recalled by the court.
5. The arrest warrant can specify the amount of bail needed by the accused to be released from custody.

An investigator making an arrest pursuant to warrant need not have the warrant in his or her possession, as long as he or she is aware of its contents. If the investigator has the warrant, he or she must display or show the warrant, if requested, to the person being arrested. If the investigator does not have the warrant in his or her possession, he or she must explain to the person being arrested the reason for the arrest.[12]

⑪ *Discuss how broadcast alarms, records inquiries, and wanted notices are used to locate suspects.*

▶ Locating the Suspect

The accused person may be known and easily located. On the other hand, the suspect's name may not be known, and he or she may have no known address or may be in hiding or in flight. Early in the investigation, an alarm or a pickup order containing only fragmentary identification is broadcast locally. Its purpose is to apprehend the perpetrator in flight. When the initial hue and cry alarm has failed, the investigators must collect and publish more detailed information about the perpetrator. This is the means by which other officers, distant in time and space from the crime, locate and identify a person in flight from justice.

The tracing of fugitives depends a great deal on the expertise with which sources of information are exploited for adequate and meaningful information about the wanted person. Although the crime and its circumstances provide the basic information, data about the suspect as a person also are available to a diligent investigator in the records of criminal justice agencies, credit reports, telephone records, employment histories, and public records. Basic research often rewards the investigator with meaningful information.

An arrest brings the investigation into close focus. The prisoner can be searched and booked, and, in the process of recording facts, fingerprinted for positive identification. Evidence that can be collected at this time will be collected, recorded, and preserved. The prisoner may be anxious to talk to the police and may deny or admit to being the criminal. This is the time to warn arrested persons of their constitutional rights to silence and legal counsel, and it is the time to ascertain if the accused person will waive such rights and participate in an interrogation session by cooperating with the investigator.

▶ The Broadcast Alarm

The initial radio transmission, or **broadcast alarms**, would alert officers in the field of the pursuit of a suspect of a crime and emphasizes the distinctive identifying characteristics of the person, vehicle, or property wanted. The first police officer on the scene of a crime or the investigator receiving the report of a crime has the responsibility of obtaining the best possible physical description of the criminal and his or her vehicle, if any. A broadcast alarm detailing a want is most effective when it is sent promptly.

Despite the urgency for broadcasting the alarm or pickup order to alert other officers, accuracy must be emphasized. Law enforcement agents no longer ask leading questions to obtain descriptions, and they emphasize in their reports that the description is a composite inasmuch as it usually is secured from both victim and witnesses. Officers do not change the composite description once it is entered in their field notes or other records, nor do they change the composite description when the wanted person is arrested or when a wanted vehicle is recovered and found to differ from the composite description.

Identifying characteristics that make a person or a vehicle different from other persons or vehicles are the basis for success in the apprehension of suspects. Partial descriptions, if distinctive, such as a damaged fender on a vehicle coupled with a fragment of the registration number, have resulted in apprehensions. In cases involving juveniles, a painted identification or other marking on the car may be very distinctive.

The content of wanted notices at this time in the investigation is oriented toward characteristics that are observable and that will guide searching police. Although a brief description of the crime (including the proceeds of a theft) is included, the major content usually is limited to describing persons, vehicles, and weapons.

The brief description of the crime is no more than the offense the offender is suspected of committing and the date, time, and location of occurrence. Stolen property is not described, but a few details of the amount of currency taken or the kind of item stolen are included. If a weapon was used, its type and description are included in the broadcast to alert police that the fleeing suspect is likely to be dangerous.

When more than one perpetrator is described, a listing by number (Suspect No. 1, Suspect No. 2, etc.) is recommended. The following characteristics, in the order listed, are standard for these notices: race, sex, adult or juvenile, age, height, weight, build, hair color, eye color, any distinguishing marks. A suspect's height and weight are usually reported in blocks or ranges: upward from 5 feet in 3-inch intervals, and from 100 pounds in 20-pound intervals.

Clothing is an observable characteristic that affords excellent opportunities for recognizing a wanted person. In the "How Dressed" section of a wanted notice, the clothing of each suspect is described, and the color, cloth, and design of the outer garments are noted. The absence of garments normally worn by others in the area is also noted. The following items, in the order listed, are standard in such alarms or pickup orders across the United States: bareheaded; hat (color and design: black, gray, porkpie, skimpy brim); cap (color); overcoat (color, cloth, design); jacket (color, cloth, windbreaker); suit (color, cloth, design); shirt (color, dress, or sport); trousers or shorts (color); dress, slacks, or shorts (color, cloth, design).

Vehicle descriptions in these alarms or pickup orders generally are limited to the following: year, make, model, color, state license number, damage or suspected damage, number and sex of occupants. The usual categories of sedan, station wagon, van, convertible, and sports car have been supplemented by pickup, "crew" pickup, jeep, and pickup with camper.

The direction of flight, if it is known, is also included. Roadblocks may be set up, and buses and other public transportation vehicles may be searched. A surveillance of the area may be conducted for criminals who seek refuge temporarily by hiding in yards, basements, hallways, and on roofs along the escape route.

The initial notices usually are concluded with a statement of the authority for the alarm or pickup order—at the local level, the name of the investigator and assignment; at other levels, the name of the issuing police department.

All broadcast alarms are distributed locally, but their coverage is expanded as the interval from the time of the crime indicates the possible enlargement of areas of flight. An **all points bulletin (APB)** is justified when adequate descriptive information is available. The geographical coverage of an APB depends on the locale and may extend to neighboring states.

As facts become available to investigators during the search, it becomes urgent to add information to what was originally broadcast. This added information may be simply a notice that the vehicle, when located, should be protected but not processed until the evidence technicians can visit the scene and search the vehicle for fingerprints and other evidence. Additional facts on the identity of a vehicle, such as the full license number and the name and description of the registered owner, may relate to information secured from the state's Department of Motor Vehicles. Additional knowledge about the suspect may relate to no more than a fragment of information about appearance, but it may be a full name and description of the perpetrator when a prompt and specific identification has been made. The objective of broadcasting facts as soon as they are available is to provide searching police with enough identification to pick out a fleeing person or vehicle with some certainty that the person or vehicle being stopped is the subject of the alarm.

Records as Sources of Information

Agencies that may provide an investigator with information useful in locating a fugitive range from criminal justice agencies that might have processed the suspect at some previous time to the vast data banks of agencies providing credit or telephone service. Investigators should develop their own ready-reference file as to sources of information. In working on an investigation, the assigned investigator has a general idea what he or she is looking for, and a ready-reference information sources file will provide information as to where such information may be found, the form in which it may be found, and how to gain access to it.

A suggested form for a file of this type includes type of information, source, name, and other identification data of a "contact" (e.g., telephone number).[13]

Among the sources of information are the following:

1. *City and County.* Vital statistics; tax, welfare, courts, schools, jurors, and voting records; prosecutor and public defender.

2. *State.* Tax and corporate records; courts and alcohol beverage records; consumer affairs data; motor vehicle license and registration files.

3. *Federal.* Federal Bureau of Investigation, and other federal law enforcement agencies such as the Secret Service, Immigration and Customs Enforcement, Postal Inspection Service, Securities and Exchange Commission, and military investigative agencies.

4. *Private.* Moving companies; telephone company (public directory and directories on file at company office) and other public utilities; credit reporting agencies; banks and finance companies; Better Business Bureau, Chamber of Commerce, business (trade) directories, industry and trade associations, professional associations, etc.[14]

5. *Fusion centers.* In a unified effort, local and federal law enforcement agencies are contributing intelligence information to combat threats from terrorism and criminal networks.

▶ Wanted Notices

A **wanted notice** should provide full information about the fugitive and about areas in which he or she is likely to be found. Copies are sent to police in neighboring areas and mailed, faxed, or sent electronically to police in areas that the fugitive is likely to visit, usually large cities and resort centers in adjacent states. If an arrest warrant has been issued for this person, an entry can be made in the National Crime Information Center (NCIC) system for this person in their wanted person's database.

The basic content of a wanted notice is a photograph or sketch of the fugitive, his or her fingerprints, and an extensive personal description (Figure 2-1). The standard mug shot taken at the time of a previous arrest is made part of the wanted notice. When this is not available, any close-up photograph from public records or from associates of the suspect may be substituted. Full-length shots of the suspect alone or with a group of associates can be used to supplement the standard front and profile photographs. Ideally, color photography and printing should be used in wanted notices because they offer a lifelike image of the wanted person.

The fingerprint classification of a fugitive in the wanted notice is a major point of identification. Often these notices contain a facsimile of the fingerprints of a suspect, and a comparison can be made by the local agency making the arrest. In recent years, the fingerprinting of persons

ARMED ROBBERY SUSPECT

Date:	**2/23/2005**
Case #	**00-0070**
Height:	**5 Feet 9 inches**
Weight:	**160**
Age:	**20**
Sex:	**M**
Race:	**White**

OTHER INFORMATION BELOW

On Monday, 2-14-05, approximately 11 P.M., a university professor was robbed on the pathway between Green and Gray Halls at Valley University. The suspects assaulted the victim with a stun gun and departed with his wallet. The suspects are described as follows:

1. White male, early 20s, 5'9" to 5'10", 160 to 180 lb., sparse, straggly beard. He was wearing a dark blue sweatshirt with some type of writing on it. (A composite of the suspect is shown above.)

2. White male, early 20s, no further description.

3. Hispanic female, early 20s, 5'0" to 5'2", 100 to 105 lb., described as "petite."

The University Police at Valley University are asking the public's help in identifying the suspects.

University Police Department, Valley University **(555) 555-5555**

TRAK (136:1.6.48) This flyer produced on a TRAK system. For more information about TRAK see www.trak.org

FIGURE 2-1 Typical Wanted Notice.

not charged with a crime has increased, and these records are available to police agencies preparing wanted notices. It is the classification and comparison of fingerprints that guarantee against the apprehension of the wrong person. Any other type of identification always includes the possibility of error. For this reason, investigators should search diligently for a fingerprint record for the wanted notice.

Observable and distinctive characteristics are used in describing a person. Identifying physical characteristics are necessary to locate the fugitive and to offer some positive identification for an arrest.

The standard base of details for describing wanted persons is race, sex, age, height, weight, color of eyes, and color of hair. Racial appearance and national origin are also identifying characteristics. Many police units use a standard listing and suggest that the most descriptive designation applicable to the fugitive be used. The usual list includes White, African American, Mexican, Indian, Chinese, and Japanese.

Observable physical characteristics found useful by police in tracing fugitives have been codified in a "relevant matter" listing of key items for a personal description. The following are the items of identity believed to be important:

1. *Face*—shape
2. *Hair*—color, type, and cut
3. *Eyes*—color, type, and defects
4. *Nose*—shape and size
5. *Mouth*—shape, size, and unusual characteristics
6. *Chin*—shape, size, and if dimpled
7. *Ears*—type, size, and defects
8. *Eyebrows and beard*—appearance
9. *Scars and marks*—location and type
10. *Amputations and deformities*
11. *Speech*
12. *Peculiarities*

In using these relevant characteristics, a person may be described in great detail—for example, round faced with long, red, wavy hair; blue, bulging, crossed eyes with hooded lids; a broken nose; a wide mouth with full lips; a receding chin; flaring ears; bushy eyebrows meeting in the center; long sideburns, mustache, and light beard; a forehead scar about one inch long over the right eye; needle marks on the left arm; and walking with a pronounced limp.

A fugitive's occupation, associates, friends, relatives, habits, and hobbies are often significant factors in a police hunt. A person's occupation or profession is often a form of habituation. Known criminal associates are likely to offer promising leads, and data on relatives and friends may suggest promising areas of inquiry. Habits and hobbies are related to places frequented or areas in which the fugitive is likely to be found. Amusement and resort areas may offer promise; theatrical and cabaret districts may also be indicated. This field is wide open to innovative practices by both the investigator preparing the wanted notice and police seeking the fugitive.

A final segment of the description of a fugitive concerns whether he or she may resist arrest. All investigators seeking the apprehension of a fugitive have a duty to specify in every wanted notice whether the fugitive is armed, whether a weapon has been used in crime, and whether the fugitive has used weapons on previous occasions to avoid capture or to escape from custody. "Armed and dangerous" may seem a cliché, but the unnecessary injury and death of arresting officers are not routine and can be avoided by adequate notice. Officers staffing roadblocks and stopping suspicious cars on the highway late at night usually are prepared for any aggressive action initiated by the occupants of a vehicle. However, on many other occasions officers likely to be met in the pursuit of a fugitive are not always as alert to possible aggression unless they are warned in advance.

Armed with the knowledge that a person is wanted, all police seek fugitives as part of the general police role. Traffic officers making so-called routine stops have apprehended fugitives. Police on patrol, in responding to a call for help or in handling a minor crime investigation, have encountered fugitives and taken them into custody. Investigators allow some time daily for inquiries about wanted persons.

Investigators, however, must exercise care in questioning people about a fugitive. They may encounter a person who knows the whereabouts of the suspect but who is more friendly with the fugitive than with the police. A warning to the suspect of the inquiries being made may result in flight, and an excellent chance for capture will be lost forever.

Traditionally, a wanted notice has always been aimed solely at locating and apprehending the fugitive. It now has an additional purpose: to discover, to collect, and to preserve evidence at the time of the arrest. The four purposes of a modern wanted notice for a fugitive from criminal justice are these:

1. To provide sufficient identifying characteristics (constituting reasonable grounds for belief) to allow other law enforcement agents to provisionally identify the fugitive upon initial contact and to make positive identification when the suspect is taken into custody

2. To alert other law enforcement officers to the nature and character of the fugitive, his or her criminal history, and if armed and dangerous

3. To suggest activities and areas in which a search or surveillance may locate the fugitive

4. To delineate the crime in sufficient detail to alert arresting officers to potential legally significant evidence available at the time of arrest

⑫ *Define the conditions under which additional items of evidence may be gathered at the time of an arrest of a suspect.*

▶ The Arrest

Investigators assemble evidence to establish probable cause before they attempt to arrest a suspect in a case. Of course, a great deal of meaningful evidence may be collected at the time of the arrest that will connect the prisoner with the crime, the crime scene, the victim, or other crimes and other criminals. The arrest is also an excellent time to guard against faulty identification of the arrestee.

All arresting officers should be alert to the nature and type of evidence that might normally be encountered at the time of arrest. In collecting evidence at this time, the finding officer must exercise the same care he or she would use if the evidence had been discovered in a crime scene search. The officer finding the evidence should make an appropriate entry in his or her field notes and in the records of the arrest, mark it for identification, and protect its integrity.

The search incidental to an arrest may not only recover the proceeds of a theft but may also produce transfer evidence that will link the suspect with the crime, the scene, or the victim. The search should be confined to the person of the arrested individual and to the vicinity of the arrest.[15] A complete body search is made at the time of booking. In serious crimes, it is not uncommon to seize the suspect's clothes for processing by a vacuum cleaner in an effort to collect dust and debris for analysis and to search the clothes for blood and other stains that may connect the defendant with the crime scene or victim.

The search of a person should not verge on conduct that shocks the conscience, such as in the case of *Rochin v. California*, in which an offender's stomach was pumped in order to recover two capsules of heroin.[16] The search should fulfill the obligation of an arresting officer by protecting the officer from harm by removing any material that might aid in the escape of the arrested person and by avoiding the destruction of evidence or the failure to collect evidence.

The doctrine of **immediate control** indicates the area in which a search is justified. If the arrest is made on the street when the suspect is walking, his or her person and the immediate public area may be searched. If the arrest takes place in a vehicle, the vehicle may be searched if the guidance established from the case of *Arizona v. Gant* is met. In this case the court allows a warrantless search of a vehicle passenger area if the arrestee has access to the vehicle at the time of the search, in other words not detained, and a reasonable belief exists that evidence related to the crime in question may be found in the vehicle.[17] If the arresting officer witnessed the jettisoning of some article just before the arrest, he or she should search for such article. If the arrest is made inside a building, the search usually is restricted to the area over which the arrested person has control. (See Appendix A: Case Briefs, Chimel.)

The police department issuing the wanted notice is notified of an arrest, cancels the want by issuing a notice of the arrest, and makes the necessary arrangements to pick up the prisoner. If the locale of the arrest is outside the state in which the crime was committed, extradition proceedings, unless formally waived by the fugitive, are required.

When a perpetrator is arrested locally, the search incidental to the arrest may involve the home of the prisoner if it is the place of arrest. Burglars and thieves in possession of recently stolen property often conceal it in their homes. Experienced detectives know that there is a great deal of promise in inspecting the residence of a suspect in burglary and theft cases. The current doctrine is to seek search warrants when looking for evidence in any building during the postarrest period unless the search is incidental to the arrest. The investigator, citing the fact that an arrest has been made, should be able to establish probable cause for a search of a specific location for particular items of evidence. The investigator can arrange for surveillance of the premises to be searched, which will secure it from disturbance while the warrant is being obtained. The search warrant prevents the tainting of evidence. It is a straightforward matter to conduct a search pursuant to a warrant and to fully report the results to the court.

An investigator may ask the arrested person to consent to a search of an office or residence. If another person has dual or joint control of such premises, consent should also be requested of such individual. Landlords and managers of multiple housing or office structures can consent to a search only of the so-called public portions of such buildings and cannot consent to the search of a room, apartment, or office under the sole control of a tenant. Since the *Miranda* decision, the compelling atmosphere of police custody has been delineated as inherently in conflict with the intelligent waiver of any constitutional right. Therefore, the waiver should be formal, should state that it is a voluntary act, and should be signed by the prisoner and by a witness. Ideally, the police should discuss with the prisoner the nature of the evidence and where in the premises it will be found. A postarrest consent to search is not illogical conduct if the arrestee is cooperating with police, and it should be requested.

▶ Case Preparation

Case preparation is organization. It is the orderly array of information collected during an investigation: all the reports, documents, and exhibits in a case. It is also the preparation of a synopsis of the individual material in the case, an abstract written without personal conclusions, opinions, or facts. A so-called final report is undesirable; the collected reports and other data constitute the final report—the package forwarded to the prosecutor. The investigator does not intrude. The case synopsis is no more than a summary of the package contents. In the evaluation of a case in this pretrial period, investigators must discriminate between evidential material and personal conclusions and opinions, between potential evidence and facts. In a criminal action, fact leads to truth, and courts admit relevant evidence at trial to determine fact.

Case preparation is the round-up time of an investigation. The investigator collates the work of the entire investigation, confers with associates, prepares the case folder and its synopsis, forwards the case to the prosecutor for preparation of the formal accusatory pleading and the legal development of the case before trial, and marks the case closed by arrest.

The Defendant's Identity

The identification of an individual as the person accused of the crime leads to an array of witnesses and evidence. Identification usually results from some combination of testimony and other evidence. This evidence structure is sometimes supported by a pretrial statement made by the accused person and is oriented toward proving the identity of the person responsible for the crime alleged in the indictment or information, the **accusatory pleading**.

Guidelines to evidence likely to have legal significance in establishing the identity of the person or persons responsible for a crime can be summarized as follows:

1. A witness (or witnesses) who has seen the suspect commit the crime or some part of it
2. A witness (or witnesses) who has seen the suspect at the crime scene at or about the time of the crime
3. A witness (or witnesses) who observed the suspect in the neighborhood of the crime at or about the time of occurrence
4. Physical evidence discovered in the crime scene search that indicates that the suspect was at the crime scene or in contact with the victim
5. Physical evidence found on the suspect or among his or her effects at the time of arrest, or secured by other lawful means, that indicates that the offender had been at the crime scene or in contact with the victim
6. Connect-ups:
   a. the suspect possessing the vehicle that witnesses will testify was used in this crime
   b. the suspect having the proceeds of the crime (in theft and burglary cases)
   c. the suspect having an unexplained injury (in assaults and homicides)
   d. the suspect having the weapon used in the crime
   e. the suspect having been interviewed by an officer at or near the crime scene at or about the time of the crime (the officer having reported it in the regular course of business and being available to so testify)

These guidelines appear to embody a potentially formidable array of witnesses and evidence, but they must be evaluated against the background of the possible defenses the accused person might raise, such as the following:

1. Variances in the original descriptions and the actual description of the accused person
2. Other errors in evidence or variances in statements of witnesses
3. A well-supported claim of **alibi**—being elsewhere at the time of the crime
4. A widespread distrust of eyewitness identification because of the many publicized mistakes in such identifications

The Defendant and the Corpus Delicti

The accusatory pleading must show that at a specified time and date in a specific place, the named person committed an act or omission in violation of a particular law specified by both name and section number and in force at the time of the act or omission. Therefore, the first major area of case evaluation is the affirmative evidence of a real-life **corpus delicti**—the classic "body of the crime" plus the identity of the person charged with it:

1. Time and date of the crime and the territorial jurisdiction in which it happened (the **venue**)
2. Name by which the accused person has been identified
3. Essential elements of the crime charged
4. Specification of the criminal agency used to accomplish the crime and of the name of the victim

This process of affirming the corpus delicti is a combining of "what happened" and "who did it" with the knowledge that the happening as reported violates a specific law and that the offender has a legal responsibility to answer to the violation.

Negative Evidence

The second major area of case preparation concerns **negative evidence** and is oriented to countering defenses to the crime charged. The following are standard negative-evidence defenses:

1. The defendant did not commit the crime. The defense allegation is that the accused person is the victim of mistaken identification, faulty police work, or pure coincidence and was somewhere else at the time.
2. The defendant did commit the crime, but
   a. it was excusable (usually a claim of self-defense or provocation).
   b. it was an accident.
   c. it was the result of legal insanity.
   d. mental factors diminished the defendant's responsibility for the act.
3. No crime was committed:
   a. attack on the sufficiency of the corpus delicti
   b. attack on the sufficiency of the evidence
   c. attack on one or more of the essential elements of the crime charged (intent, proximate cause, etc.)

If any essential element of the crime charged is not proved beyond a reasonable doubt, the defendant is entitled to acquittal.

Lawful Procedures

The third major area of case preparation concerns procedural foundations in the securing of evidence. This requires affirmative proof to dispel any allegations of unlawful activity by police that may be presented to a court. The investigator must point out the procedural lawfulness. In most cases, such evidence will show one or more of the following:

1. Nothing suggestive or otherwise improper in locating and interviewing witnesses
2. The reasonableness of the search and the integrity of collecting and preserving evidence
3. A reasonable surveillance that meets the requirements of due process
4. The voluntariness of a confession or admission, together with other due process requirements

⓭ *Explain who in the criminal justice system is responsible for making the decision to charge a suspect with a crime and what steps are involved in making this decision.*

▶ The Decision to Charge

In the office of the prosecutor, the case is reviewed and assigned to a staff member for further investigation and preparation for trial, if warranted. This review of the case by a public official trained in law is a learned review of the work of the investigator. Conferences with the investigator and witnesses usually are scheduled by this legal expert, and the physical evidence and reports of its analysis are examined. If the case is a homicide, the staff of the coroner or medical examiner and their reports may be involved in these sessions. The assigned prosecutor makes his or her decision and moves through the stages necessary for trial or recommends that no action be taken at this time and details reasons for not taking action. The decision to charge is not a function or responsibility of the investigator.[18]

Cases are not moved for trial or rejected as possible trial material solely on the basis of the work done by the investigator and the legal significance of the collected evidence. Tactical factors and the needs of law enforcement may indicate that a trial is not advisable. Prosecutors may waive prosecution in exchange for information or testimony against a more hardened criminal, and the conservation of resources may suggest a negotiated plea of guilty to a lesser charge. For example, in processing first offenders and emotionally disturbed persons, the application of the sanctions of the criminal justice process may not appear justified by the circumstances of the case.[19]

Review by the staff of the prosecutor of case preparation before arrest is not uncommon. Of course, an investigator habituated to the traditional separation of the roles of investigator and prosecutor is reluctant to ask the prosecutor to step into an ongoing investigation. However, when the measure of proof is less than the amount necessary to move the case to the prosecutor, the natural tendency to seek help arises. It is within the concept of the role of the prosecutor to accept a difficult investigation as just that—incomplete and insufficient. In such instances, and in a case with promise, the prosecutor has an ideal investigative device in the local grand jury with its powers of subpoena and the right to administer oaths and take sworn testimony. It is a route for promising cases previously marked by police with the notation "No further results possible."

⓮ *Discuss the various reasons an investigation may be closed without making an arrest.*

▶ Closing an Investigation

An investigation is successful when the crime under investigation is promptly solved and the case closed. Measurable results occur when the case is closed by the arrest of the perpetrator. Cases cleared by arrest are a statistical measure of the efficiency of the criminal investigation function of any police unit. However, case clearance may also be a statistical measure of efficiency when an investigation is terminated without an arrest. A review of reasons given by police executives for closing investigations in this manner shows the following authorized case clearances in lieu of an arrest:[20]

1. The investigation discloses that the case is unfounded; no crime occurred or was attempted. However, the return of stolen property, restitution, or refusal by the victim to prosecute does not justify this classification.
2. The offender dies.
3. The case is found to be a murder and suicide; one person kills another person and then commits suicide.
4. The perpetrator confesses on his or her deathbed.
5. Arrest and charge of an identified offender are blocked by an uncooperative victim.
6. A confession is made by an offender already in custody for another crime.
7. The person identified as the perpetrator is located in another jurisdiction, and an unsuccessful attempt is made to gain custody; or the prosecutor does not believe that the expense of an attempt to gain custody is justified.
8. Upon the decision of the assigned prosecutor, the person identified as the perpetrator is prosecuted for a less serious charge than that cited at the time of arrest.

If the investigator's case preparation reveals that the identity of the perpetrator has been definitely established, has been located, and that sufficient information and evidence exist to support an arrest and a charge of crime, no valid reason exists not to close the case by arrest if it is not covered by any of the foregoing exceptional clearances. The identification of the perpetrator solves the case and justifies such action.

An investigator should recommend, on a supplementary report, the termination of a case when no further results can be secured. In addition, a follow-up officer should have the authority to file cases in an inactive or hold file when no further results can be obtained despite due diligence.

Therefore, the criminal investigation function can be terminated in the following instances:

1. Results have been obtained in full; the case is cleared by arrest or exceptional clearance.
2. Results have been obtained in part, and no further results can be obtained.
3. No results can be obtained.

Recognition that a bona fide conclusion to a case can be achieved without an arrest is important to the new frontiers of investigation. Such action strips the dead wood from the workload of an investigator, leads to new definitions of responsibility and accountability in the criminal investigation function, and strengthens the concept that arrests are not the primary objective of criminal investigation.

In pursuing truth—the main objective of an investigation—investigators must view all aspects of a case, particularly information pointing to the innocence of the accused person. Presenting a prima facie case and hoping and trusting that it will withstand the contradiction of a defense attack are no longer sufficient. The case must be so prepared that legally significant evidence presented in court will withstand attack by the defense and establish guilt beyond a reasonable doubt.

An investigation is a search for truth in which all possible information in a post factum inquiry is searched for, collected, and analyzed. The investigative process examines all the data, both for and against the person accused of crime. Therefore, viewing a case throughout an investigation from the viewpoint of the defense is always appropriate, and particularly so in preparing the case for presentation to the prosecutor. Along with scrupulous accuracy in reporting information, viewing the defense side of a case is the ultimate technique for conducting investigations that exonerate the innocent and discover and identify the guilty.

CASE STUDY

WEEKS V. UNITED STATES 232 U.S. 383 (1914)

The defendant, Weeks, was arrested by a police officer, so far as the record shows, without warrant, at Union Station in Kansas City, Missouri, where he was employed by an express freight company. Other police officers had gone to the house of the defendant. When told by a neighbor where the key was kept, officers found it and entered the house. They searched the defendant's premises and took possession of various papers and articles found there, which were turned over afterward to the United States marshal. Later that day, police officers returned with the marshal, who thought he might find additional evidence. On being admitted by someone in the house—probably a boarder, in response to a knock—the marshal searched the defendant's room and carried away certain letters and envelopes found in the drawer of a chiffonier. Neither the marshal nor the police officers had a search warrant. The defendant filed a petition requesting the return of his private papers, books, and other property pertaining to the alleged illegal sale of lottery tickets. In his petition, the defendant contended that these items were seized in violation of the rights secured to him by the Fourth Amendment to the Constitution of the United States, which provides the following:

> The right of the people to be secure in their person, houses, papers, and effects, against unreasonable searches and seizures, shall not be violated, and no Warrants shall issue, but upon probable cause, supported by Oath or affirmation, and particularly describing the place to be searched, and the person or things to be seized.

The trial court denied the defendant's request, citing the underlying principle that the court will not take notice of the manner in which a witness has possessed himself of papers or other chattel, subjects of evidence, which are material and properly offered in evidence. Accordingly, the defendant was found guilty. He appealed to the U.S. Supreme Court.

The Court held that the letters and property in question were taken from the house of the accused by an officer of the United States, acting under color of his office, in direct violation of the constitutional

(continued)

▼

rights of the defendant; that having made a reasonable application for their return, which was heard and passed upon by the Court, there was involved in the order refusing the application a denial of the constitutional rights of the accused, and a statement that the court should have restored these letters to the accused.

The Court determined that, in holding the letters and permitting their use during the trial, prejudicial error was committed.

The judgment of the trial court was reversed, and the case was remanded for further proceedings in accordance with the opinion.

CHAPTER REVIEW

Key Terms

accusatory pleading *29*
alibi *29*
all points bulletin (APB) *24*
broadcast alarm *23*
consent search *18*
corpus delicti *29*
curtilage *20*
emergency circumstances *20*

exclusionary rule *21*
immediate control *28*
magistrate *16*
motor vehicle exception *20*
negative evidence *30*
oath or affirmation *17*
open fields *20*
plain view exception *19*

probable cause *16*
reasonable suspicion *18*
relevance *16*
search incident to a lawful arrest *19*
stop and frisk *18*
venue *29*
wanted notice *24*

Review Questions

1. _____ exists when enough facts lead a reasonable and prudent person to believe that a fair probability of criminal activity exists.
   a. Reasonable suspicion
   b. Probable cause
   c. Exigent circumstances
   d. Contingent cause

2. Which constitutional amendment provides the citizens of the United States protections against unreasonable searches and seizures?
   a. First Amendment
   b. Second Amendment
   c. Third Amendment
   d. Fourth Amendment

3. A person can waive constitutionally provided protections against unreasonable searches and seizures and allow an investigator to search home, person, and property. Such a search is known as:
   a. Consent search
   b. Plain view search
   c. Stop and frisk
   d. Search incident to an arrest

4. The U.S. Supreme Court has held that a police officer may temporarily detain a person for questioning if the officer has reasonable suspicion that criminal activity may be involved. The person may also be patted down for weapons. This police action is known as:
   a. Consent search
   b. Plain view search
   c. Stop and frisk
   d. Search incident to an arrest

5. This doctrine permits investigators to observe and seize evidence without a warrant if the officer is lawfully in a position from which an object and the incriminating character of the object are immediately apparent. This exception to the search warrant requirement is known as:
   a. Consent search
   b. Plain view search
   c. Stop and frisk
   d. Search incident to an arrest

6. Investigators who have established probable cause that evidence is likely to be at a certain place may make a warrantless entry into the premises if what type of conditions exist?
   a. Exclusionary
   b. Inclusionary
   c. Exigent
   d. Conclusively

7. The method the courts use to uphold the constitutional protections against unreasonable searches and seizures, as well as to control the investigator's actions and prevent illegally obtained evidence from being used at trial, is known as the:
   a. Exclusionary rule
   b. Inclusionary rule
   c. Emergency rule
   d. Conclusively rule
8. In the interest of public safety, vehicles are frequently taken into police custody, such as when reported stolen or when used in the commission of a crime. These vehicles may be examined, inside and out, and any evidence of a crime may be lawfully seized under which theory of law?
   a. Search incident to arrest
   b. Motor vehicle exception
   c. Procedural search
   d. Inventory procedure
9. When a wanted fugitive is apprehended in another state, the fugitive has a right to a legal hearing in which the prosecution must demonstrate the probable cause for the return of the fugitive to the state where the crime occurred. These proceedings are known as:
   a. Extraditions
   b. Extrajudicials
   c. Extrajurisdictionals
   d. Exculpatory
10. The decision to charge a suspect with a crime is the duty of which person in the criminal justice system?
   a. Judge
   b. Investigator
   c. Prosecutor
   d. Defense counsel

Application Exercise

You are on patrol and as you drive past a convenience store you notice a man standing on the sidewalk who appears to be peeking into the store window. As you drive past the store he apparently sees you and turns and walks away. Consider your course of action—are you going to stop this person and for what reason? What rules of evidence would apply to this scenario and what type of search, if any, would apply?

Discussion Questions

1. Explain the Court's reasoning behind the motor vehicle exception to the search warrant requirement.
2. Discuss the difference between probable cause and reasonable suspicion, and explain how these concepts apply in criminal cases.
3. Describe the process for obtaining a search warrant and an arrest warrant.
4. Explain in detail the various emergency situations that would justify a search without a warrant.
5. Using the case study as an example, explain how the exclusionary rule applies in criminal cases.
6. What is the rational for organizing a final review of an investigation around a theme of witnesses and exhibits of evidence?
7. Does the role of prosecutor in making the decision to prosecute an accused involve a preliminary evaluation of the evidence on the issue of guilt or innocence?
8. Present an argument in support of the validity and reliability of reviewing a case from the defense frame of reference—that is, from the point of view of the case for the accused person.

Related Websites

To review U.S. Supreme Court decisions, go to the Court's website at www.supremecourtus.gov.

For information regarding the U.S. code sections relating to crimes and criminal procedure, go to www.access. gpo.gov/uscode/title18/title18.html.

Do you want to know if federal law enforcement is looking for someone you might know? Check out the U.S. Department of Justice Most Wanted Fugitive List. This website includes persons wanted by the FBI, DEA, ATF, and the U.S. Marshal's Service: www.usdoj.gov/marshals/investigations/most_wanted.

The U.S. Marshal's Service has a wide variety of law enforcement responsibilities, one of which is fugitive investigations. To learn more about the Marshals Service as a career choice, see the website at www.usmarshals.gov/careers/index.htm

Notes

1. Stephen A. Saltzburg and Daniel J. Capra, *Basic Criminal Procedure,* 2nd ed. (St. Paul, MN: West Publishing, 1977), 77–135.

2. J. Scott Harr and Karen M. Hess, *Constitutional Law and the Criminal Justice System* (Belmont, CA: Thompson Wadsworth Publishing, 2005), 219–222.

3. Cliff Roberson, *Criminal Procedure Today: Issues and Cases,* 2nd ed. (Upper Saddle River, NJ: Prentice Hall, 2003), 148–150.

4. John N. Ferdico, *Criminal Procedure for the Criminal Justice Professional,* 7th ed. (Belmont, CA: West/Wadsworth, 1999), 352–356.

5. Thomas D. Colbridge, "Search Incident to Arrest: Another Look," *FBI Law Enforcement Bulletin* 68, no. 5 (1999): 27–32.

6. *Arizona v Gant,* 556 U.S. 332 (2009).

7. Lisa A. Regina, "The Motor Vehicle Exception: When and Where to Search," *FBI Law Enforcement Bulletin* 68, no. 7 (1999): 26–30.

8. Ferdico, *Criminal Procedure for the Criminal Justice Professional,* 385–390.

9. Roberson, *Criminal Procedure Today,* 139.

10. Edward M. Hendrie, "Creating Exigent Circumstances," *FBI Law Enforcement Bulletin* 65, no. 9 (1996): 25.

11. Michael Bulzomi, "Police Intervention Short of Arrest," *FBI Law Enforcement Bulletin* 75, no. 11 (2006): 26–27.

12. Roberson, *Criminal Procedure Today,* 98.

13. These contacts are invaluable when a speedy response to queries is necessary, despite the reciprocity inherent in these calls. Some networks include graduates of the FBI Academy, former members of the FBI and the New York City Police Department, and alumni of college/university criminal justice degree programs.

14. Herbert Edelhertz, Ezra Stotland, Marilyn Walsh, and Milton Weinberg, *The Investigation of White-Collar Crime: A Manual for Law Enforcement Agencies* (Washington, DC: U.S. Department of Justice, Law Enforcement Assistance Administration, 1977), 267–275 (Appendix B, Sample Guide to Sources of Information). For in-depth coverage of the sources on information, see Harry J. Murphy, *Where's What: Sources of Information for Federal Investigators* (Washington, DC: The Brookings Institution, 1975).

15. *Agnello v. United States,* 296 U.S. 20 (1925).

16. *Rochin v. California,* 342 U.S. 165 (1952).

17. *Arizona v. Gant,* 556 U.S. 332 (2009).

18. Wayne R. Lafave, *Arrest: The Decision to Take a Suspect into Custody* (Boston, MA: Little, Brown, 1965), S-6, 320–324.

19. Institute of Defense Analyses, *Task Force Report: The Courts—A Report to the President's Commission on Law Enforcement and Administration of Justice* (Washington, DC: U.S. Government Printing Office, 1967), 5–7.

20. International Association of Chiefs of Police, Case No. S. Criminal Investigation (Washington, DC: International Association of Chiefs of Police, Inc., 1966), 18.

3 The Crime Scene

CHAPTER OUTLINE

LEARNING OBJECTIVES

After reading this chapter, you will be able to:

1 *Identify and explain the steps investigators take in processing a major crime scene.*

2 *Describe the symbiotic relationship between the media and law enforcement at major crime scenes.*

3 *List the various methodologies available to search for evidence at a crime scene.*

4 *Define what information should be used to identify an item of evidence and the purpose of properly identifying evidence.*

⑤ *Discuss the various methods used to package various items of evidence.*

⑥ *Define what a "known standard of evidence" is and how it is used to determine the origin of other items of evidence.*

⑦ *Discuss what documentation should accompany items of evidence transported to the crime laboratory for processing.*

⑧ *Recognize the potential hazards involved in the handling of violent crime scenes where the victim may have a lethally infectious disease.*

⑨ *Explain the use of "field notes" in documenting the progress made during the course of an investigation.*

⑩ *Discuss the use of an "offense or crime report" in establishing that a crime has occurred and how it was committed.*

⑪ *Explain the types of photographs that should be taken at a crime scene to provide a pictorial representation of the scene.*

⑫ *Explain the advantage of using a crime sketch with its ability to eliminate unnecessary detail.*

⑬ *Discuss the various methods investigators use to identify and locate potential witnesses.*

Criminal investigation is a lawful search for people and things useful in reconstructing an illegal act or omission and analysis of the mental state accompanying it. It is a probing from the known to the unknown, backward in time. The objective of a criminal investigation is to determine truth as far as it can be discovered in any inquiry. Successful investigations are based upon fidelity, accuracy, and sincerity in lawfully searching for the facts and on an equal faithfulness, exactness, and probity in reporting the results.[1]

For many crimes the investigative process begins at the scene of the crime. The successful management of a crime scene involves three major functions. The first involves the responding officers whose responsibility is to render the crime scene safe and to control movement of persons and officers into and out of the area. The second function involves the crime scene investigators who conduct the search for evidence and also prepare the proper documentation of the crime scene. The third function is the search for witnesses. Witnesses may not want to come forward for a variety of reasons and often people may be unaware that what they may have witnessed is important to the ongoing criminal investigation. These witnesses must be located and their cooperation obtained.

❶ *Identify and explain the steps investigators take in processing a major crime scene.*

▶ Control of the Crime Scene

The crime scene is the focus of the preliminary investigation. A police response to a crime that has just occurred would be managed according to these guidelines.

Approach

When notified that a crime has occurred, the responding officers should be alert to any suspects or witnesses who are leaving the scene. Many crimes have been solved by an alert officer who has detained a person a short distance away from the crime scene and the investigation has determined that this is the person responsible for the crime. En route to the crime scene, the assigned investigator plans his or her action and, upon arrival reviews the problems usually connected with any crime scene. The type of crime determines the type of approach. For example, where injured victims need immediate response, lights and sirens would be appropriate. However, lights and sirens would not be appropriate for a robbery in progress, as the sirens would notify the suspect of the response and thus aid escape or encourage the taking of hostages and a hostage situation.

Safety

Upon arrival at the scene of the crime, the investigators should scan the area to determine if the crime is ongoing and if the suspect is still on the scene. It is the first responder's responsibility to **neutralize the crime scene**, making it safe for other personnel to enter the area. Neutralization of the crime scene includes the arrest of any suspects and the elimination of any hazards that might present a threat, such as a clandestine drug laboratory.

Medical Attention

The next responsibility is to ensure that medical attention is provided if required with as little impact on the crime scene as possible. The best way to minimize this impact is to work with the medical personnel so they know the importance of limiting the number of persons who enter the area and respect the need to minimize the possible destruction of evidence. The investigator, however, must be mindful that the possibility of saving a life takes precedence over the possible destruction of evidence.

Search for Witnesses

The scene of the crime is the one place where a number of witnesses will be together at the same time. The first officer on the scene should identify potential witnesses and separate them as soon as possible.[2] Witnesses should not be allowed to discuss the crime among themselves as the investigator wants only that information that the witness independently observed or experienced. When witnesses discuss the crime or overhear others talking about the crime, they tend to adopt some of this information as their own or alter their recollections to fit with those of other witnesses. This process is normal and is known as **retroactive interference**.[3]

In the process of identifying potential witnesses, the officers at the scene of a crime may encounter people who are uncooperative or state that they have no knowledge of the crime. This is not unusual. However, as soon as it is determined that these persons were in a position to be a witness to the crime, they should be identified and their refusal to give information or their statement of ignorance should be properly recorded in the police report. This process makes a record of the fact that these potential witnesses were given the opportunity to assist the investigation at the time the crime occurred. Any statement made by a potential witness refusing to cooperate or denying knowledge of the crime can be used to impeach the witness when at trial he or she becomes the star defense witness.

Broadcast Alarm

Brief contact should be made with the victim and any witnesses to obtain a suspect and vehicle description. Once this information is obtained, the investigator should broadcast this information over the police radio so other officers in the area can begin the search for the person responsible for the commission of the crime. This is only a brief contact as the victim and witnesses will be interviewed in depth at a later time. At this point time is of the essence and getting basic suspect information out to the field officers in a timely manner is of critical importance.

Scene Boundaries

The first step in processing a crime scene for clues and evidence is to make an accurate survey of the surroundings and carefully evaluate the situation—to take "a long, hard look." Deliberate action at this time guards against false moves and mistakes. The impact of the overall appearance of the scene on an experienced investigator will provide guidelines for modifying a base plan of action. The assigned investigator must ascertain as soon as possible where the crime happened. Usually the crime scene is readily discernible.

A search for evidence starts with effective protection of the crime scene. The searcher must be certain that nothing has been removed from or added to the scene since the arrival of responding police—in short, that the scene is intact. The posting of yellow "Crime Scene" barrier tape aids in delineating the crime scene area. Officers posted at the perimeter will also prevent the entry of unauthorized persons. Crime scene boundaries should be established beyond the initial scope of the crime scene with the understanding that the boundaries can be reduced in size if necessary but cannot be easily expanded.[4]

The officers guarding the perimeter of the crime scene are responsible for preparing a **chronological log** of events as they occur at the scene. This is typically a time-based log that documents when an officer enters and leaves the scene. This notation includes the time and the officer's full name, agency, rank, and reason for entering the scene. This logging process also serves to keep unnecessary officers from entering the scene just to look around.

Management Notification

Once the scene is firmly under control, it is advisable to notify those in command positions within the police agency of the circumstances of the crime. Those in charge should be kept informed as to the actions taken by their personnel and the types of crimes they are dealing with. Upon notification, the management staff members can make the decision of whether they should respond to the scene or not. If their response is not necessary, they should be fully briefed of the circumstances of the crime.

 Describe the symbiotic relationship between the media and law enforcement at major crime scenes.

Media Relations

The vast majority of crime scenes will not attract the attention of the media. However, the media's need for law enforcement is obvious: crime and the police make news. Recent studies, for example, have shown that crime reporting has made up one-third of all the coverage in local television newscasts. Newspaper, radio, and television reporters have a real hunger for news about crime and the police.

Law enforcement also needs the media. The media is essential for publicizing information on wanted suspects or alerting residents to crime trends. In addition, the news media can be a valuable tool for advertising various activities that build public support for the agency's mission.[5]

This symbiotic relationship between the media and law enforcement should be used to develop a long-term professional working relationship. The best way for law enforcement to accomplish this goal is to work with the media honestly and to provide information that can be released in a timely manner.

Usually the following information can be released to the media:

1. The type of crime committed, including a brief description of what happened, where, and when

2. Identity of the victim, which is usually not released if the victim is deceased, in which case this information would be withheld pending notification of the next of kin. (In cases of sexual assault, per applicable rape shield laws, the victim's identity is also withheld.)

3. Facts concerning the arrest of the suspect or suspects can include the name, age, and circumstances of the arrest and the time, place, resistance, and weapons involved

Information that should not be released to the media includes the following:

1. Prior criminal charges and convictions or comments regarding the reputation, character, guilt, or innocence of suspects

2. Identification of any juvenile suspects

3. Comment on any admission or confession or the fact that an admission or confession has or has not been made

4. Identity of any possible witnesses

5. Precise description of the amount of money or other items taken[6]

Officer-in-Charge

The command at a crime scene is often hectic. Most law enforcement agencies specify that the first officer to arrive at the scene is in charge until a patrol sergeant arrives. This sergeant (or officer of higher rank) is in command until he or she is relieved by a detective or an officer of even higher rank. In minor crimes, the sergeant may relinquish command by calling the dispatcher and reporting that he or she is leaving the scene and reporting the name of the officer now in charge. At the scene of a more serious crime, the sergeant waits at the scene for the detective's arrival, briefs him or her about what the police at the scene have learned about the circumstances of the crime, and turns over command of the investigation to the detective. However, the sergeant will remain at the scene in command of the uniformed personnel guarding the limits of the scene, monitoring new arrivals, and performing similar duties.

At the scene of more serious crimes, particularly homicides, larger police units field a mobile crime laboratory to process the crime scene either with detectives trained in forensic science or with crime laboratory forensic scientists. At this point, it becomes even more difficult to determine who is in charge. Despite this identification problem, most police units have men and women who are self-starters and work together to get organized and ready for the search of a crime scene.[7]

▶ Crime Scene Investigation

Typically the tasks to be performed by the crime scene investigation team start with the systematic search for evidence. Once the items of evidence have been located, they are photographed and measurements are taken for the purposes of preparing a crime scene sketch. The evidence is then collected in such a way as to not destroy the items' evidentiary value. The evidence is then packaged and transported to the crime laboratory or property warehouse where it is stored until needed in court. A chain-of-custody form is completed which documents where the item of evidence has been and who has handled it, from the time it was picked up at the scene of the crime until it is presented in court.

 List the various methodologies available to search for evidence at a crime scene.

Search Procedures

The main purpose of a search is to look for evidence of what happened during the crime. It is not a random grouping but rather a selective looking for objects and materials. The expertise of the investigator, acquired by training and experience, indicates what is to be found at the scenes of different types of crimes. For a search to be successful, its main purpose must be aligned with knowing precisely what to seek and scrutinize. Otherwise, the search lacks the necessary professional direction.

The methodology of searching depends on the case and the scene. Staffing problems in police units, as well as problems associated with the proffering of evidence in court, have brought about the development of the **single-officer search**. Associates of this single officer often assist in locating evidence, but they do not disturb it or collect it. The goal is to limit the number of officers in possession of crime scene evidence to the officer searching the scene. The use of double coverage in searching crime scenes is valuable as a double check for evidence, but it frequently results in conflicting testimony by searching officers.

When the search must cover a wide, the available investigators should be assigned in teams. One member of each team serves as the single officer collecting evidence, and each team is assigned responsibility for the search of a specified segment of the crime scene. A designated investigator or a superior officer commands the entire searching operation.

A crime scene is the place of the crime, including any adjoining entry or exit area. Therefore, prior to a search, the assigned investigator surveys the scene, noting its dimensions and the presence or absence of an adjoining entry (approach) and exit (flight) area. This evaluation is the basis for setting limits on the area of the search, for determining how to organize the search procedure, and for ascertaining what assistance is needed.

Traditionally, systematic searching has utilized the following methods (Figure 3-1):

1. A **point-to-point movement**, following a chain of objects that are obviously evidence
2. An **ever-widening circle** technique, in which the searching officer starts at the focal point of the scene or the center of the security area and works outward by circling in a clockwise or counterclockwise direction until the fringes of the protected area are reached
3. An **ever-narrowing circle**, the reverse of an ever-widening circle, in which the searching officer starts at the outskirts of the crime scene and works toward its focal point
4. A **zone or sector search** in which the scene is subdivided into segments and each sector is searched as an individual unit

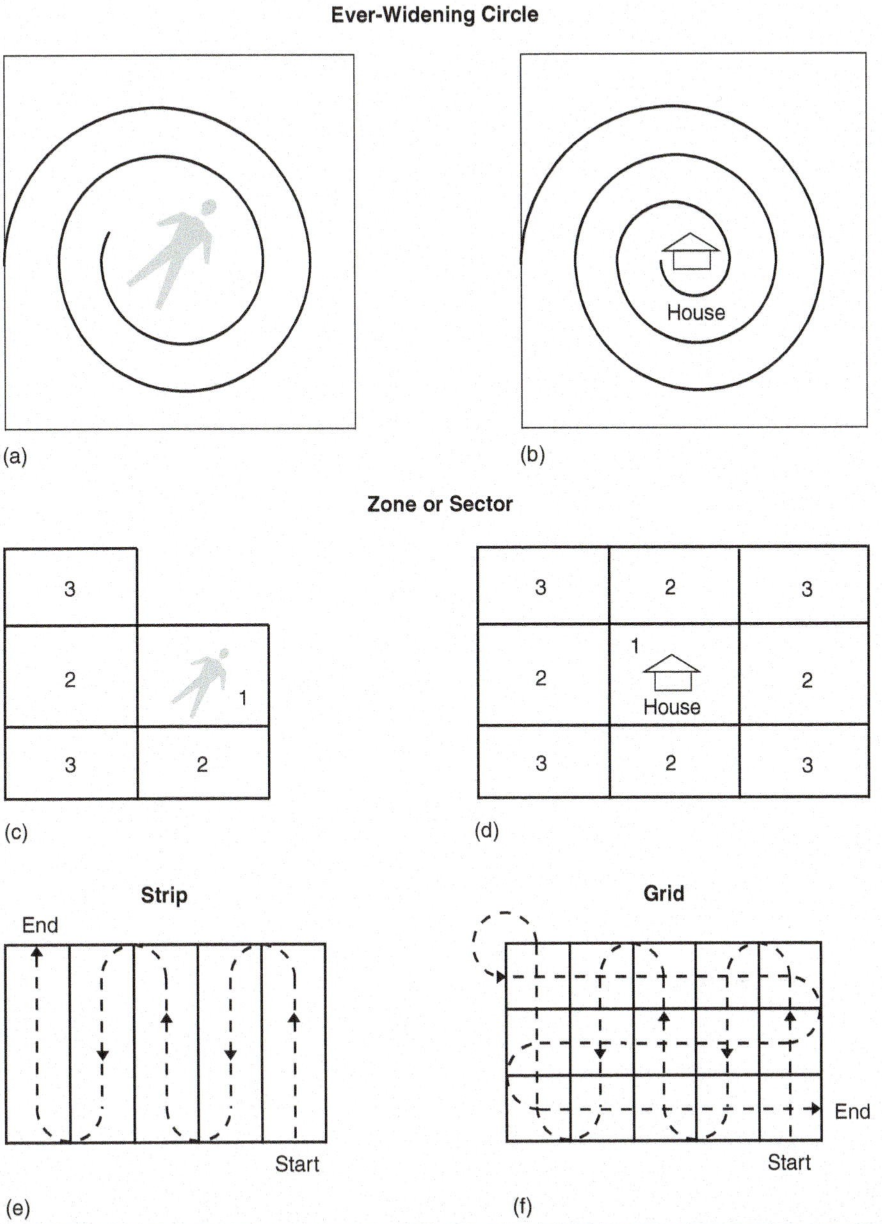

Ever-Widening Circle

(a)

(b)

Zone or Sector

(c)

(d)

Strip

(e)

Grid

(f)

FIGURE 3-1   Search Methods: (a) Indoors, (b) Outdoors, (c) Immediate Area, (d) Extended Area, (e) Strip Search of Large Area, (f) Grid Search of Large Area.

5. A **strip or grid search** for outdoor areas in which the area to be searched is plotted like a football field. Searching starts at a sideline and moves across the field to the other sideline, with searchers working back and forth across the field until the entire area is searched. The **grid search** begins after the strip search is completed. It covers the same area in a similar manner but at right angles to the previous search pattern. Metal or wood stakes and heavy cord are used to direct and control outdoor searches.

Some experienced investigators dislike describing any searching method by name because it emphasizes technique rather than purpose and has often led to criticism during cross-examination. When queried on the witness stand about searching the crime scene, investigators should state that they began the search by looking around, moved generally in a clockwise movement (if that was the technique), and made field notes as items of evidence were discovered. Their field notes then support the search as a systematic examination of the scene.

When a criminal act is suspected as being involved in a death, a search of the deceased person is often assigned to field representatives of the coroner's or medical examiner's office. In some jurisdictions, the coroner or medical examiner will permit body searches by the police upon request. In any event, the search must be methodical and thorough. Many police units require the investigator to delay such a search until it can be made in the presence of a disinterested witness and also require the investigator to record the name of such a witness in his or her field notes. A complete list of all property found on the deceased victim, as well as where it was found (e.g., right-side pocket of trousers, hidden in bra), are made part of the officer's notes.

The ability to discover and recognize evidence is a prerequisite to successful searching. As the investigator surveys the crime scene preparatory to searching, he or she develops some concept of the type and nature of evidence that should be the objective of the crime scene search. Physical evidence can be anything from massive objects to microscopic traces. The nature of the crime offers the first clue: weapons are used in assaults; an entry occurs in burglaries; a fire is set in arson cases. The victim, the **modus operandi** or method of operation of the offender, and other circumstances that can be observed during this survey may suggest possible clues.

Where to search for physical evidence is based on the type of evidence the investigator is seeking. In assaults and homicides, the injuries sustained by the victim suggest a weapon and orient the search toward it. In burglaries, the means used to gain access to the premises and the place of entrance indicates the possible location of tool marks. Tabletops, glassware, and other smooth surfaces guide the search for imprints. Soft earth, mud, and dust are known sites for foot and tire impressions.

When searching a crime scene, the investigator should be mindful of **Locard's exchange principle**, which states that suspects will bring items of evidence into the crime scene and will take items with them when they leave. This exchange of trace evidence involves such items of evidence as hairs, fibers, dirt, dust, blood, body fluids, skin cells, and other microscopic materials.[8]

Initially, it is a case of identifying the type of evidence one wants to find and its likely area of discovery, then of making a systematic search, and finally of recognizing it when it is found. The experienced investigator is always alert for evidence that may seem unimportant but is, in fact, material and relevant.

Collecting Evidence

Investigators should not rush to pick up evidence since its significance may be destroyed in doing so. The investigator's field notes should record the discovery. In addition, photographs and accurate measurements are necessary to show the original position and nature of all evidence. In searching for evidence at crime scenes, never alter the position of, pick up, or touch any object before it has been described in minute detail in an official note and photographed.

The integrity of evidence is maintained by keeping it in its original state. No alterations are made to any item that is or may be evidence. Blood, rust, grease, and dirt are not removed from objects, nor does the investigator add his or her fingerprints to the evidence or smear or wipe off

any such clues. An item of physical evidence inherently important in its own substance may have another item of evidence added to it. This can range from a fingerprint on a fragment of glass to blood and fibers on weapons.

Evidence likely to be found at crime scenes and amenable to scientific analysis is divided into seven major groups: (1) weapons, (2) blood and body fluids, (3) imprints or impressions (traces of a person or a vehicle), (4) marks of tools used to gain access to locked premises or containers, (5) dust and dirt traces, (6) questioned documents, and (7) miscellaneous trace or transfer evidence, including such items as hairs, fibers, and skin cells.

4 *Define what information should be used to identify an item of evidence and the purpose of properly identifying evidence.*

Marking Evidence

Marking evidence serves to identify it. Marking must not impair the value of the evidence or restrict the number and kind of examinations to which it might be subjected by criminalists and other experts. Consideration should also be given to the monetary value of the item of evidence and whether the item will be returned to the rightful owner when no longer needed. Will the marking of the evidence destroy or diminish the value of the item? If so, another means of marking the items should be considered. Tamperproof evidence tags and bags might suffice, as might the use of correction fluid that can be applied to the item of evidence, written on, and later removed without causing permanent damage.

Traditional marking of objects includes the investigator's initials, date, and report number if ample space is available. Counterfeit money should have a dual marking. The name of the person last in possession should be signed across a corner of the bill, or such person should be asked to scratch his or her initials on a coin. In addition, the investigator should place his or her own mark of identification on the money. When currency is mutilated by marking with a tracing powder or dye, it should not be cleaned but should be placed immediately in a sealed envelope and handled with care. Later, when no longer required as evidence, this mutilated currency should not be returned to general circulation but should be redeemed at a local bank with a statement that it contains stained material added to develop it as evidence.

Properly marking items of evidence allows the investigator to testify in court that the item to be entered into evidence was, in fact, the same object he or she found at the crime scene. On direct examination, questions usually have the following format:

Q.   Officer, I show you this revolver, now marked as people's exhibit number 7. Do you recognize it? (Officer takes the revolver, looks for his mark, finds it, and answers.)

A.   Yes, I do.

Q.   How do you recognize it?

A.   By my mark here on the butt (pointing to rear and bottom of revolver).

Q.   Where and under what circumstances did you first see this revolver?

The witness proceeds with the testimony; the identification serves as a foundation for the remainder of the testimony.

Establishing the Chain of Custody

Continuity of possession—the **chain of custody**—must be established when evidence is offered in court as an exhibit. Whenever possible, if the officer locating the evidence is not the investigator assigned responsibility for the case, the evidence should not be disturbed until its location and nature can be brought to the attention of the responsible investigator, nor should it be moved until its location and description have been noted, photographs have been taken at the scene, and measurements have been made to place it.

Adherence to standard and required procedures in every case is the best guarantee that the collection and possession of physical evidence will stand a court test of what happened—or could have happened—to it from the time of its finding to its presentation in court. Any deviation from standard procedures in processing physical evidence can affect credibility and contribute to a reasonable suspicion in the minds of the triers of fact about the entire police investigation.

In narcotics cases in many areas, investigators seal the evidence in manila envelopes, initial the sealing, and drop all the envelopes through a slot into a locked box at local headquarters. The chemist who will make the examination has the only key to this box. He or she removes the evidence by cutting open the sealed envelope, examines it, and replaces it in the original manila envelope, reseals the envelope, initials the sealing, and places the envelope in a locked box. An idea of the ritual used to prove the continuity of the possession of evidence is illustrated by the questions and responses recorded during a grand jury hearing in a case of possession and sale of narcotics. The testimony, on direct examination, of the finding investigator relative to this evidence was as follows:

Q.   I believe you found a large quantity of what you believe to be drugs in the house?

A.   Yes, sir.

Q.   Do you recognize this plastic bag as containing the quantity you discovered?

A.   Yes, sir.

Q.   Where were the drugs taken?

A.   They were brought to the station.

Q.   Where were they put?

A.   In the interrogation room and locked up.

Q.   The next day did you take the drugs from the interrogation room to the Bureau of Narcotics Enforcement?

A.   Yes, sir, I did.

Q.   In the Bureau of Narcotics Enforcement, were they put in a locker?

A.   Yes.

Q.   Was this locker locked?

A.   Yes.

Q.   Did you have a key to open it again?

A.   No, sir.

Q. Where is this locker located?

A. The chemist's office.

The chemist was then sworn and questioned.

Q. Do you recall having seen that plastic bag (indicating bag identified by previous witness) and the contents of it?

A. Yes, I have.

Q. Did you bring it with you today?

A. Yes, I did.

Q. When did you first come into contact with that particular bag?

A. On December 28 of last year.

Q. Where did you find it?

A. This was removed by me from a locked locker at the Narcotics Bureau. It is an evidence locker in my office that is used to submit evidence for analysis when I am not present to take it personally and to which I have the only key.

Q. Now, did you subsequently make an examination of those drugs in this bag?

A. Yes, I did.

Since the basic legal integrity of the evidence had been shown, the witness continued his testimony about his examination of the contents of this plastic bag.

⑤ *Discuss the various methods used to package various items of evidence.*

Packaging Physical Evidence

Evidence must be packaged to avoid breakage, loss, or contamination in transit. Tweezers, forceps, and similar tools are used to collect and place traces and small items in their containers. Latex gloves are suggested for handling some physical evidence.

An evidence box or board can be used for transporting evidence over short distances. An evidence box with pegboard sides allows for tying or wiring small- and medium-size objects in place. A series of drilled holes and appropriately sized dowels can serve the same purpose. Items of evidence that will undergo comparison analysis for possible relationships should be packaged in separate containers to obviate any allegation of cross-contamination. No wet or soiled materials or boxes or bottles should be used. Thoroughly clean and dry containers, wrapping paper, corrugated paper, boxes, and sealing tape are the basic safeguards for physical evidence in transport.

Documentary evidence is first placed in transparent envelopes without folding or bending; then between two pieces of firm, corrugated cardboard; and then in a manila envelope or other wrapper.

Plastic pill bottles or film containers with pressure lids are unbreakable; can be easily sealed with tape; and are excellent containers for hairs, fibers, and other small articles. They are also ideal for spent bullets, empty cartridge cases, and cartridges because they can be packed with cotton gauze to minimize movement of such evidence.

Plastic envelopes and bags are available in various shapes and sizes and also are easily sealed. However, when they are used to transport soil, debris, or clothing that may contain bloodstains, bacterial action contaminating the blood sample becomes a strong possibility. Use plastic containers with caution. To an unusual degree, they can act as greenhouses for the cultivation of mold that can destroy the integrity and identity of some types of evidence.

Use only the tubes or vials with stoppers found in blood collection kits for blood samples and swatches used to collect bloodstains, and follow directions on these kits for refrigeration and other care.

If the stain is on a solid object that can be moved, such as a firearm or other weapon, transport the object, protecting the area of the stain or completely enclosing the object in a package if it is small. If the stain is on clothing, wrap the garments separately in paper, mark them appropriately, and package them. This is a better procedure than any technique for removing a sample of a stain for analysis.

Articles of clothing, tablecloths, and other fabric evidence should be folded as little as possible and without applying pressure. If the areas of the fabric to be examined are known, they should be protected from friction with wrapping paper or another appropriate form of containment.

Take a soil-stained or mud-soaked object to the laboratory rather than attempting to remove and transport the soil or mud as separate items. When such traces are picked up as individual items of evidence, it is vital that every precaution be taken to keep the evidence in separate sealed containers to avoid any accidental loss or mixing in transit.

Charred wood, carpet, and drapery material from the scene of a suspicious fire may be wrapped in metal foil and sealed in an airtight container. Smaller objects, such as paper and rags, or solid samples should be sealed in the container in which they were found or placed in airtight bottles or cans. This prevents the fire accelerant and its residues from evaporating.

Pills and other noncaustic substances should be left in their original containers for transport to the laboratory. Such containers often provide useful information. The investigator should count the number of pills or capsules or accurately determine the bulk quantity of fluids or powders and should place these data in the field notes.

Caustic poison should not be transported until the investigator has made certain that the container in which it was found (or placed after its recovery from sink, bathtub, or other place) is safe for a period of time equal to at least twice the likely transport time.

Food, body substances, and fluids should be placed in as many separate moisture-proof bottles or containers as necessary to avoid any contamination of evidence. Food or other substances suspected of containing or known to contain poison should be plainly labeled as suspected or known samples of poison.

If a weapon is suspected of containing hair, blood, or fragments of flesh, it should be packaged in a sealed container of appropriate size.

Microscopic traces, hairs, and fibers should be sealed in folded paper or placed in a clean, sealed envelope or box of appropriate size.

6 *Define what a "known standard of evidence" is and how it is used to determine the origin of other items of evidence.*

Matching Physical Evidence with Known Standards

Criminalistics includes the identification of physical evidence and the finding of its origin. This individualization of evidence often requires that physical evidence collected at a crime scene be matched with a **known standard of evidence** or a control. Known standards may be collected at the crime scene, from the victim, from a suspect, or from other sources and must be collected in exactly the same manner as any other evidence because they have equal evidential value. As for other evidence, known standards must be recognized and followed so that possession is obtained legally, evidence is marked appropriately, samples are properly preserved, and the acquisition process is reported accurately.

Locating a known standard of fingerprints may require no more than a search of records for a suspect's fingerprints. Shoe prints may require the collection of a known standard of soil from the area close to a footprint or heel print for comparison with soil traces on the shoes of a suspect. Collection of a sample of hair is often required, as is the search for and the recovery of a coat or sweater or other garment that may be a known standard for fibers recovered at the crime scene.

Known samples of blood start with the victim. Samples can be secured only by a medical practitioner upon the request of the investigator. Since the *Schmerber* case, it is lawful to take a sample from an arrested person charged with a crime in which blood collected as evidence requires a known sample for comparative analysis.[9]

The self-incrimination clause of the Fifth Amendment to the U.S. Constitution protects against compelling a person or suspect to communicate or testify to matters that may incriminate him or her. However, the Fifth Amendment does not protect a person or suspect from being compelled to be the source of "real or physical evidence." The recovery of blood, clothing, and hair without consent is not prohibited by the Fifth Amendment because these are all considered "real or physical evidence" and thus are subject to the controls of the right to privacy and search and seizure clauses of the Fourth Amendment, rather than to the self-incrimination clause of the Fifth.

Handwriting analysis requires exemplars, or samples, as well as proof of authorship. These known standards are classed as either "requested" (by the investigator) or "regular course of business." In death cases in which a suicide note is found, the only exemplar possible is some "regular course of business" handwriting found on the victim or at the scene, or secured from relatives and associates and identified by a responsible person as being the victim's handwriting. In other cases, such exemplars may be available at the crime scene, at the place of employment, or in the public record. Exemplars that have been requested are often less reliable because of intentional disguising of normal writing style or distortions due to nervousness.[10]

Investigators obtaining handwriting samples from a suspect should supply him or her with paper and a pen or pencil similar to what was used for the questioned writing, dictate the material to be written or printed, and allow the suspect to spell words as he or she would usually spell them. Misspelled words can contribute to the physical **match** between sample and questioned writing.[11] In addition, the suspect should be asked to write out and sign a statement as to the validity and source of the sample or samples.

Requiring a suspect to give handwritten exemplars is not considered to be a request for communications that fall within the protection of the Fifth Amendment. The Fifth Amendment prohibits only the compulsion of communicative or testimonial evidence from a defendant. In writing to produce the exemplar for identification, the defendant is no more than the source of identification. Handwriting exemplars have been specifically held to be such an identifying physical characteristic.[12]

As with handwriting exemplars, compelling the accused to utter words spoken by an alleged thief is not within the scope of the Fifth Amendment privilege against self-incrimination. However, voice identification is subject to the Sixth Amendment's right to representation by an attorney clause and is regarded as belonging to a critical stage of the proceedings against a suspect.[13]

The justices of the U.S. Supreme Court have expressed a minority viewpoint that handwriting exemplars and voice identification are within the scope of constitutional protection. Therefore, compelling these two types of evidence against the will of a person is at least questionable if either is the key evidence in the case. It would be a better policy to obtain handwriting exemplars and speech for identification by consent and not by force. If the investigation is beyond the general inquiry stage and has focused on a suspect, the Miranda admonishment should be given to inform the person of his or her constitutional protection against self-incrimination.[14]

Many manufacturers of paint and glass provide scientific laboratories with known standards of their products, and **criminalistics** laboratories maintain many reference files of known standards. However, one should not assume that such standards are on file. It is the responsibility of the investigator to seek known standards until such time as he or she is informed that they are not required.

Because the legal significance of physical evidence often is based on comparison to a known standard, it is of vital importance that physical evidence and its collection be viewed as a dual process of collecting and preserving the basic physical evidence and of collecting and preserving the known standards of such evidence.

 Discuss what documentation should accompany items of evidence transported to the crime laboratory for processing.

Transporting Evidence

Transporting physical evidence to a laboratory, to a place of storage, or to the prosecutor's office or the courtroom is the responsibility of the investigator who found the evidence. It is usually delivered personally, but when distance is a problem, it may be shipped by registered mail, insured parcel post, or express mail. When food or physiological fluids or substances are collected, temperature control is a primary precaution. Refrigeration without freezing will prevent deterioration, and insulating containers are available for the transport of such material. Evidence should be shipped by the fastest available route. Local delivery should be made in person by the finding investigator or by authorized personnel of his or her employing agency.

When physical evidence is sent to a laboratory for scientific examination, it must be accompanied by an informative report. The report must, in effect, bring the crime scene into the laboratory. This report must be on the official letterhead of the law enforcement agency with jurisdiction in the case and should contain the following:

1. Name and address of the agency submitting the evidence
2. Crime classification of case by type and grade of offense
3. Case number of agency submitting evidence
4. Copy of the offense report, the report of the preliminary investigation, or a brief history of the case
5. List of evidence consecutively numbered by item with a brief description of each item and a notation as to (a) when and where found, (b) whether the item is a known standard for comparison, and (c) whether any change has taken place in the evidence either through accidental mishandling or because a sample is being submitted, rather than the full amount of evidence collected
6. List of suggested scientific examinations
7. Brief statement of the problems in the case
8. The name and address of the investigator to whom the exhibits should be returned upon completion of the examination

Packages in which physical evidence is to be shipped to a laboratory should be marked "Evidence for Examination" and the written request for an examination should be pasted securely to the outside of the package, with the notation "Letter" or "Invoice" indicating its location. The criminalist receiving the package can read the request letter and have some idea of the nature of the evidence before opening the package itself.

Packages containing blood or other body fluids suspected of being contaminated by a person with acquired immune deficiency syndrome (AIDS), hepatitis B, hepatitis C, or tuberculosis should be marked "CAUTION," followed by the name of the disease suspected. The technician in charge at the crime laboratory should be consulted before submitting this type of evidence.

Laboratory technicians carefully mark, tag, and otherwise identify all items of evidence while such evidence is in their custody. It is this careful handling of physical evidence by crime laboratory technicians that preserves the integrity of such evidence. Upon return of the evidence, the report of the expert examiner who conducted the laboratory examination is integrated with other information collected in the investigation to date. At no time should an investigator return any part of the evidence to its rightful claimant without the authority of the prosecutor. If the prosecutor believes that the evidence is not required in the trial of the offender, he or she has the authority to return it to the rightful owner or to store it until such time as it is disposed of according to law. When the case is completed, the prosecutor has the authority to release the evidence.

8 *Recognize the potential hazards involved in the handling of violent crime scenes where the victim may have a lethally infectious disease.*

Handling Infected Evidence

AIDS, hepatitis B, and tuberculosis are potentially lethal infectious diseases more likely to be encountered at crime scenes today than in the past. The scenes of crimes of violence involving victims with one of these diseases are likely to contain blood and possibly other infectious body fluids. Therefore, it is imperative that all possible precautions be taken.

Investigators arriving at the crime scene should question other officers as to the possibility of the victim having a lethal infectious disease. The high-risk groups include injection drug users and possibly prostitutes (male and female). A quick survey of the crime scene may indicate some warning signals—for example, condition of the victim and the presence of prescription or nonprescription drugs.

The first line of defense against infectious diseases is to wear disposable gloves. A surgical mask and protective eyewear may also be suggested with any likelihood that liquid or dried blood may come into contact with the face of the investigator or the crime scene technician. The second line of defense is to avoid cutting or puncturing a finger or other portion of the body while conducting the crime scene search and collecting evidence. A collateral line of defense is to seek

A crime scene can be well defined by using barrier tape or barricades.

medical assistance immediately if you do receive an accidental cut or other wound or believe that particles of possibly infected blood may have come in contact with your mouth or eyes.[15]

To protect others, any evidence suspected of contamination should be placed in clearly marked plastic bags and sealed. However, these bags should not be forwarded to the crime laboratory until it is certain that the laboratory will accept this type of evidence.

Because of the epidemic spread of AIDS, investigators are urged to meet with local health officials to discuss how to best protect all concerned. Health personnel should be able to outline possible signs at crime scenes that might indicate that a victim should be suspected of having an infectious disease; to explain the proper procedure for disposing of latex gloves after their use at a "suspect" crime scene; and to denote the best procedure to follow from the time an investigator or a technician believes that he or she has been in contact with blood or other body fluids likely to be infected to the time when medical assistance will be available.

Identifying Physical Changes at the Scene

Investigators search for and collect evidence of any observable damage to objects at the scene—furniture turned over, broken, or moved from its normal location at the scene and other items that are bent, broken, dented, or scratched. Disarrangement, damage, and theft may be useful in determining what happened and who did it. A fight or struggle of some kind is indicated by overturned and broken furniture. Damage may indicate the direction of force. Photographs of the scene preserve the "as is" quality of the change or disarrangement.

Not only articles taken from the scene may lead to a major suspect, but they also may supply incriminating evidence when recovered from the possession or control of a suspect at the time of arrest. The responsible investigator includes a description of the stolen property in the alarm broadcast. Even articles of little value, such as snapshots or ashtrays, have potential value as evidence when recovered.

Conducting a Final Survey of the Scene

The officer in charge should take a final survey of the scene before relinquishing control of the crime scene area. This final survey ensures that all of the evidence has been identified and collected and that the scene has been properly processed prior to release. This review of the crime scene also ensures that equipment and materials generated by the investigation are not left behind inadvertently. Investigators should keep in mind that to return to the scene for the follow-up work on items that might be inadvertently overlooked may require a search warrant, because once the area is released, it no longer carries the legal status of a crime scene.[16]

A crime scene can be anywhere, even in the middle of nowhere.

▶ Recording the Crime Scene

Field notes made during the search of a crime scene are the basic record of the search and the evidence discovered. The investigator's report is prepared from his or her field notes. The notes and report both become permanent records in the case and have the inherent integrity of records prepared in the performance of official duties.

Photographing and sketching offer opportunities to graphically portray the scene and the evidence located during the search and must be done with care to represent the subjects accurately. **Crime scene sketches and photographs** usually are offered in evidence as exhibits that are more realistic than words or that can assist jurors in understanding the case, or both. They must withstand the basic tests of relevancy and materiality. No legal presumption states that graphic representations are correct. Sketches and photos are verified as accurate by the person who made them or by any witness having sufficient knowledge of the subject who can say that the sketch or photograph is a faithful representation of what is shown.

Maps and diagrams were used to illustrate testimony long before photographs were first offered in evidence. As early as 1857, the nonphotographic drawings of a doctor illustrating the appearance of blood as seen microscopically were admitted into evidence as exhibits to clarify the verbal description of a medical witness in a Maine case. When a drawing is admitted into evidence, its ability to clarify testimony and to orient evidence to the crime scene enhances such testimony and evidence.

Videotaping is the newest use of graphics at the crime scene. Its pictorial storytelling provides substantial benefits for investigators. Likewise, the videotape may be equally useful to defense attorneys in court.

❾ *Explain the use of "field notes" in documenting the progress made during the course of an investigation.*

Field Notes

Field notes are memoranda made by the investigator during an investigation. They begin with assignment to the case and arrival at the scene; they are added to until the case is closed. That portion of field notes concerned with recording the search for evidence at a crime scene usually includes the time the search started, the names of assisting personnel, the weather and light conditions, a description of the area searched as the investigator proceeds, a note of any special equipment used, and an accurate note of the discovery of every significant item of evidence: when and where it was found, who found it, and its appearance. Any measurements that place the evidence are recorded, as is the disposition of the evidence. Sketches and diagrams drawn at the crime scene are field notes that, by their graphic portrayal of the crime scene, supplement the measurements and other data recorded.

In addition, the searching officer must record in his or her field notes any damage to objects at the scene or any disturbance of furniture and other objects. Anything unusual or foreign to the scene is also noted. Moreover, the failure to locate an item of evidence commonly found at the scene of similar crimes is noted and recorded. These factual reports may be important as clues or as negative evidence to overcome defense claims regarding the theory of the crime and its reconstruction.

Preliminary Investigative Report

The place and time to obtain data for a **preliminary investigative report** are at the crime scene during the initial investigation. Anything omitted or overlooked is either lost or must be ascertained later, which is usually a difficult and time-consuming task. Information about each item of importance must be collected if an investigation is to be comprehensive; the reports required of the officer processing the crime scene are incomplete without such information. The data in this report should include the following:

1. Victim's name, sex, age, occupation, residence and business addresses, and telephone numbers
2. Where the event took place
3. The time of occurrence
4. Who reported the event, if other than the victim, and personal data about this person
5. Date and time reported, and sometimes how reported—in person, by mail, or by telephone
6. Time that the reporting officer arrived at the crime scene
7. Witnesses—full information along with personal data
8. Arrestee, if any, and available personal data
9. Suspects, named or described, with available personal data
10. Name of the reporting officer

While at the crime scene, the reporting officer must determine the method of operation of the perpetrator and collect data about this phase of the crime. These are the modus operandi data and have a stylized form because data storage and retrieval are based on major segments of a criminal's technique. Attention to all these segments by the officer processing the crime scene ensures a thorough reporting of the technique used in the crime. The modus operandi segments include the following (Figure 3-2):

- Type of crime
- Person attacked
- How attacked
- Means of attack, weapons or bindings used
- Trademark of perpetrator (peculiarities)
- Words spoken (or the written note used)
- Vehicle used
- Property stolen
- Name or physical description of suspect

Investigators must collect pertinent data under each segment. For this reason a checklist should be prepared as a reminder of the data to be collected in various crimes. Crimes can be grouped for

| DIST. | SECT | SUB. | ☐ CUSTODY ☐ PEND.
☐ CITATION ☐ CLEARED ADULT
☐ FURTHER INVEST. ☐ CLEARED JUV. | CRIME REPORT | REPORT NUMBER |

| INDICATION OF OCCURRENCE | | REPORT DATE | DAY | TIME | EVENT NO. |

| OCC. DATE FROM | DAY | TIME | OCC. DATE TO | DAY | TIME | CONNECTED REPORT(S) — NUMBER AND TYPE |

CODE SECTION	F	M		CRIME TITLE
			A	
			B	
			C	
			D	

SPECIAL CRIME CATEGORIES EXIST?　☐ NO　☐ YES — CATEGORY FROM REVERSE _____

V | NAME (LAST, FIRST, MIDDLE) | RES. PHONE | BUS. PHONE

RESIDENCE ADDRESS　CITY　STATE　ZIP　BUSINESS ADDRESS (SCHOOL IF JUVENILE)　CITY　STATE　ZIP

| DOB | AGE | SEX | RACE | VICTIM'S VEHICLE (YR., MAKE, MODEL, LIC. NO.) | A | B | C | D | E |
| | | | | | F | G | H | I | J |

V/R | NAME (LAST, FIRST, MIDDLE) | RES. PHONE | BUS. PHONE

RESIDENCE ADDRESS　CITY　STATE　ZIP　BUSINESS ADDRESS (SCHOOL IF JUVENILE)　CITY　STATE　ZIP

| DOB | AGE | SEX | RACE | VICTIM'S VEHICLE (YR., MAKE, MODEL, LIC. NO.) | A | B | C | D | E |
| | | | | | F | G | H | I | J |

A. PLACE of CRIME
1 ☐ STRUCTURE　4 ☐ STREET/ALLEY　7 ☐ OTHER
2 ☐ VEHICLE　5 ☐ LOT/PARK
3 ☐ RES/YARD　6 ☐ BUS/STORAGE

B. DESCRIPTION OF SURROUNDINGS
1 ☐ RESIDENTIAL　4 ☐ RECREATIONAL　7 ☐ OPEN SPACE
2 ☐ BUSINESS　5 ☐ INSTITUTIONAL　8 ☐ OTHER
3 ☐ INDUSTRIAL　6 ☐ CONST. SITE

TYPE OF STRUCTURE ☐ N/A	G POINT OF ENTRY	J METHOD OF ENTRY	INVESTIGATIVE NOTATIONS
C NON-RESIDENTIAL ☐ 1 CONVENIENCE ☐ 2 FAST FOOD ☐ 3 RESTAURANT/BAR ☐ 4 DRUG/MEDICAL ☐ 5 GAS STATION ☐ 6 RETAIL ☐ 7 SCHOOL ☐ 8 FINANCIAL INST. ☐ 9 ENTERTAIN/REC. ☐ 10 PUBLIC BLDG. ☐ 11 OTHER _____ **D TARGET(S)** ☐ 1 SHOP ☐ 2 CASH REG/DRAWER ☐ 3 OFFICE ☐ 4 SAFE/BOX ☐ 5 VENDING MACHINE ☐ 6 DISPLAY ITEMS ☐ 7 CLASSROOM ☐ 8 OTHER _____	**1 ☐ N/A　4 ☐ SIDE** **2 ☐ FRONT　5 ☐ GR LEV.** **3 ☐ REAR　6 ☐ UP LEV.** **H** ☐ 1 UNKNOWN ☐ 2 DOOR ☐ 3 WINDOW ☐ 4 SLIDE GLASS ☐ 5 DUCT/VENT ☐ 6 ADJ. BLDG. ☐ 7 ROOF/FLOOR ☐ 8 WALL ☐ 9 BASEMENT ☐ 10 OTHER _____ **I ALARM SYSTEMS** ☐ 1 YES　☐ 2 NO SET OFF ☐ 3 YES　☐ 4 NO	☐ N/A . . . . ☐ 1 ATTEMPT ONLY ☐ 2 NO FORCE ☐ 3 KEY/SLIP ☐ 4 BODY/FORCE ☐ 5 SAW/DRILL ☐ 6 HID IN BLDG. ☐ 7 CHANNEL LOCK ☐ 8 PRY TOOL _____ ☐ 9 LIFT OUT ☐ 10 BRICK/ROCK ☐ 11 BOLT CUTTERS/PLIERS ☐ 12 WINDOW SMASH ☐ 13 TAPE/WIRE ☐ 14 DOOR PUNCH ☐ 15 DOOR KICK ☐ 16 OTHER _____	SUSPECT INFO PAGE (NUMBER SUSP ____) ____YES____NO PHYSICAL EVIDENCE GATHERED BY R/O ____YES____NO CSI REQUESTED ____YES____NO IDENTIFIABLE PROPERTY ____YES____NO ADDITIONAL VICTIMS/ WITNESSES ____YES____NO NEIGHBORHOOD CANV ____YES____NO PROPERTY LOSS ____YES____NO PROPERTY LIST ATTACHED ____YES____NO INVESTIGATIVE DIV. PERS. NOTIFIED
E RESIDENTIAL ☐ 1 SINGLE FAMILY ☐ 2 APT/CONDO ☐ 3 DUPLEX/TOWN ☐ 4 MOTEL/HOTEL ☐ 5 MOBILE HOME ☐ 6 OTHER _____ **F TARGET(S)** ☐ 1 STORAGE BLDG. ☐ 2 CLOSET ☐ 3 BATHROOM ☐ 4 DEN ☐ 5 FAMILY ROOM ☐ 6 GARAGE/CARPORT ☐ 7 KITCHEN ☐ 8 LIVING ROOM ☐ 9 STORAGE ROOM ☐ 10 BEDROOM ☐ 11 DINING ☐ 12 OTHER _____			

K SUSPECT'S ACTION ☐ N/A		L PROPERTY TAKEN ☐ N/A	
☐ 1 ENTERED OCCUPIED BLDG. ☐ 2 ENTERED UNOCCUPIED BLDG. ☐ 3 VACANT RES./BLDG. ☐ 4 VANDALIZED/RANSACKED ☐ 5 USED MATCHES/SMOKED AT SCENE ☐ 6 DISABLED ALARM ☐ 7 ATE/DRANK ON PREMISES ☐ 8 VEHICLES NEEDED FOR LOOT ☐ 9 USED VICTIM'S TOOLS ☐ 10 KNEW LOCATION OF HIDDEN CASH ☐ 11 SELECTIVE IN LOOT ☐ 12 USED LOOKOUT DRIVER	☐ 13 BOUND/GAGGED VICTIM ☐ 14 RIPPED/CUT CLOTHING ☐ 15 MOLESTED VICTIM ☐ 16 FORCED VICTIM TO MOVE ☐ 17 DISABLED PHONE/ELECTRIC ☐ 18 INJURED VICTIM ☐ 19 THREATENED VICTIM ☐ 20 MASTURBATED ☐ 21 DISROBED FULLY/PARTIALLY ☐ 22 FIRED WEAPON ☐ 23 SUSPECT ARMED ☐ 24 OTHER _____	☐ 1 LARGE LOSS VALUE ☐ 2 TOOK CHECKS/CREDIT CARDS ☐ 3 CONSUMABLE GOOD ☐ 4 OFFICE EQUIPMENT ☐ 5 CAMERA ☐ 6 POWER TOOLS/LAWN EQUIP. ☐ 7 FIREARMS ☐ 8 SILVERWARE ☐ 9 FINE JEWELRY ☐ 10 MONEY ☐ 21 OTHER_____	☐ 11 LARGE APPLIANCES ☐ 12 SMALL APPLIANCES ☐ 13 CLOTHING/FURS ☐ 14 DRUGS ☐ 15 CONSTRUCTION MATERIALS ☐ 16 AUTO PARTS/ACCESSORIES ☐ 17 TOOLS/CARP./MECH./ELECT. ☐ 18 GOLD/SILVER COINS ☐ 19 TV/STEREO/VIDEO ☐ 20 NO LOSS

SYNOPSIS OF CRIME

| INVESTIGATING OFFICER | BADGE | DIVISION | SUPERVISOR |

PAGE ____ OF ____

FIGURE 3-2 Crime Report—Information Called for on this Printed Form Is the Primary Record of the Circumstances of a Crime.

THIS PORTION OF THE REPORT IS REQUIRED BY LAW. REFER TO UNIFORM CRIME REPORTING STANDARDS FOUND IN THE REPORT WRITING MANUAL. IT IS **NOT** TO BE FILLED OUT ACCORDING TO CALIFORNIA PENAL CODE STANDARDS. IF YOUR CRIME CLASSIFICATION INVOLVES A BURGLARY, ROBBERY, THEFT, HOMICIDE, ASSAULT, OR RAPE, BE CERTAIN TO CIRCLE WHATEVER CATEGORY BELOW IS APPROPRIATE. CODE ONLY THE TYPE AND VALUE OF PROPERTY STOLEN AS INDICATED BELOW. RECOVERED PROPERTY IS TO BE CODED DIRECTLY ON THE RECOVERED PROPERTY REPORT, UNLESS RECOVERED SIMULTANEOUSLY AT THE TIME OF THE CRIME REPORT.

PROPERTY	Stolen Value	Recovered Value
A CURRENCY, NOTES, ETC.	$	$
B JEWELRY, PRECIOUS METALS	$	$
C CLOTHING, FURS	$	$
E OFFICE EQUIPMENT	$	$
F TV, CAMERA, STEREOS	$	$
G FIREARMS	$	$
H HOUSEHOLD GOODS	$	$
I CONSUMABLE GOODS	$	$
J LIVESTOCK	$	$
K MISCELLANEOUS	$	$
TOTAL	$	$

BURGLARY

VEHICLE AND SHOPLIFT BURGLARIES ARE TO BE CODED UNDER THEFT

ENTRY
- 051 FORCIBLE
- 052 UNLAWFUL
- 053 ATTEMPT FORCIBLE

STRUCTURE
- 1 RESIDENCE
- 2 NON-RESIDENCE (CLOSED)

ROBBERY

TYPE
- 031 FIREARM
- 032 KNIFE
- 033 OTHER WEAPON
- 034 STRONGARM

LOCATION
- 1 HIGHWAY
- 2 COMMERCIAL HOUSE
- 3 SERVICE STATION
- 4 CONVENIENCE STORE
- 5 RESIDENCE
- 6 BANK
- 7 OTHER

THEFT

TYPE
- 0610 PICKPOCKET
- 0620 PURSE SNATCH
- 0630 SHOPLIFT
- 0640 FROM VEHICLE
- 0650 AUTO PARTS & ACCESSORIES
- 0670 FROM BUILDING
- 0680 COIN-OPERATED MACHINE
- 0690 ALL OTHER

ATTEMPT VEHICLE THEFT
- 0710 AUTO
- 0720 TRUCK/BUS
- 0730 OTHER VEHICLE

A

REPORTED DATE _____
REPORTED TIME _____

DATE OCC. _____
TIME OCC. _____

FROM ___ TO ___

SPECIAL CRIME CATEGORY				NUMBER OF VICTIMS ASSAULTS	
A CRIMES AGAINST CHILDREN	0110	MURDER NON-NEG MANSLAUGHTER	0410	GUN	0440 HANDS/FEET (SERIOUS INJURY)
01 NEGLECT/ABUSE			0420	KNIFE	
02 SEXUAL	0120	MANSLAUGHTER BY NEGLIGENCE	0430	OTHER DANGEROUS WEAPON	0450 HANDS/FEET (MINOR OR NO INJURY)
B CRIMES AGAINST ELDERLY					
C DOMESTIC VIOLENCE					
D GANG AFFILIATION					
E CRIMES MOTIVATED BY:		NUMBER OF VICTIMS		RAPE	
01 RACE					
02 RELIGION	0210	FORCIBLE	0220	ATTEMPT FORCIBLE	
03 SEXUAL PREFERENCE					

ARSON

	PROPERTY CLASSIFICATION		INHABITED	UNINHABITED	TOTAL ARSON $ DAMAGE
091	SINGLE OCCUPANCY RESIDENTIAL	(House, Townhouse, Duplexes, etc.)	1	2	$
092	OTHER RESIDENTIAL	(Apartments, Tenements, Flats, Hotels, Motels, Inns, Dormitories, Boarding Houses, etc.)	1	2	$
093	STORAGE	(Barns, Garages, Warehouses, etc.)	1	2	$
094	INDUSTRIAL MANUFACTURING		1	2	$
095	OTHER COMMERCIAL	(Stores, Restaurants, Offices, etc.)	1	2	$
096	COMMUNITY/PUBLIC	(Churches, Jails, Schools, Colleges, Hospitals, etc.)	1	2	$
097	ALL OTHER STRUCTURE	(Outbuildings, Monuments, Buildings under Construction, etc.)	1	2	$

0981	MOTOR VEHICLES	(Automobiles, Trucks, Buses, Motorcycles, etc.)			
0982	OTHER MOBILE PROPERTY	(Trailers, Recreational Vehicles, Airplanes, Boats, etc.)			
0990	OTHER	(Crops, Timber, Fences, Signs, etc.)			

FIGURE 3-2 Continued

this purpose as crimes against property, crimes against persons, and other crimes. Investigators also must report the details of the crime. This segment of the crime or offense report should be structured to tell the story of the circumstances of the crime to supplement the facts contained in the primary information or the modus operandi segments of the crime report. Many police departments suggest the following organization for this segment of the preliminary investigation:

1. *Suspect(s).* Additional information should be recorded to describe the suspect or suspects, from aliases (the designation *a.k.a.,* "also known as," is used to indicate aliases) and nicknames to physical oddities and dress, including any data on employment or school attended.

2. *Property taken.* In thefts, additional descriptive data on property stolen should be recorded, including the value as set by the victim, the approximate date of original purchase or acquisition by other means ("age" of article), and the original purchase price or estimated value at the time.

3. *Physical evidence.* All items of evidence—including traces, tool marks, and other imprints or impressions—should be described in detail, along with full information as to when and where such evidence was found and who found it, handled it, and disposed of it.

4. *Victim's statement.* The victim or victims who make statements are identified by name, address, age, and employment (or school attended), and the essential facts of the victim's story are stated.

5. *Statement of witness(es).* Each witness making a statement is identified (as in item 1), and the essential facts of the story told by the witness are stated. In addition, this segment of the report should include: (a) data as to the location of the witness at the time of observation, (b) the light conditions, and (c) any relationship of the witness to the victim or suspect(s).

6. *Observations by reporting officer.* Facts are recorded that are not evidence, such as weather, conditions at the scene, and sobriety of persons contacted. Opinions based on observations are permissible in this segment, with both the opinion and its objective base being reported (opinions not based on some objective fact do not belong in a **crime report**).

⑩ *Discuss the use of an "offense or crime report" in establishing that a crime has occurred and how it was committed.*

Offense or Crime Report

The offense or crime report originates at the operational level. Its basic purpose is to record and transmit information. Such reports inform interested persons of the action taken at a crime scene by the reporting officer. They place the data reported in the possession of others who can take appropriate action, and they ensure the continuity of an investigation with little or no need to backtrack or duplicate the work of the preliminary investigator.

Primary data, modus operandi information, and the details or narrative of the crime and its circumstances must be written legibly and in clear and simple language; they must be complete in that all available and related facts are included, but they also must be brief; and they must be accurate, with all facts reported as they are known to the reporting officer, and opinions clearly noted and differentiated from the factual content of the narrative report.

⑪ *Explain the types of photographs that should be taken at a crime scene to provide a pictorial representation of the scene.*

Photographing the Crime Scene

So that the scene can be shown in its original condition, an investigator should not disturb the scene or any objects at the scene before photographing. Crime scene photography provides a permanent record of the facts at the crime scene. Photography is one means of recording facts for future use so that they can be used in reconstructing the crime scene and, sometimes, the crime. Photography is not a substitute for field notes, accurate measurements, and sketches of the scene. Pictures supplement the other forms for recording the facts of a crime scene, and they are often the best way of recording and illustrating the details of a crime scene and its evidence. Sometimes, indeed, they are the only feasible means of recording and illustrating certain features of a crime and the scene.

Photographing a crime scene serves two purposes: it provides a pictorial representation of the appearance and position of objects at the scene, and it serves as evidence to support the testimony of the investigator as to what he or she found at the scene, its location, nature, and condition.[17]

Investigators who do not take their own photographs should be on the crime scene ready to supervise the work of the photographer. As a general rule, police photographers working on crime scenes are responsive to instructions from an assigned investigator because they realize that the investigator is the person responsible for the adequacy of the photographs taken.

The camera positions and the range at which photographs are taken should take advantage of the natural composition at the scene. The story of the scene is to be told graphically, and coherence requires an orderly progression in picture taking. In this type of camera work, objects cannot be moved to gain better composition, but the camera is mobile and its mobility should be used to best advantage.

In general, the subject matter of crime scene photography should move from the general to the specific. Long-range views should tell a story of what happened at the crime scene and serve as a backdrop to locate the subjects of close-up photographs of items of physical evidence. The **long-range photos** may show the locale, the approach route, the means of ingress to the scene or its premises, a hallway, two connected rooms, or a view of the scene from the normal entrance. **Mid-range photos** (ten to twenty feet) pinpoint a specific object of evidence or a significant segment of the crime scene. **Close-up photos** are used for recording evidence in position and detail—location, nature, and condition.

One of the many uses of helicopters is to take aerial photographs of crime scenes.

Aerial photos are excellent for studying crimes in series to ascertain whether the locations of past crimes suggest a pattern of criminal behavior on which the location of the next crime in the series can be projected. They are also excellent for locating outdoor crime scenes or controlling search patterns when large areas must be searched for evidence.

To prove the **corpus delicti**, the essential elements of the crime, a close-up crime scene photograph is needed. This graphic exposition of the full story of the crime, insofar as it can be revealed from any mute viewing of the place of occurrence and its evidence, may be extremely important in preparing the case for presentation in court. Composition varies with the crime: for example, a full-length picture of the homicide victim to show the position of the body or the location of a wound or wounds, the place of forced entry in burglaries, and the point of origin of the fire in suspicious blazes. Examples of close-ups include views of the weapon and wounds in homicides, tool marks at the site of forced entrance, and a fire-setting contrivance or distinctive charring along the fire trails of the accelerant often used in arson.

Photographs also can be used to trace the modus operandi of the criminal and the continuity of crimes occurring in a series. Photographs of tool impressions record the characteristics of any tools used. Enlargements can be made, and prints can be cut in half for comparison. Quite often a jimmy or pry bar can be traced from crime to crime. Linking the impressions sometimes results in a basic lead for an investigator and often provides multiple evidence when a matching tool is found in the possession of a crime suspect.

Evidence photography of crime scenes can be used to reveal blood and hair on weapons, the trajectory of flying objects from marks on floors and walls, the location and characteristics of imprints and impressions, and the full extent of injuries and wounds. Important details can be developed from close-up photography. When a close-up view does not indicate the entire item of evidence, the photographer should show a progression from one end or side of the object to the other side, in a series of sectional views. Sectional photography reassures the triers of fact that the entire surface of the item of evidence was examined. Thus the number of photographs taken of any single item of evidence depends on the dimensions of the evidence and the need for photographic detail.

Measurements and measurement markers always have been a problem in crime scene photography because they intrude upon the photographer's reproduction of the scene as he or she found it. One acceptable procedure is to take a photograph without any change (as is) and then to take another picture with the measurement marker (a flat ruler, or the beginning section of a steel tape stretched out flat) placed in position. The use of a measurement marker is necessary to put the size of the item in the photograph in perspective.

Identification cards or markers are used in some photographs to record the date, time, location, photographer, and the agency involved. However, they are not placed on the evidence, nor do they conceal any part of the major subject of the photograph.

All photographs of a crime scene in a series are dated and numbered consecutively (starting with 1) or identified by a series of film file numbers. Information that will supply data that can be written on each photographic print should be linked with these numbers in the field notes of the photographer. Pertinent data consist of the case number and subject of the picture, the crime classification, the date and time taken, the name of the photographer, the camera's location, the direction in which the camera was aimed, and the distance (in feet) to the subject of the picture.

 Explain the advantage of using a crime sketch with its ability to eliminate unnecessary detail.

Sketching the Crime Scene

The basic reason for sketching a crime scene is to provide an in-depth understanding of the circumstances of the crime beyond the level of comprehension that can be attained solely by reading a written report or studying photographs. A sketch is more than a written report and less than a photograph in depicting a crime scene. Because of its unique virtues, it can supplement both reports and photographs. The advantage of a sketch is that unnecessary detail can be eliminated, whereas it cannot be eliminated from a photograph. Sketching a plan or diagramming the

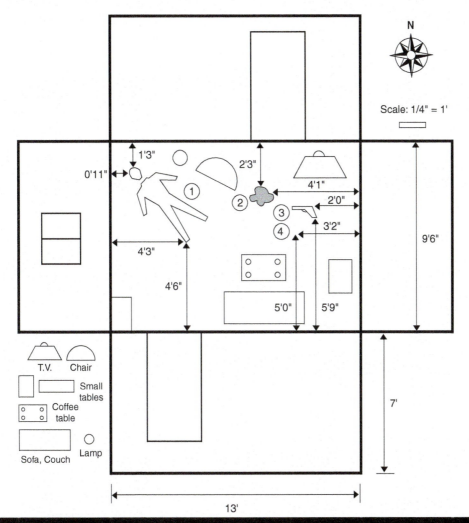

FIGURE 3-3 Floor-Plan Sketch Showing Walls of a Room and Location of (1) Body, (2) Blood, (3) Gun, and (4) Empty Cartridge Cases.

scene in the regular course of police business records the facts available to the viewer (sketcher) so that at any time in the future the assigned investigator and the triers of fact both have a graphic representation of the crime scene (Figure 3-3).

A necessary timeliness is involved in sketching a crime scene. The rough sketch must be made by the investigator as part of his or her field notes during the search of the scene. A field sketch is marked for identification by inserting the following:

1. The investigator's full name
2. The time, date, case number, and crime classification
3. The full name of any person assisting in taking measurements
4. Orientation—address; position in building; location adjacent to building; landmarks and compass direction, if outdoors

A common error in sketching the crime scene is to attempt to make an architectural reproduction or to include too many details. The crime scene sketch is not unlike the diagram of a traffic accident: items that do not aid in reproducing the accident should not be shown.[18] Standard symbols are used to indicate characteristics of the sketch, such as roads, walks, fences, common items of furniture, and evidence frequently encountered at crime scenes (Figure 3-4). A sketch shows and locates important objects at the scene; unimportant ones are omitted for simplicity. No

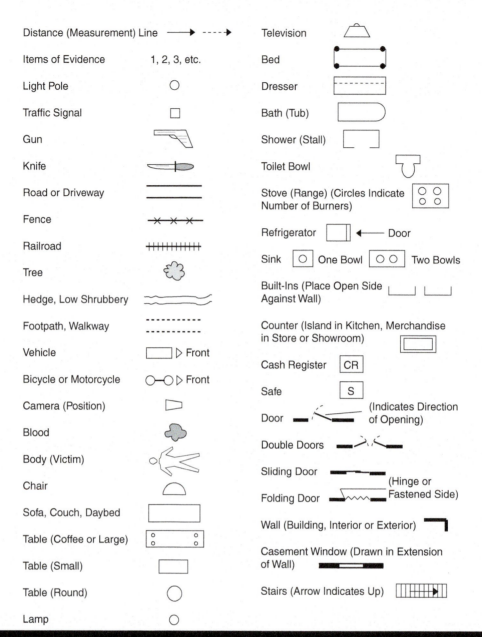

Distance (Measurement) Line		Television	
Items of Evidence	1, 2, 3, etc.	Bed	
Light Pole	○	Dresser	
Traffic Signal	□	Bath (Tub)	
Gun		Shower (Stall)	
Knife		Toilet Bowl	
Road or Driveway		Stove (Range) (Circles Indicate Number of Burners)	
Fence	×—×—×		
Railroad		Refrigerator	← Door
Tree		Sink	○ One Bowl ○ ○ Two Bowls
Hedge, Low Shrubbery		Built-Ins (Place Open Side Against Wall)	
Footpath, Walkway		Counter (Island in Kitchen, Merchandise in Store or Showroom)	
Vehicle	▷ Front		
Bicycle or Motorcycle	○—○ ▷ Front	Cash Register	CR
Camera (Position)		Safe	S
Blood		Door	(Indicates Direction of Opening)
Body (Victim)		Double Doors	
Chair		Sliding Door	
Sofa, Couch, Daybed		Folding Door	(Hinge or Fastened Side)
Table (Coffee or Large)		Wall (Building, Interior or Exterior)	
Table (Small)		Casement Window (Drawn in Extension of Wall)	
Table (Round)	○	Stairs (Arrow Indicates Up)	
Lamp	○		

FIGURE 3-4   Crime Scene Sketch Graphic Symbols.

one except the sketcher should mark or correct a field sketch in any way. This is the first permanent graphic record of the investigation. It is kept for years, beyond any possible need in court, and a photocopy is attached to the investigator's report of the case.

When a graphic illustration is meant to clarify a written report, accurate measurements are needed. Steel tapes are the approved means of measuring distances in criminal investigations. The so-called measuring wheel is an accurate device, but the investigator must show that he or she knows how to use it and did use it in a manner that produced an accurate measurement. The investigator should test it against a known distance measured with a steel tape to verify its accuracy before use. The greatest disservice an investigator can render is to record an erroneous measurement on a drawing or in his or her field notes, for in that case, no matter how many persons subsequently certify the correct measurement, a question will always remain about the initial recording and why it was erroneous.

In general, measurements are made of the area searched. They are made first with the eye. The investigator surveys the crime scene and decides what to measure and where to start. The distance lines between two objects are drawn on the sketch plan; then the actual measurements are made and recorded on the plan. Measurements should extend along and from fixed and identifiable points. Avoid any distance measurement with a floating base: that is, a reference point that may be moved or cannot be located with accuracy. Angular measurements can serve as coordinates to locate a point on the sketch only if the angle is broad and has two reference measurements (constituting a set of measurements) from identifiable fixed points or objects. Two sets of measurements are used for large items, such as a body, to fix the rotational position of that object (see Figure 3-3).

If at all possible, nothing should be moved in the process of measuring. Remember, the movement of objects changes the scene. The sketcher can claim that the object was returned to exactly the same spot, but this is an unnecessary taint of the officer's testimony.

A crime scene area diagram can supplement a crime scene diagram. The former is warranted when one or more of the basic facts in the case is beyond the crime scene itself. Such sketches pinpoint the location of shoe prints, tire tracks, weapons, and similar evidence linked to the crime scene (Figure 3-5).

Erasures may be made on such drawings. In fact, the drawings usually are completed in pencil, then inked in with a permanent ink, and the pencil marks are erased after the ink has dried completely. The drawings are identified in the same way as the crime scene sketch, and similar

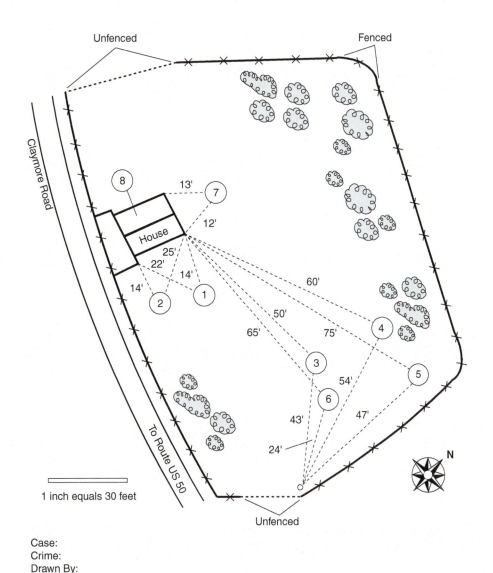

FIGURE 3-5 Crime Scene Area Diagram. Each Numbered Location Represents an Item of Physical Evidence.

symbols may be used and annotated as necessary. Colors may be used for special effects, and overlays of semitransparent paper may be used to diagram the movements of participants in the crime. Schematic diagrams are often used to show the travels (paths) of the victim, offender(s), bullets, and other moving objects.

Many graphic illustrations are drawn to scale, using the investigator's rough sketch and measurements. Recommended scales range from one-eighth of an inch equals 1 foot (1:96) for indoor scenes to 1 inch equals 20 feet (1:240) for larger outdoor areas. These scales usually permit the work to be presented on an 8 by 11-inch sheet of paper. Ideally, the investigator should select a scale that permits reproduction of the scene without completely filling the 8 by 11-inch paper and allows space for a key or legend and necessary identification.

The professional assistance of individuals with special training is often used to prepare an investigator's sketches and diagrams for use in court. These may be enlarged (blown up) but will be kept to the scale noted on the drawing. Such reproductions are usually endorsed or certified by the investigator as being a reproduction of his or her original crime scene sketch. Software is now available that will allow investigators to prepare their own sketches. These two-dimensional applications are user friendly and investigators can learn to create their own diagrams in just a few lessons.[19]

Traditionally, the crime scene sketch has been used as a single-purpose tool merely to indicate the position of physical evidence at the crime scene. Its major purpose has been to place various items of physical evidence at the crime scene rather than to serve as a complete graphic report. Basically, the objective of crime scene sketching should be to graphically present the crime scene in a manner that will permit reconstruction of the crime from the details of the sketch. Thus, an ability to draw must be placed high among the necessary skills of an investigator.

For years, sketching has been particularly effective in vehicular traffic accidents. However, it is a standard investigative technique for pictorial recording in all types of investigations.

Videotaping the Crime Scene

Videotaping is pictorial storytelling, and it offers compelling reasons for investigators to use it. The videographer is not limited by the borders of a photograph or the lens of a camera, but he or she should be more careful when using the video camera to record the graphics of a crime scene record, knowing that the defense counsel could use the videotape to discredit the police case during the trial.

Discovery is the term used for a request by the defense counsel to the prosecutor before trial for disclosure of the police case against his or her client. Its objective is to aid in making certain the defendant receives a fair trial. Detectives have become accustomed to disclosing the outcomes of their investigations, knowing that when a discovery request is made by the defense counsel in local courts, prosecutors must provide all crime reports, photos, sketches, and other pertinent materials.

Videotaping has been used to advantage by prosecutors at trial to show jurors meaningful views of the crime scene, but it has also been used by defense attorneys to destroy the credibility of investigators by using select segments of the video to contradict court testimony. The segment may show only a minor oversight on the part of the officer, but it may be enough to destroy a police case by linking suspicion to police conduct at the crime scene. Today, investigators participate in making decisions about the use of videotapes, along with prosecutors, local judiciary, and defense attorneys.[20]

Videotape has several advantages over photography: (1) it provides immediate results without the need for developing film, (2) tapes can be reused by recording over the images on the previously used tape, (3) visual movement allows the viewer to perceive the scene as it is shown, and (4) sound may be used.[21]

The low cost of camcorders, as well as their portability, user-friendly sophistication, high-quality images, and the ease with which the tape can be moved for viewing from the camcorder to a tabletop or large-screen monitor are all sound reasons for police departments to adopt this graphic system and adapt it to their needs.

In crime investigation, videotape has been used successfully in clandestine observation of suspicious places and persons, as well as transactions in "sting" operations. It is now being used more extensively to record interviews with witnesses and the built-in statement feature, which documents what was actually said, has been helpful to investigators when a witness attempts to change or deny his or her initial version of the crime's circumstances. Videotaping at crime scenes has become more commonplace.

⓭ *Discuss the various methods investigators use to identify and locate potential witnesses.*

▶ Locating Witnesses

It is the duty of the first officer at the scene of a suspected crime to "contain" it. Standard regulations require responding officers to detain witnesses and other persons at the scene. These officers secure adequate information about the identity of all persons found at a crime scene: their names, addresses, and telephone numbers; and their employers' names and business addresses. Of course, the perpetrator is arrested if he or she is at the scene and so identified, but at this time the major concern with regard to witnesses is to locate them, secure a description of the perpetrator or perpetrators and the facts of the crime, and record their identities and where they can be located.

The degree of difficulty involved in locating a particular witness is directly related to the willingness of that person to be a witness and the knowledge that person has that he or she is, in fact, a witness to a crime. A willing witness may wait at the crime scene until the police arrive or contact the police to supply information. Many willing witnesses are motivated by a sense of civic responsibility. Others may be motivated to assist the police to eliminate business competitors. It is not uncommon, for instance, for one drug dealer to inform on another drug dealer whose territory he covets. Relatives, spouses, and lovers will also provide the authorities with information regarding the whereabouts of wanted loved ones in the hope that the offender will get the necessary treatment or learn the lesson that crime does not pay. Perhaps one of the most powerful motivations is revenge: people who have been wronged by the suspect in one way or another will cooperate with the investigation to get even.

The **unwilling witness** does not want to cooperate with the investigation and will usually disappear from a crime scene when the police arrive. The motivation of such witnesses varies. It may be a simple dislike for authority or that the witness has outstanding warrants or is a suspect in a criminal act. Many unwilling witnesses will say simply that they do not want to get involved. The basis here may be selfishness or a genuine concern for loss of income or another inconvenience that might result from having to testify at a lengthy criminal trial.

Some potential witnesses may be unaware that they witnessed a crime or its circumstances. For example, the witness may have observed the arrival or departure of the suspect from the crime scene but not the crime itself. Although the nature of the crime may be unknown, this potentially important witness can place the suspect at the scene of the crime.

Revisiting the Crime Scene

Revisiting the crime scene has been effective in locating witnesses. Motorists and pedestrians who do not live or work in the area but who travel the area at about the same time daily or weekly are often witnesses, but they leave the scene prior to the arrival of responding officers, sometimes not even knowing that the event they witnessed has become a police case.

The technique of revisiting a crime scene to search for witnesses has been adapted from the investigation of hit-and-run crimes. Solving such cases, in which motorists are involved in an accident and flee the scene, usually requires locating the vehicle involved. Investigators can use only the identification potential of the physical evidence found at the scene and, when the suspect vehicle is located, the damage to the suspect car. For this reason, witnesses who can give some clue to the identity of the vehicle and its operator must be discovered. When the initial inquiry at the scene does not produce witnesses, investigators revisit the scene for a week or two for an hour or more each day, spanning the time of the accident, then revisit on the same day of the week for three or four weeks. Traffic accident investigation units have used this technique for years to find witnesses and collect information about the identity of a hit-and-run vehicle. Key witnesses have been located as much as a month after an accident. The procedure is now formalized as follows:

1. Revisit the accident scene daily for no less than a week and weekly on the day of the week of the accident for no less than a month at the same time of day that the accident occurred.

2. Question motorists and pedestrians, with particular attention to schoolchildren and service personnel, such as operators of delivery vehicles.[22]

View Area Canvass

An inquiry in the **view area** of the crime scene is also standard practice (Figure 3-6). When a crime is committed within a building, as in an office or apartment, the universe of possible witnesses may be small. When the crime is committed in a store or on the street, a large group of persons might have witnessed it. This requires a search for persons who may have been witnesses but who have not been so identified. Officers visit places of business, apartments, and residences near the scene. Customers and employees of markets, taverns, and service stations, and residents at home and their visitors, are all questioned. This is a solicitation for information about the crime and about anyone who might have seen the event, witnessed suspicious persons in the area before the crime, viewed the perpetrator's flight from the scene, heard anything unusual, or knows of someone who has or might have information.

The Neighborhood Canvass

Superior officers supervising the criminal investigation often assign additional personnel to an extensive **neighborhood canvass** in order to find a witness. The plan used in such a canvass may be based on the approach and flight route of the perpetrator, the travels of witnesses, or the path of a bullet in sniper cases. A canvass for witnesses in the neighborhood of the crime follows a pattern. It starts with revisits to persons residing or employed in the view area of the crime scene and extends to establishing contacts with employees of delivery service firms and public utilities. This canvass expands to nearby areas and bus stops and public transit stations beyond the crime scene but within a convenient distance of it. Such a canvass involves the traditional task of ringing doorbells. Often it appears to be a hopeless assignment, yet time and again an investigator canvassing an area finds a witness or, equally important, a person who knows the identity of a witness.

This knocking on doors and asking questions is a very productive source of evidence in homicide cases. The seriousness of the crime impresses most people, and they respond meaningfully when questioned. In these cases, investigators are seeking information about the victim, as well as the killer or killers.[23]

The attempt to locate witnesses in a canvass of a neighborhood includes the following steps:

1. Friends and immediate relatives of the victim living in the neighborhood are located and interviewed.

2. A house-to-house, apartment-to-apartment, door-to-door canvass is made of
   a. residents and shopkeepers and their employees
   b. delivery, utility, and other service personnel
   c. bus and taxi drivers

Supermarkets, which are isolated within the moats of their immense parking lots, have created problems in locating witnesses. The problem is not that the viewing area is curtailed, since people are still in and about this area. The problem is that the people in the view area are transients. They do not reside in it, nor is it a place of employment. They walk or drive to a view area, then leave it, and return to their homes or places of business. The tremendous population of people and vehicles in and about shopping centers complicates the problem of locating witnesses to crimes and has led to the concept of the shopping-area canvass for witnesses (Figure 3-6). Unlike the neighborhood canvass developed by detectives in large urban central cities, this shopping area canvass can be very extensive geographically. The canvass in urban centers encompasses the

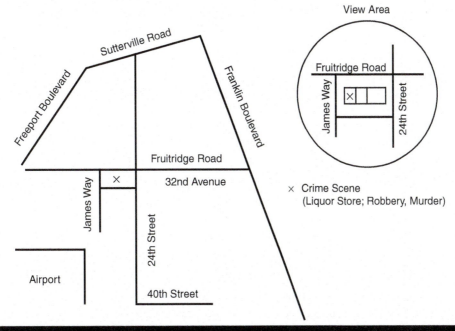

FIGURE 3-6 Shopping Area Canvass for Witnesses.

× Crime Scene
(Liquor Store; Robbery, Murder)

area in which the perpetrator may have traveled to and from the crime scene; the shopping area canvass encompasses the area in which witnesses travel to and from the crime scene.

It may seem that the distinction is highly technical or abstract, but many individuals who are otherwise very cooperative with the police reject any semblance of the informer role. These persons often feel that revealing the name or whereabouts of a witness is not in the same category as revealing the identity of a person who might have committed the crime.

Investigators successful in locating witnesses in this way are skilled in establishing liaisons with persons likely to have information and in maintaining contacts with such individuals until their cooperation is needed. This is not normally a procedure that can be developed for a specific investigation. The contacts must be established first. Then when a crime occurs, and this type of cooperation is needed, the investigator has sources of information available.

Issuing Pleas for Public Cooperation

In serious felony cases receiving unusual publicity, the police receive a great many investigative leads from members of the community. These offers of help proliferate when the crime is child molesting, a series of murders or rapes, and robberies or thefts of very large sums of money or immensely valuable jewelry. Unfortunately, the great majority of these calls are from persons justly classified as cranks. Most of the leads are useless, and the time spent making inquiries is lost entirely. An investigator cannot afford to verify every offer of information from such sources. Selectivity is necessary, and techniques for auditing these unsought messages should be developed. In the audit, all messages containing the name and address or other data identifying a potential witness are separated from letters and calls presenting theories of the crime or suspicious persons. A prompt follow-up inquiry is made on the witness leads, and the remainder is set aside for later analysis.

Police officials, in attempting to locate witnesses to crimes of importance, use all the communications media: newspapers, radio, local television outlets, and the Internet. In New York, Chicago, San Francisco, Miami, and other large cities, the standard plea to the public is to contribute any information about the case to police, and it is now made easier for them to do so by publication of a special telephone number. In some cases, the posting of a reward hastens the response to these pleas for public cooperation. However, this mercenary inducement for help should be avoided unless it is deemed absolutely necessary. For gain, some persons may supply false or meaningless information solely in the hope of making a future claim. A **silent witness program** seeks the same help but offers rewards and confidentiality.

A technique has been developed by local television stations: a telecast of clues about an unsolved and recent crime. This "clue-in" offers the viewers a minimum of facts about the case, and the core of the program is a request for listeners to call the local station if they believe they may have witnessed any of the travels of the suspected offender or offenders. Several radio stations across the country have cooperated with police in a similar fashion. Listeners in either instance are conditioned to respond by calling the station because of the growth of contests and opinion polls requiring a prompt telephone response.

In both types of clue-ins, the emphasis is not on finding people with theories of the crime or ideas of techniques the police should use in searching for the offender but rather on locating witnesses. Listeners and viewers are asked to call a specific, easily remembered telephone number under any of the following conditions:

- If you witnessed any segment of this crime, any act concerned with its preparation, any of the postcrime travels or other activities of the criminal or his or her associates
- If you know the identity of the criminal or his or her associates from other sources of information
- If you know the identity of any other person who might have been a witness or who might know the identity of the offender and his or her associates

Police in the United States have been having problems securing the cooperation of the public in solving crimes. However, when the crime is widely recognized as vicious and hurtful, the potential for community support is excellent. Persons who would not normally cooperate will do so when the atrocity of a crime inspires their sympathy for the victim and the public appeal for information orients them to the police. It is a technique in searching for witnesses that has optimum potential because everyone in the community is exposed to multimedia. Notices in the media do communicate to people and can be used successfully in discovering witnesses.

CASE STUDY

INCREDIBLE EVIDENCE

Late Sunday afternoon on June 12, 1994, Nicole Brown Simpson, the former wife of football great O. J. Simpson, attended her daughter's dance recital in West Los Angeles. Also in attendance was her former husband, who is the father of her two children. When the recital ended, Nicole, her children, and her other family members dined at the Mezzaluna restaurant near her home in Brentwood. She arrived home at approximately 8:30 P.M. and called the restaurant to inquire about her prescription sunglasses that she had left behind. A waiter friend, Ron Goldman, found the glasses and offered to bring them to her on his way home from work. Goldman left the restaurant at about 9:45 P.M.

At approximately 10:45 P.M., a limousine driver arrived at O. J. Simpson's estate to pick him up and take him to the airport. The driver noted that his passenger was "agitated and sweaty." At 11:45 P.M., Simpson's plane left for Chicago. At this time, an acquaintance noted that Simpson appeared composed and talkative about playing golf the next day in Chicago.

On Monday morning, June 13, at about 12:10 A.M., a neighbor found Nicole's dog wandering around the neighborhood. He returned the dog to Nicole's townhouse and discovered the bodies of Nicole Brown

Simpson and Ron Goldman outside the front entrance to Nicole's home. Both victims had been stabbed and had their throats slashed.

The police were notified and quickly responded to the scene. The first officer on the scene located the victims and searched the interior of the townhouse, finding Nicole's two children unharmed, asleep in their beds. The area was cordoned off and the crime scene technicians and homicide detectives were requested to respond. During the initial search for evidence at the crime scene, a bloody leather glove was found at the feet of victim Ron Goldman.

By 5:00 A.M., the detectives assigned to the case had determined the identities of the victims and decided to go to the Simpson estate a few miles away to notify him of the death of his ex-wife. Upon arrival at the estate, the detectives noticed what appeared to be blood on the driver-side door handle of Simpson's Ford Bronco, which was parked on the street outside the estate. A string of what could have been blood droplets led from the Bronco to the front entrance of the residence. The detectives received no response at the gate intercom or to follow-up phone calls to the residence. Believing the safety of O. J. Simpson and other family

(continued)

members was at risk, one of the detectives scaled over a five-foot wall surrounding the estate and opened the gate, allowing the other detectives to enter.

The detectives entered the residence, but O. J. Simpson was not there. The detectives found two navy blue socks on the floor of the master bedroom. A search of the grounds led to the discovery of a bloody leather glove, similar to the one found at the crime scene, on the rear walkway on the south side of the estate. The detectives seized these items and the Ford Bronco as possible items of evidence. These items of evidence were eventually forwarded to the crime laboratory for processing.

O. J. Simpson's whereabouts in Chicago were then determined. He was contacted by telephone in the early morning hours and informed of his ex-wife's death. Simpson arranged to catch the next flight back to Los Angeles. Upon arrival in California, Simpson was taken to police headquarters, questioned by the homicide detectives, and later released.

On June 17, Simpson was charged with two counts of murder and a warrant was issued for his arrest. On June 20, Simpson entered a plea of not guilty and his trial was scheduled to begin on January 24, 1995. During his eight-month-long trial, Simpson did not take the witness stand in his defense, and the prosecution did not use any portion of his statement given to the police on June 13. No eyewitnesses to the crime came forth, so the prosecution relied primarily on the physical evidence to make its case against the defendant, which included the following:

Simpson's Ford Bronco. A crime scene technician collected blood samples from the vehicle's interior two days after the murders. The test results on the samples indicated that these bloodstains matched the blood of both victims, as well as that of the defendant. On cross-examination, the crime scene technician who collected the samples admitted that she had used the same cotton swab on different bloodstains. This was contrary to her training, and this unapproved method of collection could have led to possible contamination of the samples.

Blood at the Crime Scene. In addition to finding the victims' blood, investigators found bloodstains at the crime scene that matched the blood of the defendant. Some three weeks after the crime was committed, a drop of Simpson's blood also was found on the rear gate at the scene of the crime. The prosecution maintained that Simpson cut himself while attacking his two victims. The defense countered that the three-week delay in finding this evidence would have given the police ample time to plant the evidence.

Navy Blue Socks. Tests revealed that the socks found in Simpson's master bedroom contained bloodstains that matched the blood of both victim Nicole Brown Simpson and the defendant.

Leather Gloves. Tests indicated that the bloodstains on the glove found at the crime scene and the glove found at the Simpson estate matched the blood of both victims and the defendant. The defense countered by suggesting that one of the gloves had been transported by the police from the crime scene and then was planted on the estate's rear walkway.

Simpson's Blood Sample. The defendant had supplied a blood sample at police headquarters shortly after being questioned by the homicide detectives. Detective Vannatter then took the sample from police headquarters to the Simpson estate. Detective Vannatter gave the sample to the crime scene technicians who were still collecting evidence. The defense argued that this was contrary to established standard procedure. The detective should have booked the blood sample at police headquarters. In addition, the defense maintained that a small quantity of this sample, 1.5 milliliters, was unaccounted for by the crime laboratory. The defense suggested that the missing blood was used by the police to plant the defendant's blood samples at the crime scene and on various pieces of evidence.

EDTA. In its analysis of blood evidence, the defense found minute quantities of a preservative known as EDTA. The defense contended that such a finding could suggest that the blood attributed to the defendant had come from Simpson's sample. The prosecution refuted this contention by arguing that had the evidence been sprinkled with blood from Simpson's reference vial, the level of EDTA would have been much, much higher.

After eight months of trial testimony, most experts expected the jury to deliberate for days, if not weeks, before reaching a verdict. However, within only a few hours, the jury completed deliberations and reached a unanimous verdict of not guilty. Juror Brenda Morgan, interviewed after the verdict was announced, told the press that the jury found Detective Vannatter's decision to carry Simpson's blood sample around with him for several hours "suspicious because it gave him the opportunity to plant evidence." Another juror put it this way: "not a conspiracy with all the police officers, but maybe with some."

Source: Adapted from Vincent Bugliosi, *Outrage: The Five Reasons Why O. J. Simpson Got Away with Murder* (New York: Norton, 1996), 309–320, 344.

CHAPTER REVIEW

Key Terms

Review Questions

1. When a witness discusses the crime or overhears others talking about the crime, he or she may unconsciously incorporate some of this information as his or her own. This process is known as:
   a. Interference
   b. Retroactive interference
   c. Reactive interference
   d. Proactive interference

2. The first officers on the scene of a crime should identify potential witnesses and_____ and them as soon as possible.
   a. Interview
   b. Separate
   c. Interrogate
   d. Dismiss

3. The essential elements of the crime are known as the:
   a. Modus operandi
   b. Corpus delicti
   c. Corpus operandi
   d. Modus delicti

4. The advantage of a crime scene sketch that cannot be accomplished with any type of photography is the:
   a. Ability to improve lighting conditions
   b. Elimination of unnecessary detail
   c. Unique ability of the artist come through
   d. Addition of missing or necessary detail

5. The crime scene search pattern that starts at one end of the scene and in which searchers work back and forth until the entire area is searched is known as what type of search?
   a. Ever-widening
   b. Ever-narrowing
   c. Zone or sector
   d. Strip

6. Being able to account for an item of evidence from the time of its finding to its presentation in court is known as:
   a. Contingency processing
   b. Chain of custody
   c. Possession accountability
   d. Chain of accountability

7. Which of the following should *not* be released to the media by investigators?
   a. Identity of possible witnesses
   b. Type of crime committed
   c. Details of the offense
   d. When and where the crime occurred

8. The first officers responding to a crime scene are responsible for making sure that the scene is safe for other personnel to enter the area. This step in the coordination of a crime scene is known as:
   a. Initializing the scene
   b. Neutralizing the scene
   c. Crime scene security
   d. Crime scene basics

9. Officers guarding the perimeter of a crime scene are responsible for maintaining a chronological log. This log is based on what?
    a. Resources expended at the crime scene
    b. Movement of persons into and out of the crime scene
    c. Time of occurrence of events at the crime scene
    d. Importance of the events that occur at the crime scene

10. The brief contact with the victim and witness for the purposes of gathering suspect information is done for what purpose?
    a. Management notification
    b. Media relations
    c. Scene safety
    d. Broadcast alarm

See Appendix D *for the correct answers.*

Application Exercise

Imagine that you are the first officer on the scene of a violent crime, a shooting that has just occurred outside of a local bar. Upon your arrival you see a person down on the ground and a weapon and other possible evidence nearby. What steps would you take to exercise control of the crime scene? How would you contain the patrons of the bar who refuse to stay out of your crime scene as they want to enter or leave the bar and really don't care for the status of the victim or your crime scene? Are there any laws in your jurisdiction that would allow you to keep a person out of a crime scene? What if the crime was committed in that person's home?

Discussion Questions

1. Explain what the first responding officers should be doing as they approach the scene of a crime that has just occurred and what they should do when they first arrive at the scene.
2. Describe the officer-in-charge concept and the logic behind this operational premise.
3. Describe standard procedures in collecting and preserving evidence.
4. Can any one rule of evidence gathering be identified as of primary importance?
5. Explain when and why known standards of evidence should be collected.
6. Discuss the concerns officers might logically have in dealing with infected evidence.
7. Discuss the importance of media relations and the purpose behind having a media spokesperson for the department.
8. Regarding the case study, discuss how a deviation from standard operating procedures in the handling of physical evidence can affect the outcome of a criminal trial.
9. Regarding the case study, is the perception of wrongdoing as persuasive to a jury as actual wrongdoing?

Related Websites

To find out more about crime scene investigation, contact the National Criminal Justice Reference Service, the research agency of the U.S. Department of Justice, at www.ncjrs.org.

To learn more about the role of public information officers (PIOs) and media relations, contact the National Information Officers Association at www.nioa.org.

New technologies are constantly being developed to help investigators to find evidence and solve crimes. Learn more about these emerging technologies at www. officer.com.

Interested in being a crime scene investigator? If so, you might be interested in some information from the International Crime Scene Investigators Association at www.icsia.org.

To learn more about crime scene photographing and sketching, visit the following site: www.crime-scene-investigator.net.

Notes

1. Hans G. A. Gross, *Criminal Investigation,* 5th ed., trans. John Adam and J. Collyer Adam, rev. R. L. Jackson (London: Sweet & Maxwell Ltd., 1962).

2. U.S. Department of Justice, Office of Justice Programs, National Institute of Justice, *Eyewitness Evidence, a Guide for Law Enforcement* (Washington, DC: Government Printing Office, 1999), 15.

3. Larry Danaher, "The Investigative Paradigm," *Law and Order* (June 2003): 134.

4. U.S. Department of Justice, National Institute of Justice, Office of Justice Programs, *Crime Scene Investigation: A Guide for Law Enforcement* (Washington, DC: Government Printing Office, 2000), 11–14.

5. Bill Toohey, "Tips from the Trenches: Advice from a PIO," *The Police Chief* (April 2001): 43.

6. D. P. Blaricom, "The Media: Enemies or Allies?" *The Police Chief* (April 2001): 52.

7. Evidence technicians are called *scenes-of-crime officers* in England. See H. J. Walls, *Forensic Science* (New York: Praeger Publishers, 1968), 4.

8. Vernon Geberth, "Physical Evidence in Sex-Related Death Investigation," *Law and Order* (July 2003): 106.

9. *Schmerber v. California,* 384 U.S. 757 (1966).

10. James P. Conway, *Evidential Documents* (Springfield, IL: Charles C Thomas, 1959), 73–83.

11. Claude W. Cook, *A Practical Guide to the Basics of Physical Evidence* (Springfield, IL: Charles C Thomas, 1984), 10–12.

12. *Gilbert v. California,* 388 U.S. 263 (1967); *United States v. Blount,* 315 F. Supp. 1321 (1970).

13. *United States v. Wade,* 388 U.S. 218 (1967). See also *United States v. Ash,* 413 U.S. 300 (1973) and *Kirby v. Illinois,* 406 U.S. 682 (1972).

14. *Miranda v. Arizona,* 384 U.S. 436 (1966).

15. Paul D. Bigbee, "Collecting and Handling Evidence Infected with Human Disease-Causing Organisms," *FBI Law Enforcement Technology,* no. 18 (October 1991): 66–70.

16. U.S. Department of Justice, *Crime Scene Investigation,* 30.

17. *Basic Police Photography,* 2nd ed. (Rochester, NY: Eastman Kodak, 1968), 16–22.

18. Paul B. Weston, *The Police Traffic Control Function,* 2nd ed. (Springfield, IL: Charles C Thomas, 1968), 196–199.

19. "The CAD Zone: Law Enforcement Drawing Software," *Police* (March 2004): 86.

20. Kenneth M. Wells and Paul B. Weston, *Criminal Procedure and Trial Practice* (Englewood Cliffs, NJ: Prentice Hall, 1977), 29–34.

21. Larry L. Miller, *Sansone's Police Photography,* 3rd ed. (Cincinnati, OH: Anderson Publishing, 1993), 111–113.

22. J. Stannard Baker, *Traffic Accident Investigator's Manual for Police,* 4th ed. (Evanston, IL: The Traffic Institute, Northwestern University, 1963).

23. Barbara Gelb, *On the Track of Murder: Behind the Scenes with a Homicide Commando Squad* (New York: William Morrow & Company, 1975), 26.

4 Physical Evidence

CHAPTER OUTLINE

LEARNING OBJECTIVES

After reading this chapter, you will be able to:

❶ *Explain the difference between class and individual evidence.*

❷ *Discuss the various types of information that can be obtained through ballistic examinations of firearms.*

❸ *Discuss the various types of tests used to identify blood and distinguish it from animal blood.*

❹ *Identify the various types of imprints and impressions found at crime scenes and the methods used to recover these items of evidence.*

❺ *Discuss the methods used for collecting tool impressions at the crime scene and the laboratory examination process.*

❻ *Discuss the importance of trace evidence such as hairs, fibers, paint, and glass.*

❼ *Explain what items a questioned documents examiner would look for in the attempt to identify the machine or person who typewrote a document.*

Two kinds of proof are used during a criminal trial to answer the question of guilt or innocence: direct evidence and circumstantial evidence. **Direct evidence** involves eyewitnesses who have, through one or more of their five senses, experienced something relative to the crime in question or its circumstances. In contrast, **circumstantial evidence** is defined as evidence from which an inference can be drawn and which includes items such as physical evidence. For instance, we can infer that the finding of a person's fingerprints at the scene of a crime would indicate that

that person was at the crime scene at some point in time even though no one actually saw that person there. The major types of circumstantial evidence include weapons, blood, imprints or impressions, tool marks, hairs, fibers, glass, paint, and questioned documents.

 Explain the difference between class and individual evidence.

▶ Class and Individual Evidence

Physical evidence can be divided into two broad categories: **class evidence** and **individual evidence**. Class evidence cannot be linked to a particular person or an object but only to a class of objects. Class evidence includes glass, paint, shoe prints, ballistics, fibers, and tool marks. This type of evidence can only link an object to a certain class of evidence; for example, a particular type of glass, such as a window glass, may be linked to a crime scene. On the other hand, individual evidence can be linked to a person or a specific object. One of the best examples of individual evidence is fingerprints. No two people have the same fingerprints, not even identical twins. Other individual evidence that would directly identify a person would include palm prints, sole prints, voice prints, bite marks, and even ear and lip prints.

Class evidence may acquire individual characteristics over time through wear and tear. For example, a new pair of shoes when first worn has class characteristics, but over time the person's distinct walk will develop a wear pattern that is unique to that person's shoes and the shoes will then have individual characteristics. A fragment of glass can take on individual characteristics when that particular piece of glass fits perfectly with the broken pieces recovered from the crime scene.[1]

❷ *Discuss the various types of information that can be obtained through ballistic examinations of firearms.*

Weapons

Firearms should be handled to preserve ballistic identity. **Ballistics** is the identification of firearms, bullets, cartridges, and shotgun shells. **Interior ballistics** refers to the functioning of firearms through the firing cycle (Figure 4-1), and **exterior ballistics** is the study of projectiles in flight. As primary sources for identification, ballistics uses the inside of the barrel (the bore, with its lands and grooves), the firing pin, the breech face in which the firing pin hole is located, the chamber, and the ejector and extractor.[2]

Investigators reject such techniques for picking up firearms as the insertion of a pencil in the barrel of a handgun and follow procedures that will not change the portions of the weapon commonly used for ballistic comparison and identification. Firearms should be picked up by their rough or checkered wooden portions, if possible, or any external metal portion except the trigger guard and trigger area, and promptly placed in a container or tied to a board or strong piece of cardboard. Firearms should not be handled unnecessarily, nor should the mechanism be actuated time and time again. Safety is of paramount importance. The minimum procedure for emptying a gun should be followed to unload a firearm. No attempt should be made to fire a gun, dismantle it, or interfere with the mechanism in any way.

A description of a firearm should start with the name of the manufacturer and the serial number. These data are necessary for tracing the weapon. Record all names and numbers stamped on the firearm, along with their locations on the gun. Some numbers are part numbers, and one- or two-digit numbers are usually model numbers. Some marks may indicate the maker, others proof testing. (Emblems and symbols are **proof marks** that indicate tests performed to prove the strength of the chamber of a firearm by actual firing with maximum loads.) All these marks help identify the gun. Sometimes a number has been obliterated by grinding, filing, or center punching. The investigator should describe the damage and its location and request laboratory services to restore the number. (It is difficult to restore when center punched, but it may be possible, and even a fragment may be helpful.)

The **caliber** of the weapon or its gauge (if a shotgun) refers to the diameter of the barrel of the gun and is also an identifying characteristic. It is often marked on the firearm in a stamping

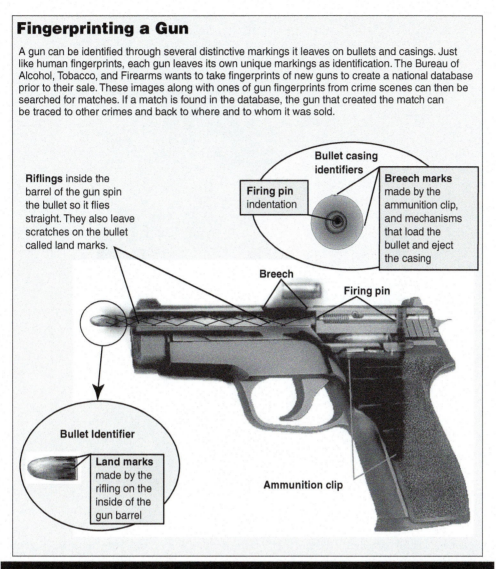

Fingerprinting a Gun

A gun can be identified through several distinctive markings it leaves on bullets and casings. Just like human fingerprints, each gun leaves its own unique markings as identification. The Bureau of Alcohol, Tobacco, and Firearms wants to take fingerprints of new guns to create a national database prior to their sale. These images along with ones of gun fingerprints from crime scenes can then be searched for matches. If a match is found in the database, the gun that created the match can be traced to other crimes and back to where and to whom it was sold.

Riflings inside the barrel of the gun spin the bullet so it flies straight. They also leave scratches on the bullet called land marks.

Bullet casing identifiers

Firing pin indentation

Breech marks made by the ammunition clip, and mechanisms that load the bullet and eject the casing

Breech

Firing pin

Bullet Identifier

Land marks made by the rifling on the inside of the gun barrel

Ammunition clip

FIGURE 4-1 Interior Ballistics Identification.

associated with the name of the manufacturer or model number. If the caliber is not marked, the investigator should qualify any estimate of the caliber by putting "unknown" in his or her field notes and noting a measurement across the bore of the weapon in fractions of an inch. This is in line with the requirement of accuracy in collecting evidence. A defense attorney can raise doubt about testimony in relation to firearms (and possibly doubt about the entire police case) by questioning failure by police to make accurate notations regarding the caliber of a weapon. Professional conduct requires an investigator to qualify any lack of knowledge, and it is more desirable to write "unknown" than to specify an approximate caliber and later to find it is grossly wrong.

Fired (empty) and unfired cartridge cases, shotgun shells, and spent bullets should also be handled with particular attention to the portions used in ballistic identification—that is, the base and the rim just above the base of the case, and the side of the cartridge or the shell immediately above the base (extractor marks). When empty cartridge cases or shotgun shells are picked up, the location should be pinpointed with measurements for future reference. Because some firearms throw out, or eject, the cartridge cases with some distinctiveness as to direction and force, the exact location of the cases can indicate the position of the person firing the gun, sometimes for each shot fired.

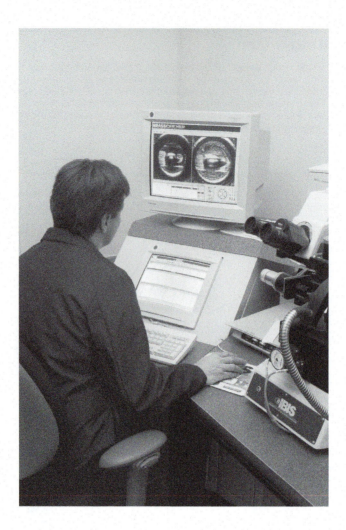

Spent bullets are excellent clues to the firearm used in the crime. They must be carefully removed from their point of impact, and the location at which they are found must be recorded accurately in the investigator's field notes. Investigators must search at crime scenes for bullets embedded in walls and furniture. A spent bullet can be ruined by digging it out with a pocket-knife. Care must be taken so that the drill or cutting instrument used in this operation does not ruin identifying characteristics on a bullet by coming into contact with the softer metal. Bullets should also be handled as little as possible and packaged to prevent movement and to protect the side portions used in ballistic comparison and identification. When the victim is dead and an autopsy is performed, one of the **postmortem forensic science** procedures is the removal of spent bullets without damage to their original condition. In the United States, physicians and surgeons are very conscious of the evidential value of spent bullets.

Because it is sometimes necessary to establish the position of a person in crimes involving a shooting, the investigator at the crime scene should look closely for places the bullet has struck in its flight.[3] These marks or holes are items of evidence and are correlated with other positioning factors, such as the location of ejected cartridge cases found at the scene and the path of a bullet in the body of a victim.

A question that must be answered concerns whether or not a victim of a suicide or the suspect of a homicide recently fired a weapon. This question can be answered through a **gunshot residue (GSR) examination**. This test starts with applying adhesive tapes to the person's hands. These tapes are then sent to the **crime laboratory** where they are examined using a scanning electron microscope interfaced with an energy-dispersive X-ray.[4] This examination is used to search for the presence of the major components in a center-fire cartridge: antimony sulfide, barium nitrate, and lead styphnate, as well as supporting metallic particles of zinc, copper, or nickel. These compounds and elements are deposited on a person's hands when they

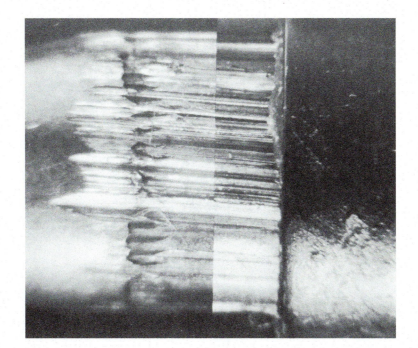

A test bullet on the right-hand side of this vertical line matches the bore marks on a bullet found at the scene of a crime.

Source: Orlando/ Three Lions/Getty Images

fire a weapon, and they undergo an intense **exothermic reaction** due to the rapid increase in temperature followed by a sharp decrease. This supercooling phenomenon leads to a unique spheroidal formation that is generally not observed in the natural environment.[5]

Other weapons commonly encountered by police investigators are knives and various blunt instruments. Accuracy in describing such evidence may depend on a general description. The presence of serial numbers is not common, and clubs and similar weapons are not stamped with the name of the maker. The lengths of a knife blade and a knife handle are easily determined without excessive handling, as are the lengths and other dimensions of clubs and bludgeons. Distinctive features of the object should be noted in the investigator's field notes. The greatest possibility of error in connection with these weapons results from the tendency, when searching, to ignore common items of furniture or equipment at the scene of the crime as suspect weapons. In one case, the bludgeon used in a killing was a piece of 2-inch by 4-inch lumber about $3\frac{1}{2}$ feet long. The scene of the crime was a lumberyard. In another case, an apparently innocuous empty soft drink bottle was collected; later, the autopsy report cited a depressed fracture of the skull of the victim as the cause of death, and laboratory tests discovered blood traces on the bottle.

 Discuss the various types of tests used to identify blood and distinguish it from animal blood.

Blood

Blood is a trace that can divulge a great deal of information about the criminal, the victim, and what happened during a crime. The police who are first to arrive at the scene of assaults are often smeared with blood in their efforts to help a victim. In some cases, it is almost impossible to walk about the scene without stepping into some trace of blood and then transporting it around the scene. Still, investigators often fail to recognize bloodstains on clothing and other objects and, therefore, fail to collect valuable evidence. To complicate the problem of blood and its stains and residues as evidence, quite frequently a mixture of this residue is found at crime scenes when both the victim and the offender have been wounded. In addition, the evidence may come from an animal source, as well as a human one, or a common liquid may dilute the blood.

Despite some of the problems associated with this type of human trace, blood drops and splashes help to narrow the size of the suspect group, support identity when a suspect is located,

The hydrodynamics of blood drops and splashes—drop size increases with the distance of the fall; the tails, or pointed ends, indicate the direction of movement; and the rounded edges face the source of bleeding.

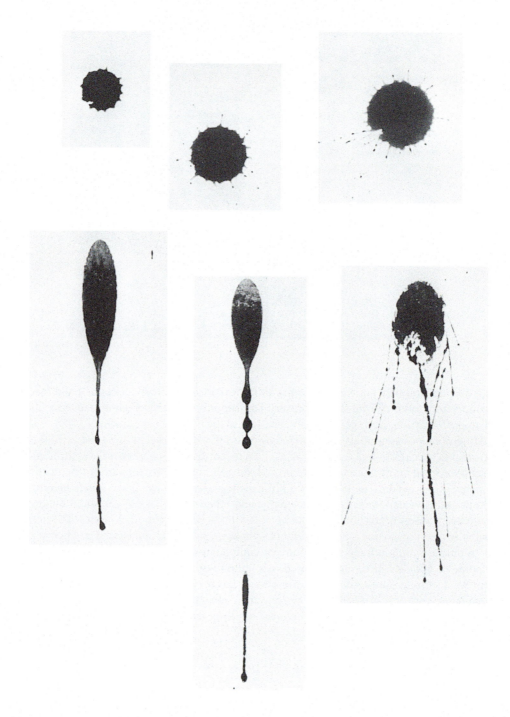

and plot the movements of the victim and the assailant (Figure 4-2). Information that can be discovered through careful bloodstain pattern analysis includes the angle of the impact; the nature of the force involved in the bloodshed and the direction from which that force was applied; the nature of any object used in applying the force; the approximate number of blows struck during the incident; and the relative position in the scene of the suspect, victim, or other related objects during the incident.[6]

Relatively fresh bloodstains generally appear to be reddish-brown in color; however, over time the stain can appear to be red to black, or appear to be green, blue, or even grayish white. The question that often must be answered is whether the stain is blood or some other substance. The determination of whether or not the stain is blood is made by means of a preliminary color test known as the **Kastle-Meyer color test**. This test is based on the reaction with the enzymes in the blood which causes the test strip to turn a deep pink color. These test strips are available under the trade name **Hemastix** and are a useful presumptive field test for blood.

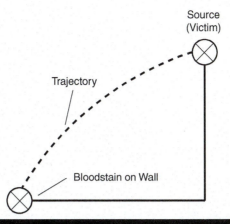

Source
(Victim)

Trajectory

Bloodstain on Wall

FIGURE 4-2 Blood Trajectory—Wall Stains.

Another question that often must be answered is whether blood was present at one time at the crime scene and has since been cleaned up. To answer this question the crime scene investigator would use another presumptive test known as **luminol**, which produces light rather than color as it reacts with blood. After spraying the suspected area with *luminol,* the room is darkened, and any blood stains present produce a faint blue glow, known as *luminescence.* A relatively new product, trade mark name of **Bluestar**, is now available and can be used in place of luminol. Bluestar has the advantage that its reaction with a bloodstain can be observed without having to create complete darkness. Both of these tests are extremely sensitive and are capable of detecting bloodstains diluted up to 100,000 times.

Once the bloodstain has been located and determined to be blood, the final determination is whether it is of human or animal origin. This question can be answered with the **precipitin test**. These tests are based on the reaction when animals, usually rabbits, are injected with human blood. The injection causes antibodies to form that react with the human blood to neutralize its presence. Another precipitin test is **gel diffusion**. This test takes advantage of the fact that antibodies and antigens diffuse or move toward one another on a plate coated with a gel medium made from a polymer called agar. If the blood is human, a line of precipitation forms where the antigens and antibodies meet. The gel diffusion test is very sensitive and requires only a small amount of blood for testing. Bloodstains which have been dried for ten to fifteen years and longer may still give a positive precipitin reaction.[7]

 Identify the various types of imprints and impressions found at crime scenes and the methods used to recover these items of evidence.

Imprints and Impressions

Personal imprints and impressions found at crime scenes identify or tend to identify a person or vehicle as having been at the crime scene. These traces hold promise as areas of inquiry, although they usually require a suspect or a suspect vehicle before their evidential value can be realized.

Imprints are markings left on a surface by protruding parts of a person or vehicle. Imprints found at a crime scene include bloody handprints or footprints, or tire tread marks left behind after the tire has been contaminated with oil or mud. Such evidence is first photographed and then may be lifted by dusting with a contrasting powder, applying a clean, sticky, transparent tape to the dusted area to pick up the markings, and then pressing the tape to a clean card to preserve it. The object with the imprint sometimes can be transported to the laboratory.

Impressions are made by a person or an object in a material softer than the item of evidence making the impression. Impressions include tire tracks or footprints left in snow or soft dirt. A trail of shoe prints or footprints offers some clues about the size or weight of the person making them, the speed of movement, and any gait abnormalities. Impressions are collected as

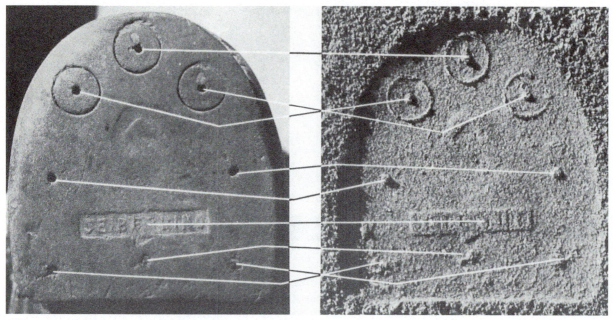

Heel of suspect's shoe (left) and heel impression taken at a crime scene (right). Lines show points of comparison—a "match."

evidence by first photographing and then casting the impression with plaster of Paris or dental plaster. Tire marks of vehicles are highly differentiated. When suspects are identified and located, vehicles used by such persons can be processed for comparison with the tire marks found at the scene. Furthermore, tire marks can be clues that aid in solving a crime inasmuch as the type of vehicle used may indicate fruitful lines of investigation. It can help to know, for example, that the vehicle was a large, late-model, high-priced car or a ten-year-old automobile. Shoe or heel prints and footprints in soft earth or other material that will take and hold a likeness are excellent to use for matching after a suspect is located.

Fingerprints can be found at crime scenes as either imprints or impressions. Bloody fingerprints left on weapons or at the scene of a crime are called **contaminated prints**. Such prints are observable with the naked eye and are collected by first photographing and then dusting and lifting with transparent tape. Fingerprints are impressions that a burglar might leave behind when his or her fingers come into contact with soft glazier's putty around the edges of a window. These are called **plastic prints** and are collected by first photographing and then casting with dental plaster. These prints can also be observed with the naked eye.

Latent prints usually cannot be seen with the naked eye and need to be developed to be seen. These fingerprints are caused by the transfer of body perspiration or oils present in finger ridges that are deposited on the surface of an object. Latent prints found on smooth nonporous surfaces such as glass can be developed by dusting with a powder, the color of which should contrast with the surface on which the print is found. Latent fingerprints on porous surfaces such as paper are developed in the laboratory through an **iodine fuming or ninhydrin process**. The iodine fumes react with the amino acids in the print and appear purple in color when developed. Prints left on smooth, slippery surfaces such as plastic bags, which are resistant to the dusting process, can be developed using the **cyanoacrylate fuming process**. Cyanoacrylate, a common glue product, is heated in a covered tank and the resulting fumes settle on the fingerprint, which is now observable and photographable.[8]

Traditionally, fingerprints were taken from persons by inking the tips of the fingers and then rolling the contaminated print onto a card. These cards were then sent to the FBI or to a state agency to be read and classified. This process took weeks or months to complete. Unclassifiable cards were returned, and often the person who supplied the prints was no longer available to supply another set of prints, resulting in loss of the opportunity to have this person's prints on file.

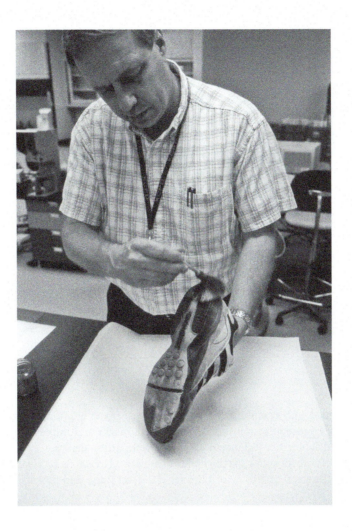

Computer technology now allows for a person's fingerprints to be captured electronically. This system is known as the Automated Fingerprint Identification System or more simply *AFIS*. When using this system, the person's hand is placed on a platen and a scanner reads and records the fingerprints digitally. The machine reads the prints and indicates, while the person is still at the machine, whether or not a classifiable set of prints has been obtained. With the touch of a button, the set of prints is electronically sent to the FBI's database, which contains 55 million sets of prints. This automated system has reduced the FBI's criminal ten-print processing time from forty-five days with the inked card system to less than two hours.[9]

5 *Discuss the methods used for collecting tool impressions at the crime scene and the laboratory examination process.*

Tool Marks

Just as weapons are likely to be found at the scene of assaults and homicides, the marks of tools are likely to be found at the scene of burglaries or other crimes in which the offender forced entry into the premises or forced open locked containers at the crime scene. The criminal must gain access by force. Windows, doors, and skylights are the traditional means of ingress for such criminals. Roofs and walls have been cut and pounded in to provide entry. In some cases the criminals exit from another area of the building. The modus operandi of many burglars is multiple entry through rows of offices or commercial establishments, with the burglars burrowing through interior walls in a molelike progress from store to store. The places of entry or exit and all the locked desks and cabinets that were forced open along the way will bear some mark of the tools used. Safes, unless

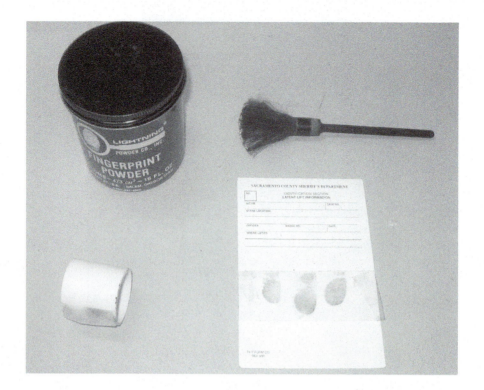

Dusting powder, brush, and tape used to develop and lift latent fingerprints.

found open or opened with a combination or key, also bear traces of prying, ripping, or battering. Scientific laboratory procedures can individualize these marks and impressions. When suspect tools are discovered, laboratory technicians can make comparison analyses.

The initial procedure for collecting the marks of tools used to gain access is to locate accurately the impression at the scene and to record the general description and measurements. Accuracy,

Criminalist applying dusting powder in search of fingerprints.
Source: © Pablo Paul/Alamy

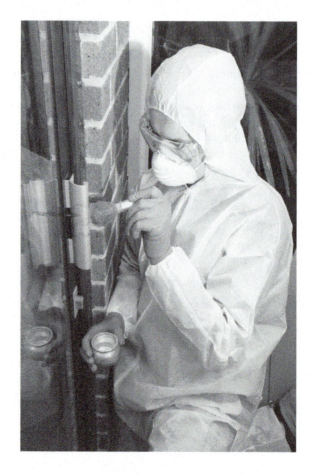

again, is the key. The impressions must be measured with an accurate rule, and the dimensions must be recorded in the investigator's field notes. Photographs of the impressions should be made. When feasible, the substance bearing the mark should be transported to the crime lab. It is sometimes possible to make a cast impression of the mark, and this will make an effective trial exhibit. Inasmuch as the mark is small, a material more costly than plaster of Paris can be used to form the impression. Various dental waxes and molding materials can be pressed into the imprint and allowed to harden. The overriding factor in reporting and collecting tool impressions at the scene of a crime is the preservation of the impression, or its reproduction, for future comparison with a suspect tool.

Quite often an investigator finds a tool that might have made an impression at the scene of the crime and attempts to match the tool visually with the impression by fitting it to the mark. This second contact of the tool to the impression ruins the evidence. Prevailing practices suggest that the best procedure is to treat any likely tool as suspect and to collect it for laboratory comparison by an expert.

Tools found on a suspect or under his or her control at the time of arrest (or traced to the suspect) become incriminating evidence when laboratory examinations show that the particularities of the suspect tool relate to the tool impressions found at the crime scene.

6 *Discuss the importance of trace evidence such as hairs, fibers, paint, and glass.*

Hair

Hair is a form of trace evidence that is transferred between individuals and objects during the commission of a crime. Hairs are typically transferred during the commission of personal crimes such as sexual assaults, physical assaults, and homicides. Hairs can also be found at crime scenes as the result of simply being shed from a person's body. A DNA analysis can be performed on hair if the root bulb is attached; see Chapter 5 for further discussion on DNA analysis. In the absence of DNA analysis the crime laboratory would conduct a microscopic analysis of the hair to determine the following.

Origin—What part of the body did the hair come from? This determination is based on the differences between head hair which shows little variation and uniform distribution of pigment compared to other body hairs. Pubic hairs, besides being short and curly, have wide variations in shaft diameter.

Racial origin—Caucasian hair is usually straight or wavy, with fine to course pigmentation which is evenly distributed. In comparison, the hair of a person of African descent is normally curly, with an uneven distribution of pigments. A cross-sectional analysis of Caucasian hair demonstrates that it is oval to round in shape, while hair from a person of African descent is flat to oval in shape. These are general observations and there is much overlap between the races, which makes racial identification difficult.

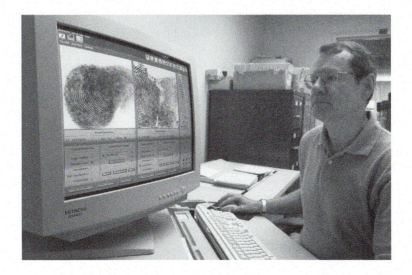

Technician using the Automated Fingerprint Identification System to compare two prints.

Source: Toby Talbot/ AP Images

Age and sex—The age and sex of a person's hair cannot be determined with any degree of certainty with the exception of infant hair which is very fine and short and has fine pigmentation. When the hair has been dyed or bleached, this processing may give a clue as to the sex of the individual, but once again there is much overlap between the sexes, which makes this identification difficult as well.

Forcible removal—an examination of the hair root and shaft may establish if the hair was pulled out or naturally fell out. The absence of adhering tissue to the bulbous-shape root is more likely to be the result of normally falling off the body than forcible removal.

Hair comparison—The most common request is whether hair recovered at the crime scene is the same as the hair obtained from the suspect. It is not yet possible to individualize a human hair to any single person through its structural characteristics. Hair tends to exhibit variable characteristics, not only from one person to another but also within a single individual. In making a comparison, the criminalist is interested in matching the color, length, diameter of the hair, as well as the color intensity. If hair has been dyed or bleached, it can be distinguished from natural hair. If the hair has grown since it was last dyed or bleached, the natural end portion will be distinct in color. An estimate as to the time since the hair was treated can be made based on the rate of hair growth of approximately one centimeter per month. Infrequent features such as abnormalities due to diseases or deficiencies as well as the presence of fungal and nit infections can further link a hair specimen to a particular individual. The examination of human hair is often most valuable in its ability to exclude someone as a suspect in the commission of a crime.[10]

Fibers

Fibers often are key items of evidence in personal crimes such as homicides, physical assaults, and sexual assaults where cross-transfer of fibers may occur between the clothing of the suspect and the victim. Fibers and whole pieces of cloth may also become embedded in part of a vehicle as a result of a hit-and-run. Fibers may also be found at the point of entry in burglary cases. In homicide and sexual assault cases where the victim has been bound with rope, twine, or cloth-backed tape, fiber analysis is important in determining the source of these materials.

The source of these fibers is all around us: in our clothing, carpets, drapes, wigs, and furniture. These fibers can be classified into two broad groups, natural and manufactured fibers. The most common natural fibers are cotton, which is a plant material, and wool from sheep. The manufactured fibers are the synthetic fibers such as nylon, polyesters, and acrylics. Laboratory analysis of these fibers includes the following.

Torn clothing—A piece of material recovered from a suspect hit-and-run vehicle or found at the point of entry in a breaking and entry case can be compared to the larger item of clothing it may have been torn from. In the laboratory the criminalist would fit together the torn edges of the two pieces of material to determine if they matched. If they can be exactly fitted together and the torn edges match, the fabrics must be of common origin.

Microscopic examination—The first step in the analysis of fibers is the microscopic examination with a **comparison microscope**, which is essentially two microscopes connected together side by side that allows two samples to be viewed simultaneously by the operator. The analysis of a fiber found on the victim with a fiber from the suspects clothing would begin with the comparison of the color and the diameter of the fibers; unless these two match, there is little reason to continue the analysis. With a match the lengthwise striations on the surface and the pitting of the fiber's surface with delustering particles would aid the operator in comparing the two samples.

Analytical techniques—The visible-light microspectrophotometer is a reliable method for analysts to compare the colors of fibers through spectral patterns. This technique is not limited by the sample size; a fiber as small as 1 millimeter can be examined by this method. In addition, before the forensic scientist can reach a conclusion that two or more fibers compare, it must be shown that the fibers in question have the same chemical composition which can be determined by the use of infrared microspectrophotometry technology.[11]

Glass

Glass evidence is often important in hit-and-run investigations, burglaries, and assault cases when the victim is struck with an instrument such as glass bottle. Glass fragments are useful in linking a suspect to a crime scene and the direction and sequence of force used to break a glass pane can be determined.

When an object breaks a glass pane, two types of fractures that form a pattern similar to a spider's web will result. These fractures are known as radial and concentric fractures. **Radial fractures** start at the center or the point of impact and run outward in a star-shaped pattern. **Concentric fractures** form concentric circular cracks in the glass around the point of impact. If a bullet perforates a pane of glass, the hole is expanded in the form of a crater on the side where the bullet exited the pane. The location where the cone-shaped crater is narrowest indicates the direction from where the bullet was fired. If a number of bullets hit the pane of glass, the sequence can be determined by examining the radial fractures. The radial fractures of the first bullet stop by themselves or run to the edge of the glass. Subsequent radial fractures produced by other bullets will stop at an already present radial fracture produced by the first bullet.

Glass splinters or shards are produced when a criminal breaks a window to gain entry in a burglary or may be produced in a hit-and-run case. When all the glass is collected and reassembled, the piece of glass found in the suspect's clothing or on the hit-and-run victim's clothing can be compared to determine if this splinter will fill the void. This type of **fracture match** will link the suspect to the crime as only one piece of glass will fill the void. Glass can also be examined for a number of physical and chemical properties. Density, refractive index, thickness, color, and chemical composition are some of the common characteristics examined to differentiate glass.[12]

Paint

Paint evidence is often important in hit-and-run investigations, burglaries, and cases where forced entry is involved. Paint evidence is usually found in the form of smears or chips. Chips tend to be more useful in that it is possible to show conclusively that the paint came from a specific location if the chips are large enough and the edges can be fitted together in a jigsaw puzzle fashion. Usually, however, only class characteristics can be determined by paint analysis.

Paint and protective coatings such as lacquer, enamel, and varnish can be identified by physical and chemical properties. Physical characteristics, such as color, layering, weathering, and texture are useful in characterizing this type of evidence. Chemical properties such as solubility and composition can indicate the type of paint and identify the pigmentation and fillers used in the manufacturing process. With automobile paints it is possible to determine the type of vehicle involved. Manufactures of automotive paints provide reference samples which can be used to determine the type of vehicle that uses that particular paint. Even if a vehicle cannot be identified as to manufacturer, known and questioned paint samples can be compared by examining their chemical and physical properties. The most that can be determined is that the paint from

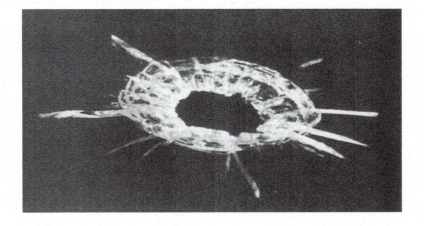

"Cratering" of a bullet hole in a glass window indicates the direction of travel. The bullet enters from the bottom, or small side of the crater, and exits from the top, or large side.

the control and questioned sources are consistent; that is, they could have come from the vehicle in question or any similarly painted vehicle. In some cases, vehicles and residences have been painted and repainted many times; in this instance the probability is greater if the two specimens share a common source.[13]

 Explain what items a questioned documents examiner would look for in the attempt to identify the machine or person who typewrote a document.

▶ Questioned Documents

In cases involving checks, the check itself is a **questioned document** and an important item of evidence. In apparent suicides, the victim may leave a note. This is an evidence item, and when found, it is often processed as a questioned document.

Documents that have been destroyed or partially destroyed by fire can sometimes be restored by laboratory technicians. Charred paper must be sprayed with a preservative and requires special packaging and transport to the place of examination. This is a critical and time-consuming process, but the potential of charred paper as evidence is worth the work involved in its recovery.

The general style of a typewritten document, margins, separation of words at the end of the typed lines, spelling errors, paragraphing, and other indentation may all contribute to identification of the person who typed it.[14] It is quite possible to match a suspect typewriter, printer, or copying machine by comparing exemplars obtained from the machine and the document under suspicion.

Indented or embossed writing is sometimes found on telephone pads, blotters, and other impressionable surfaces despite the fact that the original paper on which the writing was made has been removed.

CASE STUDY

THE BLACKEN FERN

Charlene Williams and Gerald Gallego had been together for about a year when he woke up one morning and announced that this was the day for his sexual fantasies to come true. Charlene was aware that Gerry wanted a harem, a cache of slave girls who were young and delectable who would do anything he wanted any time he wanted it. As Charlene herself would do anything he told her to do, of course she would help him. Later that day they drove to the local shopping mall, east of the city of Sacramento, to find some young girls to please Gerry. When they got to the mall, Gerry gave Charlene instructions as to the exact kind of girls he was looking for. While she entered the mall, he bought two-inch-wide tape that could be used for bindings and gags.

Charlene wandered through the mall but she was unable to choose from all the young women who were at the mall on that day. Soon Gerald was at her side telling her that she was not doing enough to help him. As they walked, he noticed two young women, teenagers ages sixteen and seventeen, outside a fast-food restaurant, and told Charlene those were the two he wanted. Gerald walked off and Charlene approached the girls. Incredibly, she convinced them to follow her to their recreational van parked outside. Charlene offered them some pot and they entered the van and got comfortable on the red carpet on the floor of the van. As soon as they were settled, Gerald entered the van and pointed a .25 caliber automatic handgun at them. Gerald got behind the wheel and drove out of the parking lot toward the interstate highway and headed east toward the Sierra Nevada Mountains. Gerry turned off the highway at Baxter, high in the mountains, and found a secluded spot. He took the girls into a tiny clearing where he repeatedly sexually assaulted both girls while Charlene waited in the van.

When it got dark, Gerald and Charlene drove the girls back to the Sacramento. They stopped at a secluded

(continued)

spot in a rural part of the county where Gerald took the girls into a farmer's field and shot them both and left them for dead. Their bodies were found a few days later. A forensic examination of the bodies disclosed some vegetable material embedded in their shoes and red fibers on their clothing. Subsequent examination of the vegetable material disclosed that it was blacken fern, a plant that grows only high in the Sierra Nevada Mountains. The investigators were unable to explain how two girls abducted from a suburban mall and found thirty miles away in a farmer's field could have blacken fern on their shoes. With few investigative leads to pursue, the case was unsolved for several years.

Within a short period after the killings, Gerald and Charlene got married and continued killing; in all they killed ten people. These killings included two similar abductions from another mall in Sacramento County, two girls in Nevada, a female hitchhiker in Oregon, a female bartender in an adjoining county, and two college students from another mall in the city of Sacramento. During the commission of the last killings a witness saw the abduction and wrote down Gerald's license plate number. When the students went missing the witness gave the plate number to the police who were able to arrest Charlene and Gerald in Omaha as they fled across the country. The pair was brought back to Sacramento and was charged only with the last two killings. The eight other killings had not been linked to them at this time as the crimes occurred in three different states—Nevada, Oregon, and California—and four counties in California representing five different law enforcement agencies.

Shortly after being in custody, Charlene requested a meeting with the investigators involved with this case. With her lawyer present, Charlene explained that she was pregnant and wanted to escape the death penalty so she could visit with her child. In exchange, Charlene would tell the investigators about all the other killings. Charlene outlined the circumstances of the killings, and when she mentioned taking the first victims to Baxter high in the Sierras, she had their attention as this information and its connection with the blacken fern had not been released to the media. The van used in these killings was located and fiber samples taken from the van matched those found on the bodies of the two young girls. Charlene also testified against Gerald at trial and he was found guilty and sentenced to death in both California and Nevada. Charlene served seventeen years in prison and visited regularly with her child who was being raised by Charlene's mother. How was she able to testify against her husband, you might ask? Small detail, but Gerald failed to divorce his previous wife and the husband/wife privilege applies only to legal marriages. Attention to detail is important.

Source: Based on data from Lt. Ray Biondi and Walt Hecox, *All His Father's Sins, Inside the Gerald Gallego Sex-Slave Murders* (Rocklin, CA: Prima Publishing, 1988).

CHAPTER REVIEW

Key Terms

ballistics   *70*

bluestar   *75*

caliber   *70*

circumstantial evidence   *69*

class evidence   *70*

comparison microscope   *80*

concentric fractures   *81*

contaminated prints   *76*

crime laboratory   *72*

cyanoacrylate fuming process   *76*

direct evidence   *69*

exothermic reaction   *73*

exterior ballistics   *70*

fracture match   *81*

gel diffusion   *75*

Gunshot Residue (GSR) examination   *72*

hemastix   *74*

impressions   *75*

imprints   *75*

individual evidence   *70*

interior ballistics   *70*

iodine fuming or ninhydrin process   *76*

kastle-meyer color test   *74*

latent prints   *76*

luminol   *75*

plastic prints   *76*

postmortem forensic science   *72*

precipitin test   *75*

proof marks   *70*

questioned document   *82*

radial fractures   *81*

Review Questions

1. The type of evidence that cannot be linked to a particular person or object is known as:
   a. Direct evidence
   b. Circumstantial evidence
   c. Individual evidence
   d. Class evidence
2. The question as to whether or not blood was present at one time and has since been cleaned up can be answered with which test?
   a. Luminol testing
   b. Hemastix testing
   c. Kastle-Meyer color testing
   d. Precipitin testing
3. Bloody fingerprints, such as those left on weapons or at the crime scene, are known as what type of prints?
   a. Contaminated
   b. Deteriorated
   c. Plastic
   d. Latent
4. Fingerprints found in soft material, such as tacky tar or glazier's putty, are known as what type of prints?
   a. Contaminated
   b. Deteriorated
   c. Plastic
   d. Latent
5. Fingerprints that cannot be seen with the naked eye and must be developed to be seen are known as what type of prints?
   a. Contaminated
   b. Deteriorated
   c. Plastic
   d. Latent
6. Approximately how many sets of fingerprints are contained within the Federal Bureau of Investigation's national fingerprint database?
   a. 55 million
   b. 80 million
   c. 160 million
   d. 320 million
7. The question of whether or not a victim or a suspect has recently fired a firearm can be answered by the examination of which of the following?
   a. Exothermic reaction
   b. Postmortem forensics
   c. Gunshot residue
   d. Heliopathic reaction
8. The crime laboratory can conduct an analysis of human hair. What cannot be determined from this analysis?
   a. Origin, the part of the body where the hair came from
   b. Racial origin
   c. Age/sex of the person who the hair belongs to
   d. Type of removal of the hair
9. Fingerprints left on smooth, slippery surfaces such as plastic bags can be developed by using which process?
   a. Dusting powder
   b. Iodine fuming
   c. Ninhydrin process
   d. Cyanoacrylate fuming
10. Fingerprints left on smooth, nonporous surfaces such as glass can be developed by using which process?
    a. Dusting powder
    b. Iodine fuming
    c. Ninhydrin process
    d. Cyanoacrylate fuming

See Appendix D for the correct answers.

Application Exercise

You are the assigned investigator of a shooting that has just occurred at a local bar. A weapon has been found at the scene and it is your responsibility to recover the weapon. What procedures should be followed to safely recover this weapon? Several spent bullets have also been found embedded in the wooden wall of the building. What are the procedures for retrieving these items of evidence? Finally, there are several spent cartridge cases on the ground. What are the procedures for retrieving these items and how should all of the items of evidence be packaged for transportations to the crime laboratory?

Discussion Questions

1. Regarding the case study, explain what type of evidence the blacken fern was and its importance to this investigation.
2. Regarding the case study, discuss the similarities and dissimilarities in the method of operation of this serial killer and how these similarities or dissimilarities would aid or hinder the investigation.
3. Discuss the various testing procedures used at crime scenes and in the laboratory to determine if a stain is blood and whether it is human or animal blood.
4. Explain the difference between internal and external ballistics as it relates to examination of firearms.
5. Describe the three types of fingerprints likely to be found at a crime scene. How are these various types of prints processed?
6. Explain the advantages of capturing a person's fingerprints electronically compared to the traditional ink-and-paper system.

Related Websites

To learn more about firearms, visit the University of Utah College of Medicine firearms tutorial at www-medlib.med.utah.edu/WebPath/TUTORIAL/GUNS/GUNINTRO.html. This site has information regarding the anatomy of firearms, ballistics, laboratory methods, and gunshot residue testing.

Tour a virtual comparison microscope used in firearms identification at www.firearmsid.com.For more information regarding the history of fingerprints, fingerprint examinations, and the legal challenges to fingerprints, visit www.onin.com/fp

Notes

1. Ayn Embar-Seddon and Allan D. Pass, *Forensics!* (Upper Saddle River, NJ: Prentice Hall, 2009), 155.
2. Urgen Thornwald, *Century of the Detective,* trans. Richard Winston and Clara Winston (New York: Harcourt Brace Jovanovich, 1965), 434.
3. J. S. Hatcher, Frank J. Jury, and Joe Weller, *Firearms Identification and Evidence* (Harrisburg, PA: Stackpole Books, 1957), 286.
4. Nicole Lundrigan, "Gunshot Residue Technology," *Law and Order* (May 2004): 66.
5. Terrence McGinn, "The Forgotten Evidence," *Law and Order* (November 2002): 30.
6. Michael Deleo, "Bloodstain Pattern Analysis," *Law and Order* (November 2002): 43.
7. Richard Saferstein, *Forensic Science: From the Crime Scene to the Crime Lab* (Upper Saddle River, NJ: Prentice Hall, 2009), 452–456.
8. Richard Saferstein, *Criminalistics: An Introduction to Forensics Science,* 5th ed. (Englewood Cliffs, NJ: Prentice Hall, 1995), 424–432; See also J. B. Wallace, "In Defense of Traditional Technology in a High-Tech World," *Journal of Forensic Identification* 43, no. 4 (July/August 1993): 378–385.
9. http://www.fbi.gov/hq/cjisd/iafis.htm.
10. Saferstein, *Forensic Science,* 368–376.
11. Ibid., 379–392.
12. Barry A. J. Fisher, *Techniques of Crime Scene Investigation,* 7th ed. (Boca Raton, FL: CRC Press, 2004), 176–182.
13. Ibid., 158–160.
14. Wilson R. Harrison, *Forgery Detection* (New York: Praeger, 1964), 209–212.

5   Laboratory and Technical Services

CHAPTER OUTLINE

LEARNING OBJECTIVES

After reading this chapter, you will be able to:

1 *Explain the fundamental scientific concepts involved in forensic science and discuss DNA profiling as it relates to criminal investigation.*

2 *Discuss the types of information a crime laboratory can supply regarding the processing of physical evidence.*

3 *Discuss the major pieces of crime laboratory equipment and their capabilities.*

4 *Explain voiceprint identification and its characteristics.*

5 *Distinguish between the various ciphers used by criminals to secure their communications.*

6 *Explain the various law enforcement databases and the specific information each provides to the investigator.*

The trustworthiness of an expert is important to the net worth of the entire investigation. Any suspicion of subjectivity or dishonesty destroys the legal significance of evidence because the average trier of fact may easily view such conduct as affecting the credibility of the entire investigation. An unusual unanimous vote for reversal of an Illinois murder conviction by the judges of the U.S. Supreme Court in the case of *Miller v. Pate* illustrates this reaction.

> Lloyd Eldon Miller, Jr., was convicted of murder in an Illinois state court in a prosecution for the death of a girl resulting from a sexual attack. A piece of compelling evidence against Miller was a pair of reddish-brown stained men's shorts found in an abandoned building a mile away from the scene of the crime and known as Van Buren's Flats.
>
> The prosecution theorized that the stains on the shorts were human blood and that the petitioner had been wearing these shorts when he committed the crime. The judgment of conviction was affirmed

on appeal by the Supreme Court of Illinois (13 Ill. 2d 84, 148 NE2d 455). On application for a writ of habeas corpus to the U.S. District Court for the Northern District of Illinois, the court granted the writ (225 F Supp 541), but the Court of Appeals for the Seventh Circuit reversed it (342 F2d 646). In the federal habeas corpus proceeding it was established that the reddish-brown stains on the shorts in question were not blood, but paint, and that counsel for the prosecution had known at the time of the trial that the shorts were stained with paint.[1]

In words of unusual bluntness the unanimous Supreme Court opinion stated:

> More than 30 years ago this Court held that the Fourteenth Amendment cannot tolerate a state criminal conviction obtained by the knowing use of false evidence. There has been no deviation from that established principle. There can be no retreat from that principle here. The judgment of the Court of Appeals is reversed, and the case is remanded for further proceedings consistent with this opinion.[2]

1 *Explain the fundamental scientific concepts involved in forensic science and discuss DNA profiling as it relates to criminal investigation.*

▶ Criminalistics: Forensic Science

The crime laboratory in which physical evidence obtained by police in the course of an investigation is examined may now be known as a **forensic science laboratory**, and laboratory technicians are often identified as **forensic scientists**. The professional group in this field, however, still identifies with the term **criminalistics**.

Criminalistics is the profession and scientific discipline directed to the recognition, identification, individualization, and evaluation of physical evidence by application of the natural sciences in matters of law and science.[3]

Identification in criminalistics is aligned with the logic of **set theory**: All objects can be divided and subdivided into various sets on the basis of their properties. Identification in relation to physical evidence and its analysis is defined as the determination of some set to which an object or a substance belongs or the determination as to whether an object or a substance belongs to a given set. Fingerprints, tool marks, blood, hair, glass, paint, and other types of evidence can be so classified. In addition, criminalistics is concerned with identity or origin. Given a bloodstain found and collected at a crime scene, the criminalist is asked to determine from whom it originated; given a spent bullet recovered from a human body, the criminalist is asked to decide if a particular firearm fired the bullet. In reaching a decision about identification, the criminalist also is asked to individualize the identification by specifying how individual or unique the item of evidence examined is within the set of its origin.

The crime laboratory is staffed by technicians educated and trained in criminalistics. Criminalistics is a subsystem in the administration of justice that studies the effect of a criminal upon a crime scene (and other sites of criminal activity) and vice versa. The informational output of a crime laboratory depends on its input: the physical evidence collected at crime scenes and forwarded to the laboratory for examination. The forensic science staff is responsible for deciding whether or not to develop information from physical evidence within a laboratory operation. Depending on the circumstances of the case, the general strategy is to order analyses so that the maximum amount of information is secured.[4]

When scientific findings are interpreted, the deductions of the criminalist reconstructing the event and the person or persons associated with it cannot be made with certainty and usually are made with prudence. Criminalists offer the most probable reconstruction on the basis of reasonable criteria and do not assign mathematical probabilities to the occurrence of two materials from different sources (two items of evidence, or one item of evidence and one known standard) having a common origin. Even the most sophisticated and specific analysis techniques do not, as a general rule, offer an opportunity for a criminalist to evaluate identification in terms of mathematical probability.

The effect on an accused person and his or her legal counsel of such identification and its individualization is considerable. Associative evidence placing a suspect at the crime scene ruins a not guilty pleading based on a general denial of presence at the crime scene or of contact with the victim at any time, and it seriously damages a defense based on an alibi. Tracing an item of evidence found at the crime scene to the accused person or an item found on the suspect back to the scene has serious implications for any successful defense unless a reasonable explanation is forthcoming. This effect is not necessarily an inducement to confess, but it does function in this fashion by its influence on the defendant and his or her legal adviser.

▶ DNA Profiling

DNA testing has become an established part of criminal justice procedure. Despite early controversies and challenges by defense attorneys, the admissibility of DNA test results in the courtroom has become routine. In the case of *Maryland v. King* the Supreme Court approved of the taking of a cheek swab of an arrestee as part of the booking procedure. The court felt that the taking and analyzing of a DNA sample obtained at the time of arrest was as legitimate as other booking procedures like fingerprinting.[5]

Understanding the importance of DNA typing to criminal investigations requires knowledge of some fundamental biological facts. Each molecule of DNA, the primary carrier of genetic information in living organisms, consists of a long, spiral structure that has been likened to a twisted ladder. The handrails of the ladder string together to form the ladder rungs. Each rung consists of a **base pair**, two of four varieties of nucleic acid, and are combined in pairs called **nucleotides**. The sequence of these base pairs constitutes the genetic coding of DNA.

DNA in humans is found in all cells that contain a nucleus—except red blood cells. Each nucleated cell (with the exception of sperm and eggs cells) usually contains the full complement of an individual's DNA, called the **genome**, that is unvarying from cell to cell. The genome consists of approximately 3 billion base pairs, of which about 3 million actually differ from person to person. However, the base pairs that vary represent a virtually incalculable number of possible combinations. Person-to-person differences within a particular segment of DNA sequence are referred to as **alleles**.

DNA typing (Figure 5-1) focuses on identifying and isolating discrete fragments of these alleles in a sample and comparing one sample with another. For example, a forensic scientist might compare a semen sample retrieved from a rape victim to a DNA sample taken from a suspect. If identical fragments appear in both samples, a match is declared. To determine the likelihood of a match being mere coincidence, a particular combination of alleles is compared to the frequency with which the combination appears in the statistical population.

Lab technician reviewing the banded DNA sequences.

Source: Tek Image/ Science Source

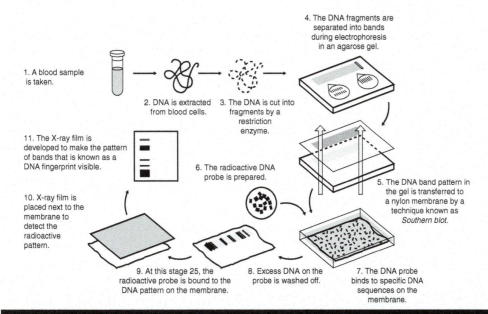

1. A blood sample is taken.

2. DNA is extracted from blood cells.

3. The DNA is cut into fragments by a restriction enzyme.

4. The DNA fragments are separated into bands during electrophoresis in an agarose gel.

5. The DNA band pattern in the gel is transferred to a nylon membrane by a technique known as *Southern blot.*

6. The radioactive DNA probe is prepared.

7. The DNA probe binds to specific DNA sequences on the membrane.

8. Excess DNA on the probe is washed off.

9. At this stage 25, the radioactive probe is bound to the DNA pattern on the membrane.

10. X-ray film is placed next to the membrane to detect the radioactive pattern.

11. The X-ray film is developed to make the pattern of bands that is known as a DNA fingerprint visible.

FIGURE 5-1   DNA Identification Process.

Many of the frequently encountered specimens found at crime scenes are either contaminated, degraded, or small in quantity. These problems are surmounted by **polymerase chain reaction (PCR) analysis**, which involves extracting DNA from a small evidence sample and then replicating it through a complex operation of repeated heating and cooling cycles and exposure to an enzyme. Because each cycle doubles the quantity of DNA, the original extraction can be replicated several million times within a short time. By examining several locations (loci) where variation occurs, a typing profile can be produced. The FBI has selected thirteen **short tandem repeats (STR)** loci to serve as a standard battery of core loci, each of which contains a short region where a sequence of three, four, or five nucleotides is repeated a different number of times in different people. Samples identified by a radioactively labeled, allele-specific probe are blotted onto a membrane, according to standard PCR protocol. Each dark spot that appears can be read as "yes" or "no" to the question of whether a particular individual possesses a given allele. When comparing DNA samples from known individuals with evidence samples, a difference of a single allele can exclude someone as the donor of that evidence sample. The more locations that show the same allele pattern, the stronger the evidence that the two samples came from the same individual.[6]

DNA is found in all body tissues and fluids. Saliva, skin cells, bone, teeth, tissue, urine, feces, and a host of other biological specimens, all of which may be found at crime scenes, are also sources of DNA. Saliva may be found in chewing gum and on cigarette butts, envelopes, and possibly drinking cups. Fingernail scrapings from an assault victim or a broken fingernail left at the scene by the perpetrator may also be useful DNA evidentiary specimens. Even hatbands and other articles of clothing may yield DNA. Because the DNA molecule is long lived, it is likely to be detectable for many years in bones or body fluid stains from older criminal cases in which questions of identity remain unresolved.

Today almost all states have legislation related to DNA data banking, most of which focuses on collecting and testing DNA from individuals convicted of sexual assaults or homicides. The FBI is supporting this effort by linking these state databases together to form a national database known as **CODIS (Combined DNA Index System)**. This system networks to link the typing results from unsolved criminal cases in multiple jurisdictions and to alert investigators to similarities among unsolved crimes.[7]

Mitochondrial DNA

Human cells contain two types of DNA, nuclear and mitochondrial. Nuclear DNA contains twenty-three pairs of chromosomes in the nuclei of the cells and each parent contributes to the genetic makeup of these chromosomes. Mitochondrial DNA (mtDNA) is found outside the nucleus and is inherited solely from the mother. Mitochondria are cell structures found in all human cells and they provide about 90 percent of the energy that the body needs to function. There are hundreds to thousands of mitochondria copies in a human cell compared to just one nuclear DNA located in the same cell.

Forensic scientists use mitochondrial DNA to identify a subject when nuclear DNA is significantly degraded, such as in charred remains. When a reference sample cannot be obtained from the individual who may be deceased or missing, a mitochondrial DNA reference sample can be obtained from any maternally related relative. However, all individuals of the same maternal lineage will be indistinguishable by mtDNA analysis. Forensic analysis of mtDNA is more vigorous, time consuming, and costly than nuclear DNA profiling. Therefore, only a handful of forensic laboratories process evidence for mtDNA determinations.[8]

❷ *Discuss the types of information a crime laboratory can supply regarding the processing of physical evidence.*

▶ Laboratory Determinations

After scientific examination of physical evidence, laboratory personnel report their findings. These determinations in past cases have led to a stylized set of expectations from field investigators. It is not always possible for a finding in a specific case to achieve the optimum expectations. As a result, the field investigator may be disappointed and, perhaps, reluctant to request such technical or laboratory assistance in the future. On the other hand, an optimistic view of the determinations that are possible through scientific aid should lead field investigators to a more extensive use of technical and laboratory services.

Great expectations may be rewarded. For this reason, an optimistic but realistic view of possible technical and laboratory determinations is necessary. The findings that possibly may result from a scientific examination of physical evidence have been organized in the following list for ready reference according to the types of evidence common to police cases:

1. Weapons—Firearms
   a. identification of bullets, shells, or cartridge cases with a specific gun
   b. operating condition of firearms, functioning of safety and trigger pull
   c. distance at which gun was fired
   d. position of the shooter at the time of firing
   e. ownership traced
   f. obliterated serial number restored
   g. imprints (latent fingerprints), impressions, or transfer evidence developed
   h. used in other crimes

2. Weapons—Knives and Bludgeons
   a. description of cutting, stabbing, or striking surfaces
   b. comparison with wounds
   c. tracing ownership
   d. imprints, impressions, or transfer evidence developed
   e. used in other crimes
   f. direction of force
   g. position of assailant
   h. identity of assailant; sex, strength, and which handheld weapon

3. Drugs and Poisons
   a. analysis by type (name)
   b. determination of quantity of fatal dose
   c. origin (purchase, manufacturer, growth)
   d. comparison with effect—wounds, body functions
   e. used in other crimes

4. Imprints and Impressions
   a. nature of object making imprint or impression
   b. identity by manufacturer or group

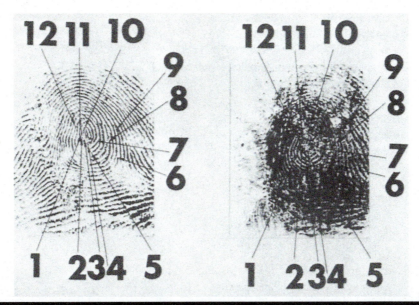

FIGURE 5-2 Latent Fingerprint Found at a Crime Scene (Left), Compared with the Rolled Fingerprint of the Suspect (Right). Twelve Points of Identity Indicate a Match.

    c. individual identity—comparison (imprint or impression made by or not made by submitted suspect object)

    d. individual identity—fingerprints (Figure 5-2)

    e. individual identity—footprints[9]

    f. direction of movement

    g. transfer evidence developed

5. Tool Marks

    a. nature of tool

    b. identity by manufacturer or group

    c. identity—for search

    d. origin (purchase)

    e. individual identity (mark made or not made by submitted suspect tool)

    f. transfer evidence developed

    g. used in other crimes

6. Traces of Identity—Blood

    a. identification as blood

    b. determination (human or animal, grouping, direction, and velocity of drops and splashes)[10]

    c. direction of force

    d. position of assailant

    e. individual identity (blood of victim or defendant)

    f. found at other crime scenes

    g. transfer evidence developed[11]

7. Blood (Test)

    a. alcohol in blood (percentage)

    b. interpretation of percentage as to degree of intoxication

8. Hairs and Fibers

    a. origin (human, head, body, pubic; animal; clothing)

    b. identity (sex, race—a broad grouping)

    c. individual identity—comparison of known standards of hair of victim with hair of defendant; comparison of fibers from clothing of victim (or found at scene) with material found on suspect

    d. dog hair (victim's pet to clothing of suspect; suspect's pet to crime scene or victim)

9. Dust, Dirt, Debris
   a. origin (locale, occupation)
   b. identity (group)
   c. individual identity or transfer evidence developed

10. Flammable Fluids—Fire and Explosive Residue
   a. identity by physical properties
   b. origin (purchase, manufacturer)
   c. direction of force (flow)
   d. used in other crimes

11. Glass
   a. identity and comparisons
   b. direction of force
   c. transfer evidence developed
   d. similar damage at other crime scenes

12. Paint
   a. identity (group)
   b. origin (purchase, usage, manufacturer)
   c. individual identity—the same as or similar to submitted sample
   d. transfer evidence developed

13. Semen Stains
   a. identity of stain as semen
   b. location and extent of stain
   c. origin—individual identity in relation to blood or other body substances or fluids of a suspect in custody[12]

14. Wood
   a. identity (type, group, name)
   b. origin (purchase, production, growth)
   c. identity—same as or similar to submitted suspect sample

15. Suspected Poisoned Food.
   a. isolation and identity of noxious or poisoned substance
   b. origin (source, process)

16. Documents
   a. authenticity of document or signature or both
   b. authorship (handwriting); authorship (typewriter); identity—"trademarks" of writer (form, spelling, vocabulary, etc.); fraudulent check "trademark"
   c. age (date written)
   d. nature of alteration or erasure
   e. copy traces, carbon paper, embossed writing, typewriter ribbons
   f. transfer evidence developed
   g. dating of ink and paper[13]
   h. used in other crimes

17. Feces
   a. comparison with samples taken from other crime scenes
   b. undigested food residues possible and informative

18. Vomit
   a. comparison for identity when suspect is located with vomit at crime scene and traces on clothing of suspect
   b. in suspected poison cases, analysis for content and identification of poison, if present

19. Urine
   a. analysis of submitted specimens (alcohol level in blood)
   b. analysis in suspected poisoning cases

Investigators should become acquainted with the language used by criminalists in reporting their determinations. If any doubts exist in the mind of the investigator as to the level of uniqueness achieved by the criminalist, a request for clarification should be made. A high level of exactness in identification is not always possible because of the nature of the evidence or the type of examination. Investigators should be particularly alert for the following phrases in the reports of technicians examining physical evidence:

1. consistent with
2. similar to
3. indistinguishable from
4. of the type used
5. matching
6. indicates that
7. has the appearance of

❸ *Discuss the major pieces of crime laboratory equipment and their capabilities.*

▶ Laboratory Equipment

The work of the criminalist concerns the physical and biological science laboratories, examination of substances involved with crimes and suspects, and the use of selected equipment normally associated with scientific techniques in such disciplines. Equipment designed especially for identification of firearms and examination of questioned documents is part of the inventory of a criminalistics laboratory.

Major items of equipment, other than the basic assortment of test tubes, retorts, burners, and the like that may be found in a modern laboratory of considerable size, range from optical equipment through X-ray and spectrographic devices to machines and measuring devices that use the latest space-age technology. Microscopes' magnification usually range from low-power instruments of comparatively low cost to high-power instruments of high cost. The comparison microscope, designed for work in the identification of firearms, and photographic equipment necessary for microphotography are common optical tools in these laboratories.

Equipment for spectrographic analysis has been part of the criminalistics scene for many years. In **spectrography**, the radiation from an incandescent gas or vapor is concentrated in certain discrete wavelengths. Such wavelengths are characteristic of the emitting elements in the gas, with each element emitting a unique and characteristic pattern of wavelengths, or **spectrum**. A spectrograph has a narrow slit to admit the radiation, a prism or grating to distribute the radiation, and a system of lenses to focus the wavelength pattern on a photographic plate. The pattern is recorded photographically as a series of short lines, each line being an image of the slit formed by the radiation of one wavelength. In analysis, the evidence sample is vaporized to incandescence by flame, arc, or spark and the radiation recorded. Evidence samples are normally composites. Therefore, spectra of all the elements comprising the evidence sample are recorded simultaneously and the criminalist analyzes the composition of the sample by sorting the recorded lines, their widths, and their positions in the spectrum. Spectra of known standards and charts of the standard wavelength of various elements are used for identification. A medium-size quartz prism instrument with a range into the ultraviolet region disperses incident light on a 10-inch photograph plate. The spectrograph, which will produce a complete elementary analysis of evidence samples containing mineral and other inorganic compounds, is an all-purpose instrument for criminalistics.[14]

Chromatography is a method of separating compounds to identify the components. Modern equipment in this area is capable of identifying compounds, such as illegal drug or poison specimens. Gas or vapor chromatography employs a columnar device in which the evidence sample is injected into the system at the opening of the column and carried along by a stream of carrier gas. Each constituent of the sample being tested is separated, emerges at a definite time from the time of injecting the sample (retention time), and is fed into a recorder. The recorder provides a trace in which the peaks and their position on a time axis (the retention time) identify each of the components of a sample. Gas chromatographs are valuable analytical tools because with them microsamples of such complex compositions as gasoline, fuel oil, perfumes,

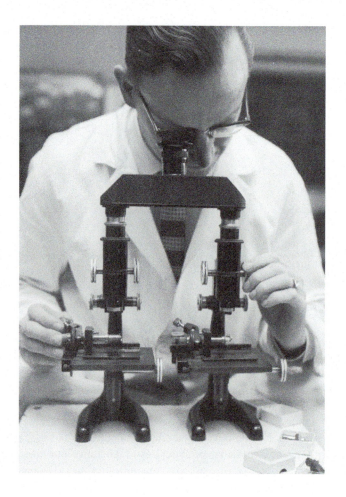

A ballistic expert adjusts a comparison microscope.

Source: Efield/Hulton Archive Photos/Getty Images

hair dressings, and paint thinners can be separated and identified from their constituents—a difficult problem with other scientific techniques when only minute quantities of evidence are available.[15]

X-ray crystallography is useful for the identification of any crystalline solid or compound from which a crystalline solid derivative can be made. **X-ray diffraction** is also of use in processing very small samples, in examining samples with noncrystalline impurities, and in identifying inorganic and mineral substances. X-ray spectra are used for analysis and identification. Equipment is based on standard X-ray devices adapted to testing and recording X-ray spectra and diffraction patterns.

The newest in laboratory equipment is a type of nuclear reactor used for **neutron activation analysis (NAA)**, a technique that can analyze samples one hundred times too small for ordinary spectrographic techniques. It is not equipment easily purchased by a local laboratory, but a centrally located radiochemistry laboratory can make this new technique available to any local criminalistics laboratory.

Neutron activation analysis is a very sensitive method of analyzing samples for the elements in their composition. It involves bombarding the samples with neutrons in a nuclear reactor, which causes the different elements in the sample to become radioactive, thus making it possible to identify the different radioactive elements present and to determine the quantity of each. The great sensitivity of this method allows the detection of mini-micro elements. The research reactor is much smaller and simpler than a nuclear power reactor. In operation, it produces vast numbers of neutrons by uranium fission chain reaction—but under precise control. When an evidence sample is inserted into this intense field of neutrons, the various elements in the sample undergo a nuclear reaction that causes some of these elements to become appreciably radioactive. After the irradiation, the activated sample is removed for counting. The different radioactive elements that are now present emit radiations of different energy levels and decay at different rates. Some die out within seconds; some within minutes or hours; some

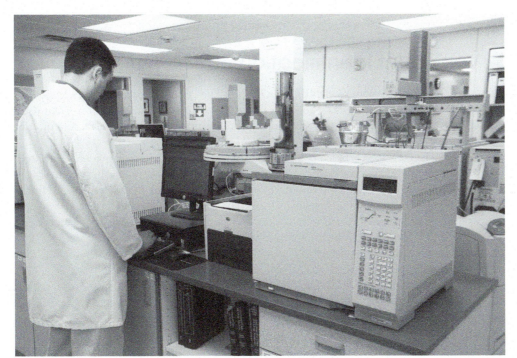

require days, weeks, or even longer. A very sophisticated apparatus, the **gamma-ray spectrometer**, is used to measure the distinctive radioactive gamma-ray emissions and thereby to identify the elements from which the rays originate. The data are printed on paper tape and are also displayed on the face of an oscilloscope. As the number of elements found at the same concentrations in two samples increases, the matching of the two samples becomes increasingly positive.[16]

The NAA technique and its application in the study of gunshot residues have returned a potential item of evidence to investigators. Testing for gunshot traces had fallen into disuse when the paraffin test was found to react to urine and a few similar substances, as well as to gunshot residues. Now paraffin-lifting kits are used on a suspect's hands, and NAA measurements for the presence of antimony and barium, which are common gunshot residues, have indicated a new and useful discrimination and particularity. Distinctive "signatures" of handguns, tools, and other metal objects are now available to investigators through an innovative **trace metal detection technique (TMDT)**, which makes the patterns of these objects visible on the skin or clothing of suspects when treated with a test solution and examined under ultraviolet light.[17]

Ultrasonic cavitation is an etching method that may replace chemical, electrolytic, and magnetic particle methods of restoring obliterated serial numbers on firearms and other metal objects. Cavitation is similar to boiling liquids in that vapor bubbles form in a liquid agitated by a vibrator. An ultrasonic generating system is used for inducing cavitation. The high-energy bubbles produced have the effect of etching a metal surface. It is a rapid and very effective method for serial number recovery.[18]

Lasers (argon-ion or copper-vapor) are widely used in the detection of latent fingerprints. Recently, laser examination of questioned documents has been found to be useful in some alteration or obliteration cases. Laser examination can reveal information unattainable by any conventional nondestructive means.[19]

The equipment found in crime laboratories is extensive. Basic cameras, microscopes, spectrographs, and fluoroscopes are being supplemented by computers and space-age devices. As new equipment is obtained and used by laboratory technicians, the director of the laboratory informs local police managers of the additional services available. Investigators should be alert to these changes in the availability of such services and use them whenever it is in the best interest of an investigation.

▶ Voiceprint Identification

Voiceprinting is the graphical identification of voices. Voiceprints are an innovative concept in personal identification and are fast becoming useful tools in criminal investigation. Their use is limited only by the adaptation of this new technique to the many areas of verbal communication encountered in an investigation.

Voiceprint identification is based on the physical characteristics of each individual's vocal cavities (the throat, mouth, nose, and sinuses) and the manner of manipulating the lips, teeth, tongue, soft palate, and jaw muscles. It is a technique of personal identification that may challenge fingerprints as the most positive means of personal identification. Chances are quite low that any two individuals have precisely the same size vocal cavities and have learned to use their articulators in the same manner. To date, this premise has survived some thousands of attempts to disprove it. Efforts to disguise the voice or to imitate the voice of another have been easily discerned. Whispering, muffling, nose holding—even filling the mouth with marbles—can be detected.

Suspect voices are recorded on a good-quality tape recorder. Known standards for comparison also are tape recorded. Tape recordings are fed into a specially designed spectrograph that reacts to the sound of the recorded voice and produces a voiceprint in much the same way as the polygraph produces a chart. The voice spectrograph reacts to voice frequency, to volume, and to the timing of a person's speech. Voiceprint techniques of identification are particularly applicable to the identification of voices involved in kidnappings, obscene language telephone calls, and telephoned threats.

Automatic methods of voice identification are being developed. This machine-aided speaker recognition will be used for naming, identifying, or distinguishing the speaker who has produced a given voice sample from other speakers. This is a mechanized, computerized extension of the ability of people to recognize voices. Speech samples will be processed for their unique features and categorized by these extracted features. Recognition will be automatic and will be based on digital computer technology rather than on the skill of a technician, a user, or an operator.[20]

❺ *Distinguish between the various ciphers used by criminals to secure their communications.*

▶ Cryptography

The use of simple ciphers and codes to protect the security of messages—**cryptography**—is increasing in the world of crime. It is common in unlawful gambling cases where records of wagers made by customers must be kept. It is used by organized crime personnel because written communications have been found to be less susceptible to investigative examination than telephone conversations. It is also likely to be used in communications among extremist groups planning crimes, as well as by various types of offenders who want to protect the security of personal telephone and memo books.

The most common cipher in use by criminals is a simple **substitution cipher** in which a symbol, letter, or digit stands for another symbol, letter, or digit. The simplistic thinking of many criminals confines the substitution to some simple order, such as 1 represents A, 2 represents B, and 3 represents C. **Transposition ciphers** are characterized by a change in the order of the enciphered material. Investigators find it fairly common in recording telephone numbers. This may be a **reversal transposition** in which the telephone number 445-1769 becomes 967-1544, or any **split combination**, for example, 176-4459, 769-4451, and 544-1769. Of help to investigators is the fact that most criminals are amateurs in cipher work, and the solution of their ciphers is a simple matter. A criminal does not have access to the few sources of information available about ciphers, and when he or she sits down to evolve a cipher, no one is there to tell the person that his or her invention is, in truth, hundreds of years old.[21]

A stolen bonds fraud case involving members of the Mafia in a typical national crime syndicate operation with international overtones was successfully solved by federal agents when a key to a code was found hidden in the wallet of one of the gang members. The code had been used in cable communications between members in New York and London to communicate secretly to name the

▼

denomination of stolen bonds available for sale and the asking price. Court action by the federal district attorney brought the records of these communications into court, and the knowledge of the code key made their content intelligible to the trial jury and showed the joint action of the conspiracy.

Investigators can learn to solve simple substitution or transposition ciphers by running down the alphabet with the first eight or ten letters of the message and then testing for substitution. This requires substituting letters one further on in the alphabet in the first run-through, then two further on in the second testing, and so on. This means to try b for a, then c for a, and so on. Julius Caesar is said to have used a cipher based on the simple substitution of a letter three letters further on in the alphabet. Simple transposition ciphers can be solved by trial and error when the enciphered work or numerical prefix in telephone numbers is known or suspected. Telephone and memo book codes usually are solved by using the local telephone exchange prefix of three numbers to break the method of transposition by trial and error. A **frequency distribution study** will solve more complex ciphers, but this requires the work of experts with tables of letter and word frequencies. However, an investigator may break a complex cipher or code if he or she has some preknowledge or can guess that a certain word is likely to appear in the message and then looks for this word.[22]

When the use of a cipher or code is suspected, the investigator should attempt to collect as much of the suspected writing as possible and to ascertain the languages and skills with which the defendant is familiar. Knowing the language fluency of the suspect and whether he or she has any particular skill, such as stenography, printing, piano playing, or the like, may be helpful in deciphering the communication because these areas of skill or experience often form the base of the cipher or code scheme. When expert assistance is required, the enciphered material should be forwarded to the police laboratory in the same manner as other questioned documents, with the relevant data noted under the details of the case, along with some of the possible words likely to be frequently used in the enciphered communications.

 Explain the various law enforcement databases and the specific information each provides to the investigator.

▶ Forensic Databases

The **National Integrated Ballistic Information Network (NIBIN)** is maintained by the Bureau of Alcohol, Tobacco, Firearms, and Explosives (ATF). In the past, unless there was a connection between cases, comparing firearms evidence from one investigation to another was usually not done. If there was a connection, the investigator could ask the firearms examiner to compare recovered bullets or shell casings. However, now with NIBIN there is a database of fired cartridge casings and bullet images used by crime laboratories. This system links firearms evidence including fired bullets, cartridge casings, shotgun shells, and recovered firearms by means of a microscope attached to a computer. The evidence is electronically scanned and stored for retrieval and comparison with other images. The system has the ability to compare images with regional and national databases.

The benefit of this system is its ability to associate firearm evidence between unrelated crimes. Test firing of confiscated firearms that come into the custody of investigators becomes important due to the possibility of developing information on cases that appear to be unrelated. Firearms evidence typically occurs in such crimes as assaults and murders.[23]

The **International Forensic Automotive Paint Data Query (PDQ)** is a database developed and maintained by the Forensic Laboratory Services of the Royal Canadian Mounted Police. The database contains chemical and color information pertaining to original (factory) automotive paint, and can determine the make, model year, and assembly plant on more than 13,000 vehicles. Contributors to the database include forensic laboratories in Canada and the United States as well as twenty-one other countries. This is a valuable source of information in hit-and-run investigations; it provides investigators with information regarding the possible make, model, and year of a suspect vehicle.

The **Shoeprint Image Capture and Retrieval (SICAR)** system is a commercially available computer database. Crime scene shoe prints can be entered into the system by scanner or digital picture. The system has a comprehensive shoe sole database that includes more than three hundred shoe manufacturers with more than eight thousand sole patterns. The system allows investigators to link crime scene footwear impressions to a particular shoe manufacturer.[24]

CHILD ABDUCTION

Twelve-year-old Courtney left home around 2:00 P.M. to go to the local convenience store two blocks away. She was reportedly seen there at about 2:15 P.M. talking to a man who was seated in a dark-colored BMW. At about 7:00 P.M., when she did not return home, her parents reported her missing. More than twenty officers and volunteers began a neighborhood search, knocking on doors in the area in an effort to find her.

Searchers did not know that Courtney's body had already been found in an adjoining county some 25 miles away. At about 5:30 P.M., some fishermen approached a spot on the river by boat, which was near the highway. As they approached, they noticed a subject running away from the beach, leaving behind a body. The beach where the body was found is a popular spot to fish, drink beer, fire guns, and dump dead bodies. The beach averages two to three bodies a year. A search of the crime scene disclosed some key pieces of evidence: a sun visor, boxer shorts, and sunglasses that the suspect had left behind.

Eight months after Courtney was slain, an arrest was made in the case. More than 1,200 possible suspects were considered and subsequently eliminated. Investigators traced the sun visor's lot number back to its source and were able to determine that twenty such visors had been sold in the area. Detectives then began tracking down the buyers through credit card receipts and by asking for DNA samples. One visor purchase

that had been made near the time of the abduction and slaying was particularly interesting. This purchaser was already under investigation for allegedly advertising in Internet chat rooms that he had child pornography to trade. When investigators went to his residence to talk to him, they determined that he had left the town and was somewhere in New Mexico.

Investigators posted a "be on the lookout" notice for this subject on the **National Crime Information Computer (NCIC) system**. When the subject, a twenty-year-old male, was arrested a few days later for walking out of a restaurant without paying for his meal, the arresting officers ran his name through NCIC, were alerted to the notice, and contacted the case investigators.

Two detectives flew to Albuquerque to question the suspect and to obtain a DNA sample. This sample was later matched to the DNA materials found at the scene where Courtney was sexually assaulted and strangled. At the time of his arrest, the suspect was driving a dark-colored BMW. The vehicle was searched and determined to contain three newspaper stories on Courtney's death. The search also revealed an adult magazine that had faces of young girls pasted over those of adult nude models. Investigators stated no evidence indicates that the suspect knew the victim prior to her death, and they speculated that she may have been abducted at random.

CHAPTER REVIEW

Key Terms

allele   88
base pair   88
chromatography   93
CODIS (Combined DNA Index System)   89
criminalistics   87
cryptography   96
forensic science laboratory   87
forensic scientist   87
frequency distribution study   97
gamma-ray spectrometer   95
genome   88
identification   87
International Forensic Automotive Paint Data Query (PDQ)   97

lasers   95
National Crime Information Computer (NCIC) system   98
National Integrated Ballistic Information Network (NIBIN)   97
neutron activation analysis (NAA)   94
nucleotide   88
polymerase chain reaction (PCR) analysis   89
reversal transposition   96
set theory   87
short tandem repeats (STR)   89
Shoeprint Image Capture and Retrieval (SICAR)   97

spectrography   93
spectrum   93
split combination   96
substitution cipher   96
trace metal detection technique (TMDT)   95
transposition cipher   96
ultrasonic cavitation   95
voiceprinting   96
X-ray crystallography   94
X-ray diffraction   94

Review Questions

1. Which piece of laboratory equipment would be used to determine the elements contained within mineral samples?
   a. Spectrograph
   b. Chromatograph
   c. Neutron activation analysis
   d. Ultrasonic cavitation

2. The laboratory equipment or method that is capable of identifying the components in compounds is the:
   a. Spectrograph
   b. Chromatograph
   c. Neutron activation analysis
   d. Ultrasonic cavitation

3. Which technique is useful in determining if a suspect or victim has recently fired a handgun?
   a. Spectrograph
   b. Chromatograph
   c. Neutron activation analysis
   d. Ultrasonic cavitation

4. Which piece of laboratory equipment would be effective for serial number recovery?
   a. Spectrograph
   b. Chromatograph
   c. Neutron activation analysis
   d. Ultrasonic cavitation

5. Criminals often use codes and ciphers to protect the security of their messages and transactions. The deciphering of such information is known as:
   a. Cavitation
   b. Crystallography
   c. Chromatography
   d. Cryptography

6. Many DNA samples are either contaminated, degraded, or small in quantity. These problems are overcome by which process?
   a. Combined Indexing System
   b. Polymerase chain reaction
   c. Short tandem repeats
   d. Base pairs nucleotides

7. Differences within a particular segment of a DNA sequence are known as:
   a. Genome
   b. Alleles
   c. Polymerase chain reaction
   d. CODIS

8. DNA is found in all cells that contain a nucleus. Each nucleated cell contains the full complement of an individual's DNA, which is called the:
   a. Genome
   b. Alleles
   c. Polymerase chain reaction
   d. CODIS

9. The state DNA data banks are linked together by the FBI to form a national DNA data bank known as:
   a. Genome
   b. Alleles
   c. Polymerase chain reaction
   d. CODIS

10. The professional name for employees in a forensic laboratory who conduct the scientific examinations is:
    a. Criminalist
    b. Criminalistics
    c. Laboratory technicians
    d. Forensic scientists

See Appendix D for the correct answers.

Application Exercise

You are investigating a recent sexual assault and murder of a college student. The forensic examination of the victim's body disclosed the presence of the perpetrator's DNA material. You do not have sufficient evidence to arrest anyone for this crime at this point; however, one male student was seen in the area at the time the crime was committed. You identify the student and his current address. You go to this address and the suspected student is not at home but his roommates invite you in and are very cooperative and allow you to look around the apartment. The roommates identify common areas that they all share, such as the bathroom and kitchen areas. What procedures should be followed to obtain the suspect's DNA material?

Discussion Questions

1. Are laboratory personnel handicapped by the legal precept that the admissibility of any scientific process in relation to evidence must be tested against acceptance of the scientific principle involved?
2. Explain the difference between the terms *forensic science* and *criminalistics*.
3. Project the likely growth and development of laboratory services.
4. Who decides the best strategy (or strategies) for the forensic science examination(s) of physical evidence?
5. Describe spectrographic analysis, trace metal detection technique, and ultrasonic cavitation.
6. Do criminalists make truly scientific and objective determinations?
7. Discuss the purposes for voiceprinting in criminal investigation.
8. Explain the meaning of one word or phrase used by criminalists in describing comparison analysis determinations.
9. Define a physical match in relation to the laboratory examination of physical evidence.
10. What was the role of DNA analysis in the case study?

Related Websites

To learn more about crime laboratory services, consult the FBI's lab home page at www.fbi.gov/hq/lab/lab-home.htm.

Interested in becoming a criminalist? The American Academy of Forensic Science lists employment opportunities on its website: www.aafs.org.

Answers to the most frequently asked questions regarding cryptography can be found at this website: www.faqs.org/faqs/cryptography-faq.

Notes

1. *Miller v. Pate,* 386 U.S. 1 (1967).
2. Ibid.
3. James W. Osterberg, "What Problems Must Criminalistics Solve?" *Law Enforcement Science and Technology* (Chicago: Thompson, 1967), 297–303. The term *forensic science* is commonly used to describe criminalistics. See Richard Saferstein, *Criminalistics: An Introduction to Forensic Science,* 5th ed. (Englewood Cliffs, NJ: Prentice Hall, 1994).
4. Brian Parker and Joseph Peterson, "Physical Evidence Utilization in the Administration of Criminal Justice," in *Sourcebook in Criminalistics,* ed. Carroll R. Hormachea (Reston, VA: Reston, 1974), 50–58.
5. *Maryland v. King,* 133 S. Ct. 1958 (2012).
6. Holly Hammond and C. Thomas Caskey, U.S. Department of Justice, National Institute of Justice, *Automated DNA Typing: Method of the Future?* (Washington, DC: Government Printing Office), 1–2.
7. Victor Walter Weedn and John W. Hicks, U.S. Department of Justice, National Institute of Justice, *The Unrealized Potential of DNA Testing* (Washington, DC: Government Printing Office, 1998), 1–8.
8. Richard Saferstein, *Forensic Science: From the Crime Scene to the Crime Lab* (Upper Saddle River, NJ: Prentice Hall, 2009), 479–481.
9. Louise M. Robbins, *Footprints: Collection, Analysis, and Interpretation* (Springfield, IL: Charles C Thomas, 1985), 183–207.
10. Herbert L. Macdonell, U.S. Department of Justice, National Institute of Law Enforcement Assistance Administration, *Flight Characteristics of Stain Patterns of Human Blood,* Stock No. 2700-0079 (Washington, DC: Government Printing Office, 1971), 1–29.
11. Federal Bureau of Investigation, "Examination of Biological Fluids," *FBI Law Enforcement Bulletin* XLI (June 1972): 12–15, 30.
12. Ibid., 15, 30.
13. Richard L. Bru Belle and Robert W. Reed, *Forensic Examination of Ink and Paper* (Springfield, IL: Charles C Thomas, 1984), 6–8.
14. H. J. Walls, *Forensic Science* (New York: Praeger, 1968), 60–61.
15. Ibid., 49–55.
16. Donald E. Bryan, et al., "High-Flux Neutron Activation Analysis as an Investigative Tool in the Field of Criminalistics," in *Law Enforcement Science and Technology* (Chicago: Thompson, 1967), 371–377.
17. U.S. Department of Justice, National Institute of Law Enforcement and Criminal Justice, Law Enforcement Assistance Administration, *Trace Metal Detection Technique*

in Law Enforcement (Washington, DC: Government Printing Office, 1970), 1–16.

18. Richard S. Treptow, *Handbook of Methods for the Restoration of Obliterated Serial Numbers* (Cleveland, OH: Lewis Research Center, prepared for the National Aeronautics and Space Administration, 1978), 73–82.

19. Ronald E. Blacklock, "The Laser: A Tool for Questioned Document Examination," *The Journal of Police Science and Administration* no. XV (July 1987): 125–126.

20. R. W. Becker, F. R. Clarke, F. Poza, and J. R. Young, U.S. Department of Justice, Law Enforcement Assistance Administration, *A Semiautomatic Speaker Recognition System* (Washington, DC: Government Printing Office, 1973), 1–26.

21. Parker Hitt, *Manual for the Solution of Military Ciphers* (Fort Leavenworth, KS: Press of the Army Service Schools, 1966), vii; David Kahn, *The Code-Breakers* (New York: Macmillan, 1966), passim.

22. Dan Tyler Moore and Martha Waller, *Cloak and Cipher* (Indianapolis, IN: Bobbs-Merrill, 1962), 17–19, 98–112.

23. Barry A. J. Fisher, *Techniques of Crime Scene Investigation* (Boca Raton, FL: CRC Press, 2004), 284–285.

24. Saferstein, *Forensic Science*, 127–128.

6 Basic Investigative Leads and Informants

LEARNING OBJECTIVES

After reading this chapter, you will be able to:

❶ *List the various basic leads and explain the origin of each.*

❷ *Discuss how the victim's background can aid in determining the who and why of an investigation.*

❸ *Define the concept of benefit as it relates to motive or why the crime was committed.*

❹ *Explain the concept of opportunity and how it relates to a suspect's alibi.*

⑤ *Discuss the line of inquiry which indicates that the suspect has specific knowledge or skill to commit the crime.*

⑥ *Appreciate the importance of field contact reports as an investigative lead.*

⑦ *Discuss the type of information that can be obtained from motor vehicle records and firearms registration.*

⑧ *Explain the different types of fingerprint searches that may be requested.*

⑨ *Explain how stolen property can be traced back to the person, or persons, responsible for its theft.*

⑩ *Explain how the modus operandi of a crime can be used to link suspects to their crimes.*

⑪ *Identify the various databases contained in the National Crime Information Center nationwide computer system.*

⑫ *Discuss how offender registration is used in the investigation of crime.*

⑬ *Discuss how photographs of known criminals can be used in the course of an investigation.*

⑭ *Explain the various methods of preparing a composite sketch.*

⑮ *Discuss how a suspect's injuries can be used to link them to a crime.*

⑯ *Describe the process that is used to identify links between persons engaged in criminal activity.*

⑰ *List the various types of informants and their motivation for informing on others involved in criminal activity.*

⑱ *Define an "accomplice witness" and explain why they might be used as an informant.*

⑲ *Distinguish between the various types of surveillance techniques and the methods employed in their application.*

⑳ *Explain the legal issues involved in audio surveillance.*

㉑ *Explain how contact surveillance might be conducted.*

㉒ *Discuss the elements required to be enumerated in the application for a search warrant.*

㉓ *Discuss the six stages involved in the police intelligence process.*

㉔ *Define proactive investigation and its use of link analysis.*

㉕ *Discuss the advantages of using undercover agents.*

㉖ *Explain the three types of lineups that might be used during the course of an investigation.*

The problem of determining "who did it?" is simple when the offender is caught in the act or apprehended in flight from the scene shortly after the crime. When the perpetrator is not promptly arrested, the direction of the investigation varies according to which of two categories the case falls into—known identity or unknown identity. The case is one of **known identity** when the perpetrator is known and has been named by the victim or witnesses. All other cases are of **unknown identity**. Cases involving named suspects constitute a high percentage of the cases cleared by arrest in any police agency. In these cases, the principal lead to the perpetrator's identity has been furnished by the victim or witnesses. The challenge to the skill of any investigator is the case without a named suspect. In such cases the basic investigative leads must be developed by the investigator to reveal the identity of the perpetrator.

Motive and opportunity (or presence) are broad areas of investigation basic to any crime. The people and things involved in a crime offer lead to the identity, motive, and opportunity of any perpetrator, known or unknown.

List the various basic leads and explain the origin of each.

▶ Basic Leads

The victim offers the initial basic lead. The background of the victim furnishes data, as do his or her activities just before the crime. A group of suspects can be developed by inquiring about who would benefit from the crime and who had the requisite knowledge about the target—the object of the crime. Field contact reports of interviews by patrol officers at and about the time and place of the crime offer data about suspects and sometimes about vehicles. When motor vehicles or weapons are involved in a crime, inquiries often link these material things with their owners or users. Latent fingerprints and other trace evidence found at crime scenes confirm that a suspect has been at the scene and indicate opportunity. Another trace of a presence at the crime scene is the manner in which the crime was committed—the modus operandi. Sometimes recovered stolen property can be traced to the thief. Police records of persons previously arrested contain photographs that can be viewed by witnesses when investigators develop suspicions about the identity of suspects. When photographs are not available, composite drawings may be used. Finally, injuries characteristic of certain crimes furnish leads that often help to link a suspect to a crime.

Experienced investigators dislike associating the development of investigation leads with any intuitive process; they believe that a hunch is out of place when dealing with people. Developing leads is a combination of know-how, the cognitive process, and an ability to work rapidly. Time is of the essence in criminal investigation and has an effect upon witnesses and investigators. It gives the criminal an opportunity to dispose of evidence, to develop defenses against the shock of being arrested, or to get farther away if he or she is in flight. No time can be lost making inquiries indicated by the basic leads of a case.

In cases of known identity, the objective is to corroborate the story of the eyewitness. The investigator follows the basic investigative leads, but particular effort is also made to corroborate the eyewitness's stories. In addition, parallel inquiries are pursued to avoid error in identity and to make the case compelling rather than subject to doubt.

In cases of unknown identity the objective is to develop suspects by following the basic investigative leads with the goal of identifying the perpetrator. The action is oriented to expanding the universe of suspects, to identifying prime suspects, and to finding the guilty person or persons among the prime suspects.

Keep in mind that determining who committed the crime should not terminate the investigation. All elements of the crime must be proved beyond a reasonable doubt. Some crimes present unique elements or possible defenses. The investigation should continue until all evidence, positive or negative, is gathered to prove the crime; to identify the perpetrator; and to disprove, when possible, defenses such as justification, excuse, lack of specific intent, lack of malice, diminished capacity, intoxication, ignorance, error, and insanity.

Basic leads suggest lines of inquiry likely to provide an investigator with information (Figure 6-1). **Active information** leads to the establishment of a group of suspects. The strength of the information accumulated against each member of this group depends on the nature of the evidence, but it may indicate prime suspects. **Passive information** is associative evidence that can be of use only if a group of suspects has been developed. Passive information often confirms suspicions against a person as a prime suspect by associating him or her with the crime scene or the victim. These basic types of information lead by two routes to sufficient evidence to reveal the person or persons who are guilty of the crime being investigated.[1]

 Discuss how the victim's background can aid in determining the who and why of an investigation.

Victim's Background

Police investigators have been criticized for cross-examining a victim and for probing his or her background and relationship to the crime. To the uninitiated, prying information from the unfortunate victim of a crime instead of promptly taking up the hue and cry for the perpetrator seems unjustifiable. However, a chase without a clearly defined objective is just aimless activity. Very

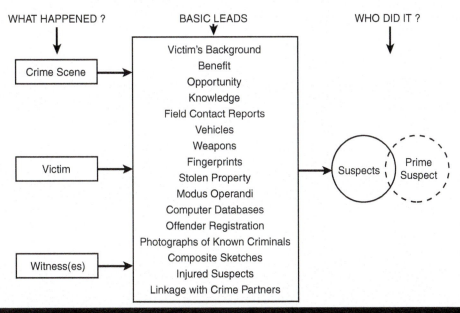

| WHAT HAPPENED ? | BASIC LEADS | WHO DID IT ? |

Victim's Background
Benefit
Opportunity
Knowledge
Field Contact Reports
Vehicles
Weapons
Fingerprints
Stolen Property
Modus Operandi
Computer Databases
Offender Registration
Photographs of Known Criminals
Composite Sketches
Injured Suspects
Linkage with Crime Partners

Crime Scene →

Victim →

Witness(es) →

Suspects | Prime Suspect

FIGURE 6-1 Basic Leads Are the Link between What Happened and Who Did It.

promising leads can be developed from a review of the background of the victim, which can give the pursuit defined goals.

Many classic avenues can be probed in regard to the victim. The following are some of these classic queries:

1. Did the victim know the perpetrator? If so, what is the relationship?
2. Does the victim suspect any person? Why?
3. Has the victim a history of crime? A history of reporting crimes?
4. Did the victim have a weapon?
5. Has the victim an aggressive personality?
6. Has the victim been the subject of any field contact reports?
7. What is the license number and description of the victim's car?
8. Was the victim mistaken for someone else?

This does not mean that an investigation of crime should boomerang into an investigation of the victim. However, any fact of significance about the victim should be unearthed at this stage of an investigation inasmuch as it may contribute a vital basic lead, and it may aid in the future evaluation of the case by the prosecuting attorney.

3 *Define the concept of benefit as it relates to motive or why the crime was committed.*

Benefit

The question of who might **benefit** from a crime provides an excellent focus for making inquiry. The factor of benefit often can provide investigative leads. In homicide cases, the motive of jealousy or elimination is a standard avenue of inquiry. Whenever a wife or husband dies and the death is unexplained, the survivor is suspect. Necessary action is taken to discover the classic love triangle. If a third party is involved, the triangle is considered a promising lead. In arson cases, the benefit may be complex: a rational motivation for financial gain in fraudulent fires of insured premises or an irrational motivation in psychopathic fire setting.

These are particularized motives in that the identity of the perpetrator can be deduced from the exposure of a relationship to the victim or the crime. Generally, the relationships between the victim in homicides and persons who might benefit from the fact of death are most productive in providing significant leads. The more universal motives of profit and sexual release common to burglaries, robberies, rapes, and other sex crimes usually do not offer investigators specific leads about the identity of the person who will benefit from the crime.[2]

4   *Explain the concept of opportunity and how it relates to a suspect's alibi.*

Opportunity

Searching for and identifying persons with the **opportunity** to commit a crime is a valid basic lead. Admitted or suspected presence at the scene of a crime at or about the time of its occurrence may be no more than an immediate investigative aid, but it is a lead.

When offenders know they are suspected of being at the crime scene and thus vulnerable to this "opportunity" line of inquiry, they often fabricate an **alibi**—a claim of being elsewhere. Investigation into an alibi will often disclose any fabrication, justifying other inquiries directed at this suspect. However, an effective alibi does not summarily exclude a suspect from further screening.

5   *Discuss the line of inquiry which indicates that the suspect has specific knowledge or skill to commit the crime.*

Knowledge

In theft cases, the victim is questioned about the identity of persons who might know their way about the premises and about the presence and location of articles of value. This inquiry is done in order to establish who may have had the **knowledge** necessary for committing the crime. In armed robberies, the victim is questioned about the identity of persons who knew of the routine of the victim or the business firm victimized. This tracing of knowledge provides a natural group of suspects, including the following:

1. Persons who have access to the premises at which the crime occurred or who are familiar with them
2. Persons who knew of the value and place of storage of property or the routine of the victim or the business victimized, such as:
   a. any present employee or spouse
   b. any former employee or spouse
   c. service and maintenance personnel (those employed in the area or the building, or those making frequent service deliveries)
   d. neighbors
   e. criminals with contacts among the persons with knowledge
3. Persons noticed in the area or on the premises recently who were:
   a. acting strangely (sex cases, fires, homicides)
   b. applying for work, soliciting sales, conducting surveys, etc.

Possession of the knowledge needed to commit a crime suggests possession also of the skill and capacity to have done it. What kind of criminal could accomplish the crime under investigation? Did it require a special (an identifying) skill, such as using a torch to open a safe or knowledge of the fast-cutting action of demolition-type burning bars? Did it require a special knowledge in a trade or occupation? The use of the hydraulic jimmy suggests a person who has worked in body and fender shops where this device is used to pry apart bent fenders and who knows about this tool's fast and powerful push-and-heave action. Did the crime require a person who was not afraid to kill, such as the cat burglar who enters occupied homes—even occupied bedrooms?

The multiple murders of the Clutter family in Kansas would have been solved months earlier if the basic lead of former employees had been pursued. Floyd Wells, a prisoner in Kansas State Prison, had worked on the Clutter ranch and had mentioned the extent of the ranch to a cell mate. The murders took place shortly after the release of the cell mate. Wells, weeks after the crime, identified himself as a former employee of the victims and supplied the authorities with a basic lead that identified one of the two killers. A check of this man's associates led to a rapid identification of his crime partner.[3]

6 *Appreciate the importance of field contact reports as an investigative lead.*

Field Contact Reports

Field contacts are an aggressive police patrol tactic. **Field contact reports** record the stop-and-frisk interviews with persons stopped in their cars or on foot because of their suspicious appearance or actions. These reports place in police records the names and the descriptions of the persons coming to police attention and the time, date, and place they were seen and interviewed. These reports are confidential in that they are not disclosed to the public but are filed in police records systems for the use of investigators. The data on who was in the vicinity and where and when are valuable aids to investigators seeking basic leads. Field contacts represent a broad surveillance involving observations of an entire patrol sector by an alert assigned officer. Often an investigator confronted with a burglary without apparent clues to the identity of the offender will find a field contact report describing a known thief being stopped in the early morning hours not more than a few blocks from the crime scene. An apparently innocent suspect in a sex case who pleads that he hardly ever leaves his home at night may be revealed, by field contacts, to be a nocturnal roamer in the city's parks.

For the purpose of revealing group identification, some police units have an automated filing system for field contact cards about youngsters under seventeen or eighteen years of age. Because most juvenile crimes are committed by groups, this cross-reference offers information about the associates of an offender. When the field contact cards of a juvenile are requested, these group associations should be probed for basic leads along the lines of race, sex, age, and associates of previous arrests.

7 *Discuss the type of information that can be obtained from motor vehicle records and firearms registration.*

Vehicles

There is no better clue to the identity of a criminal than the identification of a vehicle. True, time is important when a stolen vehicle is used because professional bank robbers and other criminals who plan their crimes with care abandon the getaway car before an alarm can be broadcast. However, two killers of a police officer were once observed as they changed cars, and thus a crucial basic lead that led to their arrest was gained.

Even a fragmentary description of a vehicle is often helpful. In a series of bank robberies in northern California, the robber walked away from his crimes. The first basic lead offering any promise followed the third robbery in which a witness noticed a man acting suspiciously while going from a bank to the parking lot. The witness could offer only a fragment of a license number: EPC. Federal Bureau of Investigation (FBI) agents sought help from the California Department of Motor Vehicles, which yielded no results. Then the "EPC" fragment was checked against reports of cars stopped at barricades set up after each robbery. The agents found one promising lead. A car with registration letters CPC had been stopped and passed through a roadblock. Again motor vehicle records were scanned. The vehicle was registered to William Liebscher, Jr., a used car dealer. Motor vehicle files provided an in-the-course-of-business exemplar of Liebscher's signature on a registration application. Agents compared it with another basic lead previously useless for lack of a suspect: the handwriting on a fictitious money order dropped by the robber at one of the crime scenes. The handwriting was similar. Other evidence corroborated these leads, and Liebscher was arrested and convicted.

Enterprising detectives scan stolen vehicle reports for similarities with the descriptions of cars used in crime. The anxious criminal who used his or her own car may become worried that the vehicle has been seen by witnesses and abandons it. Then, after an appropriate interval, he or she reports it stolen. The criminal hopes to throw off suspicion by such action if the car had been identified with the crime. Usually, the fragments of description are not enough to locate a vehicle, but they are sufficient for alert detectives when a criminal directs attention to an automobile by reporting it lost.

Motor vehicle records are statewide records filed under name and license (registration) number. Often a name not known to be used by the suspect under investigation is detected in searching for the owner of a vehicle used in a crime or known to be operated by the suspect. Motor vehicle records may contain a thumbprint or a photograph or both, and they usually will have some physical description of a licensed operator. Both owner and operator records usually contain a person's date of birth, previous residence, and dates of residence at such locations. Accident and violation reports, cross-indexed to these basic motor vehicle records, may reveal something of the activities of the suspect, such as dates and locations of accidents and driving record.

Of importance to investigators is the finality of identification possible using motor vehicles as a basic lead. Time and again the suspect's shock upon learning that he or she has been identified has led to full cooperation with police and a plea of guilty.

Weapons

Clubs and other blunt instruments are rarely engraved with an owner's name, but firearms are marked with a maker's name and a serial number, and their ownership often can be traced through sales and firearm registration records. The lead developed from such tracing may reveal that the weapon was stolen, but this fact links the crime under investigation with another crime— and that is a basic lead.

The ownership of knives often can be identified, even though knives are not marked with serial numbers. Clubs and other striking weapons often provide promising leads to identity. Poisons and drugs used in crimes sometimes can be traced, and the purchase of dynamite is often traced in bomb cases.

Bullets and fired cartridge cases, pattern wounds, and the distinctive effects of several poisons provide passive information useful for associating a suspect, when identified, with a crime.

8 *Explain the different types of fingerprint searches that may be requested.*

Fingerprints

Fingerprints found at crime scenes have a very high potential for identifying perpetrators of crime once the imprints of the victim and other nonsuspects are screened out. Searching for these chance imprints at crime scenes is emphasized more and more. Latent imprints, normally invisible, are developed by dusting various surfaces at the crime scene with contrasting fingerprint powders or by iodine fuming. The increase in the use of evidence technicians at crime scenes has resulted in more effective searches for these hidden fingerprints.

Computerized fingerprint searching systems permit a rapid scanning of thousands of ten-finger records against chance imprints found at crime scenes. Police expertise at other police agencies is developing slower, but equally effective, procedures for the rapid comparison of fingerprints found at crime scenes with the fingerprints of known offenders on file:

1. Crime-scene fingerprints are determined to be of value or of no value. Imprints of value have an adequate number of identifying characteristics.

2. Crime-scene fingerprints are compared with the imprints of persons who are legally at the scene: victim, witnesses, police, and other known visitors.

3. Fingerprints on file are searched to identify the suspect making the crime-scene fingerprint(s):
   a. **Request search**. The investigator assigned to the case names one or more suspects and asks for a search.
   b. **Single-digit search**. Identification technicians search such files as those containing other crime-scene fingerprints or the ten-digit fingerprints of repeat or career criminals.
   c. **Cold search**. Identification technicians search through an entire ten-digit fingerprint file. Unless the police agency is small or has a computerized search capability, the scope of this cold search should be reduced to (1) known criminals operating in the same geographical area or with the same modus operandi and (2) recent arrestees.[4]

Of importance is the finality of identification in this area. Fingerprints found at crime scenes reveal the opportunity or presence factor—which provides an important lead. When fingerprints pinpoint a person with a history of like crimes or link the suspect with other latents from another crime, the lead is significant.

 Explain how stolen property can be traced back to the person, or persons, responsible for its theft.

Stolen Property

A search for stolen property is a search for identifiable items. Police have been using this technique skillfully for so many years that it is sometimes overlooked as a routine, albeit successful, technique. Novice investigators are not aware of its potential value until they have worked on cases in which stolen property has been recovered. In tracing its possession, they have noted the ease with which the identity of the burglar or thief has been developed.

Tracing the proceeds of a theft is facilitated by the establishment of special investigative squads whose duties are to visit pawnshops, secondhand dealers, junk shops, and other places where stolen property is likely to be offered for sale and to coordinate the local search for locally stolen property. It is also supported by laws in many states and municipalities that require the pawnbroker to report to the police the pawning or purchase of specific second-hand merchandise (guns, watches, televisions, DVDs, computers, and other articles that are commonly stolen). These laws often require places of business handling such merchandise to maintain a log or register of their business, describing each item purchased. This record is open to police inspection at any time. The level of cooperation extended to police by many such business managers—often far above the legal demands—results in the recovery of vast amounts of stolen property. In some cities, pawnshop proprietors have personally defrayed the cost of hotlines to, and silent alarms in, nearby police stations for prompt notification of offerings by suspicious persons.

The Sacramento County Sheriff's Department has established a database of information supplied by pawnshop dealers. This information includes the date of transaction, description of the item, and name and address of the person pawning it. A compilation of all transactions for that month is printed and sent to investigators. It was noted that a woman had pawned eight different wedding rings in one month. Another individual had pawned a number of televisions and VCRs at various pawnshops around the city. This information supplied investigators with important investigative leads beyond the theft and burglary investigations that might have started a search for stolen property.

A computerized stolen property record system within a police department will make possible the following:

1. Shorten the time required to search these reports for items of stolen property
2. Allow for searches leading to the identity of persons who frequently sell or pawn used property
3. Offer opportunities—long after a crime has been committed—to locate stolen office equipment by periodic examination of the records of the repair services of manufacturers (authorized agents)[5]

Serial numbers and other positive identifying data necessary for the recovery of property are not always available from the victim of a theft. It may be necessary for the victim (or the investigator) to visit the store in which the property was purchased. Most merchants keep a detailed record of sales. When jewelry and furs are stolen, merchants can provide information regarding scratch marks on items of jewelry or hidden identifications stamped on the inside lining of fur garments or on the skins themselves. These merchants, along with pawn brokers, sometimes mark this type of property when it passes through their establishments for repair or cleaning or as collateral for a cash loan. Markings often are hidden, require information about where to look for them, or must be viewed with ultraviolet light. Fortunately, when skilled thieves believe they have removed all labels and identifying marks from stolen property, such markings may remain for the investigator's use.

No assumptions should be made in regard to describing identifying characteristics of stolen property. Recovery depends on identification. For example, when jewelry is described, it is better to state the appearance of the metal and stones than to assume a basic classification. What is described by a victim as a yellow gold ring is best detailed in a wanted notice as a yellow metal ring, and the diamonds and rubies said to be part of the setting of such rings are best described as white and red stones of a particular size and cut. Stolen property notices sometimes contain lengthy listings of stolen property, and for this reason these notices are indexed by number to each item of property listed, starting with number one. Investigators also group property within this numbered sequence in general classifications, such as jewelry, clothing, and furs. In communicating with agencies locating the property, this numbering system aids in identification and shortens the necessary communication among agencies. Know-how based on experience and some intuition can lead an investigator to the prompt recovery of stolen property and may thereby offer a valuable investigative lead.

The process for verifying the use of stolen credit cards is similar to tracing stolen goods. It is a trail that offers many opportunities for basic leads. Large commercial organizations issuing credit cards are generally not local because a central accounting office provides nationwide coverage. However, billing procedures may provide effective assistance in tracing fugitives, which more than justifies the labor of communicating with these organizations. Because gasoline is a prime credit card purchase, local service station dealers may be able to provide information about a suspect and the use of a credit card. Recent receipts, not yet forwarded to the central accounting office, may still be available at gas stations and may reveal the name of the purchaser, the credit card number, and the name of the gasoline company handling the account. Credit card accounts will reveal recent billings and may show the activity of a suspect on the days when purchases were charged to the credit card. Problems resulting from loss, theft, and misuse of credit cards have led to improved attention to security among the accounting personnel of these firms, and their cooperation with police is excellent.

🔟 *Explain how the modus operandi of a crime can be used to link suspects to their crimes.*

Modus Operandi

The choice of a particular crime to commit and the selection of a method of committing it is the **modus operandi** of a criminal. Not all criminals have a particular modus operandi, but enough of them have distinctive methods of operation to justify classifying crimes by their like characteristics. The modus operandi of a criminal is his or her **signature**.

For this reason, investigators compare the manner in which a crime was committed with relevant records stored in the modus operandi section of the police record systems. If any of these comparisons are successful, the detective secures data on possible suspects. The use of modus operandi by police agencies is both current and extensive. Its successful use in robbery, burglary, grand theft, fraud, sex offense, and fraudulent check cases amounts to a mandate to search the modus operandi files for basic leads in these crimes.

A modus operandi file contains information about the methods of operation of known criminals and the methods used in unsolved crimes. This file has three major capabilities:

1. Identifying a perpetrator by naming suspects whose modus operandi in past crimes fits the facts of the crime being investigated
2. Linking an unknown perpetrator with the modus operandi of past crimes committed by unknown perpetrators for the purpose of structuring the identity of a suspect from the modus operandi and leads from several connected crimes
3. Storing data on unsolved crimes according to modus operandi to allow comparison with the crime technique of an apprehended criminal and unresolved crimes with an arrestee

Of course, past offenses and the way they were committed must be sufficiently similar to be meaningful. They must possess a number of common features with a crime under investigation to warrant the inference that if the suspect committed the other acts, he or she must have committed the act being investigated. Similarities in methods of operation (in combination with other basic leads) also constitute an important tool in the realm of identity, for they decrease the likelihood of a claim of a mistake, or a real mistake, in suspecting a person of crime.

 Identify the various databases contained in the National Crime Information Center nationwide computer system.

Computer Databases

At the local level, the computer databases of police and sheriff's departments contain information regarding who has been victimized and where, as well as wanted person, criminal history, and stolen property information. At the state or regional level, motor vehicle files can be accessed for driver's license, registered vehicle, and stolen vehicle and vessel information. Other statewide or regional databases may contain wanted person, stolen property, and firearms registry files.

The National Crime Information Center (NCIC) is the computer system dedicated to serving the needs of law enforcement throughout the United States, Mexico, and Canada. Operated by the FBI, the system processed 2 million inquiries in its first year of operation in 1967. Today the system handles 2.5 million inquiries a day, most of which are generated by local law enforcement officials. The system was upgraded in the year 2000 and now contains files or databases on wanted persons, stolen property, criminal histories, missing and unidentified persons, convicted sexual offender registrations, and convicted persons on supervised release. This system is now supported by digital images. Upon request the system can provide mugshots; fingerprints; signature samples; and as many as ten identifying photographs on wanted, missing, or unidentified persons. Photographs can also be attached to identify stolen vehicles, boats, or other property. The system has the ability to match fingerprint records and to link related records across associated NCIC files for the same crime or criminal.[6]

The **National Integrated Ballistic Information Network (NIBIN)** is a nationwide database deploying ballistic imaging equipment. This system can compare gun evidence such as projectiles and cartridge cases that are recovered at crime scenes. The system, which is maintained by the **Bureau of Alcohol, Tobacco, Firearms, and Explosives (ATF)**, automatically compares each new entry to prior entries and generates a list of potential similar entries. A firearms examiner then examines the evidence to confirm that the cases are linked.[7]

12 Discuss how offender registration is used in the investigation of crime.

Offender Registration

In 1994, Congress passed the Jacob Wetterling Crimes Against Children and Sexually Violent Offender Registration Act. The act is name in honor of eleven-year-old Jacob Wetterling who was kidnapped while bicycling near his home in Minnesota. The act required that states create sex offender registries. Offenders who commit a criminal sexual act against a minor or commit any sexually violent offense must register for a period of ten years from the date of their release from custody or supervision. All fifty states now have sex offender registration laws. In 1996, the act was amended by establishing a national sex offender database that the FBI maintains. This national tracking system gives investigators access to sex offender registration data from all participating states.

Registry information typically includes the offender's name, address, date of birth, Social Security Number, and physical description, as well as fingerprints and a photograph. Usually, offenders must register within a certain number of days following their release from custody or placement on supervision. The registration requirement is in effect for at least ten years, with some states requiring lifetime registration for all or some offenses. Most states make it a criminal offense to knowingly fail to register or report subsequent changes in information, such as the registrant's name or address.[8]

California, the first state to pass an offender registration law in 1947, requires convicted arsonists, drug offenders, and sex offenders to register. The drug offender registration terminates five years after discharge from custody or expiration of parole or probation. However, sexual offender and arson offender registration is a lifetime requirement. This registration is required of California residents even if the crime was committed in another state or federal jurisdiction.

The nationwide **Amber Alert system** is a law enforcement tool for combating sexual predators. This system aims to assist officers in capturing kidnappers and sexual predators who have recently abducted children. The system disseminates information to the general public about the suspects and their vehicles via highway signs, television spots, and radio broadcasts. The system is named after Amber Hagerman, a nine-year-old Texas girl whose abduction and murder inspired a similar alert system in that state.[9]

⑬ *Discuss how photographs of known criminals can be used in the course of an investigation.*

Photographs of Known Criminals

A search through modus operandi records often provides photographs of suspects made at the time of a previous arrest. These photographs, or **mug shots**, are available, and if the crime being investigated has been witnessed, the investigator has an opportunity to ask an eyewitness to view them. The witness is not asked to identify any photo but is requested to scan no less than a half dozen photographs and to cast out those that offer no resemblance to the perpetrator. When one or more photographs appear to resemble the perpetrator, further inquiry is conducted. The investigator concentrates on the whereabouts of the persons selected as "possibles." It may be that the suspect was in prison, out of town, or living in a distant city at the time of the crime. Every reasonable circumstance that eliminates persons from a group of suspects reduces the group and allows concentration upon the remainder. The investigator or associates also cast out any suspect known to be working and living within his or her means and to have a reputation for no longer being involved with crime.

Mug books are often prepared for specific offenses. The FBI provides photos of known bank robbers to agents investigating bank robberies. These photographs were collected before the crime being investigated happened and thus permit a rapid viewing by an eyewitness of persons who have committed crimes similar to the crime under investigation.

As long as the photographs show five or ten suspects of various types and origins, this practice does not destroy the validity of future testimony of these witnesses. When a photograph of only one person is exhibited to an eyewitness, or when the other photos in the group are of a nature that a single suspect is isolated by some physical or racial characteristic, the future testimony of the witness is compromised. Such a viewing of photographs is likely to be criticized in

Mug shot taken at the time of arrest.

XREF#:   **5000324**
Last: **CARVER**
First: **DANIEL**
DOB: **06/06/66**
Sex: **MALE**
Race: **WHITE**
Height: **6'02"**
Weight: **210**
Hair: **BLOND**
Eyes: **GREEN**
Charges:

present-day trial procedures and likened to a conditioning process. The witness may be compromised, and his or her potential credibility toward establishing identity may be ruined. When two or more eyewitnesses are available, it is possible to use one of them to view photographs for basic leads to the identity of the offender and to reserve the remaining witness or witnesses for a later identification. Little justification can be made for ruining the potential of a major witness by having him or her confirm identification at this initial stage.

⑭ *Explain the various methods of preparing a composite sketch.*

Composite Sketches for Identification

When photographs are not available, the victim and any witnesses may be asked to collaborate with a police artist in developing a **composite sketch** of the suspect. Artists have the skills necessary to develop a portrait of a suspect from the description of a victim or witness or from the descriptions given by several witnesses. The usual procedure is for the artist to make a tentative sketch and then show it to the victim or witness and ask how closely it resembles the suspect. After some trial and error, this collaboration of the artist and the victim or witness frequently results in a drawing that is likely to be of value in identifying the suspect (Figure 6-2).

Identi-Kit is another visual means for identification through the cooperation of victims and witnesses. An Identi-Kit system consists of several hundred plastic slides containing photo reproductions of one small portion of a human face: hairstyle, forehead, eyes, nose, mouth, chin, ear, eyeglasses, and so on. Police personnel trained in the use of an Identi-Kit can work with a victim or witness in developing a composite sketch in accordance with the description and trial-and-error viewing.

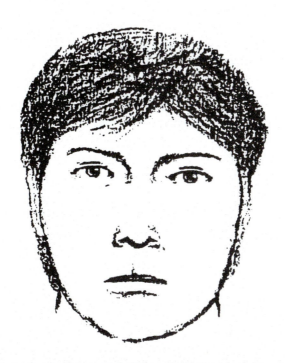

FIGURE 6-2   This Composite Sketch Resulted in Prompt Identification of a Shooter in a Double Homicide Investigation. From Fairfax County Police Department, Fairfax, VA, in "Report to the Chairman, Commerce, Consumer, and Monetary Affairs Subcommittee, Committee on Government Operations, House of Representatives: Bureau of Alcohol, Tobacco & Firearms Handling of Suspect Lead in Langley/CIA Headquarters Shooting Incident" (Washington, DC: U.S. Government Accounting Office, April 1994), 10.

Software is now available for producing composites created by a witness in response to queries in the computer program. When completed, these composites can be checked against a database of known criminal mug shots using facial recognition software. In the past, the use of composites always relied on someone recognizing that person and coming forward with that information. Facial recognition software, however, measures the spatial relationships among facial features and converts that information into a mathematical map of the face. The computer then picks the most similar set of mathematical features and displays the corresponding faces in an electronic lineup.[10]

 Discuss how a suspect's injuries can be used to link them to a crime.

Injured Suspects

In homicides, assaults, and arson cases, the criminal is sometimes bloodied or burned. An injured person may be a basic lead. In most states, physicians are required to report gunshot and knife wounds when patients seek treatment. In some cases, local hospitals are asked to be alert for persons seeking treatment for various injuries. In one case, the investigator believed that blood and a broken glass window suggested a wound with glass in it. The emergency room of the local hospital was requested to report any such wound, and forty-eight hours later a call came in describing "a wound with a great deal of powdered glass." In a rape case, the attacker was surprised in the act and ran off in the dark through a wooded area. Two days later the police received a call about "a patient… who did not seek treatment for his broken ankle for two days." An anxious suspect may wash off blood and postpone treatment for a severe injury, but chances are excellent for a basic lead if medical treatment is sought.

Searching for injured persons in developing a group of suspects is similar to an exhaustive search for witnesses. The search may or may not develop information, but this investigative work reveals a determination to follow every reasonable line of inquiry in seeking leads to the identity of the perpetrator.

Similar determination to follow every suggested line of inquiry as basic leads are developed reassures the people of a community that criminals are being sought systematically and also favors exoneration of an innocent person originally suspected of the crime. Diligent inquiry in following up basic leads gathers the active and passive information that will identify "who did it," sometimes will reveal the perpetrator's presence at the crime scene, and often will contribute to an understanding of why the crime was committed.

16 *Describe the process that is used to identify links between persons engaged in criminal activity.*

Linkage Between Suspect and Crime Partners

When more than one person is responsible for a crime, the assigned investigator must develop the identity of all the individuals involved. An arrested suspect may or may not identify his or her crime partners. An identified but unapprehended suspect may be located by identifying and locating one or more of his or her crime partners.

While crime partnerships may be based on the underworld skills of an individual (ability to neutralize burglar alarms, getaway-car driving skills, torch capability for opening safes and locked boxes), they also depend on mutual trust and compatibility. When crime is a person's business, partnerships are formed only with someone who is known, liked, and trusted.

The following are six types of relationships that form strong personal **linkages** between persons engaged in criminal activity:

1. *Neighborhood friendships.* These friendships may date from early childhood, such as from membership in a youth gang, or the social interactions among neighboring families and members of ethnic groups.

2. *Juvenile hall and prison contacts.* Incarceration in a correctional facility brings persons who are convicted of a crime, or who are adjudicated as delinquents and made wards of a children's court, into close contact. Many of these contacts ripen into friendships that

can be traced through juvenile institutions to prisons for adult offenders. Inmates band together with others they trust.

3. *Family relationships.* Many persons have a strong sense of family trust and loyalty, which may be extended to persons without kinship linkage who have exercised some form of unofficial parental control, guidance, or support.

4. *Coethnic contacts.* In ghetto neighborhoods, juvenile halls, and prisons, each ethnic group tends to band together, which is similar emotionally to family relationships.

5. *Buyer–seller interactions.* This is a business relationship between the person wanting the crime committed for profit and the criminal actor. The common types of buyer–seller relationships are the business owner and the torch, the planner of a murder and the hit man, and the receiver of stolen property and the thief.

6. *Lovers.* An identifiable and often easily traced relationship is one between husband and wife (legal or common law); a triangle relationship in which a lover of either sex is added to the husband–wife duo; and heterosexuals or homosexuals living together or otherwise identified as lovers.

When basic investigative leads do not disclose the identity of a crime partner, investigators must probe among the common kinds of relationships for "possibles."

The investigator who probes a criminal or personal relationship may gain information that is meaningful to the success of the investigation. Few relationships can survive the temptation of **"better him than me."** Ethnic gangs have their informants or potential informants; prison friendships may succumb to self-preservation; families often have hidden internal hostilities; and the instances of lovers grown cold are legion.

Social Media

Millions of people around the world use social media sites such as Facebook, MySpace, and Twitter on a daily basis. Social media is an excellent means to ask for the public's help in solving crimes. Photos of a suspect or a missing person can be transmitted over these sites asking if anyone knows of their whereabouts. Likewise photos of unidentified victims, their jewelry, tattoos, scars, and other identifying marks can be sent out via social media with a request for help in identifying the person.

Social media sites contain a wealth of information which may be important to an investigation. These sites contain photos and personal information such as the person's name, interests, employment, and relationships, including family and friends. In addition, suspects may post information that would be useful in establishing a motive for the commission of a crime, offer conflicting alibis and stories, and even confessions and photos relating to the crime. Information that is posted to a social networking site is fair game for anyone to use, including the investigator. In addition to what is publically visible, the investigator can request information from the operators of these social media sites who may have stored additional information regarding this person.

Video Surveillance Cameras

Video cameras have been used for years to monitor public places and businesses. What makes modern systems unique is that these cameras are now capable of broadcasting live via Internet connection. These video surveillance cameras are being installed just about anywhere people may gather or there is a security concern. The vast majority of these cameras are not monitored and therefore not useful in preventing crime. However, they are an effective crime solving tool as the following case illustrates.

On Monday, April 15, 2013, at 2:49 P.M. the Boston Marathon was in progress and over 5,700 runners were still on the course. Hundreds of thousands of spectators lined the 26.2 mile course. Then two explosions, 12 seconds and 214 feet apart, ripped through the crowds at the finish line on Boylston Street. Three people died and another 27 were injured. One of the first orders of police commanders on the scene was to collect all the recorded video from the surveillance cameras surrounding the scene of the blast. It took three days for the FBI to review all of the footage and to release images of the suspects, who were the only ones not to turn and look toward the

Video surveillance camera footage showing the alleged bombing suspects in the area of detonation.
Source: ©FBI/Photoshot

direction of the explosions. Investigators did not know who the suspects were until they surfaced hours later killing a police officer and were subsequently involved in an exchange of gunfire with police where one suspect was killed and another captured.[11]

Cell Phones

The great thing about cell phones is that just about everyone has one and they contain a wealth of information that may be useful in a criminal investigation. Once investigators have legal access to a cell phone a forensic analysis of the phone can be made. Cell phones usually contain information such as contacts, calendars, notes, messages, photos, and video and audio recordings. In addition, cell phones have e-mail, web browsing sites, wireless settings, social networking messages, and geographical information.

Each time a cell phone is used, a signal is sent to a cell tower which transmits the user's signal or message. These signals sent to the carrier's tower can pinpoint the user's location, a built-in feature that is part of the 911 emergency call system. When the user's signal bounces off a different site, or multiple sites, this would indicate that the person was mobile at the time of the call. This information can be obtained from the cell phone carrier and is useful in locating suspects or missing persons. In addition, alibies, that a person was not in the area of a crime at the time it was committed, can be refuted by cell phone technology that discloses that the suspect's cell phone was used in the area at the time of the crime.

 List the various types of informants and their motivation for informing on others involved in criminal activity.

▶ Informants

Informants have long been a source of information to investigators seeking basic leads to a crime under investigation (Figure 6-3). In fact, one class of informants has been termed the **basic-lead informant.** However, informants are not basic leads but rather a means through which basic leads can be developed. One criticism of criminal investigation in its early years was that police investigators were prone to rely on informants when solving crimes and paid little or no attention to processing the crime scene or to following up on available basic leads. Today, the starting point in investigating any crime is a thorough examination of the crime scene, if known, and scrutinization of the basic leads discovered in the course of this examination. The follow-up investigation picks up these data and expands and develops them. Investigators no longer depend on informants, but they do seek help from the general public in locating anyone with information about the crime under investigation.

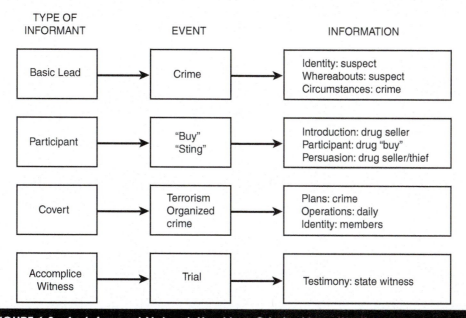

TYPE OF INFORMANT	EVENT	INFORMATION
Basic Lead	Crime	Identity: suspect Whereabouts: suspect Circumstances: crime
Participant	"Buy" "Sting"	Introduction: drug seller Participant: drug "buy" Persuasion: drug seller/thief
Covert	Terrorism Organized crime	Plans: crime Operations: daily Identity: members
Accomplice Witness	Trial	Testimony: state witness

FIGURE 6-3   An Informant Network Used in a Criminal Investigation.

Revealing other people's secrets is **snitching**. In the world of crime and criminals, snitching is a social felony. When a crime partner reveals his or her associates to police investigators and becomes a prosecution witness at subsequent court proceedings, he or she has committed treachery in the eyes of the underworld.

Words long used to describe individuals who inform police are denigrating. They tend to disparage the character or reputation of the informer: snitch, tipster, stool, stool pigeon, rat, canary. More recently, police investigators have employed *informant* as a generalized—and euphemistic—term. Anyone can be an informant. Most informants can testify in a criminal trial as long as they are acceptable as witnesses and their testimony meets the rules of admissibility.

Informants generally wish to remain anonymous. They particularly want to avoid the public identification inherent in becoming a witness for the prosecution. It is, therefore, especially important to conceal the identity of informers or to protect them from attack once their identity is disclosed because professional criminals are willing to maim or kill informants. It is difficult to conceal cooperation because criminals use every available source to learn the identity of informants.

Because the investigator relinquishes his or her basic role and seeks the help of criminals or persons associating with criminals, the use of informants is a questionable option in criminal investigation. Even noncriminal informants are often less objective than they claim. Some of their more common motivations for snitching are less than benevolent: hatred, revenge, jealousy, greed.

Informing is a dirty business because informants may lie to implicate innocent persons or to exculpate a favored crime partner. Inherent in some forms of snitching is that the snitch trades his or her version of what happened during a crime for immunity to prosecution, a reduced charge, or leniency at the time of sentencing.

Basic-Lead Informants

Despite considerations to the contrary, informants are a traditional starting point in seeking basic leads. In fact, informants sometimes offer data about an unreported or undiscovered crime or one in its planning stages.

The successful use of basic-lead informants is a complex combination of an alert and knowledgeable investigator knowing where to seek information, finding the contacts who have it, and probing and prying to gather as much meaningful information as possible.

This type of informant is motivated to divulge information to a police investigator for a multitude of reasons. He or she may have encountered it by chance or wants to do a citizen's duty by divulging it. Criminals may provide information to get rid of a competitor—a common practice in gambling, drug, and prostitution activities and not uncommon among thieves and recipients of stolen property. Jealousy and revenge sometimes motivate such informants. The "woman scorned" has done great harm to the victims of her fury by informing about their criminal activities.

Former girlfriends and wives often serve as unpaid informants. In the world of crime, the women friends of criminals often fear them with some justification. A frightened and knowledgeable ex-girlfriend or ex-wife has often allied herself in self-defense with police efforts and delivered vital information about the criminal activities of her ex-boyfriend or ex-husband.

Other informants seek pay for information leading to arrests. Investigators with unsolved jewelry thefts, suspicious fires, and homicide cases often are contacted by such informants proposing to supply information. Recently released prison inmates may be confronted with the choice of going back into crime or earning money, and they often sell information as a stopgap livelihood until they find employment or return to crime.

In many areas of the United States, "secret witness" programs sponsored by local news media are an innovative way of paying informants for basic leads. Cooperating business firms may contribute to an informant fund. Local police may request publicity about the most serious crimes or those without substantial leads. The news media involved publish the details of the crime and specify the amount of the reward (which varies by the nature of the crime). Inherent in these programs is a means by which informants, by providing a code word or number that will substantiate their claim to the reward, can contact local police investigators without revealing their identity. Rewards are paid when police have verified the information and found it meaningful and useful in the identification of a suspect, in learning the whereabouts of a known suspect, or in discovering what happened at the time of the crime.

Participant Informants

The role of the **participant informant** in enforcing the law against illegal drug sales is that of go-between: to identify the drug seller and to introduce the undercover investigator as a potential buyer, or to "instigate" the transaction in some fashion.[12]

Participant informants participate directly in gathering sufficient evidence to warrant an arrest. One type of participant informant is the special employee. He or she is paid a fee set in advance for this work. A special employee may be hired because of his or her knowledge of the local drug scene, friendships among local drug sellers and users, or the ability to deceive suspects as to his or her role.

Another type of participant informant on the drug scene is the arrestee who has been "turned," or "**flipped**," by the arresting officer. In this type of arrangement, the arrest is made on a minor charge of possessing or selling illegal drugs and the arresting officer persuades the arrestee to cooperate in identifying his or her source of drugs—in effect, to assist in a more important arrest—in return for some consideration by police, prosecutor, or court. At one time, this was an easily arranged and informal procedure, but current procedure usually requires discussion with and approval of the "deal" by the prosecutor. Often, a formal plea bargain is entered into between the prosecution and the defendant and his or her legal counsel.

Participant informants may be used by an investigator in solving crimes other than those involving the sale of illegal drugs. A few of these informants have been used as **shills** in police **sting** operations aimed at discovering burglars and thieves and recovering stolen property. This role requires the informant to sell property to the police playing the role of buyers in order to lure real burglars and thieves to do likewise.

The FBI used a participant informant to uncover political corruption in Chicago. The informant's role was to lure politicians to meetings where payoffs could be videotaped by FBI agents.[13] The sting investigation, known as ABSCAM, pioneered this videotaping of public officials accepting bribes. The name derives from the original cover story about the informant's relationship to a group of wealthy Arabs who owned "Abdul Enterprises Unlimited." In the ABSCAM prosecutions, a U.S. senator, six members of the U.S. House of Representatives, several local public officials in Pennsylvania and New Jersey, and numerous associates were found guilty. These verdicts were decided despite

▼

defense claims of unfairness and entrapment in this cash-for-political-favors "scam." The videotapes presented to the juries in these trials apparently convinced them that the government's action was not unfair, unscrupulous, or unethical.[14]

Covert Informants

Covert informants are not classified as persons who assist in developing basic leads in a criminal investigation, nor do they serve the instigator role of participant informants. They are men and women who report information to a police investigator about a terrorist or other criminal organization from a position of trust and confidence within the group. These agents-in-place are known as **moles** in the area of international espionage, as they are often in place for years before being activated.

Covert informants may or may not be remunerated for their work. They are not used for spot intelligence. The use of such persons is akin to the practice of having spies in the enemy's camp. These agents-in-place are a spin-off from military and international intelligence.[15] They can provide information over a lengthy period as long as their identities are protected. Such individuals must be developed fully, cultivated over a long time, and used only when absolutely necessary. These sources of information are not developed solely to provide information for current investigations but can be set up to provide information at a future time.

Organized crime and hate extremist groups are sites for agents-in-place. Homicides committed by hate groups are common, and organized crime is constantly expanding its operations. Hoodlums and extremists are an ever-present threat. When information is needed, after-the-fact intelligence operations are useless with either of these groups.

A man or woman may be established within a terrorist or crime group when he or she begins cooperating with an investigator. On the other hand, the investigator may recruit a person whom he or she believes to be trustworthy and capable and suggest a means by which the new covert informant can infiltrate the target organization.

A Canadian woman, a member of the Front de Liberation du Quebec (FLQ), went to the Montreal police to avoid involvement in an armed robbery planned by members of this terrorist group. She was promptly recruited as a covert informant. She was an excellent source of information for several months as she was never suspected of being an informant by any of her terrorist associates. Her police contacts avoided disclosing her identity until the day she appeared in open court as a witness.[16]

Most terrorist groups have established high thresholds to any penetration by informants; new members are always greeted with suspicion and distrust. Therefore, in seeking a productive informant, investigators should make every effort to cultivate and recruit as an informant a person who has been an active member of the group for some time.[17]

The "family" aspect of organized crime groups, regardless of its ethnic nature, is a real handicap to infiltrating an informant as a new member. However, the need for covert informants in these groups has diminished in recent years because of the success of prosecutors in turning or flipping accomplice witnesses.

 Define an "accomplice witness" and explain why they might be used as an informant.

Accomplice Witnesses

An **accomplice witness** is a person who is liable to prosecution for the identical offense charged against the defendant or defendants in a pending trial. He or she has been arrested along with one or more crime partners, and the police–prosecutor team offers leniency in return for his or her cooperation. Accomplice witnesses testify for the prosecution, identifying the defendant or defendants and testifying to acts done by them in furtherance of the crime.

Some prosecutors develop compelling evidence of guilt on the part of one person in a criminal operation, bring him or her to the prosecutor's office for a briefing on the evidence, and offer the alternatives of (1) arrest, conviction, and prison or (2) cooperation, a bargained plea to a lesser charge, and less or no incarceration.

A special state prosecutor in New York broke a complex case involving many police officers by confronting two of the police suspects with compelling evidence of guilt. Facing prison for their own crimes, these two officers flipped and agreed to inform on their coworkers in exchange for their own freedom. They continued their criminal activities (ripping off drug dealers, primarily) while being **wired** to secretly record and thereby incriminate their colleagues in crime.[18]

Recruiting a defendant in an organized crime case begins with a reiteration of the theme "every man for himself." Once the witness seeks more information, the standard deal is finalized:

1. In return for full cooperation, the witness will be given partial or full immunity.

2. After testimony is completed, the witness will be accepted in a witness protection plan (federal/state) that will furnish the witness with a new identity, funds, and assistance in relocating the witness and his or her family and will provide security measures sufficient to conceal his or her whereabouts.

When a pending case does not involve organized crime members, the accomplice witness does not usually need the protection afforded by a witness protection plan, and the prosecutor offers the potential informant only immunity or partial immunity. In a widespread diamond fraud case involving no less than $5,500,000, the mastermind (Irwin Margolies) ordered two of his crime partners killed (his accountant and her assistant). After the contract killer in this case was sentenced to over a hundred years in prison for these two homicides plus the wanton killing of three accidental witnesses to the murder of the accountant, the prosecutor was determined to indict Margolies for murder. All the evidence secured by hard-working police investigators, however, was circumstantial. Rather than allow the mastermind to avoid trial and conviction, the prosecutor offered a coconspirator in both the fraud and the murders a deal: he would be named in future indictments in the conspiracy to murder unless he freely told all he knew and agreed to testify against Margolies in any future trial. If he did cooperate, he would be granted immunity from prosecution. He did talk. Margolies was convicted of murder, primarily on the testimony of the accomplice witness, and stated that he brought Margolies and the shooter together and was a party to the murder "contract."[19]

---

⑲ *Distinguish between the various types of surveillance techniques and the methods employed in their application.*

▶ Investigative Techniques

Identifying a suspect with compelling evidence of guilt often goes beyond hours of making inquiries and miles of footwork and driving. The combination of an eyewitness, a suspect, and a police lineup may achieve this goal.

Monitoring the activities of a subject by ordinary observation can be supplemented by videotaping, court-ordered wiretaps, and fluorescent chemicals, all of which can reveal contacts and actions of great importance to an ongoing investigation—even when the suspect is aware of or fears a police interest. Patience is essential in this area: on occasion, a suspect is not as cautious as he or she should be and the investigator is able to unearth a valuable piece of information as a result.

Investigators assigned to covertly scan the activities of the known criminals of organized crime often are not the arresting officers. However, when homicides occur, the information these investigators can provide their associates can lead to arrests.

Undercover police agents assume a similar role. Seeking information in this manner can be life threatening to agents; nevertheless, facts gathered in this way can become solid evidence when the agent testifies in court.

Surveillance is observation of people and places by investigators to develop investigative leads. Often hidden—not just unobtrusive—surveillance is a seeking for specific activity and significant information rather than merely passive observation. Its basic objective is to bring an investigation into sharp focus by supplying detailed information about the activities of a person or place and about the associates of a person or the individuals who visit a place.

Visual Surveillance

Visual surveillance is nothing more than keeping watch on a particular suspect, vehicle, or place. It may be aided by binoculars or a telescope or replaced by photographic surveillance. The use of binoculars permits observation from a distance of two or three city blocks. A twenty-power telescope is effective at ten to fifteen city blocks. A robot camera can replace personnel performing fixed surveillance. Infrared viewing devices permit observation in the dark.

A **fixed visual surveillance**—a **stakeout** or plant—is located within a building, if possible, with observations made through available windows or doors. Panel trucks and campers have been converted to fixed observation posts using peepholes or curtained windows for viewing. Rooftops are excellent for long-range surveillance; stores and hallways are suitable sites for short-range viewing. Sometimes long-term positions are possible; in some instances, it is necessary to move frequently to avoid notice. The static quality of a fixed surveillance requires skilled judgment in selecting a rewarding area of observation. To be effective in scrutinizing a suspect's activities, the presence of the observing investigator must not be detected. For this reason a fixed observation post in a building is preferable because the investigator is not only concealed but, through a rental arrangement, has the rights of a resident or tenant.

Some investigators, because of their height, size, race, or national origin, may have difficulty blending into certain environments as residents or tenants. In fact, several well-hidden fixed surveillances in apartments have been compromised by the appearance of the investigator entering the premises. In the de facto segregated ghetto areas of urban centers across the United States, an investigator not conforming to the appearance of the residents or tenants is certain to be suspect.

A **moving visual surveillance**—a **tail (shadow)**—may be on foot, may be in a vehicle, or may use a combination of walking and riding. The suspect being followed is often alert and may take evasive action. Suspects "double door" the trailing investigator by entering a street-level shop and leaving by a rear, side, or basement entrance. They use the modern traffic system with its copious traffic and one-way streets to break contact or force the investigator too close to a point at which his or her presence can be noted by an alert suspect. It is difficult to supplement a moving surveillance optically, although camera equipment can be employed. A moving surveillance is a dynamic technique in that it does not depend on the appearance of the suspect at a certain place; rather, it keeps the subject in view from place to place.

To avoid detection, a mobile surveillance often uses a two- or three-person surveillance team, with members rotating in the position of closest contact. This leapfrogging technique for following persons under surveillance is useful on foot or in vehicles. Its particular value is that the chance of detection by the suspect is diminished because the same person is not following the suspect continuously. The close contact position is behind the suspect, and an alert and anxious suspect will identify a person who is in this position for an extended period. With the leapfrogging technique, the suspect just about makes an identification when a new member of the surveillance team or a new vehicle moves up and into close contact and the other team member drops back into a position well to the rear or across the street. All that is required of the personnel who drop back is to keep the contact position investigator in sight. When vehicles are used, such contact can be maintained by radio.

The position of a vehicle and its movements can be traced with the aid of a **Global Positioning System (GPS)** device. By placing a GPS device on the underside of vehicle, investigators can track the location of the vehicle. In a similar fashion cargo or contraband can also be tracked. The use of such a device has been deemed a search by the Supreme Court and therefore held to be a violation of the Fourth Amendment if conducted without a warrant.[20]

Investigators develop their own methods for blending with the surroundings on mobile surveillances. A device or technique suitable to one individual may draw attention to another. Appearances can be corrected to some extent. A change of clothing may suffice for one individual; another may use clothing to suggest a trade or service. Conduct and behavior can be coordinated with appearance to communicate some cover or excuse for being in a neighborhood. Carrying something is a common practice with some investigators adept at hiding their occupation, and most persons are not suspicious of a person carrying a bag of groceries or some similar load.

Vehicles used in mobile surveillance do not blend with surrounding traffic units if they are too distinctive in design or color. The number of occupants and the seating arrangement may also identify a vehicle to a suspect under surveillance, as will the design and position of headlights at night. Apparent changes in the number of occupants and their in-vehicle positions are a defense against identification, as are driving without lights when safe and using a vehicle with the capability to change the appearance of headlights.

Fortunately for investigators, most suspects are alert but anxious; they are on the lookout for surveillance, but they really do not want to discover it. They want to know if the police are watching them, and yet they do not want to know it. This is the only possible explanation for heavy-footed mobile surveillances going undiscovered and fixed pickup posts operating for weeks unnoticed adjacent to the meeting places of known hoodlums and crime syndicate gangsters. At Los Angeles International Airport, police intelligence unit personnel, federal agents, and state narcotics officers are frequently standing shoulder to shoulder among the throngs greeting incoming planes from Las Vegas, but the subjects of their observations never seem to notice the tail they pick up. One notorious hoodlum was so oblivious to this surveillance that he was apprehended in a minor shoplifting episode at the airport newsstand.

A combination of fixed and mobile surveillances (both on foot and by vehicle) has been found to be effective in on-the-scene apprehensions of criminals who have committed a series of crimes. The irrational arsonist who sets several fires a night and who cannot be traced by normal investigative leads can be apprehended by isolating the area of suspicious and known incendiary fires and establishing extensive surveillance. Burglars and serial rapists who enter residences and continue their operations until arrested also may be surprised in their operations by the technique of staking out an area.

The object of a surveillance is to collect information on the activities of a suspect, the persons in contact with him or her, and the places frequented. Therefore, the assigned investigator and associates must keep a running commentary, or log, of their observations. Notes are made in the field as the surveillance discloses associates of the suspect, cars used by the suspect and associates, and the ownership or reputation of places frequented. When surveillance is aligned with use of the investigator as a witness to what he or she observed, the surveillance investigator must personally verify vehicle registrations, identities of unknown persons in contact with the suspect, or data on the premises or locations frequented by the suspect or others. With such a foundation, the witness can show personal knowledge of the surveillance and the investigation that disclosed pertinent and related facts.

Visual surveillance is somewhat limited. In 1968 a federal court ruled that without a valid warrant or reasonable cause, a person should be free from the eyes of the law while within the privacy of his or her own home. Peering into the defendant's window by stealth was the complained-about action.

 Explain the legal issues involved in audio surveillance.

Audio Surveillance

Wiretapping and electronic eavesdropping are the primary forms of **audio surveillance** by listening. This observation technique has been termed a *dirty business* by the U.S. Supreme Court and is viewed with mixed emotions by law-abiding citizens who apparently see it as the epitome of an unjustified and nondirective invasion of privacy.

The interception of telephone communication is a difficult surveillance to detect. Telephone wires lead from the instrument cable to a house cable, to an area cable, to a main cable, and to a distant central office. At each point a junction box containing an array of wires and binding posts facilitates the work of the telephone company's service personnel in providing service to subscribers. The wires of an individual telephone appear in terminal boxes and are identified by pair and cable numbers located at various points from the telephone instrument to the distant central office. A telephone tap can be hooked up easily at any of these locations.

Testimony is sometimes required on the mechanics of the interception—for example, how the wires used were selected as the wires of the telephone that was meant to be tapped. A common practice is to use a regular portable telephone instrument equipped with wire clips. The investigator hooks up to the selected wires, makes certain no one is using the line, dials the subscriber's number, and hears the distinctive sound of a busy signal without conversation on the line. In other instances an associate may have to call and engage the subscriber in a simulated "survey" conversation while the listener clips in and verifies the line by recognizing the associate's voice. Tape recording devices permit direct recording of conversations and offer a verbatim record for review.

Places or people may be wired for sound. This has been termed **bugging**. When properly installed, the electronic equipment necessary for eavesdropping is almost as difficult to detect as wiretap connections and equipment. The pickup microphone may be wired directly to a tape recorder, or it may broadcast the conversation a short distance by radio to a receiver located on the person of an investigator or in a nearby car or building. Surreptitious or covert entry of private premises to install a microphone (bug) is in conflict with expectations of individual privacy. However, in *Dalia v. United States,* 441 U.S. 238 (1979), the U.S. Supreme Court ruled, "We find no basis for a constitutional rule proscribing all covert entries. It is well established that law officers constitutionally may break and enter to execute a search warrant where such entry is the only means by which the warrant effectively may be executed."

The facts of *Dalia* are that the U.S. District Court authorized the interception of specified oral communications at a particular location in compliance with Title III of the Omnibus Crime Control and Safe Streets Acts of 1958. Dalia was convicted of receiving stolen goods and conspiring to transport, receive, and possess stolen goods. At a hearing on petitioner Dalia's motion to suppress evidence obtained under the "bugging" order, it was shown that the order did not explicitly authorize entry of the petitioner's business office. However, the district court ruled that a covert entry to install electronic eavesdropping equipment is not unlawful merely because the court approving the surveillance did not explicitly authorize such an entry. (FBI agents assigned the task of implementing the court's order had entered the petitioner's office secretly and installed an electronic bug in the ceiling.)

The court considered two questions in *Dalia*: (1) May courts authorize electronic surveillance that requires covert entry into private premises for installation of the necessary equipment? (2) Must authorization for such surveillance include a specific statement by the court that it approves of the covert entry? The court held that (1) the Fourth Amendment does not prohibit per se a covert entry performed for the purpose of installing otherwise legal bugging equipment; (2) Congress has given the courts statutory authority to approve covert entries for the purpose of installing electronic surveillance equipment; and (3) the Fourth Amendment does not require that a Title III electronic surveillance order include a specific authorization to enter covertly the premises described in the order.

Audio surveillance is an investigative technique about which appellate courts have rendered many decisions. Fortunately, the U.S. Supreme Court, in *Katz v. U.S.,* 389 U.S. 347 (1967), consolidated judicial thinking in this area and established the doctrine that such eavesdropping may properly be conducted under court supervision similar to procedures now available to police in securing search warrants and warrants of arrest.

The U.S. Supreme Court reversed Katz's conviction: "Wherever a man may be, he is entitled to know that he will remain free from unreasonable searches and seizures." In this decision the Court slashed away at a confusing collection of previous decisions in this area, involving, among other things, whether or not a physical penetration or a technical trespass occurred, by pointing out that the trespass doctrine is no longer controlling "for the Fourth Amendment protects people, not places." The final words for the decision suggest that antecedent court review of the probable cause for eavesdropping and a court order similar to a search warrant would have resulted in the court's sustaining Katz's conviction. (See Appendix A: Case Briefs for a digest of *Dalia* and *Katz*.)

Consensual electronic surveillance (as opposed to nonconsensual) is also known as **participant monitoring**. Its primary use is to secure a record of a conversation in which the person wired for sound is a participant. Undercover police agents and cooperative informants, such as accomplice witnesses, can provide police with a record of conversations in which they participated. This record proves exactly what was said and is important when the substance of the conversation is later disputed by one of the other participants. Since electronic surveillance that is carried out with the consent of one of the parties to a conversation is not a "search" within the meaning of the Fourth Amendment, this type of surveillance does not require previous judicial authorization. Telephone conversations that are recorded with the consent of one participant are in this class of consensual electronic surveillance.

▼

Since a collateral purpose of consensual electronic surveillance is to expose wrongdoing, particularly in relation to an ongoing investigation, it is important that police investigators know that the Fourth Amendment does not shield a suspect–defendant from a misplaced belief that a person to whom he or she voluntarily confides wrongdoing will not reveal it.[21]

Investigators contemplating the use of audio surveillance should avoid it unless the means–end factor justifies its use. Because of the overtone of being dirty business, any results obtained by this technique are often mitigated or negated by the means used.

Any electronic eavesdropping technique may be subject to countermeasures. Technicians skilled in surveillance countermeasures make extravagant claims about **debugging**. An electronic device (bug) that is wired to its receiver is difficult to detect, as is a properly connected wiretap, or the installation of a device to record the numbers to which outgoing calls are directed. If an electronic transmitting device is used, however, its radio transmissions can be detected by other electronic devices that are commercially available.

Countersurveillance activities may also include deliberate conversations intended to be heard and recorded, such as (1) incriminating statements involving innocent persons, (2) exculpatory conversations transferring or excusing guilt or guilty knowledge, and (3) scenarios intended to reveal or "blow" the surveillance by confirming the target suspect's belief in police eavesdropping. Fortunately, police investigators carefully screen incriminating or exculpatory conversations for their basic worth, and they avoid acting on any conversation calling for police response (search, arrest) unless confirmed by other independent information.[22]

 Explain how contact surveillance might be conducted.

Contact Surveillance

Contact surveillance techniques are based on the capability of certain fluorescent preparations to stain a person's hands or clothing upon contact and thus to offer observable proof of a connection between the stained person and the object under surveillance. It is difficult to deny the connection and to offer a reasonable explanation for extensive and vivid fluorescent stains in blue, orange, or green. Contact surveillance techniques may be used alone or in supplementing a visual surveillance. They are very useful when visual surveillance is not feasible, as in cases of dishonest employees and of transactions involving the payment of money.

Tracer preparations are usually in the ultraviolet spectrum and become visible only under ultraviolet light. Persons who make contact with the object under surveillance are not aware of the treated surface nor of the transfer to their clothing or hands until questioned about the contact and examined under ultraviolet light. Tracer paste is available for objects exposed to the weather, and a marking powder is available for putting tracer powder on money or any object not exposed to weather. Felt pens are available for tracer marking of objects such as money or merchandise.

Ultraviolet light is not the only option for contact surveillance. Another choice is a dye powder that is also invisible when dry but becomes visible when wet, although it is difficult to wash off. The powder is convenient in cases of petty theft investigated in schools and business offices because a school or an office supervisor can monitor the surveillance without ultraviolet light equipment.

These tracers are available from police equipment suppliers, and most police agencies have an assortment in stock from which an investigator can select the appropriate dye, powder, paste, crayon, or pen. The selected preparation should be applied liberally to the object likely to be contacted by the suspect or suspects. It should be tested before field use for its invisibility, its ability to blend in normal light, its adhesiveness, the life of its application, and the difficulty of removing the stain by ordinary washing with soap and water.

A variation of this contact surveillance is the technique of adding a tracer substance to objects or liquids commonly subject to theft. The U.S. government has added various dyes to gasoline at federal garages to enable the ready identification of government gasoline in privately owned vehicles; state agencies have marked containers of foodstuff for state institutions (when unauthorized possession is suspected); and department stores attach tracer tags to merchandise, which alert personnel at store exits unless removed by a salesclerk upon purchase.

㉒ *Discuss the elements required to be enumerated in the application for a search warrant.*

▶ Search Warrants

The issuance of a search warrant is guided by the Fourth Amendment to the U.S. Constitution. This amendment states the following:

> The right of the people to be secure in their persons, houses, papers, and effects, against unreasonable searches and seizures, shall not be violated, and no Warrants shall issue, but upon probable cause, supported by Oath or affirmation, and particularly describing the place to be searched, and the persons or things to be seized.

Meeting the standard of probable cause requires a demonstration to the judge or magistrate that a crime has occurred, or is occurring, and that evidence relative to that crime will be found at a particular location. The investigator must swear under oath that the information establishing this probable cause is true to the best of his or her knowledge. The application for the search warrant must describe in detail the place to be searched and the items or person to be seized.

In 1968, Congress codified the requirements for obtaining court authority to intercept oral and wire communications in Title III of the Omnibus Crime Control and Safe Streets Act (Title III). This act was subsequently amended in 1994 when Congress passed the Communications Assistance for Law Enforcement Act (CALEA). Most states have enacted similar legislation regarding the issuance of search warrants for electronic surveillance. The courts and Congress have long considered any form of electronic surveillance extremely invasive. Because of this view, the prerequisites for obtaining a warrant authorizing electronic surveillance of oral, wire, and electronic communications, as well as silent video, are quite strict. Investigators must comply with the requirements of the Fourth Amendment regarding probable cause and particularity. In addition, Title III requires that the surveillance be confined to only relevant conversations or activities; specify the length of time the technique will be used; and certify that normal investigative techniques have been tried and failed, are reasonably unlikely to succeed, or are too dangerous to attempt. These requirements are designed to ensure that electronic surveillance is not used as a first resort when other standard, less intrusive investigative techniques would expose the crime.[23]

㉓ *Discuss the six stages involved in the police intelligence process.*

▶ Police Intelligence: Criminal Investigation Information

Intelligence is the secret or clandestine collecting and evaluating of information about crime and criminals not normally available to investigators through overt sources. The detection and investigation of crime and the pursuit and apprehension of criminals require reliable intelligence; otherwise, the investigator is limited to overt acts and volunteered information and thus is severely handicapped in many cases.

The collection and analysis of information discovered by undercover police agents or confidential informants usually is channeled to a special unit within a police department. There the data are analyzed and evaluated so that they may be used in current or future investigations. To a certain extent, intelligence is warehoused until it is needed.

The police intelligence process is cyclical: a series of linked activities beginning with the needs of users (consumers) and ending with intelligence reports to specific users (Figure 6-4). The following are the six stages of the police intelligence process:

1. *Needs.* Clear needs for information develop as police investigate unsolved crimes and attempt to block the commission of planned crimes. Police personnel demonstrating such needs are the users of police intelligence.

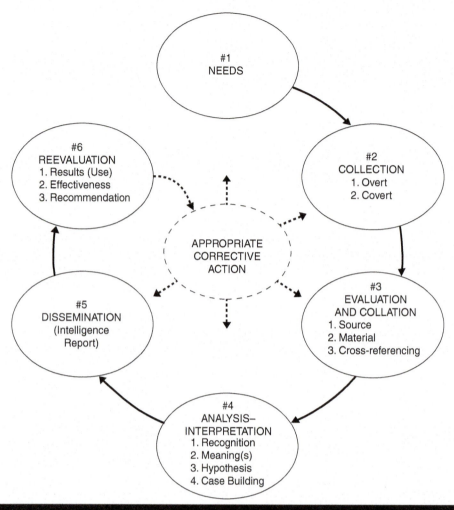

FIGURE 6-4   Six Stages of the Police Intelligence Process.

2. *Collection.* The gathering of information on matters of interest, in response to user needs, is investigatory reporting: raw intelligence (information) is reported along with a field evaluation of the information, its source, and how access to the information reported is gained. The **overt collection** of information is conducted by public sources or nonintelligence police personnel; **covert collection** of information is conducted by sources such as undercover police agents and confidential informants, or it is acquired through various types of surveillance of unaware targets.

3. *Evaluation and collation.* The **evaluation** of information screens out useless, incorrect, irrelevant, and unreliable information. **Collation** of evaluated information consists of its orderly arrangement, cross-indexing, and filing so that meaningful relationships can be developed between apparently unconnected bits and pieces of information.

4. *Analysis–interpretation.* This is the core area of the police intelligence process. This activity converts information into intelligence. Unanalyzed raw information gives little data about a developing pattern of criminal activity or a target suspect. As a result of **analysis**, a new recognition of the significance, meaning, and interrelationships of incoming information can be developed. **Interpretation** is an inseparable part of analysis—it is how collated information is related to problems requiring solutions. Interpretation also encompasses development of a hypothesis and a tentative statement about the meaning of the information involved.

5. **Dissemination.** Police intelligence reports are released to users only with a legitimate need for such intelligence. This need-to-know factor must be credibly established and strictly enforced. Unused or misused police intelligence reports sabotage a criminal investigation technique that is unique and often the only means of disclosing to police information as to ongoing and planned crimes.

6. **Reevaluation.** This is a postmortem review of the effectiveness of police intelligence reports and of subsequent action likely to improve the process and its effectiveness.[24, 25]

Criminal investigation information is police intelligence oriented to the solution of ongoing investigations. A **Criminal Investigation Information Center (CIIC)** within a police agency can assist investigators in clearing assigned cases by doing the following:

1. Reviewing and collating items of information common to police reports
2. Providing information in response to requests by investigators
3. Organizing information on criminal activities in other jurisdictions to connect it to local crime activities
4. Arranging for information "sharing" between investigators and investigative units[f]

 Define proactive investigation and its use of link analysis.

Proactive Investigation

Proactive investigation is new and innovative and moves into an attack mode long before any arrest. Cases begin with a "quiet" investigation and often move into the "hustle" mode. Proactive investigations should be based on information provided by informants, co-conspirators, and intelligence-gathering activities or on data about ongoing crimes.

Link analysis is ideal for profile work and assists in showing the relationships between a number of people and organizations in a visual form. Charting techniques have proven to be extremely valuable in clarifying or visually illustrating relationships that exist among individuals and organizations. The types of charts drawn are limited only by creativity and the needs of the user of the chart. Chart types include, but are not limited to, link charges, time line, telephone toll, case correlations, modus operandi (MO) comparison, and chronology.

㉕ *Discuss the advantages of using undercover agents.*

Undercover Police Agents

Use of police personnel as **undercover agents** is an ethical approach to the problem of securing information about criminal operations from the inside. It is surveillance from a position of advantage. It is dangerous work but is often preferable to using an underworld informant—probably the only other source of such information. Undercover agents make excellent witnesses. Unlike underworld informants whose credibility can be attacked because of criminal histories, the police agent is a person of good reputation and character. Jurors recognize the hazards of this work and tend to accept police undercover agents as very credible witnesses.

Investigators often go underground in searching out the operations of criminals. In one case, a covert investigator arranged with an underworld informant for an introduction to a gambling operator. The agent had a good cover story of being interested in gambling, and he posed as a man who had been arrested and sentenced to prison. A few weeks later, this agent was able to identify thirteen members of a gambling syndicate operating illegally and extensively and to offer legally significant evidence against them at their trial.

Many police units use young recruits fresh from police academy classes for this work because they are not known to local members of the underworld and can uncover meaningful information of help to the investigator. Statewide narcotic and alcoholic beverage control units use their young trainees during their first year or two of employment in undercover work. Federal agencies transfer suitable personnel to areas in which they are not known to facilitate the clandestine collection of information.

26 *Explain the three types of lineups that might be used during the course of an investigation.*

▶ Lineups

The **lineup** has been the traditional identification procedure used to focus a case against a suspect when eyewitnesses are available. Investigators use three different types of lineups to identify those responsible for the commission of crimes.

The **field lineup** is conducted shortly after the crime has occurred. Such lineups begin when the police have a potential suspect detained and need an eyewitness to confirm that the person being detained is responsible for the commission of the offense. Procedurally, the witnesses are brought to the suspect's location. Bringing the suspect back to the scene of the crime has been held to be too prejudicial.

The witnesses to a field lineup are asked whether or not the person they are observing is the person responsible for the crime. Based on the witnesses' responses, the suspect would be either released or held for further investigation.

A **photographic lineup** is conducted by showing a witness a number of photos, usually four to six. The photographs used in this display must be of individuals whose appearance is similar to that of the suspect's. All of the photos must be of persons of the same sex, race, approximate age, hair color, and facial characteristics, including eyeglasses, mustaches, and beards, if appropriate.

Due to the inherent suggestibility of this process, the investigator needs to advise the witness that the person responsible for the crime may or may not be among the persons present in the photographic display. The investigator should not comment when or if the witness makes a selection. The investigator should only take notes as to the witness's selection or lack thereof.

The **physical lineup** is very similar to those seen on TV and in the movies. Usually four to six persons are allowed to select their own numbered position against a wall marked clearly to indicate their height. The viewing area is well lighted, while the witness viewing area is dark, which prevents the suspects from seeing the witnesses. The individuals in the lineup may be asked to speak for identification. As in photographic lineups, great care must be given to the selection of the persons participating in the lineup. All participants must be similar in appearance, and a separate lineup must be conducted for each witness.

In 1972 the U.S. Supreme Court determined, in the case of *United States v. Wade,* 388 U.S. 218 (1967), that a lineup is a critical stage of the proceedings against the defendant and that the defendant has a right to counsel at these lineups. The presence of counsel prevents the taint of an improper lineup, and the defense counsel's role is to ensure a fair lineup. The defense counsel will request that others in the lineup be of the same general age, build, and appearance as the accused. Counsel will note the physical procedure of the lineup, should request that a photograph be taken of the lineup viewed by each identification witness, and may suggest that the accused person be allowed to change positions after each witness has viewed the lineup. He or she will request a separate lineup for any other accused persons. Counsel may object to any voice identification but, if overruled, will insist that all persons in the lineup say the same words.

Counsel will insist upon being present when each witness views the lineup and says whether he or she does or does not identify any person there. Counsel also will note any comments made by the investigator in front of the witnesses.

The presence of an attorney representing a suspect is not akin to the interrogation of suspects during which an attorney representing a suspect is likely to advise a client not to talk at all or not to answer certain questions. An attorney in this bystander role should be welcomed and used by police to strengthen their identification procedures and thus strengthen their eyewitness case at trial by foreclosing the charge of unfairness or of suggestion heretofore often raised by defense counsel.

TRACKING BAD GUYS

A federal grand jury indicted Joe Smith for assorted firearms and drug trafficking offenses. His trial will begin in a few months and he is currently being held without bail. Several government witnesses have reported that they are being harassed and threatened because of their role as potential witnesses in the upcoming trial. Unknown suspects have vandalized the witnesses' property. These incidents have occurred at random locations, including the witnesses' homes and places of employment, the residences of friends and relatives during the witnesses' visits, and the witnesses' cars. In several instances weapons have been fired at the homes where the witnesses live or were visiting. Attempts at conducting surveillance have proven to be unsuccessful and resources do not exist to offer twenty-four-hour protection to the witnesses.

It is clear that someone is engaged in witness tampering in violation of federal law, and if these activities continue, they could jeopardize the upcoming trial. Several of the defendant's close associates have been identified as likely suspects. However, there is not enough evidence that would provide the necessary probable cause to arrest these suspects at this time. The investigators decide to employ GPS tracking devices to compare the timing and location of specific future events with the movement of the suspects' vehicles.

It was determined that two of the suspects parked their vehicles on the street at night, so access to the vehicles or the installation of the tracking devices was not a problem. One suspect lives in a gated community and parks his car in his garage at night. This subject was subsequently followed to his girlfriend's apartment one night where he left the vehicle parked on the street overnight where installation of the tracking device was completed. The final subject also garages his vehicle at night, but during the day it is left unattended while he is at work and the installation is completed while the vehicle is unattended.

With the installation of the tracking devices in place, the investigators were able to track the exact location of the suspects' vehicles within a small window of time when acts of witness tampering occur. These acts include vandalism of cars, with rocks thrown through car windows, and shots fired at a witness' home. This evidence led to the indictment of two of the suspects for witness tampering and other offenses.

Source: Keith Hodges, "Tracking Bad Guys, Legal Considerations in Using GPS," *FBI Law Enforcement Bulletin* (July 2007): 27–30.

CHAPTER REVIEW

Key Terms

Review Questions

1. The claim of being somewhere else at the time the crime was committed is a defense known as:
   a. Alibi
   b. Benefit
   c. Knowledge
   d. Lack of motive

2. A police report of contact with persons who are engaged in suspicious activity not amounting to a crime is known as a:
   a. Preliminary report
   b. Progress report
   c. Field contact report
   d. Pending report

3. Electronic surveillance conducted with the consent of one party to the conversation is known as:
   a. Visual surveillance
   b. Participant monitoring
   c. Contact surveillance
   d. Bugging

4. Eyewitnesses to crimes will often be asked to look at pictures of persons arrested for similar crimes. These photos are known as:
   a. Composites
   b. Portraits
   c. Mug books
   d. rogues gallery

5. When photos are not available, an eyewitness might be asked to collaborate with a police artist in developing what?
   a. Composites
   b. Portraits
   c. Mug books
   d. Investigative leads

6. When more than one person is responsible for the commission of a crime and when one suspect is identified, the other suspects may be identified as well using which investigative lead?
   a. Mug shots
   b. NCIC

   c. Offender registration
   d. Personal linkage

7. This type of lineup is held shortly after the commission of the crime and involves bringing the witness to the suspect's location and is known as:
   a. Field lineup
   b. Photographic lineup
   c. Physical lineup
   d. Contact lineup

8. A person who has been arrested for a criminal offense and agrees to cooperate with investigators to supply information concerning others involved in criminal activity is known as what type of informant?
   a. Covert
   b. Participant
   c. Basic lead
   d. Accomplice witness

9. A person who supplies information to investigators about organized crime that is based on a position of trust and confidence from within the organization is known as what type of informant?
   a. Covert
   b. Participant
   c. Basic lead
   d. Accomplice witness

10. This type of informant is motivated to divulge information to the police for a variety of reasons, such as jealousy, greed, revenge, or to eliminate competition. Which type of informant is this?
    a. Covert
    b. Participant
    c. Basic lead
    d. Accomplice witness

See Appendix D for the correct answers.

Application Exercise

One morning a jogger running through a secluded section of a large city park discovers a female homicide victim. You as the lead investigator are assigned the case and upon examination of the victim's body notice that her underwear has been stuffed inside her mouth, that there is a flower tucked under her ear, and that her hands have been bound behind her back. You have no other physical evidence or witnesses at this point. What basic leads should you pursue in the furtherance of this investigation?

Discussion Questions

1. Regarding the case study, compare the investigative steps that would have been necessary to make an arrest in this case if GPS tracking devices were not available.
2. Explain the concept of benefit in relation to motive for a crime.
3. Is the basic lead of knowledge more likely to be concerned with motive or opportunity for a crime?
4. Discuss the role of tracing stolen property in the day-to-day investigation of crime and criminals.
5. Discuss the three major capabilities of a modus operandi file.
6. What is the common theme between the use of photographs for identification and the hue and cry for injured suspects?

Related Websites

To learn more about the history of fingerprints and the answers to the most frequently asked questions about fingerprint examination, visit this website:www.onin.com.

Want to know more about computer databases? If yes, then visit the FBI's National Crime Information Center (NCIC) web page: www.fas.org/irp/agency/doj/fbi/is/ncic.

Interested in a surveillance camera concealed in a pair of glasses or in a necktie? Check out the latest in video security www.supercircuits.com/law-enforcement.apx.

A full line of surveillance equipment can be seen at www.spybase.com.

Think your home or office is being bugged? Information on counterintelligence, bug sweeps, and surveillance countermeasures can be found at www.tscm.com.

Notes

1. M. A. P. Willmer, "Criminal Investigation from the Small Town to the Large Urban Conurbation," *British Journal of Criminology* VIII (July 1968): 259–274.
2. James W. Osterberg, "The Investigative Process," in *Law Enforcement Science and Technology* (Chicago: Thompson, 1967), 591.
3. Truman Capote, *In Cold Blood* (New York: Random House, 1965), 159–164.
4. Joan Petersilia, *Processing Latent Fingerprints: What Are the Payoffs?* (Santa Monica, CA: The Rand Corporation, 1977), 13–14.
5. John E. Eck, *Solving Crimes: The Investigation of Burglary and Robbery* (Washington, DC: U.S. Department of Justice, Police Executive Research Forum and the National Institute of Justice, 1983), 269–270.
6. Stephanie L. Hitt, "NCIC 2000," *FBI Law Enforcement Bulletin* (July 2000): 12–15.
7. Jennifer Budden, "Linking Crime Through Ballistic Evidence," *Law and Order* (November 2002): 51–54.
8. Alan Scholle, "Sex Offender Registration Community Notification Laws," *FBI Law Enforcement Bulletin* (July 2000): 17–19.

9. Juliet Eilperin, "Congress Approves 'Amber Alert' System," *Washington Post,* April 11, 2003, A2.

10. Christopher Swope, "The Digital Mugshot," *Governing* (August 1998): 54.

11. www.bostonglobe.com/metro/2013/04/28/bombreconstruc.

12. James Q. Wilson, *The Investigators: Managing FBI and Narcotics Agents* (New York: Basic Books, 1978), 62.

13. Ira Rosen, "Wheeler, Dealer, Squealer," *60 Minutes* transcript, March 6, 1988, 5–9.

14. Irvin B. Nathan, "ABSCAM: A Fair and Effective Method for Fighting Public Corruption," in *ABSCAM Ethics: Moral Issues and Deception in Law Enforcement*, eds. Gerald M. Caplan and The Police Foundation (Cambridge, MA: Ballinger, 1983), 1–16.

15. Thomas Whiteside, *An Agent in Place: The Wennestrom Affair* (New York: Viking, 1966), 150.

16. Carole De Vault (with William Johnson), *The Informer: Confessions of an Ex-Terrorist* (Toronto, Canada: Fleet Books, 1982), 115–144.

17. James M. Poland, *Understanding Terrorism: Groups, Strategies, and Responses* (Englewood Cliffs, NJ: Prentice Hall, 1988), 196.

18. Mike McAlary, *Buddy Boys: When Good Cops Turn Bad* (New York: Putnam, 1987), 25–37.

19. Richard Hammer, *The CBS Murders* (New York: William Morrow, 1987), 215–220.

20. *United States v Jones* 132 S.CT. 943 (2112).

21. Richard G. Schott, "Warrantless Interception of Communications: When, Where, and Why It Can Be Done," *FBI Law Enforcement Bulletin* (January 2003): 25–31.

22. National Commission for the Review of Federal and State Laws Relating to Wire-Tapping and Electronic Surveillance (NWC), *Electronic Surveillance* (Washington, DC: U.S. Government Printing Office, 1976), 151–152.

23. Thomas D. Colbridge, "Electronic Surveillance, a Matter of Necessity," *FBI Law Enforcement Bulletin* (February 2000): 25–31.

24. E. Drexel Godfrey, Jr. and Don R. Harris, *Basic Elements of Intelligence: A Manual of Theory, Structure and Procedure for Use by Law Enforcement Agencies Against Organized Crime* (Washington, DC: U.S. Department of Justice, Law Enforcement Assistance Administration, 1971), 11–35.

25. Don R. Harris, *Criminal Investigation Information Center: A Manual Describing the Organization and Analysis of Criminal Information* (Washington, DC: U.S. Department of Justice, 1979), 1–8.

7 Interviewing and Interrogation

LEARNING OBJECTIVES

After reading this chapter, you will be able to:

1. *Explain how conducting an interview in private will aid in the independent recall of each witness.*

2. *Define the rapport-building process and its importance in conducting a successful interview.*

3. *Explain the competency and credibility issues involved with interviewing victims and witnesses.*

4. *Discuss the four-step structure used in interviewing witnesses at crime scenes.*

5. *Realize that listening involves more than merely hearing spoken words but also a number of other means of expression.*

6. *Recognize the physical signs displayed by people who are being deceptive.*

7. *Discuss the connection between eye movement and how it is useful in detecting deception.*

8. *Evaluate the methods available to investigators to refresh a witness's recollection of an event.*

9 Explain the reasons why it is important to document the statements made by witnesses.

10 Realize that a number of Supreme Court decisions over time have led to the existing legal standards for conducting interrogations.

11 Identify the legal procedural safeguards established by the Miranda decision and how and when these safeguards apply during an interrogation.

12 Recognize the importance of conducting an interrogation in private free from distractions and the importance of being fully prepared and knowledgeable about the crime and the suspect's involvement.

13 Discuss the rationale for a person to confess to a crime.

14 Distinguish between the two types of offenders involved in the commission of a crime, and determine the best approach to be used on each during an interrogation.

15 Discuss the concept of the "suspect's dilemma" and how this situation can be used to obtain a confession.

16 Discuss the strengths and weaknesses of the various methods used to document a confession.

An **interview** is a person-to-person conversation for the purpose of obtaining information about a crime or its circumstances. Interviews should be conducted in private. The actual interview begins only after the investigator has made the person to be interviewed comfortable and has established rapport. While establishing rapport, the investigator must make assessments regarding the potential witness's competency and credibility.

The type of interview conducted at the scene of a crime is nonstructured and is used to determine exactly what happened at the crime scene. Follow-up interviews are more structured and designed to address specific areas of concern.

While conducting an interview, the investigator must listen well. This is an interactive process that involves the interpretation of both visual and verbal input. During the interview, the investigator should be mindful of the possibility of deception on the part of the person being questioned. Clues to deception can be obtained from the suspect's body language, demeanor, and comfort level during the interviewing process. A polygraph examination can be scheduled when it must be determined whether or not the person is being deceptive.

Persons who cannot recall specific details of an event can often have their recollections refreshed. When employed by a trained practitioner, investigative hypnosis can be useful in recalling memories. Another technique used to refresh a witness's recollections is the cognitive interview process. The final step in the interview process consists of transcribing the witness's oral statement to written form.

▶ Interview Essentials

1 Explain how conducting an interview in private will aid in the independent recall of each witness.

Privacy

Ideally, interviews should be conducted at the police station, but that is not always possible or practical. About 80 percent of all interviews are informal and take place outside of an office setting.[1] Even interviews conducted at the scene of a crime or at a person's home or place of work must be conducted in private. Privacy can be made possible by conducting an interview inside a patrol vehicle, in another room of a house, or any place where other witnesses or outsiders cannot overhear and possibly be drawn into the discussion.

Privacy is important as it insulates the witness from the input of others. It would be unacceptable for a witness to give a vehicle or suspect description and to have another person join the conversation to try and aid the witness's recollection. Knowing that discrepancies in testimony and differences of perception commonly occur among witnesses, it is important that the investigator obtain the independent recall of each witness. Conducting interviews in private also guards against the possibility of **reverse transference** or **retroactive interference**, which occurs when a witness overhears other witnesses discussing their observations and then takes on some, if not all, of their information as his or her own.[2]

Interviewers should not lose sight of the fact that a witness is much more likely to reveal any secrets in private rather than in the presence of additional persons.[3] Another important reason interviews are conducted in private is that privacy enhances the bonding process between the witness and the interviewer. This bonding process, known as **rapport building**, is essential if an investigator is to obtain the maximum amount of information.

 Define the rapport-building process and its importance in conducting a successful interview.

Rapport Building

Rapport is defined as developing a harmonious relationship with another person. This process begins by making the person to be interviewed comfortable. The investigator should introduce himself or herself and explain the reason or purpose of the interview. The investigator should be mindful of the witness's stress due to being a victim or a witness to a crime. As a result, this person may need reassurance as to his or her personal safety and also may need to have his or her anxiety and personal comfort issues addressed. The goal of rapport building is to make the person being interviewed feel comfortable with the interview process and with the investigator. To accomplish this, the person being interviewed should always be treated with respect and the investigator should be sympathetic and empathic when necessary. A person who is comfortable with the investigator and the interview process is more likely to become an active participant and to supply more information than someone who wants to terminate the experience as soon as possible because he or she is uncomfortable.

Prior to beginning the interview, the investigator should take a few minutes to discuss subjects unrelated to the crime. A well-rounded interviewer can always find a subject about which the witness is willing to talk. Most people like to talk about themselves, so a discussion regarding where they were born is always appropriate, as is a discussion about the weather or current events. Although this may seem like a meaningless waste of time, this step is very important. This conversational process makes the person feel comfortable talking with the investigator and more likely to answer questions. The investigator also should use this step to observe the witness when he or she is not under stress and is answering questions truthfully. This is that person's norm for truthful responses, and any deviations from this norm may be indicative of deception.

 Explain the competency and credibility issues involved with interviewing victims and witnesses.

Competency and Credibility Issues

Another benefit of the rapport-building process is that it allows the investigator to make some assessments of the person being interviewed. The investigator should be aware of competency issues as he or she relates to the person's age, intelligence, mental state, and possible intoxication. For example, no minimum age limit is set to testify in court, but a very young person must know the difference between right and wrong and that it is wrong to tell a lie; the issue for an elderly person would be soundness of mind, which can be addressed with a few questions to determine if this person is rooted in reality and if his or her answers to questions are responsive.

Like the age issue, no minimum intelligence requirements are set for a witness to a crime. However, the potential witness should be able to focus and not be easily confused. A person's mental state will affect his or her ability to testify in court. A person who hears voices or is delusional will not make a good witness, and this state should be apparent to the interviewer after a few questions. The question of intoxication is a matter of degree. Obviously a person who is intoxicated is not going to be a competent witness, but the person who has had one or two drinks might be. The standard here would be whether or not the person's speech is clear or slurred and whether or not his or her answers are responsive to questions being asked.

Credibility issues involve considerations that would make the witness's testimony unbelievable. The witness's relationship to either the victim or the suspect would affect their credibility, as testimony driven by love or hate is rightly suspect and often unbelievable. Biases and prejudices are another factor that would affect credibility. If a witness used racial slurs or other hateful epithets during the interview, this information should be noted in the official police report. Bringing a witness's biases to the attention of the prosecuting attorney will be appreciated as these officials rarely like surprises when it is time to go to trial. Other credibility issues that should be brought to the attention of the prosecutor and the defense could be any physical impairments that might affect the ability to observe an event, such as eyeglasses or hearing aids, and if they were in use at the time; conditions existing at the time of the crime, such as weather or lighting conditions that could affect a person's ability to perceive an event; and the witness's reputation for being truthful, since a person with a long criminal history is not as believable as other members of society.

 Discuss the four-step structure used in interviewing witnesses at crime scenes.

Interview Structure

The interview of witnesses conducted at the scene of a crime is a four-step process. The first step starts with the basic open-ended questions, such as "what happened?" or "what did your see or hear?" Once the question is asked, the witness should be allowed to answer without interruption. No notes or audio or visual recording is conducted at this point. Taking notes only slows down the witness and interrupts his or her concentration. Notes and recordings are also intimidating to most witnesses and will motivate them to choose their words very carefully, which is exactly what the investigator does not want.

Once the witness has told his or her story and the interviewer has a good grasp of the information given by the witness, it is time for the second step: having the witness repeat his or her story while the interviewer takes notes or records the conversation. Since the witness has already given the information to the interviewer, the taking of notes or recording will not be as intimidating to the witness. In this step, the interviewer also asks appropriate questions, addressing any competency or credibility issues that might arise, such as "do you wear eyeglasses, and were you wearing them at the time?" "were you under the influence of alcohol or drugs at the time?" "what is your relationship to the victim or suspect?" and so on.

The third step of the interview process involves the interviewer going over his or her notes with the witness. This step ensures that the interviewer accurately records or paraphrases what the witness actually said. Since this step involves action on the part of the interviewer, the pressure is off the witness. This step allows the witness to think about his or her testimony and to fill in any areas he or she might have missed.

The fourth and final step in the process involves thanking the witness for cooperating and asking for any additional information the witness wants to give at this time. The witness should be given a business card as a means of contacting the investigator in the event he or she remembers something important that was not mentioned during the interview.

Follow-up interviews are not conducted at the scene of the crime and are more structured. They occur after the event, when the investigator has a good idea of what happened and the type of questions that need to be asked of the witness.

 Realize that listening involves more than merely hearing spoken words but also a number of other means of expression.

Listening

Being a good listener is not easy. Most people speak at a speed of about 125 words a minute, which is extremely slow compared to how fast a person can think. As a result, a poor listener's thoughts drift away into daydreams or outside thoughts and fail to hear crucial spoken words.

An officer interviewing a victim of a crime.

Source: Dwayne Newton/PhotoEdit, Inc.

To aid concentration, a listener should use any extra thinking time to stay ahead of the talker, formulate ideas on where the talker is headed, and connect that information to what has already been said.

Words alone convey only part of any message. Sixty-five percent of our conversation with one another is nonverbal. Therefore, the interviewer must think beyond mere words and gather meaning from tone of voice, eye contact, facial expression, hand gestures, and body language. Remember, it is not what is said but how it is said that is important.

Being a good listener requires active involvement. The interviewer's own body movement, eye contact, hand gestures, head nodding, facial expressions, and tone of voice must convey to the witness an interest in what is being said and an interest in the witness as a person. Leaning toward the witness conveys the nonverbal signal that we are interested, even enthused, about the information being given. On the other hand, the interviewer's tone of voice, facial expression, and body movements can convey emotions of disgust, boredom, disbelief, and contempt, which can make a witness defensive or evasive.[4]

▶ Detection of Deception

Repeated studies have shown that traditional methods of detecting deception during interviews succeed only 50 percent of the time, even for experienced interviewers.[5] In spite of this, investigators still need to test the veracity of those they interview.

6 *Recognize the physical signs displayed by people who are being deceptive.*

Physical Signs of Deception

An alternative paradigm for detecting deception is based on four critical domains—comfort/discomfort, emphasis, synchrony, and perception management—and can increase the odds in the interviewer's favor.

Comfort/Discomfort

A person's level of comfort or discomfort is one of the most important clues interviewers should focus on when trying to establish veracity. People who tell the truth more often appear comfortable because they have no stress, nor do they have guilty knowledge to make them feel uncomfortable. People who are being deceptive, on the other hand, first display discomfort physiologically. Their heart rate quickens, hairs stand up, perspiration and breathing increase, all of which are autonomic responses. Nonverbally, they tend to move their bodies by rearranging themselves, jiggling their feet, fidgeting, or drumming their fingers. Deceptive people tend to distance themselves from those with whom they feel uncomfortable. They will lean away from the interviewer or create artificial barriers either with their shoulders and arms or with inanimate objects in front of them. Other clear signs of discomfort include rubbing the forehead near the temple, squeezing the face, rubbing the neck, or stroking the back of the head with the hand. Research also has shown that when people are nervous or troubled, their blink rate increases, which is a phenomenon often seen in liars under stress.

Emphasis

When people speak, they naturally incorporate various parts of their body—such as eyebrows, head, hands, arms, torso, legs, and feet—to emphasize a point. Liars, for the most part, do not emphasize with nonverbals. They will think of what to say and how to deceive, but rarely do they think about the presentation of the lie.

Synchrony

In an interview setting, the tone of both parties should mirror each other over time. A certain amount of harmony occurs in speech patterns, sitting styles, touching frequency, and general expressions. An interview that is out of sync or lacks harmony indicates that the person being interviewed is uncomfortable and possibly being deceptive. The lack of **synchrony** often occurs when people say "I did not do it" while nodding their heads up and down as if to say "Yes, I did it," or when asked "would you lie about this?" their heads again bob up and down. Synchrony should occur between what is being said and the events of the moment. The information and facts should remain pertinent to the issue at hand, the circumstances, and the questions. When the answers are asynchronous with the event and questions, the investigator may assume the possibility that something is wrong or that the person is stalling for time to fabricate a story.

Perception management

Liars will try to influence their intended targets of deception with verbal and nonverbal behavior designed to demonstrate the implausibility of their involvement in committing a crime. They may use **perception management** statements, such as "I could never hurt someone," "lying is beneath me," or "I have never lied," all of which should alert the interviewer to the possibility of deception. Statements such as "to be perfectly frank," "to be honest," "to be perfectly truthful," or "I was always taught to tell the truth" are solely intended to influence the perception of the interviewer. Nonverbal behaviors, such as yawning, indicating boredom, or stretching out on a couch, as if to demonstrate comfort, are examples of perception management.[6]

 Discuss the connection between eye movement and how it is useful in detecting deception.

Neurolinguistic Eye Movement

Research has shown that there is a direct link between brain activity and eye movement. This linkage is useful in detecting deception among people being interviewed. Approximately 90 percent of the population will move their eyes to their left when they are recalling something that they actually experienced. These same individuals' eyes will move to their right when they are creating something in their mind. The remaining 10 percent of the population who do not respond in this manner are typically left-handed people who simply reverse the movements. However, **neuro-linguistic eye movement** may be the same for both right- and left-handed people.

The observation of eye movement by an interviewer takes considerable skill. The person being interviewed should be observed closely during the rapport building phase and the person should be asked both recall and creative questions to determine how his or her eyes respond which would establish that person's behavioral norm. Sample recall questions that could be asked during the rapport building phase include the following:

Who was the first person who spoke to you this morning?

When you look at the entrance door to your home or apartment, from the outside of the door, is the door knob on the right or left side of the door?

What was the name of your fifth-grade teacher?

Sample creative questions that could be asked include the following:

What kind of paint or wall paper would you suggest if we were to decorate this room?

What would the offspring of a pig and a cow look like?

What kind of costume would you design for the next Halloween party you go to?

Once the person's behavioral norm has been established for neurolinguistic eye movements, the interviewer can ascertain whether or not the information given is being recalled or created. For investigative purposes, information that is being created is usually deceptive.[7]

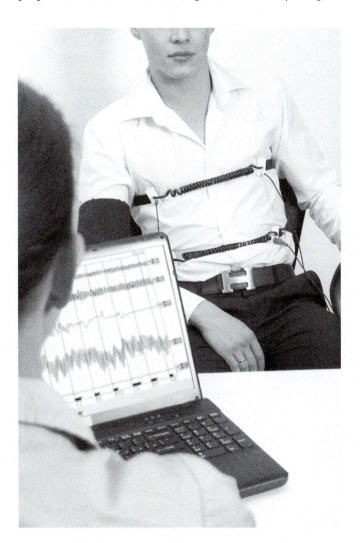

A polygraph test being administered to a subject.
Source: Andrey Burmakin/ Shutterstock

▶ Polygraph Testing

A technique useful in investigation is the instrumental detection of deception. With a cooperating subject, it is a valid investigative technique.

Modern polygraphs have three components or channels—that is, three separate capabilities for recording anatomical responses to the questioning situation. These devices and their action are as follows:

1. The **pneumograph** records respiration (breathing rate and depth).
2. The **galvanograph** records electrodermal response (skin electrical resistance changes).
3. The **cardiograph** records changes in pulse rate and blood pressure.

Generally, the cardiograph is considered to be the most reliable indicator of deception. The **galvanic skin response (GSR)**, which is measured by the resistance of the skin to the passage of a small electric current, is the least dependable.

Instrumental detection of deception is based on human anatomy. The **sympathetic division** of the **autonomic nervous system**, when stimulated by reactions such as anger and fear, mobilizes the body and its resources for emergencies. The effects are similar to those produced by adrenaline. Sugar is released from the liver for use by the muscles, the heart rate increases, and the coagulability of the blood is heightened.

Because the autonomic nervous system reacts automatically to threat in this fight-or-flight reaction, a subject cannot hide his or her involuntary responses to a situation. If the subject is threatened, fear occurs, and when a person is fearful, an involuntary, animalistic preparation occurs within the body for fight or flight—a prehistoric form of survival insurance.

A guilty subject fears relevant questions during an examination. He or she is in a stress situation: fear of telling the truth that would expose him or her as the guilty person and fear of lying that may be revealed by the measuring instrument, exposing him or her as a liar and, therefore, as a suspect in the case.

If these tests of deception are to succeed, cooperation between investigator and examiner is necessary. Just as the investigator must do an effective job of collecting evidence and delivering it to the criminalist at the police laboratory if he or she is to secure an adequate examination from the criminalist, so too must the investigator guard against contaminating the subject of a lie detection test by any action before the testing session that will make it difficult or impossible for the examiner to administer an effective test. The investigator should not discuss the lie detector or the possibility of such tests with a suspect until a decision has been made to request tests. The reason is not so much that silence is a safeguard against the subject's use of tranquilizers, since a drugged response level will be apparent when the subject is initially tested on the instrument, but rather it is a safeguard against any future allegations that the subject had been threatened with the use of this scientific device. When talking with possible subjects about the use of tests, investigators also should avoid any mention of key facts of the crime and its circumstances. Examiners use these facts for questions at the peak of tension. For example, in larcenies this might include the exact amount of money taken or perhaps the denominations of the larger bills in cash thefts, and in assaults and homicides it might include the type of weapon used or some detail about it.

The procedure in lie detection sessions may vary slightly with the examiner, but it is similar to interviews and interrogations in that these sessions have an introductory period, the actual testing phase, and a closing. During the introductory period, the examiner explains the operation of the instrument and its ability to detect bodily responses. The use of questions calling for a simple "yes" or "no" response is also explained, and the subject is instructed to remain silent if he or she does not understand the question and to reserve explanations for the period after the questioning. The subject is put at ease and allowed to ask questions to which the examiner replies in an easily understood conversational style. The transition to the testing session for suspects in criminal cases usually is accompanied by an assurance that questions will be asked only in relation to the event under investigation. The questions may even be shown to the subject before the test. Some operators believe this to be a more effective procedure. This reassures the subject that the testing period will not dig into an entire lifetime, and it validates responses as emanating from the present situation and not from any past feelings of guilt or fear about other crimes.

The testing begins after the subject is comfortably seated, and the various tubes and wires are attached securely and without discomfort. The first round of questioning contains irrelevant questions to establish a normal level of response for the individual being questioned. After these questions have established a response level, the examiner may demonstrate the capability of the machine by asking the subject to select a card from a deck of cards. The examiner directs the subject to answer "no" to questions about the value of the card. Then, by examining the graph, the examiner determines the identity of the card and tells it to the subject. The examiner is cued to its identity by the subject's reaction, which is shown on the graph made by the instrument when the subject lied by giving the required "no" response.

The core area of the testing session follows this display of the device, and the relevant questions are interspersed with irrelevant questions. The so-called peak-of-tension questions relate to the actual circumstances of the crime; the remaining relevant questions may relate to events shortly before or after the crime.

No suspect can be forced to take a lie detection test. The privilege against self-incrimination, guaranteed to individuals by the Fifth Amendment to the U.S. Constitution, protects against such coercion. However, psychological coercion is present merely in asking a suspect to take a lie detection test, and this is likely to negate any claim of voluntariness. That is, this testing has "damned if you do" and "damned if you don't" overtones.

The process of lie detection by use of instruments and a skilled examiner has not gained the general acceptance in its field needed to warrant court acceptance of the process as scientifically valid. In *Frye v. United States*, 293 Fed. 1013 (1923), this doctrine of general acceptance was established: "While courts will go a long way in admitting expert testimony deduced from a well-organized principle or discovery, the thing from which the deduction is made must be sufficiently established to have gained general acceptance in the particular field to which it belongs" (p. 1,014).

One of the major criticisms of lie detection is that the examiner's role and the mechanics of testing jeopardize the scientific aspects of the instrument. The relationship of the examiner to the instrument in the detection of deception has been compared to that of a pilot to an airplane. The emphasis on operating skill brings the entire process into question as a way to detect truth or lies.

⑧ *Evaluate the methods available to investigators to refresh a witness's recollection of an event.*

▶ Recollection Refreshment

It is not uncommon for a witness to forget some critical details of a crime. The response "I don't remember" can be overcome by refreshing the recollection of the witness through investigative hypnosis or the cognitive interview process.

Investigative Hypnosis

Hypnosis is a state resembling normal sleep. A person may be placed under hypnosis by the suggestions and operations of a **hypnotist**—a person who has studied the science or art of inducing hypnosis. Hypnosis in one form or another has been practiced for centuries, but its use in criminal investigation is a relatively recent phenomenon.

The use of hypnotically aided recall to enhance the memories of persons who have witnessed a crime but are unable to recall critical facts about the event is based on the belief that human memory is like a videotape machine that (1) faithfully records, as if on film, every perception experienced by the witness; (2) permanently stores such recorded perceptions in the brain at a subconscious level; and (3) accurately "replays" them in their original form when the witness is placed under hypnosis and asked to remember them.

This "videotape recorder" theory of law enforcement hypnotists, however, is not supported by a survey of professional literature in this area. Highlights of these writings are the following: (1) hypnosis is by its nature a process of suggestion, and one of its primary effects is that the person hypnotized becomes extremely receptive to suggestions that he or she perceives as emanating from the hypnotist; (2) the person under hypnosis experiences a compelling desire to please the hypnotist by reacting positively to suggestions, and hence to produce the particular responses that he or she believes are expected; (3) during the hypnotic session, neither the subject nor the hypnotist can distinguish between true memories and pseudomemories; and (4) neither the detail, coherence, nor plausibility of the resulting recall is any guarantee of its veracity.

The California legislature, in response to California's Supreme Court banning the testimony of witnesses who have been hypnotized to aid in recollection, enacted legislation that allows such a witness to testify under very limited circumstances. In part, the substance of the prehypnotic memory of the witness must be preserved in written, audiotape, or videotape form prior to the hypnosis session; the session must be extensively recorded; and the hypnosis can be performed only by a licensed medical doctor or psychologist experienced in the use of hypnosis and independent of and not in the presence of law enforcement officers, the prosecution, or the defense. Finally, the testimony of a witness who has undergone a memory-jogging hypnosis session is limited to "those matters which the witness recalled and related prior to the hypnosis."[8]

It is, therefore, risk-taking behavior for a criminal investigator to use investigative hypnosis. In some cases, the importance of discovering the identity of the person or persons responsible for a crime is so overriding that an investigator is justified in suggesting a hypnosis session for a witness whose recall of events appears to be blocked. Kidnappings in which the victim is still under the control of the kidnapper(s), terrorist acts, and serious crimes such as rape and murder are examples of instances in which hypnosis may be justified. In effect, the investigator sacrifices any future value of the witness in court to gain information about the identity of the criminal and associates, if any.

Cognitive Interview

Cognitive interviewing is an investigative technique used to enhance a witness's ability to recall events. This technique has proven to be as effective as hypnosis but does not jeopardize the witness's credibility in court. The witness's ability to recall events is improved by taking one or more of the following steps: reinstating the context of the event, recalling the event in a different sequence, and looking at the event from a different perspective.

Reinstating the context of an event involves having the witness recall all of his or her experiences before, during, and after the event. Instead of asking what happened, the interviewer would ask that the witness relive that part of the day surrounding the crime: how the witness got to the scene, what route was taken, what the weather was like, what was being done during and after the event, and such. This process enhances a person's retrieval of stored information: the witness can see the details of the crime in the proper sequence and context.

Changing the sequence involves having the witness recall the event in reverse order or out of order. Normally a witness is asked to recall events in chronological order, a logical sequence of events from beginning to end. By recalling the event out of order, the witness is asked to view each segment of the event independently. This process keeps the witness more focused and may reveal details that might otherwise be missed.

Changing perspective requires that the witness recall the event from the perspective of another person, such as the victim or another witness, or of an object such as a camera mounted on the wall. This technique gives the witness the opportunity to recall more of his or her experiences, and it also serves to lessen the trauma of the event.[9]

9 *Explain the reasons why it is important to document the statements made by witnesses.*

▶ Written Statement of a Witness

Statements are an excellent means of documenting the story told to the investigator by the witness. They usually consist of little more than ruled forms on which a summary has been recorded of what the witness has seen and heard and of how he or she happened to be in a position to make this observation. Investigators are expected to exercise judgment as to the number of statements taken if witnesses are numerous.

When a statement is taken, it should be accurate about both what the witness has said and what the witness is prepared to testify to, under oath, about his or her observations. If any contradiction exists, defense counsel may seize it as an opportunity to destroy the credibility of the witness.

The purpose of taking a statement from a witness is generally threefold:

1. Provide a written record that will allow a prosecutor to evaluate the case and plan its presentation at trial
2. Enable the prosecutor to monitor the testimony of the witness in court
3. "Hold" a witness—that is, discourage surprise testimony by providing a possible base for impeaching the witness

If statements are taken, or if the interview develops as a situation in which a statement should be taken in accordance with standard local operating procedures, a note of the taking of a statement, or the failure to do so when a statement is warranted, should be made part of the investigator's field notes and report to the investigation.

10 *Realize that a number of Supreme Court decisions over time have led to the existing legal standards for conducting interrogations.*

▶ Interrogations

An **interrogation** is defined as the adversarial questioning of a suspect with the goal of soliciting an admission or confession of guilt. Due to the adversarial nature of interrogations, confessions have been challenged in the courts over time. These legal challenges ultimately led to the *Miranda v. Arizona* decision that established procedural safeguards for in-custody questioning of a suspect.[10] An interrogation can be conducted only in an in-custody environment when the suspect voluntarily waives these safeguards.

Unlike an interview, an interrogation is highly structured. Prior to the interrogation, the investigator must thoroughly investigate the crime and its circumstances. As a result of this investigation and during the rapport-building process with the suspect, the investigator must make an assessment as to the kind of person to be interrogated. This assessment will determine the approach for the investigator to take during the interrogation. During the course of the interrogation, the suspect may admit guilt, give a full confession, or invoke his or her **Miranda rights** and terminate the interrogation.

11 *Identify the legal procedural safeguards established by the* Miranda *decision and how and when these safeguards apply during an interrogation.*

▶ Interrogation Law

In the case of *Brown v. Mississippi*, the defendant was suspected of murder and was picked up by sheriff's deputies and taken to the sheriff's office. Once there, Brown was stripped to the waist and forced to bend over a desk. The deputies then repeatedly whipped him with their belts until he confessed. This confession was then used to convict him of the charge of murder, and he was sentenced to death. Upon appeal to the U.S. Supreme Court, the Court determined that confessions were an essential part of the investigative process but that the confession must be made voluntarily. Accordingly, Brown's confession was invalidated and the case was returned to the state courts.[11]

Other cases dealing with police procedure include *Ward v. Texas*, which was decided in 1942. In this case, the defendant was a suspect in a murder case. He was picked up for questioning and taken out of the county. He was transported from county to county more than a hundred miles from his home over a three-day period and was not allowed to contact family or friends. He finally confessed and was found guilty of murder. Upon appeal, the Court found that holding a person incommunicado was inherently coercive.[12] In the case of *Fikes v. Alabama* (1957), the defendant was held in solitary confinement for a period of ten days until he confessed.[13] In the case of *Ashcraft v. Tennessee* (1944), the defendant was questioned for thirty-six straight hours until he confessed.[14] In both of these cases, the Court found these practices to be coercive and the confession to be involuntary.

The Court also examined the characteristics of the accused. In the 1948 case of *Haley v. Ohio* the Court determined that the questioning of a fifteen-year-old from midnight to five in the morning until he confessed was coercive.[15] In the case of *Davis v. North Carolina* (1966), Elmer Davis was a suspect of several burglaries and a homicide. He was questioned once or twice a day for sixteen straight days until he confessed. Throughout the questioning Davis was not told of the true reasons for the questioning: that he was a suspect in the homicide. Due to his low level of intelligence, having only completed the third or fourth grade of school, such questioning was determined to be coercive.[16]

The Court also examined the physical condition of the suspect. In the case of *Mincey v. Arizona* (1978), the defendant was involved in a shootout with police. One officer was killed, and the defendant was seriously wounded in the exchange of gunfire. The defendant was taken to the hospital and admitted to the intensive care unit. A short while later, a detective began to question the defendant even though a tube had been inserted in his throat to help him breathe. To answer, the defendant responded by writing his answers on pieces of paper. During questioning, the defendant lost consciousness several times and questioning was delayed for medical treatment. After four hours, the defendant finally confessed and was convicted of murder. On appeal, the Court found that the defendant's will was weakened by pain and shock and, therefore, his confession was not voluntary.[17]

In the case of *Townsend v. Sain* (1963), the defendant was a suspect in a robbery and murder. He was a heroin addict and, during questioning, began exhibiting symptoms of withdrawal from the drug. The detectives summoned a doctor who administered medication to alleviate the discomfort of the withdrawal symptoms. Unknown to the detectives, the medication had the effect of a truth serum and the defendant confessed. Upon appeal the Court determined that the confession was not the product of the defendant's free will and was, therefore, not voluntary.[18]

In 1964 the Court heard the case of *Escobedo v. Illinois*. The defendant's brother-in-law was fatally shot, and the following morning the defendant was taken into custody and questioned. He did not make a statement and was released that afternoon on a writ of habeas corpus obtained by his lawyer. A few days later his crime partner confessed and stated that Escobedo had fired the fatal shots. Escobedo was again picked up for questioning and transported to the police station. En route to the station he requested to speak to his attorney and the request was denied. Shortly after Escobedo reached the police station, his attorney arrived and was denied his request to speak with his client. After about four hours of questioning, Escobedo confessed to the crime and eventually was convicted of murder. Upon appeal, the Court held that when "the investigation is no longer a general inquiry into an unsolved crime but has begun to focus on a particular suspect, the suspect has been taken into police custody, the police carry out a process of interrogations that lends itself to eliciting incriminating statement, the suspect has requested and been denied an opportunity to consult with his lawyer, and the police have not effectively warned him of his absolute constitutional right to remain silent, the accused has been denied 'the Assistance of Counsel' in violation of the Sixth Amendment to the Constitution."[19]

Two years later the Court expanded the procedural safeguards established in the *Escobedo* decision. In the case of *Miranda v. Arizona* the Court held that when a person is taken into police custody, in which his or her freedom of movement is lost,[20] and he or she is being interrogated with questions designed to elicit an incriminating response,[21] then the police must advise the suspect of the following points of law, known today as Miranda rights:

1. You have the right to remain silent.
2. Anything you say can be used against you in a court of law.
3. You have the right to talk to an attorney and have an attorney present before and during questioning.
4. If you cannot afford an attorney, one will be appointed free of charge to represent you before and during questioning, if you desire.

The Court established that, procedurally, if a person indicates in any manner that he or she does not want to talk to the police, then the interrogation must stop. If the suspect indicates that he or she wants an attorney, then the interrogation must stop until the suspect has had the opportunity to consult with an attorney. The suspect may waive these procedural safeguards; however, the prosecution then has a "heavy burden" to prove that the waiver was freely and knowingly given.[22]

The Waiver

Police are routinely seen in the movies and on TV advising a suspect of their so-called Miranda rights while they are in the process of handcuffing a suspect. While this may be acceptable procedure, it is not required by the *Miranda* decision, and it is doubtful if anyone would agree to being questioned at this time. The so-called Miranda rights need to be given only when the two-prong test of custody and interrogation come together. A suspect may be interrogated and not be in custody, as in questioning over the telephone, or be in custody and being asked questions not designed to elicit an incriminating response. In these situations Miranda is not required. As in an interview situation, an investigator needs to build rapport prior to beginning an interrogation. Although small talk with a suspect might not be appropriate, obtaining background information is. Questions such as place of birth need to be asked and offer opportunities for other informal questions. Such questioning, which does not meet the definition of interrogation per *Innis*, allows the investigator to build rapport with the suspect.

After building rapport, the suspect should be advised of his or her Miranda rights (Figure 7-1). The Court determined that the prosecution has a "heavy burden" to prove that this waiver was freely and knowingly given. This burden can be met by the use of the Miranda Advisement form used by most police agencies in the United States. However, this form is not required by the decision, and other means such as audio or video taping can be used to meet this legal burden.

Miranda Warning

Report #_____

1. You have the right to remain silent.

2. Anything you say can and will be used against you in a court of law.

    a. Do you understand that you have the right to remain silent?

        ☐ YES_____   ☐ NO_____

    b. Understanding that right, do you wish to talk to me now?

        ☐ YES_____   ☐ NO_____

3. You have the right to talk to an attorney and have an attorney present before and during questioning.

4. If you cannot afford an attorney, one will be appointed free of charge to represent you before and during questioning, if you desire.

    c. Do you understand you have the right to talk to an attorney?

        ☐ YES_____   ☐ NO_____

    d. Understanding that right, do you wish to talk to me now?

        ☐ YES_____   ☐ NO_____

SIGNED_____

OFFICER:_____   BADGE: _____

OFFICER:_____   BADGE: _____

TIME: _____   DATE: _____

The suspect should initial the appropriate answer to each question (yes, no) and sign the waiver. The officer should then sign and date the form.

FIGURE 7-1   Miranda Warning—Action Indicating a Suspect About to be Questioned by Police While in Their Custody Has Thoughtfully Waived His or Her Miranda Rights.

⑫ *Recognize the importance of conducting an interrogation in private free from distractions and the importance of being fully prepared and knowledgeable about the crime and the suspect's involvement.*

⑭ *Distinguish between the two types of offenders involved in the commission of a crime, and determine the best approach to be used on each during an interrogation.*

▶ Interrogation Essentials

Privacy

Interrogations, like interviews, should be conducted in private. A suspect is more apt to reveal secrets, such as involvement in a crime, in the privacy of a room occupied only by himself or herself and the investigator. The room should be free from outside noises and off limits to anyone not directly involved in the interrogation. The interrogation room should not contain any ornaments, pictures, or other objects that would, in any way, distract the attention of the person being interrogated. Even small, loose objects, such as paper clips or pencils, should be out of the suspect's reach so that they cannot be picked up and fumbled with during the interrogation. These tension-relieving activities can detract from the effectiveness of the interrogation, especially during the critical phase when a person may be ready to confess.[23]

Prior to Interrogation

Prior to conducting an interrogation, the investigator needs to know as much as possible about the crime in question. What do the victim and witnesses have to say about the suspect's involvement in the crime? What evidence exists that implicates the suspect, and how does this evidence apply to the suspect? The investigator's goal here is to know as much about the crime as the suspect does. In many cases, especially homicides, the suspect may be the only person alive who knows what actually happened during the commission of the crime.

A thorough investigation is important because the suspect is going to know if the investigator is not prepared and only on a "fishing expedition." Such a lack of preparation allows the suspect to lose respect for the investigator's abilities and provides another reason to lie. To prevent this, the investigator should know the answers to the questions before asking them.

Approach

During the investigative phase and while building rapport, the investigator needs to make an assessment regarding the person to be interrogated. The investigator needs to consider the suspect's personal characteristics, the type of offense he or she is suspected of committing, the probable motivation for the commission of the crime, and the suspect's initial response to questioning. Based on this assessment, the investigator could determine if the person to be interrogated is an emotional or a nonemotional offender.

An **emotional offender** is a person who experiences considerable feelings of remorse and mental anguish as a result of committing the offense. This individual has a strong sense of moral guilt—in other words, a troubled conscience. Typically these offenders tend to commit personal crimes, such as homicides, rapes, and physical assaults, or they are first-time offenders. A sympathetic approach that uses expressions of understanding and compassion is appropriate for these offenders.

A **nonemotional offender** refers to a person who ordinarily does not experience a troubled conscience as a result of committing a crime. This offender may have developed an antisocial personality disorder—a conditioned response to repeated prior success in escaping punishment through lying—or may be the career criminal who perceives committing crimes as a business. In the latter case, the suspect approaches arrest, prosecution, and possible conviction as an occupational hazard and experiences no regret or remorse as a result of exploiting victims. The most effective tactic to use on this offender is the **factual analysis approach**. This approach appeals to the suspect's common sense and reasoning rather than emotions and is designed to persuade the suspect that his or her guilt is established and, consequently, the intelligent choice to make is to tell the truth.[24]

⑬ *Discuss the rationale for a person to confess to a crime.*

▶ Why People Confess

You would think that when suspects are taken to the police station to be questioned concerning their involvement in a particular crime, their immediate reaction would be a refusal to answer any questions. It would also seem that once a suspect senses the direction in which the interrogation is heading, the conversation would come to an end. However, for various psychological reasons, suspects continue to speak with investigators. In most cases, suspects commit crimes because they believe that it offers the best solution to their needs at the moment. If investigators are able to convince suspects that the key issue is not the crime itself but what motivated them to commit the crime, they will begin to rationalize or explain their motivating factors.

Investigators must conduct interrogations with the belief that suspects, when presented with the proper avenue, will use it to confess their crimes. Research indicates that most guilty persons who confess are, from the outset, looking for the proper opening during the interrogation to communicate their guilt to the interrogators. However, before confessing, a suspect must feel comfortable in his or her surroundings and must have confidence in the interrogator, who should attempt to gain this confidence by listening intently and allowing the suspect to verbalize his or her account of the crime.[25]

⑮ *Discuss the concept of the "suspect's dilemma" and how this situation can be used to obtain a confession.*

▶ The Suspect's Dilemma: The Crime Partner

When a suspect committed the crime with a partner, he or she has a problem: an accomplice. The suspect must decide whether or not to sacrifice a crime partner for some mitigation of his or her own involvement in the crime and must make the decision before the crime partner does. This dilemma is often thought of simply as "better him than me."

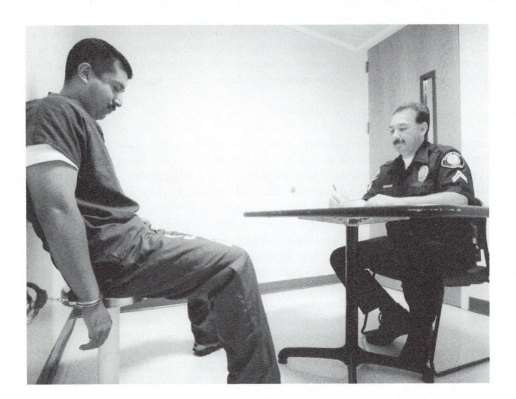

Advising a person being interrogated that a crime partner has talked is a practice that may taint an interrogation if done to persuade a suspect to waive his or her right to remain silent. If done honestly, it can, at times, be an effective technique. The offensive–defensive character of an interrogation session is replete with covert communication. The threatening aspect of the experience may be perceived with little outward awareness, but subliminally the person being interrogated experiences a strong anxiety response. The interrogator does not need to comment; the worry and concern about whether a crime partner has talked provoke a natural form of anxiety. Many offenders assume that their partner has talked or is about to talk and that the only smart thing to do is to talk first—or better, to tell everything.

16 *Discuss the strengths and weaknesses of the various methods used to document a confession.*

▶ Documenting the Confession

Three methods are used to document a suspect's confession: video recording, audio recording, and writing. Each method has its own strengths and weaknesses.

The strength of video recording is that it captures exactly what happened during the interrogation process. These video recordings can help meet the burden of proof required to demonstrate that a waiver of Miranda rights was freely and knowingly given and that no coercion was used to obtain the confession. As the video records not only what was said but how it was said, the triers of facts can view firsthand any deception on the part of the suspect.

Video recording that is done surreptitiously allows the interrogation process to be viewed by others without the suspect knowing that it is being recorded. State or local law may bar surreptitious taping. However, the U.S. Constitution should not be a bar since a suspect would be hard-pressed to prove that he or she had a "reasonable expectation of privacy" while under police interrogation in a station-house interview room. Indeed, the Miranda warning makes explicit that anything suspects say can and will be used against their interests.[26]

The covert recording of an interrogation allows other detectives to watch the interrogation and be a resource to the interrogator regarding areas of concern, deceptive movements, and officer safety issues. Such covert recording allows for the removal of two-way mirrors in interrogation rooms. These mirrors are well known by everyone who watches crime dramas on television. These mirrors work against the concept of privacy and do not aid the rapport-building process because the suspect is aware that other persons are on the other side of the mirror monitoring everything happening in the interrogation room. Another benefit of covert recording is that suspects can be left alone in the room while their activities continue to be monitored. In such situations it is not unusual for suspects to begin to talk to themselves and make incriminating statements. This tactic is even more effective when crime partners are left alone in the interrogation room and allowed to talk to one another.

One of the weaknesses of video recording is that it can be edited or altered. To guard against this allegation, the interrogation room should have a clock on the wall that is included in the recording. Any edits would be apparent to the viewer as the time would change if the tape were to be edited. Interrogation sessions often last for hours, and a drawback of using this technology is that the prosecuting attorney, the defense attorney, and the jury do not want to have to view the entire contents of the video tape of an interrogation. Another problem is that suspects, especially emotional offenders, may begin to sob or cry during the interrogation and are, therefore, difficult to understand when they are making a confession. These problems can be overcome by reducing the confession to writing.

The strength of audio recording is that this technology is available for field use for those interrogations that occur outside of an interview room setting. This technology can be used to capture the voluntary nature of the Miranda waiver, as well as the confession itself. To guard against the allegation that these tapes can be easily edited, the investigator should state the date and time the interrogation begins and ends. The lack of any time difference ensures that the tape has not been edited. However, while taping the interrogation, the investigator must not turn the recorder off and on. Taping an interrogation ensures that the investigator correctly records what the suspect has to say.

On the negative side, tape recorders have a tendency to be intimidating to some people if not used surreptitiously. Once again, the overt use of a tape recorder will work against the concepts of privacy and rapport building. The issues of using a tape recorder surreptitiously are the same as those with video recording.

The third method of documenting an interrogation is to acquire a written confession supplied by the suspect. This captures the words spoken by the suspect but not the suspect's unspoken body language. A written form documenting the waiver of Miranda rights and the written statement supplied by the suspect comprise a very effective means of documenting the voluntary nature of a waiver and confession. In the final analysis, the confession documented by video recording or audio recording must be memorialized in writing. Reducing the confession to writing allows the confession to be condensed to a concise statement of what happened, which can be included in the police report.

CASE STUDY

INTERROGATION OF A ROBBERY SUSPECT

Detectives question a suspect in an armed robbery of a credit union and obtain the following statement:

Statement of Suspect

DeRose: I am Detective Bob DeRose and this is Lieutenant Jacob Saylor. The time is now 1532 hours, the date is August 24. We would like to interview you regarding the offense today. Before doing so, I will advise you of your rights, which I will read to you from this form: "I acknowledge that I have been advised by officers Lieutenant J. Saylor and Detective R. DeRose, that I have the right to remain silent and that anything I say can and will be used against me in a court of law. I have the right to a lawyer and to have him present with me during questioning, and a lawyer will be appointed to represent me before any questioning if I cannot afford to hire one and desire to have a lawyer. Each of these rights has been explained to me, and I understand them. Having these rights in mind, I nevertheless waive them and consent to talk to the officers." Do you understand that?

(*continued*)

STRAUS: I understand them, and I waive them.

SAYLOR: You understand and you want to waive and talk to us?

STRAUS: Yes.

DEROSE: How far did you go in school?

STRAUS: Just about finished the second year of college.

DEROSE: Concerning the robbery that occurred at the credit union, could you first describe what happened from the time you got up this morning?

STRAUS: Concerning the robbery? Well, I got up, I thought, well, should I go to work? Today's the 24th and the railroad gets paid on the 24th, and people will be cashing their paychecks at the office, at the credit union office. So having made up my mind to touch and go, I called into work and told them I had a doctor's appointment and wouldn't be there until approximately 10:00 or 10:30. And I proceeded to arrange a pair of blue coveralls, a ski mask, gloves, and the piece—the pistol, the thirty-eight.

DEROSE: Where did you get the coveralls and the other stuff?

STRAUS: I bought them on the 9th of this month at the Emporium, I believe. I bought the ski hat at a sporting goods store next to Allen's Shoes on Temple Boulevard. The thirty-eight is registered to my brother-in-law, and I took it without his knowledge, hoping to return it today.

DEROSE: Then what happened?

STRAUS: Then I got into the car and went down to the credit union. It is sort of hazy from there. I circled the block a couple of times. I parked the car in a loading zone and went to see if they were open, and the door was unlocked, from which I figured they were open at the time. So I had the coveralls on and the hat on my head—I didn't have it over my face, and I had my fist in my pocket. And I heard loud noises in there—people talking—so I figured there was someone in there. I chickened out and I went back to the car and started to leave, and I said if I don't do it now, I won't do it. So I went back and parked in the parking place I showed you. Then I got out of the car. I walked over to the credit union. I went in the door and I heard the same loud male voices. There was two females. There was a couple female clerks in there. So I chickened out again, and I walked halfway back to the car. I say well, if I don't do it, I'll never do it again. And so I went back and got inside the building. I locked the door, the front double doors, behind me, went in and opened the inner door. And there was a man standing at the counter. He didn't turn around, and I put the gun—pointed the gun at the man and I said, "This is a holdup." I believe—I don't know exactly what I said.

DEROSE: Do you remember what the man looked like?

STRAUS: No. I only saw the back of his head. And I told him, "Keep quiet and everything will be all right." I said to the girl behind the counter, "Give me the money." And I had a paper bag in my hand, and I put the bag on the counter. And the man said, "Do as he says." And I was holding the gun on him.

DEROSE: Before you committed this robbery, did you anticipate what could happen?

STRAUS: No.

DEROSE: Did you ever think about getting caught?

STRAUS: No. I didn't worry about getting caught because I figured if I got caught—I got caught.

DEROSE: Well, all of the foregoing statements you have made have been given voluntarily and we haven't promised you anything?

STRAUS: No. Not yet.

DEROSE: And everything has been given of your own free volition in this statement?

STRAUS: Yeah.

CHAPTER REVIEW

Key Terms

autonomic nervous system 140	emotional offender 147	galvanograph 140
cardiograph 140	factual analysis approach 147	hypnosis 141
cognitive interviewing 142	galvanic skin response (GSR) 140	hypnotist 141

Review Questions

1. When interviewing a subject, the investigator notices that the person uses racially biased comments and slurs. The investigator should take note of these comments as they relate to that person's:
   a. Competency
   b. Credibility
   c. Veracity
   d. Truthfulness

2. When interviewing a person, the investigator should be aware that the person's age, intelligence, mental state, and level of intoxication could all affect that person's ability to testify at trial. These issues relate to the person's:
   a. Competency
   b. Credibility
   c. Varsity
   d. Truthfulness

3. Interviewing is a four-step process. At which step should the investigator begin taking notes or start recording the interview?
   a. First step
   b. Second step
   c. Third step
   d. Fourth step

4. At what step in the interview process should the investigator begin the probing process that would address any competency or credibility issues that might arise?
   a. First step
   b. Second step
   c. Third step
   d. Fourth step

5. Words alone convey only part of any conversation with another individual. What percentage of our conversations is nonverbal?
   a. 45 percent
   b. 55 percent
   c. 65 percent
   d. 75 percent

6. During the course of an interview the investigator notices that the person being interviewed begins to move around in the chair, jiggles his or her feet, and fidget. These are all signs of a lack of:
   a. Comfort
   b. Emphasis
   c. Synchrony
   d. Perception management

7. During the course of an interview, the investigator asks the subject who is responsible for the crime being investigated if he or she committed the crime. The subject states that he or she does not know who might have committed the crime, while at the same time he or she nods his or her head up and down. This combination of words and body movement is indicative of deception and an example of the lack of:
   a. Comfort
   b. Emphasis
   c. Synchrony
   d. Perception management

8. The factual analysis approach during and interrogation works best on what type of offender?
   a. Youthful
   b. Emotional
   c. Nonemotional
   d. Hardened criminal

9. A sympathetic approach that uses expressions of understanding and compassion is appropriate for what type of offender?
   a. Youthful
   b. Emotional
   c. Nonemotional
   d. Hardened criminal

10. The Supreme Court established a two-prong test that determines when the so-called Miranda warnings must be given. This two-prong test is met when which two conditions are present?
    a. Stop and frisk
    b. Custody and rapport
    c. Arrest and interrogation
    d. Custody and interrogation

See Appendix D *for the correct answers.*

Application Exercise

Develop an investigative strategy for interviewing witnesses to a crime involving the sexual assault and murder of a 5-year-old child. This strategy should address how to deal with the parents and siblings as well as willing, unwilling, and hostile witnesses. Select an approach and line of questioning to be used during the interrogation of the offender.

Discussion Questions

1. At the start of the case study on interrogation, why did the detective ask the suspect about his level of schooling?
2. At the end of the case study on interrogation, why did the detective ask the suspect about any promises being made to him?
3. Think back to the professional contacts you have had with your doctor, dentist, or lawyer. How did that professional build rapport and make you feel comfortable in his or her presence?
4. In addition to the issues addressed in this chapter, what issues affect a person's credibility as a witness?
5. Explain the similarities and differences between interviewing witnesses and interrogating suspects.
6. What is meant by *adversarial nature of interrogations*?
7. Explain the sympathetic approach used during an interrogation, and discuss the type of person with whom this approach works best.

Related Websites

Interested in becoming a polygrapher? For more information on this career choice, contact the American Polygraph Association at www.polygraph.org.

For answers to frequently asked questions regarding the polygraph, consult the following website: www.polygraphplace.com.

For information regarding the shortcomings of the polygraph, see www.antipolygraph.org.

To learn more about the Supreme Court of the United States, visit the Court's website at www.supremecourtus.gov.

Notes

1. Paul Szczesny, "Suspect Interviews: Asking for the Necessary Information," *Law and Order* (June 2002): 126.
2. Larry Danaher, "The Investigative Paradigm," *Law and Order* (June 2003): 133–134.
3. Fred Inbau, John Reid, Joseph Buckley, and Brian Jayne, *Criminal Interrogation and Confessions*, 4th ed. (Gaithersburg, MD: Aspen Publications, 2001), 51.
4. Edgar Miner, "The Importance of Listening in the Interview and Interrogation Process," *FBI Law Enforcement Bulletin* (June 1984): 12–16.
5. Paul Ekman, *Telling Lies: Clues to Deceit in the Marketplace, Politics, and Marriage* (New York: Norton, 1985), 287.
6. Joe Navarro, "A Four-Domain Model for Detecting Deception," *FBI Law Enforcement Bulletin* (June 2003): 19–24.
7. David Zulawski and Douglas Wicklander, *Practical Aspects of Interview and Interrogation*, 2nd ed. (Boca Raton, FL: CRC Press, 2002), 219–222.
8. *California Evidence Code*, sec. 795 (1984).
9. Margo Bennett and John Hess, "Cognitive Interviewing," *FBI Law Enforcement Bulletin* (March 1991): 8–12.
10. *Miranda v. Arizona*, 384 U.S. 436 (1966).
11. *Brown v. State of Mississippi*, 297 U.S. 278 (1936).
12. *Ward v. State of Texas*, 316 U.S. 547 (1942).
13. *Fikes v. Alabama*, 352 U.S. 191 (1957).
14. *Ashcraft v. State of Tennessee*, 322 U.S. 143 (1944).
15. *Haley v. Ohio*, 332 U.S. 596 (1948).
16. *Davis v. North Carolina*, 384 U.S. 737 (1966).
17. *Mincey v. Arizona*, 437 U.S. 385 (1978).
18. *Townsend v. Sain*, 372 U.S. 293 (1963).
19. *Escobedo v. Illinois*, 378 U.S. 478 (1964).
20. *Beckwith v. United States*, 245 U.S. 341 (1976).
21. *Rhode Island v. Innis*, 446 U.S. 291 (1980).
22. *Miranda v. Arizona*, 384 U.S. 436 (1966).
23. Inbau, Reid, Buckley, and Jayne, *Criminal Interrogation and Confessions*, 51–58.
24. Ibid., 209–211.
25. David Tousignant, "Why Suspects Confess," *FBI Law Enforcement Bulletin* (March 1991): 14–18.
26. U.S. Department of Justice, National Institute of Justice, Office of Justice Programs, *Videotaping Interrogations and Confessions* (Washington, DC: Government Printing Office, 1993), 4.

8 Crimes of Violence

LEARNING OBJECTIVES

After reading this chapter, you will be able to:

1 *Explain the elements of a criminal homicide and the various degrees of this crime.*

2 *Describe the autopsy procedure and the circumstances that would justify this examination.*

3 *Define the basic purpose of the medicolegal laboratory examination.*

4 *Explain how an investigation into the victim's background may indicate whether the death was a result of suicide, accident, or criminal homicide.*

5 *Discuss how the partial remains of a victim can be scientifically examined to determine the victim's identity.*

6 *List the various means that are used to establish the time of death of a homicide victim.*

7 *Define "exhumation" and the legal process to accomplish this action.*

8 *List the various stages and steps involved in the checklist for the investigation of criminal homicide.*

9 *Discuss and identify the basic patterns of a criminal homicide.*

10 *Discuss how the relationship between the suspect and victim might be a lead to the motive involved in the killing of the victim.*

11 *Compare the various types of multicide and define the dynamics of these crimes.*

⑫ *Discuss the concept of a cold case investigation and how the passage of time works in favor of the investigation.*

⑬ *List the various types of stalkers.*

⑭ *Define assault and battery.*

⑮ *Explain the telltale signs of physical child abuse and how this abuse is inflicted.*

Crimes of violence include attacks on the person that produce death or serious bodily injury. These assaults include attacks by others, self-inflicted injury, and physical abuse of children.

❶ *Explain the elements of a criminal homicide and the various degrees of this crime.*

▶ Homicide

Criminal homicides, from murder to manslaughter, and common and aggravated assault are major crimes against the person. First the crime scene and then the circumstances of the attack are the focus of investigations of these crimes.

Criminal homicide is usually divided by statute into various degrees. **First-degree murder** is defined as the premeditated killing of another human being with malice, or wrongful intent. If the death occurs as the result of the commission of a felony, such as arson, robbery, burglary, or sexual assault, then the felony murder rule would apply, which makes the killing one of the first degree regardless of the lack of intent or premeditation. **Second-degree murder** involves the killing of another but without the element of premeditation. **Manslaughter** is defined as the unlawful killing of another without malice or premeditation either voluntarily or involuntarily. Voluntary manslaughter involves a killing that is done in the heat of passion. Involuntary manslaughter is the appropriate charge when the death occurs while the perpetrator was involved in the commission of an unlawful act not amounting to a felony, such as driving while intoxicated.

The corpus delicti of all criminal homicide comprises the following: An evidentiary showing

1. of the death of a human being
2. of a criminal agency
3. that the criminal agency was the proximate cause of the death

The death must be of a human being and must occur within a certain period of time after the act causing the injury. The time may vary in different jurisdictions from one to three years. **Criminal agency** means that the death was caused by another person's unlawful act or omission.

According to the Federal Bureau of Investigation's, Uniform Crime Reporting program, there were an estimated 14,827 persons murdered nationwide in 2012, a decrease of almost 10 percent from the previous four years. The number of persons murdered equates to 4.7 murders per one hundred thousand inhabitants, the least committed of all violent crimes. Approximately 62 percent of these murders are cleared by arrest or an exceptional clearance, which is the highest clearance rate of all crimes.[1]

"Suspicious Death" Investigation

Police investigators conduct a **suspicious death** investigation in all cases in which the circumstances of the death indicate violence or **foul play**—that is, some criminal agency; when death occurs in a place other than the residence of the deceased; or when the deceased is not under the care of a physician at the time of death. From the preliminary investigation of a suspicious death, the facts may result in a decision to close the case because death resulted from natural or accidental causes or was a suicide; or a decision may be made to continue the investigation because the facts disclosed indicate a criminal—unjustified or unexcused—homicide.

The suspicious death concept is more than the traditional "foul play is suspected" in which the circumstances of a death strongly suggest murder. It is a classification of certain unexplained deaths so that they will be investigated until either the circumstances indicate that death was due to natural, accidental, or self-inflicted causes or the criminal agency is determined and the **criminal agent** is identified.

The **autopsy** is a major method of detecting murder. This postmortem examination of the victim in a suspicious death case is performed by a competent physician, generally a surgeon or pathologist specializing in this field, who determines the cause of death. If the autopsy surgeon reports that the nature of death is natural, accidental, or suicidal, then the death is not classed as a criminal homicide. When the autopsy surgeon's report states that a death resulted from a criminal agency, a criminal homicide has been detected.

Although police investigators can make no contribution to the professional conclusions of an autopsy surgeon as to the cause of death, they can assist such surgeons by supplying information related to the means used to cause death. Current prevailing practices in the detection of criminal homicide have led autopsy surgeons throughout the United States to expect a report from a police investigator before the time of the autopsy that informs the autopsy surgeon of all the facts in the case known to police at that time, including details about the scene of the crime, possible weapons, and other matters that relate to the death. The autopsy surgeon does not participate in the linking of the perpetrator to the criminal agency that caused death; that is the role of the investigator.

Thus, the detection of criminal homicide is based on finding the answers to four classic questions:

1. What was the cause of death?
2. What were the means (agency) that caused death?
3. Was the homicide excusable or justifiable?
4. Who was responsible for causing death (the agent)?

The autopsy surgeon shoulders the major responsibility in determining the cause of death. He or she and the police investigators work together to pinpoint the agency of death and define whether the agency is criminal, excusable, or justifiable. The police accept sole responsibility for identifying the person responsible for the killing.

 Describe the autopsy procedure and the circumstances that would justify this examination.

The Autopsy as an Extension of the Crime Scene

In homicide cases, the autopsy performed on the victim is an extension of the crime scene and offers an additional opportunity to search for clues and evidence useful in the investigation. For instance, the victim's body may contain bullets, the suspect's hairs, and fibers, all of which can be useful in identifying the perpetrator. This is also true, to a lesser extent, of medical testimony about examination of the wounds of a victim or injuries that occur in a rape or other sexual assault. The investigator searching the scene and the evidence technician lack the professional knowledge, skills, and experience of the medical examiner, the pathologist, and the toxicologist. Therefore, any examination of the victim in homicide cases by the investigator searching the scene must be a superficial one.

Many coroners and medical examiners consider an examination of the clothing of the victim to be a segment of the postmortem inquiry and require the same laboratory personnel processing the vital organs of the deceased to examine the clothing carefully. However, in suspicious death cases, it is the duty of the police investigator to make certain that an examination is conducted in a police laboratory.

3 *Define the basic purpose of the medicolegal laboratory examination.*

Medicolegal Laboratory Services

Most local laws governing investigative jurisdiction in cases of suspicious death require that the coroner or medical examiner be notified promptly and that the body of the victim not be moved without permission of one of these officials. The basic medicolegal service is to determine whether a death was caused by criminal agency and to identify the deceased person and the cause of death.

The report of the postmortem examination contains the autopsy surgeon's findings. Following are the five parts of this report:

1. The preamble (date, place, and identity of the deceased and of witnesses to identification)
2. External appearance (site, character, and dimensions of any wounds or marks related to the cause of death)
3. Internal examination (description of brain, spinal column, organs, and contents of body)
4. A reasoned opinion of the cause of death based on the facts found
5. Signature of examiner (title and qualifications)

Autopsy technique utilizes external examination and dissection. During this work, the pathologist may dictate his or her findings to a stenographer, an assistant, or a recorder. When transcribed, these notes, along with any sketches, diagrams, or photographs, constitute the raw notes of the examination.

The autopsy surgeon investigates all of the body cavities and makes incisions on the side of the neck to expose the neck organs for examination. A knife, saw, and chisel are used to open the head; the brain is removed and examined. The spinal cord and extremities also are examined. A microscopic examination of substances is used to search for any appearance of abnormality. The pathologist must be systematic and thorough. Recognizing the cause of death is his or her professional responsibility.

External postmortem appearances are very informative when a criminal agency is involved in the death. The areas of the body showing lividity indicate the position after death. Wounds and their appearance are particularly significant as they often assist in reconstructing the circumstances of a crime, as well as the nature of the murder weapon and the manner of its use. Significant data include an accurate description of where the wounds are situated and their shape, size, and direction.

Generally, pathologists classify and report the nature of wounds as follows:

1. *Incised Wounds.* Spindle-shaped in stabbing, linear in cutting
2. *Lacerated Wounds.* Irregularly edged, some tearing
3. *Contusions.* Bruises, discolorations, hematoma
4. *Abrasions.* Scratches, trivial wounds
5. *Gunshot Wounds.* Shotgun: "rat hole" to dispersion; rifles and pistols: contact, entrance, exit
6. *Antemortem* or **Postmortem**
7. *Age of Wound.* Signs of healing or decay
8. *Opinion About Wound.* Accidental, suicidal, or homicidal; "hesitation" wounds in suicides, and "defense" wounds in homicide

A practitioner skilled in medicolegal procedures can define the shape of the striking area of the weapon used and the degree of force in relation to the weight and striking surface of the weapon. This can mean a possible matching of a murder weapon when found and, if the offender has not been identified, possibly an estimate of the sex and size of the perpetrator.

Body temperature, lividity, and rigor mortis indicate the time of death in on-the-scene examination, but the general appearance of the body and its stomach contents afford the pathologist a means of fixing the time of death within reasonable limits. The clinical history of the case and its revelations about persons who were the last to see the victim alive and the victim's activities assist the pathologist in determining the time of death.

Classically, the autopsy report should provide information on the following:[2]

1. Cause of death
   a. Natural causes
   b. Accident
   c. Suicide
   d. Homicide
   e. Undetermined origin
2. If a weapon or substance caused death, the nature of the fatal wounds or injuries
3. Time of death in relationship to wound
4. Whether the scene where the body was discovered was the death scene; whether marks and signs indicate the victim was mobile or that the body was moved
5. Evidence of chronic illness or other disease
6. Evidence of blood, hair, or skin other than the victim's
7. Evidence of sexual knowledge or deviancy

In suspected poisoning cases, the pathologist must correlate his or her clinical postmortem findings with the history of the deceased, if available, and suggest the most promising area of investigation to the **toxicologist**, who specializes in the detection of chemical, physical, and biological toxins. The history in a medicolegal autopsy includes all available information about the circumstances of a case: (1) manner of death, (2) preceding manifestations of illness and pain, and (3) investigation at the death scene if foul play is suspected. After the toxicologist's report has been received, the pathologist first evaluates the significance of the toxicologist's findings with regard to the body conditions at autopsy and against the background of the clinical history of the deceased and then bases an opinion of the cause of death on these three types of facts.

Identification after death is determined by characteristics that distinguish the deceased from all other individuals. The usual police investigation attempts to disclose the name of the deceased to find responsible persons (relatives or friends) to view the body and identify it. The deceased person frequently is fingerprinted, and the inked impression may be forwarded through the criminal justice information system for identification or verification.

Teeth provide leads to identification, and dentists can elicit valuable clues to identity. A wealth of dental information is now in the hands of the dental profession and can be useful in the identification of deceased persons.[3]

Sex, age, marks and scars, and other physical features such as old bone fractures or deformities are also identification factors.[4] Death masks are sometimes made, photographed, and included in police bulletins when identification is a problem. These flyers are circulated in the same manner as wanted notices. Unrecognizable remains of a human body present problems. Fire, water, explosion, mutilation, and exposure to the elements and to animals often make it difficult or impossible to arrive at an identification. Nevertheless, pathologists almost always can establish some clues to identity. By correlating all available data, they may arrive at a determination of race, sex, age, and approximate height and weight.

 Explain how an investigation into the victim's background may indicate whether the death was a result of suicide, accident, or criminal homicide.

Suicide, Accident, or Criminal Homicide?

Persons who kill themselves adopt methods similar to techniques used in criminal homicides. Many suicides do not leave classic notes explaining their reasons for self-destruction and do not foreshadow their intent to commit suicide in any observable fashion. Even when the circumstances of a suspicious death reek of murder, a comprehensive investigation may indicate that the death was suicidal.

Circumstances of a suspicious death often invite an investigator's conclusion of self-destruction. However, a great number of murderers attempt to hide their crimes by cloaking them in clues and traces that will indicate suicide. The greatest problem exists when the circumstances of death show that someone has a motive, or could have a motive, for murder. An investigation into the background of a victim may indicate strongly that an apparent suicide is out of character with the victim's lifestyle—a fact that must be weighed heavily before closing a suspicious death case as a suicide.

The techniques of criminal homicide are similar to accidental causes of death. For example, death can result from a person being pushed out of a high window or from accidentally falling out of the window. It can also result from a person being shot by another person or accidentally while cleaning a firearm. Death can be caused by another's plunging a knife into a vital area or an accidental fall on a bottle driving shards of glass into the same vital area and causing similar fatal injuries. A fatal dose of poison can be administered by another or can be taken by mistake. A skull can be crushed with a blunt instrument or can result from falling down a flight of stairs.[5]

⑤ *Discuss how the partial remains of a victim can be scientifically examined to determine the victim's identity.*

Identification of the Victim

In most homicides, identifying the victim is not a problem. He or she is known and can be identified by relatives and friends. Identifying a victim becomes a problem when death occurs in a public place, a hotel, or a place other than the domicile of the victim. This is particularly true when the victim is a member of the large transient population in the United States. Although homeless men make up most of the transient population, the drug scene has contributed a great number of runaway girls and boys to the ranks of those who move about from place to place in the United States.

A major problem of victim identity occurs when the killer attempts to avoid detection by doing away with the remains of his or her victim through burning, sinking the victim in a substantial body

Human skulls can be identified through forensic dental examination.
Source: Alan Pappe/ Photodisc/Getty Images

of water, cutting up the victim, or destroying the victim's remains by chemical means. Sometimes the killer does not seek complete destruction of the body but may attempt to destroy only portions of the remains to prevent or delay identification. Scientific means for identification of the partial remains of victims in suspicious deaths include the following:

1. *Fingerprints.* If the victim had been fingerprinted in his or her lifetime, this is a positive means of identification.

2. *Dental Work.* This is a comparison identification, with the dental work of a victim being matched with the dental work of a person who has been missing from home or is otherwise unaccounted for.

3. *Bones.* Bones serve as a broad index of identification when other means are not available because of the condition of the victim's remains. They may indicate sex, height, and age and sometimes time of death, cause of death, and other features of identification.

4. *Surgical Procedures.* Surgery that took place during the lifetime of the victim may also aid in identification.

Estimates of the size, age, sex, and race of a homicide victim are possible from the study of the victim's remains, but identification of the unknown victim must depend on finding a sufficient number of unique physical characteristics for comparison with records that were made during the victim's lifetime. Insofar as skeletal remains are concerned (no fingerprints), dental records and body X-rays are the most likely means of identification. Dentists can be queried and identification made from dental records. Bone injuries severe enough to suggest hospitalization during the victim's life can lead to existing X-rays in hospital records and result in a positive identification.[6]

The major problem when dealing with burned, skeletal, or mutilated remains is locating the **ante mortem**, or before-death records of the deceased. There is no database for dental records. In order to obtain these records the deceased person's dentist must be located, and in order to do that the investigator must have an idea who the deceased person is. A starting point for this inquiry would be the missing person's reports. A forensic dentist can assist in narrowing the search of these records by providing the approximate age of the deceased. Teeth are a good indicator of age especially when the person is a child or young adult due to tooth formation. Tooth formation typically ends when a person is about 22 years of age, however, a forensic dentist can make an estimate as to a person's age based on wear on the teeth and the transparency of the roots of the teeth which occurs with age.

The forensic dentist can also supply an opinion as to the possible sex of the deceased, as generally male teeth have longer root lengths. There are also some racial differences in teeth which may lead the forensic dentist to render an opinion as to the race of the deceased. In the event no local missing person reports matches the dental profile, the investigator can use the National Crime Information Centers (NCIC) computer system to transmit this dental profile nationally to have other law enforcement agencies check their missing persons reports for a possible match.[7]

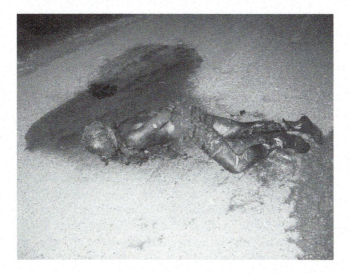

This victim was strangled, shot, and then set on fire in an apparent attempt to conceal the victims identity.

6 *List the various means that are used to establish the time of death of a homicide victim.*

Time of Death

Criminal homicide investigations have a built-in time clock keyed to the time of death. Methods for establishing this vital time, or period of time, range from the testimony of witnesses (the person who saw the killing or who last saw the victim alive, or the person who discovered and reported the crime) to the testimony of autopsy surgeons as to the condition of the body of the victim when found or examined.

The time of death connects the events that happen before the crime with the actual killing in homicide cases. The important questions related to this time-clock sequence are twofold:[8]

1. What activity was the victim engaged in at the time of the fatal assault?
2. What activity did the victim engage in immediately before death (twenty-four to forty-eight hours, and longer if warranted)?

In as much as the only certain time element in the beginning phases of a homicide investigation is the time the crime was discovered, the witness or witnesses who can testify to this aspect of the case are carefully questioned as to the circumstances that first aroused their interest or suspicions, as well as the time of that event; the time of the discovery of the victim; how the victim was found and if he or she was found dead; and the circumstances and time of reporting this discovery to police.

As a homicide investigation continues, witnesses are located who talked to the deceased victim prior to the fatal assault, either in person or over a telephone. Such witnesses can give information about the content of the conversation and its time. Sometimes the activity in which the victim was engaged prior to or at the time of death can be timed within reasonable limits. This process is known as establishing the **window of death**.

When a homicide has no witnesses, the time of death within the window of death may be established by the forensic scientist and pathologist. Estimating the time of death is important in determining opportunity to commit the crime. These estimates are based on the postmortem, or after-death, changes that occur in the body and the activity of insects that may attack the body.

After death the body begins to cool through the process of **algor mortis**. The body temperature falls until it reaches the ambient air temperature, which usually occurs within eighteen to twenty hours. Algor mortis is considered to be one of the more reliable indicators of time of death. However, due to a number of variables, including the body temperature at the time of death, clothing, surface temperature, humidity, and air movement across the body, these estimates are not exact.

Biochemical changes in the body after death produce stiffening of the muscles, or **rigor mortis**, which usually appears within two to six hours after death. The process begins in the jaw and neck and proceeds to the trunk and extremities and is complete within six to twelve hours. This rigidity remains for two to three days and disappears in the same order in which it appears.

Due to gravity, when the blood stops circulating, it begins to settle to the lowest portion of the body. This process, **postmortem lividity**, is noticeable approximately within one hour after death and is fully developed within three to four hours. Lividity appears as blue or reddish marks on the skin. Fresh livid stains are not produced by a change in position twelve hours after death. Lividity discoloration provides two types of information. The degree of discoloration is an indicator of the time of death and can indicate a change of position or movement of the body after death.

Decomposition, or **putrefaction**, begins at the time of death as a result of two processes: autolysis and bacterial action. **Autolysis** occurs by a chemical breakdown of the body that results in the softening and liquefaction of body tissue. **Bacterial action** converts body tissue into liquids and gases. Within twenty-four hours, a discoloration of the skin is noticeable. This greenish-red or blue-green color change is pronounced within thirty-six hours. Bacterial action produces gases that cause the body to swell and produces an unpleasant odor. The environment affects the rate of decomposition: colder temperatures tend to impede the process while warmer temperatures increase it.

Various kinds of insects feed on dead bodies. These insects lay their eggs, which develop into larvae, or maggots. They can reduce a body to skeletal remains in less than two months under favorable conditions. The life cycle of these insects is constant, and the forensic entomologist, a specialist in insects, can determine how long a body has been exposed to the action of these insects.[9]

7 *Define "exhumation" and the legal process to accomplish this action.*

Exhumation

A court order must be secured for **exhumation**—the removal of the body of a deceased person from its place of burial—for a medicolegal examination to disclose the presence of a previously unknown or improperly identified injuries, or to reveal the presence of a poison or other noxious substance that would indicate a criminal agency caused death.

Examination after burial is rarely as satisfactory as an autopsy before burial. However, full autopsy procedures should be carried out, and before and after the autopsy the body should be fully X-rayed and photographed.

8 *List the various stages and steps involved in the checklist for the investigation of criminal homicide.*

Checklist for the Investigation of Criminal Homicide

A checklist for a criminal homicide investigation should be divided into stages to allow for the orderly progression of the investigation from its beginning to its focusing and then to the arrest of the perpetrator and crime partners, if any (Figure 8-1).

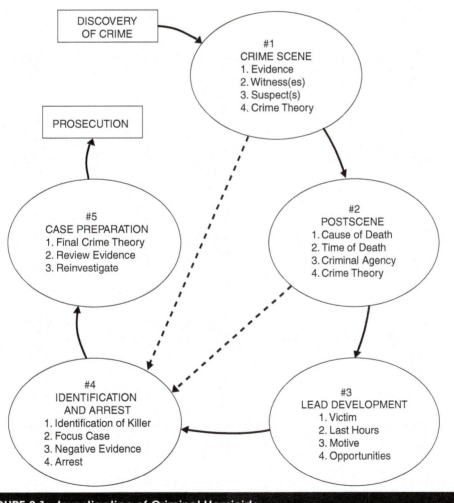

FIGURE 8-1 Investigation of Criminal Homicide.

Stage 1: Crime Scene

1. Be alert at the approach to and the entrance to the crime area for the perpetrator and others leaving the crime scene. All persons at or leaving the crime scene should be stopped and identified before they leave. Interviewing of such persons may be done at the scene or later.

2. Take a good, hard look when entering the crime scene to obtain an overview of the situation.
   a. *The Victim.* Give first aid or summon medical help, if necessary. Note if the victim is apparently dead or pronounced dead by a physician. Take a dying declaration, if possible.
   b. *The Scene.* Check entrances, exits, and extent of the scene. Protect weapons and other evidence. Prevent the entry of unauthorized persons. Call for technicians (if available) to take photographs. Process the scene for fingerprints and other physical evidence.

3. Protect the integrity of the scene by warning all present not to smoke, use any plumbing (sinks, tubs, showers, toilet) or towels, touch any objects or surfaces at the scene, or walk in or otherwise contaminate blood traces at the scene.

4. Identify witnesses, interview them, get a statement of their knowledge of the crime, and begin the search for additional witnesses.

5. If an apparent suspect is at the scene (case is focusing), warn him or her of rights; note appearance, clothing, and physical and mental condition; and record any spontaneous utterances. All present at the scene are possible suspects until the case has focused. Begin a search for suspicious persons and vehicles that were at the scene before or at the time of the crime.

6. Record the scene.
   a. Photograph the scene.
   b. Measure and sketch the scene.
   c. Make notes.
   d. Collect evidence and record where it was found and who found it. Mark the evidence, transport it, and secure it with the property officer.

7. Seal the scene: do not open it without the previous agreement of associates, technicians, and the prosecutor.

8. Identify the victim.

9. Develop a tentative crime theory.

Stage 2: Postscene

1. Determine time of death; bracket the time period.
   a. Witness(es) who saw victim alive or talked to victim by telephone before his or her death
   b. Witness(es) who discovered victim (the crime)
   c. Medicolegal testimony setting a maximum and minimum limit for time of death (report of autopsy surgeon)
   d. Other evidence

2. Determine the place of fatal assault (when different from the place of discovery of the crime).

3. Determine cause of death.
   a. Apparent cause at the scene
   b. Medicolegal autopsy report

4. Determine the means of death.
   a. Criminal agency
   b. Specific weapon
   c. Weapon recovered

5. Develop a tentative crime theory.

Stage 3: Lead Development

1. Determine the victim's background and activities.
2. Investigate the victim's last hours.
   a. Contacts
   b. Activity at time of death and before death
3. Determine the vehicle(s) used.
4. Interview injured suspects.
5. Interview informants.
6. Locate the weapon.
7. Investigate tie-ups with other crimes.
8. Determine the perpetrator's knowledge of the victim's activity and access to the premises.
9. Establish motive: the "pattern" of the criminal homicide.
10. Determine opportunity to commit the crime.
    a. Persons known to have been at the scene
    b. Persons who may have been at the scene
11. Develop a tentative crime theory to include the identification of one or more prime suspects.

Stage 4: Identification and Arrest

1. Develop evidence that will identify the killer. Review evidence for corpus delicti, identification, and consistency with the crime theory.
2. Focus the case.
3. Exonerate innocent suspects.
4. Arrest the killer and crime partner(s), if any.
5. Gather negative evidence as needed.
   a. Alibi
   b. Self-defense
   c. Intent
      i. Mental state of suspect
      ii. Sobriety of suspect
      iii. Crime record of suspect
   d. Crime or treatment (medical, psychiatric) records of witnesses and victim

Stage 5: Case Preparation

1. Reconstruct the crime.
2. Summarize the physical evidence.
3. Summarize the testimony of witness(es).
4. Review the motive (reason) and intent.
5. Confer with associates and the prosecutor.
6. Reinvestigate the crime as warranted or directed by the prosecutor.
7. Prepare the cover sheet (synopsis) for forwarding with the case records to the prosecutor.

❾ *Discuss and identify the basic patterns of a criminal homicide.*

Patterns of Criminal Homicide

The basic pattern of a criminal homicide ordinarily is disclosed in the initial investigation of a suspicious death. Even though a killer may attempt to falsify the facts of a dispute or cast the suspicion of guilt upon another person, a routine investigation should disclose the facts.

Among the basic patterns of criminal homicide are the following:

1. **The Anger Killing.** The **anger killing** pattern is an extension of the crime of assault. A dispute occurs, and anger develops. The victim is attacked, with or without weapons, and fatally injured.

2. **The Triangle Killing.** The possibility of an errant husband, a lover, or a mistress should rarely be ignored. If a wife is dead and another woman is involved in a romantic triangle, grounds exist for suspecting that the husband wished to rid himself of an unwanted wife. The reverse situation is frequently encountered: the wife is anxious to rid herself of an unwanted husband because of a developing romance. When the person who may have the motive in this triangle was also the last one to see the victim alive, the investigation starts to gather momentum in its development as a **triangle killing**.

3. **The Revenge or Jealousy Killing.** In a **revenge or jealousy killing**, the initial investigation of who the victim was and the history of the involvement between the victim and suspects usually will disclose the motive of revenge or jealousy, and thus a suspect.

4. **Killing for Profit.** The elimination of another person because the murderer would gain some benefit has long been a standard motive for murder. Who would profit? This is a splendid avenue of investigation for developing suspects. When the circumstances of a suspicious death show that persons who would profit from the death are among those who last saw the victim alive, a theory of criminal homicide along these lines can be developed. **Murder for profit** is closely aligned with the triangle-killing situation; the victim is eliminated to gain some benefit.

5. **The Random Killing.** Every killing has a motive, if **motive** is defined as a reason for the slaying. Even the **random killing**, with no previous connection or tie with the victim, has a motive. This type of killing is often termed *unmotivated* because the reason for the killing is clouded and unknown until the suspect is discovered. The killing of a complete stranger is perhaps the most difficult to solve. This pattern of murder may be disclosed by first excluding the usual or common patterns of criminal homicide.

6. **Murder–suicide.** The **murder–suicide** pattern of criminal homicide is one in which the killer self-destructs shortly after the fatal assault on the victim. In these often "compact" killings, a husband and wife, boyfriend and girlfriend, or parent and child agree that both should die with one taking the responsibility for killing the other and then committing suicide.

7. **Sex and Sadism.** The **sex and sadism murder** is marked by unusual violence. It may follow child molesting, rape, acts of perversion, or other sadistic acts. It often has bizarre overtones. In one New York case, the two female victims were stabbed repeatedly, undressed, and tied together face to face. The killer rubbed Noxzema face cream on and about the rectums of his victims. In a Nevada case, the victim's vagina and breasts were slashed deeply with a sharp instrument.

8. **Felony Murder.** In the **felony murder**, the victim's death does not result from an angered attack; a triangle, revenge, jealousy, or profit motivation; random chance; a murder–suicide compact; or sex and sadism. Rather, death results from injuries inflicted by someone in the act of committing a felony. The criminal intent of the original crime carries over to the killing.

The investigator must not close his or her mind or the investigation too quickly. A homicide investigation may appear to fit one of the criminal homicide patterns, and evidence developed in a continuing investigation may reveal sufficient data to change the murder classification to another pattern or combination of patterns. For instance, a criminal homicide case in St. Paul, Minnesota, first appeared to be a burglary gone wrong. Mrs. Carol Thompson was found semiconscious and bloody in her home. She was rushed to a hospital, where she died as a result of bleeding from multiple fractures of her skull. The death weapon was a blunt instrument, and when fragments of pistol grips were found in a pool of blood in the Thompson living room, it was assumed to be a pistol whipping. Evidence of a burglary was apparent at the crime scene in the ransacking of bureau and desk drawers. Continued inquiries developed the fact that the husband of the victim had been intimate with another woman, and a new potential pattern developed: elimination of an unwanted wife. A few days later, when local insurance executives responded to police inquiries with the news that the housewife–victim was insured for over $1 million with the husband as sole beneficiary, the "killing for profit" pattern was added as a possible motive for the crime.[10]

 Discuss how the relationship between the suspect and victim might be a lead to the motive involved in the killing of the victim.

Motive for Murder: Relationships

In a trial for murder, proof of motive is always relevant but never necessary. In a criminal homicide investigation, a motive is necessary and useful. It may surface while following the basic leads of benefit and opportunity or while reviewing the relationships of the victim. Current and former spouses and lovers of the victim promptly become suspects, as friends and relatives, not strangers, are often the killers. These relationships include the following:

1. Spouse (or ex-)
2. Common-law spouse (or ex-)
3. Boyfriend; girlfriend (or ex-)
4. Live-in boyfriend; girlfriend (or ex-)
5. Sister; brother
6. Mother; father
7. Daughter; son
8. Other relative (includes in-laws)
9. Friend of family; relative (specify)
10. Neighbor
11. Business associate (specify partner, coworker, other)
12. Acquaintance
13. Seen before (as "known from neighborhood")

The frequency of the contacts common to a relationship are classified as *live together, see daily, see weekly, see monthly,* or *hardly see at all.*

 Compare the various types of multicide and define the dynamics of these crimes.

Multicide

Multicide is the killing of a number of victims by one or more persons working in concert. Mass murder, spree murder, and serial murder are the various types of multicide.

Mass murder is the homicide of four or more victims during a single event at one location.[11] The mass murderer appears to give little thought or concern to his or her inevitable capture or death. Some are killed by police during the attack; others kill themselves once they have completed the massacre. In some cases, these killers surrender to the police and offer no resistance. Most appear to commit their crimes in public places. In cases in which families are murdered, the killer usually leaves ample evidence to lead to his or her arrest.[12]

Spree murder is the killing of three or more persons within a relatively short time frame. Most of these cases last from only a few weeks to as long as a year. The victims may be men, women, or children, and an element of randomness is present in victim selection.[13] The so-called D.C. Sniper who killed thirteen persons and wounded six others in five states and the District of Columbia during a three-week period in the fall of 2002 is an example of a spree killer.

Serial killers, by contrast, may make special efforts to elude detection. They may continue to kill for weeks, months, and often years before they are caught, if at all. The definition

Mass murderer Andrea Yates in a family portrait. She is now confined for drowning all five of her children. (One is not pictured.)
Source: © Mike Stewart/Sygma/Corbis

of a **serial murder** is two or more separate murders when an individual, acting alone or with another, commits multiple homicides over a period of time with time breaks between each murder event.[14] Several types of serial murderers have been identified based on their motivation for the killing.[15]

1. The **visionary serial killer** is propelled to kill by voices he or she hears or visions he or she sees. These breaks from reality demand that he or she kill certain kinds of people. This kind of offender is truly out of touch with reality—a psychotic. This killer's competency to stand trial for his actions is a consideration for the court to decide.

2. The **mission serial killer** feels a need on a conscious level to eradicate a certain group of people. This offender is not psychotic; he is in touch with reality but acts on a self-imposed duty to rid the world of a certain class of people: for example, prostitutes or religious or racial group members.

3. The **hedonistic serial killer**—the **lust killer** or **thrill killer**—is a subtype of this category. This killer has made a connection between personal violence and sexual gratification. These offenders murder because they derive pleasure from the act: killing for them is an eroticized experience. These killings are process focused, taking some time to complete, and include torture, mutilation, and other fear-instilling activities.

   Another type of serial killer in this category is the **comfort-oriented serial murderer** who kills for personal gain. Professional assassins and people who kill for personal gain fall under this category.

4. The **power and control serial killer** receives sexual gratification from the complete domination of his victim. He derives his gratification from the belief that he has the power to make another human being do exactly what he wants. By dominating his victims completely, he experiences a sexual pleasure. This murderer is psychologically rooted in reality: a true sociopath who lives by his own personal rules and guidelines.

The crime scene or lack of a crime scene will determine whether the killing was the work of an organized or a disorganized offender. **Organized offenders** are usually above average in intelligence. They are methodical and cunning. Their crimes are well thought out and carefully planned. They are likely to own a car in good condition. The crime is usually committed out of their area of residence or place of work. They are mobile and travel many more miles than the average person. Fantasy and ritual are important to them. They select their victims, usually strangers. Most of their victims will share some common traits. They are considered socially adept. They use their verbal skills to manipulate their victims and gain control over them until they have their victims within their "comfort zone." They are likely to follow news reports of the event and will oftentimes take a "souvenir" from the victim as a reminder, which is sometimes used to relive the event or continue with the fantasy.

Disorganized offenders are inadequate individuals who are experiencing intense sadistic sexual fantasies and may suddenly act out these fantasies on a victim of opportunity. The crime scene would be disorganized, and the perpetrator's actions and behavior could be viewed as psychotic. Offenders are usually of below-average intelligence. They generally are loners who are not married, and they either live alone or with a relative in proximity to the crime scene. They experience difficulty in negotiating interpersonal relationships and are described as socially inadequate. They act impulsively under stress and will usually select a victim from their own geographic area. In most instances, such offenders do not own a vehicle but have access to one. They use a blitz style of attack, which catches the victim off guard. This type of spontaneous action, in which the offenders suddenly acts out their fantasy, does not allow for a conscious plan or even for a thought of being detected. This is why the crime scene will be disorganized and clustered. A **clustered crime scene** involves a situation where most of the activities take place at one location: the confrontation, the attack, the assault, and sexual activity.[16]

While knowing the kind and type of serial killer involved will not tell the investigator who is committing these crimes, this information will aid the investigator in determining where to look and the type of person who may be involved. The real benefit of this information is its value at the time of interrogation. Knowing the motivation of such killers will aid in the formation of the proper questions to ask when this serial killer is caught.

The mobility of the organized offender presents a problem for the investigator as this killer may intentionally cross jurisdictional lines of authority to avoid detection. For instance, Ted Bundy, an infamous serial killer, killed twenty-nine victims in five states and was able to avoid capture for several years primarily for this reason. The **Violent Criminal Apprehension Program (VICAP)** administered by the Federal Bureau of Investigation is the clearinghouse for information regarding serial killers. Investigators send in data on their local murders, and when cases are linked, the reporting investigators in the local agencies are given each other's names so that they can coordinate their work.[17]

12 *Discuss the concept of a cold case investigation and how the passage of time works in favor of the investigation.*

Cold Case Investigations

When most people hear the term cold case investigations they think of a homicide case which is not totally accurate. A cold case investigation involves the reopening of any felony crime where prior investigative activity has exhausted all investigative leads without a resolution and the case has been inactive for some time. Time is of the essence in most investigations and generally if a crime is not solved within a few days it becomes increasingly difficult to solve. In cold case investigations the passage of time may work in favor of the investigation. Cold case investigative protocols involve three concepts:

1. *Relationships*—change over time, people who were once friends, spouses, or lovers may now be former friends, divorced or spurned lovers. The relationship that kept them from talking at the time of the crime may now the basis for telling investigators the truth as they know it.

2. *Science*—what advances in forensic technology now exists that was not available at the time the crime was committed. Advances in DNA and fingerprinting and related databases are the underlying foundation of many cold case investigations, as the following case illustrates.

> In 1978 a 61-year-old man was brutally assaulted and stabbed to death in his Omaha, Nebraska, home. Investigators recovered blood and fingerprints from the victim's home and his stolen vehicle which was recovered a few days later. The fingerprint evidence was processed but was unsuccessful in matching the prints in the fingerprint repository. Without any other investigative leads to follow, the case went cold for 30 years. On a tip from another agency the fingerprint found at the scene was searched again using new automated technology and within 5 hours a suspect was identified. The suspect was contacted and DNA tests further substantiated his involvement in the crime.[18]

3. *Fresh set of eyes*—involves investigators doing an in-depth review of all the original reports and files in the case. These new "eyes" may locate information that did not end up on the right hands at the right time during the original investigation.[19]

13 *List the various types of stalkers.*

▶ Stalking

About half of the states in the United States now have penal code provisions to combat stalking. For instance, in Kentucky, **stalking** is defined as an intentional course of conduct that does the following:

1. Is directed at a specific person or persons
2. Seriously alarms, annoys, intimidates, or harasses the victim
3. Serves no legitimate purpose

Stalking ranges from phone calls and letters through personal confrontations, to attempted murder, murder, or rape. A recently developed typology may be helpful to investigators who are suddenly confronted with the activity of a stalker:[20]

1. **Celebrity Stalker.** Victim known on an impersonal level—actor, sports star
2. **Lust.** Predatory sex (in which the victim is a stranger to the assailant), escalates to murder
3. **Hit Stalker.** Professional killer
4. **Love-scorned Stalker.** Intends violence against known victim
5. **Domestic Stalker.** Ex-lover or spouse, "get even" violence
6. **Political Stalker.** Selected victim is a stranger to the assailant

⑭ *Define assault and battery.*

▶ Assaults

An **assault** is an unlawful attempt, coupled with the present ability, to commit an injury on another person. In other words, it is an attempt to commit a **battery**: an unlawful beating or other wrongful physical harm inflicted on a human being without his or her consent.

In assaults, the victim is usually alive and willing to cooperate with investigators. In many cases, the assailant is known to the victim and the investigation becomes one in which establishing the identity of the perpetrator is not a problem. When the assailant is not known to the victim, the investigation of assault is closer to a homicide investigation than it is to any other investigation.

Assault without a weapon and in which serious injury is not inflicted on the victim is a relatively minor crime. Assault with a deadly weapon or an assault in which serious injury is inflicted with or without a weapon is **aggravated assault**—a serious crime.

Aggravated assaults are often murder attempts that have failed as a result of the intervention of witnesses, prompt medical treatment, or pure luck. For this reason, the characteristics of assailants in either crime are likely to be similar.

The term **violent injury** is synonymous with force in assault cases. It includes any application of physical force even if it entails no pain or bodily harm and leaves no marks.

The assault scene must be protected and its integrity preserved. Of course, the victim must be given first aid and prompt medical attention, if required, and furniture may have to be moved to care for the victim. The investigating officer at the scene should make note of these changes in the crime scene, and if the victim is moved from the position he or she was in at the time of the officer's arrival, the victim's original position should be noted.

The crime scene is processed for evidence that will assist in reconstructing the crime and identifying the participants as the attacker and the victim; witnesses at the scene are interviewed for the same purpose. The work of investigators at this time concentrates on securing the details of the attack and of the dispute that led to the attack.

When the victim is seriously injured and requires medical care, the investigating officer should accompany the assault victim to the hospital. The situation is flexible, but the objective is to gain as much information as possible from the victim as to the circumstances leading to the attack, the nature of the attack, and the identity of the attacker. The information provided by a victim in periods of consciousness after being seriously injured may be compelling evidence in a future trial. If a victim is in extremis and is aware of impending death, the officer may secure a dying declaration indicating the victim's mental condition and the circumstances of the attack.

If the circumstances warrant, the officer accompanying an assault victim to the hospital should collect, mark, and retain the victim's clothing as evidence. Future processing by criminalists may indicate the direction of force in bullet holes and the damage caused by knives or other sharp instruments, bloodstains and their origin, and similar evidence.

It is particularly important that the weapon or weapons involved in an assault be promptly identified, recovered, and related to a participant in the assault event. The police search of the crime scene should disclose the presence of all weapons at the scene at the time of arrival of police. Interviewing of eyewitnesses should seek disclosure of any weapons used in the attack but not found at the crime scene.

Before an assault, the offender and the victim usually have had some interaction. Generally, this was an **altercation**—a verbal dispute. The dispute's origin may range from domestic difficulties to a pushing-and-shoving situation to prove masculinity among drinking partners. Although intoxication (drugs or alcohol) may not be a factor, the high incidence of assaults during late evening and early morning hours suggests that many disputes arise during, or because of, some leisure-time pursuit. Investigators must seek out the details of the dispute in assault cases to cast some light on the reason for the attack and the roles of both the victim and the assailant.

Sometimes in the preliminary investigation of an assault case the investigating police charge both participants with assault or **disorderly conduct**. Responding police often charge the apparent victim (the one most seriously injured) with **disturbing the peace** until it can be ascertained whether the victim was responsible for the attack upon himself or herself.

Data in assault investigations are usually organized within the following major segments:

1. *The Scene.* Reconstruction of the assault event
2. *Dispute Origin.* Place, time, participants, witnesses
3. *Weapon or Weapons.* Existence or nonexistence, identified with user (attacker, victim), recovered at scene, recovered elsewhere
4. *Negative Evidence.* Whether lawful resistance, victim armed, victim previously in fear of attacker (state of mind)

⑮ *Explain the telltale signs of physical child abuse and how this abuse is inflicted.*

▶ Child Abuse

Child abuse is the intentional and deliberate assault upon a child in which serious bodily injury is inflicted by a parent, foster parent, babysitter, day-care worker, or other person in a nonparental relationship.

Serious bodily injury is a standard that excludes intervention by police in cases involving only minor assaults that could be described as corporal punishment incidental to disciplining a child.[21] In most areas of the United States, however, cases of child abuse brought to the attention of police—or discovered by them—are more properly classed as **battered child syndrome**.

Signs of physical abuse, in the absence of a reasonable explanation for the injury, include the following:[22]

1. Damage to the skin (burns, bruises, abrasions, lacerations, or swelling)
2. Brain damage (convulsions, coma, retardation)
3. Bone damage (pain on movement, deformity)
4. Internal injuries (shock, abdominal pain, signs of internal bleeding)

Burn injuries make up about 10 percent of all child abuse cases. Immersion burns result from the child's falling or being placed into a tub or other container of hot liquid. In a **deliberate immersion burn**, the depth of the burn is uniform. The wound borders are very distinct, with sharply defined edges. Little evidence indicates that the child thrashed about during the immersion, which infers that the child was held in place. **Contact burns** are caused by flames or hot solid objects. Cigarette and iron burns are the most frequent types of such injuries. Cigarette burns on a child's back or buttocks are unlikely to have been caused by walking into a lighted cigarette and are more suspect than burns to the face. Accidental burns are usually more shallow, irregular, and less well defined than deliberate burns. Multiple cigarette burns are distinctively characteristic of child abuse. Purposely inflicted branding injuries usually mirror the objects that caused the burn, such as cigarette lighters and curling irons, and are much deeper than the superficial and random burns caused by accidentally touching these objects.[23]

Shaken baby syndrome occurs primarily in children eighteen months of age or younger because their necks lack muscle control and their heads are heavier than the rest of their bodies. Such injuries are caused by a violent, sustained shaking action in which the infant's head is whipped violently forward and backward and hits the chest and shoulders. The baby begins to show symptoms such as seizures or unconsciousness within minutes of the injury being inflicted. The result may be respiratory arrest or death of the child.

A classic medical symptom associated with shaken baby syndrome is **retinal hemorrhage**, which is bleeding in the back of the eyeballs. Simple household falls and tossing a baby in the air in play are not good explanations for retinal hemorrhage. Not enough force is involved in minor falls and play activities to cause retinal hemorrhage or the kinds of severe, life-threatening injuries seen in infants who have been shaken.

Munchausen syndrome is a psychological disorder in which the patient fabricates the symptoms of disease or injury in order to undergo medical tests, hospitalization, or even medical or surgical treatment. In cases of **Munchausen syndrome by proxy**, a parent or caretaker suffering from this disorder attempts to bring medical attention to themselves by injuring or inducing illness in their children. Common occurrences in these cases include the following: the child experiences seizures or respiratory arrest only when the caretaker is there—never in the presence of a neutral third party; while in the hospital, the caretaker turns off the life-support equipment, causing the child to stop breathing, and then turns the equipment back on and summons help; or the caretaker induces illness by introducing a mild irritant or poison into the child's body.

Sudden infant death syndrome (SIDS) is not a positive finding; rather, it is a diagnosis made when no other medical explanation can account for the abrupt death of an apparently healthy infant. SIDS rarely occurs in infants older than seven months and almost never is an appropriate finding for a child older than twelve months. Before SIDS can be ruled the cause of death, the investigator must ensure that every other possible medical explanation has been explored and that no evidence points to any other natural or accidental cause for the child's death. An investigator's suspicions should be aroused when multiple alleged SIDS deaths have occurred under the custody of the same parent or caretaker.[24]

When child abuse is suspected, the assigned investigator should take the child to a local hospital for examination by a physician. This examination and the physician's report will indicate the nature of the injuries and some age dating, but the reporting physician may be reluctant to diagnose the case as child abuse.

Factors likely to influence physicians to link discovered injuries in a child with child abuse include the following:

1. Delays in seeking medical care
2. Injuries not reported by parent or guardian
3. Bruises or broken bones in an infant
4. Age dating of bruises indicating that they were sustained at different times (Figure 8-2)
5. Characteristic wraparound bruises caused by whipping with a belt, rope, or electrical cord
6. Discrepancies in the story of a parent or guardian as to how the injuries happened: described circumstances inconsistent with the nature of the injuries

When the report of child abuse originates in a hospital, the examining physician may have been alerted by one or more of these preceding factors or simply because the parent or guardian bringing the child to the hospital can be classified as a "hospital shopper" for bringing the child to a hospital outside his or her own community when a local hospital was readily available.

At this time, the investigator must make a decision as to whether or not to take the child victim into protective custody. The action taken should be in the best interest of the child. A person in the home environment of a child being a suspect in the abuse is adequate cause to remove the child from this environment. (It also warrants action as to other children in the same household, if they have been abused or may be the subject of abuse.)

During the initial contact with a child victim, while present in the hospital or following the physician's examination, the investigator must gather what facts he or she can from the child. This may be difficult when the child is very young (two to four years old) or the child has been

Determining the Age of a Bruise by Its Color	
Color of Bruise	**Age of Bruise**
Red (swollen, tender)	0–2 days
Blue, purple	2–5 days
Green	5–7 days
Yellow	7–10 days
Brown	10–14 days
No further evidence of bruising	2–4 weeks

FIGURE 8-2 Age Dating of Bruises. From U.S. Department of Justice, Office of Justice Programs, Office of Juvenile Justice and Delinquency Prevention, *Recognizing When a Child's Injury or Illness Is Caused by Abuse* (Washington, DC: U.S. Department of Justice, Office of Justice Programs, Office of Juvenile Justice and Delinquency Prevention, 2002), 5.

instructed by the person responsible for the injury either not to talk to anyone about how it happened or to repeat a false story. Once a child realizes that the investigator is truly interested in finding out the truth, the details of the assault are usually forthcoming.

The when, where, and what happened factors in these cases may cover a broad time period, several different locations, and different assaults. Once these factors have been correlated, the investigator can determine if a crime was committed, what crime, and the person or persons responsible for it.

CASE STUDY

AUTOPSY SURGEON

The witness, a physician, has been qualified at the beginning of her testimony, which has just ended the direct examination on how long the victim lived after being stabbed.

Direct-Examination Prosecutor

Q. Doctor, can you tell us what then would in your opinion be the maximum time that it could have been?

A. Well, he could not have lived an hour, I am sure, but all outside limits—I mean it could possibly be, but in my opinion it would be less than that.

Q. Less than an hour?

A. Oh, yes.

Cross-Examination Defense Attorney

Q. How long did the autopsy take?

A. About an hour and a half.

Q. Was that consistent work, or were there lapse times in the hour and a half?

A. It was consistent work going over the body, yes, sir.

Q. What did your autopsy consist of, Doctor?

A. External examination of the body.

Q. As to the external examination of the body, would you tell us what that consisted of?

A. Examining the wounds, examining the depth of the wounds, examining the positions of the wounds.

Q. You examined those by probes?

A. Yes, sir.

Q. How long did that part of your examination last, your external examination?

A. Approximately thirty minutes.

Q. How many actual—how many wounds actually penetrated into and through the lung wall into what you call "where the air would be in the lung"?

A. There were nine of them.

(continued)

Q. All nine penetrated actually?

A. Yes, sir.

Q. Were those large wounds, sir?

A. They were approximately three-eighths of an inch—approximately three-eighths of an inch in width. None greater. They were still of the stab-wound type.

Q. There were some less?

A. Yes, sir, there were. The more distant ones, there were two that were approximately a quarter of an inch. But there were nine little wounds going right down in this medial border of the lung, and each of them would have been enough to let some air into the chest cavity.

Q. Would that depend upon the position the person was in? Would that at all be a factor?

A. I don't think position would have so much—

Q. Well, would the position tend to either close or open the wounds?

A. You mean when he was standing up or lying down?

Q. Not only lying down—or curled up, or any other position.

A. I don't think position would have so much to do as possibly activity from breathing, and activity—muscular activity.

Q. But as you move, and your chest cavity moves, don't your internal organs also tend to move or contract?

A. Well, see, your lungs—when you breathe, your lungs contract and expand, the diaphragm comes up and your chest muscles contract, and there is a pumping action, like a bellows on the lung. Now, a lung that is punctured, and a lung cavity where the—instead of being a vacuum, has atmospheric air in it, and where there is a loss of blood, a rush of blood into it, that lung just contracts right down.

Q. Let's get back now to your external examination in the detail that we started with before we got off on this track—which took half an hour. Your external examination, you probed, you say, to determine the depth of the wounds, right?

A. Yes, sir.

Q. Also, Doctor, what other examinations did you make with your external examination?

A. Looking for other wounds, looking for fractures, looking for signs of trauma, and the general configuration of the body, and looking into the mouth and checking the eyes, and I was looking for any extraneous marks or anything that would give me any more of a clue as to the cause of this man's death.

Q. Did you find any except the puncture wounds and the two marks on the neck?

A. No, sir, I did not.

Q. There were no other signs of trauma?

A. No, sir.

Q. By "trauma" you mean a blow of some kind?

A. Yes, blows, bruises, any other types of mark that would, you know, have a bearing on the death of this individual.

Q. I presume you examined very closely for those kind of things.

A. Yes.

Q. You gave an opinion as to the time between the injury and death. What factors are involved to determine that particular thing?

A. The factors involved, of course, are the wounds, the number of wounds.

Q. How do you mean the wounds? That is rather a general thing.

A. Let me put it under classification of wounds, then your subheading of that would have the number of wounds, number two under that you would have the size of the wounds, number three you would have the location of the wounds, and number four you would have to figure the rate of bleeding. Then there are variable factors under that: there would come blood pressure, coagulability of the blood. That is about all, I believe, under those factors.

Q. All right, any other factors?

A. I believe that would cover just about everything, I mean when you figure time of death.

Q. Are there any others? You say just about all of them, and are there any other factors that would be important?

A. Not that I think of extemporaneously here.

Q. On what facts do you base your opinion?

A. On the above.

Q. Well, that is pretty general. Would you detail that for us, please?

(continued)

A. All right, and in doing that, of course, I would have to describe the wounds again.

Q. What I want is your detailed basis for your opinion.

A. The detailed basis of the opinion would be a description of the wounds as just described. First of all, I believe I described an incised wound, four inches long in the neck going through the skin and superficial fascia of the neck.

Q. Did that have something to do with the time of death, that particular wound?

A. Yes, it would have something to do with bleeding.

Q. All right, go ahead.

A. I would then take into consideration the wounds on the rest of the body, namely, the extremities, which, as I said before, were supplementary and contributing factors of death but not actual causes of death. Then I would take into consideration the stab wounds of the chest. And I would take into consideration the multiplicity of those wounds, their location, nine in number. Relatively an educated guess from what I have seen before, and what I know about medicine, yes.

Q. But it still would be a guess, wouldn't it?

A. Yes, sir.

CHAPTER REVIEW

Key Terms

Review Questions

1. The major method of detecting murder is the postmortem examination of the victim. These examinations, known as autopsies, are conducted by what type of physician?
   a. cardiologist
   b. pathologist
   c. neurologist
   d. forensic physician

2. The cooling of the body after death is a fairly constant process and can be used to establish the time of death. This cooling process is known as:
   a. Algor mortis
   b. Rigor mortis
   c. Autolysis
   d. Lividity

3. Biochemical changes in the body that occur after death produce a stiffening of the muscles known as:
   a. Algor mortis
   b. Rigor mortis
   c. Autolysis
   d. Lividity

4. As a result of gravity, when the blood stops circulating, it begins to settle to the lowest portion of the body. This pooling of blood is permanent and is useful in determining a change of position of the body after death. This process is known as:
   a. Algor mortis
   b. Rigor mortis
   c. Autolysis
   d. Lividity

5. After death a chemical breakdown begins that results in the softening and liquefaction of the body tissue. This process is useful in determining the time of death and is known as:
   a. Algor mortis
   b. Rigor mortis
   c. Autolysis
   d. Lividity

6. The removal of a deceased person's body from its burial place so that a medicolegal examination can be conducted to disclose the presence of previously unknown or improperly identified injuries or reveal the presence of poison or another noxious substance is known as:
   a. Autopsy
   b. Antemortem examination
   c. Postmortem examination
   d. Exhumation

7. The homicide or killing of four or more victims during a single event, usually at one location, is the definition of what type of multicide?
   a. Mass murder
   b. Spree murder
   c. Serial murder
   d. Hedonistic murder

8. The homicide or killing of two or more victims as a result of separate murders when an individual, acting alone or with another, commits multiple homicides during a period of time, with time breaks between each murder is known as:
   a. Mass murder
   b. Spree murder
   c. Serial murder
   d. Hedonistic murder

9. The killing of three or more persons within a relatively short time frame is known as what type of multicide?
   a. Mass murder
   b. Spree murder
   c. Serial murder
   d. Hedonistic murder

10. Parents or caretakers who attempt to bring medical attention to themselves by injuring or inducing illness in their children suffer from the psychological disorder known as:
    a. Sudden infant death syndrome
    b. Munchausen syndrome
    c. Munchausen syndrome by proxy
    d. Battered child syndrome

See Appendix D *for the correct answers.*

Application Exercise

One morning a jogger running through a secluded section of a large city park discovers the skeletal remains of a female. Upon your arrival at the scene you discover that this may be a homicide victim as there appears to be the remains of foreign material in the victim's mouth and that her hands are bound behind her back. In all murder investigations the identification of the victim is an important basic investigative lead. What procedures would you implement to the identity this victim? How would you determine where the information that is required to establish the victim's identity is being held?

Discussion Questions

1. Define a criminal homicide.
2. What is the role of the medical examiner (autopsy surgeon) in evaluating suspicious deaths?
3. List and describe the common patterns in criminal homicides. What patterns in criminal homicide are often related?
4. What are the possible routes (techniques) for identifying victims in suspicious deaths?
5. Why is the determination of the time of death important in the investigation of criminal homicide?
6. What procedures should be followed to protect the integrity of an autopsy in exhumation cases?
7. List five major segments of the on-the-scene phase of a criminal homicide investigation.
8. What are the similarities and differences between the investigation of criminal homicides and the investigation of criminal assaults?
9. How can a pattern of serial murders be established? Why are they difficult to close out with an arrest?
10. What circumstances are likely to indicate physical child abuse?
11. What is the goal of cross-examination in the case study?
12. The time of death is vital to this case study. Why?

Related Websites

To view homicide trends in the United States visit the Bureau of Justice Statistics at www.ojp.usdoj.gov/bjs/homicide/homtrnd.htm.

For information regarding homicide in the workplace, see www.cdc.gov/niosh/topics/violence.

Researching serial murderers? If so, you might want to take a look at *Court TV's* crime library at www.crimelibrary.com.

Notes

1. www.fbi.gov./about-us/cjis/ucr/crime-in-the-u.s./2012.
2. William F. Kessler and Paul B. Weston, *The Detection of Murder* (New York: Arco Publishing, 1961), 44–47.
3. Lowell J. Levine, "Forensic Odontology Today: A New Forensic Science," *FBI Law Enforcement Bulletin* XLI, no. 8 (August 1972): 6–9, 26–28.
4. T. D. Stewart, "What the Bones Tell Today," *FBI Law Enforcement Bulletin* XLI, no. 2 (February 1972): 16–20, 30–31.
5. Kessler and Weston, *The Detection of Murder,* 1–9.
6. Larry Miller, et al., *Human Evidence in Criminal Justice* (Cincinnati, OH: Anderson Publishing, 1983), 115–146.
7. Ayn Embar-Seddon and Allan Pass, *Forensics!* (Upper Saddle River, NJ: Prentice Hall, 2009), 192.
8. Edward A. Dieckmann, Sr., *Practical Homicide Investigation* (Springfield, IL: Charles C Thomas, 1901), 23–25.
9. Barry A. J. Fisher, *Techniques of Crime Scene Investigation* (New York: CRC Press, 2000), 445–450.
10. Donald John Geise, *The Carol Thompson Murder Case* (New York: Scope Reports, 1969), 5–20, 38–50.
11. Vernon J. Geberth, *Practical Homicide Investigation: Tactics, Procedures, and Forensic Techniques* (New York: CRC Press, 1996), 849.
12. Eric W. Hickey, *Serial Murderers and Their Victims* (Pacific Grove, CA: Brooks/Cole Publishing, 1991), 5.
13. Ronald M. Holmes and Stephen T. Holmes, *Mass Murder in the United States* (Upper Saddle River, NJ: Prentice Hall, 2001), 3.
14. Geberth, *Practical Homicide Investigation,* 348.
15. Ronald M. Holmes and Stephen T. Holmes, *Profiling Violent Crimes,* 2nd ed. (Thousand Oaks, CA: Sage Publications, 1996), 63–67.
16. Geberth, *Practical Homicide Investigation,* 419–421.
17. James B. Howleit, Kenneth A. Hanflang, and Robert K. Ressler, "The Violent Criminal Apprehension Program—VICAP: A Progress Report," *FBI Law Enforcement Bulletin* LV, no. 12 (December 1986): 14–22.
18. www.leb.fbi.gov/2013/april/iafia-identifies-suspect-from-1978-murder-case.
19. www.lawofficer.com/article/investigatio/cold-case-homicides.
20. R. M. Holmes, "Stalking in America: Types and Methods of Criminal Stalkers," *Contemporary Criminal Justice* 8, no. 4 (December 1993): 318–326.
21. Joseph Goldstein, Anna Freud, and Albert J. Solnit, *Before the Best Interests of the Child* (New York: The Free Press—Macmillan Publishing Company, 1979), 72–77.
22. California Department of Justice, *Child Abuse Prevention Handbook* (Sacramento, CA: California Department of Justice, 1982), 7–9.
23. U.S. Department of Justice, Office of Justice Programs, Office of Juvenile Justice and Delinquency Prevention, *Burn Injuries in Child Abuse: Portable Guides to Investigating Child Abuse* (Washington, DC: U.S. Department of Justice, Office of Justice Programs, Office of Juvenile Justice and Delinquency Prevention, 1997), 1–8.
24. U.S. Department of Justice, Office of Justice Programs, Office of Juvenile Justice and Delinquency Prevention, *Battered Child Syndrome: Investigating Physical Abuse and Homicide* (Washington, DC: U.S. Department of Justice, Office of Justice Programs, Office of Juvenile Justice and Delinquency Prevention, 1996), 1–11.

9 Sexual Assaults

CHAPTER OUTLINE

LEARNING OBJECTIVES

After reading this chapter, you will be able to:

1 Distinguish between forcible rape, date rape, and statutory rape.

2 Describe the steps taken in the initial response to a report of a forcible rape.

3 Explain why a follow-up interview of the victim might be postponed.

4 Define the focus of a follow-up interview of witnesses.

5 Identify and explain the various types of rapists and their personality profile.

6 Describe the evidence that might be obtained from a suspected rapist at the time of arrest.

7 Explain the obstacles involved in keeping the victim's cooperation during the case preparation phase of the investigation.

8 Explain how the transfer of physical evidence between the suspect and victim can be used to address the most common defense of mistaken identity as a problem of proof.

9 Define statutory rape.

10 List and explain the various types of nuisance sexual behavior.

11 Explain the various types of child molestation and discuss the molester's motivations.

12 Explain the structure of child molestation cases and how investigators deal with this challenge.

1 *Distinguish between forcible rape, date rape, and statutory rape.*

▶ Rape

Forcible rape is an act of violence. It is not a crime of sexual desire but an act of brutal violence, as in murder with intent and **malice**. It should be investigated in the same manner as criminal homicides and just as thoroughly.

In common law, **rape** was defined as the carnal knowledge (sexual intercourse) of a woman with force and without her consent. Consent induced by fear of violence is not consent, and it is against the woman's will if her male attacker uses an array of physical forces to overcome the victim's mind so she dare not resist. Of necessity, since force or fear is an essential element of the crime of rape, evidence should be developed of the victim's resistance or that her resistance was overcome by force or that she was prevented from resisting by threats to her safety.[1]

The means used to overcome the will of the female victim is of major importance in rape investigations:

1. Force or the threat of the use of force
2. Administration of drugs (including alcoholic beverages)
3. Incapacity to consent (victim's physical or mental condition or age)
4. In the terminology of state legislatures, rape is said to be **aggravated rape** when the rapist is armed with a dangerous weapon, kidnaps the victim, inflicts bodily injury, or is in a position of trust in regard to the victim such as official authority (custody or control) or a familial relationship.

Date rape or **acquaintance rape** is male sexual aggression in which the female half of a twosome is forced to have sexual intercourse. Sexual coercion by dates or acquaintances is really rape. This is not the blitz rape without previous interaction between offender and victim in which the offender immediately threatens or employs force to overcome his victim. In date or acquaintance rape, a previous relationship exists between the offender and the victim but the victim has been forced to have sex without her consent.

The prevalence of forced sex among dates and acquaintances may be increasing, but what is more likely is that victims are now more aware of their basic rights. This so-called simple rape, after years of underreporting, is now being reported for what it is: **forcible rape**.[2]

Although most sexual assault victims are women, a man can also be victimized sexually. However, depending on the jurisdiction, the crimes involved when a man is a victim are usually sodomy, forcible oral copulation, or both, rather than the crime of rape. The investigative protocol is the same, regardless of the victim's gender.

According to the Federal Bureau of Investigation's *Uniform Crime Reports* there were an estimated 84,376 rapes in the United States in 2012. This number was the lowest in the past twenty years. There were 52 cases of forcible rapes per one hundred thousand female inhabitants. Approximately 40 percent of these cases of reported rapes were cleared by arrest or exceptional clearance.[3]

2 *Describe the steps taken in the initial response to a report of a forcible rape.*

Initial Action

The initial task of police upon receipt of a report of a forcible rape is to aid the victim (Figure 9-1). The injured victim may require immediate transportation to a local hospital that provides emergency services; apparent shock—known as **rape trauma syndrome**—should also warrant medical attention. Men and women taking rape reports must do their best to avoid contributing to the victim's mental distress. The professional reporting officer realizes that the person reporting a forcible rape has just been through an emotionally shattering experience and acts accordingly.

Depending on the condition of the victim, the next step is the initial interview in which the victim is asked about the circumstances of the crime and the identity of the rapist. If the victim

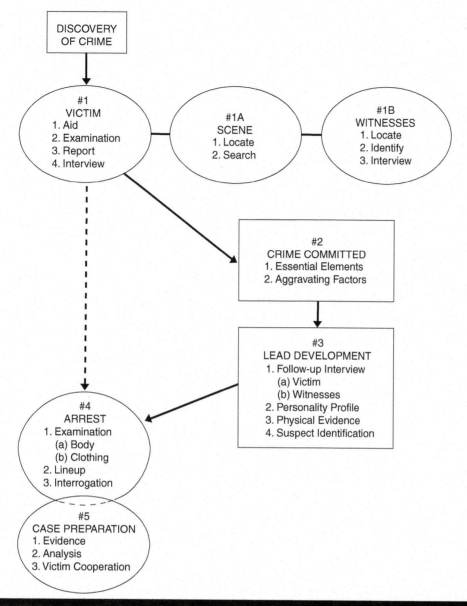

FIGURE 9-1 Investigation of Forcible Sexual Assault.

requires medical attention or is in a state of shock, questioning should be very brief and limited to the facts of the crime and a description of the rapist for a radio-broadcast alarm. If the victim can be questioned, this interview should probe all the circumstances of the crime and the identity of the rapist.

At the conclusion of this interview, the victim should be told about the necessity of a physical examination. The victim should be informed that this is voluntary but that her consent is vital to the collection and preservation of evidence that will reveal and corroborate the acts done to her and contribute to the identification of the rapist.[4]

A medical examination of a forcible rape victim may be conducted as part of the medical treatment of the victim when hospitalized or by special arrangement with the victim. The report of the examining physician becomes part of the record of the case. The report usually contains details about four specific matters:

1. Bodily injuries of the victim
2. Evidence of force in relation to the rapist's sex act

3. Evidence of the completion of the sex act to the penetration required by rape statutes

4. Evidence likely to identify the suspect

The victim of a forcible rape may not know exactly where she was when she was raped, or she may have been in the rapist's car, and the vehicle is not usually available until the rapist is arrested. If a crime scene has been located, however, it must be promptly secured until properly searched.

Correlated with the victim's telling of what happened, who did it, and where it happened is the search for witnesses. Their identity and where they can be located are important at this time in the investigation. What they observed can be secured later.

When the reporting officer believes the circumstances of the attack spell out the elements of forcible rape (lack of consent, use of force or fear, and penetration), the case will be so classified and emphasis placed on identifying and apprehending the rapist.

When the victim identifies the suspect by name or as having been seen before the rape, the emphasis will be on locating this suspect. This is also true when the victim provides information as to the color, design, or license number of a vehicle used by the rapist.

Unless the rapist is promptly identified by information supplied by the victim or witnesses or is arrested in the hot-pursuit phase of the police apprehension process, discovering the identity of the rapist is likely to be the major problem in rape investigations because, as a general rule, informants are not helpful, modus operandi files do not supply any leads unless the rapist is a repeater (serial rape cases), photographs of rape suspects are not usually available, and field interrogation reports are usually nonproductive.

Leads to the identity of an unknown rapist may be developed from the same areas as in criminal homicide investigations:

1. The victim's background

2. Persons in contact with the victim or places visited by her in the hours immediately preceding the rape

3. Weapons found at the scene

4. Persons with knowledge or opportunity—access to the victim and scene of the crime, or at or near the scene at the time of the rape

5. Injured suspects (when victim believes he or she scratched or otherwise injured the rapist)

6. Connect-ups with previous forcible rapes

3 *Explain why a follow-up interview of the victim might be postponed.*

Follow-Up Interview of Victim

If a suspected rapist is arrested before this interview, the focus of the follow-up interview is identification that will be legally significant in court at the trial of the rapist. Inquiries should concern just how the victim identifies the attacker. A lineup in which the suspect is placed among others to be viewed by the victim is warranted. All of the standard legal safeguards protecting this identification from suggestibility or other invalidating factors must be in operation.

When the victim is unable to identify the rapist at this lineup but police believe they have arrested the correct person, concentration is on other evidence of identity that will be compelling and will overcome this failure to positively identify the suspect in a lineup. Even when the victim does identify the rapist in a lineup, this other evidence of identity is important in the event that the lineup identification is attacked by defense counsel at trial.

If the rapist has not been identified, the focus of the interview is on what the victim can remember of the circumstances of the rape that will contribute to the rapist's identification. What did the rapist look like? How was he dressed? Is a vehicle included in the circumstances of this rape? These and related questions should develop the physical characteristics of the rapist, how the rapist was dressed at the time of the rape, and perhaps some vehicle identification. Investigators must probe the victim's recall of events to uncover any particular physical characteristics or article of clothing that is distinctive or unique. Even the most fragmentary description can be helpful.

Arrangements with a police artist or an Identi-Kit specialist may be indicated, with the victim cooperating and approving the final artwork as a reasonable illustration of the rapist.

Computer-based searches are now available in most state motor vehicle bureaus, and "possibles" may be obtained, indicating vehicles matched to a fragment of a license number or a partial description, or both.

Extensive searches for unidentified multiple rapists (serial rapists) by police in several urban jurisdictions have pointed to the need for information on the rapist's behavior. Therefore, investigators should question the victim as to the rapist's approach, how he exerted control of the situation, the sex acts attempted or communed, and whether or not the rapist made any effort to conceal his identity.

Was the approach friendly with sweet talk, or was it brutal and surprising? What was the victim doing during this initial conduct? What had the victim been doing just before this contact? Where had the victim been? Who had the victim seen there? Who might have witnessed this initial approach? These are some of the questions that will give behavioral dimensions to the first contact of the rapist with the victim.

Rapists control their victims by some combination of the following:

1. Verbal activity, particularly threats
2. Display of a weapon
3. Physical force

Threats and orders are the usual verbal activity, but some rapists are animated conversationalists. The essence of what was said and its pace are important aspects of the rapist's behavior.

What weapon was displayed? How does the victim describe it? What did the rapist do with it? The details of weapon display are also part of the rapist's behavior.

The use of physical force and its extent constitute one of the most important factors in defining the behavior of the rapist during the crime. A precise description of the force used should disclose whether it is minimal, excessive, or brutal. Another important factor is the rapist's reaction to resistance by the victim.

A problem area of these follow-up interviews of the rape victim may occur when the investigator seeks details of the sex acts attempted or committed by the rapist. Perhaps the best technique is to inform the victim that these queries are necessary to determine the behavioral pattern of the rapist and, possibly, to connect the rapist with other rapes.

This in-depth interview of the victim may be postponed because of injuries and mental condition of the victim, lack of a suitable private place, or a departmental ruling that such interviews be conducted by specially trained personnel.[5]

 Define the focus of a follow-up interview of witnesses.

Follow-Up Interviews of Witnesses

The police officer accepting the report of a forcible rape has the duty of securing the names and addresses of possible witnesses and, if time permits, of briefly interviewing them to know as to what they might have observed. Then, when the scene of the crime is located and the time of occurrence firmly fixed, investigators may interview or reinterview these witnesses.

Follow-up interviews of the person to whom the victim reported the rape, or from whom the victim initially sought help following the attack, are mandatory. These persons are primary witnesses to the victim's appearance and condition at the time. Of almost equal importance are witnesses who observed the victim, and possibly the rapist, just before the attack occurred.

Usually, rapists find some area in which they will not be observed when they commit this assault upon their victims. Therefore, investigators are unlikely to find witnesses to a rape. Of course, experienced investigators make every effort to find the chance onlooker who was a witness. Failing in this discovery, investigators depend on those individuals who observed the before and after phases of this crime.

The focus of these follow-up interviews of witnesses is to find evidence supportive or corroborative of the victim's report of the rape.[6]

 5 *Identify and explain the various types of rapists and their personality profile.*

Personality Profile of the Serial Rapist

The victim's description of a rapist's behavior, upon analysis by competent personnel, reflects the personality of the rapist. From data secured in the follow-up interview of the victim, a criminal personality profile may be prepared. These profiles require the services of persons trained in the behavioral sciences who can review the manner in which the rapist behaved and can portray the rapist as a person.[7] Based on the victim's description of the rapist's behavior, as well as the results of personal interviews with convicted rapists, three major types of male rapists have emerged.

The Anger Rapist or anger retaliation rapist—commits the crime of rape as a means of expressing and discharging feelings of pent-up anger and rage. The assault is characterized by physical brutality. The rapist uses far more force than is necessary to overpower the victim and achieve sexual penetration. This offender attacks his victim—grabbing her, striking her, knocking her to the ground, then beating her, tearing her clothes, and raping her. He may use a blitz style of attack or a confidence-style approach to gain access to the victim and then launch a sudden, overpowering attack. The anger rapist typically finds little or no sexual gratification in the rape. The act is more of a weapon—a means by which he can defile, degrade, and humiliate his victim. These attacks tend to be of short duration and infrequent, as it takes time for his frustrations and aggravation to reach a volatile point again. In summary, his intent is to hurt and degrade his victim; his weapon is sex and his motive is revenge.

The Power Rapist—uses sex as a means of compensating for underlying feelings of inadequacy and to express issues of mastery, strength, authority, and control over another person. His goal is sexual conquest, and he uses only the amount of force necessary to accomplish his objective. His aim is to capture and control his victim. He often is armed with a weapon for intimidation. His victim may be subjected to repeated assaults over an extended time. This offender tends to find little sexual satisfaction in the rape for it never lives up to his fantasies. The amount of force and aggression used in the assault may increase over time as the offender becomes more desperate to achieve that indefinable experience that continues to elude him.[8] Power rapists are of two types:

The Power Reassurance Rapist—is the least violent of all the rapists and the least socially competent, suffering from low self-esteem and feelings of inadequacy. The reason he rapes is to elevate his own self-status. This rapist's self-image is as a loser, and by controlling another person he hopes to make himself feel important, if only temporarily. He uses only enough force to control his victims. He may later contact his victim to inquire about her health as if he is concerned about the ill effects of the rape. He may also be convinced that his victim enjoyed being raped and may promise to return.

The Power Assertive Rapist— rapes to express his virility and personal dominance. He has a sense of superiority simply because he is a man and he rapes because he believes that he is entitled to do so. This rapist is indifferent to the comfort and welfare of his victim—she is at his mercy and she must do what he desires. He is image conscious and tends to be a flashy dresser. He is a regular at singles bars, and he is known as someone who is always trying to pick up women, and he is continually trying to validate his image as being macho.

The Sadistic Rapist—finds the intentional maltreatment of his victim intensely gratifying and takes pleasure in her torment, anguish, distress, helplessness, and suffering. The assault usually involves bondage and torture and frequently has a bizarre or ritualistic quality to it. In extreme cases—those involving sexual homicide—grotesque acts may take place, such as the sexual mutilation of the victim's body or necrophilia. Usually, the victims are strangers who share some common characteristic, such as age, appearance, or occupation. They are symbols of something the sadistic rapist wants to punish or destroy. The assault is deliberate,

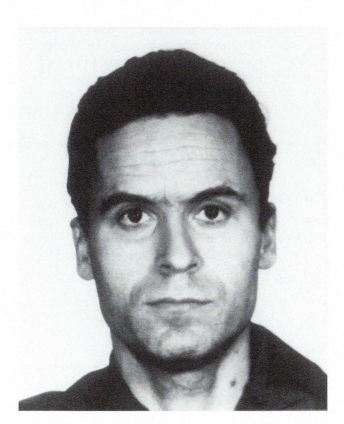

calculated, and preplanned. The offender takes precautions against discovery by wearing a disguise or blindfolding the victim. The victim is stalked, abducted, abused, and sometimes murdered. The sadistic rapist has made a connection between the infliction of pain and sexual gratification, which results in abuse and torture of the victim.

In examining the incidence of these primary patterns of rape, it appears that power rapes are the most prominent. More than half (55 percent) of the cases constitute a power rape, approximately 40 percent are anger rapes, and about 5 percent are sadistic rapes.[9] In essence, the crime of rape is primarily about anger and power and not about sexual desire. While this information may not be considered a basic investigative lead in the identification and apprehension of the rapist, it is useful information for the interrogation of the suspect when he is eventually caught.

 Describe the evidence that might be obtained from a suspected rapist at the time of arrest.

Arrest of the Suspected Rapist

Time is of the essence in arresting suspects in forcible rape cases. If the arrest is made within a reasonable amount of time after the rape, medical personnel at a local hospital should conduct a full body examination of the suspect. Most hospitals with emergency treatment facilities have kits containing the medical equipment and supplies used in rape examinations. The report of the medical personnel conducting the examination becomes part of the total investigation report. Since this report is nontestimonial evidence, no legal problems should be encountered. Delays incidental to securing a court order could result in the destruction of evidence. If the arrestee consents to this examination, appropriate forms should be prepared for his signature.

Examiners search for and report scratches, bites, bruises, and other wounds; they describe scars, moles, and tattoos; and they secure physical evidence associated with the crime of rape. In addition, samples of the suspect's blood, urine, and hair (head and pubic) are taken.[10]

If clothing worn by the suspect at the time of arrest is believed to have been worn at the time of the rape, it should be seized and sent to the forensic science laboratory for examination. If it is apparent that the clothing was not worn at the time of the rape, a prompt search should be instituted for such clothing. A search warrant may be required. All suspect clothing should be promptly forwarded to the forensic science laboratory for examination. Reports of these examinations also become part of the investigation record.

The time of arrest is when investigators search for associative evidence that will corroborate the testimony of the victim by placing the arrestee at the crime scene or in contact with the victim.

 Explain the obstacles involved in keeping the victim's cooperation during the case preparation phase of the investigation.

Case Preparation

Investigators assigned to a forcible rape investigation must develop and hold the victim as a cooperative witness for the prosecution. The reinterviewing of a victim (which is common in these cases), the time gap between arrest and trial, and the procedural safeguards protecting all accused persons dismay most men and women who have been victims of a serious, violent crime and want the criminal punished.

Lack of victim cooperation may seriously complicate case preparation and make it difficult or impossible to develop evidence proving the necessary elements of forcible rape. This aspect of forcible rape investigations, along with the humanitarian aspects of treating a rape victim decently and exhibiting a sincere concern for the victim's well-being during the postrape period, should motivate an investigator to do his or her best to close the case with an arrest and move it to trial as fast as possible.

To overcome the common defenses of a forcible rape charge, the investigator must prepare a case in which the victim is cast as the most truthful witness in the trial. Confirming and compelling evidence must be available at the trial to depict the victim in this truthful witness role.

 Explain how the transfer of physical evidence between the suspect and victim can be used to address the most common defense of mistaken identity as a problem of proof.

Problems of Proof

When a defendant denies any involvement in a rape, the most common defense is mistaken identity plus an alibi for the time of the rape (a claim of being elsewhere at or about the time of the crime).

Identification of a defendant as the rapist is a major problem of proof. Some rapists pull a pillowcase over the victim's head or cover the victim's face with an article of clothing, others wear gloves to avoid leaving conclusive physical evidence, and a few have been known to command their victim "Don't look at me!" In recent years, ski or stocking masks have become popular headgear for blitz rapists. This problem can be overcome by a combination of the victim's identification of the defendant, the testimony about the initial meeting between victim and defendant (the rapist's "approach"), and the transfer of physical evidence linking the defendant to the victim or the scene of the rape.

An investigator must be innovative. In one New York case, the defendant was convicted primarily on a voice lineup. The prosecution proved that this defendant wore a ski mask habitually, and the jurors apparently accepted the idea that the only possible identifier was his voice.

When a suspect admits to sexual intercourse with the victim, the usual defense is that of consent. This is an effective defense when the prosecution is unable to show that the victim's resistance was overcome by an immediate threat or an overwhelming use of force or that the victim did resist and did attempt to flee from the defendant.

In cases involving date or acquaintance rape, the element of consent has been a major problem. The fact of a prior relationship in these cases no longer implies such consent.

Problem-solving assistance is available from the Federal Bureau of Investigation's Investigative Support Unit (ISU), which offers profiles, assessments, and other support and may be able to take the details of the case under investigation and link them with multiple rapes elsewhere. Evidence from these other cases may provide a starting point for case development.[11]

Sperm and blood are the common forms of evidence in rape cases. In fact, these forms of evidence have become such a given that many investigators have developed a mental block with regard to other physical evidence that may be effective in proving guilt or innocence or possibly penetration in rape cases.

9 *Define statutory rape.*

Statutory Rape

Statutory rape involves consensual sex relations between two persons, in which one of the parties is a minor who, by statute, is considered incapable of consenting to a sexual act. The California penal code defines a minor as anyone under the age of 18. Many other state jurisdictions have set the age of majority lower than California.

Both men and women can be arrested and prosecuted for having sexual relations with minors. These crimes usually come to the attention of investigators when one of the parties becomes pregnant, the couple is caught in the act, or their activities are otherwise discovered. The identification of the perpetrator is usually not an issue as the minor usually knows his or her partner. When the identity of the perpetrator is unknown, the lines of inquiry are the same as for a forcible rape investigation. The most common defense in these cases is one of mistake in fact as to the victim's true age at the time of the offense. For this defense to be viable, the minor must have presented himself or herself as being an adult at the time of involvement with the perpetrator.

10 *List and explain the various types of nuisance sexual behavior.*

▶ Nuisance Sexual Behavior

Sexual acts that cause no obvious physical harm to the victim or the practitioner are known as nuisance sexual behaviors. These sexual behaviors include such acts as voyeurism, exhibitionism, obscene callers, and frottage to cite a few examples. These activities are illegal in most jurisdictions; however, they are punished less severely than other sexual crimes. While these acts may be viewed as less serious than other sexual offenses, there is an increasing amount of literature suggesting that many rapists and even sexual serial murderers had a history of nuisance sexual behavior.

Voyeurism—is the act of receiving sexual arousal by looking at private or intimate scenes which contain a sexual component. The voyeur enjoys watching people who are undressing, undressed, or in the act of sexual intercourse. It is rare that the voyeur will attempt to meet or communicate with his victim. Typically the voyeur will be involved in "peeping tom" activity, prowling around neighborhoods at night, and looking in windows. Another activity this person might engage in is the installation of a video camera in a women's restroom.

Exhibitionism—is the intentional and deliberate exposure of a person's genitalia to an unsuspecting stranger. Typically, the exhibitionist, usually a male, will expose himself to a female stranger in a public place, usually on the street, in parks, or in school yards. Exhibitionists tend to be young and many start this activity in their teenage years. The exhibitionist is not interested in sexual intercourse, but exposure. By shocking his female victim, the exhibitionist reinforces the sense of power he needs for personal fulfillment. The reaction of the victim is important; if the victim is shocked or frightened, the exhibitionist experiences sexual excitement.

Scatophilia—is the erotic gratification gained from the telephone conversation between the caller and the victim rather than from any form of sexual contact. Like the exhibitionist, the obscene phone caller wants his victim on the other end of the phone to be shocked, disgusted, or even horrified by his demeanor or words. The obscene phone caller is dependent on the reaction of the victim for erotic arousal. The obscene phone caller is more aggressive but more distant than the exhibitionist. The obscene caller typically makes his calls by dialing random phone numbers, and he seldom makes personal contact with the people he has called.

Frottage—is the realization of sexual gratification from rubbing against certain body parts of another person. The victim is usually a stranger and the activity occurs in a crowded but public place, such as a shopping center, or elevator. The frotteur experiences fantasies that are accompanied by strong irresistible urges to touch another person. The frotteur typically rubs his genitals against his victim's thighs or buttocks or fondles her genitalia or breasts. Usually the persons engaged in this activity are young, and most of the activity occurs when the offender is between the ages of fifteen and twenty-five.[12]

⑪ *Explain the various types of child molestation and discuss the molester's motivations.*

▶ Child Sexual Abuse

When children are the victims of criminal activity, they must be treated as persons to be helped (similar to victims of forcible rape). The shock of being a crime victim, particularly when it involves sex acts, is heightened by police inquiry into the circumstances of the crime. Investigators must promptly recognize that the child victim may require medical attention for possible injuries and for the emotional shock of such a crime.

Investigators serve as the community's agent in redressing the harm done to the child victims of crime. The role of investigators in cases involving child abuse, sexual exploitation, or abduction is common to all investigations: (1) reconstruct the event or events; (2) determine if a crime has been committed and, if so, what crime; (3) identify the person or persons responsible; and (4) take appropriate action. The investigator's role is not that of medical practitioner, social worker, counselor, or psychologist. The investigator does, however, have the responsibility to make referrals to such professionals whenever the investigation discloses that the child victim requires such help.

Incest

A person commits the crime of **incest** when he or she has sexual intercourse with a person known to be within the relationship of parent/child, brother/sister, uncle/aunt, or nephew/niece. Most state laws use a broad definition of incest: any sexual contact between blood-related family members who are not permitted such behavior by social norms.

So-called **psychological incest** is sexual activity between a child and a stepparent, foster parent, or a live-in boyfriend of the child's mother. It also includes such nonrelated family members as stepbrothers and stepuncles.[13] This degrading form of child sexual abuse should be investigated along the same lines as physical child abuse: fact gathering must include when, where, and what happened; the identity of the adult involved; and the adult's family relationship to the victim.

Some important validations of the fact that incest has been committed include these:[14]

1. The acts done were continuing and progressive.
2. The child's story of sexual abuse gives explicit detail in his or her own words.
3. Secrecy was encouraged, and the victim was pressured to keep silent (through gifts, threats, family disgrace).
4. The victim retracts the accusation due to familial pressure.

Child victims should be transported to a hospital for an examination similar to that conducted in cases of forcible rape. A similar examination of the suspect at the time of arrest may be warranted. Both examinations are oriented to discovering and collecting evidence supportive of the victim's story of the sexual abuse.

Pedophilia

A **pedophile** is someone who "loves" children, but this love of children—**pedophilia**—is a sexual interest that ranges from fondling to mutilation and murder. Two types of pedophiles are recognized: the situational and the preferential child molester.

Of the two, the **situational child molester** has fewer victims. This type of molester does not have a true sexual interest in children but will experiment with them when the opportunity presents itself. Following are the three types of situational child molesters:

The **regressed child molester** experiences a situational occurrence that impels this pedophile to turn to children as a temporary, not permanent, object for sexual gratification. This molester turns to children as substitute sexual partners in response to something that has occurred in the molester's life that challenges his or her self-image and results in poor self-esteem. Normally this molester would be involved with adults in normal relationships.

The **morally indiscriminate child molester** is an abuser of all available persons; children are just another category of victim. This offender has a basic motivation toward sexual experimentation and is willing to try anything; nothing is taboo for this offender.

The **naïve or inadequate child molester** includes those persons who are suffering from some form of mental disorder that renders them unable to make the distinction between right and wrong, including sexual practices with children. This type of offender does not physically harm the child and is more likely to experiment with children with sexual practices that include holding, fondling, kissing, and so forth but not sexual activity.

The **preferential child molester** views children more intensely as providers of sexual pleasure. This group prefers children as sexual partners and is the true pedophile. The preferential child molester prefers children over adults as providers of sexual satisfaction. This person's interest in children is persistent and compulsive. A large number of pedophiles can be classified as preferential child molesters, and these offenders are the most likely type to be very dangerous to children. Two types of offenders fall under this category:

The **fixated child molester** is often childlike in lifestyle and behaviors. This offender selects children as sexual objects because they are less demanding, more easily dominated, and less critical. The fixated offender is not interested in physically harming the child but rather loves children and does not want to harm them. Young boys are the preferred sexual target of this offender.

The **sadistic child molester** has made a vital connection between sexual gratification and personal violence. Typically, the child will be a stranger, and the offender may stalk the child rather than use any form of seduction. This offender will often abduct a child from places where children gather, such as playgrounds, schools, and shopping centers. This type of pedophile has no "love" for the child victim and is interested only in causing harm and death to a vulnerable victim compared to whom the offender feels great superiority.[15]

Diligent inquiry will disclose a network of other incidents, victims, and pedophiles. This **mushroom factor** links activity likely to identify a previously unknown child molester. Evidence available upon the arrest of a suspect (address book, identity of friends and associates) will often disclose the full details of a network of pedophiles and their victims. Common to this organization of pedophiles and child victims are registered sex offenders.[16]

Victims are good sources of information about pedophile networks, particularly those boys or girls who have participated in this activity voluntarily either because of their friendship with the molester or because they were paid for their services. Teenage runaways of both sexes have admitted to this type of prostitution as a survival technique in a hostile environment.

Many molesters operate in their own home or business neighborhoods, sometimes using one victim to recruit others in the age group of the molester's sexual preference. Others gain access to victims by seeking leadership positions in church or community child-centered programs. The mushroom factor in these cases takes little more than simple queries to develop: who are the victim's friends in the neighborhood, and what children's group is involved?

Criminals are also using modern technology to prey on innocent child victims. Computers and the Internet have made the predator's job easier. Historically, child predators found their victims in public places where children tend to gather such as schoolyards, playgrounds, and shopping malls. Today, with so many children online, the Internet provides predators a new place to target children. This approach eliminates many of the risks predators faced when making contact in person.[17] Investigators can learn more about this when they make their first arrest, questioning the offenders about their activities. When their acts do not imply guilt, but merely a displayed interest in the area, these offenders are likely to talk—and teach.

Police investigators have a great responsibility to detect and discover child sexual molestations. Detection may originate in a casual inquiry of a runaway child encountered in other police activity as to how they survived on the street, in the investigation of an unrelated crime, or in the willingness of a knowledgeable defendant in a case awaiting trial to reveal significant information as to child molestation in exchange for help with his or her plea negotiations.

A medical examination of the victim in these cases is more than warranted, as is a similar examination of the suspect upon arrest. This examination should be aligned with the reported sexual abuse and be focused on discovering urogenital or anal injuries, pain, irritation, and evidence of a venereal disease or any other illness related to child molestation.

Investigators should send clothing worn by the victim at the time of the attack and clothing belonging to the suspect and seized as evidence at the time of arrest or in the postarrest period to the forensic science (crime) laboratory as physical evidence. It may contain trace evidence linking the suspect to the victim or place of occurrence of the attack, or it may contain evidence of the sexual contact or contacts.

When it happened, where it happened, what happened, and who did it are the classic inquiries likely to uncover the circumstances of these crimes (Figure 9-2). If the collected evidence indicates child sexual molestation, the investigator should act promptly to identify and arrest the adult responsible. The investigator must work hard to link the suspect with other victims and other cases of child sexual abuse from evidence developed at the time of arrest or in the postarrest period.

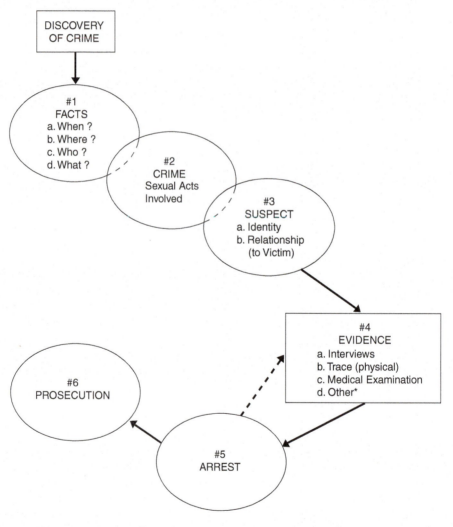

*Includes Network Development–Sex Abuse.

FIGURE 9-2 Investigation of Child Sexual Abuse.

Explain the structure of child molestation cases and how investigators deal with this challenge.

The Child as Victim–Witness

Children may testify in court in a variety of cases, but they are most likely to be classed as key witnesses in child-abuse trials. In such cases, the child is the victim and the only eyewitness. Moreover, in these criminal proceedings, police and court personnel suspect that attention is focused on protecting the constitutional rights of the defendant(s)—not because the rights of the child victim–witness will be disregarded but because the child's competence as a witness will be examined in depth and the testimony given in court will be sharply scrutinized.

Investigators usually operate on the assumption that the child is telling the truth. This behavior is desirable in any first-line agent—parent, teacher, neighbor, physician, or police officer. However, the assigned investigator must work beyond this assumption and critically appraise the story of the child during interviews and postinterview periods when evidence supporting the child's story is sought. Linked to this appraisal is an ongoing demand that the investigator in charge of carrying the case offer an opinion as to the competency of the child victim as a future key witness.

Supporting evidence of a child's story of physical or sexual abuse should develop evidence in total at the probable-cause level, along with basic leads likely to upgrade the case when fully developed. The investigator needs this for his or her decisions during the investigation; the child victim needs such support for his or her testimony in court. In forming an opinion about the child's competency, investigators should be mindful that the child must be observant and articulate, know truth as opposed to lies, and understand that a witness must testify truthfully.

California's McMartin preschool case was long and costly and a revelation to criminal investigators regarding deficiencies in their inquiries. Police investigators attempted to jump-start their investigation by sending a letter to nearly 400 parents of children enrolled in this school. This letter encouraged parents to question their children about any sexual abuse by their teachers. However, many parents promptly mentioned it to one or more of the suspect teachers, alerting them to the threat of an ongoing investigation. The case went on for several years to a very unsatisfactory conclusion: no one convicted, no truth of the accusations proved in court.[18]

Investigators need to learn the how-to of securing information from children. A nonsuggestive interview is likely to be more productive and characterized by a basic integrity. The basic structure of this interview should contain several "don'ts": (1) don't suggest anything to the child—or to his or her parent(s)—or even appear to suggest; (2) don't reveal the allegations of other children involved in the same investigation; (3) don't use dolls of any kind until subsequent interviews, and then only with good reason; and (4) avoid news releases until the crime and its facts are clear and focused.

CASE STUDY

THE EAST AREA RAPIST

The first rapes occurred in the eastern part of the county—hence the name "East Area Rapist. In all, fifty-five rapes were reported to the police in five different counties. However, many more rapes may have been committed but not reported. The rapes started in northern California and eventually ended ten years later in southern California. It is now believed that this rapist made the transition to serial killer and may be responsible for as many as ten murders. Despite investigating and eliminating 5,000 possible suspects and spending in excess of $2.5 million on the investigation,

investigators have no clear picture of the armed man in a ski mask who terrorized his victims.

The rapist cased his victims with eerie diligence, which led some to believe he had military or law enforcement training. Sometimes he would first slip into their homes, swiping a photograph or other small items that barely raised suspicion. He would gather details, like the floor plan, how the garage door operated, how an outside light timer worked, or the names and schedules of occupants. At one home, he removed bullets from a gun tucked under a mattress, then put

(continued)

it back. Then, he would come back during the night, armed with a gun or knife, carrying shoelaces to tie up his victims. He started with women living alone but soon moved to couples.

For up to three hours, he would administer terror. He kept the men from moving by putting dishes on them, threatening to kill if he heard anything break. He would then attack the women, disappear quietly in the house—eating pumpkin pie at one place—then come back again. The victims never knew for sure when he was gone. In later rapes, he grew more violent, more forceful in his threats. He was bold. He would telephone victims after the attack and would seem to know which lines were tapped. At town hall meetings set up by the authorities, as many as 700 people would jam inside. At one meeting, a couple spoke, raised doubts about the rapist's methods, and questioned his existence—and became the next victims: investigators are sure the rapist was in the audience, watching.

In southern California, this offender also invaded quiet neighborhoods. He would sometimes prowl beforehand, then slip in through unlocked windows or doors. He would bring his own cord to tie up victims. He would sexually assault the women before bludgeoning them to death. Because of the similarities in these attacks, investigators, using long-shelved DNA evidence, have connected these crimes. With this new evidence investigators are optimistic that it will lead to an identification of a suspect.

Source: Adapted from M. S. Enkoji, "New Hope in the Hunt for Rapist," *Sacramento Bee,* May 24, 2001.

CHAPTER REVIEW

Key Terms

acquaintance rape *178*
aggravated rape *178*
anger rapist *182*
date rape *178*
exhibitionism *185*
fixated child molester *187*
forcible rape *178*
frottage *186*
incest *186*
malice *178*
morally indiscriminate child
    molester *187*

mushroom factor *187*
naïve or inadequate child
    molester *187*
pedophile *186*
pedophilia *186*
power assertive rapist *182*
power rapist *182*
power reassurance
    rapist *182*
preferential child
    molester *187*
psychological incest *186*

rape *178*
rape trauma
    syndrome *178*
regressed child
    molester *187*
sadistic child molester *187*
sadistic rapist *182*
scatophilia *185*
situational child
    molester *187*
statutory rape *185*
voyeurism *185*

Review Questions

1. A person reporting a forcible sexual assault has just been through an emotionally shattering experience and may be in shock. This emotional shattering experience is known as:
   a. Victim mental distress syndrome
   b. Rape trauma syndrome
   c. Denial
   d. Victim sexual assault distress syndrome

2. What type of rapist is on a mission to get even with women for all the injustices, real or imaginary, he has suffered in his lifetime, using far more force than necessary and exceptional physical brutality?
   a. Anger retaliation rapist
   b. Power assertive rapist

   c. Power reassurance rapist
   d. Sadistic rapist

3. What type of rapist is very image conscious and believes he has a right to rape a woman because he is a man expressing his virility and personal dominance?
   a. Anger retaliation rapist
   b. Power assertive rapist
   c. Power reassurance rapist
   d. Sadistic rapist

4. What type of rapist finds the intentional maltreatment of his victims intensely gratifying and takes pleasure in tormenting his victims?
   a. Anger retaliation rapist
   b. Power assertive rapist

c. Power reassurance rapist
d. Sadistic rapist

5. What type of rapist uses a minimal amount of force and is trying to elevate his own self-status because he believes he is a loser and that controlling another person will make him important?
   a. Anger retaliation rapist
   b. Power assertive rapist
   c. Power reassurance rapist
   d. Sadistic rapist

6. What type of child molester is an abuser of all available adults and children, is basically motivated toward sexual experimentation, and does not have a preference for children?
   a. Morally indiscriminate child molester
   b. Naïve or inadequate child molester
   c. Regressed child molester
   d. Fixated child molester
   e. Sadistic child molester

7. What type of child molester has made the connection between sexual gratification and personal violence, has no love for children, and is only interested in harming or killing the child?
   a. Morally indiscriminate child molester
   b. Naïve or inadequate child molester
   c. Regressed child molester
   d. Fixated child molester
   e. Sadistic child molester

8. What type of child molester typically has normal relationships with adults but has experienced a situational occurrence that impels him to turn to children as a temporary object for sexual gratification?
   a. Morally indiscriminate child molester
   b. Naïve or inadequate child molester
   c. Regressed child molester
   d. Fixated child molester
   e. Sadistic child molester

9. What type of child molester includes persons who are suffering from some form of mental disorder that renders them unable to distinguish between right and wrong, including sexual practices with children, and finds children to be nonthreatening, which allows them to feel more in control?
   a. Morally indiscriminate child molester
   b. Naïve or inadequate child molester
   c. Regressed child molester
   d. Fixated child molester
   e. Sadistic child molester

10. What type of child molester is often childlike, selects children as sexual objects because they are less demanding and more easily dominated, is not interested in physically harming the child, truly loves children, and does not want to harm them?
    a. Morally indiscriminate c hild molester
    b. Naïve or inadequate child molester
    c. Regressed child molester
    d. Fixated child molester
    e. Sadistic child molester

See Appendix D for the correct answers.

Application Exercise

As a sexual assault investigator you have been assigned to interview a rape victim. During the night an unknown subject entered her apartment through an unlocked patio door and severely beat her and sexually assaulted her. As a male investigator what would your strategy be for developing rapport with the victim and obtaining her cooperation? As a female investigator would your strategy be any different from that of your male counterpart? Also develop a broad line of questioning designed to highlight the personality profile of the rapist.

Discussion Questions

1. What is the major responsibility of the first police officers at the scene of a forcible rape?
2. What are the aggravating factors in these cases?
3. Is the medical examination of a forcible rape victim necessary? When should it be conducted? What is its scope?
4. Outline the major factors to be covered by investigators during the follow-up interview of a victim.
5. What is the focus of the follow-up interview of a witness in forcible rape cases?
6. Does the previous relationship between victim and rapist in date rapes create a problem for the police–prosecutor team?
7. Describe network development in child sexual abuse cases.
8. Can police detect child sexual abuse? How?
9. How do child molesters use computers to find potential victims?
10. Which type of rapist is discussed in the case study? Explain and support your decision.

Related Websites

For information regarding what is a sexual assault and preventive measures, contact www.sao.co.st-clair.il.us/sexalt.asp.

To learn more about sexual assaults investigations and statistics related to this subject, contact the Rape Abuse and Incest National Network at their website www.rainn.org.

Notes

1. Paul B. Weston and Kenneth M. Wells, *Criminal Law* (Santa Monica, CA: Goodyear Publishing, 1978), 253–262.
2. Susan Estrich, *Real Rape* (Cambridge, MA: Harvard University Press, 1987), 7–26.
3. http://www.fbi.gov/about-us/cjis/crime-in-theu.s./2012.
4. Joseph A. Zeccardi and Diana Dickerman, "Medical Exam in the Live Sexual Assault Victim," in *Practical Aspects of Rape Investigation—A Multidisciplinary Approach,* eds. Robert R. Hazelwood and Ann Wolbert Burgess (New York: Elsevier Science Publishing, 1987), 315–325.
5. Lisa Brodyaga, et al., *Rape and Its Victims: A Report for Citizens, Health Facilities, and Criminal Justice Agencies* (Washington, DC: U.S. Department of Justice, Law Enforcement Assistance Administration, 1975), 37–42.
6. Jerry D. Moody and Vicki Ellen Hayes, "Responsible Reporting: The Initial Step," in *Rape and Sexual Assault: Management and Intervention,* ed. Carmen Germaine Warner (Rockville, MD: Aspen Systems Corp., 1980), 27–45.
7. Robert R. Hazelwood, "The Behavior-Oriented Interview of Rape Victims: The Key to Profiling," *FBI Law Enforcement Bulletin* LII, no. 9 (September 1983): 8–15.
8. Ronald H. Holmes and Stephen T. Holmes, *Profiling Violent Crimes: An Investigative Tool,* 3rd ed. (Thousand Oaks, CA: Sage Publications, 2002), 145–152.
9. A. Nicholas Groth, *Men Who Rape: The Psychology of the Offender* (New York: Plenum Press, 1979), 12–59.
10. Richard Braen, "Examination of the Accused: The Heterosexual and Homosexual Rapists," *Rape and Sexual Assault: Management and Intervention,* ed. Carmen Germaine Warner (Rockville, MD: Aspen Systems Corp., 1980), 85–91.
11. C. R. Van Zandt and S. E. Ether, "Real Silence of the Lambs," *Police Chief* 61, no. 4 (April 1994): 45–52.
12. Stephen T. Holmes and Ronald M. Holmes, *Sex Crimes, Patterns and Behavior,* 2nd ed. (Thousand Oaks, CA: Sage Publications, 2002), 55–75.
13. Robert J. Barry, "Incest: The Last Taboo," *FBI Law Enforcement Bulletin* LIII, no. 1 (January 1984): 2–9.
14. Marvin R. Janssen, "Incest: Exploitive Child Abuse," *The Police Chief* LI, no. 2 (February 1984): 46–47.
15. Holmes and Holmes, *Profiling Violent Crimes,* 161–171.
16. Vincent DeFrancis, *Protecting the Child Victim of Sex Crimes Committed by Adults* (Denver, CO: The American Humane Association, 1969), 1–2.
17. U.S. Department of Justice, Office of Justice Programs, Office for Victims of Crime, *Internet Crimes Against Children* (Washington, DC: Government Printing Office, 2005), 1.
18. Nancy Walker Perry and Lawrence S. Wrightman, *The Child Witness: Legal Issues and Dilemmas* (Newbury Park, CA: Sage Publications, 1991), 2–10.

10 Missing and Exploited Persons

LEARNING OBJECTIVES

After reading this chapter, you will be able to:

1. *Explain the motivations of a person involved in the abduction of an infant.*

2. *Define a family abduction and the reasons for these abductions.*

3. *Discuss the reasons why a nonfamily abduction is the most serious missing person case and explain which offenders might be responsible for the abduction.*

4. *Explain who might possess the most information regarding a missing teenager and the reasons for the disappearance.*

5. *Explain why most police agencies require a waiting period before taking a missing persons report on a missing adult.*

6. *Describe the investigative steps taken in response to a report of a missing person.*

7. *Define human trafficking and explain the various coerced activities these exploited persons are subjected to.*

8. *List the investigative leads indicative of human trafficking.*

► Missing Persons

Reports of missing persons are one of the more common types of investigations conducted by law enforcement agencies. The response to these cases is guided by a number of factors such as the missing person's age, risk factors that might apply to the missing person, and suspicious circumstances that are involved in the disappearance. Frequently, these investigations are hampered by the lack of information concerning suspicious circumstances at the onset of the investigation. For example, is a child lost or has the child been abducted? The answer to this question is not always obvious as an abductor's goal is to abduct a child without being seen. Therefore, information that affects the true nature of the investigation is not readily apparent at a critical stage of the investigation.

1 *Explain the motivations of a person involved in the abduction of an infant.*

Abducted Infants

The abduction of a newborn or infant, up to the age of six months, occurs rather infrequently. However, when a newborn or infant is abducted it is considered a major crime requiring full investigative effort. Typically the offender is a woman of child bearing age who is trying to replace an infant she recently lost or she may want to have a child but is unable to conceive or carry a child of her own. The infant may also be used as a means to maintain a relationship with the offender's "significant other."

These abductions are usually well planned as the offender must either find another person's infant to take or become familiar with a health care facility that cares for newborns. Often the offender will impersonate a nurse or other staff member and take the child away from the mother for some tests or other required activity and the offender then leaves the facility with the child. As medical facilities have made it more difficult to abduct an infant due to increased security procedures more than half of these abductions now occur outside a medical facility. The shift in location of these abductions has resulted in more direct confrontations and the risk of harm to the mother or guardian and range from the display of a weapon to killing.

It is not unusual for the offender to make prior contact with the victim's mother prior to the abduction. The suspect may contact the victim while she is in the hospital or during the pregnancy and pose as a staff member or volunteer. The offender may answer an ad to become a babysitter or nanny for the child, or be a casual acquaintance of some sort. These offenders are extremely adept at deceiving others, especially those they have interaction with on a daily basis. They have to convince others that they were pregnant when they were not or this "replacement" infant is the same one they gave birth to only a short time before. These women tend to provide good care to the abducted child as most recovered children were found to be in good physical health when found.[1]

2 *Define a family abduction and the reasons for these abductions.*

3 *Discuss the reasons why a nonfamily abduction is the most serious missing person case and explain which offenders might be responsible for the abduction.*

Missing Children

Every year approximately 325,000 children, ages 6 months to 13, are reported missing. These missing children fall within three broad categories: lost or injured, family abductions, and nonfamily abductions.

Anyone who has taken a child to a major event such as to a zoo, carnival, or state fair knows how quickly a child can become lost, blink and they are gone. Children also get injured when they wander away from home and must be taken to the hospital and the family is frantic until the child is located. Fortunately, in most of these cases the lost or injured child is located and they are reunited with their family fairly quickly.

Family abductions occur when one member of the family takes or keeps a child away from another family member in violation of that person's custodial rights. These cases come to the attention of investigators during a domestic disturbance when one family member leaves and takes a child with them; or during a hostage situation where a child is being held in violation of custodial rights; or when a child has not been returned from a visitation. Parents who are in the process of getting a divorce or any other disagreement will often use the children as pawns. Children are used by their parents as tools for retaliation and manipulation against each other.

The immediate concern in these cases is determining the status of the child's welfare. In family abductions the child's welfare should not be a concern unless the person taking the child is unstable and a possible threat to the child. Another concern is the determination of legal guardianship or custody. Parental custody rights are determined by the courts and the parent claiming a violation of those rights should have a valid copy of a child-custody order in their possession. Without a court order most states consider both parents to have equal child-custody rights. Once it is determined that one person is entitled to physical possession of the child and that the child is being kept from that person, a crime has occurred. Every state, as well as the federal government, recognizes family abduction as a crime. Also child custody orders issued in one state are given full faith and credit by the courts in all the other states.

When a family abduction is confirmed the National Crime Information Center (NCIC) should be contacted within two hours and a missing person file initiated on the child. This entry will include the child's biographical information and the circumstances of the abduction. When a vehicle is involved in the abduction, an AMBER alert can be initiated informing the public of the vehicle's identification, suspect information, crime involved, and direction of travel, if known. The media can also assist by broadcasting the missing child's photo and other pertinent information. A family abduction becomes a violation of federal law if the abduction crosses state lines or if the child has been removed from the country. As a violation of federal law the FBI and U.S. Department of State can be involved in the investigation.[2]

Nonfamily abductions occur when a child has been wrongfully taken, through the use of force, persuasion, or threat of harm, by a person who is not related to the family. While these are the least common type of abduction, they are the most serious. The fixated child molester and the sadistic child molester, as discussed in Chapter 9, may be involved in the abduction. Time is critical in this type of abduction as children face the greatest danger during the first few hours after being abducted. Investigators should plan for a worst-case scenario until the facts prove otherwise. Investigators should take a two-prong approach that would include searching for the child while preserving evidence. The primary focus is the recovery of the child and a full agency response is required. Such a response would include search and rescue experts, helicopters, search dogs, volunteers, and mutual aid from neighboring jurisdictions if appropriate.

The first investigators on the scene have the responsibility of gathering information which would substantiate a child abduction and determining any risk factors that may apply to the missing child. These **risk factors** would include the following and apply to all missing person investigations including adults where appropriate.

- Is the child thirteen years of age or younger?
- Is the child thought to be out of the zone of safety for their age and level of development?
- Does the child have any mental or behavioral disabilities?
- Is the child on medication or any illegal substance? Are they drug dependent and is this dependency potentially life-threatening?
- How long has the child been away from home?
- Do the facts in the case indicate a life-threatening situation?
- Is the missing person in the company of someone who is known to be a danger to the missing person's welfare?
- Is the absence of the missing person inconsistent with that person's established patterns of behavior?
- Are there other risk factors or circumstances involved that would be a concern for the missing child's safety?[3]

Explain who might possess the most information regarding a missing teenager and the reasons for the disappearance.

Missing Teenagers

Teenagers, ages 13–17, who voluntarily run away represent the most common missing child case. In the United States over 450,000 teenage runaways are reported each year; some are multiple offenders. While it might be tempting to not take runways seriously, investigators are aware that all missing children, including runaways, are "at-risk." Life on the run is extremely dangerous and the longer a child remains on the run, the greater the chance of falling victim to those who would exploit them.

The initial task of the first investigators on the scene would be to verify that the child is in fact missing. The parent or guardian should be asked to check their answering machine, voice mail, or any other place or person the child may have left a message that they will be arriving home later than expected. Upon confirming that the child is missing the investigator should obtain a recent photo, a DNA sample (hair or toothbrush will do), and complete a missing person report which would include a release of the name of the family dentist and authority for the release of any dental records if needed.

The family members should be interviewed to determine if the child has exhibited any personality changes recently, which might be manifested in changes in clothing or hair styles. Has the child been sneaking out at night ? Have their grades dropped? Have they displayed a need for additional money, could drugs be an issue? Has the child run away before? The child's room should be examined with the permission of the parent or guardian. Of interest would be diaries, notebooks, and letters that might outline the child's reasons for leaving the home. All electronic devices should be examined to determine if the child has met a "friend" on the Internet. The correspondence with this friend should be reviewed, especially with an older person, to determine if the child may have been misled by the intent of this person and that the friendship might lead to a dangerous situation for the child.

Investigators should also interview friends of the missing child. These friends are likely to know more about the missing child and their motivations than the child's own family. These friends may attempt to locate the missing child themselves and when that fails may become more concerned for the missing child's welfare. Investigators should remain in contact with these friends as, with the passage of time, they may be willing to provide information that they initially withheld.

When the child is located, they should be taken to a safe place away from their home and interviewed. The investigator needs to determine why the child ran away. Did they run away to escape sexual or physical abuse at home? If this is the case, then a comprehensive physical examination should be conducted and the appropriate child-protective agency notified. For the investigator it is also important to determine how the child survived on their own. Of particular concern is the commercial sexual exploitation of child. Runaways and throwaways, those children who have been told to leave the home by a parent or guardian, are particularly vulnerable to those involved in the illegal sex trade. Pimps and sex traffickers use psychological manipulation, drugs, violence, or the promise of protection and food and shelter to exploit children for the money they can earn as prostitutes. These tactics ensure that the child will remain loyal or face further victimization at the hands of the sex trafficker.[4]

 Explain why most police agencies require a waiting period before taking a missing persons report on a missing adult.

Missing Adults

Adults, people over the age of 18, are free to leave home whenever they want and they are not required to tell anyone that they are leaving. Adults in great numbers are reported missing each year and the vast majority either return home or call home within a few days. The reasons for these short disappearances are numerous; stress and anxiety, adventure, and love are just a few of the reasons given for a person's disappearance. We have all heard of people who leave their family to get a pack of cigarettes and are never heard from again. As a result of this kind of

behavior most law enforcement agencies require a waiting period before taking a missing persons report on an adult, usually twenty-four—forty-eight hours. The waiting period would be waived if any risk factors apply or there are suspicious circumstances surrounding the disappearance.

As the following case illustrates, the investigation of missing adults can be very misleading at times.

> On Tuesday afternoon Jennifer Wilbanks was reported missing from Duluth, Georgia a suburb of 22,000 people a half-hour northeast of Atlanta. Wilbanks was due to be married in four days at an elaborate wedding which was to include more than 500 guests, 14 bridesmaids and 14 groomsmen. Wilbanks disappeared after going for a jog. She left behind her keys, cellphone and her diamond ring. When she did not return from her jog fears were raised that she had been kidnapped. The ensuing search for Ms. Wilbanks involved local police from several counties, the Georgia Bureau of Investigation, the FBI and over 100 volunteers. The entire city of Duluth was searched as well as the Chattahoochee River. Family and friends who were scheduled to attend the wedding instead posted fliers and searched the woody suburb for any clues to her disappearance.
>
> On Saturday Ms. Wilbanks surfaced in Albuquerque, New Mexico and told police officers that she had been kidnapped. Under questioning by investigators Wilbanks admitted that she had taken a bus from Georgia to Las Vegas then boarded another bus to Albuquerque where she called the police from a nearby 7-Eleven. According to investigators she was concerned about the pending wedding and very nervous about it. She needed some time alone.[5]

6 *Describe the investigative steps taken in response to a report of a missing person.*

▶ Investigative Response

When a law enforcement agency receives a complaint of a missing person, there is usually no clear indication as to whether the person has wandered off or is the victim of foul play. In either case it is critical to get as much information out as soon as possible to patrol officers. The basic facts of the situation, a description of the missing person, and any vehicle or suspect information should be transmitted via police radio even before the first unit arrives on the scene. This information will allow patrol officers to begin searching their assigned areas for the missing person.

Upon arrival at the scene, the investigator must begin the process of interviewing the complainant and any potential witnesses. These interviews should be conducted separately. Did anyone see an abduction occur, is there a vehicle description, if this is a missing child what is the child's age and development stage and what is the child's zone of safety—where are they usually allowed to roam on their own and what risk factors are applicable to this case, are all questions that should be asked. Any new information that is developed during this line of inquiry should be broadcast over the law enforcement channels to keep other officers involved in the search abreast of any developments in the investigation.

Within two hours of receiving the complaint of a missing person the National Crime Information Center should be contacted and a missing person file generated on this person. The NCIC is a resource that will aid other investigators in the United States, Canada, and Mexico to be able to identify the missing person should they be located in their jurisdiction.

Investigators should obtain permission to search the home and any other areas where the missing person could be located. The search would be limited to those areas capable of containing the person being sought. A young child, for instance, may curl up and go to sleep whenever they become tired regardless of where they are at the time. Missing children have been found fast asleep under beds and in closets. This search is only to be conducted by trained investigators as the following case illustrates.

> It was Christmas night when someone sexually assaulted 6-year-old JonBenet Ramsey in her home in Boulder, Colorado. Her assailant silenced her screams by placing duct tape over her mouth, fractured her skull and strangled her with a nylon cord tightened by a wooden handle. The next morning the police received a frantic call from JonBenet's mother saying that her daughter was missing and that she had found a ransom note demanding money for the return of the child. Eight hours after the police arrived on the scene a detective suggested a search should be conducted of the 6,000 square-foot home. The child's father and a friend searched the basement of the home and in one of the rooms found JonBenet's lifeless body. The father removed the tape from the child mouth and carried her upstairs and as a result unwittingly destroyed the crime scene and potential evidence. To date this crime remains unsolved.[6]

In the event the missing person is not located after a search of the home and surrounding area the investigator should expand the search by calling in helicopters and K-9 search dogs. In addition, a neighborhood canvas would be appropriate to question persons who would have viewed any activity during the window of opportunity, from the time the person was last seen and the time they were reported missing. Most police agencies have auxiliary personnel, either volunteers or reserve officers, who can assist with the investigation. Additional personnel can also be pulled from other duties if the agency is of significant size or a call for **mutual aid** can be made, which would bring officers in from adjacent jurisdictions to assist in the investigation.

Investigators should obtain recent photographs of the missing person and copies should be distributed to those involved in the search. Has the missing person been fingerprinted and if so are those prints available? If not, the investigator should secure items recently handled by the missing person. The missing person's DNA should also be collected; items such as a toothbrush or hairbrush will suffice. Investigators should also obtain the name of the missing person's dentist and if a child is missing obtain a parental release of the dental records.

In the case of a child abduction where it is unclear whether the child is victim of a family or nonfamily abduction, the investigator should suggest a polygraph examination for those persons who may be considered suspects in the disappearance. Such an examination, while not admissible in court, is a useful tool in the elimination of possible suspects and can aid in focusing the investigation on the correct lines of inquiry.

Since the media often monitors police radio traffic they no doubt are already aware of the missing person investigation and should be contacted and asked to assist. The media can disseminate the details of the case as well as photos and physical description of the missing person and any possible suspects. The media can also put out the tip-hot-line phone number for use by anyone who has information on the case.

If during the course of the investigation the suspect's vehicle information becomes available, then an AMBER alert should be initiated.[7]

When all immediate investigative leads have been exhausted, the search for the missing person would shift to a prolonged investigative status. Search and command operations would be relocated away from the scene. A thorough review of all reports and interviews would be conducted to obtain clear insights for additional investigative follow-up. Investigators should recanvass the area of disappearance as some individuals having knowledge about the disappearance may not have been available at the time of the original canvass. Parents/guardians and witnesses should be reinterviewed for accuracy and to obtain information that may have been missed during the initial interview. Persons living in the area who may be listed in law enforcement databases as sexual predators, as well as other potential suspects who offered questionable or unsubstantiated alibies at the time of disappearance, should be contacted. What investigative leads were found from the evidence obtained at the scene and what follow-up would be appropriated based on laboratory analysis of this evidence? A missing person investigation remains open until the person is found alive or it has been determined that the person is deceased, at which time the case would become a homicide investigation. Investigators should be mindful that it is possible that a missing person may be found years after being reported missing. Investigators, like parents of missing persons, should never give up hope for a successful conclusion to a missing person's investigation.[8]

❼ *Define human trafficking and explain the various coerced activities these exploited persons are subjected to.*

▶ Exploited Persons

Human trafficking is the modern-day form of slavery—the exploitation of human beings for financial gain. Many victims are forced to work in the commercial sex trade, while others are forced to work as domestic servants, as labor in prison-like factories, or in agricultural field. The defining element of human trafficking depends not on the type of work involved but the use of force, fraud, or coercion used to compel the victim to do the work. The U.S. Congress estimates that as many as 50,000 adults and children are trafficked into this country annually. Many of these victims are lured by traffickers by promise of good working conditions and high pay. Once in this country these victims face extreme physical and mental abuse including rape, torture, starvation, and death threats against the victim and their family members. Victims are isolated and fear what would happen to them or their families if they complained or contacted the police. It is estimated that human trafficking is one of the most profitable organized crime activities and one of the fastest growing crimes.

The Thirteenth Amendment to the U.S. Constitution outlawed involuntary servitude when it was ratified in 1865. Congress again addressed this issue in the year 2000 when the Victims of Trafficking and Violence Protection Act was passed. This legislation makes it a felony to traffic in persons including the unlawful confiscation of victim's documents. Persons convicted under this statute could receive prison sentences of twenty years to life, be required to pay substantial fines, provide full restitution to victims, and be subject to forfeiture of their property. Human trafficking is also illegal by state statute as well.[9]

Trafficking in persons is an umbrella term that covers a variety of coerced activities from forced labor in agricultural fields, sweatshops, suburban mansions, brothels, escort services, bars, and strip clubs.

- **Sex trafficking**—occurs when an adult or child is coerced, forced, or deceived into acts of prostitution or other related sexual activity. An investigation of sex trafficking would include those persons involved in the recruiting, harboring, transporting, or providing persons for the purposes of prostitution. Sex trafficking includes "**debt bondage**," where a person is forced to continue to work as a prostitute to pay off a "debt" purportedly incurred through their transportation, recruitment, and substance all of which must be paid before the person can be freed.

- **Forced labor**—involves the use of force or physical threats, psychological coercion, deception, or other coercive measures to compel someone to work. Migrants are particularly vulnerable to this form of human trafficking and the victim's previous consent to work for the trafficker is irrelevant.

- **Bonded labor**—occurs when a person is working to pay off a debt owed by them or others. In South Asia there are millions of trafficking victims working to pay off their ancestors' debts. Traffickers recruit victims caught in this trap with promises of higher pay in this country.
- **Involuntary domestic servitude**—occurs in a private residence where the victim labors as a domestic laborer, nanny, or any other capacity. These victims are typically immigrants who are isolated, kept in separate living quarters, and their documents seized. These victims are easily exploited because authorities cannot inspect the home as compared to other work sites. Often these people may also be victims of sexual abuse.[10]

Approximately 80 percent of the incidents of human trafficking involved sex trafficking and 10 percent were classified as labor trafficking. The remaining 10 percent involved incidents of purchasing mail-ordered brides and child selling.[11]

⑧ *List the investigative leads indicative of human trafficking.*

▶ Investigative Leads

Human trafficking cannot be established by a single lead but the following may raise an investigative suspicion of human trafficking and are worthy of further inquiry.

- A minor, especially a runaway, involved in commercial sexual activities is being exploited through "survival sex."
- A citizen of another country is not in possession of identifying documents and claims that someone else is holding these documents.
- The person's movement, speech, and activities appear to be monitored or controlled by another person.
- Little or no compensation is paid to a person who works excessive hours.
- The person is reluctant to respond or shows fear when asked about unsafe working conditions.
- The person is unaware of their geographical location.

Home of Ariel Castro where he held three women captive for over ten years.
Source: Tony Dejak/ AP Images

- Workers who are transported to and from labor locations covertly and under controlled conditions.
- Laborers who appear to be suffering from malnutrition or physical abuse.
- Laborers quartered at or near the work site and only allowed to shop at the "company store."
- The work site is surrounded by barbed wire, may have bars on the windows, is surrounded by guards and guard dogs, and has the overall appearance of a guarded compound.
- The work site is self-contained and the workers have no access to telephones.
- Workers living in an area which is an unsuitable living space.[12]

Investigators should keep in mind that victims of human trafficking often do not consider themselves a victim. They are often completely dependent on their traffickers for their basic survival. Victims become isolated and become fearful of the criminal justice system and may be uncooperative when initially contacted by investigators.

CASE STUDY

THE CLEVELAND ABDUCTIONS

Ariel Castro moved to Cleveland, Ohio, as a child. As an adult he was employed as a school bus driver. He bought a home on Seymour Avenue where he lived with his wife and four children. When his wife left him in 1996, he continued to live in the home and maintained what appeared to be a normal lifestyle.

In 2002 Castro offered Michelle Knight, age 20, a ride. She accepted as she knew one of Castro's daughters. He drove her to his home and talked her into joining him inside, where he raped her and kept her captive for the next eleven years. In 2003 he offered sixteen-year-old Amanda Berry a ride home from her job at a fast-food restaurant. Like Knight before her, she knew Castro and his children and accepted his offer. He took her to his home where he sexually assaulted her and kept her captive as well. In 2004 Castro kidnapped fourteen-year-old Gina De Jesus who was a close friend of one of Castro's daughters.

Castro kept the women chained up in his basement and later in an upstairs barricaded bedroom where he repeatedly sexually assaulted them. When one of the women became pregnant, he beat her until she miscarried; this act would be repeated several times over.

While keeping the women captive, Castro maintained a normal lifestyle. Family members and friends visited his home, although not allowed in the basement or in the upstairs bedroom. He went to work regularly and at night he played guitar with a local band. He even attended vigils for one of his victims, Gina De Jesus, and met with members of her family.

On May 6, 2013, while Castro was away, Amanda Berry managed to escape from her chains and leave the home by kicking out the front door. Neighbors rushed to her hysterical cries for help and the police were called. The other women were rescued and on the same day Castro was arrested. Less than three months later Castro pled guilty to 937 charges, ranging from kidnapping and rape to murder of a fetus. He was sentenced to life plus an additional 1,000 years in prison. A little more than a month into serving his sentence he was found hanged in his cell. As a note of finality, his home on Seymour Avenue was torn down shortly thereafter.[13]

CHAPTER REVIEW

Key Terms

bonded labor   *200*
debt bondage   *199*
family abduction   *195*
forced labor   *199*

human trafficking   *199*
involuntary domestic
   servitude   *200*
mutual aid   *198*

nonfamily abduction   *195*
risk factors   *195*
sex trafficking   *199*

Review Questions

1. Approximately how many children, ages 6 months to 13 years, are reported missing annually in the United States?
   a. 125,000
   b. 225,000
   c. 325,000
   d. 425,000

2. What type of abduction is involved when one family member takes or keeps a child away from another family member in violation of that person's court ordered custodial rights?
   a. Newborn abductions
   b. Family abductions
   c. Nonfamily abductions
   d. Teenage runaways

3. Which group of children represents the most common missing person case?
   a. Newborn abductions
   b. Family abductions
   c. Nonfamily abductions
   d. Teenage runaways

4. The fixated child molester and the sadistic child molester are most commonly associated with which type of abduction?
   a. Newborn abductions
   b. Family abductions
   c. Nonfamily abductions
   d. Teenage abductions

5. The least reported, yet the most serious type of abduction, is the
   a. Newborn abductions
   b. Family abductions
   c. Nonfamily abductions
   d. Teenage abductions

6. While investigating a child abduction case the investigator should take a two-prong approach which would include which of the following?
   a. Searching for the child and dealing with mutual aid
   b. Searching for the child and preserving evidence
   c. Preserving evidence and dealing with mutual aid
   d. Searching for the child and dealing with the media

7. Absent any risk factors or suspicious circumstances many law enforcement agencies require a waiting period before taking a missing person report in which type of case?
   a. Missing adults
   b. Family abductions
   c. Nonfamily abductions
   d. Teenage runaways

8. How many adults and children does the U.S. Congress estimate that are victims of human trafficking each year?
   a. 15,000
   b. 25,000
   c. 30,500
   d. 50,000

9. A person who is working to pay off a debt owed by their ancestors is said to be a victim of which type of human trafficking?
   a. Sex trafficking
   b. Forced labor
   c. Bonded labor
   d. Involuntary domestic servitude

10. Which type of human trafficking is by far the most common?
    a. Sex trafficking
    b. Forced labor
    c. Bonded labor
    d. Involuntary domestic servitude

Application Exercise

Consider that you are investigating a case of a missing child, under ten years of age, with behavioral disabilities. What procedures would you use to determine whether you are dealing with a family or nonfamily abduction? What would be the investigative response to a family abduction of this child? Develop an investigative response to a nonfamily abduction of this child.

Discussion Questions

1. In the Cleveland abduction case study which involved both adult and teenage missing persons discuss the steps involved in each of these investigations and contrast any differences due to the victim's ages.

2. In the case study discuss the common link in this case, the fact that all three missing persons knew the suspect and his daughters prior to their abductions. Had investigators known of this common link would it have made a difference?

3. In the Jennifer Wilbanks case explain whether or not you believe that law enforcement agencies involved in the exhaustive search for her should demand restitution for the costs incurred during this investigation.

4. In the case of six-year-old JonBenet Ramsey case explain the impact the family's wealth may have played in the initial response to this missing person case.

5. Outline and explain the "risk factors" that may apply to all missing person cases.

6. Small law enforcement agencies occasionally must deal with a major investigation, such as a missing child case; explain how a small agency would be able to obtain the resources necessary to conduct an exhaustive search for a missing child.

Related Websites

For more information on human trafficking contact the Polaris Project, a nonprofit organization that focuses on ending human trafficking. www.polarisproject.org/about-us/overview.

The U.S. Department of Justice's Civil Rights Division is actively involved in the prosecution of human trafficking and their website offers information on victims' rights and resources. www.justice.gov/crt/about/crm/htpu.php.

The U.S. Department of Immigration and Customs Enforcement is on the frontlines of suppressing human trafficking. To receive e-mail updates on their activities contact them at www.ice.gov/human-trafficking.

Notes

1. U. S. Department of Justice, Office of Juvenile Justice and Delinquency Prevention, *Missing and Abducted Children: a Law-Enforcement Guide to Case Investigation and Program Management,* 4th ed. (Washington, DC: Government Printing Office, 2011), 33–120.
2. Ibid., 81–90.
3. Ibid., 38–39.
4. Ibid., 111–120.
5. www.nytimes.com/2005/05/01/national/01bride.
6. www.nytimes.com/1997/01/10/us/colorado-murder-mystery-lingers-as-police-press.
7. Ibid., 33–45.
8. Ibid., 70–74.
9. www.dol.gov/wb/media/reports/trafficking.
10. www.state.gov/j/tip/what/index.
11. www.victimsofcrime.org/library/crime-information-and-statistics/human-trafficking.
12. www.doj.state.wi.us/cvs.
13. www.biography.com/people/ariel-castro-21311121.

11   Robbery

CHAPTER OUTLINE

LEARNING OBJECTIVES

After reading this chapter, you will be able to:

1. *Define the elements of robbery and distinguish between the various degrees of this offense.*

2. *Explain the various tactics or styles of robbery.*

3. *Describe the different persons who may be involved in the commission of a robbery and their roles.*

4. *Discuss the signature aspects of robbery and how this is an aid to investigators.*

5. *List the various robbery targets and explain the various preventive measures.*

6. *Discuss the use of surveillance cameras as a means of identifying robbers.*

7. *Describe the steps investigators take in the investigation of robbery.*

8. *Define what a career criminal is and their relationship to robberies.*

9. *Define carjacking.*

10. *Discuss the steps involved in a carjacking investigation.*

11. *Discuss the problems of proving a robbery case.*

❶ *Define the elements of robbery and distinguish between the various degrees of this offense.*

❷ *Explain the various tactics or styles of robbery.*

❸ *Describe the different persons who may be involved in the commission of a robbery and their roles.*

❹ *Discuss the signature aspects of robbery and how this is an aid to investigators.*

▶ Components of Robbery

To substantiate charging a suspect with robbery, the investigation must uncover legally significant evidence that a crime was committed, that this crime was robbery, and that the defendant committed it. In such investigations, the basic evidence must range through each of the essential elements of the crime of robbery. The essential elements of **robbery** are as follows:

1. Taking of personal property from the person or presence of a possessor
2. Taking against the possessor's will
3. Taking by force or fear

Taking "from the person" means from the victim's body or his or her clothing, and "from the presence of a possessor" means within sight or hearing of the victim. It is in the nature of robbery that an offender not only takes personal property with intent to steal but also carries it away. Taking a possession away from the victim and into the control of the robber is sufficient. Control by the robber rather than the distance moved is the issue. "Against the possessor's will" is implied in the force and fear element of robbery, which must be adequate to frighten the victim and make the victim part with his or her property against his or her will.

According to the Federal Bureau of Investigation *Uniform Crime Reports*, there were an estimated 354,000 robberies in the United States in 2012. The robbery rate was 112 per one hundred thousand inhabitants. Losses due to robbery were estimated at $414 million; the average loss per robbery was $1,167. Only 28 percent of the robbery cases were cleared by and arrest or exceptional clearance.[1]

Robbery is generally divided into degrees to express the legislative intent that armed robberies are more serious than unarmed robberies:[2]

1. *First Degree.* Robbery while armed with a dangerous or deadly weapon likely to cause death or serious wounding.
2. *Second Degree.* Robbery accomplished by physical force or its threat but without a weapon, including purse snatching.

Robbery is a felony-level crime likely to result in a convicted robber receiving a lengthy sentence. It may be aggravated robbery (leading to a longer sentence) when the robber has an armed crime partner at the scene and either of them inflicts serious bodily injury against the victim or any witnesses.

Related crimes, such as kidnapping, must be substantiated in a similar manner. However, larceny and assault merge with robbery. Kidnapping, on the other hand, may not merge with robbery. In 1969, the top court in California repudiated the doctrine that any movement of the robbery victim amounted to kidnapping. In *People v. Timmons*, the court held that the true test was whether the movement of the victim substantially increased the risk of harm beyond that inherent in robberies.[3] If it did, kidnapping would be added to the charges against the robber or robbers; if not, the "movement" would be considered part of the robbery activity.

During the robbery investigation, the investigator need not decide whether these crimes join with the robbery or are separate crimes; the investigator's role is simply to collect all available evidence and develop the existence of related crimes from the array of collected evidence.

A video surveillance camera picture of a robbery in progress.

Another area of concern is the difference between robbery and extortion. One of the essentials of robbery is consent resulting from force or fear; in **extortion**, the victim consents more willingly. Consent may be induced by persuasive threats that are related to future harm or disgrace rather than here-and-now harm. A close call for investigators is a **scam** described in 1890 by Chief of Detectives James Byrnes of the New York City Police Department as the **badger game**. This is an extortion scheme in which a woman places a selected victim in a comprising position (nude, in bed, in a hotel room) and then victimizes him by demanding money. Next, her male accomplice breaks in and pretends to be an outraged husband threatening violence, scandal, or the like. The harassment of the victim is the key to the success of this scheme. It has been successful over the years with only minor changes.

The identification in an armed robbery case often relates to the tactics or style of the robbery. Robbery has been categorized as having three styles: (1) the ambush, (2) the selective raid, and (3) the planned operation. The **ambush robbery** is the least planned of all and is based on the element of surprise. The **selective-raid robbery** involves a minimum of planning but involves some casing, checking out or visiting and observing the robbery scene. The **planned-operation robbery** is carefully structured: the robbery group examines all aspects of the situation and plans for all foreseeable contingencies. In fact, the group may engage in practice runs in this style of robbery.

Crime partners in a robbery group form a loose partnership that provides the skills for the various tasks necessary to carry out different types of robberies. They participate in planning the robbery, including the basic decision about whether or not a certain target can be successfully robbed. Crime partners usually are associates from spontaneous play groups in the underworld: persons who live in or frequent the same neighborhood, who purchase drugs from the same source, or who have served sentences together in juvenile or adult institutions.

New York's notorious "Robert's Lounge Gang" was composed of customers frequenting a small bar near the cargo area of John F. Kennedy International Airport (JFK). This was a gang of varying size—depending on the availability of targets—but in total its membership was drawn from the **spontaneous play group** that assembled daily in this popular drinking place. Seven members of this gang carried out a robbery at the Lufthansa air cargo terminal at JFK. Their loot totaled $8 million in cash, jewels, and gold. Investigators were frustrated in their probing, until one of the suspects led them to Robert's Lounge and the gang associates.[4]

Investigators assigned a single robbery or series of robberies should search for **link-ups** or **connect-ups** that will indicate the operations of a group. In many instances, a gang of two to six robbers will not allow more than two robbers to be on the scene of a robbery. A Chicago robber, whose robbery group specialized in ambushing lone pedestrians late at night on streets and in alleys, explained this switching of the group's membership in various robberies: "Now we never did nothing with the four of us together, always two. I'd be with George when we'd get one guy, and next I'd be with Percy."[5] Linking or connecting several robberies may lead to the identification of four or five members of a gang, and such data may lead the investigator to some clues about the style of a particular robbery gang.

The fact that a robbery mob may be involved in a robbery or series of robberies can be developed by the investigator through a study of the style of the robbery: whether it was a selective raid or a planned operation, whether a getaway driver aided the robbery, and whether backup people were present at the scene. Inquiry may develop data identifying one or two persons who are not similar in description to the armed robber or robbers who committed the crime but were loitering about the premises and inquiring about employment or making other inquiries that would permit them access to the premises and that would allow them to scan (case) the scene of the crime before the robbery.

The presence of a getaway driver may be established from witnesses who can offer data as to how the robber or robbers who committed the actual robbery fled the crime scene. A **getaway driver** is a specialist who remains in the escape vehicle until the robbers have completed the robbery, then picks them up and flees the scene.

A **backup person** is a member of the gang who remains in the background unnoticed and, in case of trouble, supports the members of the gang who are actually committing the robbery. The presence of a backup person may be more difficult to discover because he or she often does not flee from the scene in the same car as the armed robber or robbers. Since the backup person has not been identified with the crime, he or she may stay at the scene for some time and then walk away to meet with his or her crime partners at some prearranged location. The role of the backup person in modern robbery gangs is to protect his or her crime partners from the unexpected. He or she is "buried" in the store (when customers are not the victims) or outside the robbery scene, from where the crime scene and its approaches can be viewed. The backup person's job is to fight off police who might chance on the scene or respond to a silent alarm.

Some signature aspects are typical of robberies. These trademarks are part of the modus operandi of a crime and distinguish it as work of a specific robber or robbery group who have committed previous crimes in which the same identifying circumstances occur. The investigating officers pick out from the modus operandi the most likely identifying signature characteristic and develop their investigation to identify the robber group. For instance, the "paper bag robber" carried a brown paper bag to the scene of the robbery and told the victims to put their money and valuables in it. The "lover's-lane robber" frequented lover's lanes and always victimized a boy and girl. The "Mutt and Jeff" robbers were always described as a tall man and a short man.

Traditionally, weapons indicate violence, but violence is used in robberies only as a tool of the robber in carrying out the robbery itself. Only in recent years has a new measure of violence in robberies indicated some hostility on the part of the robber. Such hostility can serve as a signature characteristic to identify suspects because it is unusual among robbers. Most robbers view the employment of violence to overcome resistance only as a self-defense measure, but today the number of wanton pistol whippings or shootings of victims is increasing. This use of force is beyond what is necessary to control the robbery victim or victims. As one convicted robber expressed it, "The last thing you want is trouble. If you gotta shoot somebody you gotta run, and you don't get any money. The thing is to get in and get what you are after and get out with the least trouble possible."[6]

The use of addicting and dangerous drugs by a robber is indicated when the modus operandi reveals restricted drugs are part of the proceeds of a robbery. Even when restricted drugs are not acquired during a robbery, an investigator can identify the robberies of a drug addict by the time span between robberies and the proceeds of each crime. This assumption is based on (1) other modus operandi information identifying a series of robberies as the work of one or more robbers, (2) the amount of money stolen, and (3) the date of the next robbery of the robber or robbers under investigation. The time gap between the robberies is extended when a good score allows the robber to buy sufficient drugs for a specific habituation level ($100-a-day habit, $200-a-day habit).

A characteristic of the addict–robber is that robberies are not committed when the addict is high on a drug but rather when he or she needs money to purchase drugs.

Robbery investigators must realize the potential for conflict between data contained in police reports and the testimony of witnesses in court. Accuracy in recording the statements of witnesses is of primary importance. Investigators should not encourage a witness to guess or record a guess as a fact and should not suggest facts to a witness who is unsure but rather should let the witness describe the person, car, weapon, clothes, disguise, marks, hair, speech, and the like in his or her own terms. Investigators should record the description in the witness's terms and not interpret them. Mistakes will be made, but the investigator should not compound them by adding to or interpreting the witness's descriptions.

⑤ *List the various robbery targets and explain the various preventive measures.*

▶ The Target in Robberies

The determination of a criminally oriented person to rob a specific and predetermined person or place, when and how to do it, and whether he or she cruises to find a place to rob are mental processes of considerable interest to an investigator. The selection of a target in robberies offers clues about who did it. In planned robberies, whatever was done before the crime can suggest suspects or indicate persons in the suspect group who are unlikely suspects. In the unplanned robberies of the cruising criminal, an investigator can develop a theory of who did it solely on the basis of the target selection.

In planned robberies, the offender considers not only the victim of the robbery but also such operational facts as the number of accomplices necessary, the weapons selected, the number of persons likely to be present during the robbery, and the escape route. In unplanned robberies, the offender acts on impulse, generally selects a weapon based on its availability, and haphazardly cruises an area in search of a victim.[7] Nevertheless, the "cruiser" does avoid victims likely to be armed or places that might be wired for a silent alarm that will alert police to a robbery in progress or equipped with video cameras.

In using the target aspects of a crime to further an investigation, the investigator first attempts to determine if the robbery was planned or unplanned. Beginning with information about the victim and whether he or she was alone at the time, plus information about where the crime occurred, the investigator tries to evaluate the need for precrime planning. The cruising robber seeks out victims who will present little or no operational problem, such as resistance or activating an alarm. Lone victims are symptomatic of unplanned robberies, although the location of the robbery may offer a more substantial clue to target selection and to the planning of the crime.

People who commit robberies have a wide variety of targets to choose from and each has its own level of risk and reward involved. The most commonly committed types of robberies include the following:

Bank robbery—People rob banks simply because that's where the money is. Bank "take over" robberies, where a number of people enter and rob the bank, occur infrequently. The typical bank robber of today is a single individual who passes a "note" to the teller demanding money. This is usually done in such a low key manner that the other people standing in line might not even know the bank is being robbed. Since the robbery of a federally insured bank is a federal crime, the FBI conducts the investigation and collects these notes. Robberies are serial type of crime, in that they occur over and over again until the suspect is caught. However, these robbers always use the same wording, use the same spelling, and make the same grammatical errors in each note. Therefore, it is possible to link these crimes together through the similarity of the notes the robbers use. Even years later, after being released from prison, the robber will begin robbing again and will use essentially the same wording in these notes.

In response to the number of robberies that occur each year, banks have instituted a number of measures to prevent or reduce the number of robberies.

- *Video surveillance cameras*—record the robbery as it occurs. These videos are released to the media and shown on news programs in the hope of identifying the robber.

- *Alarm systems*—connect directly to a police dispatch center or to a manned offsite security office. These systems allow for immediate notification of law enforcement and improve response time.

- *Double entry door systems*—require a person to be "buzzed" through one locked door into a waiting area; once this door is closed and locked the second locked door will open allowing entry to the interior of the bank. The same procedure is used to exit the bank. The waiting area is a great place to hold a suspected robber until the police arrive.

- *Bullet proof glass/plastic*—is often erected between the customer and the teller. While effective in reducing robberies the downside is that the transaction becomes impersonal, very similar to an ATM transaction.

- *Bait money*—included in the money given to a robber would be bills that the bank has previously recorded the serial number, usually by photocopy. This allows the bank to identify these bills as money belonging to the bank and only issued during a robbery. During an interrogation it is very difficult, if not impossible, for a robber to explain how he or she came into possession of these bills.

- *Dye packs*—each teller at a bank has a stack of bills that conceal a dye pack. Once opened, the pack explodes, coating the money and everything nearby with bright florescent paint. The money is virtually useless and the person walking around in brightly colored clothing should be considered a suspect.

- *GPS devices*—similar to dye packs, these locator devices can be concealed in stacks of money given to a robber. Law enforcement agencies have the ability to trace these devices.

- *Armed guards*—have been used since the very first robbery and serve as an effective deterrent. Most robbers want access to quick and easy money, not a shootout with an armed guard.

- *Training*—bank employees are taught to be on the alert for specific modus operandi of potential robbers and how to be a good witness. Typically people are not good witnesses but with a little training a person can learn to make a mental note of a suspect's clothing and personal identifying marks.

Business robberies—would include just about any business worthy of being robbed. A business once robbed is highly likely to be robbed again. In response, most business have responded to robberies by increasing staff, employee training, limiting cash availability with a drop safe, and video cameras.

Home invasion *robberies*—an unintended consequence of banks and businesses increasing their security is that would-be robbers have gone to less secure targets, such as the family home. While this type of robbery is relatively rare it can be very lucrative. New immigrants, senior citizens, and others who either don't trust banks or don't have access to banks are easy targets as they keep their valuables in their homes. Most robberies occur in public or semipublic places; however, the home invasion robbery occurs in the privacy of someone's home. The robber has time to threaten and use violence if necessary to have the homeowner turn over their hidden valuables. Typically these robbers will talk their way into a home or use force to break or push their way into the home.

Drug house robberies—this is a high-risk high-gain proposition for the robber. Drug houses have lots of drugs and money, but they also have guns and security personnel. A drug house cannot call the police for protection so they must be prepared against rival drug dealers and anyone else who would want to rob them.

Street robberies—are the most commonly committed form of robbery and the targets are frequently pedestrians as this is a crime of opportunity. Another popular target are bicyclists who are knocked off their bikes and the robber rides off on with the bike which will then be sold. These robbers are often armed or of sufficient physical size that resistance is rare. These types of robberies often occur at night and happen so quickly that suspect descriptions are often incomplete or vague.

Carjacking—a form of robbery where the robber uses force or the threat of force to have the driver relinquish control of his or her vehicle. The robber then drives off with the vehicle, usually a luxury model, that will bring a good price when disposed of.

6 *Discuss the use of surveillance cameras as a means of identifying robbers.*

▶ Identification Evidence

In robberies in which the victim is not killed, identification is made through facial characteristics, identifying natural marks or tattoos, hair line and color, race, clothing, speech characteristics, and unusual habits or nervous spasms. In robberies in which the victim is killed or is unable to see the robber's face, identification can be made by general physical build, fingerprints, footprints, type of disguise, recovery of the loot, means of escape (automobile license, model, or year, if an automobile is used), and type of weapon used. A sufficiently compelling combination of these factors will convince a court or jury of the identity of the robber. Facial characteristics, fingerprints, or an auto license may be sufficiently persuasive without additional factors.

Grounds for attacking the credibility of the identification evidence may be any of the following:

1. Suggestive use of photographs
2. Failure to safeguard the rights of the accused in placing a suspect or an arrestee in a police lineup (see Appendix A for a case brief of *U.S. v. Wade*)
3. Conflict between the physical description given by witnesses and the actual appearance of the defendant in court
4. Conflict between the weapon described by witnesses, or "constructively described" by the nature of injuries inflicted on victim, and the weapon presented in court as the robbery weapon
5. Conflict between the vehicle, if any, involved in the robbery as described by witnesses and the actual vehicle used in the robbery

Fixed TV surveillance cameras have become an increasingly important tool in the identification of robbers. This photographic surveillance frequently captures identifiable photographs of persons engaged in a robbery. Such photographs are used in identifying suspects, in their apprehension, and as identification evidence at trial. Banks pioneered the use of overt, fixed surveillance cameras, but the rise in robberies of stores and other businesses has expanded the use of these cameras in both overt and covert installations.[8]

7 *Describe the steps investigators take in the investigation of robbery.*

▶ Checklist for the Investigation of Robbery

A prompt response by police to the scene of a robbery, a fast-breaking search for the robber or robbers, and a continuing investigation aimed at identifying the person or persons responsible are the basic routine for successful robbery investigations (Figure 11-1). The following is a checklist for the investigation of robbery:

1. Assume the suspect is present and make an arrest.
2. Ascertain if the suspect has left the scene and, if so, how; obtain descriptions of the suspect and any vehicle.

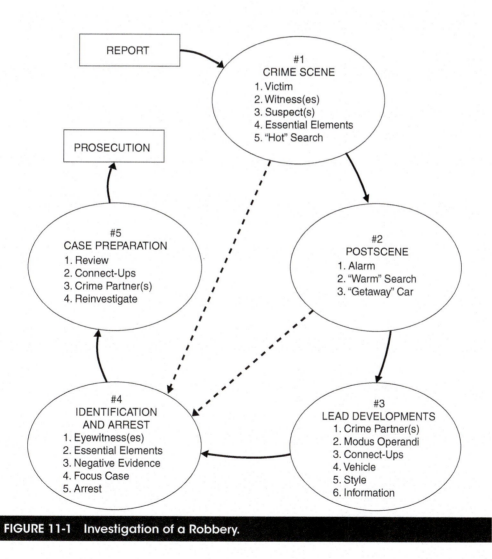

FIGURE 11-1 Investigation of a Robbery.

3. Provide a description of the suspect to the dispatcher; also provide the following information:
   a. Nature of the offense
   b. Weapon involved
   c. Direction of flight
   d. Description of vehicle
   e. Loss, if any
4. Search for the suspect.
   a. Escape route
   b. Refuges (theater, tavern)
   c. Hiding places (stairways, cellars, yards, trash bins)
   d. Prowler calls
   e. Stolen cars
5. Search the crime scene for evidence.
   a. Protect the area
   b. Call in a technician
   c. Extend the crime scene to the "discard" area where masks and clothing may be discarded
6. Search the scene for witnesses.
   a. Include latecomers and onlookers
   b. Canvass the view area and the neighborhood
7. Advise the superior officer of the following
   a. Details of offense
   b. Identification of victim and witnesses
   c. Personnel at scene and assignments
   d. Progress of preliminary investigation
8. Prepare a report on the preliminary investigation.
9. Compile a physical description of the suspect(s) and vehicle, if any.
10. Ascertain the modus operandi.
    a. Target
    b. Bindings (tape, wire)
    c. Weapon(s)
    d. Plus rape
    e. Plus kidnapping
    f. Narcotics taken
    g. Signature traits
11. Locate and interview informants.
12. Identify robbery groups.

    a. Number in group
    b. Connect-ups
    c. Spontaneous play groups
       i. Prison
       ii. Neighborhood
       iii. Same drug dealer
       iv. Same teen center
    d. Presence of getaway driver
    e. Presence of backup person or people
13. Identify the style of the robbery.
    a. Ambush
    b. Selective raid
    c. Planned operation; inside information
14. Identify other basic leads.
15. Identify and arrest the offender(s).
16. Prepare the case.

8 *Define what a career criminal is and their relationship to robberies.*

▶ Repeat-Offender Cases

Career criminals are offenders who have had previous arrests, have one to two cases pending in the local courts, and are on the street on some form of conditional release at the time of their latest arrest. While other violent serious crimes may be committed in a series of two or more, the series assailant or rapist is not usually a career criminal.

Career criminals comprise a high percentage of armed robbers. Aggravated robbery is the violent crime favored by repeat offenders. As a result, many prosecutors have established special units to concentrate on the prosecution of recidivists, particularly armed robbers. From a crime-control standpoint, priority for such repeat-offender cases is now established as an appropriate strategy for prosecutors.

In the past, prosecutors expended effort based on the strength of the evidence in a case, the probability of conviction, or the leverage of plea bargaining. More recently, prosecutors have been realizing that repeat offenders are inherently more convictable. Witnesses are generally more cooperative in repeat-offender cases, and the factors leading to the frequent arrests of such robbers also contribute to the weight of evidence indicating guilt.[9] Of course, investigators must make every effort to build a strong case against a repeat offender to maximize the probability of conviction, but they must also do so as rapidly as possible to get repeat offenders off the street and into an effective corrections program.

9 *Define carjacking.*

▶ Carjacking

Carjacking—the theft or attempted theft of a motor vehicle by force or threat of force from the person or the immediate presence of the victim—is armed robbery and a felony-level crime. Even when the carjacker has not displayed a weapon, the force and fear required for robberies is present (a forced entry of the driver's-side door, followed by a rude command to leave the car). When the circumstances and conditions of the robbery lead to a reasonable belief in the victim's mind that he or she may suffer injury unless he or she complies with the robber's demand, the fear required in such a robbery is present. The most common carjacking is described as one committed by an assailant in his or her twenties with a pistol or revolver and a crime partner. Auto thieves, on the other hand, commit crimes of stealth without violence and without the owner's presence. When the thieves no longer need the car, they abandon it. Investigators in police agencies should stop treating carjackings as they would auto theft (by closing out the case when the car is recovered) and should treat them as crimes of violence primarily against the person, not against property.

10 *Discuss the steps involved in a carjacking investigation.*

Outline of a Carjacking Investigation

The carjacking investigation is structured around a multiscene routine focused on using the recovery of the car not as a goal but as an aid in the identification of the offender. When the offense runs true to form, the carjacking has taken place, the first officers and associates have secured a physical description of the carjacker from the victim along with data on his or her car, and the investigation is turned over to an assigned detective or detectives. The outline of the investigation suggested is as follows:

1. *The Crime Scene.* Investigation of a carjacking crime scene is the same as for a robbery crime scene, plus an expanded canvass for witnesses to the offender's, and possibly the crime partner's, precrime activity; the vehicle used; and the offenders' conduct while selecting a victim.

2. *The In-Progress Crime Scene.* An in-progress crime scene includes places such as the gas station where the fleeing offenders purchased gasoline and the area in which the offenders were involved in a traffic accident. Likewise, if the owner's cell phone was left in the car, calls made on the phone should be investigated.

3. **The Dump Scene.** Prior notice should be given to patrol units to secure the car where it is "dumped" and to not touch it. The finder should be asked to notify the assigned detective or command. Arrangements should be made to tow the car to the crime lab, where fingerprint examination of the interior and exterior of the car should be requested. Any damage to the car and any other possible physical evidence should be noted.

4. **The Prearrest Scene.** A modus operandi search for "similars" in the past year should be conducted, and incoming crime reports on carjackings, ATM heists, and fast-food restaurant robberies should be scanned hourly. Composite sketches and photo spreads should be arranged. Inquiries should be made in line with relevant basic leads. (The investigator's hunch should be used as a guide to the suspect's home neighborhood and why the crime scene location was selected—for example, the suspect might have been a former employee of fast-food restaurants in the crime scene area.)

5. **The "Receiver" Scene.** The receiver scene is where the car parts are sold. The investigator should trace the car parts to buyers and thus seek the offender's identity.

6. **The "Fraud" Scene.** If the victim had a handbag in the car at the time of the crime, the carjacker may use the victim's credit cards, pass them to family or friends, or sell them on the street. Each transaction should be traced to determine the offender's identity.

7. **Postarrest.** The investigator should try to develop the crime partner, if he or she was arrested with the carjacker, receivers of car parts, and credit card abusers as witnesses against the carjacker at trial.

⑪ *Discuss the problems of proving a robbery case.*

▶ Problems of Proof

The first major problem of proof in robbery cases concerns the defendant: identifying him or her as the robber. The second major problem is how to show conclusively that the crime committed is a robbery in which the victim was separated from his or her valuables through force or against the victim's will.

The victim is expected to testify as a major identification witness. After all, the confrontation in robberies is between robber and victim. If a victim's testimony is weak and inconclusive, supporting witnesses need to be positive in their identification of the robber. Often, the defendant not only denies the act done but also claims mistaken identity and offers an alibi in support of this claim. If the alibi has strength and the identification evidence is weak, many jurors will think that this constitutes reasonable doubt.

The victim of a robbery is also mandated by the elements of the crime of robbery to testify that he or she handed over to the robber money and other valuables out of fear. Threats alone are not legally significant unless the victim testifies that he or she believed the robber had the intent to carry them out, as well as the apparent ability to do so promptly.

CASE STUDY

CHESHIRE HOME INVASION

In the afternoon of July 22, forty-eight-year-old Jennifer Petit and her eleven-year-old daughter went to a grocery store in Cheshire, Connecticut. In the parking lot at the time was Joshua Komisarjevsky, age 22, who took notice of the nice car driven by Petit. Komisarjevsky had a lengthy history of burglary and car theft. When the Petits left the store, he followed them home. Later in the day he contacted Steven Hayes, age 44, a fellow criminal he had met in a drug treatment center in Hartford. The two men had burglarized several homes over the weekend and the Petits would be their next target.

The next morning, around 3 A.M., the two men entered the Petit home through an unlocked basement door. On the first floor they found Dr. William Petit asleep in a chair. One of the pair hit him on the head

(continued)

with a baseball bat they had found in the basement. They then took Dr. Petit to the basement where they tied him up. In the upstairs bedrooms they found the Petits' two daughters and Mrs. Petit and tied them up in their respective bedrooms.

Hayes and Komisarjevsky then searched the house and were disappointed with what they found. They did locate a checkbook and they saw that the Petits had a large sum of money in a local bank. Later that morning Hayes took Mrs. Petit to the bank and had her withdraw $15,000 from her account while he waited in the parking lot. Mrs. Petit told the teller that the reason for the withdrawal was that she and her family were being held hostage and that if the police were called they would all be killed. After Mrs. Petit left the bank the police were notified of the suspicious transaction.

Upon his return to the Petit home Hayes learned that Komisarjevsky had sexually assaulted one of the daughters while he was away. Hayes responded to this news by rapping Mrs. Petit. Afterwards they decided to destroy any DNA evidence of the sexual assault by pouring gasoline on the still-restrained hostages and setting them on fire. At about the same time the father escaped from his bounds and stumbled outside and began yelling for the neighbors to call 911.

A few moments before Dr. Petit escaped the police had arrived on the scene and were working to secure a perimeter around the home. After lighting the fire the two suspects jumped into the Petits' family vehicle and tried to flee from the scene. After crashing into several police vehicles they were taken into custody and eventually tried, convicted, and sentenced to death for their crimes.[10]

CHAPTER REVIEW

Key Terms

ambush robbery *206*
backup person *207*
badger game *206*
carjacking *213*
connect-ups *207*

extortion *206*
getaway driver *207*
home invasion *210*
link-up *207*
planned-operation robbery *206*

robbery *205*
scam *206*
selective-raid robbery *206*
spontaneous play group *206*

Review Questions

1. Residential robberies are also known as
   a. cruising robberies
   b. domestic robberies
   c. home invasion robberies
   d. lone victim robberies

2. Crime partners, who commit robberies, are usually associates who live in the same neighborhood, purchase drugs from the same source, or have served time together. These groups of criminal are known as:
   a. organized crime
   b. criminal enterprise groups
   c. robbery cabals
   d. spontaneous play groups

3. A member of the robbery group that remains in the background unnoticed and whose job it is to fight off the police who might arrive on the scene is the:
   a. Robber
   b. Getaway driver

   c. Backup person
   d. Decoy

4. Lone victims of a robbery are symptomatic of _____ robberies.
   a. Ambush robberies
   b. Selective-raid robberies
   c. Planned-operation robberies
   d. Unplanned robberies

5. A person armed with a note and some threat of force that victimizes one teller is known as the _____ robbery.
   a. home invasion
   b. cruising
   c. single-teller bank
   d. selective-raid

6. The type of robbery that is based on the elements of surprise and is the least planned of all types of robbery is the:
   a. Planned operation
   b. Ambush

c. Scam

d. Selective raid

7. The most carefully planned robbery is the:

a. Planned operation

b. Ambush

c. Scam

d. Selective raid

8. The type of robbery that involves a minimal amount of planning, such as casing of the scene, is the:

a. Planned operation

b. Ambush

c. Unplanned operation

d. Selective raid

9. The single-teller bank robbery is what type of robbery?

a. Planned operation

b. Ambush

c. Scam

d. Selective raid

10. The most common defense in a robbery case is one based on:

a. Alibi

b. Improper lineup procedures

c. Mistaken identification

d. Improper Miranda waiver

See Appendix D for the correct answers.

Application Exercise

Imagine that you are investigating a single-teller bank robbery where a suspect displayed a weapon and passed a note to the teller demanding money. After placing the money in his briefcase the suspect left the bank on foot and has not been apprehended. What procedures should be employed in the collection of evidence and how should this evidence be used to identify the robber? Develop a line of questioning of witnesses that might indicate whether this robbery was done by an amateur or a serial robber.

Discussion Questions

1. What are the various styles of robbery?
2. What are the essential elements of robbery that distinguish this crime from theft?
3. Describe the role of a backup person in a robbery.
4. What facts likely to be disclosed in a robbery investigation can serve as identification of a robber?
5. Discuss the groups from which robbers generally recruit crime partners.
6. What are the signature aspects of the modus operandi of robbers?
7. Why is it useful to determine whether a robbery suspect may be addicted to restricted drugs?
8. What is the role of fixed surveillance cameras in the investigation of robbery?
9. Discuss the physical evidence involved in the case study.
10. Describe in detail at least three ways the home invasion robbery outlined in the case study could have been prevented.

Related Websites

For charts and tables about robbery trends in the United States, consult this website: www.ojp.usdoj.gov/bjs/glance/rob.htm.

To view robbery surveillance photos and robbery prevention tips, check out the Colorado Association of Robbery Investigators website at www.co-asn-rob.org.

Notes

1. www.fbi.gov/ucr/cius2008/offenses/violent_crime/robbery.html.

2. Kenneth M. Wells and Paul B. Weston, *Criminal Law* (Santa Monica, CA: Goodyear, 1978), 200–211.

3. *People v. Timmons*, 482 F.2d 648 (1971).

4. Ernest Volkman and John Cummings, *The Heist: How a Gang Stole $8,000,000 at Kennedy Airport and Lived to Regret It* (New York: Franklin Watts, 1986), 1–27.

5. Henry Williamson, *Hustler* (New York: Doubleday, 1965), 117.

6. John Bartlow Martin, *My Life in Crime: The Autobiography of a Professional Criminal* (New York: Harper & Brothers, 1952), 68.

7. Gerald D. Wolcott, "A Typology of Armed Robbers" (Master's thesis, Sacramento State College, 1968), 30.

8. U.S. Department of Justice, Law Enforcement Assistance Administration, *Selection and Application Guide to Fixed Surveillance Cameras* (Washington, DC: U.S. Department of Justice, Law Enforcement Assistance Administration, 1974), 1–5; *United States v. McNair,* 439 F. Supp. 103 (1977).

9. U.S. Department of Justice, Law Enforcement Assistance Administration, *Curbing the Repeat Offender: A Strategy for Prosecutors* (Washington, DC: U.S. Department of Justice, Law Enforcement Assistance Administration, 1977), 16–17.

10. www.nytimes.com/2007/08/07/nyregion/07slay.

12 Arson, Bombings, and Hate Crimes

CHAPTER OUTLINE

LEARNING OBJECTIVES

After reading this chapter, you will be able to:

1. *Distinguish between the legal concepts of arson and aggravated arson.*

2. *Explain the distinction between a naturally occurring fire and a suspicious fire.*

3. *Discuss the motivation that compels a pyromaniac to set fires.*

4. *Describe the typical burn pattern of a structural fire and explain the factors that may retard or alter this pattern.*

5. *Discuss the burn pattern in a nonstructural fire and the factors that influence this pattern.*

6. *Explain how intentional fire setting devices are deployed.*

7. *List the items of evidence that an investigator should be looking for at a fire scene.*

8. *List the steps taken in a continuing arson investigation.*

9. *Describe the six stages of a bombing investigation.*

10. *Evaluate the problems investigators face in proving arson and bombing cases.*

❶ *Distinguish between the legal concepts of arson and aggravated arson.*

▶ Arson and Arson Law

Fires set by arsonists and explosives placed to damage property and kill or inflict injury on people are crimes against both person and property. Because great secrecy usually surrounds the fire setting or the placing of explosives, these crimes create problems for investigators.

The great eighteenth-century British jurist Sir William Blackstone, in his *Commentaries on the Laws of England*, defined **arson** as the "malicious and willful burning of the house or outhouse of another man."[1] In common law, arson was considered an offense against the home (habitation). Arson was defined as the malicious and willful burning of a dwelling (house or outhouse) of another, and extended to structures within the curtilage (enclosed space around building) of the dwelling.

Arson law in the United States has taken many twists—depending on the individual state law examined. Arson may include the burning of buildings other than houses or outhouses, personal property, and crops. The law may distinguish between burning in the day and at night and between vacant and occupied buildings. The degree of arson may depend on the value of what is burned. Such laws generally make the burning of one's own insured property, with intent to defraud, a crime within the general scope of arson. Common, however, to all arson or arson-type crime is the element of burning and the malicious intent of the person setting the fire.

The corpus delicti in arson cases requires that the burning be the result of a criminal agency and that there be actual burning—a consuming-type fire—although the fire need not in fact consume, for a charring is usually sufficient.[2] Thus, the facts that must be proved in any prosecution for arson are as follows:

1. The fire occurred—a burning, a charring.
2. The burning was not accidental; its origin was the result of a criminal agency.
3. The person who appears as a defendant in court in an arson case is identified as the person who set the fire, or caused it to be set, or otherwise acted in furtherance of a criminal plan for the fire setting.

The term **aggravated arson** reflects public and legislative concern with arson as a crime against people as well as property. It is best described as any arson in which the following are true:

1. Explosives are used.
2. People are present at the site or are placed in danger.

Aggravation occurs when explosives are used to injure or harm people or property or, if at the time of fire or explosion, a person other than the arsonist is within or upon the structure damaged. Inherent in the present or placed-in-danger element of aggravated arson is the fact that actual physical harm can result from the fire or explosion. Some states use aggravation as essential to first-degree arson; others cite it as adding to the seriousness of arson and, if proven at trial, as calling for additional years to be added to the sentence linked to basic arson.[3]

Although motive is an important element in the continuing phase of an arson investigation, it is not necessary to prove motive in an arson prosecution in order to convict the defendant as long as the defendant can be identified as the fire setter and his or her intent to set the fire is established.

According to the FBI's *Uniform Crime Reports* there were 52,600 cases of arson in the United States in 2012. Arsons involving structures (including residential, storage, and public), accounted for 47 percent of the total arson offenses; arsons involving mobile property accounted for 23 percent of the total; and other types of property (such as crops, timber, and fences) accounted for 30 percent of the reported cases. The average dollar loss per offense was estimated at $12,800. Nationwide the rate of arson was 18.7 per every one hundred thousand inhabitants.[4]

② *Explain the distinction between a naturally occurring fire and a suspicious fire.*

③ *Discuss the motivation that compels a pyromaniac to set fires.*

The Suspicious Fire Concept

In investigating a burning, the investigator must first seek evidence to prove whether the fire was of natural or accidental origin. When little or no evidence can be secured to identify the fire as accidental, the second step is to seek evidence to eliminate all possible causes except **incendiarism**. The investigator must evaluate the possibility of persons smoking in bed, of spontaneous combustion, of a pilot light igniting fumes from flammable liquids, of electrical storms, or of faulty construction or maintenance of a building (electrical wiring, motors, space heaters, furnaces, and flues). Next, the investigator must review the possibility of children, the elderly, intoxicated individuals, and the mentally ill being involved in a noncriminal incendiary fire through carelessness or misfortune.

The third step is to seek evidence that will prove that the fire was of incendiary origin. Investigators seek such evidence as separate and distinct fires in different areas of the premises: the residue of inflammables; the odor of petroleum and similar fire starters; holes in plaster walls; windows and doors shaded and locked to prevent discovery and retard entry of firefighters; removal of personal effects before a fire; owner or occupant not present, or absent when normally present; excessive insurance; and the presence of ignition devices or **fire sets**.

Once the suspicious nature of the fire has been revealed, the investigator attempts to classify the burning as a rationally or irrationally motivated fire. Rational motivation is based on hate, profit, or the desire to conceal a crime. In rationally motivated fires, the suspects are those people who would want the fire. Irrationally motivated arsonists are pathological fire setters.[5]

Hate fires are set because of some dispute. The work of the investigator is to question the victim as to his or her suspicions and any recent arguments. Landlords may need questioning to help recall a dispute over an unfulfilled tenant request. Querying employers about recently discharged employees or customers with complaints may help them recall a few names. Persons who set hate fires have emotional problems. An unimportant event to an average person may be overemphasized by these individuals and trigger their need to set a fire for spite or for revenge. Religious, racial, and political disputes may be involved. Although the identity of the **arsonist** or **incendiary** is not as apparent in these disputes, suspects may be identified in the opposition group involved in the dispute if the investigator probes and pries.

For-profit fire setters are not difficult to expose once hate has been eliminated as motivation. The first step is a general inquiry about the company insuring the building and its contents, followed by a more specific inquiry into the insurance and the record of the policyholder. Collaterally, a general inquiry as to the financial status of the insured and his or her business is appropriate and often rewards the investigator with information that the insured "needed" a fire.

Representatives of the national crime syndicate have been linked to arson with great frequency in recent years. They buy into a legitimate business and turn it into an illicit operation. The general procedure in these cases is for the new owners to manipulate the firm's operations to gain full control from the previous owners; to take all readily available assets in merchandise, services, and credit from the business; and then to set a fire for the insurance money.[6]

A fire may have originated as an attempt to conceal a major crime. This is not a difficult evaluation. What crime could be involved? Was a human a victim of the fire? Was murder involved? Was any property missing? Did a robbery occur? Were the record books destroyed, found partially burned, or tented (spread half open with the bound edge up and the leaves spread out for burning)? Is tax fraud an issue? What about embezzlement? Sometimes the seriousness of the basic crime does not appear to warrant arson, but people in trouble do strange things.

Pyromania is the obsessional impulse to set fires or a preference for arson as an instrument of damage. **Pyromaniacs**, the "firebugs" who terrorize entire neighborhoods by their fire-setting activities, repeat their crimes unless they are apprehended and placed in a correctional setting oriented to their needs. These individuals may claim rational motivation, but they set fires for no practical reason and receive no material profit from their incendiarism.[7] Motive in these cases is some sensual satisfaction resembling an irresistible impulse—the act of setting a fire solves the fire setter's problems more efficiently and often more pleasurably than any other means available.[8]

The pathological fire setter usually does not have any relationship with the victim or the place of burning. A "pyro" fire is similar to a "psycho" murder case in this respect. The fire scene search may reveal a clue to personal identity. The suspect may attract attention by his or her overt and suspicious conduct in the crowd watching the fire. These irrationally motivated incendiaries have a tendency to act out the role of hero at the fire scene. In seeking a solution to these fires, it is possible to develop suspects by reviewing records of suspicious juvenile vandals, sex psychopaths, known pyromaniacs, and others with a history of weird behavior or bizarre acts. When fires occur in a series within reasonable geographic limits, the technique of working out the pattern of the fire setter and organizing surveillance for his or her apprehension is sometimes successful.

4 *Describe the typical burn pattern of a structural fire and explain the factors that may retard or alter this pattern.*

▶ Burn Patterns: Structural Fires

Structural fires form a pattern that is determined chiefly by evaluating the physical layout of the building involved, the available combustible material, and ventilation. Simply stated, the fire burns upward from its original ignition in an inverted conical shape with the apex of the cone at the place of origin—where the fire was ignited. Physical characteristics of a building may retard a fire or change its direction. Ventilation will cause a fire to spread away from this conical fire pattern: open doors, open windows, chimney like physical characteristics (stairways or elevators), and holes in a floor, wall, ceiling, or roof (either caused by the fire or caused by some other means) contribute to the spread of a fire and its rate of burning (Figure 12-1). Another variation of the classic fire pattern is caused when the fire encounters highly combustible materials that burn more vigorously and thus radically modify the direction of a fire.[9]

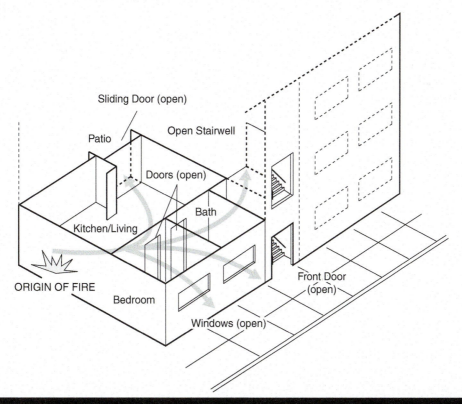

FIGURE 12-1   Normal Fire Path in Structural Fires. Arrows Indicate Spread of Fire from Origin in Kitchen.

Combustibility in structural fires usually is defined in terms of ignitability, rate of heat release, and total heat release. It is a function of the physical characteristics of the furnishings and building materials at the fire scene, their spatial relationships, and the structural features of the place of occurrence.[10] A little-known aspect of structure fires is room **flashover**—a rapid development of the fire that occurs when the volume of active fire becomes a significant portion of the room volume. At flashover, all the previously uninvolved combustibles in a room suddenly ignite. The rate of the heat release at this time is high and usually a flaming spreads across the ceiling of the room.[11] A basic key to determining the pattern of a structure fire is to note the approximate time between ignition and flashover in the room in which the fire originates.[12] A fire initially may be classified as suspicious when its pattern suggests more than one place of origin, when an inexplicable or unexplained deviation from a fire pattern is common to the structural characteristics and ventilation of the place burned, or when a rapid buildup of a room fire is not in harmony with the known combustibility of the room and its contents.

⑤ *Discuss the burn pattern in a nonstructural fire and the factors that influence this pattern.*

▶ Burn Patterns: Nonstructural Fires

In outdoor fires in which a structure is not involved, a predominant horizontal spread characterizes the fire, rather than the typical cone pattern of structural fires. The factors that influence fire patterns in outdoor fires are the wind and terrain. On level ground—in the absence of wind—a fire will spread from the point of origin in all directions. In the absence of a strong wind, the partial vacuum created by the fire, which permits air to flow into the fire's base, has a tendency to retard the spread of the fire. Wind spreads the fire in a fan shape with the apex of the fan closest to the source of the wind. On terrain with an uphill slope, the fire will burn uphill from the point of origin. The combination of wind and terrain may produce a fire that burns uphill and is canted to the left or right because of the direction and velocity of the wind at the time of the fire. A strong wind sometimes can override the influence of terrain and cause a fire to burn laterally across a sloping hillside. In some cases, fires have been spread downhill by a very strong wind.[13]

A wind condition in southern California known as the **Santa Ana winds** contributes to the ignitability of forest-fire fuels. These winds, by their strong airflow associated with very low humidity, quickly dry out forest fuels. When a fire is started in the presence of these conditions, the increased ignitability of these fuels accounts for a rapid spread in all directions and, due to wind-driven embers, the occurrence of many spot fires ahead of the main fire. Under Santa Ana conditions, fire can spread quickly and violently in any direction. A surge or slackening in the airflow or a sudden change in wind direction, rapid heat release, and the mountainous southern California terrain, characterized by numerous canyons that act as chutes or chimneys, all contribute to sudden changes in the pattern of the fire.[14]

⑥ *Explain how intentional fire setting devices are deployed.*

▶ Fire Ignition and Place of Origin

One of the major differences between an accidental fire and an incendiary fire is that accidental fires frequently burn themselves out because of a lack of proper ventilation or combustible material. On the other hand, the set fire is planned. The fire setter places his or her fire so that it will burn vigorously after being ignited. He or she may use a fire **accelerant** or may depend on ventilation and the combustible material normally present at the fire scene.

Sparks, matches, mechanical lighters, friction, radiant heat, hot objects, and chemical reactions can cause fire. The primary source of ignition can be manual, as in striking a match; mechanical, as in a spark device used by welders; electrical, as in faulty wiring or defective appliances; or chemical, as in spontaneous combustion.

When matches or other simple devices are used to set a fire, little evidence points to the means of ignition. However, many arsonists construct various mechanical delay devices to afford themselves a few hours in which they can establish an alibi of being elsewhere at the time the fire was started. Candles provide another delay factor for the arsonist. The time lag depends on the diameter and height of the candle above the **plant**, which is the fire-boosting material such as newspapers used to spread the fire. An alarm clock is another common mechanical device used to start fires. Both clocks and candles leave traces at the fire scene—when the debris and rubble at the fire scene are searched, some evidence of their use is often located. Electrical fire starters often make a fire appear to be accidental because faulty wiring and careless handling of electrical appliances often cause fires. Spontaneous combustion from items such as oily rags is often claimed as a cause of fire, but ideal conditions are needed to generate enough heat for self-ignition. In some industrial fires, however, spontaneous combustion can result from the chemical reaction of various volatile oils with air.[15]

Where a fire was ignited is classified as the place of origin. Fire setters set fires in more than one place to get a rapid buildup of the fire. **Trailers** are often used to spread fires from a point of ignition and can be considered a secondary incendiary device, carrying the fire from the original place of ignition to other parts of the room or building. The trailer may be nothing more than a rope or a ropelike string of toilet paper, newspaper, or rags soaked in fire accelerant. Sometimes a fire accelerant is simply poured across the floor in a pattern similar to the spokes of a wheel, with each trail radiating outward from the original source of ignition.[16] The major indication of a set fire is the fact that the source of ignition is such that the fire spreads rapidly, indicating the use of a trailer and a fire accelerant or that several different places constitute the points of origin.

The investigator should study the lower regions of a fire for the place or places of origin. However, the place of origin may be higher than some of the burned portions of a building because the fire accelerant that spread the flames from the original place of ignition might have dripped downward through holes or crevices in the floor before the fire secured enough heat to change the fire accelerant from its liquid state.

 List the items of evidence that an investigator should be looking for at a fire scene.

▶ The Fire Scene

The best-case scenario in arson investigation is when the investigator arrives at the fire scene while the fire is still in progress. All the firefighters are still on the scene then, and occupants of the premises (or the owner of the land on which the fire started), onlookers, and other witnesses are also available at this time. Under these circumstances, the investigator can conduct on-the-scene interviews of persons knowledgeable about the fire and its circumstances (Figure 12-2). These interviews should point toward securing the following data:

1. Who reported the fire
2. The color and volume of flames and smoke: natural materials such as wood and grass typically produce white smoke and petroleum-based products produce black smoke
3. Whether anyone reported the odor of gasoline or other fire accelerant
4. Where and when the fire started
5. The movements of occupants and others involved in the fire
6. Anything unusual at the fire scene

After the fire is over and the investigator can enter the fire scene—which is when most investigators arrive at the fire scene—the onset of the fire and its circumstances can be reconstructed. Unfortunately, fire investigators usually are faced with various disturbances or changes in the original fire scene caused by the need of firefighters to overhaul after extinguishing a fire. **Overhauling** is the examination and search by firefighters for hidden flames or sparks that might rekindle the fire. To accomplish this, firefighters often throw the contents of a room outside the building and frequently rip cabinets and paneling from walls to expose the space between the studs.

Tracing the root of a fire by examining the manner and direction of burning from the point of origin is the primary means of reconstructing the fire scene.[17] Basically, reconstruction of a fire scene requires the investigator to secure data on how a fire started, how it burned, and whether it was accelerated.

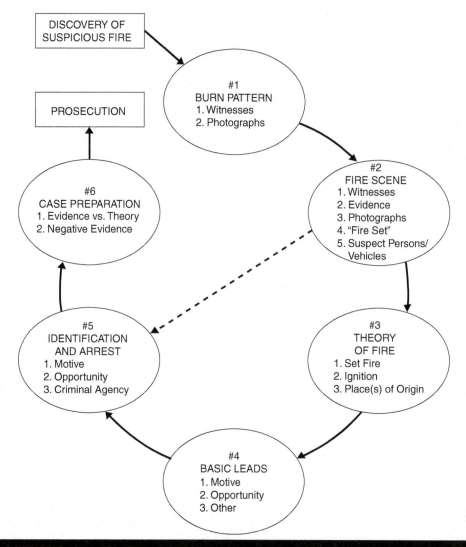

FIGURE 12-2 Investigation of Arson.

Once an investigator has reconstructed a fire, he or she can develop a theory about it. This theory may be backed up by various items of evidence, such as empty containers of flammable fluid found at the scene, traces of fire accelerants, or the remains of a fire-setting device in the rubble of a fire. It is primarily concerned, however, with the pattern of a fire: how it was ignited, the point of origin, and the source and direction of its burning.

Searching a fire scene is similar to searching any crime scene, with the exception that a lengthy period of freezing the scene is necessary to protect physical evidence until the searchers can find it among the rubble and debris of a fire. Although the fire scene search is pointed toward discovery of the means of ignition and the point or points of origin of a fire, the searchers also look for anything unusual or foreign to the fire scene, evidence that will connect a suspect to the scene by revealing his or her presence at the scene (the opportunity to set a fire), clues to the motive of a fire setter, or evidence of the fire setter's intent to set a fire.

Items of evidence suspected of containing volatile substances commonly used to accelerate fires must be found and sealed quickly to prevent loss by evaporation. Such items must be transported to the crime laboratory in airtight containers.

Liquid fire accelerants (e.g., kerosene, gasoline) can and do survive fires. The areas most likely to contain residues of these accelerants are the low points at the fire scene: floors, carpets, or soil. When a suspect is arrested shortly after the fire at or near the scene, the suspect's outer clothing and shoes may contain residual traces if the fire setter used a liquid fire accelerant. The human nose can detect the distinctive odor of a liquid fire accelerant at the scene or on a suspect, but it is best supplemented by detectors of flammable vapors. These "sniffers" operate on several principles. The most common type operates on the catalytic combustion principle. However, the recovery and individualization of fire accelerant residues require the services of forensic scientists in a crime laboratory and the use of solvent extraction devices.[18]

One popular method for separating flammable and combustible liquid residues from fire debris is the **passive headspace concentration method**. In this method, an adsorbent material such as activated charcoal is used to extract the residue from the static headspace above the sample, then the adsorbent is eluted with a solvent. Results of studies have demonstrated that multiple separations can be performed without jeopardizing the recovery and identification of volatile residues.[19] The headspace concentration method is best used when a high level of sensitivity is required because of a low concentration of ignitable liquid residues in the sample. Several variations on this method have also been developed and are effective for separating residues from fire debris.

Solvent-extraction devices support the work of fire scene searches by recovering flammable fluids from fire rubble (wood, cloth, and paper). The searchers find and recover the material suspected of containing residues of a fire accelerant and transport it to the crime laboratory for processing by criminalists. Later, the report of these laboratory technicians may contribute to the development of the case, and their expert evidence in court at the trial of the offender offers testimony in support of the prosecution's case.

Photographs of the Fire Scene

Fires and fire scenes are ideal subjects for photo essays that communicate otherwise undetectable facts about a fire, its origin, and its pattern of burning. In-progress photos are seldom taken by assigned investigators, but they are taken by the news media, fire personnel, and amateur photographers and can be secured by investigators. Such in-progress photographs, particularly when in color, identify the location of a fire, reveal its spread and intensity, identify the color of the smoke, and detail the mixture of smoke and flames. In addition, such photographs sometimes reveal the presence of a suspect at the fire scene; identify one or more vehicles parked at or entering or exiting from the scene; and reveal signs of forced entry, attempts to bar firefighters from the structure, or methods used to prevent prompt discovery of the fire.

Investigators and assisting personnel assigned to process the scene of a suspicious fire should take both color and black-and-white photographs of the fire scene and of items of evidence found at the scene. Inasmuch as the corpus delicti of arson is the burning (charring) of a portion of a structure, this burning should be photographed from its place of origin to wherever the fire caused damage to the structure or its contents, both in overall views and in close-ups. Overall pictures reveal a fire's patterns and offer some clues to its ignition and origin, but it is the close-up photography in

the area or areas of the origin of the fire that is of particular importance in revealing any ignition device and the use of a fire set with trailers and accelerants. Although the ignition device itself may have been consumed in the fire, mute evidence of its use to set the fire may be developed from such photographs.

Photographs taken during the postfire processing of the scene of a suspicious fire may exonerate innocent suspects or serve as the only corroboration of an investigator's testimony as to things found, or not found, at the fire scene and their application to the prosecution's theory of the fire, the criminal agency, and the identity of the defendant on trial as the fire setter.

8 *List the steps taken in a continuing arson investigation.*

▶ The Continuing Arson Investigation

The preliminary investigation of a suspicious fire is complete when the fire scene examination is recorded and the theory of an incendiary fire has been developed, and when it can be proved by available evidence that the fire was not accidental.

The investigator assigned to the continuing investigation uses the following lines of inquiry as to motive and opportunity (presence at crime scene):

1. Who would want or benefit from the fire?
2. Who would have the opportunity to set the fire?

The specific lines of inquiry suggested by the basic investigative leads are not exhausted until the dual inquiry as to motive and opportunity is fully developed. The specific areas of inquiry in the continuing investigation of an arson case depend on the individual characteristics of each case, but the following major areas of inquiry should be explored in developing an arson investigation:

1. Burn pattern (whether in harmony with structure and contents)
2. Fire scene
   a. Examination for source of ignition
   b. Determination of place or places of origin
   c. Physical evidence

3. Witnesses
   a. Person discovering fire
   b. Fire personnel
   c. Eyewitnesses
   d. Occupants (and owner of premises or place)
   e. Others (onlookers, neighbors, and relatives of person discovering fire)
4. Suspicious persons
   a. At fire scene
   b. At fire scene but left before arrival of investigators (e.g., children playing, strangers in area, transients or homeless persons, former occupants, discharged employees)
5. Suspicious vehicles
   a. At fire scene
   b. Usually parked at fire scene but not present now
   c. At fire scene but departed before arrival of investigators
6. Theory of fire
   a. Rationally motivated
      i. Hate
      ii. Profit
      iii. Concealment of a crime
   b. Pathological fire setter
      i. Lack of rational motive
      ii. Fire in series
      iii. Neighborhood involved
      iv. Known pyromaniacs
   c. Criminal agency
      i. Not caused by accident
      ii. Means of ignition
      iii. Place of origin(s)
      iv. Proof fire was set
   d. Physical evidence
   e. Witnesses
   f. Other (e.g., motive, opportunity)
5. Identification of fire setter
   a. Scene
   b. Witnesses
   c. Suspicious person or vehicle
   d. Inquiries—basic leads
6. Review of evidence disclosed by the following:
   a. Burning pattern
   b. Examination of fire scene
   c. Witnesses
   d. Suspicious persons and vehicles
   e. Basic leads
7. Compatibility of evidence—identifying fire setter
   a. Burning pattern
   b. Evidence at fire scene
   c. Testimony of witnesses
   d. Results of investigation
8. Case preparation; compatibility of identification of fire setter with theory of fire
   a. Criminal agency
   b. Motive (rational, irrational)
   c. Review of negative evidence (block common defense of accident, alibi, mistaken identification, or lack of motive)

▶ Bombings

Many fires result from explosions. Criminal investigation techniques used in arson investigation can be applied to bombings despite the fact that a fire may not result from the explosion.

The investigation of bombings takes place in six stages (Figure 12-3):

1. **Determination of Cause.** An accidental origin, such as a gas explosion or an explosion resulting from the misuse of chemicals, must be eliminated as the cause of the explosion.

2. **Scene Investigation Pattern.** The pattern of the explosion must be determined—high or low explosive; approximate amount used (damage).

3. **Scene Processing.** The bombing scene is processed by police (responding officers and bomb squad personnel, if available) to locate and interview witnesses and victims, to find and preserve physical evidence, and to identify any suspicious persons or vehicles.

4. **Case Building.** The investigator develops a theory of the bombing target, opportunity, motive, and technical know-how.

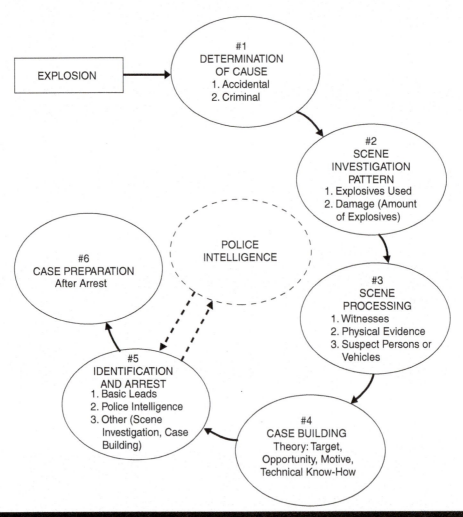

FIGURE 12-3 Investigation of Bombings.

5. **Identification and Arrest.** Inquiries are initiated to exploit any basic leads, police intelligence, and other clues and traces (scene investigation and processing, case building) likely to result in the identification and arrest of the person or persons responsible for the bombing.

6. **Case Preparation.** The case is prepared immediately after the arrest of the bomber and any associates.

Because the nature of an explosion destroys traces of the explosives used, explosive **tagging** offers future promise that the scene of investigation of a bombing will hold identifiable traces of the explosives used. An explosives tagging program developed at the federal level involves the addition of coded microparticles or **taggants** to explosives during their manufacture. The taggants survive detonation, can be recovered at the bombing scene, and can be decoded by crime laboratory examination to show where and when the explosives were made.

The use of police intelligence reports may be the most important factor contributing to the success of a bombing investigation. These reports can provide information that will link suspects to prior bombings and provide data on the associates and possible whereabouts of suspects and associates. In addition, a police intelligence unit may initiate preventive intelligence operations to disclose the identity of persons involved in the planning of future bombings (see Chapter 6).

Individuals or groups who use explosives as the ultimate weapon against persons or property may be linked to any of the following:

1. Politically motivated groups (extremists, radicals) (see Chapter 17)

2. Organized crime (bombings involving known criminals, informants for police, and witnesses or potential witnesses against members of crime syndicates)

3. Mentally ill persons (including bombers motivated by hate, anger, and revenge).

❿ *Evaluate the problems investigators face in proving arson and bombing cases.*

▶ Problems of Proof in Arson and Bombing Cases

Two common defenses create problems of proof in prosecuting arson cases: (1) a claim that the fire resulted from an accident, a misfortune, or a natural cause and (2) if the fire did result from a criminal agency, the defendant was not that agent.

To prove that a criminal agency was responsible for the fire, the police prosecutor team must foreclose all possibilities that the fire resulted from any other cause (accident, misfortune, natural cause) by a strong showing of evidence linking the fire to a single cause: someone set it.

Identifying the defendant as the fire setter is a problem that is generally attacked along the dual lines of motive and opportunity. The prosecution must, at the least, produce evidence showing that the defendant wanted the fire or would benefit from it, and that by his or her presence at the fire scene, not only had the opportunity to set the fire but did so, or that the defendant contracted a crime partner to set the fire.

While cases involving explosive devices may be linked to fires, their investigation is hampered by the fact that the explosion usually destroys most of the physical evidence at the bombing scene. When these cases are prosecuted, the motive and opportunity factors are important. In political bombings, anyone proven to be a member of a terrorist group is assumed to have a motive for the bombings of that group.

▶ Hate Crimes

Hate crimes are committed by individuals or organizations of people who engage in antisocial and illegal behavior and pose a danger to agents of the criminal justice system and to the general public. Add to this definition is the fact that the hate–violence is commonly directed at African

Americans, Asians, Hispanics, Jews, gays, and even at the U.S. government itself—for example, the Oklahoma City bombing.

Hate groups include organizations such as the Ku Klux Klan (KKK), Aryan Nation, and **skinheads**. In some locales, various militias demonstrate against the government for a specific reason.[20]

Alan Berg, a controversial talk-show host, was shot dead not far from his home on the outskirts of Denver. His killers were members of a neo-Nazi group aligned with the Aryan Nation. Berg was Jewish and openly challenged neo-Nazi and other hate groups. Killing Berg was murder—but also a hate crime. He was killed because he was "different" in the eyes of his murderers.

A hate crime is not usually so closely identified with a **community threat group**. It is usually a single offender acting out his or her particular hate. Arson and bombing are common, and often fires and bombings occur in a series a few days apart. Although the motivation is irrational, suspects can be found and evidence can be developed for a trial.

Cults range from groups preaching revolution or resistance to taxation or similar governmental activity to those preaching from the Bible and performing good works among the sick and the poor. These groups may have other problems linked, for example, to the children of the group or the lifestyle of the group. Some cults have been targeted for allegations of **mind control**, which is the use of undue influence and unethical means to recruit and retain members.

Despite the negative public perception of groups labeled as cults, police investigators must remember that the United States has a longtime commitment to religious tolerance and freedom. Investigators should not probe and pry into any such group unless a crime has been reported or discovered and unless there is strong probable cause to warrant police action.[21]

CASE STUDY

MOTIVE FOR ARSON

The defendant was convicted by a jury of the crime of arson. In April 1995, defendant secured fire insurance in the sum of $141,000 on a home located in Corona, California (comprising rooms numbered on a diagram in evidence at trial as 1 to 10, inclusive). Title to the property was formerly in the name of defendant's son, who, with defendant, was one of the co-beneficiaries of the policy. The house was leased to a Mr. Keys, who resided in it from April 1995 to November 1998. During that period, defendant listed the property for sale at $160,500.

On January 5, 1998, defendant came to Corona from her home in Santa Clara where she lived with her husband. She stayed in the Corona house on the nights of January 5 and 6. On January 7, defendant's insurance agent received a telephone call from defendant informing him that she wanted $10,500 additional insurance. The agent notified the head office to increase the insurance accordingly, effective January 7, 1998. Defendant spent the night of January 9 with a friend in Corona.

A neighbor, living next door to defendant's property, testified that he saw defendant carry an amber-colored gallon bottle into the house on January 7 and saw her again at the house on the morning of January 10; that he saw lights in the back part of the house about 6:00 P.M. that night; that he retired about 9:00 P.M.; and that at 2:30 A.M. on January 11 he was awakened by flames coming from the gabled ends of the defendant's house. The fire department was called. The firemen forced open the backdoor and saw no flames in rooms 8, 9, 3, or 4. One fireman saw evidence of separate fires in rooms 5, 6, and 10. In room 1, other firefighters found an open-faced gas heater on which the valve was open and gas was coming into the house. After the fire was subdued, the fire chief discovered that one of the backdoors had been left open.

On January 11, a deputy state fire marshal and others investigating the fire discovered that the heaviest fire occurred in room 10—a closet—which was separated from room 1 by a door. The fire in that area had burned down through the floor and up through the ceiling, resulting in considerable fire damage to the house and roof. Directly across from room 10, in room 1, an area about 36 inches wide had been burned on

(continued)

the wall. Apparently, the fire at that point started from the floor and burned up because the baseboard was entirely gone.

Prosecution

The district attorney focused on the incendiary origin of a fire, which is generally established by circumstantial evidence, such as the finding of separate and distinct fires on the premises. Evidence of four separate, simultaneous, and unrelated fires was found in the house in question; holes were found in the plaster behind two of the fires; boxes of combustibles were in front of the holes; papers were stuffed between the laths in one of the holes; and debris smelling of petroleum products was near another hole in the plaster. The facts amply justify an inference that the fire was of incendiary origin and that it was neither accidental nor from natural causes and that the jury could reasonably infer that the fire was willfully and maliciously set for the purpose of burning the house.

In the opinion of duly qualified experts who testified at the trial, there was no communication or connection between the fire causing the charred condition in room 5 and the burned areas in rooms 10 and 1, nor between the burned area in room 6 and the burned area in rooms 10 and 1, nor between the fires causing the burns in rooms 5 and 6.

Defense

Counsel for defendant contended that the evidence of the corpus delicti was insufficient because it had not shown that the defendant was present when the fire was set, nor that the defendant was the means by which the fire occurred. No evidence connects the defendant to the crime.

The identity of the defendant as the person who committed the crime may be proved by circumstantial evidence connecting her to the crime, but circumstantial evidence must consist of proof of the defendant's motive and conduct that connects her with the crime and statements that show a consciousness of guilt.

Comment

The jury was justified in believing the defendant had offered the house for sale and that it had not been sold. This fact and evidence of several points of origin, coupled with the fact that defendant had secured an increase in the insurance on January 7, three days before the fire, justify the inference that she had a motive in burning the building and collecting the insurance.

CHAPTER REVIEW

Key Terms

accelerant *222*
aggravated arson *219*
arson *219*
arsonist *220*
combustibility *222*
Community Threat Group *230*
cult *230*
fire set *220*
flashover *222*

hate crime *229*
hate fire *220*
incendiarism *220*
incendiary *220*
mind control *230*
overhauling *223*
Passive Headspace Concentration
   Method *225*
plant *223*

pyromania *220*
pyromaniac *220*
Santa Ana Winds *222*
skinhead *230*
taggants *229*
tagging *229*
trailer *223*

Review Questions

1. _____ is any arson in which explosives are used and people are present or placed in danger.
   a. Serious
   b. Aggravated
   c. Accelerated
   d. Severe

2. When investigating a burning, the investigator must first seek evidence to prove whether the fire was of _____ or _____ origin.
   a. Rational/irrational
   b. Natural/accidental

c. Intentional/rational
d. Incendiarism/irrational

3. A fire that is started due to some real or imagined dispute with another person is an arson motivated by _____ reasons.
   a. Greed
   b. Sex
   c. Hate
   d. Fear

4. A person who has an obsession to set fires or has a preference for arson as an instrument of damage is known as a/an _____.
   a. Pryomaniacs
   b. Terrorists
   c. Deviant
   d. Paranoia

5. At _____, all the previously uninvolved combustibles in a room suddenly ignite. At this time, the rate of the heat release is high and flaming spreads across the ceiling of the room.
   a. Combustibility
   b. Overhauling
   c. Flashover
   d. Incendiarism

6. Factors that influence patterns of outdoor fires are _____ and the.
   a. Wind/humidity
   b. Weather/terrain
   c. Humidity/precipitation
   d. Wind/terrain

7. _____ are often used to spread fires from a point of ignition.
   a. Accelerants
   b. Taggants
   c. Trailers
   d. Plants

8. Coded microparticles are added to explosives at the time of manufacture. These _____ survive detonation, can be recovered at the bombing scene, and can be decoded to indicate where and when the explosives were made.
   a. Accelerants
   b. Taggants
   c. Trailers
   d. Plants

9. _____ crimes are committed by individuals or organizations of people who engage in antisocial and illegal behavior and who pose a danger to agents of the criminal justice system and to the general public.
   a. Arson
   b. Pyromania
   c. Incendiary
   d. Hate

10. Pathological fire setters are motivated by _____ reasons to set their fires.
    a. Rational
    b. Irrational
    c. Hateful
    d. Prejudiced

See Appendix D for the correct answers.

Application Exercise

As an arson investigator you have been advised of an ongoing structure fire in an area where a number of suspicious fires have occurred recently. Develop a strategy for determining the place of origin and the source of ignition. What questions should be asked of the first responders to the scene and other witnesses in order to determine if this is an accidental or intentional fire. What evidence would you be looking for and where might it be found and from whom?

Discussion Questions

1. Define a suspicious fire.
2. How does the burning pattern in structural fires differ from that of nonstructural (field and forest) fires?
3. What is a fire set? A fire trailer? A fire accelerant?
4. What basic factors should be considered in investigating fires set because of hate (revenge or jealousy), for profit, or to conceal a crime?
5. What are the basic characteristics of fires set by pyromaniacs?
6. What are the six stages of a bombing investigation?
7. What individuals or groups may be involved in a bombing?
8. What is explosives tagging?
9. Has the corpus delicti been established in the case study?
10. How was the fire in the case study started?

Related Websites

For information regarding arson investigation, recent events, and related sites, consult www.firehouse.com.

The Inter Fire resource center contains useful information for the arson investigator. This site contains information on arson evidence collection, methods used to determine the origin and cause of fire, and links to related websites. You can access this site at www.interfire.org/resourcecenter.asp.

The International Association of Arson Investigators website contains information regarding fire investigation, career opportunities, and arson related publications. You can visit this site at www.firearson.com/home.aspx.

Statistics on hate crime in the United States can be found at this website: www.fbi.gov/hq/cid/civilrights/hate.htm.

Notes

1. William Blackstone, *Commentaries on the Laws of England* (Oxford, England: Clarendon Press, 1765–1769), bk. 4, chap. 16.
2. Kenneth M. Wells and Paul B. Weston, *Criminal Law* (Santa Monica, CA: Goodyear, 1978), 221–228.
3. *Kehoe v. Commonwealth,* 149 Ky. 400 (1912).
4. www.fbi.gov//about-us/cjis/ucr/crime-in-the-u.s./2012
5. Brendan P. Battle and Paul B. Weston, *Arson: Detection and Investigation* (New York: Arco, 1978), 30–42.
6. "Fire Marshalls on Duty: The Intelligence Unit in Fire Investigation," *The Fire Journal* LXIV (September 1970): 92–93.
7. Noland D. C. Lewis and Helen Yarnell, *Pathological Firesetting: Pyromania* (New York: Nervous and Mental Disease Monographs, 1951), 86–134.
8. W. Hurley and T. M. Monahan, "Arson: The Criminal and the Crime," *British Journal of Criminology* IX (1969): 4–21.
9. Paul Kirk, *Fire Investigation* (New York: Wiley, 1969), 71–81.
10. Edwin E. Smith, "An Experimental Determination of Combustibility," *Fire Technology* VII, no. 2 (May 1971): 109–119.
11. T. E. Waterman, "Room Flashover: Criteria and Synthesis," *Fire Technology* IV, no. 1 (February 1968): 25–31.
12. T. E. Waterman and W. J. Christian, "Characteristics of Full-Scale Fires in Various Occupancies," *Fire Technology* VII, no. 3 (August 1971): 205–217; and "Fire Behavior of Interior Finish Materials," *Fire Technology* VI, no. 3 (August 1970): 165–178.
13. Kirk, *Fire Investigation,* 82–88.
14. C. M. Countryman, M. A. Fosberg, R. C. Rothernel, and M. J. Schroeder, "Fire Weather and Fire Behavior in the 1966 Loop Fire," *Fire Technology* IV, no. 2 (May 1968): 126–141.
15. Bruce V. Etting and Mark F. Adams, "Spontaneous Combustion of Linseed Oil and Sawdust," *Fire Technology* VII, no. 3 (August 1971): 225–236.
16. Battle and Weston, *Arson,* 17–29.
17. Richard D. Fitch and Edward A. Porter, *Accidental or Incendiary* (Springfield, IL: Charles C Thomas, 1968), 3–26; and John J. O'Connor, *Practical Fire and Arson Investigation* (New York: Elsevier, 1987), 81–105.
18. John F. Boudreau, Quon Y. Kwan, William E. Faragher, and Genevieve C. Denault, *Arson and Arson Investigation: A Survey and Assessment* (Washington, DC: U.S. Department of Justice, Law Enforcement Assistance Administration, 1977), 77–89.
19. L. V. Waters and L. A. Palmer, "Multiple Analysis of Fire Debris Samples Using Passive Headspace Concentration," *Journal of Forensic Sciences* 18, no. 1 (January 1993): 165–183.
20. Jack Levin and Jack McDevitt, *Hate Crimes: The Rising Tide of Bigotry and Bloodshed* (New York: Plenum, 1993), 1–5.
21. James D. Tabor and Eugene V. Gallager, *Why Waco? Cults and the Battle for Religious Freedom in America* (Los Angeles: University of California Press, 1995), 147–148.

13 Property Crimes

CHAPTER OUTLINE

LEARNING OBJECTIVES

After reading this chapter, you will be able to:

1 *Explain the elements of burglary and the aggravating factors that would increase the degree or seriousness of this crime.*

2 *List the various methods burglars use to enter buildings to commit a felony or theft.*

3 *Describe the five-step behavioral cycle in burglary.*

4 *Explain the methods safe burglars use to attack a safe.*

5 *Describe the three major phases of the burglary scene investigation.*

6 *Describe the methods investigators use to develop leads during the postscene investigation.*

7 *Describe the investigative procedures that would be employed regarding known burglars.*

8 Define the elements of theft or larceny and explain the method and items attacked as investigative leads.

9 Define modus operandi searches and how they relate to a suspect's decision-making pattern.

10 Describe how investigators work with other investigators and other sources of information to whittle down the universe of suspects responsible for a specific crime.

11 Explain how investigators posing as receivers of stolen property gain information useful in identifying thieves active in the community.

12 List the various types of auto thieves.

13 Explain the three types of employee theft and how these crimes are investigated.

14 Describe how organized retail theft occurs.

15 Define cargo theft and the methods used to steal containers and truckloads of goods.

16 Explain why cases of fraud go unreported.

17 Define the four elements of fraud.

18 Identify the more common swindles or con games used to defraud unsuspecting victims.

19 Discuss how a bank examiner fraud works.

20 Describe the steps involved in passing fraudulent checks.

21 Explain how thieves obtain the credit cards they will use to commit a fraud.

22 Discuss the common consumer frauds.

23 Define workplace fraud and embezzlement.

24 Explain how thieves obtain personal identification numbers (PIN) in order to commit ATM fraud.

Property crimes are committed for the personal gain of the perpetrator. These crimes include **burglary**, theft, and fraud. While burglary, by definition, is the entering of a structure for the purpose of committing a felony or theft therein, the crime of burglary is almost predominantly a crime wherein the object of the crime is the breaking and entering of a structure for the purpose of committing a theft.

1 Explain the elements of burglary and the aggravating factors that would increase the degree or seriousness of this crime.

▶ Burglary

In the past, conviction of common-law burglary required the proof of six essential elements:[1]

1. A breaking
2. An entry
3. In the nighttime
4. Of a dwelling house
5. Belonging to another
6. An intent to commit a felony

In most jurisdictions today, conviction for burglary requires only three basic or essential elements:[2]

1. Entry
2. Of a building (or other structure, place, or thing described by the particular penal code section)
3. With intent to steal or commit another felony

Burglary is usually separated into first-, second-, and possibly third-degree burglary. Some of the old essential elements of common-law burglary are used to divide the modern crime of burglary into degrees. The division into degrees may be based on whether the crime occurs in a dwelling house; whether such a dwelling is inhabited by a person actually present at the time; whether it is entered in the nighttime; or whether the act is committed by a person who is armed with a deadly weapon or who, while in the commission of a burglary, arms himself or herself with such a deadly weapon, depending on the state in which the crime is committed. In recent years, the use of explosives has increased the degree of burglary.[3]

The allied misdemeanor offense of possession of burglar tools assists police in apprehending burglars and in preventing burglaries. Any person who has on his or her person or in his or her possession a picklock or other instrument with intent to feloniously break into or enter any building is guilty of a misdemeanor in California. So is any person who knowingly makes or alters any picklock or other instrument so that it can be used to open the lock of any building without the specific consent of a person having control of such building.[4]

According to the FBI's *Uniform Crime Reports* there were an estimated 2,103,787 burglaries in the United States in 2012. Fifty-nine percent of these burglaries involved forcible entry; 34 percent, unlawful entries (without force); and the remaining 6 percent, attempted forcible entry. Burglaries of residential properties accounted for 74 percent of all burglaries. In all, the estimated loss for all burglaries was in excess of $4.7 billion. Approximately 12.7 percent of the burglaries were cleared by arrest or exceptional clearance.[5]

Burglary is a crime of opportunity, a crime of easy opportunity. Although many burglars limit their activities to a certain area and thus reduce the scope of their burglaries, every area has many easy opportunities.

Investigators should try to develop some insight into how a burglar selects a site for his or her crime. Why the choice of one area? Why the selection of one house as opposed to a neighboring house? The probability of profit and safety is perhaps at the core of this site-selection process, with burglars having a large physical area in which they evaluate (by search) the opportunity for a successful burglary.[6] If this insight can be developed, a roving stakeout of an area may be successful in apprehending the burglar.

Burglary is usually a passive crime in that the burglar normally tries to avoid contact with victims. The chances of getting caught in an unoccupied structure are lower than the chances of being apprehended in an occupied structure. Persons who are not present at the scene of a burglary can never be eyewitnesses to the identity of a burglar in court. Without an alarm to alert police of a crime in progress, no "hot" search can take place. In more public crimes, when a criminal has fled the scene shortly before the arrival of police, the victim may give the police a physical description of the criminal, of a vehicle, and of the direction of flight, thus giving the police the opportunity for a "warm" search. This is not possible when the victim does not even know that his or her premises have been burglarized until some time after the burglar has fled the scene. This restricts the police apprehension process to the "cold" portion of this crime-solving process, commonly termed the **investigative phase**. In other words, burglars usually are not apprehended at the scene of their crime or in flight but must be apprehended as a result of an investigative process (Figure 13-1).

The objective of burglars may be something other than theft. It may be assault—usually rape. Sometimes theft and assault are joint goals. Both larceny and rape or any other crime involved is investigated along with the basic burglary. The investigator must be alert to obtain evidence of each essential element of the additional crimes, as well as the essential element of the burglary.

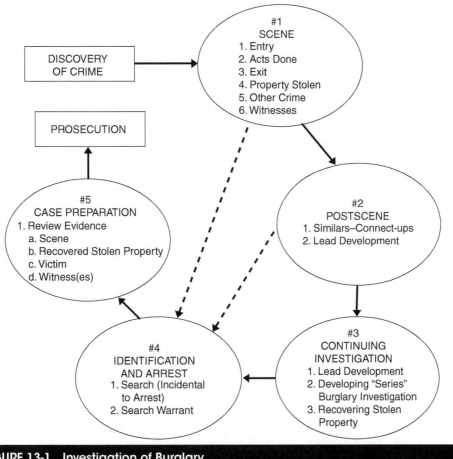

FIGURE 13-1   Investigation of Burglary.

❷   *List the various methods burglars use to enter buildings to commit a felony or theft.*

Types of Burglars

For years, police schools have taught about two general types of burglars: (1) the amateur and (2) the professional. **Professional burglars** are defined as those persons who work at burglary as a trade, making their living by burglary and larceny alone and having no other means of income. Other burglars are loosely grouped beneath this plateau of "professionalism." The **amateur burglar** includes the burglar who commits crimes primarily to secure money for drugs.

Because burglary is probably the most common serious crime in the United States, it is timely to reconstruct a typology of burglars that will encompass skill levels. This typology categorizes the skills of a burglar on two levels:

1. The ability to gain entry to a premises
2. The business sense of the burglar in regard to the selection of loot and the method of disposing of the proceeds of the crime (i.e., selling the stolen property)

The skill required to gain entry to a premises may be limited to forcing open a door or window, but it can extend to the use of lock-picking tools, which keeps pace with the art of the locksmith in providing security against thieves, and to the skill that opens locked containers such as safes. The business sense of a burglar depends on his or her ability to distinguish between

Burglars often gain entry by prying or kicking doors open.
Source: Stuart McClymont/Getty Images, Inc.

valuable and worthless items at the time of the burglary, the burglar's contacts with receivers of stolen property, and whether he or she needs desperately (common with drug addicts) to sell the stolen property.

This new typology of burglars describes a burglar as being in one of the following categories:

1. Unskilled
2. Semiskilled
3. Professional

The fact that such a typology of burglars exists does not mean that investigators should discount the classic modus operandi criteria used to describe various types of burglars. These specifics have served as a working typology for many years, as follows:[7]

1. Type of premises entered
2. Means of entry
3. Type of loot (stolen property)
4. Time of operation
5. Presence of crime partners

It does mean, however, that these basic items of modus operandi information should be reviewed from the viewpoint of discovering the skills demonstrated in gaining entry to the premises and the business sense demonstrated to some extent by the nature of the property taken at the time of the burglary, its quantity, and its value.

The **means of entry** differ in various burglaries and are related to the skill of a burglar. The various known means of entry include the following:

1. *Open Door or Window Entry.* The burglar roams residence areas, apartments, and hotels looking for open doors or windows.

2. *Jimmy Entry.* The burglar forces a door or window with a tool such as a tire iron, screwdriver, or small crowbar or box opener.

3. *Celluloid Entry.* The burglar forces open a door's spring lock with a small piece of celluloid.

4. *Stepover or Human Fly Entry.* The burglar is an aerialist; the **stepover burglar** steps from a fire escape, balcony, or other building to a nearby window; the **human-fly burglar** can progress upward or downward on the sides of a building to a selected point of entry.

5. *Roof Entry.* The burglar breaks into a premises through a skylight or air conditioning duct on the roof or by cutting a hole in the roof of a building.

6. *Hide-In Entry.* The burglar hides in a commercial premises until all employees have left, then breaks out with the stolen property.

7. *Cut-In Entry.* The burglar uses tools of various kinds to cut through the floor, ceiling, or wall of a store or office to another store or office.

8. *Hit-and-Run Entry (Smash and Grab).* The burglar breaks a window of a ground-floor store and takes property from a window or nearby portions of the premises, then flees before police can be alerted to the crime.

9. *Key Entry.* The burglar uses a key. The key may have been given to him or her by an informant, it may have been stolen, or the burglar may have obtained a duplicate or master key by various means.

It is apparent that most unskilled or semiskilled burglars are prowlers who enter a residence and search very rapidly for cash or property that is easily transported and quickly converted into cash. Whether they succeed in finding it or not, they will leave without any loss of time, taking with them the portable wealth of the householder—usually stereo systems, DVD players, computers, and other items that are easily sold to individuals seeking bargains or to persons who deal in and sell drugs and are willing to exchange the drugs for the stolen merchandise.

The semiskilled and the professional burglars also deal in articles of value, but those articles are not as easily converted into cash and generally require the services of a **fence**, a receiver of stolen property. The loot of such thievery ranges through jewelry, furs, clothing, liquor, tobacco, meat, and textiles.

❸   *Describe the five-step behavioral cycle in burglary.*

Burglary as a Behavioral Concept

Burglarizing is the behavior of committing a burglary and, most likely, another and another and another. Burglaries usually are crimes in a series.

Like all behavior, burglary involves needs and the opportunity to satisfy these needs. It also involves a common decision about whether or not to take advantage of opportunities. The five-step **behavior cycle in burglary** is as follows:

1. Needs

2. Opportunities

3. Means (skills)

4. Satisfaction

5. Choice

To understand the elements in this burglary cycle is to understand the behavior of burglars. Among burglars whose goals are theft (profit), the economic needs are met through successful burglaries, the successful taking away of stolen property, and its profitable disposition. The opportunity to commit a burglary is perceived; the burglary and its profit will meet the needs of the burglar; the burglar has the necessary "technology" to enter a premises successfully to take away the proceeds of a crime and to sell it. The individual with these needs who makes a choice of burglary over other possible activities to meet unmet needs not only receives satisfaction from the work but also a reinforcement of this behavior, thus increasing the probability of the recurrence of this behavior—more burglaries and theft.[8]

Many years ago burglars stole primarily for economic reasons. Today, the same economic reasons may be complicated by an addiction to drugs. Although the need for funds to buy drugs is an economic need, a more urgent compulsion is related to the need for the drugs and their effect on the drug user.

Rapist–burglars exhibit needs to satisfy various psychological and physical desires. These burglars are abnormal in selecting forcible rape as an outlet, but they follow the burglar's typical cycle of behavior—and each successful crime is reinforcement for continuing this pattern of behavior.

4 *Explain the methods safe burglars use to attack a safe.*

Safe Burglars

Burglars often demonstrate skill at opening locked desks, file cabinets, safes, and other containers. It may be that such entry to locked containers will be made by basic tools such as a jimmy or screwdriver or tools picked up on the premises and used by the burglars. Most safe burglars, however, will bring to the crime scene whatever special tools they need: torch, sectional crowbar, and so on.

Force used to attack safes generally follows one of the following patterns:

1. *Punching*—a manner of entry, where a sledge hammer and a drift punch are used to knock the combination dial from the safe and drive the spindle back into the safe. This makes the release mechanism of the lock accessible and allows the safe to be opened.

2. *Pulling*—a device similar to a gear or wheel puller is used to pull the dial or spindle completely out of the safe door, thus allowing the safe to be opened (similar to punching).

3. *Peeling*—involves prying off the outer surface of the safe door so that the locking mechanism of the safe is exposed and can be pried open, allowing entry to the safe.

4. *Ripping*—invovlves the battering of the top, bottom, or sides of a safe with a chisel or other metal cutter such as a ripping bar (burglar's tool) or the hydraulic ramming device used in a body-and-fender shop.

5. *Drilling*—one or more holes are drilled in the door of the safe to expose the lock mechanism, allowing the safe breaker to align the lock tumblers manually and open the door of the safe.

6. *Burning*—the safe is attacked with an oxygen-acetylene torch, and a section of the safe is burned out to allow entry. When bank vaults are involved, a variation of this burning technique is the use of a thermal-burn burning bar that makes the original oxygen-acetylene torch much more efficient so that it is possible to burn through 6-inch tempered steel in fifteen to twenty seconds.

7. *Blasting*—is the use of explosives to open safes.

8. *Carrying Away*—occurs when the burglar removes a safe in order to open it at a more convenient location.

Intruders often open a safe without force, by means of its combination. It may be that the burglar found the safe open, but when no physical force is used to open a safe, investigators assume it was opened by using the combination. In such cases, the burglar may have found the combination written on the side of a drawer in a nearby desk, in an account book, or in another convenient place, or he or she may have been given it by a dishonest employee.

⑤ *Describe the three major phases of the burglary scene investigation.*

The Burglary Scene Investigation

The purpose of the burglary scene investigation is to ascertain what clues or traces at the scene may identify the burglar and crime partner(s). The burglary scene investigation has three major phases:

1. The means of gaining entry
2. What the burglar did while in the premises
3. How the burglar exited the premises

The place of entry and tool marks are the classic identifying characteristics found at the scene of burglaries. The burglar's ability to break into any locked containers at the scene is a demonstration of a skill in the use of tools.

Acts done while at the crime scene may be no more than necessary to accomplish a theft. On the other hand, the acts of a rapist–burglar spell out the essential elements of a second major crime. In addition, some acts may aid in identifying the burglars. The property stolen is another useful factor in identifying the burglar.

The burglar's means of exit rounds out what can be gleaned from a burglary scene by investigators. The burglar may simply have exited from a rear door after a roof entry. In the course of determining this fact, however, investigators may find significant clues or traces in and about the place of exit.

However, none of the evidence likely to be found at burglary scenes will actually identify a burglar by name or as a person. Factors related to the burglar's modus operandi may contribute to developing one or more suspects. Therefore, this on-the-scene evidence should be preserved for future use. When suspects are uncovered, the clues and traces can be related to these suspects by the investigator.

If the investigator has good reason to believe that a suspect is still in possession of stolen property from one or more recent burglaries, and the investigator can secure reliable information describing this stolen property and where it is located, such data can be tied to the victim's reports of what was stolen and developed into an application for a search warrant. The execution of the search warrant and the recovery of the stolen property in premises controlled by the suspect will support other evidence identifying him or her as the burglar.

⑥ *Describe the methods investigators use to develop leads during the postscene investigation.*

The Postscene Investigation

The postscene investigation is the development of leads from connect-ups and a comparison of modus operandi with other crimes either solved or unsolved, which tends to identify one or more suspects as the offender in a series of crimes of which the burglary being investigated is the latest. The investigation often involves the use of informants or identification through recovery of the stolen property and a tracing back to the burglar.

Although connect-ups and the use of informants are classic avenues of investigation to identify suspects in burglary investigations, they offer little or no admissible prosecution evidence that a particular suspect committed the particular burglary under investigation.

The identification of the seller of stolen property through a questioning of the receiver of stolen property has a more promising potential as evidence. When a person is known to be in possession of stolen property, a search warrant can be secured. The resultant seizure of stolen property is lawful, and such evidence can be used in court against the receiver or against the person who sold the stolen goods to him or her—if there is testimony or other evidence that connects the seller to the stolen property.

Describe the investigative procedures that would be employed regarding known burglars.

Known Burglars

When an investigator has developed a suspect known to police to be a burglar but is unable to develop evidence likely to serve as probable cause for an arrest, then he or she must continue the connecting-up of subsequent burglaries until sufficient evidence is accumulated to supply probable cause for the arrest of the suspect.

Innovative surveillance procedures have been used in recent years in many police departments to clear burglary cases when a known burglar is identified as the suspect in a series of burglaries. An around-the-clock surveillance of the known burglar (and usually a crime partner or partners) is established and continued until such time as the burglar enters a building under circumstances that indicate his or her intent to commit a crime. This type of arrest is opportune and timely.

 Define the elements of theft or larceny and explain the method and items attacked as investigative leads.

▶ Theft

In common law, *larceny* was defined as a trespassory taking and carrying away of personal property belonging to another with an intent to deprive the owner of such property permanently. Currently, **larceny** (theft) is defined in most states as the unlawful taking or stealing of property or articles without the use of force or violence. It includes shoplifting, pocket picking, purse snatching without strong-arm tactics, thefts of and from vehicles, and taking property or cash from a home.

New terms used in criminal justice statistics describe the scope of common larceny:[9]

1. *Household Larceny*—theft or attempted theft of property or cash from a residence or the immediate vicinity of the residence is household larceny. The thief must have a legal right to be in the house—as a guest or maid, for example.
2. *Personal Crimes of Theft (Personal Larceny)*—the theft or attempted theft of property or cash by stealth, in either of the following manners:
   a. with contact but without force or threat of force
   b. without direct contact between the victim and the offender
3. *Personal Larceny with Contact*—the theft or attempted theft of property or cash directly from the victim by stealth but not by force or the threat of force.

According to the FBI's *Uniform Crime Reports* there were over 6.1 million larceny-thefts nationwide in 2012. The rate of thefts was 1,959 per one hundred thousand inhabitants. This is the most commonly committed crime in the United States, without exception. These thefts account for approximately 68 percent of all property crimes. The average loss was $987 per offense; with a total loss of over $6 billion. Approximately 22 percent of these cases are cleared by arrest or exceptional clearance.[10]

Thieves steal money, vehicles, and other property from rightful owners. They sell it to individuals (bargain seekers) or criminal receivers of stolen goods (fences). The profit motive in thefts is too general to offer any promising leads. The solution of these crimes begins with a prompt alarm for the stolen property and an examination of the crime scene to determine the circumstances of the crime and to search for and collect physical evidence. Victims are interviewed to develop suspects, and witnesses to some preparatory or postcrime activity are sought and their help solicited. Extensive modus operandi comparisons are made. Information about the work of known thieves suspected of operating locally is correlated with the facts known about the crime being investigated. Thieves can be traced when the proceeds of the crime are sold and recovered by police. Persons who buy stolen property quite frequently reveal the

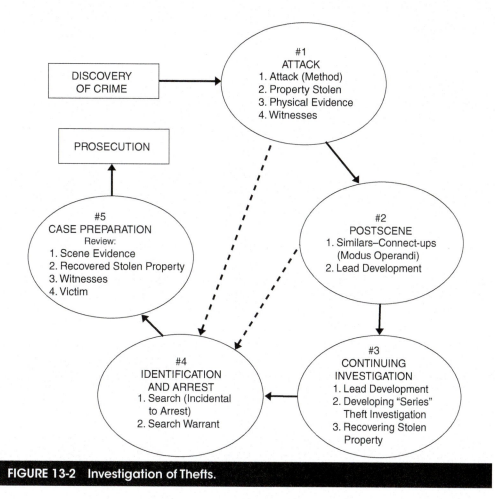

FIGURE 13-2 Investigation of Thefts.

identity of the thief. However, theft cases are difficult to solve because of the lack of eyewitnesses. They generally are unknown-identity investigations characterized by the absence of a named suspect (Figure 13-2).

Before recovering the stolen property, investigators attempt to identify the perpetrator by seeking a characteristic signature in the modus operandi of the crime or a basic lead from field interview reports and tips from underworld sources of information. The value of physical evidence found and collected at the scenes of thefts has a growing importance. It is not likely that such scientific evidence will serve to name a suspect, but it can serve as an identifier when the foregoing techniques bring together a group of persons who are all equally suspect.

Most investigations of thefts involve past thefts. The police patrol force sometimes detects a thief at work or responds to a theft-in-progress call. Quite often when investigating prowler calls, the responding officers discover a thief, but usually the victims of these crimes do not discover the prowler until after the crime has been attempted or is completed. One of the unfortunate aspects of thefts is that police have to bracket the occurrence between the time of discovery and the time at which the stolen property was last seen or otherwise noticed.

Time is likely to favor a criminal. It may blur the focus of an investigation and can aid the thief's escape and the safe disposal of stolen property. The time element in past crimes does not encourage the assigned investigator and probably serves as a passive means of discouragement. Crimes of violence have an inherent motivation for any investigator. In thefts, the investigator must seek motivation within his or her personal experience and occupational goals for effective work.

The Attack

Money and valuable property are usually safeguarded. To steal either or both requires planning, direction, and operating skills. This is the attack of the thief. To be considered are the premises attacked, the method of the attack itself, and the means used to dispose of the proceeds of the crime—the loot or swag. In fact, the proceeds of a crime are the objective of the attack, and they are an important highlight in viewing the attack as an event.

The property stolen is a major clue. The broadcast and computer generated alarms announce to all cooperating law enforcement agencies the fact of the crime and identifying data on the property taken begin the tracing that often leads to recovery of the property and a backtracking to the thief. The characteristics of stolen property are listed by quantity, kind, material, physical description, serial numbers, and value. Many investigators at crime scenes have discovered that victims cannot describe the stolen property. Therefore, investigators often must question the victim about the stolen property item by item—what each item is used for, what it is made of, whether it is a man's or woman's item, what marks are on it, and its value (cost and estimated current value).

The characteristics of the stolen property have long been used as part of modus operandi searches, but they are gaining new significance as indicative of the routine decision making of a particular thief. The property stolen is now recognized as part of the attack event that can serve to name a suspect. It is part of the criteria used to evaluate a target. Some thieves steal money only, which is not grossly incriminating even minutes after a theft. Other thieves consider a proposed theft and reject it because of the difficulty of disposing of the property that will be the proceeds of the crime. Thieves who have an established disposal route with customers such as housewives, employees of gas stations and drive-ins along a highway, and small merchants in nearby towns and villages reject all proposals unless the property is suitable for their customers. Other thieves use wholesalers of the underworld—the fences—and tend to specialize in property that can be legitimized by removing all identifying marks. A few professional thieves have the necessary friendships among members of the organized crime syndicate to dispose of jewelry, furs, bonds, electronics, and other merchandise with retail values in the tens of thousands of dollars and higher.

 Define modus operandi searches and how they relate to a suspect's decision-making pattern.

Modus Operandi Searches

Modus operandi searches are rewarding in theft investigations because thieves are known as single-pattern offenders. Modus operandi searching will identify a group of suspects as persons actively engaged in committing property crimes and will produce a number of suspects for the crime being investigated. Computerized record searches allow the scanning of a huge number of past crimes for the purpose of modus operandi identification.

A great deal of personal satisfaction can be gained by solving a theft in the early stages of a continuing investigation before the proceeds of the crime have been recovered and the process of tracing back has been initiated. It is a possibility that is not being exploited to its fullest extent; the lack of a named suspect often relegates a theft investigation to a category of "no results possible" until there is some feedback about the stolen property being recovered.

The key to an early break in property crime investigation is the expanded modus operandi search to include the decision-making processes exhibited by the criminal in his or her operations. By developing an understanding of how thieves make decisions and the nature of the thought processes that underlie this decision making, an aware investigator can learn a great deal about these criminals. Interpreting selected modus operandi data of a theft under investigation provides clues about a thief's decision routines for dealing with each of the components of the overall task. Then it is the role of the investigator to develop an "identifier" based on the thought streams of individual thieves. Each person's decision making exhibits a pattern because each person learns how to deal with a particular aspect of any task in an individual way. The investigator's use of this decision pattern may disclose the who, when, where, or how, making it possible to identify, trap, or find the thief before or during his or her next crime.

 Describe how investigators work with other investigators and other sources of information to whittle down the universe of suspects responsible for a specific crime.

The Universe of Suspects

Each member of a criminal investigation division should be able to recognize information that is of importance to all members of the division and to advise coworkers of possible suspects in current or future crimes. In solving thefts, unlike the pursuit of a named suspect in crimes of violence, one must engage in a battle for information, and every investigator needs the help of associates. Although mainly concerned with general information about individuals who are suspected of earning the major portion of their incomes from criminal operations, this information can sometimes isolate a number of persons as suspects in a specific crime.

Field interview reports placed into police records systems may hold meaningful data about persons and vehicles stopped and questioned by police officers on patrol. However, a great deal of data about people living and working in a patrol sector is stored in the minds of the officers working the sector with some regularity. Often, this useful information never gets into the police records system. At one time, local police communicated this type of information to federal agents and uniformed police supplied local detectives with similar data about persons considered suspects because of their activity. More recently, the upward supply of information from local levels has been noticeable in its absence. An investigator must work to correct this situation, allocating time on a daily basis to developing liaisons with local sources of information among fellow police officers, to finding out the names and descriptions of persons known to be well supplied with money but without a known source of income, to noting the automobile make and license number of a newly arrived hoodlum or a recently released felony parolee, to learning the consensus in regard to a merchant suspected of buying and selling stolen property, and to hearing about a host of seemingly unimportant items shared among police officers in friendship and appreciation of mutual occupational objectives.

Work also must be devoted to remedying current practices about credit and reward for information received. Entries should be made in the service records of the helping officers when such leads assist in breaking a case. More important, such fellow workers may be assisted when their ambition is to step up into investigative work. Willingness to help an investigator is a good recommendation about a person's basic worth for this type of duty.

Investigators also must allocate time regularly to frequent the haunts of known thieves. Taxi drivers, waitresses, cocktail hostesses, bartenders, and tavern owners in such areas are potential sources of information about persons who are new to the area and apparently well supplied with money. Persons in these occupations are less reluctant to talk about thieves than they are about people who rob and are assaultive. Underworld informants interviewed clandestinely can give supplementary information for a better understanding of data already collected; they can assist in interpreting information, and they can offer leads that may be developed by inquiries in the known hangouts of these criminals. This is necessarily a discreet inquiry in order not to compromise any ongoing investigation. The investigator's relations with such sources of information are guarded ones, quite different from the friendships necessary to develop information from among local police officers.

Learning to appreciate the significance of an apparently minor item of information is a developed skill. However, it is a learned skill that will enhance the value of other information collected during an investigation. It will also increase the universe of suspects and the probability that the group of suspects will contain the person responsible for the crime under investigation. Because of the lack of eyewitnesses in crimes against property, the ability to solve a crime is likely to rest on the necessary information getting into the police system without loss or distortion and being used to the best advantage.[11]

Explain how investigators posing as receivers of stolen property gain information useful in identifying thieves active in the community.

Criminal Receivers of Stolen Property

Theft investigators would be seriously handicapped if the proceeds of all thefts were cash or its equivalent. Most thefts are of various goods and merchandise. Unfortunately, the market for stolen property is stable and continuous.

The real success in stealing is not the completion of the crime itself but the disposal of the stolen property at a profit—without leaving the trace that so often identifies the perpetrators of these crimes. Criminals who commit property crimes are repeaters. It may be that they are fatalistic about this Achilles' heel of property crimes and consider it a permanent occupational hazard, but not many of them blithely pawn their loot or sell it to someone likely to identify them to police.

Initially, the receiver of stolen property insulates the thief from identification and arrest. As soon as the property transfer is made, the thief can no longer be caught with the stolen property in his or her possession. However, when police detect and apprehend a receiver with stolen property, the potential for tracing it back to the thief is always present. This tracing from receiver to thief is an effective investigative technique for theft. It is the only method to use when a thief does not leave any fingerprints or "signature" (modus operandi) at the crime scene, when the thief is not observed or apprehended while the crime is in progress, or while the thief is in possession of recently stolen property.

When the stolen property is purchased by an individual seeking a bargain, this tracing is relatively easy. The receiver is informed of the possible criminal implications of possessing stolen property. Usually, the price and the circumstances of purchase create a reasonably probable cause to assume the purchaser knew the property was stolen. In disclaiming any criminal responsibility, this type of receiver either identifies the seller–thief or gives sufficient information about the purchase to enable the investigator to identify the thief.

When the stolen property is purchased by a professional receiver (a fence), tracing from receiver to thief becomes a problem. Fences with long-standing business dealings with a thief are unlikely to reveal the circumstances of how they received the stolen property.

Fences are the intermediaries of larceny. They buy and sell stolen property regularly. They are in direct contact with thieves and with possible purchasers. Most of them have acquired a reputation ("rep") on both sides of this business loop, and depend on this "goodwill" for third-party referrals of new business. This rep is that the fence will not, under any circumstances, inform police of the identity of a thief or a purchaser of stolen property.[12]

The **storefront or "sting" technique** is an investigative technique in property crimes aimed at the wholesale identification and apprehension of thieves. Police investigators pose as fences for the purpose of "buying" stolen property.[13] Since the prices paid to thieves by a real fence are copied by the police, the cost of this technique is not a real problem. The problem is whether such police activity may encourage local thieves to take more and more—as long as a thief has the ability to convert merchandise into cash will the thief be encouraged to steal more.

12 List the various types of auto thieves.

Auto Theft

The theft of cars, trucks, and motorcycles is common throughout the United States. According to the FBI's *Uniform Crime Reports* an estimated 721,053 motor vehicles were stolen in 2012. More than $4.3 billion was lost due to motor vehicle thefts, with an average loss of approximately $6,020. The vast majority, 73 percent, of the vehicles stolen were automobiles. Approximately 12 percent of all motor vehicle thefts are cleared by arrest or exceptional clearance.[14] **Auto theft** is the term generally used by police in describing this form of larceny. The universe of auto thieves is comprised of both amateurs and professionals.

1. *The Joyriding Juvenile.* Joyriding juveniles are usually host to several other juveniles. They abandon the vehicle when it runs out of gas or they tire of it.

2. ***The Transportation Thief.*** The transportation thief "borrows" a car for transportation, sometimes to cross state lines or for a lengthy period and abandons the vehicle when it has served the thief's purpose.

3. ***The Use-in-Crime Thief.*** Use-in-crime thieves steal a car for the sole purpose of using it in the commission of another crime, such as a robbery. Again, this type of thief abandons the vehicle when it has served its purpose.

4. ***Insurance-Fraud Swindlers.*** Insurance-fraud swindlers abandon automobiles in ghetto areas where they know they will be stripped promptly for parts, or they have an automobile dismantled or "squished" in a junkyard or will arrange for its burning. The vehicle owner claims—and usually receives—the current *Blue Book* value of the vehicle from the insurance company.

   In a spin-off of this fraud, the swindler registers and insures a "paper" car (forged title to a nonexistent vehicle), reports it stolen, and puts in a claim to the insurance carrier for the current *Blue Book* value of the phantom car.

5. ***Strippers and Dismantlers.*** **Strippers** usually attack a parked car, taking a variety of parts readily disposed of on the local black market. Stereos, CDs, batteries, bucket seats, transmissions, rear ends, generators, wheels and tires, and even motors have been stripped from automobiles in public places.

   Dismantlers steal a car, tow or drive it to a "chop shop," and have it cut up for most of its parts. The stolen car's body (sometimes even minus fenders, doors, headlights, front grill, and motor hood) is abandoned some distance from the shop, usually in a remote area. These thieves work fast. A parked car can be stripped in place in less than an hour, and dismantlers can chop up a car, dispose of the leftover body, and move the parts to be sold to another location all within an hour or so.

6. ***Professional Auto Thieves.*** The "pro" auto thief steals late-model automobiles and resells them. Sometimes the stolen car is transported to another state and registered in that state with forged or fraudulent papers prior to resale. A contemporary practice is to ship the stolen car out of the country (Mexico and South America are favorite destinations) and sell it on arrival. Some of these professional thieves have developed a new trade: stealing cars to order for "chop shops."

Many auto thieves now use weapons to gain possession of a car. **Carjacking** is the armed robbery of a person in possession of an automobile or other motor vehicle. One or more thieves confront a car's driver with a gun, knife, or other weapon and demand the car's keys, then drive off.

While amateur car thieves (joyriders and transportation thieves) sometimes seek automobiles with the keys in the lock or the car doors unlocked, the professionals use tools such as dent pullers and slide hammers or a set of master keys to enter a locked car and defeat the ignition lock. Of course, many amateur thieves are as skilled at hot-wiring a car's ignition as are the professionals.

An auto theft investigation has the following stages:

1. ***Preliminary Investigation.*** The preliminary investigator accepts the report of a stolen vehicle from the owner or his or her representative. The report must contain the name, address, and telephone number of the owner; a full description of the vehicle, including registration number and public and other identification numbers; the time and place of the theft and the location of the vehicle when stolen; and assurance that the vehicle was not repossessed by a finance company or other legal owner. Any distinctive features about the stolen vehicle (e.g., design, color, damage) will be entered on this report to aid in its location as promptly as possible.

2. ***Alarm.*** Information from the preliminary investigation report—particularly the distinctive characteristics of the stolen vehicle—is transmitted to all members of the police agency and sent to cooperating agencies, by Teletype or other means, and reported to state and national computerized records systems.

3. ***Recovery.*** Auto thefts for convenience or joyriding are usually identified by prompt recovery of the stolen auto without any evidence of stripping. This is also true of the

use-in-crime theft, with the time of recovery usually occurring shortly after the crime. Citizens often notice these parked vehicles and assist the patrol force in locating them.

The recovery of a stripped or "chopped" vehicle identifies the work of strippers and dismantlers. The nonrecovery of the stolen vehicle tends to identify the other types of auto thieves.

4. *Continuing Investigation.* Arrest of an auto thief while in possession of the stolen vehicle or its recovery is usually what prompts a probe into the circumstances of an auto theft. When the vehicle is not recovered within a reasonable time, investigators prowl auto accessory and salvage yards and body and fender shops proactively to locate stolen vehicles. Local laws usually require proprietors to allow police inspection.

5. *Case Preparation.* Cases involving the theft of a *single* vehicle closed out by arrest are simple: the appropriation of another's property to the thief's own use without permission of the owner. Cases involving *multivehicle* thefts require extensive evidence not only to show the larceny but possibly to assemble a conspiracy case against all offenders involved. In either event, inquiries along the basic leads common in property crimes give initial direction to any continuing investigation of auto theft.

The reality of auto theft is that the current high prices for vehicle accessories and components contribute to the growth of "hot parts" dealers. This ready market for the proceeds of crime assures strippers and dismantlers of better-than-average prices in comparison with thieves stealing other goods and merchandise. In fact, the growing market for such goods has attracted many segments of the national crime syndicate to this lucrative field.

In preliminary or continuing investigations of auto theft, primary identification of a stolen vehicle is made by the public vehicle identification number (PVIN), motor number, and confidential vehicle identification number (CVIN) at various hidden locations on the vehicle. (Vehicle manufacturers and the National Automobile Theft Bureau supply police agencies with information about the location of such numbers on cars, trucks, and motorcycles.)

 Explain the three types of employee theft and how these crimes are investigated.

Theft by Employees

Businesses in the United States lose billions of dollars annually as a result of employee theft. **Shrinkage** is the term business uses for the loss of inventory from employee theft. The resulting loss is transferred to the consumer in the form of higher costs for products and services. Many large firms employ security personnel who are trained in employee theft investigations. However, the criminal investigator may be involved when the loss is extensive and criminal prosecution is desired or when the business does not have access to an investigative staff. A thorough investigation is required in these cases because the suspected employee may be fired and subject to criminal prosecution. Generally, employee theft falls within three categories: incidental, situational, and continual theft.

Incidental theft involves those instances when employees consume the employer's product while on the job or take home items such as pens and pencils at the end of the day. The cost to the employer is relatively minor. Most businesses deal with this type of employee theft through disciplinary measures and assume the loss as the price of doing business.

Situational theft involves those instances when the employee is presented with an opportunity for theft that, in the employee's mind, must be acted on. Truck drivers, for instance, who at the end of their route have extra merchandise that has not been charged out to them, have an excellent opportunity to take that merchandise. The restaurant manager who is called away to handle an emergency while counting the previous day's receipts inadvertently leaves the office door open. An employee acts on the opportunity, and the manager returns to find that some or all of the money is missing. In both of these instances, the criminal investigator may become involved and presented with the challenge of having a number of potential suspects.

The missing merchandise could have been put on any one of a number of trucks, and any of the restaurant's employees could have entered the manager's office while he or she was gone.

The initial goal for the investigator is to reduce to a manageable total the number of possible suspects who will ultimately be interrogated or asked to submit to a polygraph examination. Accomplishing this task requires that each suspect be interviewed individually. Each suspect is asked a predetermined set of questions designed to evaluate his or her reaction to each question. An example of the type of questions the investigator might ask would include the following:

Do you know why I am talking to you?

Do you have any idea of who may be responsible for the loss?

Is there anyone you would eliminate as a suspect?

The guilty and innocent employees have different motivations concerning the responses to these questions. The innocent employee wants to aid the investigation and knows he or she is there to help the investigator. The innocent employee wants the responsible person caught so that the innocent employee will no longer be a suspect and life at work will return to normal. The innocent person, therefore, will identify the most likely suspects for the investigator and will eliminate those above suspicion. In contrast, the guilty person will want to expand the list of possible suspects as much as possible. The missing merchandise could have been put on anyone's truck or could have been a clerical error; anyone in the area at the time could have access to the manager's office and the missing money. The guilty would not eliminate anyone from suspicion; after all, everyone could use some extra cash. The guilty would pretend not to know why the investigator is talking to him or her, since he or she would not want to be considered to be a suspect. When the employee's reactions indicate guilt, the investigator may switch to an interrogation mode or, possibly, may schedule the suspect for a voluntary polygraph examination.

Continual theft involves ongoing, constant acts of theft by an employee. This type of theft is usually motivated by the need to support a vice of the employee, such as gambling, drugs, or alcohol. In California, the theft of money, labor, or real or personal property valued at more than $400 in any twelve-month consecutive period is a felony.

The investigator usually starts the investigation by charting the known dates and times of the losses and comparing this information with employee attendance records. A reasonable match, over a sufficient amount of time, of a specific employee who was on the job when the losses occurred would qualify him or her for closer scrutiny. Trusted supervisors and managers should also be consulted to determine any reason that the suspected employee may be responsible for the losses. Finally, the suspected employee would be subjected to surveillance, either by visual or contact method, until a loss occurs. Once the surveillance confirms that the employee is the responsible party, the employee should be confronted while still in possession of the money or merchandise and then questioned.

 Describe how organized retail theft occurs.

Organized Retail Theft

The thieves involved in **organized retail theft** go way beyond the activities of an ordinary shoplifter. These thieves fill a shopping cart up with expensive goods, such as DVDs or baby formula, or simply grab an arm full of expensive clothing and walk out of the store without paying for the merchandise. What they steal is often directed by the needs of fences, people who buy stolen merchandise. Fences are interested in merchandise that they can get rid of quickly at their retail stores, at the flea market, or through online action. Typically, the fence will pay 30 cents on the dollar for stolen goods. According to the FBI the loss in merchandise is between $30 and $37 billion a year, more than the loss due to burglary, larceny, robbery, and auto theft combined.[15]

⓯ *Define cargo theft and the methods used to steal containers and truckloads of goods.*

Cargo Theft

This type of theft involves the taking of an entire truck or cargo container full of merchandise. The more common methods of committing this type of crime include the following:

- *Highjacking*—the thieves follow a targeted truck and wait for the driver to stop or force the driver to stop the vehicle. The thieves, who may be armed, board the truck and order the driver out of the vehicle and then drive off with the truck and merchandise.
- *Truck Stops*—when the driver pulls off the highway to eat, rest, or get fuel, they may be approached by thieves and offered money to give up their truck. The thieves may also wait until the driver is away from the vehicle then break in, manipulate the ignition system, and drive off with the vehicle.
- *Dropped or unattended trailers*—sit in transportation yards waiting to be unloaded or transported to another location. Thieves with their own stolen truck pull up to the trailer, hook it up to their tractor, and drive off.
- *Deceptive pickups*—the thieves assume the identity of a legitimated cargo carrier and have a cargo container loaded on their stolen tractor and drive off with the contents.

Cargo thieves can steal any product but the most popular targets are shipments of pharmaceuticals, consumer electronics, clothing, and food. Cargo thieves are responsible for stealing an estimated $30 billion in merchandise annually.[16]

⓰ *Explain why cases of fraud go unreported.*

▶ Fraud

Fraud is nothing new. It is defined as a nonviolent crime involving elements of intentional deceit, concealment, corruption, misrepresentation, and abuse of trust to gain the property of another, and it is often facilitated by the willing cooperation of unaware or unknowing victims.

The guile, deception, and trickery common to frauds often silence the victim. Either the victim does not realize a theft has occurred or is unwilling to report it for fear of being involved in a crime or of publicly admitting to being a "sucker" who has been duped. In addition, police frequently fail to discover unreported frauds because fraud is a covert scheme with a lower profile than overt thefts or violent crimes.

Fraud in the United States is on the increase. Swindlers use simple bunco or complex confidence (con) games to steal from unknowing victims. Fraudulent check writers menace the integrity of banks. White-collar criminals operating in both the marketplace and the workplace abuse the trust common to merchant–customer and employee–employer relations.

Fraud investigations usually begin with a citizen's complaint or a police probe. A preliminary investigation should disclose whether the act or acts done to further the objective of the fraud are a crime under state laws. Such investigation should spell out the time, place, and modus operandi of the fraud, along with data on the victim, property lost, witnesses, and suspects.

Continuing investigations are the action phase in which suspects are identified, pursued, and apprehended, and the case is prepared for criminal prosecution. When a fraud case reveals substantial economic loss to a victim but cannot be developed for criminal prosecution, it is best referred to state or federal regulatory agencies for possible civil action, a cease-and-desist order, or other appropriate remedial action (Figure 13-3).

Fraud auditing is a new occupational specialty in commercial and industrial employment. Fraud auditors are assigned the task of detecting and preventing frauds in commercial transactions. Job descriptions in this role call for the skills of a well-trained auditor and an experienced criminal investigator. Fraud auditors examine the covert aspects of employee behavior and the barriers established to prevent fraud. Can the barriers be breached? When? How? By whom?[17]

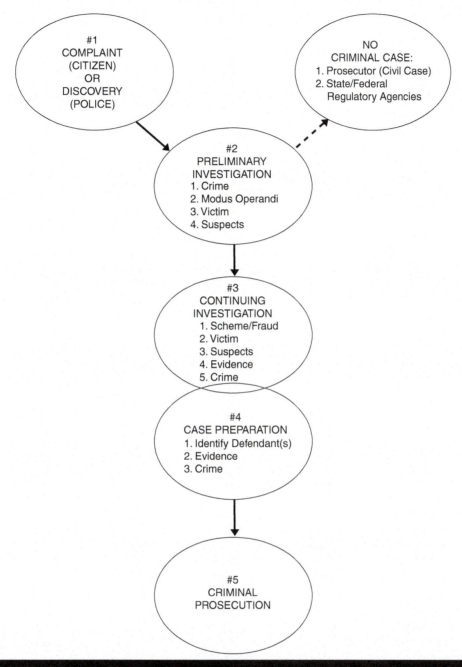

FIGURE 13-3 Investigation of Fraud.

⑰ *Define the four elements of fraud.*

Elements of Fraud

Investigators must seek evidence of four common characteristics of fraud:

1. Criminal intent (mens rea)
2. Wrongful objective (deprive true owner of property)
3. Disguise or concealment of objective (wrongful)
4. Reliance on victim's cupidity, carelessness, or compassion

The criminal intent is to achieve the wrongful objective of the scheme. The act or acts done to implement the scheme spell out the disguise or concealment of the scheme's unlawful objective.

Thieves who profit from fraudulent schemes must induce the victim to part voluntarily with his or her property. This may be accomplished by the signing of a contract or the actual payment of money or transfer of property ownership.

 Identify the more common swindles or con games used to defraud unsuspecting victims.

Bunco Schemes and Con Games

Bunco schemes and **con games** are frauds based on promises of unusual returns: something for nothing, double your money, or income for life. The false hopes of the victim are fostered by assurances that the risk is minimal. The scheme is usually described as a "sure thing."

Some of the more common swindles classed as bunco or con games are (1) pigeon drop, (2) payoff, and (3) carnival bunco. The **pigeon drop, or pocketbook drop** (Figure 13-4), is street bunco that requires a minimum number of "props": pocketbook or envelope and a sizable amount of cash. The **pigeon** is the victim, and no more than two or three swindlers participate in this crime. This is a scheme in which a victim is conned into withdrawing a large sum of money from a bank account to show financial responsibility. In the presence of the potential victim, one of the swindlers apparently "finds" a pocketbook or envelope filled with money (from $500 to $2,500 usually). The approach to the victim is disarming, combining happiness at finding the money along with the query, "What do I do now?" As the victim starts to discuss the swindler's apparent good fortune, the second swindler shows up. Assuming the role of a stranger who just happened to witness the "find" and wants to be part of it, the second swindler joins in the excited talk that makes the victim a partner in a plan to withhold the money from its owner until the origin of this amount of cash can be determined. Since this will take time, the two swindlers team up to convince the victim that he or she should hold the find, but to assure them of the victim's good faith, they ask the victim to show cash equal to the amount found (or close to it). Faced with the possible loss of one-third of the found money, the gullible victim goes to a bank, gets the cash, and reveals it to the swindlers. They go through the motions of counting it, advising the victim of their satisfaction, and bundling the found money with the victim's cash and arranging to meet again with the victim the next day. After this parting, the natural curiosity of the victim leads to an examination of the bundle of money. It turns out to be paper cut to size. The swindlers switched the bundle just before they parted from the victim.[18]

The **charity switch** is a variation of the pigeon drop used by swindlers who have a potential victim unlikely to be motivated by greed. The pitch in the charity switch is to a victim's compassion. The swindlers convince the victim (often a clergyman or nurse) to hold money ($500 to $2,500) for a sick or dying person. If the owner of the money does not recover, the victim can use the money for his or her favorite charity. However, to show good faith, the victim is asked to show financial responsibility. At this point, the routine of the pigeon drop occurs, with the swindlers taking off with all of the money.[19]

The **payoff** is a swindle in which the swindler claims to have access to information regarding fixed horse races. In its simple street bunco form, the swindler acts out the role of **tout**, a person who, by false misrepresentation, persuades another to bet on a horse race. Three or four bettor–victims place large bets on horses that the swindler believes will win a selected race. If one of the swindler's horses wins, the winning bettor shares the winnings with the swindler. In its more elaborate form, victims are identified by **ropers** and are put in contact with men who pose as representatives of the fixed-race conspiracy. Another man poses as the manager of the bogus horse room used in this swindle. In a carefully orchestrated scheme, the **sucker, or mark**, is allowed to win at first, but he or she loses the final large bet. In breaking away with their loot, the swindlers "cool" the victim by implying that he or she is equally guilty of violating federal or state communications laws or participating in a criminal conspiracy.[20]

Carnival bunco is street bunco in which each victim may be "taken" only for small amounts of money, but the overall profit to these swindlers is huge. Customers pay a 10- to 50-cent fee to play these games, hoping to win one or more of the better-quality prizes exhibited,

487 PC PIGEON DROP

Date: **6/22/2005**

Case #: **01-6956 / 01-7010**

Name: **UNKNOWN**

Height: **5 Feet 8 Inches**

Weight: **180**

Age: **40**

Sex: **M**

Eyes: **BROWN**

Hair: **BLACK**

Complexion: **CLEAR**

Race: **BLACK**

OTHER INFORMATION BELOW

On 6-20-2005 at 1400 hours, (S) took up conversation with Asian (V) at Valley Shopping Center. (S) told victim he was new in the U.S. and stated he was not trusted since he was black. (S) asked (V) to withdraw money ($6,700) from (V)'s bank account to prove his point. The (V) withdrew the money. The (S) then asked (V) to trust him to walk around the block with the (V)'s money. (S) told (V) that if he did that and if the (S) returned, the (S) would give the (V) double his money. The (V) agreed and the (S) left with the money and never came back.

On 6-21-2005 at 1446 hours, the same (S) made another attempt at the Cheapcost Store. In that crime, a second suspect (BMA) was used. Police were called by the (V) while he was in the bank conducting the withdrawal. (S)s fled the area prior to police arrival.

Please BOL and contact me with any similars.

Officer John Smith   Valley Department of Public Safety
(555) 555-5555

TRAK (59 -> 131:1.70.66) This flyer produced on a TRAK System. For more information about TRAK see www.trak.org

FIGURE 13-4   Pigeon Drop Con Game Wanted Notice.

but they cannot win those better prizes. Customers are encouraged to try and try again by allowing them to win minor prizes (cheap merchandise) and fast counting their scores: operators total up a customer's score above what has been achieved to convince the victim that he or she is really close to winning a better prize. Of course, the games are rigged so that these scores can never be attained. Trick balls, weighted dolls, underinflated balloons, and oversized marbles are some of the mechanical aids used to defraud gullible carnival goers.

Discuss how a bank examiner fraud works.

The Bank Examiner Fraud

Bank examiner fraud is an ego-building swindle based on the hidden desire of many people to serve as a secret agent for the police. Victims are located through telephone books or pseudo-surveys. The first telephone call to the victim is double-talk, alleging some problem with his or her account at the local bank. The next call is allegedly from an officer of the bank. The story told is that one of the bank's employees has been tampering with accounts of depositors, they want to catch him, and they need the victim's help to do so. Cooperative victims are then informed they should go to the bank, withdraw a specific sum (usually just short of the victim's total deposited funds), and bring it home. The victim is assured that the withdrawal will be watched secretly by an armed agent who will follow the victim home to make certain the money is safe. A few moments after arrival at home with the money, the victim is visited by the swindler posing as the armed agent. After some double-talk, the swindler counts the victim's money, gives him or her a signed deposit slip, and takes the money. Hours, days, and even weeks later, the victim finds out that the name on the deposit slip is fictitious, the bank knows nothing of any dishonest employee, and the money given to the swindler is a total loss.

 Describe the steps involved in passing fraudulent checks.

Fraudulent Checks

Passers of forged checks have always concerned police forgery squads. However, it is the unusual fraudulent check writers who attempt to pass off a signature as genuine. It is true that they sign names other than their own, but this is just the first step in a fraud that also involves (1) false or stolen identification cards, (2) a story that overcomes a merchant's reluctance to cash a check upon presentation of minimal identification, and (3) a bunco or a con artist's sense of the right time, place, and victim to conclude this fraud successfully. Fortunately, the modus operandi of these check passers identifies them to investigators. Sometimes, a victim will assist in identification, but since the identification documents are spurious and the contact at the time of check cashing is short, victims have recall problems.

NSF (not sufficient funds) check writers are overt thieves, signing their name to a worthless check and cashing it. Willingness to repay the loss to the victim and an active checking account can overcome the perception of fraud. So-called occasional fraudulent check writers can postpone criminal prosecution on a promise of restitution. The true fraud investigation in this area focuses on the "chronic" fraudulent check writer and the extent of his or her theft when more than one NSF check has been cashed.

 Explain how thieves obtain the credit cards they will use to commit a fraud.

Credit Card Fraud

Credit card fraud is emerging as a popular form of theft. Fraudulent use of credit cards provides the thief with various goods and services, and credit cards can easily be converted into cash by sale on the street—the illegal marketplace. Thieves obtain credit cards by theft (from mail, the person to whom the card belongs, a residence, an auto, a place of business, a hotel, or other location), by fraudulent application to the issuing firm, or by counterfeiting. Credit cards stolen from the mail, intercepted en route to the legitimate receivers, are sought on the illegal market because they have not been reported as lost or stolen. If the card requires a signature, the illegal owner can sign the card in the name of the legitimate card owner and in a style he or she can readily replicate (despite disguising the handwriting).

Credit card thieves may be discovered on the complaint of merchants who call for an authorization because of the amount of a purchase and discover that the card is on the "hot card list," on the complaint of those who become suspicious because of alterations on the card itself, during legal searches, or in the course of other investigations. In one Los Angeles case, the investigation of a group forging motor vehicle driver's licenses led to several credit card thieves who bought forged licenses to show additional identification when "running a card."

 Discuss the common consumer frauds.

Consumer and Business Fraud

Consumer and business frauds are marketplace swindles in which the buyer or investor is defrauded by the swindler's misrepresentations.[21] Common consumer frauds include these:

1. *Bait and Switch*—advertised merchandise bargains lure customers into a merchant's place of business. Sales personnel then run down the advertised merchandise and switch the customer to a higher-priced item of allegedly better quality.

2. *Repair Fraud*—includes overcharging for services performed; charging for services not performed or parts not replaced; failing to provide labor and materials as agreed; and charging for labor or materials not needed or discussed with the customer, or within the scope of the customer's agreement.

3. *Misrepresentation*—is failing to give the true facts about product performance, warranties, credit charges, or other hidden costs.

The **Ponzi scheme, or kiting,** is the base of all investment frauds; securities frauds are get-rich-quick schemes; land frauds have a similar scheme along with the promise of a future home in a desirable climate; and advance fee swindles offer assistance in securing huge loans to poor-risk credit applicants.

In a Ponzi scheme (named after its originator) the swindler uses money invested by new victims to pay a high interest on the investments of earlier victims—whose money the swindler has appropriated to his or her own use, rather than investing it as claimed in the sales pitch given the victim. A Ponzi scheme collapses when the swindler runs out of victims.

Securities frauds are based on promises to victims of rapid capital growth and a high and quick rate of returns in dividends, as well as special advantages such as tax shelters. Victims are selected on the basis of their liquid or convertible assets. High-income professionals and persons approaching the threshold of retirement are common victims.

Land-sales frauds are based on the swindler's misrepresentations about the value and future development of worthless, unimproved land. Fraudulent land sales have involved the sale of property at inflated prices in which the swindler had no existing title or interest. Undeveloped property owned by the swindler, but without roads, water, or other improvements, is sold because of false statements of current or future development (e.g., roads, water) that does not exist and that the swindler has no intention of providing.

Advanced-fee frauds victimize businesspeople who are having problems securing loans from local banks or other lending institutions. The swindler claims to have access to loan officers or out-of-town banks or the mortgage loan officials of a labor union pension fund. The advance fee is up-front money to motivate the loan arranger (swindler) to arrange the loan. The swindler has no intention of performing as promised but will make any misrepresentation to secure the victim's money. This swindle is common in the United States because the reality of securing loans by poor-risk applicants is that up-front money has been used to influence bank loan officers and officials of union pension funds.

Home-improvement frauds victimize homeowners by false claims that the work is necessary or that the cost of the proposed work is much below its real worth and will add to the homeowner's basic equity. Gangs of home-improvement swindlers move from town to town, transferring their accounts payable to a local bank at a discount and moving to new areas. These frauds include one or more of the following characteristics:

1. Misrepresentation of the need for labor or materials
2. Poor workmanship
3. Substandard materials
4. Gross overpricing

5. Failure to provide paid-for labor and material

6. Concealment of the cost of credit, as well as the fact that failure to pay will result in a lien on the victim's home

Bankruptcy frauds involve false claims of insolvency. The planned bankruptcy or scam has been used by organized crime personnel to loot the assets of a business. In bankruptcy fraud, the swindler either conceals or diverts to friends and associates the major assets of a business so that they cannot be sold to pay off creditors or uses previously established credit to secure huge amounts of merchandise and then conceals or converts such merchandise to his or her own use just prior to the bankruptcy—and without paying the supplier's bills.

Insurance frauds are not uncommon in the world of commerce and business. They are in a class by themselves because the swindler must be the insured, and the victim is the insurer. The swindler may have crime partners, but only the insured can profit from defrauding an insurance company. The filing of false claims is the fraud. In some fraudulent fire cases, sham mortgages are used fraudulently to raise the value of a building. As a result, insurance policies are issued in amounts far in excess of the true value of the insured building. An arson investigation into a series of fires in an urban ghetto area found that the insured owner had engaged in selling to friends and business associates a number of times, with little or no cash involved in the transfer of ownership. Each time, the seller took a new second mortgage to artificially inflate the building's value.[22]

 Define workplace fraud and embezzlement.

Workplace Fraud

Major frauds in the workplace are embezzlement and computer frauds. Investigations are usually initiated upon discovery of the fraud, with investigators following leads about the identity of employees having the necessary access to the funds or the computer.

Embezzlement is the conversion of another's property over which the thief has custody or control. Victims are the employers of these dishonest employees, with the scope of the theft depending on the position held by the employee and his or her ability to conceal the theft or thefts. Investigators should be alert for money losses reported as armed robberies to cover up embezzlement.

The newest fraud in the workplace involves computers and has frightening potential for victimization. The Equity Funding fraud exemplifies use of a computer as an essential tool for accomplishing a theft that totaled a $100 million loss to customers, stockholders, and others. To sustain its image as a successful insurance company, Equity Funding produced fake insurance policies, which were recorded in the computer as new business and sold for cash to reinsurance firms. In this case, the computer was also programmed to conceal the fraud: a special code was used to skip the usual premium procedures on the fake policies. At least seventy-five employees served as accomplices and participants in this crime. So-called creative accounting covered up this fraud for many years until a fired employee talked about it.[23]

 Explain how thieves obtain personal identification numbers (PIN) in order to commit ATM fraud.

ATM Fraud

Thieves find automated teller machine (ATM) cards in the wallets and pocketbooks of their victims. They also find driver's licenses, sometimes checkbooks, and, often, photographs or papers with the names of family members. All this material used to be worthless; today, it has become the basis for finding the personal identification number (PIN) that validates the ATM card. ATM card holders seem to have a subliminal fear of forgetting their "secret" PIN numbers and use easily remembered numbers, such as birth date or anniversary date, a fore-and-aft series of numbers from their bank account or driver's license number, a simple 1-2-3-4 code based on their name or the names of children or grandchildren, or a transposition of a home or office telephone number.

Now in possession of the ATM card and the correct PIN number, the thief tries to get to the machine before the rightful owner of the card contacts the bank and cancels his or her card. Withdrawing whatever the cash limit is for a single transaction, thieves have hit an ATM, walked away, come back for another withdrawal, continuing until the account is empty or the card is reported stolen and the machine retains the card.

Thieves are aware of the surveillance cameras at these machines but knowingly discount any in-court identification at trial and openly scoff at the possibility of arrest. However, police and bank fraud investigators struggle with the "gotcha" problem in these cases:

1. They move fast upon a stolen card cancellation notice, study the rhythm of the withdrawals by the thief from the ATM transaction record, and, as long as funds remain in the account, wait until the thief arrives to hit the machine again.

2. When credit cards from the same source have been used successfully, they interview the salesclerks who wrote up the sales, asking for a good physical description and knowledge of the suspect. They also request the cooperation of one or two of these individuals to help produce a composite sketch.

3. When forged checks begin to appear, they interview the endorser for help in identification of the suspect.

4. They send cards and checks to the crime lab to lift latent fingerprints.

5. If they have partial identity, they seek out ex-lovers, ex-spouses, and former friends or crime partners for help in making a full identification from photos or the composite sketch. If any one of these individuals is in jail awaiting trial, the investigator may have the classic leverage to secure cooperation.

Investigation of Fraud

Since crime scenes are usually nonexistent in fraud cases, the investigator must concentrate on securing facts about the crime from the victim and witnesses and from the records or other documents prepared and used by one or more of the participants.

Collected evidence should be organized under the following major headings:

1. *Description of the Offense.* How was the scheme conceived, what was its nature, where was it placed in operation, and what dates was it in operation?

2. *Victim.* How was the initial contact made? Subsequent contacts? Where? Who was involved? Who made what representations? What was the victim's reliance on such representations? What was the extent of the loss? How was payment made to the swindlers?

3. *Suspect–Defendant.* When available, what are the name, address, occupation, date and place of birth, physical description, associates, and criminal history of the suspect–defendant? What is the identity of the suspect–defendant who may cooperate with the investigation, possibly serving as an accomplice witness in a criminal trial?

4. *Evidence.* What data on witnesses, victim, documentary, and other physical evidence are available, and how were they obtained?

5. *Crime.* What are the essential elements of the crime or crimes that might be charged along with (a) major misrepresentations, false pretenses, false promises used by the suspect–defendant in obtaining the victim's money and (b) presentation of evidence in support of the investigator's conclusion that such evidence supports a belief in the criminal intent of the suspect–defendant and sets out the fraud involved?

Identification should not be a major problem in fraud investigations once a suspect is located and apprehended. The pursuit and apprehension of swindlers is often handicapped by the inability of victims to properly describe the swindler and others involved. Once the swindler is apprehended, however, the victim can usually identify him or her.

The investigation of credit card frauds provides a splendid opportunity to uncover more serious crimes and to apprehend crime partners. A credit card is unusual in that the issuing firm (the theft victim in extensive frauds) will aid the investigation by tracing and reporting the activities associated with the illegal use of the credit card. As a result, investigators may secure the following:

1. Samples of handwriting in the form of signed sales drafts and applications
2. License plate numbers recorded on gasoline sales drafts at service stations
3. Driver's licenses on car rental contracts or on sales drafts for which further identification was requested
4. Credit card imprint on copies of sales drafts, airline tickets, hotel bills, or car rental contracts
5. Description of a rented motor vehicle that the subject had in his or her possession at any particular time
6. Description of merchandise on a sales slip, which could reveal the purchase of guns, knives, or items identifiable by serial numbers, as well as distinctive clothing and wigs

Decoy vehicles and appliances have opened up new horizons for proactive, as well as reactive, investigations of consumer frauds. The **decoy vehicle** or appliance is in good working order except for some minor or easily discovered and repaired fault. When the repair personnel entrusted with the decoy vehicle or appliance lie about needed repairs, or charge for repairs not done or for parts not supplied, the investigator can begin developing a fraud case.

CASE STUDY

COSTLY CRUSH

Carl Miller, age 77, is more than $200,000 in the hole after falling victim to a classic "sweetheart" scam. In the course of a two-and-a-half-year relationship, Miller financed his home to help him provide cash and gifts, including a car, to a woman who is half his age. Miller met the woman in the parking lot of a local bank. The detective explained that the suspect started off by telling the victim that she was very upset because the creditors were after her. Then she brought her kids around to start working him.

According to the detective, younger women stake out places where they might find elderly men. Sometimes it's the bank where they can overhear them make a deposit or a withdrawal. Other times the women will scan the obituaries to find men whose wives have recently passed away. Once a scammer spots a potential mark, she will try to figure out his financial situation through casual conversation. Then the scammer will exchange phone numbers with the potential victim.

The scammer will start by calling or showing up at the victim's home. The scammer will usually present a tale of woe, escalating it each time to extract more money from the victim. Health issues, their family, they need money for tests, cancer, and sending money to their home country are a partial list of the lines used on these victims. Sometimes sweetheart scammers will go as far as marrying their victims. However, one sure sign that it's a scam marriage is the lack of sexual relations.

The detective added that the sad part is that these victims are lonely. It's not so much about a romantic relationship; it's about companionship and someone to talk to. Then, thousands of dollars later, they realize that they have been duped.

Source: Stan Oklobdzija, "Costly Crush, Woman pulls 'sweetheart' scam on man, 77, stealing more than $200,000, officials say," *Sacramento Bee,* October 9, 2007, B3.

CHAPTER REVIEW

Key Terms

advanced-fee fraud   *255*
amateur burglar   *237*
auto theft   *246*
bait and switch   *255*

bank examiner fraud   *254*
bankruptcy fraud   *256*
behavior cycle in burglary   *239*
blasting   *240*

bunco scheme   *252*
burglarizing   *239*
burglary   *235*
burning   *240*

Review Questions

1. Burglary is usually a _____ crime in that the burglar normally tries to avoid contact with victims.
   a. Passive
   b. Personal
   c. Property
   d. Aggressive

2. The real success in stealing is not the commission of the crime, but the _____ of the stolen property at a profit.
   a. Removal
   b. Concealment
   c. Disposal
   d. Conversion

3. What type of employee theft occurs when the employee takes items home, such as pens or tools?
   a. Situational theft
   b. Incidental theft
   c. Continual theft
   d. Grand theft

4. What type of employee theft occurs when the employee is presented with an opportunity for theft that in the employee's mind must be acted upon?
   a. Situational theft
   b. Incidental theft
   c. Continual theft
   d. Grand theft

5. What type of employee theft is usually motivated by the need to support a vice such as gambling, drugs, or alcohol?
   a. Situational theft
   b. Incidental theft
   c. Continual theft
   d. Grand theft

6. In what type of fraud does the swindler use money invested by new victims to pay high interest rates on the investments of earlier victims?
   a. Bait and switch
   b. Ponzi scheme
   c. Securities fraud
   d. Embezzlement

7. In what type of fraud is advertised merchandise used to lure customers into the place of business where sales personnel then bad-mouth the advertised merchandise and sell higher-priced merchandise to the customer?
   a. Bait and switch
   b. Ponzi scheme
   c. Securities fraud
   d. Embezzlement

8. In what type of fraud are victims promised rapid capital growth, a high and quick rate of return on dividends, or special advantages such as tax shelters on their investments?
    a. Bait and switch
    b. Ponzi scheme
    c. Securities fraud
    d. Embezzlement
9. What type of theft involves the conversion of another person's property over which the thief has custody or control and victimizes employers of dishonest employees?
    a. Bait and switch
    b. Ponzi scheme
    c. Securities fraud
    d. Embezzlement
10. The intermediaries of larceny, the people who buy and sell stolen property regularly, are known as_____.
    a. Embezzlers
    b. Burglars
    c. Fences
    d. Ponzis

See Appendix D for the correct answers.

Application Exercise

Assume that you are a burglary detective and you have submitted a proposal to open and run a "sting operation." Your proposal calls for a storefront operation where detectives acting as fences buy stolen merchandise. Other agencies have used similar sting operations in their jurisdictions and have had a great deal of success in identifying active thieves and burglars. While your chain of command likes your proposal they doubt if it can be implemented due to the lack of funding. Your agency can provide the necessary detectives to staff the operation but they do not have the necessary seed money to buy stolen merchandise. You have been advised that if you can secure the necessary funding from private sources, your agency will back your efforts. Develop a strategy to find the necessary money to implement your proposal.

Discussion Questions

1. After reading the case study can you think of any way law enforcement can prevent this type of fraud?
2. List and describe five means of entry common to burglars.
3. Explain the Achilles' heel of stealing and the bland acceptance of this occupational hazard by thieves.
4. What circumstances may induce a receiver of stolen property to reveal the true circumstances of its purchase?
5. What are the advantages of a storefront or sting program to recover stolen property? The disadvantages?
6. What is a chop shop?
7. What are the four elements of fraud?
8. Describe the bank examiner fraud.
9. Define embezzlement.
10. What are decoy vehicles? Appliances?

Related Websites

For charts and tables about burglary trends in the United States see www.ojp.usdoj.gov/bjs/glance/burg.htm.

For information about mail fraud, mail theft, identity theft, and becoming a U.S. Postal Inspector contact the Postal Inspection Service website. www.postalinspectors.uspis.gov.

To learn more about Internet fraud, such as charity scams, online auctions, and pyramid and other schemes, check out this website: www.fraud.org/internet/intinfo.htm.

Notes

1. *State v. Wiley,* 173 Maryland 119 (1937).
2. California Penal Code, sec. 459.
3. Ibid., sec. 461.
4. Ibid., sec. 459.
5. www.fbi.gov/ucr/cius2008/offenses/property_crimee/burglary.
6. George Rengert and John Wasilchick, *Surburban Burglary: A Time and a Place for Everything* (Springfield, IL: Charles C Thomas, 1985), 53–75.
7. Maurice J. Fitzgerald, *Handbook of Criminal Investigation* (New York: Arco, 1960), 131.
8. Harry A. Scarr, et al., *Patterns of Burglary* (Washington, DC: U.S. Department of Justice, Law Enforcement Assistance Administration, National Institute of Law Enforcement and Criminal Justice, 1972), 4–5.
9. U.S. Department of Justice, *Criminal Victimization in the United States: 1992* (Washington, DC: U.S. Department of Justice, 1994), 154–155.
10. www.fbi.gov/ucr/cius2008/offenses/property_crime/larceny-theft.
11. M. A. Wilmer, "Criminal Investigation from the Small Town to the Large Urban Conurbation," *British Journal of Criminology* VIII, no. 3 (July 1968): 259–274.
12. Darrel J. Stefensmeier, *The Fence: In the Shadow of Two Worlds* (Totowa, NJ: Rowman & Littlefield, 1986), 13–35, 157–186.
13. U.S. Department of Justice, Law Enforcement Assistance Administration, *Strategies for Combating the Criminal Receiver of Stolen Goods: An Antifencing Manual for Law Enforcement Agencies* (Washington, DC: U.S. Department of Justice, Law Enforcement Assistance Administration, 1976), 89–97. Also see Ron Shaffer and Kevin Kloss (with Alfred R. Lewis), *Surprise! Surprise! How the Lawmen Conned the Thieves* (New York: Viking Press, 1977).
14. www.fbi.gov/ucr/cius2008/offenses/propeerty_crime/motor_vehicle_theft.
15. www.fbi.gov/news/stories/2007/april/retail040607.
16. www.inboundlogistics.com/cms/article/the-cargo-theft-threat.
17. G. Jack Bolongna and Robert J. Lindquist, *Fraud Auditing and Forensic Accounting: New Tools and Techniques* (New York: Wiley, 1987), 27–42.
18. Mary Carey and George Sherman, *A Compendium of Bunk: Or, How to Spot a Con Artist—A Handbook for Fraud Investigators, Bankers, and Other Custodians of the Public Trust* (Springfield, IL: Charles C Thomas, 1976), 9–20.
19. Ibid., 28–38.
20. David W. Maurer, *The American Confidence Man* (Springfield, IL: Charles C Thomas, 1974), 30–47.
21. See Herbert Edelhertz, Ezra Stotland, Marilyn Walsh, and Milton Weinberg, *The Investigation of White-Collar Crime: A Manual for Law Enforcement Agencies* (Washington, DC: U.S. Department of Justice, Law Enforcement Assistance Administration, 1977).
22. Brendan P. Battle and Paul B. Weston, *Arson: Detection and Investigation* (New York: Arco, 1979), 108.
23. Edelhertz, et al., *The Investigation of White Collar Crime,* 200; and Lee J. Seidler, Fredrick Andrews, and Marc J. Epstein, *The Equity Funding Papers: The Anatomy of a Fraud* (New York: Wiley, 1977), 3–19.

14 Cybercrime

LEARNING OBJECTIVES

After reading this chapter, you will be able to:

1 *Define an internal threat to a computer system and explain the different motivations of those involved.*

2 *Define an external threat to a computer system and discuss the motivations of those involved.*

3 *Discuss the different forms of computer fraud.*

4 *Explain how identity theft occurs.*

5 *Describe the problem of child pornography and the Internet.*

6 *Explain how child molesters use the Internet to find victims.*

7 *Outline the growing problem of contraband sales on the Internet.*

8 *Discuss the reasons why cyber terrorism is an attractive option for terrorists.*

9 *Explain the investigative process involved in cybercrime.*

Computers, as we know them today, were developed during World War II in response to the need to decrypt enemy communications. These early computers contained over twelve thousand vacuum tubes and occupied approximately a thousand square feet of floor space, the size of an average 25 × 40 college classroom. These computers were not only expensive to build but also used a tremendous amount of energy to operate and had less computing capacity than today's handheld cell phone. The vacuum tube was replaced by the transistor in the 1950s which resulted in smaller, faster computers that had greater computing capacity which used far less energy to operate. In 1959 IBM released their first line of mainframe computers which were primarily used by research universities, governments, and major corporations. These mainframes were stand-alone systems and were not interconnected; as such the security threats to these computers were limited to disgruntled or dishonest employees.

Early computers were as large as the average college classroom.

Source: University of Pennsylvania/AP Images

In 1981 IBM released its personal computer designed for use by small business and home use. These computers ran word processing and spreadsheet applications and little else. These were also stand-alone computers with limited security issues. As silicone technology advanced, the personal computer became faster and capable of running more and more applications. With the advent of the World Wide Web, or Internet, in the 1990s virtually all computers became interconnected and the security threat was now a global one as criminals became computer literate just like everyone else.[1]

Computer crime, or **cybercrime**, is distinguishable from other forms of crime in that a computer is either the target or the means to commit the crime. The Internet unintentionally aided criminals in two ways. First, it presented the opportunity for new forms of crime such as hacking which is a major worldwide problem. Second, the Internet has made it easier and safer for someone to commit a crime. A child molester, for instance, no longer has to risk detection by hanging around school yards and other places where children congregate in order to find a potential victim. With access to the Internet a child molester can meet possible victims online via chat room. From the safety of their own home, the molester can befriend a child and eventually arrange a meeting with the child for unlawful purposes. In addition to child molestation, cybercrime also includes the crimes of theft, fraud, vandalism, child pornography, illicit sales of contraband, and terrorism.

❶ *Define an internal threat to a computer system and explain the different motivations of those involved.*

▶ Internal Threats

Employees and contractor's employees who have direct access to the employer's computer system are the internal threat. While the overwhelming number of employees is not a cause for concern, a lone rogue employee can do irreparable harm. These employees not only have the necessary passwords to access the system, they also have the direct working knowledge of the interactions of the system. These rouge employees are motivated by different reasons as follows:

> The **dishonest employees** motivation is one of personal gain. These employees can do a number of things to gain financial advantage depending on their level of access to various databases. One common scheme is to establish fictional suppliers and employees who are paid for nonexistent

service and supplies. The payments for these services and supplies are then directed to a bank account or address which is under the control of the employee. Employees can also sell the employer's customer lists, trade secrets, and research and development progress. As insurance a dishonest employee may install a **logic bomb** which is a program within a program that perform destructive acts based on a trigger event. The trigger event might be a significant future date or an act such as the removal of a person's name from a payroll database, indicating that he or she has either been fired or laid off.

Exiting employees are those who are leaving their current employment voluntarily. The employees are a potential threat because their loyalty may be shifting from their current employer to their future employer or in the case of self-employment to themselves. An **exit interview** should be conducted to determine why the employee is leaving. Is the employee going into business for themselves and therefore be a potential competitor or are they going to work for an existing competitor? Exiting employees have been known to take the employer's trade secrets and customer lists with them when they leave in order to better themselves or to make a good impression with their new employer. Any concerns raised during the exit interview may result in limiting the exiting employee's access to vulnerable databases.

The *disgruntled employee* is one who is motivated by striking back at their employer as the result of some real or imagined wrong on the part of the employer. Their motivation is to get even, to do harm, as they feel they have been harmed. As a means of getting even these employees abuse their access to a computer system and obtain sensitive and potentially embarrassing information and then send it to others outside the organization.

❷ *Define an external threat to a computer system and discuss the motivations of those involved.*

▶ External Threats

Hackers are, in essence, trespassers—intruders who enter into another's computer system without authorization. A distinction has been made between good and bad hackers. Using terminology from Western movies, good hackers are known as **white hat hackers,** as the good guys always wore white hats. In contrast, the bad guys wore black hats and their intentions were more sinister. All hackers possess a high level of expertise with a computer. White hat hackers are motivated to test their skill against those who design a computer systems security features. Since the formation of the Internet these hackers have played a crucial role in the development of Internet security. They have tested various computer systems and found their flaws and as a result code writers were forced to develop higher standards of security. Through the years these white hat hackers have been recruited by governments and major corporations to help identify system vulnerabilities and weaknesses that might be subject to attack.[2]

The **black hat hacker,** on the other hand, is a cyber-criminal. Their motivation is either to circumvent a computers security for personal gain or vandalism. This hacker may sabotage a system's databases, or attempt to shut down the entire Internet. The tools of these vandals include the following:

Viruses are a type of malicious code that replicates itself and inserts copies or versions of itself in other programs. A virus requires some action on the part of the user, such as opening an e-mail attachment to be activated. A virus may do something as simple as to let the user know that it exists or as malicious as to destroy the entire contents of the computer's memory.

Worms are like viruses, but spread with no human interaction after they are started.[3]

Bot-nets are malicious malware programs that a user unknowingly downloads on to their computer. This software turns the user's computer into a "zombie" or "slave computer." The bot-net usually remains dormant awaiting instructions from its controller and the user is unaware that their computer is infected. Typically these zombies or slaves are home PCs and laptops which are not properly protected against such malware. A number of attacks are possible with a bot-net arrangement; however, the most destructive is the *distributed denial of service* attack (DDOS). In such an attack the controller of the bot-net unleashes a number of the bots to create more inbound traffic than the targeted system can handle. The largest known bot-net system in the world is thought to have between 1 and 50 million infected computers under their control.[4]

Most black hat hackers are motivated by money rather than vandalism; they are the mercenaries of cyberspace. Like a cat burglar they hope to gain access to a computer system, commit their crime, and leave without being detected. These thieves frequently target intellectual property, including new product plans, new product description, research marketing plans, prospective customer lists, and similar information. The theft of trade secrets, also known as **economic espionage**, occurs when someone takes this information for the benefit of someone other than the owner, and many of these thefts are accomplished by hackers. U.S. businesses, academic institutions, defense contractors, and government agencies are targeted for economic espionage and it is estimated that this form of espionage costs the American economy over $19 billion annually. Often this form of hacking is sponsored by foreign governments as a means of avoiding the expense and difficulty doing basic research and product development themselves.[5]

Another, and even a greater threat to the economy, is the theft of credit card and customer personal information. This information is then sold to other thieves engaged in identity theft activities as the following case illustrates.

> During the busy holiday shopping season hackers hit the Target store chain and stole data on over 40 million customers. Hackers normally attack databases where credit card information is stored and where most companies concentrate their intrusion security. This attack differed in that it was a point-of-sale breach, meaning that customer information was sent directly from the store's cash registers to the hackers. This allowed the hackers to collect "track data," which includes the cardholders name, credit card number and expiration date. Armed with this information criminals can sell this data on the black market where credit card numbers sell for $1 each. With this information criminals, with a minimal equipment investment, can print cards for people to use at cash registers or simply purchase items on-line.[6]

❸ *Discuss the different forms of computer fraud.*

▶ Fraud

The Internet is a perfect forum for committing basic to complex frauds. Simple business frauds include offering items or services for sale and either supplying worthless goods or not sending the merchandise or providing the service. The Federal Bureau of Investigation (FBI) in conjunction with the Department of Justice's Bureau of Justice Assistance (BJA) has established the Internet Fraud Complaint Center. The center receives over a quarter of a million complaints a year representing an annual loss in excess of a half a billion dollars. Each complaint is analyzed for similarities and this collated information is then referred to law enforcement agencies for further action. Some of the more common complaints include the following.

Auto Fraud—criminals advertise on classified ad sites that they have a vehicle for sale, usually priced below market value. The perpetrators claim they are forced to sell because they are relocating for work, being deployed by the military, or have a family emergency and they are urgently in need of money. Due to the circumstances of the emergency the seller is unable to meet directly with the buyer or to allow inspection of the vehicle. The seller attempts to make the arrangement appear legitimate by having the victim wire full or partial payment to a fictitious third-party agent. The seller keeps the money and never delivers the promised vehicle. Frauds of this type represent an annual loss to victims of over $65 million.

FBI Impersonation—the name of the FBI director and other high ranking government officials have been used in e-mails sent to potential victims. While the government does not send unsolicited e-mails, these fraudulent notices incorporate many of the elements of the

Nigerian letter scam. These e-mails inform the victim of get-rich inheritance scenarios, bogus lottery winnings notifications, and occasional extortion threats. Victims lose an estimated $4.6 million a year to these types of scams.

Scareware/Ransomware—in this scenario the victim receives a pop-up message that advises the victim that their computers have been infected with a virus. These scareware notifications cannot be easily closed and the victim is directed to a website to purchase software that would allegedly remove the virus. While the website looks reputable it is not and once the victim pays for the software they find out that the related links to download the software are nonoperational.

The Citadel malware is another similar scheme where the victim's computer freezes and a warning of a violation of U.S. law displays on the monitor. To add to the intimidation the logo of the FBI, or other federal agency, appears on the screen with the message that the victim's **Internet protocol** or IP address was identified as recently visiting a child pornography website.

The user is instructed to pay a fine to the government via prepaid money card services before service can be restored. Once payment has been made the service is not restored. Victims have lost over 130,000 dollars each year on these types of scams.

Real Estate/Timeshare—information from legitimate homes for rent listings is posted on an online classified section under the perpetrator's e-mail address. The home is listed at a below-market price as the owner must rent the home quickly as he or she has been transferred overseas. The victim is instructed to send the first and last month's rent, via wire service. Renters might also be asked to complete a credit application which asks for personal information including Social Security numbers and work history, information which is then used to commit identity theft.

A variation of this scheme involves timeshare resale representatives who contact the victim with an offer that is too good to be true. They have a buyer who wants to buy the victim's timeshare and they must move quickly as the buyer is either on the line or in the office and wants to close the deal today. If the victim agrees to the sale they are asked for a credit card to pay up-front fees to cover the cost of the listing, advertising fees, and closing costs. Shortly after the transaction is completed the company fades away and the victim is defrauded. The reported loss to these types of scams is in excess of $15 million a year.

Romance Scams—perhaps the cruelest fraud of all is this one as it victimizes the most vulnerable in our society, the lonely. Perpetrators of this scam locate potential victims in chat rooms, on dating sites, and on social media networks. The victim is seduced with small gifts, claims of common interests, friendship, and possible companionship. Once they have the victim's trust they request money, usually for an operation for a family member who is in another country. Victim's losses totaled more than $55 million, not to mention the emotional and mental implications as well.[7]

Warning Signs

- The scammer professes love quickly and uses terms of endearment such as "sweetie, honey, and baby."

- Their e-mails contain bad grammar and spelling errors and they are unfamiliar with typical American slang terms, which would tend to indicate they are communicating from another country.

- They state that they are professional people assigned to projects that take them away from home.

- Soon into the relationship they claim that they have lost a love one, possibly a child, due to a serious accident or have family members who are seriously ill. They ask for financial help to get through the emergency and promise to pay the money back.

- They want the money sent by wire transfer, and always have a reason why their repayments haven't arrived.

- They request that the relationship be kept secret.[8]

The incidence and cost of computer fraud as "reported" to the Internet Crime Complaint Center does not reflect the true picture of computer fraud that occurs annually in the United

States. Many victims are reluctant to report that they have been defrauded as they may not want others to know that they got duped and that they lost some of their hard-earned money, and in some cases their life savings, to a complete stranger. However, these statistics do serve a useful purpose in that they provide a reference point or benchmark each year that allows for the comparison of the rate of increase or decrease of this crime from year to year.

4 *Explain how identity theft occurs.*

▶ Identity Theft

Basically identity theft is nothing more than a criminal assuming another's identity for the purposes of obtaining credit and buying merchandise with no intention of making payment. To assume another's identification the criminal needs at minimum a name, date of birth, and address. All of this information is included on the magnetic strip on the back of each credit card. The hacking of Target store's credit card information highlights the methods this information becomes available to identity thieves. Unfortunately, some people inadvertently post this information on their social networking sites.

Phishing is another method identity thieves use to collect personal data. In this scheme a victim is sent an official-looking e-mail from a bank requesting verification of personal information for security purposes. The victim is informed that this information is required in order to continue online banking. When the victim responds and clicks the provided link to the bank a fictitious official looking banking page opens with instructions to provide personal information including name, address, dates of birth, Social Security number, driver's license number, and account numbers as well as passwords. The identity thief now has all the information necessary to access the victim's bank account as well as apply for credit cards and loans in the victim's name.[9]

5 *Describe the problem of child pornography and the Internet.*

▶ Child Pornography

The First Amendment's protections of free speech do not apply to child pornography. It is a violation of most state, as well as federal law to produce, distribute, receive, or have in their possession any visual depiction of sexually explicit conduct involving a minor, someone under eighteen years of age. The child pornography market increased drastically with the advent of the Internet. Sexually explicit images of children can be produced in one country and easily viewed in another and these investigations often cross international jurisdictions. It is estimated that there are more than a million pornographic images of children on the Internet and 200 new images are posted daily. The number of offenders worldwide is estimated to be between 50,000 and 100,000 and that a third of these offenders operate in the United States.[10]

This is an offense that occurs not in public but in a location where the offender feels safe and away from public view. These cases come to the attention of investigators in a variety of scenarios.

Informants—are people who are aware of the offender's involvement in child pornography and provides investigators with information necessary to begin an investigation.

Computer technicians—while servicing an offender's computer discover files containing child pornography and as a result contact investigators.

Search incident to an arrest—a suspect of one crime may have their computer seized as a result of that offense and a forensic examination of the computer discloses evidence of child pornography.

Chat rooms—the offenders frequently contact various forums such as chat rooms to share their experiences and interest in this form of pornography in order to network with other offenders. Investigators also visit these chat rooms and engage with these offenders in order to identify them and their activities.

6 *Explain how child molesters use the Internet to find victims.*

▶ Child Molesters

As child molesters do not form lasting relationships they are constantly in search of new victims. In the old days these offenders would frequent places where children were known to be, such as school yards and after-school activities. At these locations the molester would use child lures, such as stories of needing help finding a lost puppy, as a means of attracting a child. This action on the part of the molester was always risky, but a risk the molester had to take in order to find a victim. Today, such risks need not be taken as these offenders use the Internet and visit child-friendly chat rooms from the comfort of their home. Once in a chat room, the offender attempts to befriend a child, often by posing as a child themselves, and set up a time and place to meet the child. Tragically these offenders are adept at manipulation and another child becomes a victim.

Investigators, often with the assistance of citizens groups, search child-friendly chat rooms looking for signs of child molester activity. Posing as a child, an investigator will agree to meet a suspect at a specified time and place. When the suspect arrives at the location he can be arrested as they have taken the necessary steps to further the crime of child molestation.

7 *Outline the growing problem of contraband sales on the Internet.*

▶ Contraband Sales

Sales of **Contraband**, or illegal goods, have been carried out on the Internet since its inception. The specific sites were usually short lived as they were easily located and shut down by investigators. The ease of identifying these sites is becoming more difficult with the release of **Deep Web** technology. In 1996 scientists with the U.S. Naval Research Laboratory developed a system which allowed users to access the Internet without divulging their identities. They called this system "**onion routing**" because of the various layers of encryption that surrounded the data being transmitted over a specific branch of the Internet that search engines don't or can't index. The Deep Web requires specific software that is free and takes less than three minutes to download. With this software in place a user's data is wrapped in layers of encryption to hide the sender's location. The data is sent through a network of relays, specifically other computers using this same software. Each relay peels away a layer of encryption before forwarding the data, thereby providing complete anonymity for the user. The developers of the Deep Web wanted to provide a secure means of covert communication for military, intelligence, and law enforcement agencies.

Unfortunately, the Deep Web did not remain a secret for long. Today the Deep Web is a potential haven for thieves, child pornographers, and the sale of contraband. One recently discovered site was a clearinghouse for an estimated million users. Over a two-year period these users purchased over $1 billion worth of contraband, mostly illegal drugs. The administrator of the site earned $80 million in fees which were payable in **Bitcoins**, a digital form of currency. The bitcoin is traded on the Internet and unlike bank transactions these transactions are unregulated and are virtually anonymous.[11]

8 *Discuss the reasons why cyber terrorism is an attractive option for terrorists.*

▶ Terrorism

Our critical national infrastructure, such as the energy grid, transportation, financial institutions, stock exchange, and government services, are dependent on computer networks that are connected to the Internet for their operation. For the cyber terrorist these systems are attractive targets due to the potential to inflict massive damage and psychological impact. While no incident of cyber terrorism has been reported in this country, the threat of such attack is real and one that numerous government agencies are working hard to prevent. While cyber terrorism has not happened here, it has occurred elsewhere. In 2007 a confrontation between Russia and Estonia triggered a denial-of-service cyber-attack that caused Estonian governmental websites and financial institutions to shut down.

Cyber terrorism is an attractive option for the terrorists for several reasons:

- It is inexpensive; all the terrorist needs is a computer and an online connection.
- Less personal risk as there are no physical barriers, no borders to cross or customs agents to deal with.
- The Internet offers a wide variety of targets with weakness and vulnerabilities to exploit.
- Cyber terrorism requires less training time and involves less personal risk or physical harm to the terrorist.
- Cyber terrorism has the potential to directly affect a large number of people and generate extensive media coverage, the primary goal of any terrorist organization.

A distinction should be noted between **hacktivism** and cyber terrorism. While their actions may be similar, the distinction is that the hacktivist is politically motivated, and wants to protest and to disrupt Internet functions; however, they do not want to kill, maim, or terrify as the cyber terrorist would.[12]

9 *Explain the investigative process involved in cybercrime.*

▶ Investigation

A forensic examination of the computer involved in a cybercrime, including desktops, laptops, tablets, and cell phones, is standard procedure in these investigations. Other crimes such as homicides, terrorist attacks, arsons, illicit drugs cases, and other crime that may indirectly involve a computer may require a forensic examination as well. A suspect who enters a crowded movie theater and begins shooting people may not have used a computer to commit this crime; however, his motivations for the commission of the crime might be spelled out in a word processing document contained on their computer.

The first step in the forensic examination process would be the seizure of the suspect's computer. As the Fourth Amendment provides protection against the unreasonable search and seizure of a person's papers a search warrant or permission from the suspect would be required. An application for a search warrant would have to outline the relevance of the forensic examination and how the targeted evidence would be directly linked to the question of guilt or innocence.

With the approval of the suspect or the issuance of a warrant by a judge the next step in the process is determining whether the computer is password protected. Obtaining the password from a suspect who gives permission to examine their computer in the first place would not be an issue. Without the luxury of having the password provided there are two methods available to determine the password.

Blunt force attack—involves the use of software that systematically enters every combination of letters, characters, and numbers until the password is discovered. The success of this option is dependent on the level of sophistication of the password. Lengthy passwords containing a combination of letters, numbers, and characters may be very difficult to successfully determine. Fortunately for the forensic examiner most computer users are not overly sophisticated or may be too lazy to be bothered with lengthy passwords.

Social engineering—relies on the shortcomings of human nature. This method involves the critical observation of the environment where the targeted computer is located at the time of seizure. Since people often have a number of different passwords they often write their computer passwords in their address book, day planner, or some other location near their computer. An application for a search warrant should include any of the areas where a suspect might conceal a password.[13]

Once the password has been obtained the search for evidence can begin. The investigator should have a thorough understanding of the type of case they are dealing with and the type of evidence that would likely to be involved as well as potential investigative leads. An examination of the contents of the computers files would include:

- Internet history/favorites—once logged on to the Internet the history bar will display the visited websites for the past three weeks. The favorites bar will display those websites the users most frequently visits on the web. Noting the websites the suspect has visited may provide possible investigative leads, such as banking activity, and sites relative to criminal activity are worthy of follow-up.

- Calendars—may provide insight into where the suspect may have gone, with whom, and when.

- E-mail—review of the content of the suspect's e-mail might provide links to other person's knowledge of the crime as well as their involvement. A review of the suspect's "address book" might provide links to other coconspirators as well as persons who should be contacted in furtherance of the investigation. Address books may contain information such as the person's name, address, phone numbers, and aliases.

- Spreadsheets—can be set up to display a variety of information. Of interest to the investigator may be financial spreadsheets. Criminals involved in illicit drug dealing, gambling, and loan sharking activities have a need to keep track of their financial dealings.

- Word documents—each file should be opened and examined to reveal information relative to the commission of the crime in question. Documents relative to the suspect's mental state and any documents relative to the commission of the crime implicating the suspect or indicating premeditation of the crime would be an important find for the investigator.

- Picture files—the finding of child pornography on the suspect's computer is a prima facie demonstration of the commission of this crime; the mere possession of child pornography is a crime. Pictures also provide insights into the places and people the suspect is involved with. In the day-and-age of the "selfie" it is within the realm of possibility that the suspect may have taken a picture indicating their involvement in the crime in question.

- Deleted files—may be recovered. When someone deletes a file, that file is relocated as a fragment and stored in slack or unused space on the hard drive. Forensic tools allow the investigator to recover these fragments to a readable file.

The forensic examination of a computer should only be conducted by an investigator who possesses the necessary education, training, and experience to conduct the examination. The forensic examination must be conducted according the established professional standards. The forensic examination should be able to withstand a rigorous independent examination by a third party who should come to the same conclusion regarding the recovery of the evidence. The investigator conducting the examination must know the applicable rules of evidence and be prepared to testify in court as to the actions taken to recover the evidence from the computer. Recovered evidence must be protected from change or destruction and a documented chain-of-evidence should be established to account for the evidence from the time of recovery to the time it is presented in court.[14]

CASE STUDY

THE CASE AGAINST PFC. BRADLEY MANNING

As a military analyst PFC. Bradley Manning had access to classified government information. While stationed in Iraq, this low level analyst amassed hundreds of thousands of diplomatic cables, files on detainees being imprisoned at Guantanamo Bay, Cuba, and hundreds of thousands of incident reports from the wars in Iraq and Afghanistan. Included in this material was a video depicting a helicopter attack on a group of believed insurgents in Baghdad; among the dead were several children and two journalists. While Manning was disturbed by this incident a Pentagon review concluded that U.S. forces acted appropriately and had mistaken the journalist's camera equipment for weapons.

(continued)

Manning eventually contacted a well-known whistleblower website "Wikileaks" and offered his collection of classified material for release to the media. The subsequent release of this information was the largest breach of classified information in U.S. history. In e-mail conversation with former hacker Adrian Lamo, Manning, using the name "bradass87," revealed his reasons for divulging this information. He was disdainful of the feeble computer security at his post in Baghdad. He was also struggling with a recent breakup with his boyfriend and the difficulty he was having as an intelligent, awkwardly effeminate homosexual trying to survive in the military. Manning confided that he was in the desert with a bunch of hyper-masculine trigger-happy ignorant rednecks as neighbors and that the only place he felt comfortable was at his computer and Internet connection. Lamo passed this information on to the FBI and Army CID investigators and Manning was arrested on 22 counts of disseminating classified information, including six counts of violating the Espionage Act and one count of aiding the enemy.[15]

Three years after his arrest Manning was found guilty on most of the charges against him but was acquitted of the most serious charge of aiding the enemy. He was sentenced to thirty-five years in prison. In addition, he was dishonorably discharged and reduced in rank to private, the lowest military rank and would forfeit his pay. During his trial his attorney had argued that his client had leaked this information in order to begin a public debate on the government's actions as a means of bringing about change. His client therefore was a well-intentioned whistleblower.[16]

PFC Bradley Manning, responsible for the largest illegal release of "classified" documents in U.S. history.

Source: Patrick Semansky/AP Images

CHAPTER REVIEW

Key Terms

Review Questions

1. Rouge employees who have access to the employer's computer system may install a logic bomb as insurance for their own protection. The rouge employee who is most likely to employ a logic bomb is which kind of employee?
   a. Dishonest
   b. Exiting
   c. Disgruntled
   d. Activist

2. A hacker who uses a distributed denial of service attack is most likely to use which of the following:
   a. Viruses
   b. Worm
   c. Bot-nets
   d. Economic espionage

3. The fraud scheme where the victim's computer freezes and the monitor displays a logo of a federal investigative agency with the message that the computer has been involved in criminal activity and a fee is required to unlock the computer is known as:
   a. Phishing
   b. Time share
   c. FBI impersonation
   d. Citadel malware

4. Identity theft involves criminal activity where one person assumes another person's identity for the purposes of obtaining credit and goods without making payment. The victim's personal information may have been obtained by which of the following?
   a. Viruses
   b. Phishing
   c. Worms
   d. Bot-nets

5. In the United States, child pornography involves the visual depiction of sexually explicit content involving a minor, a person who is under what age?
   a. 12
   b. 14
   c. 16
   d. 18

6. Internet sales of contraband, or illegal goods, have become more difficult to identify and investigate due to the encryption technology known as:
   a. Onion routing
   b. Bitcoins
   c. Bot-nets
   d. Phishing

7. The distinction between a hacktivist and a cyber-terrorist is that the hacktivist
   a. Is politically motivated
   b. Uses disruptive hacking techniques
   c. Uses Black Hat tactics
   d. Does not want to kill or maim

8. During the investigation of a cybercrime a blunt force attack would be useful in determining what?
   a. Victim's identification
   b. Suspect's identification
   c. A computer's password
   d. A computer Internet protocol

9. Relying on the shortcomings of human nature to gain information through the process of critical observation of a suspect's environment is known as?
   a. Skeptical observation
   b. Forensic observation
   c. Personal engineering
   d. Social engineering

10. Prior to the 1990s computer security issues were mainly centered around which types of threats?
    a. Internal
    b. External
    c. National
    d. International

Application Exercise

As a cybercrime investigator you are aware that many people do not report the fact that they have been a victim of a fraud, or that they have been solicited to be part of a fraud scheme. What these victims and potential victims fear is the stigma that is attached to being the victim of such a crime. Rightly or wrongly, these victims believe that others will view them as being gullible and easily duped out of their hard-earned money. As a result of these beliefs people often do not talk of these crimes and this lack of knowledge works in favor of the rip-off artists.

You have just discovered a new Internet fraud scheme that is aimed at the most vulnerable members of our society, the elderly. This scheme, if successful, will strip elderly victims of their life savings and virtually destroy their lives forever. Develop a strategy that will get the information you have on this fraud out to the community so that potential victims will be aware of this fraud and can protect themselves.

Discussion Questions

1. Define the types of questions an employer should ask an employee during the course of an exit interview and the reasons why these questions should be asked.
2. An employee who installs a logic bomb on their employer's computer system does so for protection. Discuss the protections a logic bomb might provide an employee.
3. Explain how hackers are a threat to the economic viability of the Internet and what can be done to limit the hacker's potential for harm.
4. Discuss the reason why a victim of a computer fraud may not want to report this crime to law enforcement.
5. Define the other aspects of social engineering, in addition to critical observation, that can be used to obtain information in furtherance of an investigation.

Related Websites

Want more information regarding Internet crime that has been reported nationally and by state? Visit the Internet Crime Complaint Center at http://www.ic3.gov/about/default.aspx.

To review the latest information regarding e-scams go the Federal Bureau of Investigation's (FBI) website at http://www.fbi/scams-safety/e-scams.

To see what the U.S. Department of Immigration and Customs Enforcement (ICE) is doing to combat cybercrime visit their website at http://www.ice.gov/predator.

Notes

1. http://www.computerhistory.org/timeline/?category=cmptr.
2. David S. Wall, *Cybercrime, the Transformation of Crime in the Information Age* (Cambridge, UK: Polity Press, 2007), 55.
3. Bernadette H. Schell and Clemens Martin, *Cybercrime a Reference Handbook* (Santa Barbara, CA: ABC-CLO, 2004), 1–9, 61.
4. Aaron Philipp, David Cowen, and Chris Davis, *Hacking Exposed Computer Forensics second edition* (New York, NY: McGraw-Hill, 2010), 454–456.
5. http://leb.fbi.gov/2013/october-november/economic-espionage-competing-for-trade-by-ste.
6. http:///www.nbcnews.com/technology/massive-target-credit-cad-breach-new-step-security.
7. http:www.ic3.gov/media/annualreport/2012.
8. Claudia Buck, "Romance Scams Heating Up," *Sacramento Bee,* January 29, 2013.
9. Will Gragido and John Pirc, *Cybercrime and espionage an Analysis of Subversive Multivector Threats* (Amsterdam: Elsevier, 2011), 69.
10. U.S. Department of Justice, Community Oriented Policing Services, *Child Pornography on the Internet* (Washington, DC: U.S. Department of Justice, Community Oriented Policing Services, 2010), 8–12.
11. Lev Grossman and Jay Newton-Small, "The Deep Web," *Time* 182, no. 20 (November 11, 2013): 25–33.
12. http://www.usip.org/publications/cyberterrorism-how-real-the-threat.
13. Michael Sheetz, *Computer Forensics an Essential Guide for Accountants, Lawyers, and Managers* (Hoboken, NJ: John Wiley & Sons, 2007), 49–50.
14. Eoghan Casey, *Handbook of Computer Crime Investigation* (London, UK: Academic Press, 2002), 7.
15. http://www.armytimes.com/article/20111213/NEWS/112130319/Hero-traitor-View-Bradl.
16. http://www.nytimes.com/2013/08/22/us/manning-sentenced-for-leaking-government-secret.

15 Dangerous Drugs

CHAPTER OUTLINE

LEARNING OBJECTIVES

After reading this chapter, you will be able to:

1. Define the major defense of entrapment as it would apply in cases involving the sale of controlled substances.

2. Describe the major kinds of dangerous drugs and the effects these drugs have on the user.

3. Identify the organizations responsible for the manufacture or importation of dangerous drugs into the United States.

4. Define the legal test of the "reasonable person" as it applies to a pickup arrest of person suspected of transporting illegal drugs.

5. Explain how an arrest based on the purchase of dangerous drugs is conducted to withstand legal challenge.

6. Outline the steps involved in the application and execution of a search warrant in drug cases.

7. Recognize those circumstances in dangerous drug investigations for which a search without a warrant would be appropriate.

8. Explain how investigators work up the drug-selling marking pyramid to arrest the major suppliers or importers of illegal drugs.

9 *Discuss the anticipated problems associated with a raid and entry into a building where dangerous drugs are being sold.*

10 *Discuss the problems of proving an illegal drug case.*

The possession of dangerous and restricted drugs or narcotics is prohibited. Exceptions are made when such dangerous drugs or narcotics are possessed through a lawful medical prescription. Previous conviction of one or more offenses related to possession of dangerous drugs or narcotics generally adds to the basic penalty imposed on conviction. Many jurisdictions specify that a convicted offender may not be eligible for release on parole or on any other basis until he or she has served a stated minimum number of years in prison. The basic law prohibits the unlawful possession of drugs and narcotics, transporting, importing, selling, furnishing, administering, or giving away of a dangerous drug or narcotic.

The word *possession,* in statutes forbidding the possession of drugs and narcotics, means an immediate and exclusive possession under dominion and control with intent to exercise control.[1] Persons having such control must have knowledge of the presence of drugs or narcotics, and such knowledge must precede the intent to exercise, or the exercise of, such control. Knowledge is a basic element of crimes related to illegal drugs and narcotics. This also means that knowledge of the character of the substance is essential to the offense of possession of narcotics.

In a prosecution for possession of dangerous drugs and narcotics, the burden is on the prosecution to prove knowledge of the presence of the drugs or narcotics. The prosecution must also show that a defendant charged with possession of illegal drugs and narcotics knew that the objects in his or her possession were drugs and narcotics. However, the burden of proof may be satisfied by facts that infer such knowledge (circumstantial evidence).

The events leading up to a suspect's arrest should show a state of facts amply sufficient to constitute reasonable cause for arrest (Figure 15-1). Reasonable and probable cause for an arrest without warrant, on justified belief that a suspect has committed a violation of illegal drugs and narcotics laws, can be based on an officer's past experience, knowledge of the suspect, and observation of suspicious and furtive conduct.

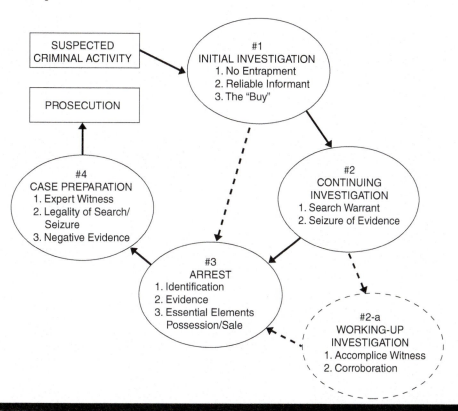

FIGURE 15-1   Investigation of Illegal Drugs and Narcotics.

The following instances are illustrative of evidence sufficient to arrest:

1. Investigators knew of a suspect's previous arrest and conviction for possession of narcotics; learned from the manager of suspect's apartment building that a good deal of suspicious traffic had been going in and out of suspect's apartment; and overheard occupants' references to funnels used in preparation of narcotics and balloons commonly used as containers for narcotics. The officers had reasonable cause for belief that occupants were committing a felony, and an arrest without warrant was proper.

2. In a prosecution for possession of heroin, the evidence indicated that the arresting officer had known the informant for approximately one year, that the informant had given information of a detailed nature and a complete description of the defendant and his or her modus operandi, and that such information had been independently verified in substantial part. This was reasonable cause to arrest the defendant without warrant.

The fact that a person is a drug addict, a "user" of drugs, does not justify arresting him or her. In *Robinson v. California,* the U.S. Supreme Court ruled that drug addiction is an illness, drug addicts are sick people, and their capacity to form the necessary criminal intent is diminished.[2] Before this case, California had a law that allowed police to arrest drug addicts just for being addicted—for a condition rather than commission of an act. In *Robinson,* the Court ruled the California law to be unconstitutional.

❶ *Define the major defense of entrapment as it would apply in cases involving the sale of controlled substances.*

▶ Entrapment

Any conviction for the possession (or sale or transport) of illegal drugs should be for a wrongful act voluntarily committed and not for an act induced by the investigator or his or her "special employee," which would not have occurred without such urging. It is not simple to determine whether, in a particular case, facts suggest the unlawful **entrapment** of an individual who might otherwise have gone through life without an arrest.

For instance, one defendant charged with the possession for sale of narcotics was not a user.[3] No evidence indicated that he was regularly engaged in the traffic of narcotics, and he did not have previous arrests of any kind. The sale of illegal narcotics, which was admitted, was consummated only after constant urging by a federal agent over a period of three months.

To avoid a defense claim of entrapment, no more pressure or persuasion can be exerted than that ordinarily occurring between willing buyer and willing seller. However, a defense of entrapment is not available to persons charged with possession of heroin when a suspect suggested to the police investigator that he could obtain illegal drugs or narcotics, and where no persuasion or allurement had been used by the officer who had merely furnished an opportunity for the suspect to acquire illegal drugs or narcotics to sell to the undercover investigator.[4] It is not the purpose of the law to prevent the unwary criminal from being trapped in a crime; it is instead the purpose of the law to prevent the police officer from inducing crime—that is, from seducing the unwary, innocent person into a career of crime.

❷ *Describe the major kinds of dangerous drugs and the effects these drugs have on the user.*

▶ The Drug Scene

Numerous restricted drugs and narcotics, from marijuana to heroin, are being used by millions of people. The most common drugs that can lead to drug dependence or addiction fall into four major groups:

1. *Narcotics*—drugs that depress the central nervous system. They usually lead quickly to both psychological and physical dependence.

2. *Sedatives*—like narcotics, cause both psychological and physical dependence, but the dependence develops more slowly. They are also central nervous system depressants.

3. *Stimulants*—amphetamines and methamphetamines. These drugs cause a rapid buildup of tolerance so that additional quantities are needed to achieve the same stimulating effects. Stimulant use quickly leads to psychological dependence.

4. *Hallucinogens*—cause sensory distortions and result in illusions and delusions. They are the psychedelic, or "mind-expanding," drugs.

Eight types of drugs are commonly encountered on the drug scene. Each is described next.

Heroin

Heroin is derived from a morphine base to produce diacetylmorphine (the chemical name for heroin), which, when blended with hydrochloric acid, forms into a salt (heroin hydrochloride) that is easily soluble in water. It usually consists of crystals so small as to resemble powdered sugar or flour. Heroin ranges in color from white to ivory, through dull or brownish gray, to tan or brown. Heroin is usually administered intravenously. Narcotics have four main characteristics: First, they kill pain—that is, they have an **analgesic** effect. Second, they are

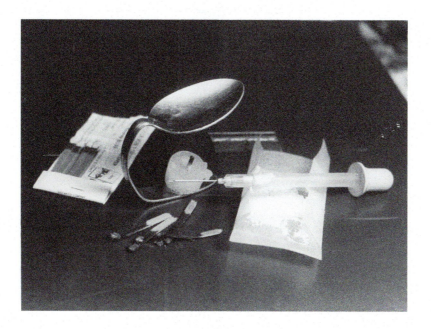

soporific agents, which means they induce drowsiness, lethargy, and sleep. Third, used with time, they produce physical and psychological dependency. Fourth, they generate a sense of **euphoria**—a feeling of well-being and tranquility.

Cocaine

Cocaine is a stimulant, usually derived from the leaves of the South American coca bush, and sometimes from bushes grown in the West Indies, Java, India, and Ceylon. The alkaloid is extracted from the leaves and treated with hydrochloric acid to form cocaine hydrochloride, a salt easily soluble in water. It is encountered as fine, fluffy white crystalline powder, and (depending on the degree of refinement) may resemble snowflakes, camphor, sugar, or Epsom salts. It is sometimes found in tablet form. Cocaine produces feelings of exhilaration and euphoria, and it increases the user's energy level and suppresses fatigue. Cocaine is usually administered by snorting through the nose and produces a psychological dependency. Cocaine is also smoked in two forms.

1. *Freebase.* When cocaine is freebased, it is dissolved in ether and then heated to boil off the impurities. What remains is a pure form of cocaine which is then ground up and smoked. Because smoking is a more effective means of administration, the user feels a more intense "rush," which often leads to heavy chronic use.

2. *Crack.* Also known as **hubba** or **rock, crack** is made by soaking cocaine in baking soda and water. The mixture is then heated until the water is driven off. During the heating process, the mixture makes a crackling sound, hence the name. The resulting crystals—or pea-sized "rocks"—are crushed, heated, and smoked in a crack pipe. This smokable form of cocaine gives the user a "rush" that lasts as long as two minutes, followed by an afterglow that lasts ten to twenty minutes.

Marijuana

Marijuana, or **pot**, consists of the leaves and flowering tops of the female hemp plant (*Cannabis sativa, C. indica*) cultivated in many temperate zones of the world. Crude marijuana contains parts of the leaves, tops, stems, and seeds (fruit) of the plant; "manicured" marijuana

A "Bong" used to smoke marijuana. What does the number 420 represent?

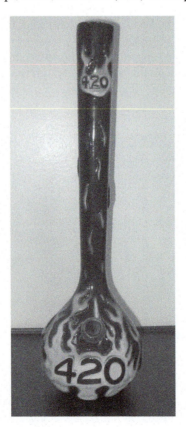

consists of smaller particles of the leaves and tops, from which almost all the stems and seeds have been removed. Fresh marijuana is dark green and turns brown with age and exposure. It may be packaged in tobacco tins, cellophane, paper bags, tissue paper, or cigarettes. Bricks of crude marijuana are about three inches by five inches by ten inches and weigh about two pounds. There are approximately four hundred and twenty different chemicals in marijuana; however, the psychoactive agent is delta-9-tetrahydrocannabinal, or **THC**. Wild, or uncultivated, marijuana may have a 1 percent THC level. Proper cultivation will raise the THC level to 3 percent. Marijuana grown in Colombia or Hawaii may have a THC level between 4 and 6 percent. Sinsemilla, a hybrid without seeds, may have an 8 to 14 percent THC content. Two derivatives of marijuana are hashish and hash oil:

1. *Hashish.* The resin of the marijuana flower is dried and compressed to make hashish, which has a THC level of 8 to 14 percent.
2. *Hash oil.* Amber to dark brown, hash oil is produced by boiling hashish in alcohol. It is sold as a viscous liquid with a THC level between 15 and 50 percent.

Amphetamine and Methamphetamine

Amphetamine and methamphetamine are synthetic substances usually produced in clandestine labs. The most common form of these substances is **methamphetamine**, also known as **speed, crank,** and **meth**. It has the same effects as cocaine and is often referred to as **poor man's cocaine**. Injected meth usually produces a "flash" or "rush" and is taken every four to eight hours, which leads to a "run"—a period of wakefulness lasting two to five days followed by a long period of sleep. A chronic user is known as a **tweaker**.

Ice is a purified form of methamphetamine that is usually smoked in a glass pipe. When ice is heated, the crystals melt and vaporize and the vapor is inhaled by the user. One gram of ice is enough for 10 to 25 hits. The physical and mental effects are similar to those of crack cocaine, with one exception; the effects of crack wear off within ten to twenty minutes, while the effects of ice last for eight hours or more. As the name implies, ice is similar in appearance to broken pieces of ice or glass. Initially ice showed up in Hawaii and on the West coast. Its use is now gradually spreading across the mainland of the United States.

Clandestine laboratories produce all of the illicit methamphetamine that is consumed in the United States. Federal, state, and local law enforcement agencies seize almost four thousand meth labs annually. Most of these labs were relatively small operations, producing one to four ounces per batch. Super labs, that can produce 100 to 200 pounds of meth in each production cycle, require large quantities of **pseudoephedrine** to operate. When the source of pseudoephedrine, which is a major component in many allergy and cold medications as well as in the manufacture of methamphetamine, dried up in this country, the number of super labs declined sharply. These labs were relocated to Mexico where pseudoephedrine could more easily be imported from India and China. Today Mexican drug traffickers control approximately 80 percent of all the meth sold in the United States.

Clandestine laboratories pose a significant threat to neighborhoods, to law enforcement, and to the environment. The production of each pound of meth produces an estimated five to six pounds of hazardous waste. Lab operators, known as **cookers**, routinely dump this hazardous waste on the ground, into streams, or into sewage systems. As Americans consume over twenty-two tons of meth a year, this creates between 110 and 150 tons of hazardous waste that is dumped into the environment. The average cost of cleaning up a small lab is between $3,500 and $4,500. The cost of cleaning up a super lab site can cost as much as a quarter of a million dollars.[5]

Phencyclidine

Phencyclidine has the street names **angel dust, dust,** and **PCP**. It was originally developed as a general anesthetic for surgical procedures. However, its use for this purpose was abandoned because of the ability of the drug to produce hallucinogenic side effects. For a while, it was used in veterinary medicine to tranquilize large animals but was removed from the market in 1978 and is now made in clandestine labs. PCP is a white, crystalline powder that readily dissolves in water. It is commonly applied to tobacco or marijuana cigarettes and smoked. In the right dose, PCP will produce hallucinations and, in some users, will evoke violent suicidal impulses. Because of the anesthetic effect of his drug, the user may display a total disregard for personal safety coupled with a lack of sensation.

Lysergic Acid Diethylamide

Lysergic Acid Diethylamide or LSD is a semisynthetic drug derived from a fungus that contaminates rye bread. Although LSD was first synthesized in 1938, its psychoactive properties were not discovered until 1943. LSD is usually swallowed in the form of impregnated paper, tablets, or thin squares of gelatin. A dose equal to a few grains of salt can produce hallucinations lasting ten to twelve hours. The drug is ambivalent, in that the users experience both good and bad sensations.

Ecstasy

Ecstasy is methylenedioxymethamphetamine (MDMA). First developed in 1912 as an appetite suppressant, it is a stimulant like meth and a hallucinogenic like LSD. It produces a warm, fuzzy sense of well-being and the manic energy to dance all night. Most of the drug is produced in Europe, although it can be made in clandestine U.S. labs. It is usually consumed at "raves," where the user spends the night dancing to music.

Rohypnol

A sleeping pill not licensed in the United States, **Rohypnol** is legal in Europe, South America, and Asia. It is also known as **roofies**. In the United States, the drug is most frequently used with alcohol—the synergistic effect produces disinhibition and amnesia. Because of these effects, Rohypnol is known as the **date rape drug**.

 Identify the organizations responsible for the manufacture or importation of dangerous drugs into the United States.

▶ Drug-Selling Organizations

Knowledge of the organizational setup of criminals engaged in selling illicit drugs is important to investigators working on the drug scene. The traditional sales–marketing pyramid of manufacturer, importer (source of supply), distributors, wholesalers and jobbers, and retailers (peddling mobs, or pushers) has not changed a great deal in the last quarter century.[6] "The boss" is still at the top of the pyramid, whether he or she is a major dealer or importer, or both. Today a few more levels can be found in the distribution network, generally based on the volume of sales (multikilo, kilo, fractional kilo). The formerly lowest level—street dealers—has been augmented by lookouts and runners. **Lookouts** inform street dealers about any police presence. **Runners** transport small quantities of drugs from the **stash** of the dealer to wherever the drugs are being sold (Figure 15-2).

Twenty-five years ago, most of these sales–marketing pyramids were headed by the leaders of Italian crime "families" or their "underbosses," and importation of drugs into the United States was mainly in the hands of Europeans (French, Corsicans, Italians). Today criminal organizations have expanded, and importation routes originate in South America, Central America, and Mexico. Cocaine and its derivative crack are immensely popular in the United States, and both are readily sold at high profits. In addition, the pyramid networks have become more sophisticated in their sales–marketing and in avoiding police interference with their daily sales. Currently, the following are the known criminal organizations engaged in major dealings in illicit drugs:

- Mafia (La Cosa Nostra) crime families
- Mexican cartels

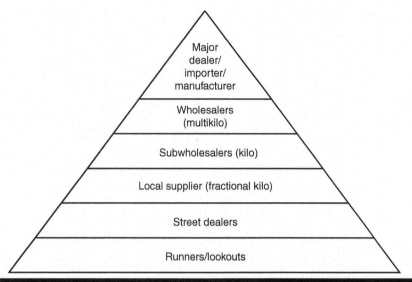

FIGURE 15-2 The Marketing Pyramid—Illegal Drugs and Narcotics.

- Colombians
- Jamaican ("posses")
- Asian (Chinese, Vietnamese, Korean)
- Motorcycle gangs
- Prison gangs
- Street gangs (Crips, Bloods)

The Mafia, Mexican Cartels and Colombians are generally organized along "family" lines, with roles in the sales–marketing pyramid resulting from recommendations from internal sources. The Jamaican "posses" are sophisticated crime mobs dealing primarily in crack in major U.S. cities. Personnel are recruited from Jamaica and other countries in the Caribbean basin. They are a hardball organization characterized by ruthless and extensive violence.[7]

Asian criminal organizations have kept a low profile. Not much is known about the extent of their operations, but a great deal is suspected. Because they operate in their own ethnic neighborhoods, investigators have had little success in developing informants or making buys. Youth gangs are often the source of personnel for these networks.

Motorcycle gangs have been involved in general misbehavior and traffic in firearms for some time. In recent years, they have developed tightly organized drug-selling networks.[8] These are nationwide groups with major dealers in most of the large urban centers. They are disciplined groups, with death a common form of punishment for violations of gang rules.

Prison gangs originated in prisons and sold drugs to inmates. Released members of these gangs were soon employed as street dealers in illicit drugs. In the U.S. Southwest, the Mexican Mafia is a major prison gang selling drugs both inside and outside prison walls. Various prison gangs (neo-Nazis, Aryan Brotherhood, and others.) operate in other areas of the United States.

Street gangs are a new addition to the drug-selling field. They do not usually buy as a gang but rather as individual members or small groups of gang members. They do sell drugs ("sling dope"), but their manner of purchasing drugs and selling them usually reflects the loose organizational structure of these street gangs.[9]

All these drug-selling gangs commit murder as a business technique to (1) eliminate competition, (2) protect their territory from the competition of rival gangs, (3) discipline suspected informants, and (4) protect their cash and illicit drugs from rip-offs by armed robbers.

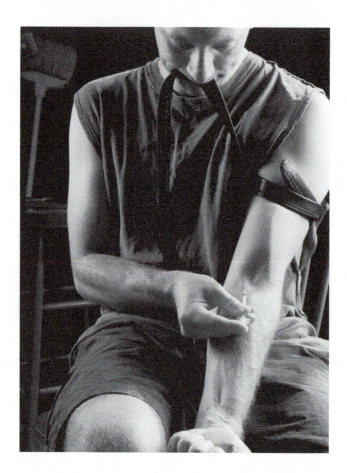

④ *Define the legal test of the "reasonable person" as it applies to a pickup arrest of person suspected of transporting illegal drugs.*

▶ Drug Investigations

Pickup Arrests

In warrantless arrests for the possession of dangerous drugs or narcotics or both, the investigator must act within the legal image of a "reasonable person." The test is this: would the facts from which the arresting officer acted warrant a person of reasonable caution to believe that a crime was committed? The court usually takes into consideration police expertise from training or experience in determining whether the arrest was reasonable. An important case in this area of pickup arrests is *Draper v. United States*.[10] In *Draper*, a federal narcotics of considerable experience (Marsh) had been informed by a special employee (Hereford), an informant, who had always been found to be accurate and reliable, that Draper was peddling narcotics and that he had gone to Chicago and would return by train with three ounces of heroin on the morning of September 8 or 9. The informant gave a physical description of Draper and said that he would be carrying a "tan zipper bag" and that he habitually "walked real fast." The agent kept the incoming trains from Chicago under surveillance, and on the morning of September 9, observed a person fitting the description given by the informant walking "fast" toward an exit and carrying a tan zipper bag. This person was Draper, and he was arrested by the officer.

The information about Draper given to narcotics agent Marsh by "special employee" Hereford may have been hearsay to Marsh, but coming from one employed for that purpose and whose information had always been found accurate and reliable, it is clear that Marsh would have been derelict in his duties had he not pursued it. And when, in pursuing that information, he saw a man—having the exact physical attributes, and wearing the precise clothing, and carrying the tan zipper bag that Hereford had described—alight from one of the very trains from the very place stated by Hereford and start to walk away at a "fast" pace toward the station, Marsh had personally verified every facet of the information given to him by Hereford except whether the petitioner had accomplished his mission and had the three ounces of heroin on his person or in his bag. Surely, with every other bit of Hereford's information being thus personally verified, Marsh had "reasonable grounds" to believe that the remaining unverified bit of Hereford's information—that Draper would have heroin with him—was likewise true.

In some instances, officers discover contraband in the form of illegal drugs or narcotics in searches incidental to an arrest or in the normal course of executing a search warrant. In such cases, the legality of the basic arrest and search or the search under the authority of a warrant must be demonstrated and supported by evidence before the illegal drugs or narcotics case can be developed for prosecution.

❺ *Explain how an arrest based on the purchase of dangerous drugs is conducted to withstand legal challenge.*

Arrests Based on "Buys"

The investigation of cases involving the possession or sale of dangerous drugs or narcotics usually is developed by one or more "buys" of these illegal substances. An undercover police investigator (sworn officer) or an informant (special employee) buys a quantity of dangerous drugs or narcotics from a suspect; the transaction often is witnessed by officers conducting surveillance of the undercover agent or special employee and of the suspect. The integrity of the informant's buy is preserved by a pretransaction and posttransaction search of the informant; compelling evidence often is secured by prior registration by the investigators of the serial numbers of the money used for the "buy." The substance purchased is marked for identification and transported to a local police (or state) narcotics laboratory for examination and identification and is retained as evidence of the sale of drugs or a narcotic substance to the informant or employee.

The informant, under supervision, sets up the "buy." The suspect may be identified by police and the informant asked to develop a case, or the informant may identify to the police a suspect known to him or her as a drug seller. After the "buy," the informant details the circumstances of the transaction to his or her police associates, turns over the substance purchased, and returns any unused money advanced for the "buy."

The usual procedure in making a "buy" is as follows:

1. The informant is advised to avoid any taint of entrapment.
2. The informant, under police supervision, makes contact with the subject and arranges the "buy."
3. The police arrange surveillance of the informant and possibly of the suspect.
4. The police search the informant to make certain that he or she is not carrying any drugs or any substantial amount of money. They also provide the informant with "state" money (serial numbers recorded) for the "buy."
5. The police maintain contact with the informant to the scene of the transaction.
6. The police watch the transaction as closely as possible.
7. When the informant returns to his or her police associates, he or she informs them of the transaction, turns over the purchase and any unspent funds, and is again searched (to allow police investigators to testify that the informant had none of the funds given him or her or any other drugs).
8. The purchased substance is marked as evidence and transported to a laboratory.
9. A laboratory analysis is sought to confirm the illegal nature of the substance as drugs or narcotics, the type of drug, and the amount of drug.
10. The case is prepared for (a) an arrest warrant, (b) an arrest (with or without warrant) on subsequent "buy," and (c) an application for a search warrant.

When an undercover police agent participates in a "buy," he or she conceals his or her identity as a police officer. A crewcut police recruit can become in a few weeks a long-haired participant in the search for drug sellers. The ability to act out his or her new identity without revealing police employment ensures continuation in this undercover role until the officer must reveal his or her identity as the investigation is terminated.

Successful undercover police operations in the drug scene usually require that an informant introduce and vouch for the undercover agent. The undercover agent's identity is revealed only when the agent has developed cases against a number of sellers of narcotics and the department decides to make all the appropriate arrests simultaneously.

 Outline the steps involved in the application and execution of a search warrant in drug cases.

Search Warrants

A "buy" is a normal prelude to an application for a search warrant in illegal drug and narcotics cases. The purpose of the search warrant is to gain judicial authorization to enter a place in which the suspect from whom the "buy" was made has his or her stash of drugs, to seize these drugs, and to arrest the suspect.

The past criminal record of a suspected person, his or her association with known narcotics users, and the fact that another person (usually the informant) was found to be in possession of a narcotic after leaving the premises of a suspected drug seller may be taken into account in determining whether probable cause exists for issuance of a search warrant (Figure 15-3).

In many instances, the report of an informant in relation to his or her purchase of drugs will identify a specific room, or portion of a room, from which the drug seller procured the drugs. This identification allows the application for the search warrant to contain the necessary particulars about the place or places to be searched.

To be constitutionally sufficient, an affidavit (accompanying an application for a search warrant) based solely on an unnamed informant's tip must set forth some underlying circumstances that reveal the source of the informant's information pertaining to the criminal activity, and it must present sufficient objective evidence to enable the magistrate to conclude that the unnamed informant is credible or that his or her information is reliable.[11] The report of the chemist examining the substance purchased can be used to establish the fact that before the transaction or transactions ("buys") the suspect had possessed illegal drugs or narcotics.

Unlike an application for search warrants in burglary and theft cases where specific articles of stolen property must be identified in the application, drugs may be described in general terms as contraband and by common names. Although returns to the issuing magistrate must contain a specific inventory of the drugs and narcotics seized under the authority of the search warrant, the drugs or narcotics seized do not need to "match" the drugs or narcotics in the application for the warrant.

⌐⌐ No. ███████████

STATE OF CALIFORNIA – COUNTY OF SACRAMENTO
SEARCH WARRANT AND AFFIDAVIT
(AFFIDAVIT)

JIMMY ████, being sworn, says that on the basis of the information contained within this Search Warrant and Affidavit and the attached and incorporated Statement of Probable Cause, comprising a total of __14__ pages, he/she has probable cause to believe and does believe that the property described below is lawfully seizable pursuant to Penal Code Section 1524, as indicated below, and is now located at the location(s) set forth below. Wherefore, affiant requests that this Search Warrant be issued.

Night Search Requested YES [X] NO [ ] (Justification on page(s) { 9)

_____   Reviewed by __Michael a. reve_____
(Signature of Affiant - after having been sworn)   (Deputy District Attorney)

(SEARCH WARRANT)

THE PEOPLE OF THE STATE OF CALIFORNIA TO ANY SHERIFF, POLICEMAN OR PEACE OFFICER IN THE COUNTY OF SACRAMENTO:

proof by affidavit having been made before me by JIMMY ████, that there is probable cause to believe that the property described herein may be found at the locations set forth herein and that it is lawfully seizable pursuant to Penal Code Section 1524 as indicated below by "x" (s) in that it:

_____ was stolen or embezzled

___X____ was used as the means of committing a felony

___X____ is possessed by a person with the intent to use it as means of committing a public offense or is possessed by another to whom he or she may have delivered it for the purpose of concealing it or preventing its discovery.

___X____ tends to show that a felony has been committed or that a particular person has committed a felony.

YOU ARE THEREFORE COMMANDED TO SEARCH:

███ Arcade Boulevard located in the City and County of Sacramento. It is a single story, single family residence, beige in color with brown trim and a brown composition roof. The numbers ████ are affixed to the front of the residence and are visible from the street. The single car attached garage is to the right (west) of the residence and the house is on the south side of Arcade Boulevard, between Colfax Street and Edgewater Road. Also to include all attics, basements, rooms, garages, outbuildings, storage sheds, inoperative vehicles, garbage cans and containers located with in the property boundaries.

FOR THE PERSON(S) OF:

████, Dennis Michael aka Dennis Michael ████, DOB: 10-4-54.

FIGURE 15-3 Search Warrant Issued by a California Court in an Illegal Drug Case. The Request for This Warrant Totaled Fourteen Pages. Magistrates are Aware of Their Responsibility for This Prior Approval of Police Action and Scan These Requests with Great Care. If They Do Not Understand It or Believe It Is Inaccurate, They Will Deny the Request.

FOR THE FOLLOWING VEHICLE(S):

A white with blue trim motor home, California license ████ and also request authorization to search the 1978 Datsun Pickup, California license ████, registered to ████████.

FOR THE FOLLOWING PROPERTY:

Methamphetamine and paraphernalia associated with its use, sales, transportation and manufacture, including; measuring and weighing devices, milk sugar, baggies, paper bindles, funnels, syringes, bent spoons, chemical formulas, phenylacetic acid, phenyl-2-propanone, methylamine, benzyl chloride, acetaldehyde, formamide, ephedrine, ether, acetone, lye, mercuric chloride, magnesium filings, sulfuric and hydrochloric acid, sodium acetate, chloroform, methanol, ethanol, red phosphorus, palladium black, and acetic anhydride, funnels, flasks, distillation flasks, various types of heaters and heating mantles, hot plates, various types of crystallizing dishes, desiccators, distilling apparatuses, extractors, vacuum dryers, beakers, jars, condensers, graduated cylinders, vacuum pumps, shakers and stirrers, thermometers, transformers, ovens, regulators, glass tubing, hoses, scales, filter papers, PH papers, plastic containers, gloves, masks, fans, air conditioners, generators, bills, receipts, ledgers, maps, charts, buyers lists, seller lists and recordation of sales, personal telephone books, address books, telephone bills, papers and documents containing lists of names, addresses and phone numbers, utility company receipts, rent receipts, addressed envelopes, keys and photographs. Searching officers are directed to answer the phone and converse with callers who appear to be calling in regard to drug/narcotic sales and note and record the conversation without revealing their true identity. They are also directed to note and record phone numbers or other messages received on telephonic pagers for the purpose of calling those persons paging the suspect(s) to determine if the page was regarding an intended purchase or delivery of drugs/narcotics.

AND TO SEIZE IT IF FOUND and bring it forthwith before me, or this court, at the courthouse of this court. This Search Warrant and incorporated Affidavit was sworn to and subscribed before me this ___5___ day of _____January_____, 19_89_, at __8:04__ AM./P.M. Wherefore, I find probable cause for the issuance of this Search Warrant and do issue it.

_____   Night Search Approved YES [X]   NO [_____]
(Signature of Magistrate)   (Magistrates' initials)
Judge of the Superior Court [X] Municipal Court—Sacramento Judicial District [ ].

Executed by _____████████   Date ___1·5·89___   Hr. __10:45 P.M.__

FIGURE 15-3 Continued

An outline of the usual procedure in this major type of investigation follows:

1. The case against the suspect is developed by one or more "buys" and information from a reliable informant.

2. The investigator makes observations supporting the transactions and information as evidence of the suspect's criminal behavior and is prepared to show the reliability of the informant.

3. Application is made to the magistrate for a search warrant, naming the suspect and the place or places to be searched, and citing dangerous drugs or narcotics, or both, as the object of the search.

4. A warrant is executed, the suspect is arrested, and the "return" is made to the magistrate.

5. The substances are seized and analyzed, and the fact that the substances are illegal drugs or narcotics, or both, is revealed and reported to the magistrate in a supplementary "return."

6. The case is prepared against the arrestee for presentation to the prosecutor.

In the investigation of a major drug seller, the "buy" is the preliminary investigation. With this transaction, and any subsequent "buys," accumulating evidence is likely to support an application for a search warrant. In preparing and executing the search warrant, investigators are conducting a continuing investigation that will identify the drug seller as the person in possession of a quantity of drugs or narcotics.

❼ *Recognize those circumstances in dangerous drug investigations for which a search without a warrant would be appropriate.*

Warrantless Searches

Reasonableness is the constitutional test of any warrantless search. Exigent circumstances are often present in drug cases. Drug possession for the purpose of sale is an ongoing crime; drug sellers do not suspend their activity while police do the necessary paperwork involved with obtaining a search warrant. Evidence that might be sufficient to convict them may be destroyed if police do not take prompt action.

An example of this reasonableness is a case in which a police officer observed a crime in progress inside a building (narcotics "cutting" and packaging operation—a "factory") and contraband (drugs) in plain view.[12] An appellate court ruled that the police were fully authorized under these circumstances to enter the premises, make arrests, and seek contraband. The police officer in this case, acting on an anonymous tip, went to a certain address, looked through a basement window, and saw the major narcotics-packaging operation in progress. He then sought the aid of other police officers. With this additional help, the officer subsequently (within thirty to forty minutes) entered and searched the premises without a warrant. Searching officers found the "cutting" mirror (used for mixing the illegal drugs with cheaper adulterants) on a table, along with plastic bags and measuring spoons and pans. Nearby, the officers found a large quantity of narcotics packaged for distribution. Four persons found on the premises were arrested.

❽ *Explain how investigators work up the drug-selling marking pyramid to arrest the major suppliers or importers of illegal drugs.*

Working-Up Investigations

Working up the drug-selling marketing pyramid necessitates both buy-and-bust arrests and arrests and seizures under the authority of a search warrant. An arrest is first made at the sales level of the pyramid (Figure 15-2), the street seller of illicit drugs. Then the supplier of this dealer is arrested, and onward and upward until a major supplier or importer is arrested.

Informants in these **working-up investigations** are arrestees who have agreed to cooperate in revealing their suppliers in return for leniency in drafting the indictment or at the time of sentencing. This is often termed **working off a beef**. However, investigators must be cautious in these cases because many arrestees make a deal with the arresting officer (and prosecutor) but have no intention of informing on their true source of supply. They engage in **lateral snitching**, informing only on drug sellers who are equal to or lower than themselves in the drug-marketing pyramid. In this fashion, an arrestee manipulates an investigator, informing primarily on his or her competition.[13]

Lengthy investigations probing upward in a drug-marketing network can develop a case against a manufacturer, a major dealer, or an importer. To be successful, such investigations require (1) a criminal associate of the "targeted" major manufacturer, dealer, or importer and (2) evidence corroborating the expected testimony of the accomplice witness.

Arrestees situated above the street-dealer level in a drug-marketing pyramid are more difficult to "turn" than are lesser network members. When a man or woman close to a major manufacturer, dealer, or importer is arrested, the "boss" commonly provides legal counsel, bail, and other assistance pending trial.

In addition, the past-performance record of informants being murdered while in prison or out on bail is an ongoing deterrent to cooperating with the police. As a result, an investigator needs a strong case against an arrestee to entertain any hope of turning him or her into an accomplice witness.[14] When an accomplice witness can provide data as to the date and time of a future delivery of drugs, an arrest and seizure based on this information and involving the major dealer or importer are most compelling evidence. Usually, corroboration results from an investigator collecting bits and pieces of information from techniques such as the following:

- Physical and electronic surveillance
- Tally analysis of telephone records of outgoing calls from a "suspect" telephone

- A survey of car rental contracts, credit card purchases, hotel and motel registrations, and major cash purchases
- Tracing "laundered" cash

Corroborating the expected testimony of an accomplice witness against a major manufacturer, dealer, or importer is more or less a "paper chase." Ideally, the observations made by investigators of the activities of the suspect will reveal the linkage between others in the drug-marketing network. The observations are supported by these persons contacting the suspect from time to time by telephone. Renting cars, registering in hotels, and buying items—from gasoline to mansions—tend to place the suspect in various locations on specific dates. Finally, money can be traced. The Bank Records and Foreign Transactions Act requires bank officials to report deposits and withdrawals by their customers of over $10,000. It is difficult to conceal millions of dollars in drug-selling profits.

It is a long and difficult investigation when a major manufacturer, a dealer, or an importer is targeted for arrest and prosecution. Suspected informants are immediately murdered, both to negate their services to police and to build up a long-time creed of organized crime: "death to the informer." Confidential police files and operations are compromised by bribery of public employees in order to learn what evidence the police have to date and the scope of their existing plans.[15]

 9 *Discuss the anticipated problems associated with a raid and entry into a building where dangerous drugs are being sold.*

Raids

A **raid** in drug-law enforcement is an entry into a building for the purpose of seizing illicit drugs and arresting one or more drug dealers and associates. Entry may be gained by subterfuge (a tale to gain entry without force) or by the use of force (sledge hammer, battering ram, kicking).

Commonly, raids are no longer the combined effort of several investigators. They are now a major action of the investigating unit with a superior officer designated as the overall commanding officer. Most departments now require all members of a raiding party to wear bulletproof vests. In fact, the expectation of a shoot-out during a raid is today integrated with raid planning. Special weapons teams are frequently assigned to back up the investigators, particularly when the place to be raided is a "rock house" from which crack is sold—such premises are heavily armored, and automatic weapons fire from the premises being raided is more than a possibility.

A great deal of responsibility rests with the leadership of a raid on the drug scene. Fears are of "hitting the wrong door," of having a member of the raiding party injured or killed, of failing to identify the major suspect among the occupants, of not finding any drugs at all (or only a small amount), and of not finding the **trap**—a built-in hiding place usually constructed by a skilled carpenter—containing the major stash.

Legally, the authority for a raid is a search warrant authorizing police officers to enter a specific premises to seize illicit drugs believed to be in the described premises. These warrants or local laws will provide for a "no-knock" entry. In past years, the notice-and-demand factor slowed up raiding parties to such an extent that drug sellers and associates had time to get rid of the incriminating evidence, usually flushing the illicit drugs down the toilet. Today, aware jurists and legislators have recognized the need of police for speedy entry.

Armoring the place from which drugs are sold is the drug seller's response to the capability of police to gain speedy entry and to seize drugs before they can be destroyed. Sheet-steel panels are screwed or bolted to entry doors, and windows are covered with steel panels and heavy iron gratings. Drug sellers claim that this armoring is necessary to protect them from rip-offs, but it has a valuable side action in preventing speedy entry by police.

Once entry is made and the occupants have been placed under control (and disarmed, if carrying weapons), the commanding officer of the raiding party supervises a methodical search for illicit drugs and weapons and oversees a thorough scanning of the identity of the occupants.

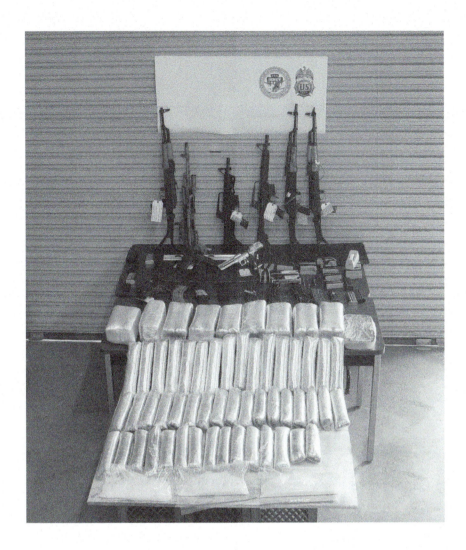

A sample of some of the drugs and weapons seized by agents of the Drug Enforcement Administration during "Project Coronado," which also resulted in the arrest of over 1,100 people for trafficking in controlled substances. *Source:* DEA.

⑩ *Discuss the problems of proving an illegal drug case.*

▶ Problems of Proof

The classic defense claim in drug-selling cases is entrapment: that the investigator or police agent (special employee, informant) urged and persuaded the defendant to sell the drugs and that the sale itself was solely to recover the cost of the drugs to the defendant. This entrapment defense has many variations, but it has been successful in many jury trials. It is likely to continue as a successful defense unless prosecutors can affirmatively show that no coercive persuasion or allurement was used on the defendant.

In cases involving only a small quantity of illicit drugs, a defendant may claim that he or she was **flaked** by the police investigator or his informant partner—that is, the illicit drugs were planted by the informant or the arresting officer. Unfortunately for the prosecution in these trials, one or more jurors may have heard of the police practice of flaking and may be willing to give greater credence to the claim than to the denial.

The compulsion of immunized testimony by an accomplice witness is an in-court problem of credibility. This person is not a sympathetic witness to whom jurors might relate but rather a person who has turned state's witness to save his or her own skin. The problem is that many jurors are ready to believe that such a witness is prone to lie, and they are repeatedly told this by the defense counsel.

To many jurors, undercover investigators appear to be individuals who have used friendship, deceit, and persuasion in making arrests. Defense attorneys' allegations of entrapment—that their client did no more than "accommodate" a friend by getting him or her illicit drugs—cater to this conscious or subliminal belief. The legal significance of most of the evidence may rest on the prosecutor's ability to somehow insert a "victim" into the case—but this is difficult to do because drug selling is one of the so-called victimless crimes.

CASE STUDY

DANGEROUS DRUGS LAW ENFORCEMENT—ROLES AND STORY LINES

SCENE: Extracts from the testimony of police investigators tell the story of a major investigation into drug selling.

The first witness was a state chemist who testified that the substances examined by him (a bottle of orange tablets and balloons containing a white powder) were dangerous drugs—amphetamines—and a quantity of narcotics—heroin.

The next witness was one of the police investigators, Sergeant Charles Nekola of the City Police.

Direct Examination by the Assistant District Attorney (ADA)

Q: Sergeant Nekola, directing your attention to last April 13, did you have or were you present at an address, 150 "E" Street, here in the city on that date?

A: Yes, sir, I was.

Q: What was the purpose of being out there?

A: We went out there to serve a warrant of arrest on Robert Rodriquez at his residence at 150 "E" Street and a search warrant for the premises.

Q: Was the arrest warrant in relation to the recent grand jury indictment of the defendant?

A: Yes, sir.

Q: Who were you in company with?

A: I was in company with Sergeant James Larson.

Q: Did you approach the door of the residence?

A: Yes, I did.

Q: What did you do, if anything, at that time?

A: I knocked on the front door and waited approximately fifteen seconds. A female I later identified as Alice Rodriquez came to the window just north of the door.

Q: Did you observe her through the window?

A: Yes, sir, I did.

Q: What, if anything occurred at that time?

A: I told her to open the door, and she said, "What for?" I told her we were police officers and we had a search warrant for the house.

Q: Did you in any way identify yourself other than to say you were police officers?

A: Yes, sir. I had my badge in my right hand.

Q: Could you hear her through the window?

A: Yes, sir, I could.

Q: And what occurred, if anything, at that time?

A: I waited a short moment, and then she turned and appeared to run toward the back of the house.

Q: Could you hear noise coming from inside the house?

A: Yes, sir, I could.

Q: What, if anything, happened at that time?

A: Sergeant Larson started kicking the door, and he forced the door open with his foot.

Q: You have been a police officer for approximately thirteen years?

A: Yes, sir.

Q: Did you feel it was necessary to force the door open?

A: Yes, sir, I did.

Q: Would you explain why?

A: Usually, in a case when we are serving a search warrant on a residence and we know that the residents are people involved in the sale of drugs, they will recognize the agents and will flush the drugs down the toilet.

Q: Have you ever had this personally happen to you?

A: Yes, sir.

Q: Approximately how many times?

A: Oh, I'd say more than twenty times.

Q: Did you later enter this residence?

A: Yes, I did.

Q: And this young lady you indicated, who you observed in the window, was she present inside the residence?

A: Yes, sir, she was.

Q: After you entered?

A: Yes, sir.

ADA: No further questions, Your Honor. (Witness was excused.)

(continued)

Direct Examination of Sergeant James Larson by the Assistant District Attorney

Q: Sergeant Larson, where are you employed?

A: The City Police Department.

Q: How long have you been so employed?

A: Nine and a half years.

Q: Where do you work within the City Police?

A: I'm on assignment to the narcotics detail.

Q: Direct your attention to last April 13. Did you have occasion to be at a residence in the city, specifically 150 "E" Street?

A: I did.

Q: What was your purpose in being there?

A: We were going to make a warrant arrest and execute a search warrant on the residence.

Q: Were you present when a forced entry was made?

A: I was.

Q: Were you through the door first or were you the second one or—

A: (Interposing) I believe I was the first officer through the door.

Q: What did you observe immediately on entry?

A: There was no one in the front room or in the kitchen, that I could see. I went to the hallway and turned left. As we were entering, I had heard some doors closing in this direction. The door to the bathroom was closed. It opens off this hallway.

Q: Had you ever been in that house before?

A: I had been in it in February.

Q: What, if anything, did you do at this time?

A: I tried to open the bathroom door, and I couldn't get it open. I then knocked on it and pounded on it. I said, "Police officer. Open up." They didn't open up, so I then kicked in the door of the bathroom.

Q: You kicked in the door of the bathroom?

A: I did.

Q: After you kicked in the door what did you find, if anything?

A: Rodriguez was against the wall in the bathroom. He had a bag in one hand, which he dropped to the floor.

Q: Now, let me show you an item marked previously, marked No. 1 for identification. It is a brown manila envelope, and contained within there appears to be a brown leather bag. Does that in any way resemble the bag that you saw Mr. Rodriquez holding?

A: Yes, it does.

Q: When you entered the bathroom did he have it in his hand?

A: He had it in his right hand.

Q: Then what happened?

A: He dropped it to the floor as I entered.

Q: Then what occurred?

A: I then turned him against the wall, searched him, and placed him under arrest.

Q: Had you seen Mr. Rodriguez on previous occasions?

A: I had.

Q: You knew him?

A: I did.

Q: And what was your purpose for being there—in this house at this time?

A: To place Rodriguez under arrest on an arrest warrant we had in our possession, and also to serve a search warrant.

Q: What was the arrest warrant based on?

A: It was two counts of sales of narcotics. We made "buys."

Q: Grand jury indictments?

A: That's correct.

Q: Let me show you this brown leather purse. It is marked No. 1-A for identification. Would you examine the contents contained therein?

A: Yes, sir.

Q: Do you recognize the contents contained therein?

A: Yes, sir. This is the brown leather purse that was on the floor in the bathroom when I arrested Robert Rodriguez, and I seized it as evidence.

Q: How about the other items contained therein? Do you recognize any of those?

A: All of these items were contained inside the purse.

Q: Specifically, would you elaborate for the record what items we are talking about?

A: Yes, sir. This is a bottle of orange tablets.

Q: How about the brown paper bag. Do you recognize this item?

A: Yes, sir.

(continued)

Q: Let me open up the contents of the brown paper bag. By the way, does it bear your initials?

A: Yes, sir. It has the initials J. L. on it for my name.

Q: How about any of the contents contained within the brown paper bag?

A: All the items have my initials, J. L., written on them.

Q: Just briefly describe what was contained in this brown paper bag.

A: There were thirteen green balloons containing a powdery substance.

Q: What did you do with these items?

A: I retained them in my possession until such time as marked and submitted to the state chemist's locker.

Q: How long have you been an agent with this special squad?

A: A little over one year.

Q: Approximately how many arrests and investigations involving narcotic or restricted dangerous drugs have you participated in?

A: I would have to estimate over a hundred.

Q: Have you personally made "buys" of heroin?

A: Yes, sir, I have.

Q: On more than one occasion?

A: Numerous occasions.

Q: Assuming these items, that is the thirteen balloons, do contain heroin, do you have an opinion as to whether that is an amount sufficient to constitute a possession for sale?

A: Yes, it is.

Q: What do you base that opinion on?

A: On the method of packaging, the quantity contained inside, and the number of balloons.

Q: Have you ever seen heroin packaged in balloons before?

A: Yes, sir, I have.

Q: On numerous occasions?

A: Yes, sir.

CHAPTER REVIEW

Key Terms

analgesic   *277*
clandestine laboratories   *279*
cookers   *279*
crack (hubba, rock)   *278*
ecstasy   *280*
entrapment   *276*
euphoria   *278*
flaked   *289*
hallucinogens   *277*
ice   *279*
lateral snitching   *287*
lookout   *280*
Lysergic Acid Diethylamide
    or LSD   *280*

marijuana (pot)   *278*
methamphetamine (speed, crank,
    meth)   *279*
narcotics   *276*
Phencyclidine (angel dust, dust,
    PCP)   *279*
poor man's cocaine   *279*
pseudoephedrine   *279*
raid   *288*
rohypnol (roofies, date rape
    drug)   *280*

runner   *280*
sedatives   *277*
soporific agent   *278*
stash   *280*
stimulants   *277*
THC   *279*
trap   *288*
tweaker   *279*
working off a beef   *287*
working-up investigation   *287*

Review Questions

1. What controlled substance kills pain, induces drowsiness, produces physical and psychological dependency, and generates a sense of euphoria?
   a. Heroin
   b. Cocaine
   c. Phencyclidine
   d. Ecstasy
   e. LSD

2. What controlled substance produces a warm, fuzzy sense of well-being and the manic energy to dance all night?
   a. Heroin
   b. Cocaine
   c. Phencyclidine
   d. Ecstasy
   e. LSD

3. What controlled substance is commonly applied to tobacco or marijuana cigarettes and smoked, produces hallucinations, and—because of its anesthetic effect—may result in the user displaying a total disregard for his or her personal safety?
   a. Heroin
   b. Cocaine
   c. Phencyclidine
   d. Ecstasy
   e. LSD

4. What controlled substance produces feelings of exhilaration and euphoria, increases the user's energy level, and suppresses fatigue?
   a. Heroin
   b. Cocaine
   c. Phencyclidine
   d. Ecstasy
   e. LSD

5. What controlled substance produces hallucinations lasting ten to twelve hours and is ambivalent in that the user may experience both good and bad sensations?
   a. Heroin
   b. Cocaine
   c. Phencyclidine
   d. Ecstasy
   e. LSD

6. The drug that is most frequently used with alcohol has a synergistic effect that produces disinhibition and amnesia and, because of these effects, is known as the _____ drug.
   a. Love
   b. Date rape
   c. Feel good
   d. Poor man's

7. A/An _____ is a normal prelude to an application for a search warrant in illegal drug and narcotics cases.
   a. Informant
   b. Information
   c. Buy
   d. Drug analysis

8. The purpose of the _____ law is not to prevent the unwary criminal from being trapped in a crime; instead, it is to prevent the police officer from manufacturing crime.
   a. Entrapment
   b. Corroboration
   c. Entitlement
   d. Cultivation

9. When cocaine is dissolved in ether and then heated to boil off the impurities, the resulting drug is known as _____.
   a. Speed
   b. Crank
   c. Freebase
   d. Crack

10. When cocaine is mixed with baking soda and water and then heated to drive off the impurities, the resulting drug is known as _____.
    a. Speed
    b. Crank
    c. Freebase
    d. Crack

See Appendix D for the correct answers.

Application Exercise

As the supervisor of the drug unit you have been given information regarding possible illegal drug sales being conducted at a specific location. Your investigators have gone to that location and observed frequent in-and-out activity indicative of drug sales. These new investigators have an informant they can work with but they have not conducted a "buy" before. Draft a procedure for these investigators to follow in making a purchase of illegal drugs that will stand up in a court of law.

Discussion Questions

1. What drugs are common on the drug scene?
2. Briefly describe the drug-marketing pyramid (network).
3. Under what circumstances of investigation is a pickup arrest justified?
4. Name and describe the participants in a buy of illegal drugs.
5. In working-up investigations, what investigative techniques have proven useful in discovering evidence to corroborate the testimony of an accomplice witness?
6. What are the story lines of each witness in the case study?

Related Websites

Want to know what American national drug control policy is? If so, you should visit the Office of National Drug Control Police's website. This site contains information on drug facts, enforcement, prevention and treatment programs: *www.whitehousedrugpolicy.gov.*

To learn more about dangerous drugs as a global problem, visit the United Nations Office on Drugs and Crime website: *www.unodc.org.*

Notes

1. *People v. Martinez,* 256 P.2d 1028 (Dist. Ct. App. 1953).
2. *Robinson v. California,* 370 U.S. 660 (1962).
3. *People v. Monteverde,* 46 Cal. Rptr. 2–7 (1965).
4. *People v. Muñoz,* 18 Cal. Rptr. 82 (1962).
5. "Drug Identification Bible, 2008 ed." (Grand Junction, CO: Amera-Chem, 2008), 276–282.
6. Paul B. Weston, "The Illicit Traffic in Drugs," *Narcotics, U.S.A.* (New York: Greenberg, 1952), 127–140.
7. Phillip C. McGuire, "Jamaican Posses: A Call for Cooperation Among Law Enforcement Agencies," *The Police Chief* LV, no. 1 (January 1988): 20–27.
8. William D. Hyatt, "Investigation of Major Drug Distribution Cartels," in *Critical Issues in Criminal Investigation,* 2nd ed., ed. Michael J. Palmiotto (Cincinnati, OH: Anderson, 1988), 113–139.
9. Scott H. Decker and Barrik Van Winkle, "Sling Dope: The Role of Gang Members in Drug Sales," *Justice Quarterly* 11, no. 4 (December 1994): 583–604.
10. *Draper v. United States,* 358 U.S. 307 (1959).
11. *Aguilar v. Texas,* 378 U.S. 108 (1964); *Spinelli v. United States,* 393 U.S. 410 (1969); *United States v. Garrett,* 565 F. 2nd 1065 (1977).
12. *United States v. Johnson,* 561 F. 2nd 832 (1977).
13. Peter K. Manning, *The Narcs' Game: Organizational and Informational Limits on Drug Law Enforcement* (Cambridge, MA: The MIT Press, 1980), 161.
14. Mark Harrison Moore, *Buy and Bust* (Lexington, MA: D. C. Heath, 1977), 135.
15. James Mills, *The Underground Empire: Where Crime and Government Embrace* (New York: Doubleday, 1986), 72–113, 283–394, 520–618.

16 Special Investigations

LEARNING OBJECTIVES

After reading this chapter, you will be able to:

❶ *Discuss the various types of prostitution activity and the investigative steps needed to deal with them.*

❷ *Describe the operational structure of organized crime in the United States and the problems associated with achieving successful prosecution of the criminals involved in it.*

❸ *Summarize the characteristic activities of an organized crime syndicate.*

❹ *Describe the activities which would alert investigators that organized crime is doing business in their jurisdiction.*

❺ *Discuss the different criminal gangs and the types of crimes they are involved with.*

❻ *Understand the various motivations of the hit-and-run driver.*

❼ *Discuss the investigatory process involved in the apprehension of hit-and-run drivers.*

Many times during an investigator's career, he or she will be involved in cases that are outside or beyond his or her field of expertise. Even so, the investigator will be expected to contribute to the investigative efforts of these cases. This scenario is often played out in the area of the highly specialized investigations involving vice and gambling and hit-and-run accidents. Investigators should have a basic understanding of the underlying concepts involved in these investigations so they can be contributing members of the investigative team.

▶ Vice and Gambling

Vice laws, which regulate standards for public morals, are not usually aggressively enforced unless someone is offended and lodges a complaint or unless the activity occurs publicly. For example, most of the efforts of vice cops are directed toward the highly visible street-level prostitute. Prostitution that has gone underground, or become invisible, generates little attention. The same is true of gambling and other forms of immoral conduct. The degree to which these laws are enforced can easily bring forth criticism. A department that aggressively pursues enforcement of public morals laws may be criticized for squandering resources that could be used to control far more serious forms of crime. Too little effort in this area is often cited by critics as a graphic example of the corrupt nature of local law enforcement agencies. Somewhere between these two extremes is the fine line that most agencies follow in an effort to control vice in their community.

Gambling

The social harm of gambling has diminished with the added convenience of legal betting and a public awareness of the "fairness" of state-run lotteries, horse betting at tracks with a pari-mutuel setting system—even at "ghost" tracks (without horses but using video systems linked to other tracks with betting hooked to a central computer system and payoff the same as if the races were run locally). Some states offer off-track betting, which also affords the appeal of convenience and track odds.

Sports gambling's main events are professional and college basketball and football games; baseball is a poor second. A new interest is visible in soccer games among fans at local sports taverns. All sports wagering is aided by the local press, which gives the day's **line**, or betting odds for these events. Boxing is a suspect sport since it lacks the basic fairness of team sports.

Some **bookies**, people who take illegal bets on these events, are very quick to take a game **off the board**, or stop taking bets, with the knowledge that a **fix** is in, or the outcome of the event is predetermined. This they consider to be only good business—no morality is involved.

Casino gambling run by American Indian tribal enterprises that are not controlled by crime bosses brings Las Vegas–type table games to the local level. These gambling establishments establish a new horizon on the question of fairness: is it better for the local compulsive gambler to be able to satisfy his or her needs at local tables rather than at the hands of the local crime boss?

Illegal gambling is big business, often with interstate connections to organized crime. Investigators need to think big and be proactive in their investigative actions. Once probable cause exists to believe that illegal gambling is occurring, it is time to gather information and evidence, which often involves court-ordered eavesdropping. A task-force approach is an excellent way to gather the necessary personnel and resources to address this problem.

 Discuss the various types of prostitution activity and the investigative steps needed to deal with them.

Prostitution

Most cities are large enough to support a variety of prostitution activities most of which are outlined as follows:

> *Street level prostitution*—is considered to be lowest in status for this type of crime. Prostitutes stand on the sidewalk or in the street and wait for a potential client to stop. These women, and sometimes men, are readily identifiable due to their choice of clothing, or lack thereof, that is clearly the calling card of the profession. The prostitute will ask the potential client if they want to party. The two will agree to the type of sex to be performed and the price to be paid. The agreed-to act will then be performed in the client's vehicle or in a cheap nearby motel or hotel room.

Bar girls—hang around bars with the approval of the owner or bartender. These girls encourage men to buy them drinks, usually made of the most expensive liquor of course. The girls will also provide sex for money usually in a nearby back room.

Escort services—the phone numbers for these services are usually included in the phonebook or the classified sections of some newspapers. The services provide women for the purposes of prostitution if the client has a hotel or motel room available. These services usually take credit cards and provide a male escort for the prostitute as a form of protection. The male escort usually collects the money and sets the level of services to be provided.

Cat houses—are a permanent location where prostitution service are provided. This location is usually run by a **madam** who provides clients as well as shelter and protection for the prostitutes. The madam handles the financial transactions and keeps a percentage of the fee to pay her overhead costs as well as a healthy profit. The whereabouts of the cat house is not generally known to the average citizen. The cat house survives on a word of mouth referral basis which not only provides clients but a level of protection from law enforcement due to its anonymity.

Massage parlors—the vast majority of massage therapists, and massage parlors they work in, are honest hard working people and businesses. However, some are nothing more than a front for prostitution. The operational procedures for these massage parlors are similar to a cat house; however, these are storefront operations that take walk-in clients. As such these operations are more visible and more vulnerable to law enforcement.

Day trippers—these women ride the train or other conveyances into the city, or may be city dwellers. They wait in hotel lobbies until the bell captain gives them a room number to go to and ply their trade. These women work without protection as the status of the hotel and the screening provided by the bell captain are usually enough to avoid any potential problems. The only overhead for the prostitute is the fee charged by the bell captain for his services.

Call girls—are considered to operate at the highest level of the prostitution trade. These women only provide services to clients they know or who have been referred to them by a person they know and trust. These women are usually attractive, well dressed, and classy and therefore can command huge fees for their services.

Pimps are men and madams are women who live off the proceeds of one or more prostitutes. The activities of these people are a clear sign that someone is testing the no-tolerance rule of local law enforcement. Prompt action to arrest these people for their hustling activities sends a clear message that this behavior will not be tolerated. Similar prompt action should be taken against hotel/motel and tavern employees who act out the role of a pimp or madam on a part-time basis.[1]

Prostitution is known as the world's oldest profession. What the investigator should take away from this statement is that it would be unrealistic to expect to totally eliminate all prostitution activity. However, it is realistic to contain this criminal activity and even relocate it to another location. What is at issue here is street level prostitution; it is highly visible and this activity must be addressed for the good of the community. A number of law enforcement tactics can be employed to address street level prostitution.

Decoys—both men and women are used as decoys in the process of controlling prostitution. The male decoys are used to arrest the females supplying the prostitution services and female decoys are used to arrest the **Johns**, who are the clients seeking the services of a prostitute. The crime involved is known as the **solicitation** of sexual services for money. The crime of solicitation is completed when the prostitute or John agrees to have sex for money and then does some overt act in furtherance of this solicitation, such as the prostitute getting into the John's vehicle or the John going to the prostitute's hotel or motel room where they would be arrested.

High visibility enforcement—involves assigning numerous police officers to actively identify prostitutes and their prospective clients before they can engage in any sexual activity. The objective of this type of police effort is to deter potential clients by the sight of numerous police officers and their vehicles in the area. The downside to this tactic is that it is very labor intensive and expensive to operate.

Court orders—in some jurisdictions judges have issued orders to keep a prostitute from being in specific locations known to be frequented by prostitutes. This is known as a **restraining order** and the person being restrained can be arrested for violating the court order by merely being in the restricted area. Judges may be reluctant to use such orders to control prostitutes unless it can be shown that the prostitute is known to be infected with a communicable disease, such as AIDS, and continues to ply their trade despite being told that such activity is dangerous to the welfare of others.

Health and Safety Code enforcement—prostitution often flourishes in areas that have cheap hotel and motel rooms. These businesses are usually in a state of decline and may be operating in violation of health and safety codes. Actively enforcing these codes can be used to apply legal pressure on the owners of these businesses. The owners can either bring their property up to code specification. Which would increase the cost of the rooms, or to close the business. Once the price of the room increases or the business is closed, the prostitution activity may move into another area, which was the ultimate goal to begin with.

❷ *Describe the operational structure of organized crime in the United States and the problems associated with achieving successful prosecution of the criminals involved in it.*

▶ Organized Crime

Fighting regional organized crime is more than solving a single murder case, raiding a house of prostitution, or exposing an illegal bankruptcy ring. The investigation must be pursued beyond the operational level of the local overlords of crime to their allies in local government who have been well bribed.

The characteristic that most distinguishes the crime syndicate (organized crime) is unity of action. Criminal actions are dictated by executive and management personnel and are performed by subordinates in the organization. Little freelancing takes place; crime is almost always a franchise operation.

The hierarchy of command (the lines of authority) begins with the regional boss or chief, then extends to the underbosses who exercise a functional supervision over a group of activities, and then to the "owner" of an activity, such as a bookmaking enterprise, a ring of prostitutes, or other such activity. Authority is clearly delineated, and orders and suggestions are obeyed without question. The severity of supervision prompts an adherence to direction difficult to attain otherwise.

A second major characteristic of syndicate operations is the corruption of weak and foolish public officials to secure immunity from arrest and successful prosecution. This protection allows the open and notorious operation of both criminal and quasi-legal enterprises.

A third major characteristic of syndicate operations is the extension of the creed of death to the informer to justify the killing of anyone who interferes with the operations of organized crime. As a business technique, this may have originated as the only feasible means of settling disputes and silencing witnesses. Witnesses who have been connected with the syndicate do not talk to police investigators and are unlikely to talk even under the threat of legal action because other witnesses who have talked have died—usually in a very unpleasant manner.

Nature of Operations

An emerging characteristic of considerable importance to investigators is the wraparound nature of syndicate operations. Organized crime members involved in prostitution have expanded from the traditional role of madam or pimp—enjoying a profit from the earnings of a prostitute. They also control the booking of prostitutes from one area to another (a change of merchandise for local customers) and provide them with medical and legal talent as necessary. In labor racketeering, the labor unions are infiltrated for the basic enterprise, but the operation of nonunion shops and the control of employee associations provide fringe profits. In the infiltration of legitimate business, in addition to a planned bankruptcy or monopolistic activity, in-plant gambling and assignment of all freight business to syndicate trucking firms are organized until the organized crime operation is wrapped around every possible means for making money.

Convicted organized crime boss John Gotti listens to opening arguments in his New York State Supreme Court trial for racketeering.

Source: Richard Drew/AP Wide World Photos

③ *Summarize the characteristic activities of an organized crime syndicate.*

Characteristic Activity

Unity of action, immunity from governmental action, murder as a technique of business, and expansionistic methods summarize the characteristics that have made the crime syndicate a successful business in which large regional groups operate with nationwide unity.

Participant informant Salvatore "Sammy the Bull" Gravano testifies against his boss, John Gotti, in New York State Supreme Court.

Source: Steven Purcell/Getty Images

A significant factor in syndicate activity is whether an enterprise can be operated without interference from law enforcement agencies. The syndicate does not dislike sharing its profits with its allies in government, but corrupt politicians and police officers often make distinctions among different types of corruption. Syndicate members know that they must operate in areas such as their initial business of bootlegging—that is, in activities having a modicum of public approval. This often constitutes a black market of consumer services and sales in which the fixers and hookers of the crime syndicate corrupt politicians and police with the plea that nothing is wrong with a little prostitution, gambling, money lending at high rates of interest, or manufacturing and selling a good grade of untaxed alcohol. Of course, the enterprise has to be illegal to ensure a lack of competition by legitimate business groups, but it cannot be "too illegal" because then immunity is not only costly but may not be purchasable.[2]

The syndicate also operates in other areas of crime, such as selling narcotics, receiving and selling stolen goods, labor racketeering, infiltrating legitimate business, and having hidden ownerships in casinos in Nevada and other areas in which gambling is legalized by state or local law.

 Describe the activities which would alert investigators that organized crime is doing business in their jurisdiction.

Investigative Alerts

A lead alerting an investigator to local activity by members of an organized crime syndicate may originate in a federal or local agency. Personnel of the U.S. Drug Enforcement Agency (DEA) alert the local police when they believe the syndicate has started a new operation—and the locals work closely with informants who have in-depth knowledge of the lower-echelon members of the syndicate. The FBI continuously inventories the operations of organized crime and its allies in government. The work of FBI agents in clearing cases involving the interstate transportation of stolen goods has made this bureau very knowledgeable about the massive fencing operation of the syndicate. Local police intelligence units collect and interpret all incoming information from their own and the foregoing sources and compile their own files on the resident representatives of organized crime and the transients who display interest locally.[3]

In their work on other cases, investigators often encounter facts indicating that organized crime is developing a local interest—the changeover of a cabaret or roadhouse to a strip joint, the opening of an after-hours club, or the expansion of local sales of pornographic material. A little probing may indicate that these places of business are employing persons with police records or that ex-convicts are involved in management through a hidden ownership shield if licenses are required. The investigator has a lead to some of the initial operations of the syndicate when a restaurant owner complains of being pressured into buying meat from one firm or leasing linens from a particular concern, or when a bartender mentions that he or she and the owner of the bar were "asked" to use a certain vending machine firm. These danger signals are probable cause to inquire into the pressure and its origin. The inquiry may reveal the monopolistic control of a legitimate business and isolate and identify some of the resident members of the syndicate.

Arrests for illegal gambling, prostitution, and violations of state laws regulating the sale of alcoholic beverages can be audited by supervisors of the criminal investigation unit for traces that indicate syndicate takeover, such as a new pattern of arrests (mere increase or decrease is not significant) marked by continuing operations and the use of a small group of bail bondsmen and attorneys after arrests. Reports of the patrol force about suspicious persons and premises—whether increasing or diminishing—should be integrated to see what patterns emerge.

Because syndicate members are today closely involved with business, the initial alert may originate with the rank and file of a union, a trade association, or the Better Business Bureau and may be little more than an allegation of unfair treatment or competition or a complaint of in-plant gambling. Quite frequently, syndicate activity can be detected because of a killing, a suspicious fire, or an aggravated assault. Because of the massive fencing operation developed by organized crime, the presence of organized crime in an area may be determined from the activities of burglars and thieves who appear to operate without selling their loot. The alert may result from some suspicion or knowledge that the police agency has been penetrated (for information) or infiltrated (for protection), based on evidence that suspected personnel are living above their wage levels or of other suspicious behavior.

⑤ *Discuss the different criminal gangs and the types of crimes they are involved with.*

Gang Activity

Motorcycle ("biker") gangs have an organization similar to regional organized crime (La Cosa Nostra, the Mafia) but tend to specialize in peddling firearms and illicit drugs.[4] The bikers confront police officers with their crimes rather than attempting to conceal them or secure approval for their commission. Police surveillance can easily reveal the bikers' lifestyle.

Asian criminal organizations, made up primarily of Chinese and Vietnamese persons, are ethnic crime groups that closely resemble other "families" of organized crime in terms of their possible relationship to other social business groups of the same ethnic composition, in this case called **tongs**. The crimes of these groups are concentrated on extortion of local illegal gambling groups and legitimate business owners.[5]

Prison gangs operating outside prisons are somewhat similar to organized crime, although they also have a limited range of criminal activities—primarily drug selling—as do other drug-selling organizations, such as those composed of Colombians and Jamaicans.

Ideally, the person to lead a comprehensive investigation into the operations of organized crime is the local prosecutor or U.S. attorney. These public officials can develop a special investigation that combines the interrogation of witnesses with the examination of subpoenaed or seized records. Witnesses can be called before grand juries by prosecutors and placed under oath when they are questioned. Witnesses fearful of the syndicate may talk when granted immunity or threatened with jail for contempt if they refuse to testify or for perjury if they lie when they do testify. Despite the fact that members of the hierarchy of organized crime rarely become informants, this dilemma of cooperation or jail for contempt or perjury can be effective to make otherwise mute witnesses talk. Police investigators do not wield this power, but prosecutors can do so in their role as legal advisor to a public investigative body.

Problems of Proof

Witnesses are the major source of evidence in a case. They are commonly available when none of the defendants have links to organized crime or other crime groups, such as bikers, prison gangs, and other such organizations. Any link to a crime group on the part of a defendant usually means that witnesses will be threatened and intimidated—if they are not previously conditioned by the "death to the informer" stance of most of these groups. Usually, all of the co-conspirators know of potential witnesses who have been killed or so intimidated that they moved out of town without leaving a forwarding address. This disposal of witnesses by death or intimidation tends to silence anyone thinking of becoming a witness for the prosecution.

Investigative Tactics

Recognizing that organized crime poses a severe threat to society the U.S. Congress passed legislation specifically designed to address this threat. Congress passed laws making it illegal to be involved in organized crime or **racketeering**, addressed the financial incentives by restricting the movement of money and asset forfeiture, and dealt with the practice of killing the informant through the witness protection program.

The Racketeer Influence and Corrupt Organization Act (RICO) was passed with the declared purpose of seeking to eradicate organized crime. To successfully prosecute a person under this statute the government must prove that first, an organized criminal enterprise existed; second, that the enterprise affected interstate commerce; third, the defendant was associated with or employed by the enterprise; forth, the defendant engaged in a pattern of racketeering activity; and fifth, that the defendant conducted or participated in at least two acts of racketeering activity within ten years of each other. Under RICO the crimes related to racketeering activity are drawn from a list of 35 crimes—27 federal crimes and 8 state crimes. A person found guilty under this statute can be fined up to $25,000 and sentenced to twenty years in prison for each racketeering count. In addition, the racketeer must forfeit all ill-gotten gains and interest in any business gained through a pattern of racketeering activity.

The RICO statute also allows the U.S. Attorney the option of seeking a pretrial restraining order or injunction to temporarily seize the defendant's assets to prevent the transfer of potentially forfeitable property.[6]

Money laundering—organized crime is heavily involved in cash-only activities such as gambling, prostitution, loan sharking, and illegal drugs. These activities generate large amounts of cash and the challenge for organized crime bosses is to convert this money into what appears to be legitimate sources of income, or to launder the money as to make it look legitimate. One way to launder money is to pass it through a legitimate cash business such as vending machine business, or casino that the organization owns. Another option is to send the money offshore and get it into banking systems that do not come under the control of U.S. banks or the purview of the Internal Revenue Service (IRS) to ask questions regarding the legitimacy of these funds.

To prevent the movement of large amounts of money financial institutions are now required to report any transaction larger than $10,000 to the IRS. In addition, it is illegal to move money with the intent to disguise the source or ownership of the money.

Asset forfeiture—is an effective tool in reducing the incentive for illegal conduct. Any money directly or indirectly traceable to a crime is subject to forfeiture. In addition, money earned during the commission of a crime that was used to purchase any product or property is subject to forfeiture as well. Also, any item or property used in the furtherance of a crime is subject to forfeiture, regardless of the source of the money used to purchase the item or property. Therefore, a vehicle used to transport illegal drugs could be seized regardless of who purchased, or owns the vehicle.[7]

Witness protection—the U.S. Marshal's Service provides protection for witnesses and their immediate family whose lives are in danger as a result of their testimony against organized crime and other major criminals. Witnesses are given round-the-clock protection prior to testifying and are given new identities and are relocated after testifying. Since this program began in 1971 the Marshal's Service has provided protection to over 8,500 witnesses and 9,900 of their family members. No participant who followed security guidelines has been harmed while under the active protection of this program.[8]

6 *Understand the various motivations of the hit-and-run driver.*

▶ Hit and Run

Investigators have difficulty avoiding personal involvement when attempting to solve a crime without motive and usually without witnesses. Standard police procedure calls for the issuance of a prompt alarm for the fleeing vehicle, an extensive crime scene search, and assignment of police investigators to the accident-and-crime scene around the time of occurrence, and on days following the accident, in a search for witnesses.

The Hit-and-Run Operator

Hit-and-run drivers have been grouped into three categories based on possible psychological explanations for their motivation for flight:

1. The apprehensive, panic-driven, fearful driver
2. The projectionist—projects guilt
3. The sneak—inflicts minor property damage

The **apprehensive driver** has a greater sin to hide, either morally or criminally. This individual typically flees the scene for one or more of the following reasons: (1) driving while intoxicated, (2) operating without a license, (3) having no insurance, (4) being a companion in the car who is not the driver's mate or who is the mate of another, (5) driving a stolen car, (6) possessing stolen goods in the car, (7) leaving the scene of another accident, (8) fleeing a crime scene, (9) being wanted for some crime, or (10) just being fearful.

(a) This vehicle was involved in a hit and run of a pedestrian.

(b) Note the victim's eyeglasses in the door frame of the suspect's vehicle.

The **projectionist driver** tries the case—sitting as judge and jury, he or she finds the other driver at fault, refuses to be a party to the accident, and drives off as the offended person.

The **sneak operator** is one that crushes a fender and smashes grillwork as daily occupational activities and chalks up the action as the calculated risk shared by all vehicle owners who place their vehicles on the roadway.

Fortunately, hit-and-run operators do not have the attitudes of a professional criminal, nor are they skilled at concealing damage to a vehicle. They will usually be cooperative when found, and traces of vehicle damage can be easily located, even if recently repaired.

Discuss the investigatory process involved in the apprehension of hit-and-run drivers.

The Alarm

The basic line of investigation in hit-and-run cases must be along the lines of opportunity: (1) what car was at the scene? and (2) who operated it? The ideal time of apprehension is while the fugitive car is being operated by the hit-and-run driver. For this reason, time is most important in determining that the accident is a hit-and-run case and in getting a broadcast on the air.

When investigators find that the scene of an accident is a hit-and-run case, their first effort is to obtain from available witnesses a full description of the vehicle involved. This should include all odd or unusual details. Even noises heard are sometimes useful clues. Descriptive items that may prove extremely valuable in locating the vehicle are (1) stickers on windows or windshield, (2) dented fenders, (3) fancy wheel covers, (4) broken radio aerials, (5) distinctive ornaments and fixtures, (6) broken window glass, (7) unusual colors and body styles, and (8) out-of-state license plates that are easily recognizable.

These data, together with a description of the occupants and the direction of the vehicle when last seen, should be immediately broadcast in a police radio alarm to all members of the department and to nearby police units. The alarm alerts police on patrol to look for abandoned vehicles or vehicles in transit with such damage and as described. Particular attention is usually directed along the possible escape routes of the fleeing vehicle.

Garages, parking lots, used car lots, and other places where a vehicle might be stored or taken for repairs should be promptly checked by police. Generally, if a vehicle is not located within a reasonable time after the accident occurred, it may be assumed that the driver removed it from the streets and placed it in a private garage. A prearranged list of all public garages and other likely storage places will facilitate the police in conducting preliminary inquiries. Prearranged contacts with garages may result in immediate reporting of a damaged vehicle.

Officers at the accident scene should also check suspicious persons at the scene or inquisitive passersby. Sometimes hit-and-run drivers return to the scene, curious to find out how much evidence the police have discovered. In many cases the hit-and-run driver stops from habit, examines the injuries of the victim, stays a few minutes, and then flees. This habit should be kept in mind when questioning witnesses about persons who were at the scene but drove away.

Police officers should be alert for vehicles reported stolen after the time of the hit-and-run case and that fit the description of the fugitive car. When no description is available, all these cases of reported thefts should be investigated for possible involvement. It is a common technique of the hit-and-run driver, in attempting to explain vehicle damage and the presence of his or her vehicle at the scene, to flee and then park the vehicle in some out-of-the-way area and report it stolen so that he or she can explain any damage and the presence of the vehicle at the scene without implicating himself or herself.

The Scene Search

Transfer evidence is important in hit-and-run investigations. Since the only investigative leads are along the line of opportunity, it is vital to search for evidence at the accident scene that will identify the vehicle and the driver involved. This search should not be limited to prime identification that will lead to prompt recognition of either the vehicle or operator but should extend to any evidence that will connect the vehicle and its driver to the scene when the suspect vehicle is located or the fleeing operator is apprehended.

The search for physical evidence at the scene should be thorough. It should be planned so that every part of the area is carefully and methodically searched. A haphazard search procedure may frustrate the entire investigation by failing to discover evidence or by destroying or impairing the value of evidence. This is a most important step in the investigation. The scene must be protected and safeguarded, and then the search must be pointed toward broken headlight glass, door handles, hubcaps, paint marks or scrapings, soil and mud fallen from cars at impact, and any other debris. Objects carried in or on a hit-and-run vehicle are of value. Damage to fixed objects can also be studied for traces of paint and indication of damage to the vehicle.

Whenever the scene search reveals the nature of the damage to the vehicle or the probable make or model of the vehicle, this information should be added immediately to the alarm and broadcast to all units aiding in the search. Several police agencies use an artist or a special-effects photographer to prepare a graphic illustration of the wanted vehicle on the basis of known information secured in the investigation and of probable damage, based on the damage sustained by vehicles involved in previous accidents of a similar nature.

Experienced hit-and-run investigators attempt to identify the original purpose of the hit-and-run driver. What brought the driver into the neighborhood of the accident scene? What brought him or her into this area at the time of the accident, on the day of the week on which the accident happened? This assumption of purposefulness is coupled with the habits of drivers who utilize the same routes to and from work or for leisure activity. This is the basis for the concept of returning to the accident scene on stakeout duty in a quest for witnesses. It is also an emerging concept for locating the vehicle involved in a hit-and-run case and for evidence that will connect the suspect with the scene or vice versa.

Stakeouts

Investigators should regularly return to the scene to look for new witnesses. The return should be at the same time of day and day of week as the accident. The neighborhood of the accident, route of travel, and other possible areas should be canvassed thoroughly for new witnesses. Perseverance is the rule, not the exception in locating witnesses.

Transfer Evidence

Science has provided the police with one of their most effective weapons against hit-and-run cases. The scientific analysis of evidence found at an accident scene sometimes identifies the make and model of the wanted vehicle. Comparison analysis of such evidence with that recovered from a suspect's automobile provides data placing the vehicle at the crime scene. Some of the most common types of evidence found in hit-and-run accident investigations are amenable to scientific analysis.

Since the advent of sealed-beam headlights, glass fragments found at accident scenes are not as productive of results as in former years. However, they are still excellent evidence for proving that a suspect vehicle, when located, was at the accident scene. Broken or damaged automobile parts, paint, soil, hairs, fibers, bloodstains, and tire marks all lend themselves to the identification of the type and make of vehicle in the first phase of searching for the vehicle, as well as to later comparison analysis when the suspect vehicle is located.

When a suspected vehicle is located, it should be impounded for an immediate search for evidence. All exterior parts of the vehicle should be carefully examined. Special attention should be given to all protruding parts where hairs or fibers might have been caught. All damaged parts should be noted and inspected for traces of blood or signs of contact with other objects. No foreign material should be discarded from consideration until its source is definitely determined. Evidence of recent damages, repairs, new paint, or wash jobs should be carefully noted. If damaged parts have been replaced, attempts should be made to obtain the original parts.

The undercarriage of the vehicle should receive special attention. The vehicle should be placed over a mechanic's pit or up on a rack for a proper search. Spots that appear to have been brushed by an object and all protruding parts should be thoroughly examined for hairs, fibers, and blood spots.

The possibility of developing latent fingerprints to identify the driver of a vehicle must always be attempted. Frequently a suspect denies having driven the vehicle, and it may in fact have been driven by a thief. Fingerprints may tell the story.

All evidence should be properly preserved and compared with evidence found at the scene of the accident so that the investigating officer can prove that the suspect's vehicle was at the accident scene and was involved in the accident.

The vehicle is the key to the criminal in these cases. If transfer evidence will connect the vehicle with the accident scene, then police can look to its owner for honest answers in a fact-finding inquiry about the operator.

A common explanation by the owner of the vehicle is that his or her car may be involved, but he or she denies driving it at the time and claims it was loaned to a friend of recent acquaintance known only as "Joe." Investigators should not believe it until "Joe" is identified, is found, and confesses.

Accountability

Apprehension of a hit-and-run driver is difficult because information can be secured only from victims and witnesses and from physical evidence found at the scene. Informers are of little use in such cases. No modus operandi is available to identify the criminal, and the suspect usually does not have a record of previous offenses and could be any member of the community.

Motive is not a potential line of inquiry in these cases insofar as a desire to kill or injure the victim. Motivation is only for flight from the scene and has no connection with the victim. Therefore, the line of inquiry as to who wanted to kill the deceased, which frequently leads to the criminal in homicide cases, is useless in hit-and-run cases.

Car dealers and motor vehicle license authorities can supply either the names and addresses of persons who recently purchased a vehicle similar to the wanted vehicle or a license number close to the license number of the wanted vehicle. Apprehension can be accomplished, but a great deal depends on chance.

Hit-and-run investigations should be conducted by accident investigators. When this work is assigned to detective units, it is only human for a detective working on criminal homicides, felonious assaults, kidnappings, and bank robberies to assign a role of lesser importance to hit-and-run cases. Yet in this field of traffic safety, the people of a community can be won over to the police side by the quick solution of these cases and prompt apprehension and trial of the offenders. Much of this work can be accomplished by accident investigators working in uniform, but permission should be granted to assigned investigators working out of uniform when necessary. Accident investigators are key personnel in getting these investigations started promptly. A prompt alarm and search will result in an apprehension before a vehicle can be hidden and the damage repaired. It will also result in an emotional shock to the fleeing driver, which results in an offender's waiving the right to silence and legal counsel and making a prompt and full admission of fleeing the scene and the reasons for such flight.

Possible Murder

Infrequently, a pedestrian, walking or jogging on a sidewalk or the side of a road, is struck by a fast-moving vehicle and is dead on arrival at the local hospital before police arrive. The case usually goes into the hit-and-run routine without producing results. The local homicide investigators should be notified whenever the slightest evidence of murder is noted and asked to run a regular homicide check on who might profit from or want the victim dead. In the meantime, the hit-and-run investigator concentrates on finding the damaged vehicle and witnesses.

CASE STUDY

HIT AND RUN

June 8

2045 Hours. The city police dispatch center receives a 911 call of a pedestrian versus vehicle accident at 21st and Jay Streets. Patrol and medical units are dispatched to the scene.

2052 Hours. The first police unit arrives on the scene and confirms that a pedestrian has been struck by a vehicle and that the victim is critically injured. According to witnesses, the vehicle involved has left the scene. The vehicle is described as a tan four-door sedan, last seen heading west on 21st Street. All available units are updated with this information and requested to search the area for the suspect vehicle.

2054 Hours. An ambulance arrives on the scene and begins emergency medical treatment. The victim is transported to the nearest hospital, code 3: red lights and siren.

2105 Hours. The highway patrol transfers a cellular 911 call to the city dispatch center. A young woman advises that she and her boyfriend are following a tan sedan that was just involved in an accident at 21st and Jay Streets in the city. The caller states that they were in light traffic when they observed the car in front of them run the light at the intersection and hit a pedestrian. The force of the impact caused the pedestrian to strike

(continued)

the windshield and be thrown over the roof of the vehicle and land in the street. As other drivers stopped to aid the victim, the couple decided to follow the suspect as he fled from the scene. The couple is now a few car lengths behind the suspect vehicle, headed east on the freeway toward the suburbs. The dispatcher asks the caller to stay on the line and to continue to follow the suspect at a discreet distance. The dispatcher obtains the suspect's license plate number from the caller and runs the number through the Department of Motor Vehicles (DMV) database.

2110 Hours. Patrol units are advised of the suspect's location and possible destination. The DMV inquiry discloses that the suspect's vehicle is registered to a location in the eastern part of the county. As the suspect's residence is located in the jurisdiction of the sheriff's department, this department is advised.

2117 Hours. The couple following the suspect advises that the vehicle has stopped at a residence and that the suspect has parked the vehicle and gone inside. The address given by the couple matches the address supplied by DMV records.

2120 Hours. Police and sheriff's units arrive at the suspect's residence and secure the area to prevent escape. Officers knock at the suspect's door, but no one responds to open the door.

2135 Hours. The telephone number for the residence is obtained from the reverse directory and the dispatcher places a call to the suspect's residence. After a few minutes, a male answers the telephone and is advised to step outside to talk to the officers. When he opens the door and steps outside, he is taken into custody.

2215 Hours. Crime scene technicians arrive at the suspect's residence and begin to photograph and process the vehicle for evidence. The victim's eyeglasses are recovered from the door frame of the vehicle.

2230 Hours. The officer at the hospital advises that the victim was just pronounced dead as a result of the injuries sustained in the accident. The suspect is subsequently booked at the county jail for vehicular homicide.

September 12

During a formal ceremony at City Hall, the young couple is presented with a citation from the chief of police commending their actions leading to the apprehension of this hit-and-run driver.

CHAPTER REVIEW

Key Terms

apprehensive driver   *302*
asset forfeiture   *302*
bar girls   *297*
bookie   *296*
call girls   *297*
cat houses   *297*
code enforcement   *298*
court orders   *298*
day trippers   *297*
decoys   *297*

escort services   *297*
fix   *296*
high visibility enforcement   *297*
john   *297*
line   *296*
madam   *297*
massage parlors   *297*
money laundering   *302*
off the board   *296*
pimp   *297*

projectionist driver   *303*
racketeering   *301*
restraining order   *298*
sneak operator   *303*
solicitation   *297*
street level prostitution   *296*
tong   *301*
vice law   *296*
witness protection   *302*

Review Questions

1. Female undercover officers, or volunteer decoys, are used to arrest ____, who solicit females for prostitution.
   a. Strolls
   b. Pimps
   c. Madams
   d. Johns

2. The first characteristic that most distinguishes organized crime is ____ of ____.
   a. Hierarchy/command
   b. Unity/action
   c. Corruption/officials
   d. Death/informants

3. A second major characteristic of syndicate operations is the ____ of weak and foolish public officials to secure immunity from arrest and successful prosecution.
   a. Threatening
   b. Corruption
   c. Ignorance
   d. Timidness

4. A third major characteristic of syndicate operations is the extension of the creed of ____ to the informer.
   a. Death
   b. Expulsion
   c. Expellant
   d. Exposure

5. Which type of prostitution activity is considered to be the lowest in terms of professional status?
   a. Street level
   b. Escort services
   c. Day trippers
   d. Call girls

6. Which type of prostitutes are considered to be operating at the highest professional status?
   a. Street level
   b. Escort services
   c. Day trippers
   d. Call girls

7. The law enforcement tactic which is most likely to have prostitution relocated involves the enforcement of which laws?
   a. Vehicle codes
   b. Health and safety codes
   c. Penal codes
   d. Business and professions codes

8. The type of hit-and-run driver involved in a hit and run because he or she has a greater sin to hide, either morally or criminally, such as drunk driving is known as the:
   a. Apprehensive driver
   b. Alarmist driver
   c. Projectionist driver
   d. Sneak operator

9. The type of hit-and-run driver involved in a hit and run because he or she has tried the case in his or her mind and has found the other driver at fault, refuses to be a party to the accident, and drives off is known as the:
   a. Apprehensive driver
   b. Alarmist driver
   c. Projectionist driver
   d. Sneak operator

10. The type of hit-and-run driver involved in a hit and run because he or she has justified the accident as the result of the calculated risk shared by all vehicle owners who place their vehicle on the roadway is known as the:
   a. Apprehensive driver
   b. Alarmist driver
   c. Projectionist driver
   d. Sneak operator

See Appendix D for the correct answers.

Application Exercise

A section of your community has been in decline for a number of years and recently street level prostitution has established a foothold in the area. Citizens groups are demanding that something be done to address this problem. As the lead investigator of the special investigations unit you have been tasked with this issue. Accordingly, draft a proposal that you think would be most successful in bringing this problem under control.

Discussion Questions

1. Describe how a police agency can be criticized for actively enforcing vice laws in the community.
2. Explain how an agency can be criticized for not actively enforcing these very same laws?
3. Define organized crime.
4. What is an accomplice witness? Why do accomplice witnesses agree to cooperate with the police investigator? Do they require protection? Why?
5. Discuss how, as in the case study, the witnesses' use of a cell phone facilitated the suspect's identification and arrest.
6. Discuss how investigators can use other technology, such as security cameras, in solving hit-and-run cases.

Related Websites

To get up-to-date information about organized crime, go to *www.ganglandnews.com*.

For the history of organized crime, including biographies, pictures, mugshots, and more, go to *www.gangrule.com*.

Notes

1. Frederick W. Egen, *Plainclothesman: A Handbook of Vice and Gambling Investigation* (New York: Arco, 1968), 3–104.
2. Donald R. Cressey, *Theft of the Nation* (New York: Harper & Row, 1969), 248–289.
3. Drexel Godfrey, Jr. and Don R. Harris, *Basic Elements of Intelligence: A Manual of Theory, Structure and Procedures for Use by Law Enforcement Agencies Against Organized Crime* (Washington, DC: U.S. Department of Justice, Technical Assistance Division, Law Enforcement Assistance Administration, 1971), 11–35.
4. James Burro, *Mob Rule: Inside the Canadian Mafia* (Toronto: Macmillan, 1985), 256–258.
5. Francis M. Roache, "Organized Crime in Boston's Chinatown," *The Police Chief* 45, no. 1 (January 1988): 48–51.
6. www.justice.gov/usao/eousa/foia-reading-room/usam/title9/crm00109.
7. Douglas Leff, "Money Laundering and Asset Forfeiture, Taking the Profit Out of Crime," *FBI Law Enforcement Bulletin* 81, no. 4 (April 2012): 23–32.
8. www.usmarshals.gov/witsec.

17 Terrorism

CHAPTER OUTLINE

LEARNING OBJECTIVES

After reading this chapter, you will be able to:

1 *Define terrorism.*

2 *List the various criminal acts committed by terrorists.*

3 *Explain the historical development of domestic terrorism in the United States and identify the groups involved.*

4 *Discuss the historical development of terrorism in the Middle East and the events that led to the formation of the groups involved.*

5 *Define what the weapons of mass destruction are and explain why terrorists would want to use these weapons.*

6 *Appreciate the efforts toward counterterrorism in the United States and the role of the agencies involved.*

7 *Discuss the role of police operations units in dealing with terrorists' threats and events.*

8 *Discuss the activities the investigator would be engaged in during the course of a terrorist investigation.*

9 *Explain the problems of proving a case of terrorism.*

Prior to the attacks on the World Trade Center and the Pentagon on September 11, 2001, counterterrorism efforts in the United States were fragmented. After these attacks, Congress passed legislation, such as the Patriot Act, which removed the barriers preventing counterterrorist agencies from working together and sharing information. The Joint Terrorism Task Force concept was expanded, and now investigators from the state, federal, and local levels work together to respond to terrorist activity and prevent future attacks. The United States is a prime target for terrorists both from within its borders and from international terrorists groups.

1 *Define terrorism.*

▶ Defining Terrorism

Title 18, section 2331, of the United States Code defines **terrorism** as a "violent act or an act dangerous to human life in violation of the criminal laws of the United States or of any state to intimidate or coerce a government, the civilian population, or any segment thereof, in furtherance of political or social objective." More simply put, a terrorist is someone who commits criminal acts in furtherance of a political or social agenda.

The United States and other Western countries have an enormous capacity to conduct conventional warfare, and any direct confrontation on the battlefield would be fruitless. Therefore, dissident individuals and groups use unconventional means to strike symbolic blows designed to break the will of the stronger power and to advance the terrorist political agenda. Democracies, throughout history, have been the targets of terrorist attacks because democratic systems are expected to play by the rules and, therefore, cannot respond in comparable fashion to these attacks. Autocracies and totalitarian systems are able to respond more easily to terrorist attacks with terrorist acts of their own, which sometimes serves as effective deterrents, but democracies cannot respond in similar fashion.[1]

2 *List the various criminal acts committed by terrorists.*

▶ Terrorist Acts

The crimes a terrorist group chooses to commit may be based on a political agenda or some other factor specific to that group. For instance, bombings are a common form of terrorist activity, yet some terrorist groups may prefer arson because the killing of human beings is inconsistent with the political agenda of those groups. The following are some of the more common crimes committed by terrorist groups:

1. *Bombings* are the most common terrorist tactic because a properly placed bomb can inflict massive numbers of casualties. For example, the 1995 bombing of the Murrah Federal Building in Oklahoma City killed 168 people and injured 500 others.

2. *Hijackings* of airliners, cruise ships, and other means of mass transportation have been committed primarily for their propaganda value. Such scenarios are played out in the media on a daily basis for the duration of the event and bring the terrorists' names and objectives to the world's attention.

3. *Kidnapping* is committed for several reasons. As a maintenance function, the kidnapping of a wealthy subject may be a means of collecting ransom monies that terrorists then use to support their daily expenses and to finance future terrorist activity. Kidnapping is also useful as a propaganda tool, especially if the subject is a well-known individual or a member of the media.

4. *Physical assaults* such as **kneecapping** was a technique developed by the Irish Republican Army to cripple rather than kill. The process involves shooting an informant in the back of the knee and making that person a cripple for the rest of his or her life. A person in such a condition sends a strong visual message and thus becomes an example to others of the terrorists groups' power and the cost of informing on them.

5. *Arson*, unlike bombs, is designed to destroy property and not people. Arson has been a crime of choice for animal rights groups, such as those who set fire to and destroyed the animal research lab at the University of California at Davis.

6. *Vandalism* is a crime of choice for **ecoterrorists** who are dedicated to destroying the lumber industry due to its perceived negative impact on the environment. Damage to logging equipment is a prime objective. A favorite tactic known as **tree spiking** involves driving metal spikes into trees in logging areas for the purpose of damaging logging equipment.

The damaged Pentagon building in Virginia surrounded by fire trucks and ambulances in the aftermath of the terrorist hijacking and airliner crash of September 11, 2001.

Source: US NAVY/ Alamy

7. *Assassinations* are usually carefully planned and executed. Victims are selected for both their symbolic and their publicity value.

8. *Robbery* is another crime committed for the maintenance of terrorists and their operations. Banks and armored cars are popular targets, and the money gained in the commission of these crimes is used to support terrorist groups' daily existence and future terrorist activities.

9. *Narcoterrorism* is another source of revenue for the terrorist. In the Middle East, narcoterrorists are involved in the production of opium, and in South America they are involved in the production of cocaine.

10. *Cyberterrorism* involves the hacking into automated control systems that run networks for electricity, water, gas, oil, communications, and more. Where such control systems are connected to the Internet, they are vulnerable. According to the FBI, terrorist groups have shown an interest in either developing hacking skills or hiring hackers to work for them.[2]

▶ Terrorist Atrocities

Terrorist atrocities, such as the events of September 11, 2001, serve several essential objectives for the terrorist. First and foremost, they can produce pure terror or paralyzing fear. A second major purpose is to attract attention and gain sympathy through publicity. The purpose of an atrocity is to attract widespread attention; thus, the more spectacular the act of terroristic violence, the more interest it arouses in the general population. Viewing the atrocity may lead one audience to supply recruits, another to supply material aid, and yet another to offer encouragement. In addition, the terrorist atrocity may increase the prestige of the terrorist group and strengthen its acceptability and influence among other terrorist groups. The boldness of the act of terrorism may also strengthen a terrorist group's claim that it is the only legitimate representative of "the people."

The third purpose of terrorist atrocities is to provoke the existing political establishment to commit counteratrocities. If the government is seen as employing the same tactics as the terrorist group, then potential sympathizers become allies and the strength of the terrorist group grows. The aim of the terrorist group is to enrage the establishment.[3]

❸ *Explain the historical development of domestic terrorism in the United States and identify the groups involved.*

▶ Domestic Terrorism

According to Title 18, section 2331(5), of the United States Code, **domestic terrorism** refers to terrorist activities that occur primarily within the territorial jurisdiction of the United States. Domestic terrorists are active on the far left and the far right of the political spectrum in America.

The beginnings of the **Ku Klux Klan** can be traced back to 1865 in Pulaski, Tennessee, when a small group of Confederate veterans gathered together to form a social club. To show off their new club, the members disguised themselves in sheets and rode through the main street, which created quite a stir in the small town. The men adopted the sheets as official regalia and eventually added tall hats and masks. As the club grew, the men's actions began to have a chilling effect on the local blacks, an effect that was noted by the more violent members of the group.

Soon the hooded riders began intimidating night raids to homes of blacks and advised blacks against exercising their newfound rights. As the Klan became more violent over time, its night rides included hangings, acid branding, tar and feathering, and other forms of terror. The numbers of Klan victims will never be known since many victims were too afraid to report their victimization. However, between 1889 and 1941 some 3,811 blacks were lynched by Klansmen for "crimes" and alleged "crimes" ranging from attempting to vote to being disrespectful to a white person. The image of a black male hanging from a tree by a rope became a symbol of the worst of the Klan violence.[4]

A typical Ku Klux Klan rally includes white robes and hats and a cross burning.
Source: © Jim McDonald/ CORBIS-NY

A second Klan movement emerged in 1915 and lasted until 1945. This new Klan, in addition to holding its prior beliefs of white Protestant supremacy, added Catholics, Jews, and foreigners to its hate list. The Klan's membership was estimated to be between four and five million. The Klan controlled not only state and local politics but included at least two U.S. senators among its ranks. During World War II, the group's close association with the Nazi party became known and the Klan fell into disrepute.

The Klan reemerged a third time between 1960 and 1975 in response to the civil rights movement. In Birmingham, Alabama, more than a hundred bombs were detonated by Klan members in the early 1960s to intimidate blacks and civil rights workers. By 1966 the level of violence had overwhelmed local law enforcement, so the federal government stepped in and began to prosecute the top leadership of the Klan for the slaying of civil rights workers. Today Klan membership has dwindled, and many of its former and potential new members have been drawn to other groups committed to **white supremacy**.[5]

In 1985 William Pierce, a white supremacist headquartered in West Virginia, wrote a novel under the pseudonym of Andrew MacDonald. ***The Turner Diaries***, as he named it, is a fictionalized account of an international white revolution and a how-to manual for terrorism. The book discusses the proper methods for making bombs and attacking targets. With is frequent diatribes against minorities and Jews, the book has become the philosophical standard for many antigovernment white supremacist groups. The lone wolf Timothy McVeigh, who was responsible for the Oklahoma City bombing of the Murrah Federal Building, had a well-worn copy of *The Turner Diaries* in his possession at the time of his arrest in 1995.[6]

In 1983 Robert Jay Mathews, inspired by *The Turner Diaries*, founded the Order, a violent white supremacist group. The Order's war against the "Zionist Occupation Government" included counterfeiting, bank robbery, armored car robberies, and murder. The Order was responsible for the 1984 murder of talk radio host Alan Berg, who regularly lambasted the **neo-Nazi** movement. Also in 1984 the group robbed an armored car in Ukiah, California, and made off with $3.6 million. Matthews was traced to Whidbey Island in Washington, where he died in an FBI-led siege. Mathews is considered a martyr and an inspiration to other hate groups.[7]

Domestic terrorist Timothy McVeigh was convicted of bombing the Murrah Federal Building in Oklahoma City.

Source: © Bob E. Daemmrich/Sygma CORBIS-NY

On the political left, two violent single-issue groups have surfaced that focus on one particular issue to the exclusion of all others. The **Animal Liberation Front (ALF)** and the **Earth Liberation Front (ELF)** have committed numerous acts of violence, including arson and vandalism. ALF members favor direct action to protest animal abuse, with the objective of saving as many animals as possible. ELF was founded in England by activists who split from the environmentalist group EarthFirst! because of its decision to abandon criminal activities. ALF and ELF have coordinated their activities and have made joint claims about taking responsibility for property damage and other acts of vandalism. Both groups have been nonviolent toward humans, but they have committed many incidents of property destruction. ALF/ELF actions have included the following:

- Destruction of a forest station in Oregon
- Destruction of the University of California at Davis livestock research laboratory
- Tree spiking; this involves pounding metal staves into trees in logging areas for the purpose of destroying logging equipment
- "Liberating" minks in Wisconsin
- Arson at a ski resort in Vail, Colorado

The FBI estimates that ELF alone has caused about $100 million in property damage since 1996. In one particularly destructive incident in August 2003, the group caused $50 million in damages to a condominium complex under construction in San Diego, California.[8]

In the 1960s there were public protests to the Vietnam War and a call for social change. The group Students for a Democratic Society (SDS) was promoting these demonstrations. When the SDS collapsed in 1969, a more violent group, the **Weather Underground**, emerged and they embraced communist ideologies and violence as a way to protest the war. In 1974 the group took credit for an explosion at the headquarters of the State Department in Washington, DC, that caused extensive damage to the building but no injuries. Hours later a second bomb was found at as military induction center in Oakland, California. By 1978 the FBI had identified and arrested five members of the group who were plotting to bomb a political office. An accident at the group's bomb factory in New Jersey and subsequent arrests of other members of the group led to their demise by the mid-1980s.[9]

On February 4, 1974, Patty Hearst, the granddaughter of newspaper magnet William Randolph Hearst, was kidnapped from her apartment in Berkeley, California. It was determined that the **Symbionese Liberation Army** (SLA) was responsible for the abduction. The group led by a hardened criminal by the name of Donald DeFreeze wanted to incite guerilla warfare against the government and to destroy the "capitalist state." Soon after the abduction the group released audio tapes demanding millions of dollars in food donations in exchange for Hearst's release. The donations were made yet a tape released by the SLA had Hearst saying that she had joined the group and their fight to free the oppressed.

The SLA took responsibility for the killing of two school officials in Oakland, California, and supported themselves by robbing banks. A bank robbery in Carmichael, California, a suburb of Sacramento, resulted in the death of an innocent customer. A few months later in Los Angeles two members of the group attempted to steal an ammunition belt from a local store and were almost caught. Their getaway van was located by the police at an SLA safe house. The house was surrounded by the police and a massive shootout ensued and six members of the group, including DeFreeze, were killed. Several months later Hearst was captured in San Francisco. Other members of the group went underground and assumed new identities and would not turn themselves in for another twenty-five years.[10]

Lone Wolf terrorists operate on the fringes of extremist movements and they act alone. Examples of lone wolf terrorists include U.S. Army Major Nidal Hassan who shot and killed 13 soldiers and injured 30 others at the Fort Hood Army base in 2009; the Boston Bombers where allegedly brothers Tamerlan and Dzhokhar Tsanaev detonated two pressure cooker bombs near the finish line of the Boston Marathon in 2013 that killed three and injured another 260; and Timothy McVeigh who was responsible to the Oklahoma City bombing of the Murrah federal building that killed 168 and injured another 680 more in 1995. What these incidents have in common is that these terrorists acted alone and had no connection to any known terrorist groups.

The Internet is making it easier for these lone wolves to become radicalized. On the Internet they can find sites supporting extremist ideologies. In addition, these sites advocate the use of force and offer technical support on tactics, weapons use, and bomb making. The Internet also offers important investigative leads as these lone wolves often express their radical beliefs on-line. They will use chat rooms, social media, and e-mail to share their intentions to act on their beliefs and to brag about their efforts.[11]

④ *Discuss the historical development of terrorism in the Middle East and the events that led to the formation of the groups involved.*

▶ International Terrorism

Title 18, section 2331(1), of the United States Code defines **international terrorism** as occurring primarily outside the territorial jurisdiction of the United States or transcending national boundaries. The U.S. State Department has identified thirty-six groups as foreign terrorist organizations. The most dangerous of these is **Al Qaeda**, which means "the base" or "the base of Allah's support."

Al Qaeda was founded by Osama bin Laden in the early 1980s to support the effort in Afghanistan against the invasion by the former Soviet Union. These holy warriors, or **Mujahedeen**, were supported by the United States, and in 1989 the Soviets retreated. Bin Laden, born in 1957, is one of fifty-two siblings of a business tycoon who made billions of dollars in the construction business on the Arabian Peninsula. After the death of his father, bin Laden allegedly inherited over $300 million. He studied engineering at a Saudi university where he was exposed to the writing and teachings of radical Muslim concepts.

In 1990 Iraq invaded Kuwait and the American-led coalition drove the invaders out in what was known as Operation Desert Storm. Radical Muslims, such as bin Laden, were appalled to find Muslims fighting Muslims under American leadership. In addition, Al Qaeda opposed the United States for its support of Israel and because of its perceived decadent society. Bin Laden declared war on the United States and began training his followers in terrorist tactics in training

Now deceased international terrorist Osama bin Laden was the leader of the Al Qaeda network, which was responsible for the events of 9/11.

Source: AFP/Getty Images

camps in Somalia and Afghanistan. Al Qaeda's presence has been confirmed in at least fifty-five countries and is believed to be responsible for the following terrorist attacks:[12]

1992 Bombed hotel in Yemen housing U.S. troops

1993 Bombed the World Trade Center in New York City

1993 Somalia firefight; eighteen U.S. soldiers killed by Al Qaeda–trained extremists

1995 Bombed National Guard building in Riyadh, Saudi Arabia; five U.S. soldiers killed

1996 Bombed U.S. military housing known as Khobar Towers in Dharan, Saudi Arabia; nineteen Americans killed

1998 Suicide bombings of U.S. embassies in Nairobi and Dar Es Salaam, Tanzania; more than 230 killed and 5,000 injured

1999 Planned "Millennium Bombing" attacks in Jordan and the Los Angeles airport; prevented by arrests

2000 Suicide bombing of the destroyer *U.S.S. Cole* in Aden, Yemen; seventeen sailors killed, thirty-nine injured

2001 Suicide bombing of the World Trade Center and Pentagon; 3,000 killed

2003 Multiple suicide bombing in Morocco; thirty-two killed at five locations

2003 Multiple suicide bombings in Saudi Arabia; four killed

Almost ten years after the attack on the World Trade Center Osama bin Laden was located in Pakistan and killed in a shootout with U.S. Special Forces. Despite the death of its leader the Al Qaeda continues to function as an international terrorist organization.

When Israel invaded Lebanon in 1982, Iran responded by sending its Revolutionary Guards to Lebanon, which led to the creation of a new terrorist network called **Hizbollah**, or "the party of God." In the same year, French paratroopers and U.S. marines arrived in Beirut as part of a multinational peacekeeping force. Hizbollah viewed the peacekeeping force as an act of aggression, and on October 23, 1983, two suicide bombers driving vehicle bombs simultaneously struck the marine barracks and the paratroopers' headquarters; 241 marines and 58 paratroopers were killed. The remaining peacekeeping forces were withdrawn in early 1984.[13]

With the bombing of the marine barracks, Hizbollah introduced a new terrorist tactic, the suicide bomber that has plagued the Middle East since that time. Hizbollah kidnapped dozens of Western hostages from numerous countries for economic and political gain. Eighteen Americans were held hostage from 1983 until the release of the final hostage in 1991. During that time, three American hostages were killed. Hizbollah transcended Lebanon's borders in 1992 when it bombed the Israel embassy in Buenos Aires. It struck again two years later with the truck bombing of the Argentine–Jewish Mutual Association, which claimed the lives of nearly a hundred persons.[14]

Hizbollah continues to conduct military provocations by firing into Israel's territory and conducting cross-border raids. The kidnapping of three Israel soldiers in the summer of 2006 provoked a month-long war between Hizbollah and Israel.

One of the most volatile militant organizations in the Middle East is the Islamic Resistance Movement, better known as **Hamas**. Unlike Hizbollah, this group grew from the Palestinian liberation movement. Hamas's position is that the State of Israel should not exist. In its view the only acceptable solution to the Palestinian problem is to eliminate Israel and create a united Arab realm. According to Hamas, the State of Israel and anyone who supports it are abominations to Islam.

To understand Hamas, it is necessary to go back to the events right after World War I. Because of British promises, many Arabs felt that the entire Middle East would be united under one great Arabic banner, from North Africa to the Iranian border, known as **dar al-Islam**. When the European powers divided the area, taking control of some regions and placing their Arab allies in control of others, many Arabs were infuriated. One group, the Muslim Brotherhood, founded in 1925, rejected the new territorial lines and called for the unification of the entire Arab realm under the control of Islam.

The Muslim Brotherhood registered as a religious organization with the Israeli government in 1978 and attempted to convert followers into a more pristine version of Islam. In the 1980s as

Yasser Arafat, the leader of the Palestinian Liberation Organization, moved toward moderation, the Muslim Brotherhood maintained its rigid views on the unification of the realm of Arabs and the necessity to rule through Islamic law. When the call for self-government began to dominate the Palestinian liberation movement, the Muslim Brotherhood rejected the idea because no nation should exist outside dar al-Islam. In 1987 the Muslim Brotherhood formed Hamas, an Arabic acronym for Harakat al-Muqawama al-Islamiyya, or "Islamic Resistance Movement."

Hamas states that it is at war with the Jewish people and the State of Israel. Its purpose is to kill Jews and drive the Zionist settlers and their allies from the area. The only acceptable outcome for Hamas is the united realm of Islam. Hamas is well financed, and its tentacles reach outside of the Middle East, including support bases in the United States. So far Hamas has been successful in disrupting the peace process and is engaged in a constant barrage of terrorist activities against the State of Israel, including suicide bombings and the shelling of Jewish settlements.[15]

5 *Define what the weapons of mass destruction are and explain why terrorists would want to use these weapons.*

▶ Weapons of Mass Destruction

The rationale for a terrorist to use weapons of mass destruction at the most basic level is simply the desire to kill as many people as possible. Chemical, biological, radiological, and nuclear weapons could give a terrorist group the ability to kill thousands, possibly even hundreds of thousands of people in a single strike.

Chemical agents include choking gases such as phosgene and chlorine, blood agents including hydrogen cyanide and cyanogen chloride, blister agents such as mustard gas, and nerve agents such as sarin. Due to the difficulty in obtaining these chemicals, terrorists would most likely reject most of them. However, sarin is relatively easy to make, and the Japanese terrorist group Aum Shinriko used this agent to attack the Tokyo subway system in 1995, killing 12 and injuring more than 5,000 others.

Biological agents are available to terrorists in a number of different ways, such as purchasing from one of the world's 1,500 germ banks, theft from a research laboratory, isolation and cultivation from natural sources, or through a rogue state or a state sponsor of terrorism. The principal obstacle in the use of biological agents is the development of sufficient quantities to cause mass casualties. In October 2001, a series of anthrax-laced letters were mailed to political and media targets, including two U.S. senators and news anchor Tom Brokaw. Although these letters did not reach their intended targets, five people who handled the letters died.

Radiological terrorism involves the dispersion of **radioactive agents** by conventional means, most commonly known as a "dirty bomb." The sources of material for such a device would include nuclear waste from fuel processing and radiological medical isotopes from hospitals or research laboratories. Such a weapon would have the ability to kill a large number of people, and the resulting panic would be devastating. In 2002 José Padilla, a follower of Osama bin Laden, was arrested in Chicago for allegedly planning a dirty-bomb attack.

Nuclear terrorism involves the detonation of a nuclear device in a major metropolitan city causing massive casualties. With the fall of the former Soviet Union, such materials were stolen from military bases and became available on the black market. Another possible source is a rogue nation with nuclear capabilities, such as North Korea. Due to the unthinkable destructive power of nuclear devices, this is the worst-case scenario.[16]

6 *Appreciate the efforts toward counterterrorism in the United States and the role of the agencies involved.*

▶ Counterterrorism

The lack of a coordinated response to terrorism became evident in the analysis of the attack on the World Trade Center and the Pentagon on September 11, 2001. In response to these events, the FBI expanded the use of the Joint Terrorism Task Force concept to include a joint task force in each of its fifty-six field offices. These task forces include investigators from other federal, state, and local law enforcement agencies who bring a variety of skills to the task force environment. These field investigators have immediate access to the National Joint Terrorism Task Force located at FBI headquarters in Washington, D.C. The national task force includes members from the Central Intelligence Agency (CIA) and FBI, as well as agents and officers from the Naval Criminal Investigative Service, Transportation Security Agency, U.S. Coast Guard, U.S. Bureau of Prisons, and approximately fifty other significant contributors to the national counterterrorism mission.[17]

The purpose of these organizations is to gather information, or intelligence, in order to have the ability to anticipate the behavior of terrorists and to thereby predict future terrorist incidents. The basis for these predictions is from two sources: signal and human intelligence.

With proper court authorization, **signal intelligence** is used to intercept financial data and to monitor communications such as land-line and cell phones and e-mail messages. Satellite imagery is also used, as are sophisticated computers that specialize in code breaking.

Due to the cellular organization of terrorist groups and their insular interactions, technology alone cannot provide a sufficient counterterrorism response. **Human intelligence** is a critical component, therefore, and the first step in this process is a cooperative venture with intelligence agencies and law enforcement investigators, which is the purpose of the Joint Terrorism concept. Another source of human intelligence includes the development of informants affiliated with terrorist organizations or their support groups. The use of undercover police officers is not only dangerous but usually not productive as the members of terrorist cells are made up of individuals who know each other very well.

The United States has a number of intelligence-gathering agencies. The director of national intelligence is responsible for coordinating the various components of the intelligence community, which include the following agencies:[18]

> **The Central Intelligence Agency (CIA)** is responsible for collecting intelligence outside the borders of the United States. The agency uses covert human and technological assets to gather information on terrorist activity.

> **The Federal Bureau of Investigation (FBI)** is within the U.S. Department of Justice and is charged with conducting domestic counterterrorism efforts. The agency engages in domestic intelligence collection efforts and has agents deployed to U.S. embassies around the world.

> **The National Security Agency (NSA)** is the technological unit of the intelligence community. Its primary mission is to collect communications and signal intelligence and to conduct code-breaking activities.

> Each branch of the military collects intelligence, and the **Defense Intelligence Agency (DIA)** coordinates and analyzes this information.

7 *Discuss the role of police operations units in dealing with terrorists' threats and events.*

▶ Role of Police Operations Units

Operations units of a police agency have responsibility for controlling the acts of terrorists once they are threatened or in progress. Patrol units are the first line of defense in these instances, with specialists available to them. Specialists in threat analysis will pass on the credibility and potential of the threat. Bomb detection and disposal specialists will direct the search for explosives and incendiary devices and effect their disposal if found. Hostage negotiators will establish communications with terrorists in hostage–kidnapping cases and conduct negotiations leading to termination of the event.

The commanding officer of the operational units also has the responsibility of the preliminary investigation:

Threats

1. Date and time of threat, how it was received, and who received it
2. Nature of act threatened, including target, time element, and weapon (e.g., fire, bomb)

3. Demands or grievances accompanying threat

4. Stated political or organizational affiliation of threat maker, including any claims of responsibility for prior terrorist threats or acts

5. Other data, such as background noises (telephone threat, speech characteristics, and apparent personal characteristics of threat maker)

Events

1. Arrest any terrorist at scene; identify; collect data and prepare "alarm" for terrorists who have fled scene.

2. Assign personnel to interview victims and witnesses and to search scene for evidence likely to identify the terrorists and modus operandi.

3. Assign personnel to protect the scene until qualified personnel can assist in the search for physical evidence.

4. Assign a sworn officer or supervisor to collate all collected information and evidence, and to prepare the preliminary report.

8 *Discuss the activities the investigator would be engaged in during the course of a terrorist investigation.*

▶ Role of the Criminal Investigator

The role of a criminal investigator in relation to terrorist acts can be summed up as follows:

1. Identification of responsible parties—co-conspirators

2. Reinterview of victims and witnesses to get statements, check stories; follow-up on physical evidence and laboratory examinations

3. Identification of aiders and abettors—individuals on the fringes of the crime or criminal conspiracy

4. Pursuit of unapprehended terrorists and co-conspirators

5. In kidnapping cases, immediate organization of pursuit in the attempt to locate victim and terrorists; immediate action seeking the identity of the terrorists and the hideout in which the captive is held; participating in rescue planning; and, if ransom is paid, probing for clues to the kidnappers during ransom negotiations and the ransom payment and on release of the person kidnapped

6. Apprehension of all persons wanted in connection with the terrorist act or conspiracy

7. Investigation of all arrestees to disclose associations, past history, and potential for cooperation: (a) to serve as an accomplice witness and (b) to provide information

8. Upgrading of preventive intelligence surveillance to secure more information on suspects

9. Case preparation highlighting the relevancy and probative value of various items of evidence in relation to prosecution for a specific crime or crimes

An investigation should be considered incomplete until evidence, direct or circumstantial, has been secured of an overt act that constitutes a "substantial step" in furtherance of the conspiracy (Figure 17-1). Forming or planning a conspiracy is not a true overt act, nor are acts done merely to cement the agreement.

A social network analysis is useful in investigating terrorism. This is a linking of known members of a group (or "cell") with suspected members or just a linking of suspects believed to be joined in a group. First, the individual suspects are linked to each other, then to the group, and then to incidents and their scenes.[19]

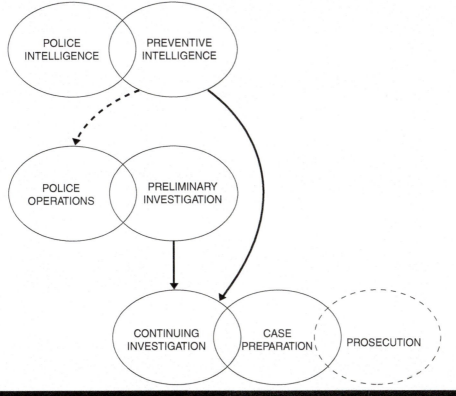

FIGURE 17-1 Investigation of Terrorist Activity.

Another network analysis is how the terrorists secured reliable information about the targets of their attacks, particularly the targets to be killed or kidnapped. The link-up here relates to who was the source of information: members, sympathizers, collaborators, dissidents, and so on. The names of these individuals should be worked into the social network analysis for the development of connections between known members of a group and sources of information.[20]

Investigators assigned to the activities of terrorists require all the standard skills of criminal investigators, plus a high level of integrity and an appreciation for the legal significance of collected evidence. One guarantees against illegal shortcuts that may ruin evidence; the other is a safeguard against building a case on evidence of little relevance or probative value.

9 *Explain the problems of proving a case of terrorism.*

▶ Problems of Proof

Trials of terrorists in the United States have survived or perished on the issue of the legality or illegality of the means used by investigators to gather evidence. Electronic eavesdropping evidence has been attacked as an unreasonable and a broad invasion of privacy; undercover agents have been described as partisan witnesses, unworthy of belief; and informants (and the rare accomplice witness) are perceived as persons of no credibility, intent on getting some benefit from the prosecution for their testimony. Unless the police–prosecutor team can overcome the damage wrought by these accusations, any jurors will downgrade the legal significance of the prosecution's evidence in these areas and conclude that a reasonable doubt of guilt exists.

JOINT TERRORISM TASK FORCE

On February 23, 1997, a seventy-year-old Palestinian visited the observation deck of the Empire State Building in New York City. Shortly after arriving he opened fire with a handgun, killing one person and wounding seven others, before killing himself. A search of his clothing revealed a long rambling letter that expressed anti-U.S. and anti-Israel sentiments, along with a Florida identification card and a receipt for the weapon.

The FBI–New York City Police Department Joint Terrorism Task Force (JTTF) responded to the scene. The task force command center opened, and the various agencies that comprise the task force began working to ascertain the shooter's identity, his origin, and his ties to terrorist groups, if any.

Within hours, the command center had answers. The FBI dispatched its legal attaché in Israel to the Gaza Strip to interview the subject's family.

The FBI and the local police in Florida interviewed several people who could help identify the shooter and track his movements while living in that state. It was determined that he had fulfilled the residency requirement and that he had legally purchased the murder weapon one month after arriving in the United States.

The task force concluded that the shooter seemed mentally unstable. He had expressed hatred of Israel and the United States; however, he had no connection to any organized international terrorist group and had committed the attack alone. The speed at which these conclusions were reached is a testament to the effectiveness of the joint task force concept. According to investigators, had the JTTF not been in place, the investigation might have taken days or weeks, rather than hours, to complete.

Source: Robert A. Martin, "The Joint Terrorism Task Force: A Concept That Works," *FBI Law Enforcement Bulletin* 68, no. 3 (1999): 23–24.

CHAPTER REVIEW

Key Terms

Al Qaeda *316*

Animal Liberation Front
(ALF) *315*

biological agent *318*

Central Intelligence Agency
(CIA) *319*

chemical agent *318*

dar al-Islam *317*

Defense Intelligence Agency
(DIA) *319*

domestic terrorism *313*

Earth Liberation Front (ELF) *315*

ecoterrorist *311*

Federal Bureau of Investigation
(FBI) *319*

Hamas *317*

Hizbollah *317*

human intelligence *319*

international terrorism *316*

kneecapping *311*

ku klux klan *313*

lone wolf *315*

Mujahedeen *316*

narcoterrorist *312*

National Security Agency
(NSA) *319*

neo-Nazi *314*

nuclear terrorism *318*

radiological agent *318*

signal intelligence *319*

Symbionese Liberation Army *315*

terrorism *311*

The Turner Diaries *314*

tree spiking *311*

weather underground *315*

white supremacy *314*

Review Questions

1. When Israel invaded Lebanon in 1982, Iran responded by sending its Revolutionary Guards into Lebanon, which led to the creation of a new terrorist network known as:
   a. Hamas
   b. Mujahedeen
   c. Al Qaeda
   d. Hizbollah

2. The group formed in Palestine to resist the moderate view of the acceptance of a separate Palestinian state is one of the most volatile militant organizations in the Middle East and is known as:
   a. Hamas
   b. Mujahedeen
   c. Al Qaeda
   d. Hizbollah

3. The group founded in the early 1980s, by Osama bin Laden, to support the Muslim effort in Afghanistan against the invasion by the former Soviet Union is known as:
   a. Hamas
   b. Mujahedeen
   c. Al Qaeda
   d. Hizbollah
4. The agency responsible for collecting intelligence on terrorists groups inside the borders of the United States is known as the:
   a. Central Intelligence Agency
   b. Federal Bureau of Investigation
   c. National Security Agency
   d. Defense Intelligence Agency
5. The agency responsible for collecting intelligence outside the borders of the United States by the use covert human and technological assets to gather information on terrorist activity and is known as the:
   a. Central Intelligence Agency
   b. Federal Bureau of Investigation
   c. National Security Agency
   d. Defense Intelligence Agency
6. The technological unit of the intelligence community whose primary mission is to collect communications and signal intelligence and conduct code-breaking activities is known as the:
   a. Central Intelligence Agency
   b. Federal Bureau of Investigation
   c. National Security Agency
   d. Defense Intelligence Agency

7. The group founded after the Civil War that used intimidating night raids to discourage newly freed blacks from voting is known as the:
   a. Ku Klux Klan
   b. Pierce Movement
   c. Order
   d. ALF/ELF
8. The group founded by Robert Mathews, who was inspired by the novel *The Turner Diaries*, has waged war against the U.S. government through counterfeiting, bank robberies, and murder and is known as the:
   a. Ku Klux Klan
   b. Pierce Movement
   c. Order
   d. ALF/ELF
9. The group concerned with a single issue that has committed numerous acts of arson and vandalism estimated in excess of $100 million since 1996 is known as the:
   a. Ku Klux Klan
   b. Pierce Movement
   c. Order
   d. ALF/ELF
10. The holy warriors supported by the United States for the purpose of repelling the invasion of Afghanistan by the Soviet Union in the early 1980s are known as the:
    a. Hamas
    b. Mujahedeen
    c. Al Qaeda
    d. Hizbollah

See Appendix D for the correct answers.

Application Exercise

Recently several members of a radical group have been spotted in your community. Your initial investigative efforts disclosed that these people have moved into a rented home in your area. Since their arrival your agency has been receiving calls that indicated that this group is holding meetings and is actively recruiting new members.

Hate literature and posters usually associated to this group have been found within the last few days. In other parts of the country this group has been responsible for hate motivated arsons and even bombings. Develop a plan to deal with this potential problem and address the pros and cons of each proposed course of action.

Discussion Questions

1. Explain what a dirty bomb is and why terrorist groups would want to deploy such a weapon.
2. Define signal intelligence and explain how this information is gathered.
3. Define human intelligence and explain how this information is gathered.
4. What were the origins of the terrorist group Al Qaeda, and who is this group's founder?
5. Discuss the history of the Ku Klux Klan and the possibility of a reemergence of this group.
6. Explain the concept of the joint terrorism task force.
7. In the case study, explain why the Joint Terrorism Task Force was able to resolve the issues in this investigation so quickly.

Related Websites

For in-depth information on terrorism incidents and the groups responsible for them, visit the website of the Memorial Institute for the Prevention of Terrorism at *www.mipt.org*.

The Department of Homeland Security posts up-to-date information on the national threat level, press releases, current issues of national security, and employment opportunities on its web page at *www.dhs.gov*.

You can go to the Central Intelligence Agency's web page for information on its history, mission, values, and employment opportunities: *www.cia.gov*.

For information on foreign terrorist organizations and their activities, as well as a list of the most wanted terrorists, go to the United States Department of State website at *www.state.gov/s/ct*.

Notes

1. Cindy C. Combs, *Terrorism in the Twenty-First Century,* 3rd ed. (Upper Saddle River, NJ: Prentice Hall, 2003), 9.
2. Robert Lenzner and Nathan Vardi, "The Next Threat," *Forbes,* September 20, 2004, http://www.forbes.com/forbes/2004/0920/070.html.
3. James M. Poland, *Understanding Terrorism, Groups, Strategies and Responses,* 2nd ed. (Upper Saddle River, NJ: Prentice Hall, 2005), 17.
4. Clifford E. Simonsen and Jeremy R. Spinlove, *Terrorism Today: The Past, the Players, the Future* (Upper Saddle River, NJ: Prentice Hall, 2000), 39–43.
5. Poland, *Understanding Terrorism, Groups, Strategies and Responses,* 29–31.
6. Jonathan R. White, *Terrorism: An Introduction,* 4th ed. (Belmont, CA: Thompson, 2003), 229–230.
7. Gus Martin, *Understanding Terrorism,* 2nd ed. (Thousand Oaks, CA: Sage, 2006), 459–460.
8. Ibid., 447.
9. www.fbi.gov/news/tories/2004/january/weather-012904.
10. www.fbi.gov/about-us/history/famous-cases/patty-hearst-kidnapping.
11. www.policemag.com/channel/patrol/articles/2013/10/beware-the-lone-wolf.
12. Poland, *Understanding Terrorism, Groups, Strategies and Responses,* 102–107.
13. Martin, *Understanding Terrorism,* 385.
14. Poland, *Understanding Terrorism, Groups, Strategies and Responses,* 93–95.
15. White, *Terrorism,* 159–161.
16. Yonah Alexander and Milton Hoenig, *Super Terrorism: Biological, Chemical, and Nuclear* (Ardsley, NY: Transnational Publishers, 2001), 12–17.
17. James Casey, "Managing Joint Terrorism Task Force Resources," *FBI Law Enforcement Bulletin* 76, no. 11 (2004): 1–6.
18. Martin, *Understanding Terrorism,* 495–497.
19. Christopher A. Hertig, "The Investigation of Terrorist Activity," in *Critical Issues in Criminal Investigation,* ed. Michael J. Palmiotto (Cincinnati, OH: Anderson, 1988), 235–245.
20. Walter Laqueur, *The Age of Terrorism* (Boston: Little, Brown, 1987), 109–111.

18 The Investigator as a Witness and Ethical Awareness

CHAPTER OUTLINE

LEARNING OBJECTIVES

After reading this chapter, you will be able to:

❶ *Recognize the steps investigators take to prepare themselves for testifying in court.*

❷ *Identify the condition of stage fright that a witness may experience and how to deal with it.*

❸ *Discuss the role nonverbal communication plays in a witness's testimony.*

❹ *Explain the distinction between the unethical behaviors of corruption and misconduct.*

❺ *Discuss in what circumstances, or types of investigations, money becomes available to corrupt investigators.*

❻ *Discuss the concept of reasonable care and how it can be used to define standards of conduct for the criminal investigator.*

❶ *Recognize the steps investigators take to prepare themselves for testifying in court.*

▶ The Investigator as a Witness

At the conclusion of an investigation, an investigator does know the victim, the circumstances of the crime, the identity of the offender, and sometimes possesses data on the motive for the crime. He or she has collected facts, linked them together, and mentally shaped a pattern of the crime and a narrative of the event with form and order. However, the events and incidents of a crime are known to the investigator only indirectly, through the interviewing of witnesses and other techniques of investigation. No matter how much intelligence and honesty went into the many decisions common to any investigation, the sum total is a subjective impression in the mind of the investigator.

The investigator as a witness is confined to the same narrow band of personal knowledge as any other witness, and he or she is under the same requirement to establish a proper foundation to show personal knowledge prior to giving any oral evidence.

Criminal investigators have a basic obligation to court and community when testifying as a witness in a criminal case: to tell the truth as they have found it. They also have a basic obligation to themselves and their employing agency not to allow any item of their appearance or any act done within the courtroom to affect adversely their testimony on the witness stand. The legal significance of an investigator's testimony can be damaged by behavior not in harmony with his or her role as impartial fact finder and reporter. Men and women serving as trial jurors evaluate witnesses on what they say, how they say it, and their overt behavior while saying it.

❷ *Identify the condition of stage fright that a witness may experience and how to deal with it.*

Action Prior to Court Appearance

Investigators should review the substance of their testimony before the trial of the defendant. Investigators can easily review areas of likely inquiry in direct examination by a friendly associate—the prosecutor. Unfortunately, investigators can never prepare fully for cross-examination, which is usually hostile questioning by the defense counsel. Major areas for this self-analysis are the following:

1. Is the possible testimony arrayed in a manner that allows the investigator to relate it simply and convincingly so that the triers of fact will both understand it and believe it?

2. Is the investigator willing to state that he or she does not know or cannot recall certain facts?

3. Is the investigator ready to acknowledge mistakes made in the investigation when questioned, and is he or she prepared to answer questions truthfully and directly, without hedging?

4. Is the investigator prepared to refute and rebut any allegation of "improving" the case against the defendant?

5. Is the investigator prepared for being a witness by refreshing his or her memory immediately prior to trial?

The legal significance of evidence demands a pretesting for credibility. Self-analysis is often difficult, but it is vital to the integrity of an investigator's testimony. The facts stated by the investigator as a witness will be tested in court against standard bases of credibility.

A short time prior to the date of court appearance, investigators should confer with the assigned prosecutor for a last-minute check. No doubt the prosecutor is well informed as to the expected testimony and possible areas of difficult cross-examination. A brief review just before a court appearance can be helpful to the investigator–witness. Ethical prosecutors will make certain that any conference with witnesses does not degenerate into a coaching session, and an investigator–witness should promptly admit to any such meetings under questioning, as they are normal case-preparation procedures.

On the date that an investigator is scheduled for a court appearance, he or she should allow a generous amount of time for the trip to the courthouse. This is a safeguard against unexpected traffic delays or other events that make the trip longer than anticipated. In court appearances, it is better to be very early than to rush in at the last minute.

On arrival at the courthouse and prior to opening of court, the investigator should sign in or check in as required by local regulations and make contact with the assigned prosecutor. If witnesses are excluded from the courtroom until they have testified and been excused, the investigator must wait outside the courtroom until a bailiff calls his or her name. If witnesses have not been excluded, the investigator should take a seat within the courtroom and await his or her call.

This is an excellent time to get rid of the **stage fright** not uncommon among witnesses about to testify. This is a nebulous fear, often based on no more than a reluctance to get up and talk in front of a group of people. With investigator–witnesses, it may be complicated by knowledge that the presiding judge is known to have a short-fuse temper or by the unpleasant memory of a previous experience with an aggressive cross-examiner.[1]

Stage fright is often cumulative. Initially, blood pressure and respiration rate of the witness increase, producing a feeling of being "charged up." This is accompanied by a noticeable dryness of the mouth and sometimes a shaking of the hands. This is unusual and uncomfortable, and the common reaction is greater anxiety.

Stage fright can be controlled. Planning ahead is the first step. Therefore, quickly review the substance of the case and possible questions. Second, mentally scan past experiences that can be termed "satisfactory" or better, and relax in the thought that such past experiences will be helpful in successfully concluding the forthcoming session as a witness. Finally, remember that anxiety at this time is nothing more than the witness's body preparing the person to do his or her best.[2]

General Behavior

Upon being called as a witness, the investigator walks promptly to the front of the courtroom. He or she stops in the "well" of the court, usually in front of the witness stand, to take the oath to tell the truth. This is an important stop on the way to the witness stand. A court officer proffers a Bible. The witness-to-be places his or her hand on it. The court officer then administers the oath (usually slowly and clearly), and the witness-to-be replies in the affirmative. The investigator's behavior during this portal ceremony should reflect a deep and sincere belief in the oath.

The first questioning of a witness that is not within the scope of any previous examination of the witness is the **direct examination** conducted by the party calling the witness (by subpoena). In the case of investigator–witnesses, this is most often the prosecutor. This questioner guides the witness to prevent deviation from relevant facts. This stage of the examination is followed by **cross-examination** by defense counsel. Cross-examiners are likely to be aggressive. In either stage of this examination, a witness is expected to be responsive to questions.

Cross-examiners often prefer to limit the responsiveness of a witness by phrasing questions calling for a yes-or-no answer. A "yes" means that the witness accepts the idea expressed in the question; a "no" indicates that the witness rejects the idea. If a cross-examiner does not use simple language in his or her query, then "yes" or "no" is not a simple response. Therefore, if a witness does not fully agree with the idea expressed in the question, he or she should give a negative response: "no." A "qualified yes" is often a responsive answer, but it is not usually allowed because the scope of the question may be extended when the witness explains the need to qualify the answer. As a general rule, the investigator–witness is not alone at this time. The prosecutor usually speaks out and asks the court to have the question withdrawn, reworded, or thrown out. Any witness who does not understand a question has the right to ask that the question be repeated, and it usually is read by the court reporter. Sometimes, when this request is made, the questioner withdraws the question and rephrases it.

How is it best to answer questions? Speak up! Speak clearly and loudly enough for everyone in the courtroom to hear all the testimony, and use simple language in making responses.

Simple language is plain talk. It helps people to understand the meaning of each answer. Beyond the limits of a yes-or-no answer, an investigator–witness should speak in complete sentences rather than sentence fragments. Normally, each sentence should express no more than one idea. Short sentences spread out ideas so that jurors, as well as others in the courtroom, get a breathing spell between them.[3]

Open-ended questions are often asked of investigator–witnesses during direct examination. These queries detail one segment of the investigation and ask the witness to respond in his or her own words. The key to a responsive answer, and one that will usually be understood by all listeners, is to use short sentences arranged in chronological order.

The time element in responding to questions is also important in any evaluation of a witness by in-court listeners. A short pause before responding is good behavior. It allows the prosecutor to interpose an objection to the question if he or she wishes. It also indicates a thoughtful reflection upon the substance of the question and the response.

Investigator–witnesses should avoid using underworld slang and police lingo. Jurors are unfamiliar with such language and will not understand it—and possibly will not understand a good portion of witnesses' responses in which this language is used. To many jurors a "hit" does not mean to kill, a "piece" does not indicate a pistol or revolver, and a "scam" does not describe a criminal conspiracy. Jurors also have little understanding of words common among police personnel—for instance, "pinch" (arrest), "frisk" (search), "DOA" (dead on arrival), and "FOA" (for other authority).

An investigator–witness must be courteous to questioners. It is an imperative rule, even with difficult defense attorneys. Questioners should be carefully addressed. Avoid the prefix "Mister," as it may be viewed as sarcasm. Be cautious of "Madam," as it not only means a lady but also is the title given to a woman in charge of a brothel. "Counselor" seems to be fairly safe as a general term for either the prosecutor or defense counsel, man or woman.

The apogee of discourtesy is to interrupt a questioner when he or she is phrasing a question. An interruption usually damages the ability of jurors to understand the question and any response made by the witness when the question is finally completed. Jurors, as well as others in the courtroom, view this conduct as argumentative. This evaluation can be harmful to the goals of the prosecution.

Another caution for any investigator–witness is not to argue with the defense counsel. Arguing destroys the image of the witness as an impartial fact finder and reporter. Jurors do not expect investigators to be "friendly with" the defendant or his or her counsel, but any argument during cross-examination can antagonize many jurors. It projects a hostility toward the defense beyond the expectations of these men and women. Remember: defendants are innocent until proven guilty.

A final caution is not to lie or misrecollect on the witness stand. Unfortunately, many investigator–witnesses are sensitive about one or more areas of the investigation in which they failed to perform up to standard or were overzealous in their performance. Rest assured that no circumstance of this area of the investigation will be left unexplored when a cross-examiner detects this sensitivity. It is also reasonably certain that any attempt to stonewall or cover up can be disastrous to the credibility of the witness.

If any sensitive areas do exist, the best procedure is to discuss them with the assigned prosecutor prior to trial and then to obtain his or her guidance. These guidelines will probably be to admit to any substandard practice, inefficiency, or incompetence if questioning begins to exploit one or more of these areas. It is better to have the jurors think of a witness as a bungler (a common human condition) rather than a perjurer (an unacceptable human condition).

One survival technique for withstanding the most aggressive and belligerent cross-examination is to think and rethink constantly the fact that cross-examination of a witness is a constitutional right of all defendants—an absolute right.

 Discuss the role nonverbal communication plays in a witness's testimony.

Nonverbal Communication

Nonverbal communication is a process of a person transmitting unspoken cues that have potential meaning to one or more observers.[4] It includes anything someone does that another person finds meaningful. Nonverbal communication is body language, and body movement and eye behavior send signals to observers.

In the drama of witness and questioner as it is staged in U.S. courtrooms during criminal trials, the observers and listeners are jurors. These men and women are alert to what each witness is saying, and they are also alert to any body language signs that will help them to better understand the testimony of the witness and evaluate his or her credibility. Certainly many jurors mentally note what they do not hear to evaluate fully the net worth of what they do hear from a witness.

Communication without speech is transmitted through body movements and eye behavior. Facial expressions (smiles to frowns), head nods and shoulder shrugs, gestures (clenched fists to folded arms), leg crossing, and toe tapping are all body movements. The direction of eye movement and the frequency and duration of eye contact sum up common eye behavior.

A good portion of body language is involuntary and difficult or impossible to control. On the other hand, anyone can learn to mask some basic emotions.

Investigator–witnesses can easily learn the rudiments of masking nonverbal communication that indicates to observers that the witness is bored, impatient, anxious, surprised, angry, or fearful. Then a conscious effort to avoid these indicators while testifying should not interfere with the testimony of an investigator–witness.

As far as any body movement is concerned, most basic police academy lectures on being a witness have long emphasized "Don't fidget." Sit down. That's what witnesses are supposed to do on witness stands. Better yet, sit still.

Eye behavior is a nebulous area. "Do what comes naturally" is generally good advice. In making eye contact initially, the eyes should move casually to the presiding judge, the jury, prosecutor, defense counsel, defendant, and the spectators. When asked a question, make eye contact with the questioner. In answering, the eye contact moves from the questioner toward the jury, where the witness scans the jury box as he or she responds. If reading from notes or exhibits, the investigator–witness should look upward toward the jury box now and then and briefly make eye contact with one or two jurors. When extensive answers are called for by questions, the witness may pick out jurors who he or she believes to be more attentive than others and make eye contact without staring.

Clothing is also nonverbal communication, but investigator–witnesses are usually police officers, and most police departments have established rules for the appearance of their members in court. If a man or woman is working in uniform, these rules usually require court appearance in uniform. For members working as investigators in an out-of-uniform assignment, a dress code is usually specified—or stylized by custom—for appearance in so-called plainclothes. To identify the latter group as police officers, most departments require that badges or identification cards be pinned to the outer garment of the witness. Many badge cases are designed so that one-half of the case slips into the breast pocket of a coat and the other half hangs out and over the pocket, displaying the badge or ID card as if pinned to the coat.

To be identified as a police investigator by uniform or badge is not out of order. After being sworn in, a police witness must give his or her name, assignment, and the name of his or her employing agency. What may be considered a negative nonverbal communication is to stress this class membership by displaying a holstered revolver or pistol through an open jacket.

Conduct After Testifying

After testifying, the investigator–witness should make a graceful exit from the courtroom. Stopping to shake hands or chat with the prosecutor on the way out is definitely taboo. If the witness has not been excused by the court, he or she should wait in the hallway until the next recess prior to speaking to the prosecutor in low-key conversation. Also, this is the time for the witness to speak to the prosecutor about segments of his or her testimony about which the witness may be concerned.

Many prosecutors want the investigator–witness to be available for recall to the witness stand, and they will make whatever arrangements are necessary. While in or near the courtroom during this period, the investigator should not discuss his or her testimony with anyone except the prosecutor assigned to the case or a person designated by this official.

At this time, or shortly thereafter, the investigator should review in his or her own mind as much of the given testimony as possible. These are self-teaching sessions in which the investigator impartially examines his or her performance on the witness stand. In this fashion, every minute spent on the witness stand can be educational and serve as a means of improving future performance in court.

④ *Explain the distinction between the unethical behaviors of corruption and misconduct.*

▶ Ethical Awareness

Ethics is used as a euphemism for corruption and crime in U.S. police and law enforcement agencies. (A euphemism is the substitution of an inoffensive word or expression for one that might offend or suggest something unpleasant.) Law enforcement ethics includes two distinguishable topics: corruption and noncorrupt misconduct. The term **corruption**, as used in its traditional sense, involves an officer's misuse of police authority for personal gain; police **misconduct** may involve issues such as excessive use of force, violation of a suspect's constitutional rights, and a variety of other misdeeds.[5]

Dealing with these concerns can be called *ethical awareness*, as this term deals with some of the influences likely to cause criminal behavior and gets all the issues out on the table. **Ethical awareness**, even at average levels, warns a person that criminal behavior is "wrong," as well as unlawful, and warns that misconduct on the job is "wrong," substandard conduct. It also activates inner indications that it is not "right" for criminal investigators to use the wrong means to gain a desired result, the right means to achieve a wrong end, or to act out anything that is immoral or unprincipled.

⑤ *Discuss in what circumstances, or types of investigations, money becomes available to corrupt investigators.*

Crime and Outrageous Conduct

Corrupt conduct has a rich history in America's police establishment. Years ago, the locus of this corruption was vice and gambling. Madams, bookmakers, and other gambling-game operators paid police officers on vice squads for **protection** each month to avoid arrests. Today, the money tree includes narcotics and drug dealers and the thing of value is money—big money.

The money tree has shifted to narcotics law enforcement. Corrupt narcotics officers do not have a monthly "pad," similar to vice and gambling payments, for so-called protection. These agents depend on deals made at the time of the arrest or other threat to a drug dealer's business. It is a deal with the thing of value being money or drugs. Those deals, in fact, have the essential element of armed robbery![6]

Impact of Misconduct on Criminal Investigation

A major result of disclosures of misconduct is that the labor pool of men and women who want to become police officers will decrease and the most desirable candidates will not apply. Recruitment of working police officers will become more difficult as many applicants may now have records of prior misconduct.

Investigators have become aware of a change from the good old days when witnesses were not reluctant or unwilling to talk to investigating officers. They have identified this unfriendliness as a general mistrust of police, which indicates that simply blaming "a few bad apples" in a department cannot erase all of its recent transgressions. Investigators also are aware that the term **jury nullification** is becoming more common in the courthouses of America: the jury's not-guilty verdict is influenced by mistrust of police witnesses.

⑥ *Discuss the concept of reasonable care and how it can be used to define standards of conduct for the criminal investigator.*

Standards for Criminal Investigators

Investigators have obligations that derive from common membership in the community of investigators. A basic responsibility is to conform to prevailing practices and to be accountable when behavior is strange and unusual. In general, the behavior expected is that of a reasonable person exercising reasonable care, prudence, self-discipline, and judgment in his or her work. *Reasonable care*—in its legal definition—is care fairly and properly taken in response to the circumstances of a situation, such care as an ordinary prudent person would take in the same time frame,

▼

conditions, and act(s). *Self-discipline* and *judgment* mean jump-starting an inner moral sense in decisions on the moral quality of actions and discriminating between right and wrong.

Conforming to professional standards of conduct and having an appreciation of the ethical viewpoint of a reasonable person present a profile of an investigator who is conscientious, reliable, and responsible without regard for varying situations. It also describes a person who can justify, warrant, or excuse his or her conduct.

Prevention of Misconduct

Officers live and work in a constantly changing and dynamically social context in which they are exposed to a myriad of ethical conflicts. Those officers who are unprepared to meet these challenges are more likely to succumb to pressure from unethical peers and become compromised. The progression is predictable and for the most part preventable. If officers are going to survive ethical dilemmas, they need to be as mentally prepared as they would be for tactical encounters.

To be mentally prepared requires credible ethical instruction, proactive supervision, and continual ethical awareness. Ethical instruction begins at the academy and should continue throughout an officer's career. Ethical training taught in the academy should be reinforced by field training officers who have been selected as ethical role models and who have been provided with specific ethical awareness training. Ethical training should continue through ongoing professional training sessions and should be relevant, job-specific training on ethics rather than a knee-jerk reaction to some recent event.

Proactive supervision involves an acknowledgment of the existence of the **continuum of compromise** and the need to be ever vigilant for even the most minor unethical acts. Supervisors must be committed to acting quickly and must be held responsible for the unethical conduct of the officers under their command. Supervisors should strive to prevent small infractions of unethical conduct from becoming major problems. Proactive supervision also includes walking one's talk by setting the example of ethical professional conduct.[7]

CASE STUDY

THE SPECIAL CRIME SQUAD

Cast of Characters

Judge:	Anonymous
Defense Counsel:	Anonymous
Assistant District Attorney:	Anonymous
Defendant:	Bob (not otherwise identified)
Prosecution Witness:	Detective Sergeant Daniel Costello

SCENE: A courtroom. There is a high judicial bench, an adjacent witness stand and a chair, and a table and two chairs in front of the bench and witness stand. As the scene opens, the judge is seated on the bench, the two chairs are occupied by the defendant and his counsel, the witness chair is empty, and the assistant district attorney is standing in front of it.

ASSISTANT DISTRICT ATTORNEY: I would like to call my first witness—Detective Sergeant Daniel Costello. (Sergeant Costello appears, is sworn in, and sits down in witness chair.)

ASSISTANT DISTRICT ATTORNEY: What is your name and occupation?

DETECTIVE COSTELLO: Daniel Costello. I am a sergeant of detectives—all detectives are sergeants—and I work for the police force of this city.

ASSISTANT DISTRICT ATTORNEY: How long have you been in this occupation and rank?

DETECTIVE COSTELLO: Ten years in the police department, four years in the rank.

ASSISTANT DISTRICT ATTORNEY: About two years ago, I understand you were assigned to this new unit, the Organized Crime Suppression Squad, the OCSS, and that within a few days of working in your new job you visited a high official of your police force. Do you recall this event?

DETECTIVE COSTELLO: Yes, I do.

ASSISTANT DISTRICT ATTORNEY: When was it, and who was involved?

DETECTIVE COSTELLO: It was just after St. Patrick's Day, March 18, of this year. It was about 10:00 in the morning, and the person involved was Captain Richard Jones of the Police Academy.

ASSISTANT DISTRICT ATTORNEY: Tell us in your own words what happened on this occasion.

(continued)

DETECTIVE COSTELLO: I knew Captain Jones from the Academy—he was my instructor. He was a lieutenant, and I was a recruit. I told him I thought the OCSS, the whole group, was infiltrated or penetrated by the mob, the hoodlums, and drug pushers. He listened—I talked. His advice was to take it up with higher authorities in the department. He made a phone call arranging a meeting for me, and I thanked him and left the office.

ASSISTANT DISTRICT ATTORNEY: What happened next in direct relation to this talk?

DETECTIVE COSTELLO: I met a captain from the Internal Security Division that night, at a few minutes after 10:00, in the parking lot of the golf course—the city one.

ASSISTANT DISTRICT ATTORNEY: Please identify this man and tell us, again in your own words, what happened at this meeting.

DETECTIVE COSTELLO: His name is Captain John Behan. He works directly under the chief. He came over to my car, and I told him substantially what I had told Captain Jones. He told me that I had no specific evidence that he could use, but that if I was willing to work with him, I could get the evidence. Captain Behan gave me his home phone number and told me to call him. He said we would meet again where we were, in the golf course parking lot. That was for when I had something to tell him. We shook hands and split.

ASSISTANT DISTRICT ATTORNEY: Did you meet the captain again in this golf course parking lot? That is, Captain Behan?

DETECTIVE COSTELLO: Yes, I did. All told, I met with him about seven or eight times.

ASSISTANT DISTRICT ATTORNEY: At any of these meetings did Captain Behan spell out in any way what your job was in this new arrangement with him?

DETECTIVE COSTELLO: Yes, he did. Thoroughly. I was to work undercover, for him and the chief. I was to act as if nothing was out of order and to come up with some specific evidence of what I had said about dishonesty.

ASSISTANT DISTRICT ATTORNEY: In this new role, did you know the defendant?

DETECTIVE COSTELLO: Yes, he was one of my associates, another detective sergeant—a member of OCSS.

ASSISTANT DISTRICT ATTORNEY: During this time of your association with the defendant, did you at any time participate with the defendant in any event that led you to make a report about him to Captain Behan?

DETECTIVE COSTELLO: Yes, and it was on the Monday after I first met Captain Behan. That would be March 21 of this year.

ASSISTANT DISTRICT ATTORNEY: Tell us, in your own words, what happened at this time—on this occasion.

DETECTIVE COSTELLO: I met the defendant, Bob, in the Nitro Bar and Grill on Seventh and Main Streets. It was about 11:00 A.M. He had a hoodlum with him who I knew as Big Bart, Bart Nino, and he introduced us. Nino took some money from his pocket right away and handed some bills to me. I said, "What's that for?" Nino said, "Get yourself a hat." I said, "I don't wear a hat," and gave him back the money.

ASSISTANT DISTRICT ATTORNEY: Do you know the amount of money?

DETECTIVE COSTELLO: No, I don't. Several bills, folded up. No, I do not.

ASSISTANT DISTRICT ATTORNEY: What happened next?

DETECTIVE COSTELLO: Nino shrugged his shoulders and gave the money to Bob, the defendant. Then, Nino talked a little bit about nothing much, ball games and girls, and he left. I asked Bob, "What's he buying?" He said, "Not much." Then I said something like, "Why me?" He said, "Why not? You don't use money?" Then he told me that Nino wanted to get some records taken out of our squad files about his brother—his younger brother. Bob said the kid was trying to go legit, and our records were bugging him in getting a job. I heard him out, then left and went back to the office.

ASSISTANT DISTRICT ATTORNEY: Did you do anything in relation to this conversation?

DETECTIVE COSTELLO: Yes, I did. I went to our files. Everyone went out to lunch. I got young Nino's file folder out, looked at it, found he was wanted for suspicion of receiving stolen property and for suspicion of homicide in another case. I photocopied the file papers, and I put the photocopies copies in my desk drawer—which I locked—put the record file back in our filing cabinet, and then I went out to lunch myself.

(continued)

ASSISTANT DISTRICT ATTORNEY: Now, at any future date, did you have anything to do with this record again?

DETECTIVE COSTELLO: Yes. It was the following Saturday—that's March 26, this year. I went into the office early, went to our files, and looked for young Nino's record. I took it out and examined it, and I found that the photo had been changed. Big Bart's photo was substituted for his brother's picture, and the wanted cards were missing.

ASSISTANT DISTRICT ATTORNEY: I show you a folder marked "Nino, Alberto," and I ask you, do you recognize it?

DETECTIVE COSTELLO: (Reading) Yes, it's the fixed-up, tampered-with folder.

ASSISTANT DISTRICT ATTORNEY: In relation to this photocopy of the original folder in your squad files about this young Nino—what happened to that?

DETECTIVE COSTELLO: I have that here (showing file folder) with me now.

ASSISTANT DISTRICT ATTORNEY: Your Honor, can I have both these files marked for identification? Thank you. Your witness (to defense counsel), counselor. (Defense counsel stands and begins cross-examination.)

DEFENSE COUNSEL: Are most of your fellow police officers honest?

DETECTIVE COSTELLO: Yes. Most of them are honest—and hardworking.

DEFENSE COUNSEL: How many officers, in your knowledge, entered the police department for the purpose of becoming dishonest?

DETECTIVE COSTELLO: None, to my knowledge—not to my knowledge.

DEFENSE COUNSEL: I gather from your prompt answers that you know a great deal about your fellow police officers. Is that true?

DETECTIVE COSTELLO: Well—I guess I do. They're my coworkers. Why not?

DEFENSE COUNSEL: Now—tell the court if any conduct of yours has bothered or upset your fellow coworkers.

DETECTIVE COSTELLO: I don't—I don't understand the question.

DEFENSE COUNSEL: It's a simple question, but let me withdraw it, and phrase it in this fashion: To your knowledge has any of your conduct upset your fellow police officers?

DETECTIVE COSTELLO: Oh sure! That's a different thing. Sure, yes.

DEFENSE COUNSEL: Tell us of such an incident that you consider important.

DETECTIVE COSTELLO: Well—when I was transferred out of uniform, from patrol to the OCSS in plainclothes, I grew a beard (puts hands to face, indicating beard) and wore some clothes—well, the kind of clothes I used to wear only on my day off, kind of sharp, I suppose. The guys in the squad used to tell me, "What a disguise!"

DEFENSE COUNSEL: And that upset you, bothered you—emotionally disturbed you?

DETECTIVE COSTELLO: Well, I don't know all that. You asked the question. Say it bugged me a bit.

DEFENSE COUNSEL: Why? Why would this remark bother you—this "What a disguise!"?

DETECTIVE COSTELLO: It wasn't any makeup, really a disguise. It was just the clothes I liked. That's why it bothered me.

DEFENSE COUNSEL: Oh, I'm beginning to understand. Now—tell me this: in relation to the charges of dishonesty against my client, your fellow police officer, did you ever get any feedback from him about yourself as a person or as a police officer?

DETECTIVE COSTELLO: Yes, a few times, mostly about—or along the lines of—something like "why don't you go along with the guys?" or "why do you have to be different?"

DEFENSE COUNSEL: This was in relation to your manner of dress, your appearance?

DETECTIVE COSTELLO: No, it wasn't. It was in relation to the money he was making and that I didn't want to take—like from Nino.

DEFENSE COUNSEL: Your Honor, would you direct the witness just to answer the question?

JUDGE: No, I don't think I will. You asked the question, and it was open-ended. Let it stand along with its answer.

DEFENSE COUNSEL: Thank you, Your Honor.

DEFENSE COUNSEL: Did the defendant or any of your coworkers in this Organized Crime Squad ever actually do anything to indicate any dislike for you?

DETECTIVE COSTELLO: They—they sure did. All of them did. They stopped talking to me. Except when they had to, like a phone call for

(continued)

me, then it was a "Here, you—." Real brief. And they would stop talking to one another when I came in the room or walked up to them on the street.

DEFENSE COUNSEL: This animosity resulted from your dirty work—the role of informer or spying on your fellow workers?

DETECTIVE COSTELLO: No, counselor. At that time, no one knew of what you term "dirty work." All they knew was that I wouldn't do any business with the hoodlums—that I wanted to do my job just like I get paid for it.

DEFENSE COUNSEL: There is entrapment in your role, is there not?

ASSISTANT DISTRICT ATTORNEY: Your Honor, I object. The question—

JUDGE: (Interrupting) Sustained.

DEFENSE COUNSEL: (Resuming questioning) Since you place such a premium on doing what you get paid for, did you ever counsel or advise my client to do the same thing?

DETECTIVE COSTELLO: You sure you want to hear this?

DEFENSE COUNSEL: I asked the question.

DETECTIVE COSTELLO: Just before I left the Nitro Bar on the day we met Big Bart Nino, I said to Bob, the defendant, "My God, you're making good money as a police detective. You could never make this kind of money on the outside doing any other kind of work. You know you have a family, kids. Don't be stupid. Think about it." That was how it ended.

DEFENSE COUNSEL: Was there any response to these words of yours—any words said at all by my client?

DETECTIVE COSTELLO: No, not much. Something like "If I really did think about it, I'd blow my brains out."

Source: Paul B. Weston, *Criminal Justice and Law Enforcement: Cases* (Englewood Cliffs, NJ: Prentice Hall, 1972). Reprinted by permission of Prentice Hall.

CHAPTER REVIEW

Key Terms

Review Questions

1. The hostile questioning by the defense counsel is known as ____.
   a. Nonverbal communication
   b. Direct examination
   c. Cross-examination
   d. Redirect examination

2. The first questioning of a witness that is conducted by the attorney calling the witness is known as ____.
   a. Nonverbal communication
   b. Direct examination
   c. Cross-examination
   d. Redirect examination

3. A short ____ before responding to a question allows the prosecution to offer an objection to the question.
   a. Chuckle
   b. Pause
   c. Smile
   d. Smirk

4. An officer's misuse of his or her police authority for personal gain is known as ____.
   a. Corruption
   b. Misconduct
   c. Ethical awareness
   d. Unethical behavior

5. Police use of excessive force or the violation of a suspect's constitutional rights are both examples of police ____.
   a. Corruption
   b. Misconduct
   c. Ethical awareness
   d. Unethical behavior
6. A jury's not-guilty verdict that is influenced by the mistrust of police witnesses is known as jury ____.
   a. Disbelief
   b. Disappointment
   c. Equalization
   d. Nullification
7. Ethical training should begin as part of the ____ curriculum.
   a. College
   b. High school
   c. Prehiring
   d. Academy
8. Ethical training should be reinforced by ____ who have been selected as ethical role models.
   a. Peers
   b. Field training officers
   c. Supervisors
   d. Managers
9. Ethical training should continue throughout an officer's career with specific professional training sessions based on relevant ____ training.
   a. Job-specific
   b. Theoretical
   c. Scenario
   d. Field
10. The progression of a compromised officer is predictable and, therefore, ____.
    a. Concerning
    b. Troubling
    c. Preventable
    d. Acceptable

See Appendix D for the correct answers.

Application Exercise

Assume that you are a police officer who has an excellent reputation for honesty, both on and off the job. Your chief has recognized your high level of ethical awareness by selecting you to address an academy class of new recruits on this subject. What information regarding the standards for criminal investigators and the insights relative to the continuum of compromise would you share with these students?

Discussion Questions

1. Can stage fright be controlled? How?
2. Why are investigator–witnesses advised not to argue with a cross-examiner?
3. Define nonverbal communication.
4. What body movements indicate boredom, impatience, anxiety?
5. Do you believe eye contact between an investigator–witness and jurors in a criminal trial is important? Why?
6. Sum up the recommended behavior for investigator–witnesses following their appearance on the witness stand.
7. Do the facts of this case study justify a conclusion that police dishonesty is an inescapable part of the "system"?
8. In the case study, is the "thing of value" in this attempt to corrupt Detective Costello the money that would be given to him or the approval of his associates?
9. If you were a member of the jury in the case study, would you consider Detective Costello to be a credible witness and his testimony truthful?

Related Websites

The U.S. Department of Justice (DOJ), Civil Rights Division, Special Litigation Section, seeks court orders to address systemic cases of police misconduct. To review the types of complaints addressed by this agency, consult the DOJ website at www.usdoj.gov/crt/split/police.htm.

The FBI's Civil Rights Division is responsible for investigating citizens' allegations of police misconduct, known as "color or law" violations. The FBI website can be accessed at www.fbi.gov/hq/cid/civilrights/color.htm.

Notes

1. John J. Burke, "Testifying in Court," *FBI Law Enforcement Bulletin,* XLIV, no. 9 (September 1975): 8–13.
2. John F. Wilson and Carroll C. Arnold, *Dimensions of Public Communication* (Boston: Allyn and Bacon, 1976), 34–36.
3. Rudolf Flesch, *The Art of Plain Talk* (New York: Harper & Brothers, 1946), 31–56.
4. Loretta A. Malandro and Larry Barker, *Nonverbal Communication* (Reading, MA: Addison-Wesley, 1983), 4–28.
5. William Geller, ed., *Local Government Police Management* (Washington, DC: The International City Management Association, 1991), 239.
6. James Lardner and Thomas Reppetto, *NYPD: A City and Its Police* (New York: Henry Holt, 2000), 276–277.
7. Kevin Gilmartin and John Harris, "The Continuum of Compromise," *The Police Chief* (January 1998): 25–28.

Appendix A   Case Briefs

▶ A. Search and Seizure

Fourth Amendment of the U.S. Constitution

Mapp v. Ohio, 367 U.S. 643 (1961)

Facts: Miss Dolly Mapp was convicted of the possession of lewd and lascivious books, pictures, and photographs. At her trial, evidence seized during a forcible search of her home without a warrant was admitted into evidence and was the primary evidence leading to her conviction.

Issue: Can evidence seized during an illegal search be admitted as evidence to convict a defendant?

Decision: No evidence seized illegally may be admitted in evidence in any case. It must be excluded as evidence in any state or federal court. The exclusionary sanction is to deter the police from unlawful acts and preserve the integrity of the court.

Katz v. United States, 389 U.S. 347 (1967)

Facts: Charles Katz was convicted in a U.S. district court of transmitting wagering information by telephone. At his trial, the prosecution was permitted to introduce evidence of Katz's portion of telephone conversations, despite defense counsel's objection. Eavesdropping was by agents of the Federal Bureau of Investigation, who had attached an electronic eavesdropping and recording device to the outside of the public telephone booth used by Katz.

Issue: Was the evidence obtained through a legal surveillance (electronic eavesdropping)?

Decision: It was reversible error to admit such evidence, in view of the lack of prior judicial authorization (search warrant).

Dalia v. United States, 441 U.S. 238 (1979)

Facts: Pursuant to Title III of the Omnibus Crime Control and Safe Streets Act of 1968, the federal district court found probable cause and authorized the government to intercept all oral conversations taking place in the suspect's business office. Even though the court order did not specifically authorize entry of the suspect's business office by government agents, FBI agents did secretly enter the business office at midnight and install an electronic bug.

Issue: Was the secret entry of the specified office a violation of the Fourth Amendment or the federal statute?

Decision: Secret entry to install an electronic device pursuant to a lawful search warrant is not a violation of the U.S. Constitution or the statute.

Terry v. Ohio, 392 U.S. 1 (1968)

Facts: A revolver was introduced in evidence at the trial of John W. Terry for carrying a concealed weapon unlawfully (after failure of a pretrial motion to suppress). A police officer had observed unusual conduct by Terry and two other men, and—concluding that they were contemplating a robbery—he stopped and frisked them, discovering the weapon carried by Terry and seizing it.

Issue: Is the police stop-and-frisk procedure constitutional?

Decision: The police stop-and-frisk procedure does not violate the Fourth Amendment rights of Terry (under the circumstances of the case), and the revolver seized from Terry was property admissible at his trial for carrying a concealed weapon unlawfully.

Chimel v. California, 395 U.S. 752 (1969)

Facts: Police officers armed with an arrest warrant but not a search warrant were admitted to Chimel's home by his wife in his absence. The officers awaited Chimel's arrival and then arrested him when he entered his home. Chimel refused consent to the officers' search of his home (to "look around"). Despite this refusal, officers searched the entire home on a claim that the lawful arrest justified the search. Chimel was convicted on burglary charges; items taken from his home during the police search having been admitted into evidence despite counsel's objection on constitutional grounds.

Issue: What is the scope of a search incidental to a lawful arrest?

Decision: Under the circumstances of this case, the scope of the police search was unreasonable under the Fourth and Fourteenth Amendments.

Gustafson v. Florida, 414 U.S. 260 (1973)

Facts: James F. Gustafson was convicted for unlawful possession of marijuana. The state introduced in evidence several marijuana cigarettes found in a box in Gustafson's coat pocket when a municipal police officer conducted a full body search of Gustafson after a lawful arrest for driving an automobile without having his driver's license in his possession.

Issue: Was the scope of this search connected with a lawful traffic arrest reasonable?

Decision: The scope of the search was reasonable under the Fourth and Fourteenth Amendments of the Constitution.

Rochin v. California, 342 U.S. 165 (1952)

Facts: Having "some information" that Rochin was selling narcotics, officers went to his home and found the defendant in bed. On the nightstand were some capsules, and when the officers asked what they were, Rochin put them in his mouth and swallowed them. He was taken to the hospital where his stomach was pumped against his will. Two capsules that contained morphine were recovered, and he was convicted for possession of narcotics.

Issue: Was the scope of this search—the pumping of his stomach—unreasonable?

Decision: The court found that this search was unreasonable as it runs counter to the decencies of civilized conduct and, as such, shocks the conscience of the court and society.

▶ B. Interrogation

Payne v. Arkansas, 356 U.S. 560 (1958)

Facts: The suspect confessed to murder, was convicted by this and other evidence of murder in the first degree, and was sentenced to death. Undisputed evidence in this case showed that Payne, a mentally dull nineteen-year-old youth, (1) was arrested without a warrant; (2) was denied a hearing before a magistrate, at which he would have been advised of his right to remain silent and of his right to counsel, as required by Arkansas statutes; (3) was not advised of his right to remain silent or of his right to counsel; (4) was held incommunicado for three days, without counsel, advisor, or friend, during which time members of his family tried to see him but were turned away and he was refused permission to make even one telephone call; (5) was denied food for long periods; and finally, (6) was told by the chief of police "that there would be thirty or forty people there in a few minutes that wanted to get him."

Issue: Did the acts and statements of the police deprive the suspect of due process of law?

Decision: The use in a state criminal trial of a defendant's confession obtained by coercion—whether physical or mental—is forbidden by the Fourteenth Amendment.

Lego v. Toomey, 404 U.S. 477 (1972)

Facts: The suspect was arrested and made a confession to the police. Evidence was conflicting on the issue of voluntariness (coercion) of the confession. The trial court admitted the confession into evidence.

Issue: What is the burden of proof necessary to admit a confession into evidence? Who determines the admissibility of the confession?

Decision: "By a preponderance of the evidence" is a constitutionally permissible burden of proof. Admissibility of evidence is a determination for the court, not the jury.

Miranda v. Arizona, 384 U.S. 436 (1966)

Facts: Ernesto A. Miranda was arrested by police for kidnapping and rape and taken to an interrogation room in a police building. In response to police questioning, Miranda signed a confession containing a typed paragraph stating that the confession was made voluntarily with full knowledge of his legal rights and with the understanding that any statement he made therein might be used against him. This confession was admitted in evidence at his trial on kidnapping and rape charges, and Miranda was convicted as charged.

Issue: Were Miranda's constitutional rights to counsel and against self-incrimination violated?

Decision: In the absence of intelligent waiver of the constitutional rights involved, confessions and other statements obtained by custodial police interrogation are inadmissible in evidence, where the suspect (as Miranda) was not informed of his right to counsel, or of his right to be silent, or of the possible use of his statements as evidence against him.

▶ C. Right to an Attorney

Gideon v. Wainwright, 372 U.S. 335 (1963)

Facts: The defendant was charged and convicted of the felony of breaking and entering a poolroom with intent to commit a misdemeanor. The trial court denied defendant's request for an appointed attorney pursuant to Florida law, which allowed appointed attorneys for indigent defendants in capital cases only. The defendant proceeded to trial and was convicted without an attorney to represent him.

Issue: Does the Constitution require the appointment of an attorney for indigent defendants accused of crime?

Decision: The Sixth Amendment requires appointment of counsel unless waived for indigents accused of crime. The provision is obligatory on the states by the Fourteenth Amendment.

United States v. Wade, 388 U.S. 218 (1967)

Facts: Several weeks after Wade's indictment for robbery of a federally insured bank and for conspiracy, Wade was, without notice to his appointed counsel, placed in a lineup in which each person wore strips of tape on his face, as the robber allegedly had done and, on direction, repeated words like those the robber allegedly had used. Two bank employees identified Wade as the robber. At the trial, when asked if the robber was in the courtroom, they identified Wade. The prior lineup identifications were elicited on cross-examination. Urging that the conduct of the lineup violated his Fifth Amendment privilege against self-incrimination and his Sixth Amendment right to counsel, Wade filed a motion for judgment of acquittal or, alternatively, for a ruling to strike the courtroom identifications. The trial court denied the motions, and Wade was convicted.

Issue: Are courtroom identifications of an accused at trial to be excluded from evidence because the accused was exhibited to the witnesses before trial at a postindictment lineup conducted for identification purposes without notice to and in the absence of the accused's appointed counsel?

Decision: In-court identification by a witness to whom the accused was exhibited before trial in the absence of counsel must be excluded, unless it can be established that such evidence had an independent origin or that error in its admission was harmless beyond a reasonable doubt.

Appendix B Federal Controlled Substances Law*

▶ Title 21, USC *Section 812*

The five schedules of controlled substances and placement into any one of these schedules are as follows:

Schedule I

a. The drug has a high potential for abuse.
b. The drug has no currently accepted medical use in treatment in the United States.
c. There is a lack of accepted safety for use of the drug under medical supervision.

Schedule I Controlled Substances

Heroin

Lysergic acid diethylamide (LSD)

Marijuana

Mescaline

Peyote

Psilocybin

Schedule II

a. The drug has a high potential for abuse.
b. The drug has a currently accepted medical use in treatment in the United States or a currently accepted medical use with severe restrictions.
c. Abuse of the drug may lead to severe psychological or physical dependence.

Schedule II Controlled Substances

Cocaine

Opium

Fentanyl

Methadone

Injectable Methamphetamine

Schedule III

a. The drug has a potential for abuse less than the drugs in Schedules I and II.
b. The drug has a currently accepted medical use in treatment in the United States.

---

* This section has been edited, and for a full understanding of the law in this area your attention is directed to Title 21 of the United States Code, sections 812–844.

c. Abuse of the drug may lead to moderate or low physical dependence or high psychological dependence.

Schedule III Controlled Substances

Amphetamine

Methamphetamine

Barbituric acid

Phencyclidine

Codeine

Anabolic steroids

Schedule IV

a. The drug has a low potential for abuse relative to the drugs in Schedule III.
b. The drug has a currently accepted medical use in treatment in the United States.
c. Abuse of the drug may lead to limited physical dependence or psychological dependence relative to the drugs in Schedule III.

Schedule IV Controlled Substances

Barbital

Chloral hydrate

Schedule V

a. Any compound, mixture, or preparation containing limited quantities of narcotic drugs, such as the following:

Codeine

Dihydrocodeine

Ethylmorphine

Opium

▶ Title 21, USC *Section 841: Prohibited Acts*

It shall be unlawful for any person knowingly or intentionally to manufacture, distribute, dispense, or possess 1 kilogram or more of heroin, 5 kilograms or more of cocaine, 100 grams or more of phencyclidine (PCP), 10 grams or more of lysergic acid diethylamide (LSD); 1,000 kilograms or more of marijuana, or 1,000 marijuana plants; 50 grams or more of methamphetamine. Such person shall be sentenced to a term of imprisonment that may not be less than ten years or more than life, and if death or serious bodily injury results from the use of such substances shall be not less than twenty years or more than life, a fine not to exceed $4,000,000 if the defendant is an individual or $10,000,000 if the defendant is other than an individual.

After a prior conviction for a felony drug offense, such person shall be sentenced to a term of imprisonment that may not be less than twenty years and not more than life imprisonment, and if death or serious bodily injury results from the use of such substances shall be sentenced to life imprisonment, a fine not to exceed $8,000,000 if the defendant is an individual or $20,000,000 if the defendant is other than an individual, or both.

► Title 21, USC *Section 844: Penalties for Simple Possession*

It shall be unlawful for any person knowingly or intentionally to possess a controlled substance unless such substance was obtained directly, or pursuant to a valid prescription or order, from a practitioner, while acting in the course of his or her professional practice. Any person who violates this subsection may be sentenced to a term of imprisonment of not more than one year and shall be fined a minimum of $1,000 or both. A person with a prior conviction shall be imprisoned for not less than fifteen days but not more than two years and shall be fined a minimum of $2,500. After two prior convictions, the person shall be imprisoned for not less than ninety days but not more than three years and shall be fined a minimum of $5,000. Notwithstanding the preceding sentence, a person convicted under this section for the possession of a mixture or substance that contains cocaine base shall be imprisoned not less than five years and not more than twenty years and fined a minimum of $1,000.

Appendix C   Identity Theft: What to Do If It Happens to You

This guide provides victims of identity theft with the major resources to contact for help. Unfortunately, at this time, victims themselves are burdened with resolving the problem. It is important to act quickly and assertively to minimize the damage.

In dealing with authorities and financial institutions, keep a log of all conversations, including dates, names, and phone numbers. Note time spent and any expenses incurred. Confirm conversations in writing. Send correspondence by certified mail (return receipt requested). Keep copies of all letters and documents.

▶ What to Do

Once you discover you are a victim of identity theft, you should do the following:

1. ***Credit Bureaus.*** Immediately call the fraud units of the three credit-reporting companies: Experian (formerly TRW), Equifax, and Trans Union. Report the theft of your credit cards or numbers. Ask that your account be flagged. Also, add a victim's statement to your report, using up to one hundred words. (Example: "My ID has been used to apply for credit fraudulently. Contact me to verify all applications.") Be sure to ask for how long the fraud alert will be posted on your account and how you can extend it if necessary. Be aware that these measures may not entirely stop new fraudulent accounts from being opened by the imposter. Ask the credit bureaus, in writing, to provide you with free copies every few months so you can monitor your credit reports.

   Ask the credit bureaus for names and phone numbers of credit grantors with whom fraudulent accounts have been opened. Ask the credit bureaus to remove inquiries that have been generated as a result of the fraudulent access. You may also ask the credit bureaus to notify those who have received your credit report in the last six months to alert them to the disputed and erroneous information (two years for employers).

2. ***Creditors.*** Immediately contact by phone and in writing all creditors with whom your name has been used fraudulently. Get replacement cards with new account numbers for your own accounts that have been used fraudulently. Ask that old accounts be processed as "Account closed at consumer's request." (This is better than "Card lost or stolen," because when this statement is reported to credit bureaus, it can be interpreted as blaming you for the loss.) Carefully monitor your mail and credit card bills for evidence of new fraudulent activity. Report it immediately to credit grantors.

   Creditors' requirements to verify fraud. You may be asked by banks and credit grantors to fill out and notarize fraud affidavits. This could become costly. The law does not require that a notarized affidavit be provided to creditors. A written statement and supporting documentation should be enough (unless the creditor offers to pay for the notary).

3. ***Stolen Checks.*** If you have had checks stolen or bank accounts set up fraudulently, report it to the check verification companies. Put "stop payments" on any outstanding checks about which you are unsure. Cancel your checking and savings accounts and obtain new account numbers. Give the bank a secret password for your account (*not* your mother's maiden name).

4. *ATM Cards.* If your ATM card has been stolen or compromised, get a new card, an account number, and a PIN. Do not use your old password. When creating a password, do not use common numbers such as the last four digits of your Social Security Number or your birth date.

5. *Fraudulent Change of Address.* Notify the local postal inspector if you suspect an identity thief has filed a change of your address with the post office or has used the mail to commit check or bank fraud. (Call the local postmaster to obtain the phone number.) Find out where the fraudulent credit cards were sent, and notify the local postmaster for that address to forward all mail in your name to your own address. You may also need to talk with the mail carrier.

6. *Social Security Number Misuse.* Call the Social Security Administration (SSA) to report fraudulent use of your Social Security Number. As a last resort, you might want to change your number. The SSA will change it only if you fit its fraud victim criteria. Also order a copy of your Earnings and Benefits Statement and check it for accuracy.

7. *Passports.* If you have a passport, notify the passport office in writing to be on the lookout for anyone ordering a new passport fraudulently in your name.

8. *Phone Service.* If your long-distance calling card has been stolen or you discover fraudulent charges on your bill, cancel the account and open a new one. Provide a password that must be used any time the account is changed.

9. *Driver's License Number Misuse.* You may need to change your driver's license number if someone is using yours as identification on bad checks. Call the Department of Motor Vehicles (DMV) to see if another license was issued in your name. Put a fraud alert on your license. Go to your local DMV to request a new number. Also, fill out the DMV's complaint form to begin the fraud investigation process. Send supporting documents with the complaint form to the nearest DMV investigation office.

10. *Law Enforcement.* Report the crime to the law enforcement agency within the jurisdiction for your case. Give the agency as much documented evidence as possible. Get a copy of your police report. Keep the phone number of your fraud investigator handy and give it to creditors and others who require verification of your case. Credit card companies and banks may require you to show the report to verify the crime. Some police departments have been known to refuse to write reports on such crimes. Be persistent!

11. *False Civil and Criminal Judgments.* Sometimes victims of identity theft are wrongfully accused of crimes committed by the imposter. If a civil judgment has been entered in your name for actions taken by your imposter, contact the court where the judgment was entered and report that you are a victim of identity theft. If you are wrongfully prosecuted for criminal charges, contact the Department of Justice in your state and the FBI. Ask how to clear your name.

12. *Legal Help.* You may want to consult an attorney to determine legal action to take against creditors or credit bureaus if they are not cooperative in removing fraudulent entries from your credit report or if negligence is a factor. Call the local bar association to find an attorney who specializes in consumer law and the Fair Credit Reporting Act.

13. *Dealing with Emotional Stress.* Psychological counseling may help you deal with the stress and anxiety commonly experienced by victims. Know that you are not alone.

Appendix D Answers to Chapter Review Questions

▶ Chapter 1

1. a   2. a   3. c   4. c   5. a   6. c   7. b   8. d   9. c   10. c

▶ Chapter 2

1. b   2. d   3. a   4. c   5. b   6. c   7. a   8. d   9. a   10. c

▶ Chapter 3

1. b   2. b   3. b   4. b   5. d   6. b   7. a   8. b   9. c   10. d

▶ Chapter 4

1. d   2. a   3. a   4. c   5. d   6. a   7. c   8. c   9. d   10. a

▶ Chapter 5

1. a   2. b   3. c   4. d   5. d   6. b   7. b   8. a   9. d   10. a

▶ Chapter 6

1. a   2. c   3. b   4. c   5. a   6. d   7. a   8. b   9. a   10. c

▶ Chapter 7

1. b   2. a   3. b   4. b   5. c   6. a   7. c   8. c   9. b   10. d

▶ Chapter 8

1. b   2. a   3. b   4. d   5. c   6. d   7. a   8. c   9. b   10. c

▶ Chapter 9

1. b   2. a   3. b   4. d   5. c   6. a   7. e   8. c   9. b   10. d

▶ Chapter 10

1. c   2. b   3. d   4. c   5. c   6. b   7. a   8. d   9. c   10. a

▶ Chapter 11

1. c   2. d   3. c   4. d   5. c   6. b   7. a   8. d   9. d   10. b

▶ Chapter 12

1. b   2. b   3. c   4. a   5. c   6. d   7. c   8. b   9. d   10. b

▶ Chapter 13

1. a   2. c   3. b   4. a   5. c   6. b   7. a   8. c   9. d   10. c

▶ Chapter 14

1. a   2. c   3. d   4. b   5. d   6. a   7. d   8. c   9. d   10. a

▶ Chapter 15

1. a   2. d   3. c   4. b   5. e   6. b   7. c   8. a   9. c   10. d

▶ Chapter 16

1. d   2. b   3. b   4. a   5. a   6. d   7. b   8. a   9. c   10. d

▶ Chapter 17

1. d   2. a   3. c   4. b   5. a   6. c   7. a   8. c   9. d   10. b

▶ Chapter 18

1. c   2. b   3. b   4. a   5. b   6. d   7. d   8. b   9. a   10. c

Chapter 1

Anthropometry. An early system of human identification based on eleven measurements of the human body.

Blood-feuds, or vendettas. An ongoing situation where the family of the offender retaliates against the victim for the unjust punishment of a crime.

Bobbies. The nickname of the London police which is used in reference to the founder, Sir Robert Peel.

Civil Service System. A fair and open system of testing new hires and those seeking promotion to ensure that only the best candidates are selected for government positions.

Constable. Supervised night watchmen and brought arrested offenders before a magistrate.

Criminalistics. Individualization of physical evidence in a crime lab; also referred to as forensic science.

Exchange principle. An early French researcher, Edmond Locard, believed that when a criminal came in contact with another object or person, a cross-transfer of evidence may occur, primarily of hairs and fivers.

Forensics. The use of science to answer legal questions.

Hue-and-cry. The call for assistance from citizens to aid the night watchmen, or police.

Patronage. A corrupt system of hiring only friends or supporters for government jobs.

Police Gazette. Established by Magistrate John Fielding (1721–1780), the gazette published information about criminal activity, names and descriptions of wanted criminals, and descriptions of stolen property.

Posse comitatus. The legal requirement that all available citizens are expected to respond to protect the community.

Sheriff. Provide law enforcement–related functions to those areas in the county that are located outside the jurisdiction of city police departments.

Spoils system. A corrupt system where politicians extort money from people wanting to do business with the government.

Statute of Winchester. Passed in 1285, this English law required all towns to have men on the street after dark to provide for safety of travelers and inhabitants.

Toxicology. The study of the effects of poisons on the human body.

Chapter 2

Accusatory pleading. The court proceeding where the defendant responds to the accusation that a crime has been committed and he or she is the person responsible for the commission of the crime.

Alibi. The defense to the charge of criminal wrongdoing as the defendant was elsewhere at the time of the crime.

All points bulletin (APB). Distributed when coverage is expanded as the interval from the time of the crime indicates the possible enlargement of areas of flight, and when adequate descriptive information is available.

Broadcast alarms. Alert other police units of the recent crime; usually are done first by radio and then by Teletype, fax, or mail.

Consent search. A person can voluntarily consent to the police to search his or her person, home, and property. Any evidence found as a result is admissible in court.

Corpus delicti. Body of a crime; essential elements.

Curtilage. The area immediately surrounding a dwelling.

Emergency Circumstances. Justification to make a warrantless entry and search of a premise based on the belief that a delay would result in evidence destruction, hot pursuit, protection of life, or the threat to the safety of the officers conducting the search.

Exclusionary rule. Prevents illegally obtained items from being admitted into evidence.

Immediate control. The extent of the area that may be searched is restricted to that area which the arrested person has control.

Magistrate. A judge.

Motor vehicle exception. An exception to the search warrant that requires the existence of probable cause to believe that the vehicle contains evidence of a crime, or contraband, and that the searching officers have lawful access to the vehicle.

Negative evidence. Oriented to countering defenses to the crime charged.

Oath or affirmation. When an officer raises his or her hand before a magistrate and swears or affirms that the information given to the court is true.

Open fields. Not protected by the Fourth Amendment and that investigators may enter and search unoccupied or undeveloped areas without a search warrant.

Plain view exception. Permits investigators to observe and seize evidence without a warrant if the officer is lawfully in a position to view an object and if the incriminating character of the object is immediately apparent.

Probable cause. Exists when enough facts are determined that would lead a reasonable and prudent person to believe that criminal activity is fairly probable.

Reasonable suspicion. Belief that criminal activity is occurring, is about to occur, or has recently occurred, and that the person or vehicle to be detained is related to that criminal activity.

Relevance. The connection between a fact offered in evidence and the issue to be proved.

Search incident to a lawful arrest. Includes the person of the arrestee, including a wallet or purse immediately associated with the arrestee, which is conducted without a warrant.

Stop and frisk. A person may be patted down for weapons if the officer has the additional reasonable suspicion that the pat-down was necessary for officer safety. Such a temporary detention is not considered to be an arrest.

Venue. The territorial jurisdiction in which the crime occurred.

Wanted notice. Provides full information about the fugitive and about areas in which he or she is likely to be found.

Chapter 3

Aerial photo. Crime scene pictures taken from a helicopter or airplane.

Chain-of-custody A written document that can account for an item of evidence from the time it came into an agency's possession to the time it is presented in court.

Chronological log A record of events as they occur at the scene of a crime.

Close-up photo. Crime scene pictures taken for detail, within a few feet of the subject.

Corpus delicti Body of a crime; essential elements.

Crime report. The report written by investigators at the crime scene which documents any action taken and establishes modus operandi information, the details of the crime and its circumstances.

Crime scene sketches and photographs. Exhibits that are offered in evidence, that can assist jurors in understanding the case.

Criminalistics. Individualization of physical evidence in a crime lab; also referred to as forensic science.

Discovery. A request by the defense counsel, which is made before the trial to the prosecutor, in order to review the evidence against the defendant.

Ever-narrowing circle. A crime scene search method where the officer starts at the outskirts of the crime scene and works in a circle pattern toward the focal point of the crime scene.

Ever-widening circle. A crime scene search method where the searching officer starts at the focal point of the crime scene and works outward in a circular pattern toward the fringes of the crime scene.

Field notes. Memoranda made by the investigator during an investigation.

Known standard of evidence. Evidence collected from a known source.

Locard's exchange principle. An early French researcher, Edmond Locard, believed that when a criminal came in contact with another object or person, a cross-transfer of evidence may occur, primarily of hairs and fibers.

Long-range photo. Pictures of the crime scene that show the locale, the approach route, the means of ingress and exit to the scene.

Match (matching). Most favorable term in a crime lab report of a comparison analysis of evidence submitted by police investigators.

Mid-range photo. Pictures of the crime scene, taken ten to twenty feet away, showing specific objects of evidence or a significant segment of the crime scene.

Modus operandi. Involves the choice of a particular crime to commit and the selection of a method of committing it.

Neighborhood canvass. A method of contacting people in the area of a crime scene to locate potential witnesses.

Neutralize the crime scene. Making the crime scene safe for other personnel to enter the area.

Point-to-point movement. A crime scene search method that follows a chain of objects that are obviously items of evidence.

Preliminary investigative report. Another name for a crime report, which establishes that a crime has been committed, who the victim is, and any suspect and witness information.

Retroactive interference. When witnesses discuss the crime or overhear others talking about the crime, they tend to adopt some information as their own.

Silent witness program. Seeks witness cooperation by offering rewards and confidentiality.

Single-officer search. Limits the number of officers in possession of evidence and the possibility of conflicting testimony by searching officers.

Strip or grid search. The strip search is a crime scene search method used outdoors where the searching officers move back and forth across the area until the area is searched. The grid search pattern, also used outdoors, starts when the strip search method is completed. It covers the same area at a right angle to the previous search pattern.

Unwilling witness. A witness that does not want to cooperate with the investigation.

View area. The universe of possible witnesses that may have seen or heard anything related to the investigation.

Zone or sector search. A crime scene search method where the scene is divided into segments and each sector is searched as an individual unit.

Chapter 4

Ballistics. The identification of firearms, bullets, cartridges, and shotgun shells.

Bluestar. An alternative test for luminol.

Caliber The diameter of the barrel of a gun.

Circumstantial evidence. Evidence from which an inference may be drawn.

Class evidence. Evidence that cannot be linked to a particular person or an object but only to a class of objects.

Comparison microscope. Essentially two microscopes connected together side by side that allows two samples to be viewed simultaneously by the operator.

Concentric fractures. On broken glass they form concentric circular cracks around the point of impact.

Contaminated prints. Prints that are observable with the naked eye, such as bloody fingerprints.

Crime laboratory. A facility equipped for the scientific examination of evidentiary material submitted by police evidence gatherers, staffed by qualified forensic scientists or criminalists; has the capacity to provide reports explaining what was discovered in the lab, by whom, relevancy to the issue of guilt or innocence, and whether examiner is qualified as an expert witness in court in the scientific area of the examination.

Cyanoacrylate fuming process. Used to develop fingerprints left on smooth, slippery surfaces such as plastic bags.

Direct evidence Witness testimony as it relates to what they saw or heard.

Exothermic reaction. Compounds that are deposited on a shooters hands in a unique spheroidal formation due to the rapid increase and decrease in temperature when a firearm is discharged.

Exterior ballistics. The study of bullets after they leave the barrel of the gun, projectiles in flight.

Fracture match. Reassembling a broken pane of glass, or similar object, to determine if a suspected piece will fill the void.

Gel diffusion. A laboratory test used to determine whether blood is of human or animal origin.

Gunshot residue (GSR) examination. An examination of a person's hands to determine whether or not they have recently fired a hand gun.

Hemastix. A presumptive field test for blood.

Impressions. Occur when an object comes into contact with a softer material, such as footprints in snow.

Imprints. Markings left on a surface by protruding parts of a person or vehicle, such as bloody handprints.

Individual evidence. Evidence that can be linked to a person or a specific object.

Interior ballistics. Refers to the functioning of firearms through the firing cycle.

Iodine fuming or ninhydrin process. A laboratory process used to develop fingerprints left on paper.

***Kastle-Meyer* color test.** Used to determine whether or not a stain is blood.

Latent prints Must be developed or dusted as cannot be seen with the naked eye.

Luminol. The faint blue glow that blood stains present after a suspected area is sprayed and the room is darkened.

Plastic prints. Prints left in soft material such as tar or tacky paint.

Postmortem forensic science. Removal and analysis of spent bullets from a victim's body.

Precipitin test. Used to determine whether a blood sample is of human origin.

Proof marks. Stamped into the metal of a firearm that indicate tests have been performed to prove the strength of the chamber by actual firing of the weapon.

Questioned document. Paper evidence which may have been forged, destroyed, or of questionable origin.

Radial fractures. On broken glass they start at the center or the point of impact and run outward in a star-shaped pattern.

Chapter 5

Allele. The person-to-person differences within a particular segment of a DNA sequence.

Base pair. Part of the DNA molecule the sequencing of which constitutes genic coding.

Chromatography A laboratory method of separating compounds to identify the components.

CODIS (Combined DNA Index System). The FBI is supporting the effort of linking the state DNA databases together to form a national database.

Criminalistics. Individualization of physical evidence in a crime lab; also referred to as forensic science.

Cryptography. Ciphers and codes (cloak and dagger) used to protect the security of underworld communications; decoding.

Forensic science laboratory. Crime laboratory where physical evidence is processed.

Forensic scientist. The name of the technicians who conduct the laboratory tests on physical evidence; also known as criminalists.

Frequency distribution study. Used to solve more complex ciphers and codes.

Gamma-ray spectrometer. A sophisticated piece of laboratory equipment that measures the distinctive radioactive gamma-ray emissions and thereby identifies the elements within a test item.

Genome A full complement of an individual's DNA.

Identification. All objects can be divided and subdivided into various sets on the basis of their properties.

Lasers. Used in the crime laboratory in the detection of latent fingerprints.

National Crime Information Computer (NCIC) system. Administered by the FBI, this database provides law enforcement information regarding wanted persons, stolen property, criminal histories, missing and unidentified persons, and sexual offender registration.

Neutron activation analysis (NAA). A laboratory technique used to determine the presence of gunshot residue on a subject's hands; can detect the presence of antimony and barium, common gunshot residues.

Nucleotide. Part of the DNA molecule, composed of varieties of nucleic acid.

Polymerase chain reaction (PCR) analysis. Used to replicate DNA samples that are contaminated, degraded, or small in quantity.

Reversal transposition. A simple means of hiding a telephone number by reversing the numbers or writing it backwards.

Set theory. All objects can be divided and subdivided into various sets on the basis of their properties.

Short tandem repeats (TR). A standard battery of core loci used to produce a typing profile.

Spectrography. A piece of laboratory equipment used to identify the elements contained in a test item.

Spectrum. Characteristic pattern of wavelengths.

Split combination. Commonly used to hide telephone numbers.

Substitution cipher. A simple code or cipher in which one symbol or letter stands for another symbol or letter.

Trace metal detection technique (TMDT). A test used to determine if a person has handled metal objects.

Transposition cipher. A cipher or code characterized by a change in the order of the enciphered material.

Ultrasonic cavitation. A method of restoring obliterated serial numbers on firearms and other metal objects.

Voiceprinting. The identification of an individual based on the unique characteristics of each person's vocal body formation and manner of speaking.

X-ray crystallography. A laboratory process used for the identification of any crystalline solid or compound from which a crystalline solid derivative can be made.

X-ray diffraction. A laboratory process of examining noncrystalline impurities and identifying inorganic and mineral substances.

Chapter 6

Accomplice witness. A person who is liable to prosecution for the identical offense charged against the defendant.

Active information. Establishes a group of suspects.

Alibi. The defense to the charge of criminal wrongdoing as the defendant was elsewhere at the time of the crime.

Amber alert system. A system that disseminates information regarding child abductions to the general population, suspects, and their vehicles via highway signs and the media.

Analysis. The interpretation of intelligence information as to its significance, meaning, and interrelationships.

Audio surveillance. Wiretapping and electronic eavesdropping.

Basic-lead informant. People who offer information that are not directly linked to the crime.

Benefit. A basic lead linked to who might gain from the commission of the crime.

"Better him than me." Crime partner agrees to testify for prosecution in return for a reduced charge or reduced sentence.

Bugging. Secret wiring of suspect's home, office, or car with electronic eavesdropping device—bug.

Bureau of Alcohol, Tobacco, Firearms, and Explosives (ATF). The federal agency that administers the national ballistic database.

Cold search. A fingerprint comparison without a suspect, searching an entire database with prints found at the scene.

Collation. The orderly arrangement, cross-indexing, and filing of intelligence information used to develop meaningful relationships.

Composite sketch. Likeness of the suspect prepared by an artist with the collaboration of a witness.

Contact surveillance. The use of fluorescent preparations used to stain a person's hands or clothing upon contact.

Covert collection. Hidden or concealed sources of information.

Covert informants. Persons who provide information from a position of trust and confidence within a criminal group.

Criminal Investigation Information Center (CIIC). The focal point of police intelligence, where information is applied to solve crime.

Debugging. Surveillance countermeasures.

Evaluation. A screening process of intelligence information that eliminates useless, incorrect, irrelevant, and unreliable information.

Field contact report. A report of a suspicious occurrence not amounting to a crime.

Field lineup. Conducted shortly after the crime has occurred.

Flipped. Confronted with evidence of his or her guilt, suspect agrees to become accomplice witness in return for reduced charge or lesser sentence.

Fixed visual surveillance. Keeping watch from one physical location, in person or by video camera.

Global positioning system (GPS) device. Tracking device that uses satellite technology.

Identi-kit system. Used to help a witness develop a likeness of a suspect of a crime.

Interpretation. Part of the intelligence analysis process that determines how collated information is related to problems requiring solutions.

Knowledge. Basic investigative lead regarding the identification of the person who had the knowledge, skill, or capacity to commit the crime in question.

Known identity. When the perpetrator has been identified by the victim or witness.

Lineup. An eyewitness identification procedure used to focus a case against a suspect.

Link analysis. A charting technique useful in showing the relationship between a number of people and organizations in a visual form.

Linkage. Relationship formed between persons engaged in criminal activity.

Modus operandi. Involves the choice of a particular crime to commit and the selection of a method of committing it.

Mole. Agents in place who provide information.

Moving visual surveillance. Following a suspect who may be on foot or in a vehicle, or other conveyance.

Mug shot A photograph taken of a suspect at the time of arrest.

National Integrated Ballistic Information Network (NIBIN). A nationwide database deploying ballistic imaging equipment, which is maintained by the ATF.

Opportunity. A basic investigative lead that places the suspect at the scene of a crime at or about the time of its occurrence.

Overt collection. Public sources of information.

Participant informant. A person working for an investigator who is actively engaged in gathering evidence to warrant an arrest.

Participant monitoring. Consensual electronic surveillance.

Passive information. Data are useful when a group of suspects is developed in a crime investigation.

Photographic lineup Conducted by showing a witness a number of photos, usually four to six.

Physical lineup. An eyewitness identification procedure where the suspect is directly viewed by the witness.

Request search. Having the fingerprints found at the scene compared to the fingerprints of one or more suspects.

Shill. A person who works for the police to aid an investigation.

Signature. The so-called trademark that is part of the modus operandi of a crime and distinguishes it as the work of a specific criminal or group of criminals who have committed previous crimes in which the same identifying circumstances occurred.

Single-digit search. Comparison of one fingerprint found at the scene against the ten-digit fingerprints on file.

Snitching. Revealing other people's secrets.

Stakeout (plant). Fixed visual surveillance.

Sting. Police-operated "fencing" operation to trap thieves as they sell their stolen property to undercover police; thieves are videotaped and identified for future arrest at completion of operation; also modified and used to trap graft-taking public officials and others.

Surveillance. The observation of people and places by investigators to develop investigative leads.

Tail (shadow). A moving visual surveillance.

Undercover agent. Use of police personnel to gather information about criminal operations from the inside.

Unknown identity. When the identity of the perpetrator is not known.

Visual surveillance. Keeping watch on a particular suspect, vehicle, or place.

Wired. A person who is secretly carrying a recording device or transmitter to gather information.

Chapter 7

Autonomic nervous system. Governs respiration, heartbeat, and perspiration.

Cardiograph. Part of a polygraph machine that records pulse rate and blood pressure.

Cognitive interviewing. An investigative technique used to enhance a witness's ability to recall events.

Emotional offender. A person who experiences considerable feelings of remorse and mental anguish as a result of committing the offense.

Factual analysis approach. Appeals to the suspect's common sense and reasoning rather than emotions.

Galvanic skin response (GSR). The skin's resistance to the passage of electric current.

Galvanograph. Part of a polygraph machine that records electrodermal response or sweating.

Hypnosis. A state resembling normal sleep that can be used to refresh the recollections of a witness.

Hypnotist A person trained to induce hypnosis.

Interrogation. The adversarial questioning of a suspect with the goal of soliciting an admission or confession of guilt.

Interview. A person-to-person conversation for the purposes of obtaining information about a crime or its circumstances.

Miranda rights. When a person is in police custody and prior to an interrogation the investigators must advise the suspect of their constitutional rights, among which is the right to remain silent.

Neurolinguistic eye movement. The link between brain activity and eye movement that is useful in detecting deception.

Nonemotional offender. A person who does not experience a troubled conscience as a result of committing a crime.

Perception management. A process of verbal and nonverbal behavior liars use to influence their intended targets of deception.

Pneumograph. Part of a polygraph machine that records respiration.

Rapport. Developing a harmonious relationship with another person.

Rapport building. A bonding process based on developing a harmonious relationship with another person.

Retroactive interference. Witnesses' tendency to adopt information from other witnesses as their own or alter their recollections to fit with those of other witnesses.

Reverse transference. A witness who overhears other witnesses discussing their observations may take some or all of their information as their own.

Sympathetic division. Part of the autonomic nervous system when stimulated mobilizes the body and its resources for emergencies.

Synchrony. A certain amount of harmony occurs when people talk with one another. The lack of harmony indicates that the person being interviewed is uncomfortable and possibly being deceptive.

Chapter 8

Aggravated assault. The use of force against another with a weapon or the infliction of serious bodily injury without a weapon.

Algor mortis. The cooling of a body after death.

Altercation. A verbal dispute.

Anger killing. As the result of a dispute the victim is attacked and fatally injured.

Ante mortem. Before death.

Assault. The attempt to commit a battery, or the attempted unlawful beating of another.

Autolysis. A chemical breakdown of the body that results in the softening and liquefaction of body tissue after death occurs.

Autopsy. The postmortem examination of the victim in a suspicious death case that is performed by a pathologist who determines the cause of death.

Bacterial action. Converts body tissue into liquids and gasses after death occurs.

Battered child syndrome. Child abuse resulting in serious bodily injury.

Battery. The unlawful beating or infliction of physical harm to another person without their consent.

Child abuse. The intentional and deliberate assault upon a child in which serious bodily injury is inflicted.

Clustered crime scene. Involves a situation where most of the activities take place at one location, the confrontation, the attack, the assault, and sexual activity.

Cold Case. The reopening of any felony crime where prior investigative activity has exhausted all investigative leads without resolution and the case has been inactive for some time.

Comfort-oriented serial murderer. A person who kills for personal gain, professional assassins, and others.

Contact burn. Caused by flames or hot solid objects, such as cigarette burns.

Criminal agency. That the death was caused by another person's unlawful act or omission.

Criminal agent. The person responsible for the death of another person by an unlawful act or omission.

Deliberate immersion burn. A form of child abuse where the child is placed into hot water and burned.

Disorderly conduct. Behavior that is contrary to law and disturbs the public peace.

Disorganized offender. Inadequate individuals who are experiencing intense sadistic sexual fantasies and may suddenly act out these fantasies on a victim of opportunity.

Disturbing the peace. Interruption of the peace and quiet of a neighborhood.

Exhumation. A court order for the removal of a body of a deceased person from its burial place for a medicolegal examination.

Felony murder. Death resulting from injuries inflicted by someone in the act of committing a felony.

First-degree murder. The premeditated killing of another human being with malice, or wrongful intent.

Foul play Some criminal agency is involved when the death occurs.

Hedonistic serial killer. Lust or thrill killer derives pleasure from the act of killing another; for them the killing is an eroticized sexual experience.

Lust killer. Derives pleasure from the act of killing another; an eroticized experience.

Manslaughter. The unlawful killing of another without malice or premeditation either voluntarily or involuntarily.

Mass murder. The homicide of four or more victims during a single event at one location.

Mission serial killer. Feels the need on a conscious level to eradicate a certain group of people.

Motive. The cause or reason why a person acted as they did.

Multicide. The killing of a number of victims by one or more persons working in concert.

Munchausen syndrome by proxy. A psychological disorder in which parents or caretakers attempt to bring medical attention to themselves by injuring or inducing illness in their children.

Murder for profit. The elimination of another person because the murderer would gain some benefit.

Murder-suicide. After killing the victim the murderer then commits suicide.

Organized offenders. These offenders are usually above average in intelligence, methodical, and cunning. Their crimes are well thought out and carefully planned.

Postmortem lividity. After death the blood stops circulating and begins to settle to the lowest portion of the body.

Power and control serial killer. Receives sexual gratification from the complete domination and killing of his victim.

Putrefaction. The decomposition of the body which begins at the time of death.

Random killing. The killer has no previous connection or tie with the victim.

Retinal hemorrhage. Bleeding in the back of the eyeballs associated with shaken baby syndrome.

Revenge or jealousy killing. Occurs when the suspect and the victim have a prior relationship that has soured.

Rigor mortis. Body appearance after death—stiffening; factor in determining time of death in criminal homicides.

Second-degree murder. The killing of another without the element of premeditation.

Serial killer. A person who commits two or more separate murders, acting alone or with another, commits multiple homicides over a period of time with time breaks between each murder event.

Serial murder. Two or more separate murders when an individual, acting alone or with another, commits multiple homicides over a period of time with time breaks between each murder event.

Serious bodily injury. Includes damage to the skin, burns or cuts, brain damage, bone damage or internal injuries causing shock, or internal bleeding.

Sex and sadism murder. The killer has made the connection between sexual gratification and personal violence; they will torture and mutilate their victims.

Shaken baby syndrome. Injuries caused by a violent sustained shaking action in which the infant's head is violently whipped forward and backward, hitting the chest and shoulders; occurs primarily in children eighteen months of age or younger because their necks lack muscle control and their heads are heavier than the rest of their bodies.

Spree murder. The killing of three or more persons within a relatively short time frame.

Stalking. Aggressive and threatening pursuit of a victim selected because of celebrity status, past relationship, or some irrational motive; initial harassing letters and telephone calls escalate to threats and demands and then to serious injury or even fatal attack.

Sudden infant death syndrome (SIDS). Not a positive finding but rather is a diagnosis made without other medical explanation for the abrupt death of an apparently healthy infant.

Suspicious death. Whenever the circumstances of the death indicate violence or foul play, that some criminal agency was involved when the death occurred.

Thrill killer. This killer has made the connection between personal violence and sexual gratification.

Toxicologist. A scientist who specializes in the detection of chemical, physical, and biological toxins.

Triangle killing. Death is the result of a romantic triangle; for example, wife and new boyfriend kill the husband.

Violent Criminal Apprehension Program (VICAP). Administered by the FBI, this is a clearinghouse for information regarding serial killers.

Violent injury. Synonymous with force in assault cases.

Visionary serial killer. Propelled to kill by voices he or she hears or visions he or she sees.

Window of death. The time between when the victim was last known to be alive and when the death was discovered.

Chapter 9

Acquaintance rape. Male sexual aggression where the female is forced to have sexual intercourse against her will and a previous relationship exists between the offender and the victim; also known as date rape.

Aggravated rape. Occurs when the rapist is armed with a dangerous weapon, kidnaps the victim, inflicts bodily injury, or is in a position of trust in regard to the victim such as official authority.

Anger rapist. Someone who commits the crime of rape as a means of expressing and discharging feelings of pent-up anger and rage.

Date rape. Prior relationship between rapist and victim.

Exhibitionism. The intentional and deliberate exposure of a person's genitalia to an unsuspecting stranger.

Fixated child molester. Loves children and does not want to harm them; young boys are the preferred target.

Forcible rape. An act of sexual intercourse where the victim's will is overcome by the threaten use of force or the actual use of force.

Frottage. The realization of sexual gratification from rubbing against certain body parts of another person.

Incest. Sexual intercourse with a person known to be a blood-related family member.

Malice. An offender's inexcusable, unjustified, unmitigated, person-endangering state of mind.

Morally indiscriminate child molester. An abuser of all available persons; children are just another category of victim for this offender.

Mushroom factor. Diligent investigation of child molester likely to lead to exposure of a network of these offenders.

Naïve or inadequate child molester. This offender is suffering from some form of mental disorder that renders them unable to make the distinction between right and wrong, including sexual practices with children.

Pedophile. A person who has a sexual interest in children that ranges from fondling to mutilation and murder.

Pedophilia A sexual perversion in which children are the preferred sexual object.

Power assertive rapist. Rapes to express his virility and personal dominance and believes that he is entitled to do so as a man.

Power rapist. Uses sex as a means of compensating for underlying feelings of inadequacy and serves to express issues of mastery, strength, authority, and control over another person.

Power reassurance rapist. The least violent of all rapist; suffers from low self-esteem and rapes to elevate his own self-status.

Preferential child molester. Prefers children as sexual partners and his interest in children is persistent and compulsive.

Psychological incest Sexual activity between a child and a non-blood related family member.

Rape. The act of sexual intercourse of a woman without her consent.

Rape trauma syndrome. Apparent shock a victim might experience after an emotionally shattering experience.

Regressed child molester. This offender experiences a situational occurrence that impels him to turn to children as a temporary, not permanent, object for sexual gratification.

Sadistic child molester. This offender has made a vital connection between sexual gratification and personal violence.

Sadistic rapist. Finds the intentional maltreatment of the victim intensely gratifying and takes pleasure in victim's torment, anguish, distress, helplessness, and suffering.

Scatophilia. The erotic gratification gained from the telephone conversation between the caller and the victim rather than from any form of sexual contact.

Situational child molester. Does not have a true sexual interest in children but will experiment with them when the opportunity presents itself.

Statutory rape. Consensual sexual relations between two persons, in which one of the parties is a minor who, by statute, is considered incapable of consenting to a sexual act.

Voyeurism. The act of receiving sexual arousal by looking at private or intimate scenes which contain a sexual component.

Chapter 10

Bonded labor. Occurs when a person is working to pay off a debt owed by them or others.

Debt bondage. Occurs when a person is forced to continue to work as a prostitute to pay off a "debt" purportedly incurred through their transportation, recruitment, and substance costs.

Family abduction. Occurs when one family member takes or keeps a child away from another family member in violation of that person's custodial rights.

Forced labor. Involves the use of force or physical threats, psychological coercion, deception, or other coercive measures to compel someone to work.

Human trafficking. The exploitation of human beings for financial gain, a modern-day form of slavery.

Involuntary domestic servitude. Occurs in a private residence where the victim is compelled to labor as a domestic worker, nanny, or any other capacity.

Mutual aid. An interagency agreement whereby officers from adjacent jurisdictions can be requested to assist in major investigations.

Nonfamily abduction. Occurs when a child has been wrongfully taken, through the use of force, persuasion, or threat of harm, by a person who is not related to the child's family.

Risk factors The existence of these factors would elevate the seriousness of the missing person's status.

Sex trafficking. Occurs when a person is coerced, forced, or deceived into acts of prostitution or other related sexual activity.

Chapter 11

Ambush robbery. The least planned of all types of robberies and is based on the element of surprise

Backup person. Shooter for a robbery gang. Mixes with bystanders as robbery is in progress; acts only when police or armed guards appear and threaten overt robbers.

Badger game extortion. Male and female crime partners operate a three-act scam: (1) victim (sucker) is placed in compromising position; (2) offender discovers, claims to be husband or lover of female, screams and threatens, demands money; (3) goes to bank with victim to get cash.

Carjacking. Vehicle taken from driver by force or fear; handgun most popular weapon; if handbag left in car, contents may be "bonus" loot.

Connect-ups. A series of robberies should reveal similarities that would lead to links to other robberies and suspects.

Extortion. The obtaining of personal property from another, with his consent induced by force or fear.

Getaway driver. A member of the robbery team who remains in the escape vehicle until the robbers have completed the robbery, then picks them up and flees the scene.

Home invasion (robbery). A vicious and violent robbery of a family in its home. Pistol whipping and threats to kill force victims into disclosing hiding places of cash, jewelry, and other valuables.

Linkup. A series of robberies should reveal similarities that would lead to links to other robberies and suspects.

Planned-operation robbery. Carefully structured; the robbery group examines all aspects of the situation and plans for all foreseeable contingencies.

Robbery. The taking of personal property from another against their will by the means of force or fear.

Scam. Fraud, rip-off often based on the promise of high profit on a "sure thing."

Selective-raid robbery. Involves a minimum of planning but involves some casing or checking out or visiting and observing the robbery scene.

Spontaneous play group. A group of robbers assembled from a common meeting place, such as a bar.

Chapter 12

Accelerant. Combustible material used to enhance the fire.

Aggravated arson. Whenever explosives are used or when people are present or placed in danger.

Arson. The willful and malicious setting of fire to, or burning of, any structure, forest land, or property.

Arsonist. The person responsible for an arson fire.

Combustibility. Defined in structure fires in terms of ignitability, rate of heat release, and total heat release.

Community threat groups. Organizations engaging in hate crimes and their advocacy (e.g., Klu Klux Klan, skinheads, Aryan Nation).

Cult. An organization, a group, or a sect (not a gang) bound together by a charismatic leader and his or her spin on one or more segments of the Bible or areas of religious worship; often accused of child abuse, unorthodox lifestyles, misuse of funds, and undue influence in recruiting members and adopting mind-bending techniques to retain them.

Fire Set. An ignition device.

Flashover. A rapid development of the fire that occurs when the volume of active fire becomes a significant portion of the room volume.

Hate crime. Vandalism and violent crime motivated by apparent hate of victim's religion, race, ethnic heritage, or sexual orientation; may be linked to offender's membership in community threat group.

Hate fire. A fire set because of some dispute.

Incendiarism. The act of setting a fire, arson.

Incendiary. The person responsible for setting the fire.

Mind control. Some cults use undue influence and unethical means to recruit and retain members.

Overhauling. The examination and search by firefighters for hidden flames or sparks that might rekindle the fire.

Passive Headspace Concentration Method. Crime laboratory method for separating flammable and combustible liquid residues from fire debris.

Plant. Fire-boosting material such as newspapers used to spread the fire.

Pyromania. Obsessional impulse to set fires; a *pyro* is a fire bug, a pyromaniac.

Pyromaniac. A person who sets a fire in order to experience some sensual satisfaction.

Santa Ana Winds. A wind condition in southern California.

Skinhead. An antisocial person whose hairless head is a symbol of rebellion or anarchy.

Taggants. Coded microparticles added to explosives during manufacture; these particles survive detonation, can be recovered at the bombing scene, and can be decoded by the crime laboratory to indicate where and when the explosives were made.

Tagging. The addition of coded microparticles to explosives during their manufacture. These particles survive detonation and can be decoded to show where and when the explosives were made.

Trailers. Used by arsonists to spread fires from a point of ignition to other parts of a room or building; the trailer may be nothing more than a rope or ropelike string or toilet paper, newspaper, or rags soaked in a fire accelerant.

Chapter 13

Advanced-fee fraud. Fee is up-front money to motivate the loan arranger who has no intention of arranging the loan.

Amateur burglar. One who commits crimes primarily to secure money for drugs.

Auto theft. A form of larceny.

Bait and switch. Sales personnel demean the quality of the advertised merchandise and then switch the customer to a higher-priced item.

Bank examiner fraud. An ego-building swindle based on the desire of many people to serve as a secret agent in locating employees tampering with depositors' accounts. The victim puts up money to entice the dishonest employee only to find that their money is long gone.

Bankruptcy fraud. The swindler either conceals or diverts the major assets of a business so that they cannot be sold to pay off creditors.

Behavior cycle in burglary. A five-step process involving the burglar's needs and the opportunity to meet those needs.

Blasting. The use of explosives to open a safe.

Bunco scheme. Frauds based on promises of unusual returns.

Burglarizing. The act of committing a burglary.

Burglary. The entry of a building with the intent to steal or commit another felony.

Burning. Using a torch a section of a safe is burned out to allow entry.

Cargo theft. Involves the theft of entire trucks, trailers, and cargo containers full of merchandise.

Carjacking. Vehicle taken from driver by force or fear; handgun most popular weapon; if handbag left in car, contents may be "bonus" loot.

Carnival bunco. Rigged carnival games that cannot be won by the participant.

Carrying away. The removal of a safe from its location in order to open it at safer location.

Charity switch. A variation of the pigeon drop where the victim is asked to hold money for a sick of dying person, after putting up "good faith" money. The hold money is fake and the swindler leaves with the "good faith" money.

Con (confidence) game. Fraud, rip-off, or scam based on promise of high profit in a "sure thing."

Continual theft. An ongoing act of employee theft.

Credit card fraud. The use of stolen credit cards, or card numbers, to purchase goods and services without intent to pay.

Decoy vehicle. A proactive tactic where a vehicle in good working condition is taken to a repair shop to see if the shop will give an honest estimate of repairs.

Dismantler. Steals vehicles that will be then taken apart and sold for parts.

Drilling. Holes are drilled in the door of the safe to expose the locking mechanism.

Embezzlement. The theft of another's property over which the thief has custody or control.

Fence. Professional receiver of stolen property.

Fraud. The intentional deceit, concealment, corruption, misrepresentation, and abuse of trust to gain the property of another.

Fraud auditing. Assigned the task of detecting and preventing frauds in commercial transactions.

Home-improvement fraud. Victimizes homeowners by false claims that work is necessary.

Household larceny. The theft of property from inside a residence.

"Human-Fly" burglar. Moves upward or downward on the sides of a building to a selected point of entry.

Incidental theft. Minor level theft committed by employees.

Insurance fraud. Fake or false claims; the swindler must be insured and the victim is the insurer.

Investigative phase. That part of the burglary investigation that occurs after the crime has been committed.

Land-sales fraud. Worthless, unimproved land sold by misrepresentation of future development and potential value.

Larceny. The taking and carrying away of the personal property belonging to another with the intent to deprive.

Means of entry. How did the burglar enter the structure.

Misrepresentation. Failing to give the true facts about product performance, warranties, credit charges, or other hidden costs.

Organized retail theft. Thieves walk into a store, fill up a cart with expensive items, and then leave without paying for the merchandise.

Payoff. The swindler claims to have access to information regarding fixed horse races.

Peeling. Prying off the outer surface of the safe door to get at the locking mechanism.

Personal larceny. Theft of property from another by stealth, with contact but without force, and without direct contact between the victim and the offender—purse snatching.

Personal larceny with contact. The theft of property directly from the victim by stealth but not by force or the threat of force—pickpocket.

Pigeon. The victim of a fraud.

Pigeon drop, or pocketbook drop. The victim is asked to hold recently found money so the finder can look for the real owner and the victim is asked to put up "good faith" money. The hold money is fake and the swindler leaves with the "good faith" money.

Ponzi scheme or kiting. A con in which the swindler uses money invested by new victims to pay high interest on the investments of earlier victims whose money the swindler has appropriated to his or her own use.

Professional burglar. People who work at burglary as a trade, making their living by committing burglaries.

Property crime. Committed for personal gain and includes burglary, theft, and fraud.

Pulling. Use of a gear or wheel puller to pull the safe's dial out of the locking mechanism.

Punching. Use of a sledge hammer and punch to drive the locking mechanism back into the safe.

Repair fraud. Overcharging for services performed or charging for services not performed.

Ripping. Attacking the top, bottom, or sides of a safe with a chisel or other metal cutting devise to expose the interior of the safe.

Roper. The person who identifies potential victims, horse racing bettors, for the "payoff" swindle.

Securities fraud. A scheme based on promises to victims of rapid capital growth and high rate of return on investment.

Shrinkage. The loss on inventory from employee theft.

Situational theft. Those instances when the employee is presented with an opportunity for theft that, in the employee's mind, must be acted on.

"Stepover" burglar. Steps from a fire escape, balcony, or other building to a nearby window.

Storefront or sting technique. Investigators pose as fences for the purpose of "buying" stolen property.

Stripper. Usually attack parked cars and take a variety of parts that can be readily disposed of.

Sucker, or mark. The potential victim of a fraud.

Tout. A person who, by false misrepresentation, persuades another to bet on a horse race.

Chapter 14

Bitcoins. A digital form of currency.

Black hat hackers. Cyber criminals whose motivation is to circumvent a computer's security for personal gain.

Blunt force attack. Involves the use of software that systematically enters every combination of letters, characters, and numbers until a password is discovered.

Bot-nets. This malware turns the user's computer into a "zombie" or "slave computer."

Contraband. Illegal or banned goods.

Deep Web. Allows users to access the Internet without divulging their identities.

Distributed denial of service. The control of the bot-net unleashes a number of the bots to create more inbound traffic than the targeted system can handle.

Economic espionage. The theft of trade secrets.

Exit interview. Used to determine why the employee is leaving the company and take appropriated action if necessary.

Hacktivism. Politically motivated hackers that want to protest and to disrupt Internet functions; however, they do not want to kill, maim, or terrorize.

Internet protocol. The computer's identification or address.

Logic bomb A computer program that performs destructive acts based on a trigger event.

Onion routing. Various layers of encryption surround the data being transmitted over a specific branch of the Internet.

Phishing. A scheme to obtain personal information to be used in identity theft.

Social engineering. Relies on the shortcomings of human nature to determine a person's password.

Viruses. Malicious computer code that replicates itself and inserts copies or versions of itself in other computers.

White hat hackers. Motivated to test their skill against those who design computer security systems and do no harm in the process.

Worms. Similar to viruses, but spread with no human interaction after they are started.

Chapter 15

Analgesic. Pain killer.

Clandestine laboratories. Produce the illicit drugs, usually methamphetamine.

Cookers. Lab operators who run clandestine laboratories producing illegal drugs.

Crack (hubba, rock). A smokable form of cocaine.

Ecstasy. A stimulant like methamphetamine and a hallucinogenic like LSD.

Entrapment. A crime or wrongful act that was induced by the investigator and otherwise would not have occurred.

Euphoria. A feeling of well-being and tranquility.

Flaked. The allegation that illegal drugs were planted on the defendant by the police.

Hallucinogens. Cause sensory distortions and result in illusions and delusions.

Ice. A purified form of methamphetamine.

Lateral Snitching. Informing only on drug sellers who are equal to or lower than themselves in the drug-marketing pyramid.

Lookout. Inform street dealers about any police presence.

LSD. Lysergic acid diethylamide; a semisynthetic drug derived from a fungus.

Marijuana (pot). Most popular illegal drug in the United States, and usually the most available and inexpensive.

Methamphetamine (speed, crank, meth). An illegal drug. A stimulant, popular because of "hit," low price, and availability. Usually made in clandestine labs or at home (kitchen lab) from legal substances. Also known as crank, speed.

Narcotics. Drugs. See Appendix B.

Phencyclidine (angel dust, dust, PCP). Developed as a general anesthetic for surgical procedures; however, produces hallucinogenic side effects.

Poor man's Cocaine. Methamphetamine; also known as speed, crank, and meth. Its effects are similar to cocaine.

Pseudoephedrine. A major component in many allergy and cold medications; also the main precursor to making methamphetamine.

Raid. A law enforcement entry into a building for the purpose of seizing illicit drugs and arresting drug dealers.

Rohypnol (roofies, date rape drug). A sleeping pill when taken with alcohol produces disinhibition and amnesia and is known as the date rape drug.

Runner. Transport small quantities of drugs for drug dealers from the stash to the point of sale.

Sedatives. Central nervous system depressants.

Soporific agent. Induces drowsiness, lethargy, and sleep.

Stash. Hiding place of a drug seller's inventory of drugs; generally, hiding place of cash, weapons, and stolen property.

Stimulants. Increases the central nervous system.

THC. The psychoactive agent in marijuana.

Trap. A built-in hiding place for illegal drugs.

Tweaker. A chronic user of methamphetamine.

Working off a beef. The process of an arrestee making a deal with the arresting officers and prosecutor for exchanging information and cooperation in an investigation in return for leniency in drafting the indictment or at the time of sentencing.

Working-up investigation. The use of arrestees who have agreed to cooperate in revealing their suppliers in return for leniency.

Chapter 16

Apprehensive driver. Hit-and-run driver who flees the scene due to issues unrelated to the accident—having no insurance, driving without a license, driving a stolen car, etc.

Asset forfeiture. Any money directly or indirectly traceable to a crime is subject to forfeiture.

Bar girls. Hang around bars with the approval of the owner or bartender and provide sex for money.

Bookie. People who take illegal bets on sporting events.

Call girls. Operate at the highest level of the prostitution trade on a referral basis.

Cat houses. Permanent location where prostitution services are provided.

Code enforcement. Used to address cheap and rundown hotel and motel room where prostitution flourishes.

Court orders. Restrain prostitutes from frequenting areas where prostitution is occurring.

Day trippers. Women who come into a city to work as prostitutes during the day.

Decoys. Both men and women work as agents of the police to arrest suspects for the solicitation of sex for money.

Escort services. Arrive at the client's hotel/motel room and may offer prostitution services.

Fix. The outcome of a sporting event is predetermined.

High visibility enforcement. Involves assigning numerous police officers to actively engage prostitutes and their prospective clients before they can engage in any sexual activities.

John. Men who solicit females for the purposes of prostitution.

Line. Betting odds for a specific sporting event.

Madam. A woman who lives off the proceeds of one or more prostitutes.

Massage parlors. May be a front for prostitution.

Money laundering. Pass money through a legitimate business to make it appear to have been legally earned.

Off the board. Stop taking bets with the knowledge that the game may be fixed.

Pimp. Men who live off the proceeds of one or more prostitutes.

Projectionist driver. Hit-and-run driver who finds the other operator in fault and refuses to be a party to the accident.

Racketeering. To be involved in organized crime.

Restraining order. Court order prohibiting a person from doing something or being in a certain place.

Sneak operator. Hit-and-run driver that believes a dented fender and other damage are all part of calculated risk shared by all vehicle owners.

Solicitation. The agreement between two or more people to provide sex in exchange for money.

Street level prostitution. The lowest level of prostitution where people stand on the sidewalk or street and offer to provide sex in exchange for money.

Tong. Asian criminal organizations.

Vice laws. Regulate standards for public morals.

Witness protection. Provides protection for witnesses whose lives are in danger as a result of their testimony.

Chapter 17

Al Qaeda. Which means "the base," is an international terrorist group founded by Osama bin Laden.

Animal Liberation Front (ALF). A domestic terrorist group dedicated to direct action to protect animal abuse.

Biological agent. The use of germ warfare, such as anthrax-laced letters being sent to politicians.

Central Intelligence Agency (CIA). Responsible for collecting terrorism related intelligence outside the boarders of the United States.

Chemical agent. Includes choking gases, blood agents, blister agents, and nerve agents.

Dar al-Islam. A united Arabic country from North Africa to the Iranian border.

Defense Intelligence Agency (DIA). Coordinates and analyzes information collected by the various branches of the military.

Domestic terrorism. Refers to terrorist activities that occur primarily within the jurisdiction of the United States.

Earth Liberation Front (ELF). A domestic environmental terrorist group.

Ecoterrorist. Dedicated to environmental causes.

Federal Bureau of Investigation (FBI). The federal agency charged with conducting domestic counterterrorism efforts.

Hamas. An Islamic terrorist group centered in Palestine.

Hizbollah. An Islamic terrorist group centered in Lebanon.

Human intelligence. Information gain from informants affiliated with terrorist groups.

International terrorism. Occurs primarily outside the territorial jurisdiction of the United States.

Kneecapping. A terrorist tactic designed to cripple a person rather than kill them.

Ku Klux Klan. A domestic terrorist organization dedicated to white supremacy.

Lone wolf. A terrorist working alone and not affiliated with any terrorist group.

Mujahedeen. Holy warriors fighting in Afghanistan against the former Soviet Union.

Narcoterrorist. Terrorist activities supported by the narcotic activity.

National Security Agency (NSA). The technological unit of the intelligence community that deals with signal intelligence and code-breaking activities.

Neo-Nazi. Recent followers of Adolph Hitler's Nazi party.

Nuclear terrorism. Involves the detonation of a nuclear device and causing massive casualties.

Radiological agent. Involves the dispersion of radioactive materials by conventional means, a "dirty bomb."

Signal intelligence. Intercepted landline, cell phone, e-mail messages and satellite imagery.

Symbionese Liberation Army. A domestic terrorist group dedicated to inciting a guerrilla war against the U.S. government and destroying the "capitalist state."

Terrorism. A violent act committed to intimidate or coerce a government or the civilian population in furtherance of political or social objective.

The Turner Diaries. A novel written about an international white revolution and a how-to manual for terrorists.

Tree spiking. Involves driving metal spikes into trees in logging areas for the purpose of damaging logging equipment.

Weather underground. A domestic terrorist group that embraced violence and crime as a way to protest the Vietnam War, racism, and other left-wing aims.

White supremacy. Belief in the superiority of the white race.

Chapter 18

Continuum of compromise. Small infractions of unethical conduct leading to becoming major ethical problems.

Corruption. The misuse of police authority for personal gain.

Cross-examination. Questioning conducted by the party calling the witness to testify.

Direct examination. Questioning conducted by the party that did not call the witness to testify.

Ethical awareness. An alertness to behavior that is wrong, immoral, unprincipled, substandard, and criminal.

Ethics. Used as a euphemism for corruption and crime in the United States.

Jury nullification. Jury verdict apparently influenced by mistrust of police witnesses or testimony.

Misconduct. Involves issues such as excessive use of force, violation of a suspect's constitutional rights, and a variety of other misdeeds.

Nonverbal communication. A process of transmitting unspoken cues that have potential meaning to one or more observers.

Protection. Money paid to police officers to avoid being arrested.

Stage fright. The fear or reluctance to get up and talk in front of a group of people.

Index